Institutional Investment Management

The Frank J. Fabozzi Series

Fixed Income Securities, Second Edition by Frank J. Fabozzi
Focus on Value: A Corporate and Investor Guide to Wealth Creation by James L. Grant and James A. Abate
Managing a Corporate Bond Portfolio by Leland E. Crabbe and Frank J. Fabozzi
Real Options and Option-Embedded Securities by William T. Moore
Capital Budgeting: Theory and Practice by Pamela P. Peterson and Frank J. Fabozzi
The Exchange-Traded Funds Manual by Gary L. Gastineau
Investing in Emerging Fixed Income Markets edited by Frank J. Fabozzi and Efstathia Pilarinu
Handbook of Alternative Assets by Mark J. P. Anson
The Global Money Markets by Frank J. Fabozzi, Steven V. Mann, and Moorad Choudhry
The Handbook of Financial Instruments edited by Frank J. Fabozzi
Interest Rate, Term Structure, and Valuation Modeling edited by Frank J. Fabozzi
Investment Performance Measurement by Bruce J. Feibel
The Handbook of Equity Style Management edited by T. Daniel Coggin and Frank J. Fabozzi
The Theory and Practice of Investment Management edited by Frank J. Fabozzi and Harry M. Markowitz
Foundations of Economic Value Added, Second Edition by James L. Grant
Financial Management and Analysis, Second Edition by Frank J. Fabozzi and Pamela P. Peterson
Measuring and Controlling Interest Rate and Credit Risk, Second Edition by Frank J. Fabozzi, Steven V. Mann, and Moorad Choudhry
The Handbook of European Fixed Income Securities edited by Frank J. Fabozzi and Moorad Choudhry
The Handbook of European Structured Financial Products edited by Frank J. Fabozzi and Moorad Choudhry
The Mathematics of Financial Modeling and Investment Management by Sergio M. Focardi and Frank J. Fabozzi
Short Selling: Strategies, Risks, and Rewards edited by Frank J. Fabozzi
The Real Estate Investment Handbook by G. Timothy Haight and Daniel Singer
Market Neutral Strategies edited by Bruce I. Jacobs and Kenneth N. Levy
Securities Finance: Securities Lending and Repurchase Agreements edited by Frank J. Fabozzi and Steven V. Mann
Fat-Tailed and Skewed Asset Return Distributions by Svetlozar T. Rachev, Christian Menn, and Frank J. Fabozzi
Financial Modeling of the Equity Market: From CAPM to Cointegration by Frank J. Fabozzi, Sergio M. Focardi, and Petter N. Kolm
Advanced Bond Portfolio Management: Best Practices in Modeling and Strategies edited by Frank J. Fabozzi, Lionel Martellini, and Philippe Priaulet
Analysis of Financial Statements, Second Edition by Pamela P. Peterson and Frank J. Fabozzi
Collateralized Debt Obligations: Structures and Analysis, Second Edition by Douglas J. Lucas, Laurie S. Goodman, and Frank J. Fabozzi
Handbook of Alternative Assets, Second Edition by Mark J. P. Anson
Introduction to Structured Finance by Frank J. Fabozzi, Henry A. Davis, and Moorad Choudhry
Financial Econometrics by Svetlozar T. Rachev, Stefan Mittnik, Frank J. Fabozzi, Sergio M. Focardi, and Teo Jasic
Developments in Collateralized Debt Obligations: New Products and Insights by Douglas J. Lucas, Laurie S. Goodman, Frank J. Fabozzi, and Rebecca J. Manning
Robust Portfolio Optimization and Management by Frank J. Fabozzi, Peter N. Kolm, Dessislava A. Pachamanova, and Sergio M. Focardi
Advanced Stochastic Models, Risk Assessment, and Portfolio Optimizations by Svetlozar T. Rachev, Stogan V. Stoyanov, and Frank J. Fabozzi
How to Select Investment Managers and Evaluate Performance by G. Timothy Haight, Stephen O. Morrell, and Glenn E. Ross
Bayesian Methods in Finance by Svetlozar T. Rachev, John S. J. Hsu, Biliana S. Bagasheva, and Frank J. Fabozzi
The Handbook of Municipal Bonds edited by Sylvan G. Feldstein and Frank J. Fabozzi
Subprime Mortgage Credit Derivatives by Laurie S. Goodman, Shumin Li, Douglas J. Lucas, Thomas A Zimmerman, and Frank J. Fabozzi
Introduction to Securitization by Frank J. Fabozzi and Vinod Kothari
Structured Products and Related Credit Derivatives edited by Brian P. Lancaster, Glenn M. Schultz, and Frank J. Fabozzi
Handbook of Finance: Volume I: Financial Markets and Instruments edited by Frank J. Fabozzi
Handbook of Finance: Volume II: Financial Management and Asset Management edited by Frank J. Fabozzi
Handbook of Finance: Volume III: Valuation, Financial Modeling, and Quantitative Tools edited by Frank J. Fabozzi
Finance: Capital Markets, Financial Management, and Investment Management by Pamela Peterson Drake and Frank J. Fabozzi
Leveraged Finance: Concepts, Methods, and Trading of High Yield Bonds, Loans, and Derivatives by Stephen J. Antczak, Douglas J. Lucas, and Frank J. Fabozzi
Modern Financial Systems: Theory and Applications by Edwin H. Neave

Institutional Investment Management

Equity and Bond Portfolio Strategies and Applications

FRANK J. FABOZZI

John Wiley & Sons, Inc.

Copyright © 2009 by John Wiley & Sons, Inc. All rights reserved.

Published by John Wiley & Sons, Inc., Hoboken, New Jersey.
Published simultaneously in Canada.

No part of this publication may be reproduced, stored in a retrieval system, or transmitted in any form or by any means, electronic, mechanical, photocopying, recording, scanning, or otherwise, except as permitted under Section 107 or 108 of the 1976 United States Copyright Act, without either the prior written permission of the Publisher, or authorization through payment of the appropriate per-copy fee to the Copyright Clearance Center, Inc., 222 Rosewood Drive, Danvers, MA 01923, (978) 750-8400, fax (978) 646-8600, or on the web at www.copyright.com. Requests to the Publisher for permission should be addressed to the Permissions Department, John Wiley & Sons, Inc., 111 River Street, Hoboken, NJ 07030, (201) 748-6011, fax (201) 748-6008, or online at http://www.wiley.com/go/permissions.

Limit of Liability/Disclaimer of Warranty: While the publisher and author have used their best efforts in preparing this book, they make no representations or warranties with respect to the accuracy or completeness of the contents of this book and specifically disclaim any implied warranties of merchantability or fitness for a particular purpose. No warranty may be created or extended by sales representatives or written sales materials. The advice and strategies contained herein may not be suitable for your situation. You should consult with a professional where appropriate. Neither the publisher nor author shall be liable for any loss of profit or any other commercial damages, including but not limited to special, incidental, consequential, or other damages.

For general information on our other products and services or for technical support, please contact our Customer Care Department within the United States at (800) 762-2974, outside the United States at (317) 572-3993, or fax (317) 572-4002.

Wiley also publishes its books in a variety of electronic formats. Some content that appears in print may not be available in electronic books. For more information about Wiley products, visit our web site at www.wiley.com.

ISBN: 978-0-470-40094-4

Printed in the United States of America.

10 9 8 7 6 5 4 3 2 1

FJF
To my wife Donna, and my children
Francesco, Patricia, and Karly

Contents

Preface	xv
Acknowledgments	xix
About the Author	xxiii

CHAPTER 1
Overview of Investment Management — 1
Setting Investment Objectives	2
Establishing an Investment Policy	4
Selecting a Portfolio Strategy	9
Constructing and Monitoring the Portfolio	10
Measuring and Evaluating Performance	11
References	11

PART ONE
Portfolio Theory and Asset Pricing — 13

CHAPTER 2
Theory of Portfolio Selection — 15
Some Basic Concepts	16
Measuring a Portfolio's Expected Return	19
Measuring Portfolio Risk	21
Portfolio Diversification	26
Choosing a Portfolio of Risky Assets	30
Index Model's Approximations to the Covariance Structure	36
Summary	39
References	40

CHAPTER 3
Applying Mean-Variance Analysis — 41
Using Historical Data to Estimate Inputs — 42
Application of Portfolio Theory to Asset Allocation — 46
Implementing the Optimal Portfolio — 53
Summary — 56
References — 57

CHAPTER 4
Issues in the Theory of Portfolio Selection — 59
Quick Review of Probability Theory — 60
Limitations of the Variance as a Risk Measure — 64
Desirable Features of Investment Risk Measures — 68
Alternative Risk Measures for Portfolio Selection — 74
Extensions of the Theory of Portfolio Selection — 77
Behavioral Finance Attack on the Theory of Portfolio — 80
Summary — 82
References — 84

CHAPTER 5
Asset Pricing Theories — 89
Characteristics of an Asset Pricing Model — 90
Capital Asset Pricing Model — 91
Arbitrage Pricing Theory Model — 102
Some Principles to Take Away — 107
Summary — 108
Appendix — 109
References — 117

PART TWO
Common Stock Analysis and Portfolio Management — 119

CHAPTER 6
The U.S. Equity Markets — 121
Exchange Market Structures — 121
The U.S. Stock Markets: Exchanges and OTC Markets — 125
Off-Exchange Markets and Alternative Electronic Markets — 134
Evolving Stock Market Practices — 138
Basic Functioning of Stock Markets — 140

Summary	145
References	145

CHAPTER 7
Common Stock Strategies and Performance Evaluation — 147

Market Efficiency	147
Stock Market Indicators	149
Top-Down vs. Bottom-Up Approaches	152
Fundamental vs. Technical Analysis	153
Strategies Based on Technical Analysis	154
Strategies Based on Fundamental Analysis	161
Equity Style Investing	166
Passive Strategies	169
Measuring and Evaluating Performance	176
Summary	187
References	189

CHAPTER 8
Financial Analysis — 193

Financial Ratio Analysis	194
Cash Flow Analysis	223
Usefulness of Cash Flows in Financial Analysis	235
Summary	241
References	242

CHAPTER 9
Applied Equity Valuation — 245

Discounted Cash Flow Models	245
Relative Valuation Methods	266
DCF vs. RV Methods	272
Summary	275
References	276

CHAPTER 10
Forecasting Stock Returns — 277

The Concept of Predictability	279
A Closer Look at Pricing Models	286
Predictive Return Models	287
Is Forecasting Markets Worth the Effort?	293
Summary	295
References	297

CHAPTER 11
Managing a Common Stock Portfolio with Fundamental Factor Models — 299
Tracking Error — 300
Fundamental Factor Model Description and Estimation — 309
Risk Decomposition — 312
Applications in Portfolio Construction and Risk Control — 316
Summary — 329
References — 330

CHAPTER 12
Transaction Costs and Trade Execution in Common Stock Portfolio Management — 331
Trading Mechanics — 332
Trading Arrangements for Institutional Investors — 335
A Taxonomy of Transaction Costs — 340
Liquidity and Transaction Costs — 347
Market Impact Measurements and Empirical Findings — 349
Forecasting and Modeling Market Impact — 352
Incorporating Transaction Costs in Asset-Allocation Models — 355
Optimal Trading — 356
Integrated Portfolio Management:
   Beyond Expected Return and Portfolio Risk — 359
Summary — 360
References — 362

CHAPTER 13
Using Stock Index Futures and Equity Swaps in Equity Portfolio Management — 365
Derivatives Process — 366
Basic Features of Futures Contracts — 367
Basic Features of Stock Index Futures — 373
Applications for Stock Index Futures — 381
Equity Swaps — 393
Summary — 394
References — 395

CHAPTER 14
Using Equity Options in Investment Management — 397
Basic Features of Options — 397
Basic Features of Listed Equity Options — 400
Risk and Return Characteristics of Listed Options — 402

The Option Price	410
Use of Listed Equity Options in Portfolio Management	415
OTC Equity Options: The Basics	421
Use of Exotic Equity Options	425
Summary	426
References	427

CHAPTER 15
Equity Option Pricing Models — 429

Put-Call Parity Relationship	429
Option Pricing Models	431
Sensitivity of the Option Price to a Change in Factors	447
Estimating Expected Stock Return Volatility	452
Summary	453
References	454

PART THREE
Bond Analysis and Portfolio Management — 455

CHAPTER 16
Bond Fundamentals and Risks — 457

Features of Bonds	457
Risks Associated with Investing in Bonds	467
Summary	482
Appendix: Calculating Accrued Interest	484
References	486

CHAPTER 17
Treasury and Agency Securities, Corporate Bonds, and Municipal Bonds — 487

Treasury Securities	487
Federal Agency Securities	490
Corporate Bonds	491
Municipal Bonds	495
Non-U.S. Bonds	501
Summary	504
References	505

CHAPTER 18
Structured Products: RMBS, CMBS, and ABS — 507
Agency Residential Mortgage-Backed Securities — 509
Private-Label Residential MBS — 528
Mortgage-Related, Asset-Backed Securities: Subprime MBS — 533
Commercial Mortgage-Backed Securities — 537
Nonmortgage Asset-Backed Securities — 540
Summary — 546
References — 547

CHAPTER 19
The Structure of Interest Rates — 549
The Base Interest Rate — 549
The Risk Premium Between Non-Treasury and Treasury Securities with the Same Maturity — 550
Factors Affecting the Risk Premium — 551
Term Structure of Interest Rates — 555
Summary — 564
References — 565

CHAPTER 20
Bond Pricing and Yield Measures — 567
Pricing of Option-Free Bonds — 567
Conventional Yield Measures — 576
Portfolio Yield Measures — 583
Total Return — 585
Summary — 592

CHAPTER 21
Bond Price Volatility and the Measurement of Interest Rate Risk — 593
Price Volatility Properties of Option-Free Bonds — 593
Factors that Affect a Bond's Price Volatility — 596
Measuring Interest Rate Risk Using the Price Value of a Basis Point — 596
Measuring Interest Rate Risk Using Duration and Convexity — 598
Measuring Exposure to Yield Curve Changes Key Rate Duration — 610
Summary — 611
References — 612

CHAPTER 22
Valuing Bonds with Embedded Options — 613
The Interest Rate Lattice — 614
Calibrating the Lattice — 618
Using the Lattice for Valuation — 622
Using the Lattice Model to Value Bonds with Embedded Options — 625
Extensions — 630
Summary — 634
References — 634

CHAPTER 23
Bond Portfolio Strategies — 635
Bond Market Indexes — 635
The Spectrum of Strategies — 640
Value-Added Strategies — 647
Using Factor Models to Manage a Portfolio — 658
Liability-Driven Strategies — 672
Summary — 680
References — 682

CHAPTER 24
Using Derivatives in Bond Portfolio Management — 683
Using Treasury Bond and Note Futures Contracts in Bond Portfolio Management — 683
Use of Interest Rate Options in Bond Portfolio Management — 692
Using Interest Rate Swaps in Bond Portfolio Management — 704
Using Stock Index Futures and Treasury Bond Futures to Implement an Asset Allocation Decision — 715
Using Credit Default Swaps to Manage Credit Risk — 716
Summary — 720
References — 722

PART FOUR
Investment Companies, Exchange-Traded Funds, and Alternative Investments — 723

CHAPTER 25
Investment Companies, Exchange-Traded Funds, and Investment-Oriented Life Insurance — 725

Investment Companies	725
Exchange-Traded Funds	739
Investment-Oriented Life Insurance	744
Summary	764
References	765

CHAPTER 26
Alternative Assets — 767

Hedge Funds	767
Private Equity	786
Commodity Investments	798
Summary	806
References	807

APPENDIX
Measuring and Forecasting Yield Volatility — 809

Calculating the Standard Deviation from Historical Data	809
Modeling and Forecasting Yield Volatility	814
Summary	825
References	825

Index — 827

Preface

The job of planning, implementing, and overseeing the funds of an individual investor or an institution is referred to as investment management. The purpose of this book is to describe the process of investment management.

There are many excellent investment management books available. In deciding whether another book on the same topic merited publication, I drew upon my experience in the training of portfolio managers at various seminars I have taught throughout the world and my experience as an advisor and board member of several financial institutions. Moreover, I drew heavily from my writings with other professionals and academics whose contribution I have acknowledged elsewhere in this book.

This book differs from other investment management books in four fundamental ways. First, I felt that the focus of an investment management book should be on the management of funds of institutional investors (depository institutions, insurance companies, investment companies, pension funds, and endowment funds and foundations), not on individual investors. Although many of the principles are equally applicable to the investments of individual investors, there are nuances that are unique to the management of institutional funds. Hence, the title for the book: *Institutional Investment Management*.

Second, there should be greater emphasis on bond analysis and strategies. This reflects my bias that many students entering the investment management profession will be employed by institutions that concentrate on these products. Historically, common stock portfolio management has been emphasized in books, leaving the student who ventures into the field of bond portfolio management to learn on the job. I, as well as employers of college graduates majoring in finance, have been astonished at the lack of training that students receive in the area of bond portfolio management, particularly structured bond products.

Third, the use of derivative instruments—options, futures, and swaps—should be emphasized. Often the focus when derivatives are covered in investment management books is on pricing. However, a portfolio manager can effectively use derivatives without being an expert in pricing. The approach I have taken in this book is how derivatives can be used to effectively control a portfolio's risk and how they may be used to reduce the cost of implementing investment strategies. Illustrations are provided.

Finally, an investment management book should tie together theory and practice. Investing in a theoretical world is simple; investing in a world where there are client-imposed or regulatory constraints, and in which there are transaction costs and other market imperfections, means that theory must be adapted to real-world conditions.

The book has 26 chapters and one appendix, and is divided into four parts. Chapter 1 explains the investment management process, explaining the major tasks in managing money.

Part One covers theories about portfolio selection and asset pricing. Chapter 2 covers what is now popularly known as *modern portfolio theory* as developed by Professor Harry Markowitz, the 1990 corecipient of the Nobel Memorial Prize in Economic Sciences. This theory, also referred to as mean-variance analysis, provides a framework for the construction of efficient portfolios—portfolios that offer the maximum expected return for a given level of risk. The implementation of mean-variance analysis is not straightforward. There are issues associated with the estimation of the inputs required in the optimization model that must be employed to obtain efficient portfolios. These implementation issues are explained in Chapter 3. There are other issues surrounding the theory of portfolio selection and the implementation of the model that are covered in Chapter 4. In that chapter, the empirical evidence and the theoretical evidence that challenges the widely accepted notion in traditional finance that return distributions are normally distribution are reviewed. A distribution that has been proposed as an alternative to the normal distribution because it better characterizes the behavior of real-world asset returns is explained. Alternative risk measures are provided, as well as an attack on portfolio selection theory by those who are advocates of a branch of finance known as *behavioral finance*. In Chapter 5, the fundamentals of asset pricing models—economic models that describe the relationship between risk and expected return—are explained. The two most well-known asset pricing models—the capital asset pricing model and the arbitrage pricing theory model—are covered in the chapter.

The 10 chapters in Part Two cover common stock analysis and portfolio management. Coverage of this asset class begins with a discussion of the U.S. equity markets in Chapter 6: the structure and different venues and practices for trading. The wide spectrum of common stock strategies are covered in Chapter 7, along with a discussion of the concept of market efficiency and its implications for trading strategies, and the measurement of investment performance. Stock analysts rely on financial analysis in evaluating the operating performance and financial condition of a company. The tools of financial analysis are covered in Chapter 8. Practical methods of valuing a company's stock based on discounted cash flow models and relative valuation models are explained in Chapter 9.

One of the key tasks in seeking to generate attractive returns is producing realistic and reasonable return expectations and forecasts. In Chapter 10, the issue of whether forecasting stock returns can be done so as to generate trading profits and/or excess returns is examined. A brief description of the relevant concepts in probability theory and statistics is provided as background before discussing the different types of predictive return models that are used by portfolio managers. Common stock portfolio managers who pursue a quantitative-oriented common stock strategy typically employ a multifactor equity risk model, commonly referred to as factor models, in constructing and rebalancing a portfolio. The most popular type of factor model used in practice is a fundamental factor model. In Chapter 11, the use of a fundamental factor model is illustrated. Because trading is an integral component of the investment process, Chapter 12 provides a simple taxonomy of trading costs and the linkage between transaction costs and liquidity, as well as the measurement of these quantities. Portfolio managers and traders need to be able to effectively model the impact of trading costs on their portfolios and trades. Several approaches for the modeling of transaction costs are described in the chapter, as well as a brief introduction to optimal execution strategies.

Derivative instruments are contracts that essentially derive their value from the behavior of cash market instruments such as stocks, stock indexes, bonds, currencies, and commodities that underlie the contract. In the last three chapters of Part Two, we describe equity derivative instruments, their use in portfolio management, and how they are valued. Chapter 13 begins with a description of the derivatives process that should be used before deciding to employ derivatives in investment management and then focuses on stock index futures and equity swaps. Chapter 14 covers the use of options and Chapter 15 explains the how to determine the fair value or theoretical value of an equity option.

In Part Three the focus is on the other major asset class: bonds. This nine-chapter part begins with bond fundamentals and the risks associated with investing in bonds in Chapter 16. The various sectors of the bond market are the subjects of Chapters 17 and 18. In Chapter 17, debt instruments issued by the U.S. Department of the Treasury, its agencies, corporations, and municipalities are explained. Structured products are more complex bond structures. They include residential mortgage-backed securities, commercial mortgage-backed securities, and asset-backed securities and are described in Chapter 18. Obviously, there is not one interest rate in a country's financial market. Rather there is a structure of interest rates and the factors that affect this structure are explained in Chapter 19.

How to determine the price of a bond, the relationship between price and yield, and the various yield measures used by bond market participants are covered in Chapter 20. The characteristics of a bond's price that affect its price volatility and how to quantify a bond's price volatility (i.e., interest rate risk) are explained in Chapter 21. One of the more popular measures of interest rate risk, duration, is explained in this chapter. In the discussion on bond pricing in Chapter 20, the focus is on simple, option-free bonds. The complication in valuing bonds with embedded options (e.g., callable and putable bonds) is that the bond's cash flows depend on interest rates in the future. Thus valuing such bonds requires that the valuation model capture the stochastic behavior of interest rates. The lattice framework described in Chapter 22 provides a means for implementing interest rate models and thereby allowing for the valuation of bonds with embedded options.

The last two chapters in Part Three cover bond portfolio strategies and the use of derivatives. As in the case of equity portfolio strategies, bond portfolio strategies can be classified as active strategies and passive strategies. Both types of strategies are discussed in Chapter 23. The chapter begins with a discussion of the various bond market indexes and then explains how the spectrum of bond portfolio strategies can be understood in terms of the degree of mismatch that is permitted between a bond index and the managed portfolio. Several value-added strategies are described. As done in Chapter 11, where an equity factor model is illustrated, in Chapter 23 a bond factor model is illustrated. How interest rate derivatives—Treasury futures, Treasure futures options, and interest rate swap—and credit derivatives (specifically credit default swaps) are used in bond portfolio management are described and illustrated in Chapter 24. Also explained in the chapter is the difficulty of applying equity option models to value options on bonds.

Part Four covers other investment vehicles that offer an alternative to the direct investment in stocks and bonds. Chapter 25 covers investment companies, exchange-traded funds, and investment-oriented insurance. Three types of the best known alternative assets—hedge funds, private equity, and commodities—are described in Chapter 26.

In the appendix to the book, we explain how to measure and forecast yield volatility.

I hope that the approach presented in this book provides a more appealing alternative for teaching investment management.

Frank J. Fabozzi

Acknowledgments

In writing this book, I drew from my joint writings over the past 15 years with experts from academia and industry. Below I have identified my coauthors of chapters in the book. Any errors are mine and should not be attributed to my coauthors.

Chapter 2   *Theory of Portfolio Selection*
Francis Gupta, Ph.D., Director, Research, Dow Jones Indexes.
Harry M. Markowitz, Ph.D., Consultant.

Chapter 3   *Applying Mean-Variance Analysis*
Francis Gupta, Ph.D., Director, Research, Dow Jones Indexes.
Harry M. Markowitz, Ph.D., Consultant.

Chapter 4   *Issues in the Theory of Portfolio Selection*
Sergio Focardi, Ph.D., Partner, The Intertek Group, France.
Petter N. Kolm, Ph.D., Clinical Associate Professor and Deputy Director of the Mathematics in Finance M.S. Program, Courant Institute, New York University.
Christian Menn, Ph.D., Senior Equity Derivatives Trader, DZ Bank AG, Frankfurt, Germany.
Svetlozar T. Rachev, Ph.D., Dr. Sci., Chair-Professor, Chair of Econometrics, Statistics and Mathematical Finance, School of Economics and Business Engineering, University of Karlsruhe and Department of Statistics and Applied Probability University of California, Santa Barbara, and Chief Scientist, Finanalytica.

Chapter 6   *The U.S. Equity Markets*
Frank J. Jones, Ph.D., Professor, Accounting and Finance Department, San Jose State University and Chairman of the Investment Committee, Salient-Wealth Management, LLC.

Chapter 8   *Financial Analysis*
Pamela P. Drake, Ph.D., CFA, J. Gray Ferguson Professor of Finance and Department Head of Finance and Business Law, James Madison University.

Chapter 9 *Applied Equity Valuation*
Pamela P. Drake, Ph.D., CFA, J. Gray Ferguson Professor of Finance and Department Head of Finance and Business Law, James Madison University.
Glen A. Larsen Jr., Ph.D., CFA, Professor of Finance, Kelley School of Business, Indiana University–Indianapolis.

Chapter 10 *Forecasting Stock Returns*
Sergio Focardi, Ph.D., Partner, The Intertek Group, France.
Petter N. Kolm, Ph.D., Clinical Associate Professor and Deputy Director of the Mathematics in Finance M.S. Program, Courant Institute, New York University.

Chapter 11 *Managing a Common Stock Portfolio with Fundamental Factor Models*
Frank J. Jones, Ph.D., Professor, Accounting and Finance Department, San Jose State University and Chairman of the Investment Committee, Salient-Wealth Management, LLC.
Raman Vardharaj, CFA, Principal, OppenheimerFunds.

Chapter 12 *Transaction Costs and Trade Execution in Common Stock Portfolio Management*
Sergio Focardi, Ph.D., Partner, The Intertek Group, France.
Petter N. Kolm, Ph.D., Clinical Associate Professor and Deputy Director of the Mathematics in Finance M.S. Program, Courant Institute, New York University.

Chapter 13 *Using Stock Index Futures and Equity Swaps in Equity Portfolio Management*
Bruce M. Collins, Ph.D., Professor of Finance, Western Connecticut State University.

Chapter 14 *Using Equity Options in Investment Management*
Bruce M. Collins, Ph.D., Professor of Finance, Western Connecticut State University.

Chapter 18 *Structured Products: RMBS, CMBS, and ABS*
Anand K. Bhattacharya, Ph.D., Professor in the Practice, Department of Finance, Carey School of Management, Arizona State University.
William S. Berliner, President, Berliner Consulting & Research.

Chapter 22 *Valuing Bonds with Embedded Options*
Michael Dorigan, Ph.D., Senior Quantitative Analyst, PNC Capital Advisors.
Andrew Kalotay, Ph.D., President, Andrew Kalotay Associates.

Acknowledgments

Chapter 25 *Investment Companies, Exchange-Traded Funds, and Investment-Oriented Life Insurance.*
Frank J. Jones, Ph.D., Professor, Accounting and Finance Department, San Jose State University and Chairman of the Investment Committee, Salient-Wealth Management, LLC.

Chapter 26 *Alternative Assets*
The sections on hedge funds and private equity are coauthored with:
Mark J. P. Anson, Ph.D., J.D., CPA, CFA, CAIA, President and Executive Director of Nuveen Investment Services.
The section on commodities is coauthored with:
Roland Füss, Ph.D., Professor of Finance, Endowed Chair of Asset Management, European Business School (EBS), International University School Reichartshausen.
Dieter G. Kaiser, Ph.D., Director Alternative Investments, Institutional Advisors GmbH Research Fellow, Centre for Practical Quantitative Finance, Frankfurt School of Finance Management.

Appendix *Measuring and Forecasting Yield Volatility*
Wai Lee, Ph.D., Managing Director, Head of Quantitative Investment, Neuberger Berman.

The following sections in Chapters 7 and 24 draw from my work with others:

- The section on equity style investing in Chapter 7 is coauthored with **Eric H. Sorensen**, Ph.D., President and CEO, PanAgora Asset Management.
- The section on passive strategies in Chapter 7 is coauthored with **Bruce M. Collins**, Ph.D., Professor of Finance, Western Connecticut State University.
- The section on hedging with interest rate swaps in Chapter 24 is coauthored with **Shrikant Ramamurthy**, Managing Director, RBS Greenwich Capital.

The illustration in Chapter 23 on the use of a bond factor model was provided by **Vadim Konstantinovsky**, Ph.D., CFA, Director, Quantitative Portfolio Strategy, Fixed Income Research at Barclays Capital.

Peter Ru of Morgan Stanley provided the hedging illustration using futures and futures options in Chapter 24.

I am grateful to these individuals for allowing me to use our joint work in this book.

About the Author

Frank J. Fabozzi is Professor in the Practice of Finance and Becton Fellow in the Yale School of Management. Prior to joining the Yale University faculty, he served for six years as a Visiting Professor of Finance in the Sloan School of Management at MIT. Professor Fabozzi is a Fellow of the International Center for Finance at Yale University and on the Advisory Council for the Department of Operations Research and Financial Engineering at Princeton University. He is an affiliated professor at the Institute of Statistics, Econometrics and Mathematical Finance at the University of Karlsruhe (Germany).

Professor Fabozzi is the editor of the *Journal of Portfolio Management*, an associate editor of the *Journal of Fixed Income, Journal of Asset Management*, and *Journal of Structured Finance*, and on the advisory board of the *Review of Futures Markets*. He is on the board of directors of the BlackRock complex of closed-end funds where he chairs the performance committee and is a member of the audit committee. He has also served on the board of directors of the Guardian Life complex of mutual funds.

He earned a doctorate in economics from the City University of New York in 1972 and a BA (*magna cum laude*) and an MA in economics from the City College of New York both in 1970. He was elected into the Phi Beta Kappa Society in 1969.

In 2002, Professor Fabozzi was inducted into the Fixed Income Analysts Society's Hall of Fame and is the 2007 recipient of the C. Stewart Sheppard Award given by The CFA Institute. He earned the designations of Chartered Financial Analyst and Certified Public Accountant. He is the recipient of an Honorary Doctorate of Humane Letters from Nova Southeastern University (June 1994).

He has authored and edited numerous books on finance including three books coauthored with the late-Franco Modigliani and a book coedited with Harry Markowitz. His book *Mortgage-Backed Securities: Products, Structuring, and Analytical Techniques* (with Anand Bhattacharya and William Berliner) was selected by RiskBook.com for "Best of 2007 Book Awards," his book *Financial Modeling of the Equity Market* (with Sergio Focardi and Petter Kolm) was selected by *Financial Engineering News* as one of the top 10 technical books in 2006, and his book *The Mathematics of Financial*

Modeling and Investment Management (with Sergio Focardi) was selected by RiskBook.com for "Best of 2004 Book Awards" and by *Financial Engineering News* as one of the top three books in 2005.

Research papers by Professor Fabozzi have appeared in leading finance and economics journals, including the *Journal of Finance, Journal of Financial and Quantitative Analysis, Journal of Banking and Finance, Journal of Empirical Finance, Quantitative Finance, Applied Mathematical Finance, Applied Financial Economics, Journal of Economic Dynamics and Control, Operations Research, Economic Letters, Econometric Journal,* and *Studies in Nonlinear Dynamics and Econometrics.*

CHAPTER 1

Overview of Investment Management

Investment management is the process of managing money. Other terms commonly used to describe this process are *portfolio management*, *asset management*, and *money management*. Accordingly, the individual who manages a portfolio of investments is referred to as an investment manager, portfolio manager, asset manager, or money manager. We will use these terms interchangeably throughout this book. In industry jargon, an investment manager "runs money." The investment process requires an understanding of the various investment vehicles, the way these investment vehicles are valued, and the various strategies that can be used to select the investment vehicles that should be included in a portfolio in order to accomplish investment objectives.

Investors can be classified as either individual investors or institutional investors. The purpose of this book is to describe the process of investment management—that is, how investment managers run money. Our primary focus in this book is on the management of institutional investors' portfolios, although the basic principles of are applicable to retail investors as well. In practice, the management of portfolios for institutional investors is typically done by a portfolio team.

The *investment management* process involves the following major activities:

- Setting investment objectives
- Establishing an investment policy
- Selecting an investment strategy
- Constructing and monitoring the portfolio
- Measuring and evaluating investment performance

This is a cyclical process where performance evaluation may result in changes to the objectives, policies, strategies, and composition of a portfolio.

This chapter briefly describes these activities because it will allow us to see the major activities involved in managing a portfolio and, therefore, the significance of the topics that we describe in later chapters.

SETTING INVESTMENT OBJECTIVES

Setting investment objectives starts with a thorough analysis of the investment objectives of the entity whose funds are being managed. These entities can be classified as individual investors and institutional investors. Within each of these broad classifications is a wide range of investment objectives.

The objectives of an individual investor may be to accumulate funds to purchase a home or other major acquisition, to have sufficient funds to be able to retire at a specified age, or to accumulate funds to pay for college tuition for children. An individual investor may engage the services of a financial advisor/consultant in establishing investment objectives.

Institutional investors include:

- Pension funds
- Depository institutions (commercial banks, savings and loan associations, and credit unions)
- Insurance companies (life companies, property and casualty companies, and health companies)
- Regulated investment companies (mutual funds and closed-end funds)
- Hedge funds
- Endowments and foundations
- Treasury department of corporations, municipal governments, and government agencies

Classification of Investment Objectives

In general we can classify the investment objectives of institutional investors into the following two broad categories:

1. Nonliability-driven objectives
2. Liability-driven objectives

As the name indicates, those institutional investors that fall into the first category can manage their assets without regard to satisfying any liabilities. An example of an institutional investor that is not driven by liabilities is a regulated investment company.

The second category includes institutional investors that must meet contractually specified liabilities. A *liability* is a cash outlay that must be made at a specific future date in order to satisfy the contractual terms of an obligation. An institutional investor is concerned with both the *amount* and *timing* of liabilities, because its assets must produce the cash flow to meet any payments it has promised to make in a timely way. Here are two examples of institutional investors that face liabilities:

- Life insurance companies have a wide range of investment-oriented products. One such product is a *guaranteed investment contract* (GIC). For this product, a life insurance company guarantees an interest rate on the funds given it to by a customer. With respect to the GIC account, the investment objective of the asset manager is to earn a return greater than the rate guaranteed.
- There are two types of pension plans offered by sponsors. The sponsor can be a corporation, a state government, or local government. The two types of pension plans that can be sponsored are a defined contribution or a defined benefit plan. For defined contribution plans, the sponsor need only provide a specified amount for an employee to invest and the employee is responsible for investing those funds. The plan sponsor has no further obligation. However, in the case of a defined benefit plan, the plan sponsor has agreed to make specified payments to the employee after retirement. Thus, the plan sponsor has created a liability against itself and in managing the assets of the pension plan, the asset manager must earn a return adequate to meet those future pension liabilities.

Keep in mind that some institutional investors may have accounts that have both nonliability-driven objectives and liability-driven objectives. For example, a life insurance company may have a GIC account (which as explained above is a liability-driven objective product) and a variable annuity account. With a variable annuity account, an investor makes either a single payment or a series of payment to the life insurance company and in turn the life insurance company (1) invests the payments received and (2) makes payments to the investor at some future date. The payments that the life insurance company makes will depend on the performance of the insurance company's asset manager. While the life insurance company does have a liability, it does not guarantee any specific dollar payment.

Benchmark

Regardless of the type of investment objective, to evaluate the performance of an asset manager, a *benchmark* will be established. The determination of a benchmark is in some cases, fairly simple. For example, in the case of a liability-driven objective, the benchmark is typically an interest rate target. In the case of a nonliability-driven objective, the benchmark is typically the asset class in which the assets are invested. For example, later in this chapter we describe the major asset classes. One such asset class is large capitalization stocks. There are several benchmarks for that asset class and the client and asset manager will jointly determine which one to use.

It is not always simple to determine the benchmark. A client and the asset manager may decide to develop a customized benchmark.

ESTABLISHING AN INVESTMENT POLICY

The second major activity in the investment management process is establishing policy guidelines to satisfy the investment objectives. Setting policy begins with the *asset allocation decision*. That is, a decision must be made as to how the funds to be invested should be distributed among the major asset classes.

The term "asset allocation" means different things to different people in different contexts. Arnott and Fabozzi (1992) divide asset allocation into three types: (1) policy asset allocation, (2) dynamic asset allocation, and (3) tactical asset allocation. The *policy asset allocation decision* can loosely be characterized as a long-term asset allocation decision, in which the investor seeks to assess an appropriate long-term "normal" asset mix that represents an ideal blend of controlled risk and enhanced return. The strategies that offer the greatest prospects for strong long-term rewards to accomplish the investment objectives tend to be inherently risky strategies. The strategies that offer the greatest safety tend to offer only modest return opportunities. The balancing of these conflicting goals is what is referred to as the policy asset allocation. In *dynamic asset allocation* the asset mix (i.e., the allocation amongst the asset classes) is mechanistically shifted in response to changing market conditions.

Once the policy asset allocation has been established, the investor can turn attention to the possibility of active departures from the normal asset mix established by policy. That is, suppose that the long-run asset mix is established as 60% equities and 40% bonds. A departure from this mix under certain circumstances may be permitted. If a decision to deviate from this mix is based upon rigorous objective measures of value, it is often called *tactical asset allocation*. Tactical asset allocation is not a single, clearly defined strategy.

Many variations and nuances are involved in building a tactical allocation process. One of the problems in reviewing the concepts of asset allocation is that the same terms are often used for different concepts. The term "dynamic asset allocation" has been used to refer to the long-term policy decision and to intermediate-term efforts to strategically position the portfolio to benefit from major market moves, as well as to refer to aggressive tactical strategies. Even the words "normal asset allocation" convey a stability that is not consistent with the real world. As an investor's risk expectations and tolerance for risk change, the normal or policy asset allocation may change. It is critical in exploring asset allocation issues to know what element of the asset allocation decision is the subject of discussion, and to know in what context the words "asset allocation" are being used.

Tactical asset allocation broadly refers to active strategies that seek to enhance performance by opportunistically shifting the asset mix of a portfolio in response to the changing patterns of reward available in the capital markets. Notably, tactical asset allocation tends to refer to disciplined processes for evaluating prospective rates of return on various asset classes and establishing an asset allocation response intended to capture higher rewards.

Asset Classes

In most developed countries, the four major asset classes are (1) common stocks, (2) bonds, (3) cash equivalents, and (4) real estate. Why are they referred to asset classes? That is, how do we define an asset class? There are several ways to do so. The first is in terms of the investment attributes that the members of an asset class have in common. These investment characteristics include (1) the major economic factors that influence the value of the asset class and, as a result, correlate highly with the returns of each member included in the asset class; (2) have a similar risk and return characteristic; and (3) have a common legal or regulatory structure. Based on this way of defining an asset class, the correlation between the returns of different asset classes would be low.

Kritzman (1999) offers a second way of defining an asset class based simply on a group of assets that is treated as an asset class by asset managers. He writes

> ... some investments take on the status of an asset class simply because the managers of these assets promote them as an asset class. They believe that investors will be more inclined to allocate funds to their products if they are viewed as an asset class rather than merely as an investment strategy. (Kritzman 1999, 79)

Kritzman then goes on to propose criteria for determining asset class status which includes the attributes that we mentioned above and that will be described in more detail in later chapters.

Based on these two ways of defining asset classes, the four major asset classes above can be extended to create other asset classes. From the perspective of a U.S. investor, for example, the four major asset classes listed earlier have been expanded as follows by separating foreign securities from U.S. securities: (1) U.S. common stocks, (2) non-U.S. (or foreign) common stocks, (3) U.S. bonds, (4) non-U.S. bonds, (5) cash equivalents, and (6) real estate.

Common stock and bonds are commonly further partitioned into more asset classes. For U.S. common stocks (also referred to as U.S. equities), the following are classified as asset classes in two ways:

1. *Market capitalization*, that is, large capitalization stocks (more than $10 billion), mid-capitalization stocks (between $2 billion and $10 billion), and small capitalization stocks (between $300 million and $2 billion)
2. Growth stocks and value stocks

The market capitalization of a firm is the total market value of its common stock outstanding. For example, suppose that a corporation has 300 million shares of common stock outstanding and each share has a market value of $40. Then the market capitalization of this company is $12 billion (300 million shares times $40 per share). A firm's market capitalization is commonly referred to as its *market cap*.

While the market cap of a company is easy to determine given the market price per share and the number of shares outstanding, how does one define "value" and "growth" stocks? We describe how this done in Chapter 7.

For U.S. bonds, also referred to as fixed income securities, the following are classified as asset classes: (1) U.S. government bonds, (2) corporate bonds, (3) U.S. municipal bonds (i.e., state and local bonds), (4) residential mortgage-backed securities, (5) commercial mortgage-backed securities, and (6) asset-backed securities. In turn, several of these asset classes are further segmented by the credit rating of the issuer. (We discuss credit ratings in Chapter 16.) For example, for corporate bonds, investment-grade (i.e., high credit quality) corporate bonds and non-investment grade corporate bonds (i.e., speculative quality) are treated as two asset classes.

For non-U.S. stocks and bonds, the following are classified as asset classes: (1) developed market foreign stocks, (2) developed market foreign bonds, (3) emerging market foreign stocks, and (4) emerging market foreign bonds. The characteristics that market participants use to describe emerging markets is that the countries in this group:

- Have economies that are in transition but have started implementing political, economic, and financial market reforms in order to participate in the global capital market.
- May expose investors to significant price volatility attributable to political risk and the unstable value of their currency.
- Have a short period over which their financial markets have operated.

Loucks, Penicook, and Schillhorn (2008, 340) describe what is meant by an emerging market as follows:

> Emerging market issuers rely on international investors for capital. Emerging markets cannot finance their fiscal deficits domestically because domestic capital markets are poorly developed and local investors are unable or unwilling to lend to the government. Although emerging market issuers differ greatly in terms of credit risk, dependence on foreign capital is the most basic characteristic of the asset class.

With the exception of real estate, all of the asset classes we have identified above are referred to as *traditional asset classes*. Real estate and all other asset classes that are not in the above list are referred to as *nontraditional asset classes* or *alternative asset classes*. They include hedge funds, private equity, and commodities, all of which we describe in Chapter 26.

Along with the designation of asset classes comes a barometer to be able to quantify the performance of the asset class—the risk, return, and the correlation of the return of the asset class with that of another asset class. The barometer is called a "benchmark index," "market index," or simply "index." An example would be the Standard & Poor's 500. We describe many more indexes in later chapters. The indexes are also used by investors to evaluate the performance of professional managers that they hire to manage their assets.

Investment Constraints

In the development of an investment policy, the following factors must be considered:

- Client constraints
- Regulatory constraints
- Tax considerations

Client-Imposed Constraints

Examples of client-imposed constraints would be restrictions that specify the types of securities in which a manager may invest and concentration limits on how much or little may be invested in a particular asset class or in a particular issuer. Where the objective is to meet the performance of a particular market or customized benchmark, there may be a restriction as to the degree to which the manager may deviate from some key characteristics of the benchmark.

For example, throughout this book we will discuss certain portfolio risk measures that are used to quantify different types of risk. The three major examples are tracking error risk for any type of asset class and market risk as measured by beta for a common stock portfolio and duration for a bond portfolio. These portfolio risk measures provide an estimate of the exposure of a portfolio to changes in key factors that affect the portfolio's performance—the market overall in the case of a portfolio's beta and the general level of interest rates in the case of a portfolio's duration.

Typically, a client will not set a specific value for the level of risk exposure. Instead, the client restriction may be in the form of a maximum on the level of the risk exposure or a permissible range for the risk measure relative to the benchmark. For example, a client may restrict the portfolio's duration to be +0.5 or –0.5 of the client-specified benchmark. Thus, if the duration of the client-imposed benchmark is 4, the manager has the discretion of constructing a portfolio with a duration between 3.5 and 4.5.

Regulatory Constraints

There are many types of regulatory constraints. These involve constraints on the asset classes that are permissible and concentration limits on investments. Moreover, in making the asset allocation decision, consideration must be given to any risk-based capital requirements. For depository institutions and insurance companies, the amount of statutory capital required is related to the quality of the assets in which the institution has invested. For example, for regulated investment management companies, there are restrictions on the amount of leverage that can be used.

Tax Considerations

Tax considerations are important for several reasons. First, certain institutional investors such as pension funds, endowments, and foundations are exempt from federal income taxation. Consequently, the asset classes in which they invest will not be those that are tax-advantaged investments.

Second, there are tax factors that must be incorporated into the investment policy. For example, while a pension fund might be tax-exempt, there may be certain assets or the use of some investment vehicles in which it invests whose earnings may be taxed.

SELECTING A PORTFOLIO STRATEGY

Selecting a portfolio strategy that is consistent with the investment objectives and investment policy guidelines of the client or institution is another major activity in the investment management process. Portfolio strategies can be classified as either active or passive.

An *active portfolio strategy* uses available information and forecasting techniques to seek a better performance than a portfolio that is simply diversified broadly. Essential to all active strategies are expectations about the factors that have been found to influence the performance of an asset class. For example, with active common stock strategies this may include forecasts of future earnings, dividends, or price/earnings ratios. With bond portfolios that are actively managed, expectations may involve forecasts of future interest rates and sector spreads. Active portfolio strategies involving foreign securities may require forecasts of local interest rates and exchange rates.

A *passive portfolio strategy* involves minimal expectational input, and instead relies on diversification to match the performance of some market index. In effect, a passive strategy assumes that the marketplace will efficiently reflect all available information in the price paid for securities. Between these extremes of active and passive strategies, several strategies have sprung up that have elements of both. For example, the core of a portfolio may be passively managed with the balance actively managed.

A useful way of thinking about active versus passive management is in terms of the following three activities performed by the manager: (1) portfolio construction (deciding on the stocks to buy and sell), (2) trading of securities, and (3) portfolio monitoring. Generally, active managers devote the majority of their time to portfolio construction. In contrast, with passive strategies managers devote less time to this activity.

In the bond area, there are several strategies classified as *structured portfolio strategies* that are a type of liability-driven strategy. A structured portfolio strategy is one in which a portfolio is designed to achieve the performance of some predetermined liabilities that must be paid out. These strategies are frequently used when trying to match the funds received from an investment portfolio to the future liabilities that must be paid and are therefore referred to as *liability-driven strategies*.

Given the choice among active and passive management, which should be selected? The answer depends on (1) the client's or money manager's view of how "price efficient" the market is, (2) the client's risk tolerance, and (3) the nature of the client's liabilities. By marketplace price efficiency, we mean how difficult it would be to earn a greater return than passive management after adjusting for the risk associated with a strategy and the transaction costs associated with implementing that strategy. In our discussion of secondary markets in Chapter 7, we will discuss the different forms of market efficiency.

CONSTRUCTING AND MONITORING THE PORTFOLIO

Once a portfolio strategy is selected, the investment manager must select the assets to be included in the portfolio. The following are involved in this major activity of the investment management process:

- Producing realistic and reasonable return expectations and forecasts
- Constructing an efficient portfolio
- Monitoring, controlling, and managing risk exposure
- Managing trading and transaction costs

In seeking to produce realistic and reasonable return expectations, the investment manager has several tools available that we describe in this book. An active portfolio manager will seek to identify mispriced securities or market sectors. This information is then used as inputs to construct an *efficient portfolio*. An efficient portfolio is defined as a portfolio that offers the greatest expected return for a given level of risk or, equivalently, the lowest risk for a given expected return. The specific meaning of return and risk cannot be provided at this time. As we develop our understanding of investment management throughout this book, we will be able to quantify what we mean by these terms.

Once a portfolio is constructed, the investment manager must monitor the portfolio to determine how the portfolio's risk exposure may have changed given prevailing market conditions and information about the assets in the portfolio. The current portfolio may no longer be efficient and, as a result, the investment manager is likely to rebalance the portfolio in order to produce an efficient portfolio.

Transaction costs critically impact performance and we discuss them in Chapter 12. They must be considered not only in the initial construction of the portfolio but when the portfolio must be rebalanced.

MEASURING AND EVALUATING PERFORMANCE

The measurement and evaluation of investment performance involves two activities. The first activity is performance measurement, which involves properly calculating the return realized by an investment manager over some time interval referred to as the *evaluation period*. It may seem that this would be a straightforward calculation, but, as we will see in Chapter 7, there are several important issues that must be addressed in developing a methodology for calculating a portfolio's return. Different methodologies can lead to quite disparate results, making it difficult to compare the relative performance of different investment managers.

The second activity is performance evaluation which is concerned with two issues: (1) determining whether the investment manager added value by outperforming the established benchmark and (2) determining how the investment manager achieved the calculated return. For example, in Part Two of this book we describe several strategies the manager of a stock portfolio can employ. Did the investment manager achieve the return by market timing, by buying undervalued stocks, by buying low-capitalization stocks, by overweighting specific industries, and so on? The decomposition of the performance results to explain the reasons why those results were achieved is called *performance attribution analysis*. Moreover, performance evaluation requires the determination of whether the asset manager achieved superior performance (i.e., added value) by skill or by luck.

REFERENCES

Arnott, R. D., and F. J. Fabozzi. 1992. The many dimensions of the asset allocation decision. In *Active asset allocation*, edited by R. Arnott and F. J. Fabozzi. Chicago: Probus Publishing.

Kritzman, M. 1999. Toward defining an asset class. *Journal of Alternative Investments* 2, no. 1: 79–82.

Mednikov Loucks, M., J. A. Penicook, and U. Schillhorn. 2008. Emerging markets debt. In *The handbook of finance*, vol. 1, edited by F. J. Fabozzi (pp. 339–346). Hoboken, NJ: John Wiley & Sons.

Part One

Portfolio Theory and Asset Pricing

CHAPTER 2

Theory of Portfolio Selection

In the four chapters that comprise Part One, we set forth theories that are the underpinnings for the management of portfolios: portfolio theory and capital market theory. Portfolio theory deals with the selection of portfolios that maximize expected returns consistent with individually acceptable levels of risk. Using quantitative models and historical data, portfolio theory defines "expected portfolio returns" and "acceptable levels of portfolio risk," and shows how to construct an optimal portfolio. Capital market theory deals with the effects of investor decisions on security prices. More specifically, it shows the relationship that should exist between security returns and risk if investors constructed portfolios as indicated by portfolio theory. Together, portfolio and capital market theories provide a framework to specify and measure investment risk and to develop relationships between expected security return and risk (and hence between risk and required return on an investment). Moreover, these theories provide a framework for measuring the performance of managed portfolios.

The goal of portfolio selection is the construction of portfolios that maximize expected returns consistent with individually acceptable levels of risk. Using both historical data and investor expectations of future returns, portfolio selection uses modeling techniques to quantify "expected portfolio returns" and "acceptable levels of portfolio risk," and provides methods to select an optimal portfolio. The theory allows investment managers to quantify the investment risk and expected return of a portfolio, providing a scientific and objective complement to the subjective art of investment management. More importantly, whereas at one time the focus of portfolio management used to be the risk of individual assets, the theory of portfolio selection has shifted the focus to the risk of the entire portfolio. This theory shows that it is possible to combine risky assets and produce a portfolio whose expected return reflects its components, but with the potential for

---

This chapter is coauthored with Francis Gupta and Harry M. Markowitz.

considerably lower risk. In other words, it is possible to construct a portfolio whose risk is smaller than the sum of all its individual parts.

In this chapter, we present the theory of portfolio selection as formulated by Markowitz (1952). This theory is also referred to as *mean-variance portfolio analysis* or simply *mean-variance analysis*.

SOME BASIC CONCEPTS

Portfolio theory draws on concepts from two fields: financial economic theory and probability and statistical theory. This section presents the concepts from financial economic theory we use in portfolio theory. While many of the concepts presented here have a more technical or rigorous definition, the purpose is to keep the explanations simple and intuitive so the reader can appreciate the importance and contribution of these concepts to the development of modern portfolio theory.

Utility Function and Indifference Curves

In life there are many situations where entities (i.e., individuals and firms) face two or more choices. The economic "theory of choice" uses the concept of a utility function developed by von Neuman and Morgenstern (1944), to describe the way entities make decisions when faced with a set of choices. A *utility function* assigns a (numeric) value to all possible choices faced by the entity. The higher the value of a particular choice, the greater the utility derived from that choice. The choice that is selected is the one that results in the maximum utility given a set of (budget) constraints faced by the entity.

In portfolio theory too, entities are faced with a set of choices. Different portfolios have different levels of expected return and risk. Also, the higher the level of expected return, the larger the risk. Entities are faced with the decision of choosing a portfolio from the set of all possible risk-return combinations: where return is a desirable that increases the level of utility, and risk is an undesirable that decreases the level of utility. Therefore, entities obtain different levels of utility from different risk-return combinations. The utility obtained from any possible risk-return combination is expressed by the utility function. Put simply, the utility function expresses the preferences of entities over perceived risk and expected return combinations.

A utility function can be expressed in graphical form by a set of indifference curves. Figure 2.1 shows indifference curves labeled u_1, u_2, and u_3. By convention, the horizontal axis measures risk and the vertical axis measures expected return. Each curve represents a set of portfolios with different combinations of risk and return. All the points on a given indifference curve

Theory of Portfolio Selection

FIGURE 2.1 Indifference Curves

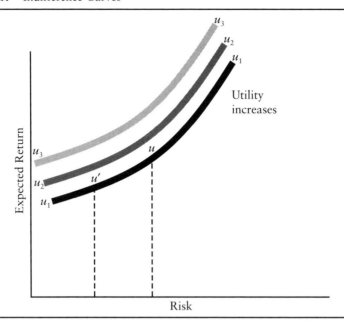

indicate combinations of risk and expected return that will give the same level of utility to a given investor. For example, on utility curve u_1, there are two points u and u', with u having a higher expected return than u', but also having a higher risk. Because the two points lie on the same indifference curve, the investor has an equal preference for (or is indifferent to) the two points, or, for that matter, any point on the curve. The (positive) slope of an indifference curve reflects the fact that, to obtain the same level of utility, the investor requires a higher expected return in order to accept higher risk.

For the three indifference curves shown in Figure 2.1, the utility the investor receives is greater the further the indifference curve is from the horizontal axis, because that curve represents a higher level of return at every level of risk. Thus, for the three indifference curves shown in the exhibit, u_3 has the highest utility and u_1 the lowest.

The Set of Efficient Portfolios and the Optimal Portfolio

Portfolios that provide the largest possible expected return for given levels of risk are called *efficient portfolios*. To construct an efficient portfolio, it is necessary to make some assumption about how investors behave when making investment decisions. One reasonable assumption is that investors are *risk averse*. A risk-averse investor is an investor who, when faced with choosing between two investments with the same expected return but two different risks, prefers the one with the lower risk.

In selecting portfolios, an investor seeks to maximize the expected portfolio return given his tolerance for risk. Alternatively stated, an investor seeks to minimize the risk that he is exposed to given some target expected return. Given a choice from the set of efficient portfolios, an *optimal portfolio* is the one that is most preferred by the investor.

Risky Assets vs. Risk-Free Assets

A risky asset is one for which the return that will be realized in the future is uncertain. For example, an investor who purchases the stock of Pfizer Corporation today with the intention of holding it for some finite time does not know what return will be realized at the end of the holding period. The return will depend on the price of Pfizer's stock at the time of sale and on the dividends that the company pays during the holding period. Thus, Pfizer stock, and indeed the stock of all companies, is a risky asset.

Securities issued by the U.S. government are also risky. For example, an investor who purchases a U.S. government bond that matures in 30 years does not know the return that will be realized if this bond is held for only one year. This is because changes in interest rates in that year will affect the price of the bond one year from now and that will affect the return on the bond over that year.

There are assets, however, for which the return that will be realized in the future is known with certainty today. Such assets are referred to as *risk-free* or *riskless assets*. The risk-free asset is commonly defined as a short-term obligation of the U.S. government. For example, if an investor buys a U.S. government security that matures in one year and plans to hold that security for one year, then there is no uncertainty about the return that will be realized.[1] The investor knows that in one year, the maturity date of the security, the government will pay a specific amount to retire the debt. Notice how this situation differs for the U.S. government security that matures in 30 years. Whereas the 1-year and the 30-year securities are obligations of the U.S. government, the former matures in one year so that there is no uncertainty about the return that will be realized. In contrast, while the investor knows what the government will pay at the end of 30 years for the 30-year bond, he does not know what the price of the bond will be one year from now.

---

[1] Here "return" refers to the nominal return. The "real" return, which adjusts for inflation, is uncertain.

MEASURING A PORTFOLIO'S EXPECTED RETURN

We are now ready to define and measure the actual and expected return of a risky asset and a portfolio of risky assets.

Measuring Single-Period Portfolio Return

The actual return on a portfolio of assets over some specific time period is a weighted average of the returns on the individual assets in the portfolio, and is straightforward to calculate using the following:

$$R_p = w_1 R_1 + w_2 R_2 + \ldots + w_G R_G \tag{2.1}$$

where

R_p = rate of return on the portfolio over the period
R_g = rate of return on asset g over the period
w_g = weight of asset g in the portfolio (i.e., market value of asset g as a proportion of the market value of the total portfolio) at the beginning of the period
G = number of assets in the portfolio

In shorthand notation, equation (2.1) can be expressed as follows:

$$R_p + \sum_{g=1}^{G} w_g R_g \tag{2.2}$$

Equation (2.2) states that the return on a portfolio (R_p) of G assets is equal to the sum over all of the product of the individual assets' weights in the portfolio and their respective return. The portfolio return R_p is sometimes called the *holding period return* or the ex post return.

For example, consider the following portfolio consisting of three assets:

Asset	Market Value at the Beginning of Holding Period	Rate of Return over Holding Period
1	$6 million	12%
2	8 million	10%
3	11 million	5%

The portfolio's total market value at the beginning of the holding period is $25 million. Therefore,

w_1 = \$6 million/\$25 million = 0.24, or 24% and R_1 = 12%
w_2 = \$8 million/\$25 million = 0.32, or 32% and R_2 = 10%
w_3 = \$11 million/\$25 million = 0.44, or 44% and R_3 = 5%

Notice that the sum of the weights is equal to 1. Substituting into equation (2.1), we get the holding period portfolio return,

$$R_p = 0.24(12\%) + 0.32(10\%) + 0.44(5\%) = 8.28\%$$

Note that since the holding period portfolio return is 8.28%, the growth in the portfolio's value over the holding period is given by (\$25 million) × 0.0828 = \$2.07 million.

The Expected Return of a Portfolio of Risky Assets

Equation (2.1) shows how to calculate the actual return of a portfolio over some specific time period. In portfolio management, the investor also wants to know the expected (or anticipated) return from a portfolio of risky assets. The expected portfolio return is the weighted average of the expected return of each asset in the portfolio. The weight assigned to the expected return of each asset is the percentage of the market value of the asset to the total market value of the portfolio. That is,

$$E(R_p) = w_1 E(R_1) + w_2 E(R_2) + \ldots + w_G E(R_G) \qquad (2.3)$$

The $E(\ )$ signifies expectations, and $E(R_p)$ is sometimes called the *ex ante return*, or the expected portfolio return over some specific time period.

The expected return, $E(R_i)$, on a risky asset i is calculated as follows. First, a probability distribution for the possible rates of return that can be realized must be specified. A probability distribution is a function that assigns a probability of occurrence to all possible outcomes for a random variable. Given the probability distribution, the expected value of a random variable is simply the weighted average of the possible outcomes, where the weight is the probability associated with the possible outcome.

In our case, the random variable is the uncertain return of asset i. Having specified a probability distribution for the possible rates of return, the expected value of the rate of return for asset i is the weighted average of the possible outcomes. Finally, rather than use the term "expected value of the return of an asset," we simply use the term "expected return." Mathematically, the expected return of asset i is expressed as:

$$E(R_i) = p_1 R_1 + p_2 R_2 + \ldots + p_N R_N \qquad (2.4)$$

TABLE 2.1 Probability Distribution for the Rate of Return for Stock XYZ

n	Rate of Return	Probability of Occurrence
1	12%	0.18
2	10	0.24
3	8	0.29
4	4	0.16
5	–4	0.13
Total		1.00

where

R_n = the nth possible rate of return for asset i
p_n = the probability of attaining the rate of return n for asset i
N = the number of possible outcomes for the rate of return

How do we specify the probability distribution of returns for an asset? We shall see later on in this chapter that in most cases the probability distribution of returns is based on historical returns. Probabilities assigned to different return outcomes that are based on the past performance of an uncertain investment act as a good estimate of the probability distribution. However, for purpose of illustration, assume that an investor is considering an investment, Asset XYZ, which has a probability distribution for the rate of return for some time period as given in Table 2.1. The asset has five possible rates of return and the probability distribution specifies the likelihood of occurrence (in a probabilistic sense) for each of the possible outcomes.

Substituting into equation (2.4) we get

$$E(R_{XYZ}) = 0.18(12\%) + 0.24(10\%) + 0.29(8\%) + 0.16(4\%) + 0.13(-4\%)$$
$$= 7\%$$

Thus, 7% is the expected return or mean of the probability distribution for the rate of return on asset XYZ.

MEASURING PORTFOLIO RISK

The dictionary defines risk as "hazard, peril, exposure to loss or injury." With respect to investments, investors have used a variety of definitions to describe risk. Markowitz (1952, 1959) quantified the concept of risk using the well-known statistical measures of variances and covariances. He defined the risk of a portfolio as the sum of the variances of the investments and covariances among the investments. The notion of introducing the covariances among returns of the investments in the portfolio to measure the risk of a portfolio forever changed how the investment community thought about the concept of risk.

Variance and Standard Deviation as a Measure of Risk

The variance of a random variable is a measure of the dispersion or variability of the possible outcomes around the expected value (mean). In the case of an asset's return, the variance is a measure of the dispersion of the possible rate of return outcomes around the expected return.

The equation for the variance of the expected return for asset i, denoted $\sigma^2(R_i)$, is

$$\sigma^2(R_i) = p_1[r_1 - E(R_i)]^2 + p_2[r_2 - E(R_i)]^2 + \ldots + p_N[r_N - E(R_i)]^2$$

or

$$\sigma^2(R_i) = \sum_{i=1}^{N} p_n[r_n - E(R_i)]^2 \qquad (2.5)$$

Using the probability distribution of the return for asset XYZ, we can illustrate the calculation of the variance:

$$\sigma^2(R_{XYZ}) = 0.18(12\% - 7\%)^2 + 0.24(10\% - 7\%)^2 + 0.29(8\% - 7\%)^2$$
$$+ 0.16(4\% - 7\%)^2 + 0.13(-4\% - 7\%)^2$$
$$= 24.1\%$$

The variance associated with a distribution of returns measures the compactness with which the distribution is clustered around the mean or expected return. Markowitz argued that this compactness or variance is equivalent to the uncertainty or riskiness of the investment. If an asset is riskless, it has an expected return dispersion of zero. In other words, the return (which is also the expected return in this case) is certain, or guaranteed.

Standard Deviation

Since the variance is squared units, it is common to see the variance converted to the standard deviation (σ) by taking the positive square root of the variance:

$$\sigma(R_i) = \sqrt{\sigma^2(R_i)}$$

For asset XYZ, then, the standard deviation is

$$\sigma(R_{XYZ}) = \sqrt{24.1\%} = 4.9\%$$

The variance and standard deviation are conceptually equivalent; that is, the larger the variance or standard deviation, the greater the investment risk.

There are two criticisms of the use of the variance as a measure of risk. The first criticism is that because the variance measures the dispersion of an asset's return around its expected return, it treats both the returns above and below the expected return identically. There has been research in the area of behavioral finance to suggest that investors do not view return outcomes above the expected return in the same way as they view returns below the expected return. Whereas returns above the expected return are considered favorable, outcomes below the expected return are disliked. Because of this, some researchers have argued that measures of risk should not consider the possible return outcomes above the expected return.

Markowitz recognized this limitation and, in fact, suggested a measure of downside risk—the risk of realizing an outcome below the expected return—called the *semivariance*. The semivariance is similar to the variance except that in the calculation no consideration is given to returns above the expected return. However, because of the computational problems with using the semivariance and the limited resources available to him at the time, he used the variance in developing portfolio theory.

Today, practitioners use various measures of downside risk. However, regardless of the measure used, the basic principles of portfolio theory developed by Markowitz and set forth in this chapter are still applicable. That is, the choice of the measure of risk may affect the calculation but doesn't invalidate the theory. This is discussed further in Chapter 4.

The second criticism is that the variance is only one measure of how the returns vary around the expected return. When a probability distribution is not symmetrical around its expected return, a statistical measure of the skewness of a distribution should be used in addition to the variance. This is discussed further in Chapter 4.[2]

Because expected return and variance are the only two parameters that investors are assumed to consider in making investment decisions, the Markowitz formulation of portfolio theory is often referred to as a *two-parameter model*. It is also referred to as *mean-variance analysis*. There have been models that propose including additional measures of a return distribution into the portfolio selection model.[3]

---

[2]See Ortobelli et al. (2005).
[3]See Fabozzi, Forcardi, and Kolm (2007) for a discussion of these models.

Measuring the Portfolio Risk of a Two-Asset Portfolio

In equation (2.5), we provide the variance for an individual asset's return. The variance of a portfolio consisting of two assets is a little more difficult to calculate. It depends not only on the variance of the two assets, but also upon how closely the returns of one asset track those of the other asset. The formula is

$$\sigma^2(R_p) = \sigma^2(R_i) + \sigma^2(R_j) + 2w_i w_j \operatorname{cov}(R_i, R_j) \qquad (2.6)$$

where

$\operatorname{cov}(R_i, R_j)$ = covariance between the return for assets i and j

In words, equation (2.6) states that the variance of the portfolio return is the sum of the squared weighted variances of the two assets plus two times the weighted covariance between the two assets. We will see that this equation can be generalized to the case where there are more than two assets in the portfolio.

Covariance

Like the variance, the covariance has a precise mathematical translation. Its practical meaning is the degree to which the returns on two assets covary or change together. In fact, the covariance is just a generalized concept of the variance applied to multiple assets. A positive covariance between two assets means that the returns on two assets tend to move or change in the same direction, while a negative covariance means the returns tend to move in opposite directions. The covariance between any two assets i and j is computed using the following formula:

$$\operatorname{cov}(R_i, R_j) = p_1[r_{i1} - E(R_i)][r_{j1} - E(R_j)] + p_2[r_{i2} - E(R_i)][r_{j2} - E(R_j)] \\ + \cdots + p_N[r_{iN} - E(R_i)][r_{jN} - E(R_j)] \qquad (2.7)$$

where

r_{in} = the nth possible rate of return for asset i
r_{jn} = the nth possible rate of return for asset j
p_n = the probability of attaining the rate of return n for assets i and j
N = the number of possible outcomes for the rate of return.

The covariance between asset i and i is just the variance of asset i.

Theory of Portfolio Selection

TABLE 2.2 Probability Distribution for the Rate of Return for Asset XYZ and Asset ABC

n	Rate of Return for Asset XYZ	Rate of Return for Asset ABC	Probability of Occurrence
1	12%	21%	0.18
2	10	14	0.24
3	8	9	0.29
4	4	4	0.16
5	−4	−3	0.13
Total			1.00
Expected return	7.0%	10.0%	
Variance	24.1%	53.6%	
Standard deviation	4.9%	7.3%	

To illustrate the calculation of the covariance between two assets, we use the two assets in Table 2.2. The first is asset XYZ from Table 2.1 that we used earlier to illustrate the calculation of the expected return and the standard deviation. The other hypothetical asset is ABC whose data are shown in Table 2.2. Substituting the data for the two assets from Table 2.2 in equation (2.7), the covariance between assets XYZ and ABC is calculated as follows:

$$\text{cov}(R_{XYZ,ABC}) = 0.18(12\% - 7\%)(21\% - 10\%) + 0.24(10\% - 7\%)(14\% - 10\%)$$
$$+ 0.29(8\% - 7\%)(9\% - 10\%) + 0.16(4\% - 7\%)(4\% - 10\%)$$
$$+ 0.13(-4\% - 7\%)(-3\% - 10\%)$$
$$= 34$$

Relationship between Covariance and Correlation

The *correlation* is analogous to the *covariance* between the expected returns for two assets. Specifically, the correlation between the returns for assets i and j is defined as the covariance of the two assets divided by the product of their standard deviations:

$$\text{cor}(R_i, R_j) = \text{cov}(R_i, R_j) / [\sigma(R_i)\sigma(R_j)] \qquad (2.8)$$

The correlation and the covariance are conceptually equivalent terms. Dividing the covariance between the returns of two assets by the product of their standard deviations results in the correlation between the returns of the two assets. Because the correlation is a standardized number (i.e., it has been corrected for differences in the standard deviation of the returns), the correlation is comparable across different assets. The correlation between the returns for asset XYZ and asset ABC is

$$\text{cor}(R_{XYZ}, R_{ABC}) = 34/(4.9 \times 7.3) = 0.94$$

The correlation coefficient can have values ranging from +1.0, denoting perfect comovement in the same direction, to −1.0, denoting perfect comovement in the opposite direction. Because the standard deviations are always positive, the correlation can only be negative if the covariance is a negative number. A correlation of zero implies that the returns are uncorrelated. Finally, though causality implies correlation, correlation does not imply causality.

Measuring the Risk of a Portfolio Comprised of More than Two Assets

So far we have defined the risk of a portfolio consisting of two assets. The extension to three assets—i, j, and k—is as follows:

$$\sigma^2(R_p) = w_i^2 \sigma^2(R_i) + w_j^2 \sigma^2(R_j) + w_k^2 \sigma^2(R_k) \\ + 2w_i w_j \text{cov}(R_i, R_j) + 2w_i w_k \text{cov}(R_i, R_k) + 2w_j w_k \text{cov}(R_j, R_k) \quad (2.9)$$

In words, equation (2.9) states that the variance of the portfolio return is the sum of the squared weighted variances of the individual assets plus two times the sum of the weighted pairwise covariances of the assets. In general, for a portfolio with G assets, the portfolio variance is given by,

$$\sigma^2(R_p) = \sum_{g=1}^{G} \sum_{h=1}^{G} w_g w_h \text{cov}(R_g, R_h) \quad (2.10)$$

In (2.10), the terms for which $h = g$ results in the variances of the G assets, and the terms for which $h \neq g$ results in all possible pairwise covariances amongst the G assets. Therefore, (2.10) is a shorthand notation for the sum of all G variances and the possible covariances amongst the G assets.

PORTFOLIO DIVERSIFICATION

Often, one hears investors talking about diversifying their portfolio. An investor who diversifies constructs a portfolio in such a way as to reduce portfolio risk without sacrificing return. This is certainly a goal that investors should seek. However, the question is how to do this in practice.

Some investors would say that including assets across all asset classes could diversify a portfolio. For example, an investor might argue that a portfolio should be diversified by investing in stocks, bonds, and real estate. While that might be reasonable, two questions must be addressed in order to construct a diversified portfolio. First, how much should be invested in each asset class? Should 40% of the portfolio be in stocks, 50% in bonds, and 10% in real estate, or is some other allocation more appropriate? Second, given the allocation, which specific stocks, bonds, and real estate should the investor select?

Some investors who focus only on one asset class such as common stock argue that these portfolios should also be diversified. By this they mean that an investor should not place all funds in the stock of one corporation, but rather should include stocks of many corporations. Here, too, several questions must be answered to construct a diversified portfolio. First, which corporations should be represented in the portfolio? Second, how much of the portfolio should be allocated to the stocks of each corporation?

Prior to the development of portfolio theory, while investors often talked about diversification in these general terms, they did not possess the analytical tools by which to answer the questions posed above. For example, in 1945, D. H. Leavens (1945) wrote:

> An examination of some fifty books and articles on investment that have appeared during the last quarter of a century shows that most of them refer to the desirability of diversification. The majority, however, discuss it in general terms and do not clearly indicate why it is desirable.

Leavens illustrated the benefits of diversification on the assumption that risks are independent. However, in the last paragraph of his article, he cautioned:

> The assumption, mentioned earlier, that each security is acted upon by independent causes, is important, although it cannot always be fully met in practice. Diversification among companies in one industry cannot protect against unfavorable factors that may affect the whole industry; additional diversification among industries is needed for that purpose. Nor can diversification among industries protect against cyclical factors that may depress all industries at the same time.

A major contribution of the theory of portfolio selection is that by using the concepts discussed above, we can provide a quantitative measure of the diversification of a portfolio, and it is this measure that we can use to achieve the maximum diversification benefits.

The Markowitz diversification strategy is primarily concerned with the degree of covariance between asset returns in a portfolio. Indeed a key contribution of Markowitz diversification is the formulation of an asset's risk in terms of a portfolio of assets, rather than in isolation. Markowitz diversification seeks to combine assets in a portfolio with returns that are less than perfectly positively correlated, in an effort to lower portfolio risk (variance) without sacrificing return. It is the concern for maintaining return while lowering risk through an analysis of the covariance between asset returns, that separates Markowitz diversification from a naive approach to diversification and makes it more effective.

Markowitz diversification and the importance of asset correlations can be illustrated with a simple two-asset portfolio example. To do this, we will first show the general relationship between the risk of a two-asset portfolio and the correlation of returns of the component assets. Then we will look at the effects on portfolio risk of combining assets with different correlations.

Portfolio Risk and Correlation

In our two-asset portfolio, assume that asset C and asset D are available with expected returns and standard deviations as shown:

Asset	E(R)	σ(R)
Asset C	12%	30%
Asset D	18%	40%

If an equal 50% weighting is assigned to both assets C and D, the expected portfolio return can be calculated as shown:

$$E(R_p) = 0.50(12\%) + 0.50(18\%) = 15\%$$

The variance of the return on the two-asset portfolio from equation (2.6) is

$$\sigma^2(R_p) = w_C^2 \sigma^2(R_C) + w_D^2 \sigma^2(R_D) + 2w_C w_D \text{cov}(R_C, R_D)$$
$$= (0.5)^2 (30\%)^2 + (0.5)^2 (40\%)^2 + 2(0.5)(0.5)\text{cov}(R_C, R_D)$$

From equation (2.8),

$$\text{cor}(R_C, R_D) = \text{cov}(R_C, R_D)/[\sigma(R_C)\sigma(R_D)]$$

so

$$\text{cov}(R_C, R_D) = \sigma(R_C)\sigma(R_D)\text{cor}(R_C, R_D)$$

Since $\sigma(R_C) = 30\%$ and $\sigma(R_D) = 40\%$, then

$$\text{cov}(R_C, R_D) = (30\%)(40\%)\,\text{cor}(R_C, R_D)$$

Substituting into the expression for $\sigma^2(R_p)$, we get

$$\sigma^2(R_p) = (0.5)^2(30\%)^2 + (0.5)^2(40\%)^2 + 2(0.5)(0.5)(30\%)(40\%)\text{cor}(R_C, R_D)$$

Taking the square root of the variance gives

$$\begin{aligned}\sigma(R_p) &= \sqrt{(0.5)^2(30\%)^2 + (0.5)^2(40\%)^2 + 2(0.5)(0.5)(30\%)(40\%)\text{cov}(R_C, R_D)} \\ &= \sqrt{625 + (600)\text{cor}(R_C, R_D)}\end{aligned} \quad (2.11)$$

The Effect of the Correlation of Asset Returns on Portfolio Risk

How would the risk change for our two-asset portfolio with different correlations between the returns of the component assets? Let's consider the following three cases for $\text{cor}(R_C, R_D)$: +1.0, 0, and –1.0. Substituting into equation (2.11) for these three cases of $\text{cor}(R_C, R_D)$, we get:

$\text{cor}(R_C, R_D)$	$E(R_p)$	$\sigma(R_p)$
+1.0	15%	35%
0.0	15	25
–1.0	15	5

As the correlation between the expected returns on assets C and D decreases from +1.0 to 0.0 to –1.0, the standard deviation of the expected portfolio return also decreases from 35% to 5%. However, the expected portfolio return remains 15% for each case.

This example clearly illustrates the effect of Markowitz diversification. The principle of Markowitz diversification states that as the correlation (covariance) between the returns for assets that are combined in a portfolio decreases, so does the variance (hence the standard deviation) of the return for the portfolio. This is due to the degree of correlation between the expected asset returns.

The good news is that investors can maintain expected portfolio return and lower portfolio risk by combining assets with lower (and preferably negative) correlations. However, the bad news is that very few assets have small to negative correlations with other assets! The problem, then, becomes one of searching among large numbers of assets in an effort to discover the portfolio with the minimum risk at a given level of expected return or, equivalently, the highest expected return at a given level of risk.

The stage is now set for a discussion of efficient portfolios and their construction.

CHOOSING A PORTFOLIO OF RISKY ASSETS

Diversification in the manner suggested by Professor Markowitz leads to the construction of portfolios that have the highest expected return at a given level of risk. Such portfolios are called *efficient portfolios*. In order to construct efficient portfolios, the theory makes some basic assumptions about asset selection behavior by the entities. The assumptions are as follows:

Assumption 1: The only two parameters that affect an investor's decision are the expected return and the variance. (That is, investors make decisions using the two-parameter model formulated by Markowitz.)

Assumption 2: Investors are risk averse. (That is, when faced with two investments with the same expected return but two different risks, investors will prefer the one with the lower risk.)

Assumption 3: All investors seek to achieve the highest expected return at a given level of risk.

Assumption 4: All investors have the same expectations regarding expected return, variance, and covariances for all risky assets. (This is referred to as the *homogeneous expectations assumption*.)

Assumption 5: All investors have a common one-period investment horizon.

Constructing Efficient Portfolios

The technique of constructing efficient portfolios from large groups of assets requires a massive number of calculations. In a portfolio of G securities, there are $(G^2 - G)/2$ unique covariances to calculate. Hence, for a portfolio of just 50 securities, there are 1,224 covariances that must be calculated. For 100 securities, there are 4,950. Furthermore, in order to solve for the portfolio that minimizes risk for each level of return, a mathematical technique called *quadratic programming* must be used. A

TABLE 2.3 Portfolio Expected Returns and Standard Deviations for Five Mixes of Assets C and D

Portfolio	Proportion of Asset C	Proportion of Asset D	$E(R_p)$	$\sigma(R_p)$
1	100%	0%	12.0%	30.0%
2	75	25	13.5%	19.5%
3	50	50	15.0%	18.0%
4	25	75	16.5%	27.0%
5	0	100	18.0%	40.0%

Asset C: $E(R_C) = 12\%$, $\sigma(R_C) = 30\%$
Asset D: $E(R_D) = 18\%$, and $\sigma(R_D) = 40\%$
Correlation between Asset C and D = $cor(R_C, R_D) = -0.5$

discussion of this technique is beyond the scope of this chapter. However, it is possible to illustrate the general idea of the construction of efficient portfolios by referring again to the simple two-asset portfolio consisting of assets C and D.

Recall that for two assets, C and D, $E(R_C) = 12\%$, $\sigma(R_C) = 30\%$, $E(R_D) = 18\%$, and $\sigma(R_D) = 40\%$. We now further assume that $cor(R_C, R_D) = -0.5$. Table 2.3 presents the expected portfolio return and standard deviation for five different portfolios made up of varying proportions of C and D.

Feasible and Efficient Portfolios

A *feasible portfolio* is any portfolio that an investor can construct given the assets available. The five portfolios presented in Table 2.3 are all feasible portfolios. The collection of all feasible portfolios is called the *feasible set of portfolios*. With only two assets, the feasible set of portfolios is graphed as a curve that represents those combinations of risk and expected return that are attainable by constructing portfolios from all possible combinations of the two assets.

Figure 2.2 presents the feasible set of portfolios for all combinations of assets C and D. As mentioned earlier, the portfolio mixes listed in Table 2.3 belong to this set and are shown by the points 1 through 5, respectively. Starting from 1 and proceeding to 5, asset C goes from 100% to 0%, while asset D goes from 0% to 100%—therefore all possible combinations of C and D lie between portfolios 1 and 5, or on the curve labeled 1–5. In the case of two assets, any risk-return combination not lying on this curve is not attainable, since there is no mix of assets C and D that will result in that risk-return combination. Consequently, the curve 1–5 can also be thought of as the feasible set.

FIGURE 2.2 Feasible and Efficient Portfolios for Assets C and D

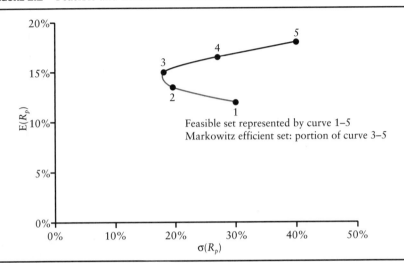

In contrast to a feasible portfolio, an *efficient portfolio* is one that gives the highest expected return of all feasible portfolios with the same risk. An efficient portfolio is also said to be a *mean-variance efficient portfolio*. Thus, for each level of risk there is an efficient portfolio. The collection of all efficient portfolios is called the *efficient set*.

The efficient set for the feasible set presented in Figure 2.2 is differentiated by the bold curve section 3–5. Efficient portfolios are the combinations of assets C and D that result in the risk-return combinations on the bold section of the curve. These portfolios offer the highest expected return at a given level of risk. Notice that two of our five portfolio mixes—portfolio 1 with $E(R_p) = 12\%$ and $\sigma(R_p) = 20\%$ and portfolio 2 with $E(R_p) = 13.5\%$ and $\sigma(R_p) = 19.5\%$—are not included in the efficient set. This is because there is at least one portfolio in the efficient set (for example, portfolio 3) that has a higher expected return and lower risk than both of them. We can also see that portfolio 4 has a higher expected return and lower risk than portfolio 1. In fact, the whole curve section 1–3 is not efficient. For any given risk-return combination on this curve section, there is a combination (on the curve section 3–5) that has the same risk and a higher return, or the same return and a lower risk, or both. In other words, for any portfolio that results in the return/risk combination on the curve section 1–3 (excluding portfolio 3), there exists a portfolio that dominates it by having the same return and lower risk, or the same risk and a higher return, or a lower risk and a higher return. For example, portfolio 4 dominates portfolio 1, and portfolio 3 dominates both portfolios 1 and 2.

FIGURE 2.3 Feasible and Efficient Portfolios with More Than Two Assets[a]

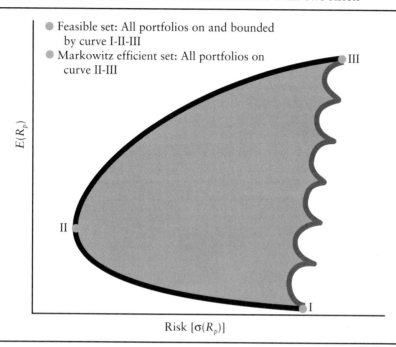

[a]The picture is for illustrative purposes only. The actual shape of the feasible region depends on the returns and risks of the assets chosen and the correlation among them.

Figure 2.3 shows the feasible and efficient sets when there are more than two assets. In this case, the feasible set is not a curve, but an area. This is because, unlike the two-asset case, it is possible to create asset portfolios that result in risk-return combinations that not only result in combinations that lie on the curve I–II–III, but all combinations that lie in the shaded area. However, the efficient set is given by the curve II–III. It is easily seen that all the portfolios on the efficient set dominate the portfolios in the shaded area.

The efficient set of portfolios is sometimes called the *efficient frontier*, because graphically all the efficient portfolios lie on the boundary of the set of feasible portfolios that have the maximum return for a given level of risk. Any risk-return combination above the efficient frontier cannot be achieved, while risk-return combinations of the portfolios that make up the efficient frontier dominate those that lie below the efficient frontier.

Choosing the Optimal Portfolio in the Efficient Set

Now that we have constructed the efficient set of portfolios, the next step is to determine the optimal portfolio.

Because all portfolios on the efficient frontier provide the greatest possible return at their level of risk, an investor or entity will want to hold one of the portfolios on the efficient frontier. Notice that the portfolios on the efficient frontier represent trade-offs in terms of risk and return. Moving from left to right on the efficient frontier, the risk increases, but so does the expected return. The question is which one of those portfolios should an investor hold? The best portfolio to hold of all those on the efficient frontier is the *optimal portfolio*.

Intuitively, the optimal portfolio should depend on the investor's preference over different risk-return trade-offs. As explained earlier, this preference can be expressed in terms of a utility function.

In Figure 2.4, three indifference curves representing a utility function and the efficient frontier are drawn on the same diagram. An indifference curve indicates the combinations of risk and expected return that give the same level of utility. Moreover, the farther the indifference curve from the horizontal axis, the higher the utility.

FIGURE 2.4 Selection of the Optimal Portfolio

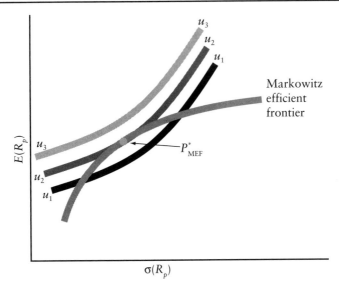

u_1, u_2, u_3 = indifference curves with $u_1 < u_2 < u_3$
P^*_{MEF} = optimal portfolio on Markowitz efficient frontier

Theory of Portfolio Selection

From Figure 2.4, it is possible to determine the optimal portfolio for the investor with the indifference curves shown. Remember that the investor wants to get to the highest indifference curve achievable given the efficient frontier. Given that requirement, the optimal portfolio is represented by the point where an indifference curve is tangent to the efficient frontier. In Figure 2.4, that is the portfolio P^*_{MEF}. For example, suppose that P^*_{MEF} corresponds to portfolio 4 in Figure 2.2. We know from Table 2.3 that this portfolio is made up of 25% of asset C and 75% of asset D, with an $E(R_p)$ = 16.5% and $\sigma(R_p)$ = 27.0%.

Consequently, for the investor's preferences over risk and return as determined by the shape of the indifference curves represented in Figure 2.4, and expectations for asset C and D inputs (returns and variance-covariance) represented in Table 2.2, portfolio 4 is the optimal portfolio because it maximizes the investor's utility. If this investor had a different preference for expected risk and return, there would have been a different optimal portfolio. For example, Figure 2.5 shows the same efficient frontier but three other indifference curves. In this case, the optimal portfolio is P^*_{MEF}, which has a lower expected return and risk than P^*_{MEF} in Figure 2.4. Similarly, if the investor had a different set of input expectations, the optimal portfolio would be different.

FIGURE 2.5 Selection of Optimal Portfolio with Different Indifference Curves (Utility Function)

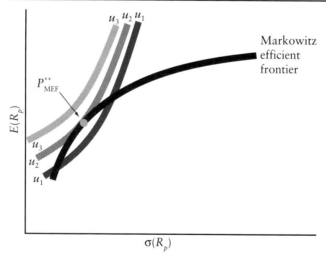

u_1, u_2, u_3 = indifference curves with $u_1 < u_2 < u_3$
P^*_{MEF} = optimal portfolio on Markowitz efficient frontier

At this point in our discussion, a natural question is how to estimate an investor's utility function so that the indifference curves can be determined. Unfortunately, there is little guidance about how to construct one. In general, economists have not been successful in estimating utility functions.

The inability to estimate utility functions does not mean that the theory is flawed. What it does mean is that once an investor constructs the efficient frontier, the investor will subjectively determine which efficient portfolio is appropriate given his or her tolerance to risk.

Adding Constraints

In our theoretical derivations above, we imposed no restrictions on the portfolio weights other than having them add up to one. In particular, we allowed the portfolio weights to take on both positive and negative values; that is, we did not restrict short selling. (As explained in Chapter 6, short selling involves the sale of assets not owned in anticipation of profiting from a decline in the value of that asset.) Nor did we impose constraints on the maximum or minimum allocation to an asset or asset class. As explained in the next chapter, in practice many portfolio managers do impose restrictions. For example, a portfolio manager may not be allowed to sell assets short. This could be client imposed as set forth in investment guidelines or legal reasons, or sometimes just because particular asset classes are difficult to sell short such as real estate. Portfolios that are restricted to only owning assets or asset classes and therefore do not allow selling short are called "long-only portfolios." When there is no restriction on short selling, a portfolio may contain long and short positions and is therefore referred to as a "long-short portfolio."[4]

INDEX MODEL'S APPROXIMATIONS TO THE COVARIANCE STRUCTURE

The inputs to mean-variance analysis include expected returns, variance of returns, and either covariance or correlation of returns between each pair of securities. For example, an analysis that allows 200 securities as possible candidates for portfolio selection requires 200 expected returns, 200 variances of return, and 19,900 correlations or covariances. An investment team tracking 200 securities may reasonably be expected to summarize their analyses in terms of 200 means and variances, but it is clearly unreasonable for them to produce 19,900 carefully considered correlations or covariances.

---

[4] For an explanation of how to deal with portfolios that can have both long and short positions, see Jacobs, Levy, and Starer (1999) and Jacobs, Levy, and Markowitz (2005).

It was clear to Markowitz that some kind of model of covariance structure was needed for the practical application of normative analysis to large portfolios. He did little more than point out the problem and suggest some possible models of covariance for research.

One model Markowitz proposed to explain the correlation structure among security returns assumed that the return on the ith security depends on an "underlying factor, the general prosperity of the market as expressed by some index." Mathematically, the relationship is expressed as follows (Markowitz (1959, pp. 96–101):

$$r_i = \alpha_i + \beta_i F + u_i \qquad (2.12)$$

where

r_i = the return on security i
F = value of some index
u_i = error term[5]

The expected value of u_i is zero and u_i is uncorrelated with F and every other u_j.

The parameters α_i and β_i are parameters to be estimated. When measured using regression analysis, β_i is the ratio of the covariance of asset i's return and F to the variance of F.

Markowitz further suggested that the relationship need not be linear and that there could be several underlying factors.

Single-Index Market Model

Sharpe (1963) tested equation (2.12) as an explanation of how security returns tend to go up and down together with general market index, F. For the index in the market model he used a market index for F. Specifically, Sharpe estimated using regression analysis the following model:

$$r_{it} = \alpha_i + \beta_i r_{mt} + u_{it} \qquad (2.13)$$

where

r_{it} = return on asset i over the period t
r_{mt} = return on the market index over the period t
α_i = a term that represents the nonmarket component of the return on asset i

---

[5]Note that Markowitz (1959) used the notation I in proposing the model given by equation (2.12).

β_i = the ratio of the covariance of the return of asset i and the return of the market index to the variance of the return of the market index

u_{it} = a zero mean random error term

The model given by equation (2.13) is called the *single-index market model* or simply the *market model*. It is important to note that when Markowitz discussed the possibility of using equation (2.12) to estimate the covariance structure, the index he suggested was not required to be a market index.

Suppose that the Dow Jones Wilshire 5000 is used to represent the market index, then for a portfolio of G assets regression analysis is used to estimate the values of the β's and α's. The beta of the portfolio (β_p), is simply a weighted average of the computed betas of the individual assets (β_i), where the weights are the percentage of the market value of the individual assets relative to the total market value of the portfolio. That is,

$$\beta_p = \sum_{i=1}^{G} w_i \beta_i$$

So, for example, the beta for a portfolio comprised of the following:

Company	Weight	β
General Electric	20%	1.24
McGraw-Hill	25%	0.86
IBM	15%	1.22
General Motors	10%	1.11
Xerox	30%	1.27

would have the following beta:

Portfolio beta = 20%(1.24) + 25%(0.86) + 15%(1.22) + 10%(1.11) + 30%(1.27)
= 1.14

Multi-Index Market Models

Sharpe concluded that equation (2.12) was as complex a covariance as seemed to be needed. This conclusion was supported by research of Cohen and Pogue (1967). King (1966) found strong evidence for industry factors in addition to the marketwide factor. Rosenberg (1974) found other sources of risk beyond a marketwide factor and industry factor.

One alternative approach to full mean-variance analysis is the use of these multi-index or factor models to obtain the covariance structure.

SUMMARY

In this chapter, we have introduced portfolio theory. Developed by Markowitz, this theory explains how investors should construct efficient portfolios and select the best or optimal portfolio from among all efficient portfolios. The theory differs from previous approaches to portfolio selection in that he demonstrated how the key parameters should be measured. These parameters include the risk and the expected return for an individual asset and a portfolio of assets. Moreover, the concept of diversifying a portfolio, the goal of which is to reduce a portfolio's risk without sacrificing expected return, can be cast in terms of these key parameters plus the covariance or correlation between assets. All these parameters are estimated from historical data and other sources of information and draw from concepts in probability and statistical theory.

A portfolio's expected return is simply a weighted average of the expected return of each asset in the portfolio. The weight assigned to each asset is the market value of the asset in the portfolio relative to the total market value of the portfolio. The variance or the standard deviation of an asset's returns measures its risk. Unlike the portfolio's expected return, a portfolio's risk is not a simple weighting of the standard deviation of the individual assets in the portfolio. Rather, the covariance or correlation between the assets that comprise the portfolio affects the portfolio risk. The lower the correlation, the smaller the risk of the portfolio.

Markowitz has set forth the theory for the construction of an efficient portfolio, which has come to be called a efficient portfolio—a portfolio that has the highest expected return of all feasible portfolios with the same level of risk. The collection of all efficient portfolios is called the efficient set of portfolios or the efficient frontier.

The optimal portfolio is the one that maximizes an investor's preferences with respect to return and risk. An investor's preference is described by a utility function, which can be represented graphically by a set of indifference curves. The utility function shows how much an investor is willing to trade off between expected return and risk. The optimal portfolio is the one where an indifference curve is tangent to the efficient frontier.

REFERENCES

Cohen, K. J., and G. A. Pogue. 1967. An empirical evaluation of alternative portfolio selection models. *Journal of Business* 40, no. 2: 166–193.

Jacobs, B. I., K. N. Levy, and D. Starer. 1999. Long-short portfolio management: An integrated approach. *Journal of Portfolio Management* 25, no. 2: 40–51.

Jacobs, B. I., K. N. Levy, and H. M. Markowitz. 2005. Portfolio optimization with factors, scenarios, and realistic short positions. *Operations Research* 53, no. 4: 586–599.

King, B. F. 1966. Market and industry factors in stock price behavior. *Journal of Business* 39, no. 1 (Part 2: Supplement on Security Prices): 139–190.

Leavens, D. H. 1945. Diversification of investments. *Trusts and Estates* 80: 469–473.

Markowitz, H. M. 1952. Portfolio selection. *Journal of Finance* 7, 1: 77–91

Markowitz, H. M. 1959. *Portfolio selection: Efficient diversification of investments.* Cowles Foundation Monograph 16, New York: John Wiley & Sons.

Ortobelli, S., S. T. Rachev, S. Stoyanov, F. J. Fabozzi, and A. Biglova. 2005. The proper use of risk measures in portfolio theory. *International Journal of Theoretical and Applied Finance* 8, no. 8: 1–27.

Rosenberg, B. 1974. Extra-market components of covariance in security returns. *Journal of Financial and Quantitative Analysis* 19, no. 2: 23–274.

Sharpe, W. F. 1963. A simplified model for portfolio analysis. *Management Science* 9, no. 2: 277–293.

von Neumann, J. and O. Morgenstern. 1944. *Theory of games and economic behavior.* Princeton, NJ: Princeton University Press.

CHAPTER 3
Applying Mean-Variance Analysis

In the previous chapter, we explained mean-variance analysis for constructing efficient portfolios. In this chapter, we move from theory to practice by illustrating how mean-variance analysis is applied. Figure 3.1 shows a schematic view of the portfolio selection process. The inputs to the process are estimates of the expected returns, volatilities, and correlations of all the assets together with various portfolio constraints. An optimization software package is then employed to solve a series of optimization problems in order to generate the efficient frontier. Depending upon the complexity of the portfolio, the optimizations can be solved either with a spreadsheet or with more specialized optimization software.[1]

FIGURE 3.1 Schematic Presentation of the Portfolio Selection Process

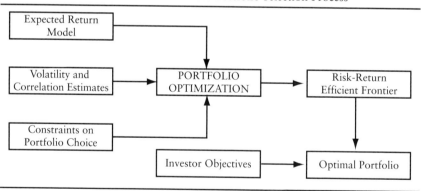

Source: Exhibit 2 in Fabozzi, Gupta, and Markowitz (2002, 8).

---

[1]For a comprehensive discussion of optimization software, see Fabozzi, Kolm, Pachamanova, and Focardi (2007).

This chapter is coauthored with Francis Gupta and Harry M. Markowitz.

We begin this chapter with the problem of using historical data to estimate the inputs required by the model. The application we employ is to asset allocation among asset classes.[2] We then explain how to implement the optimal portfolio. Other issues arising in implementation of the mean-variance model are described in the next chapter.

USING HISTORICAL DATA TO ESTIMATE INPUTS

The inputs required for portfolio theory are generally estimated from historical observations on the rate of returns. The assumption is that the values obtained from historical observations are reasonable estimates for the expected returns, standard deviations, and correlations in the future. Or, in some case, the time period chosen to obtain the estimates may indeed be the best representation of the beliefs of the future performance of the asset classes.

Historical returns are calculated from either monthly data or weekly data. Table 3.1 uses monthly returns over different and varying time periods to present the annualized historical returns for four market indexes. Market indexes are used to broadly represent the performance of a market portfolio that is made up of a set of predefined securities. The Lehman Brothers Aggregate Bond Index (now the Barclays U.S. Aggregate since the acquisition of Lehman Brothers by Barclays) represents the U.S. government and corporate bond market and will be discussed in Part Three of this book. The S&P 500 index is made up of 500 stocks and is supposed to closely mimic the performance of large U.S. firms. The Morgan Stanley Capital International (MSCI) EAFE index represents the performance of the equity markets in Europe and Japan, while the EM Free index captures the performance of equity markets of the emerging economies.

TABLE 3.1 Annualized Returns Using Historical Performance Depend on the Time Period

Period	Lehman Aggregate	S&P 500	MSCI EAFE	MSCI EM Free
5-year				
1991–1995	9.2%	15.9%	10.5%	16.3%
1996–2000	6.3	18.3	8.2	0.1
10-year				
1991–2000	7.7	17.1	9.3	8.2

---

[2] In Chapters 11 and 23 we will see how multifactor risk models are used to select individual securities in the management of common stock and bond portfolios, respectively.

One drawback of using the historical performance to obtain estimates is clearly evident from Table 3.1. Based on historical performance, a portfolio manager looking for estimates of the expected returns for these four asset classes to use as inputs for obtaining the set of efficient portfolios at the end of 1995 would have used the estimates from the five-year period, 1991–1995. Then according to the portfolio manager's expectations, over the next five years, only the U.S. equity market (as represented by the S&P 500) outperformed (i.e., had the highest return), while U.S. bonds, Europe and Japan, and emerging markets all underperformed. In particular, the performance of emerging markets was dramatically different from its expected performance (actual performance of 0.1% versus an expected performance of 16.3%). This finding is disturbing because if portfolio managers cannot have faith in the inputs that are used to solve for the efficient portfolios, then it is not possible for them to have much faith in the outputs (i.e., the makeup and expected performance of the efficient and optimal portfolios).

Portfolio managers who were performing the exercise at the beginning of 2001 faced a similar dilemma. Should they use the historical returns for the 1996–2000 period? That would generally imply that the optimal allocation has a large holding of U.S. equity (since that was the asset class that performed well), and an underweighting to U.S. bonds and emerging markets equity. But then what if the actual performance over the next five years is more like the 1991–1995 period?[3] In that case, the optimal portfolio is not going to perform as well as a portfolio that had a good exposure to bonds and emerging markets equity. (Note that emerging markets equity outperformed U.S. equity under that scenario.) Or should portfolio managers use the estimates computed by using 10 years of monthly performance?

There is no right answer. This is because we are dealing with the world of uncertainty. This is also true for the cases of obtaining estimates for the variances and correlations. Table 3.2 presents the standard deviations for the same indexes over the same time periods. Though the risk estimates for the Lehman Aggregate and EAFE indexes are quite stable, the estimates for the S&P 500 and EM Free are significantly different over different time periods. However, the volatility of the indexes does shed some light into the problem of estimating expected returns as presented in Table 3.1. MSCI EM Free, the index with the largest volatility, also has the largest difference in the estimate of the expected return. Intuitively, this makes sense—the greater the volatility of an asset, the harder, or longer the data required to predict its future performance.

---

[3]Similarly, there are other methods for estimating the variances and covariances. See Chapters 11 and 23 on multifactor risk models. See also Chan, Karceski, and Lakonishok (1999).

TABLE 3.2 Annualized Standard Deviations Using Historical Performance Depend on the Time Period

Period	Lehman Aggregate	S&P 500	MSCI EAFE	MSCI EM Free
5-year				
1991–1995	4.0%	10.1%	15.5%	18.0%
1996–2000	4.8	17.7	15.6	26.6
10-year				
1991–2000	3.7	13.4	15.0	22.3

Figure 3.2 shows the five-year rolling correlation between the S&P 500 and MSCI EAFE. In January 1996, the correlation between the returns of the S&P 500 and EAFE was about 0.45 over the past five years (1991–1995). Consequently, a portfolio manager would have expected the correlation over the next five years to be around that estimate. However, for the five-year period ending December 2000, the correlation between the assets slowly increased to 0.73. Historically, this was an all-time high. In January 2001, should the portfolio manager assume a correlation 0.45 or 0.73 between the S&P 500 and EAFE over the next five years? Or does 0.59, the correlation over the entire 10-year period (1991–2000) sound more reasonable?

FIGURE 3.2 Correlation Between Returns of the S&P 500 and MSCI EAFE Indexes

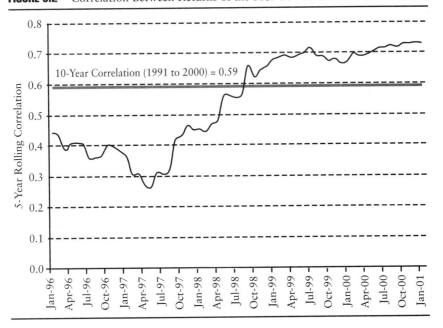

Again, there is no right answer. In reality, as mentioned earlier, if portfolio managers believe that the inputs based on the historical performance of an asset class is not a good reflection of the future expected performance of that asset class, they may objectively or subjectively alter the inputs. Different portfolio managers may have different beliefs, in which case the alterations will be different.[4] The important thing here is that all alterations have theoretical justifications, which in turn ultimately leads to an optimal portfolio that closely aligns to the future expectations of the portfolio manager.

When solving for the efficient portfolios, the differences in precision of the estimates should be explicitly incorporated into the analysis. But modern portfolio theory assumes that all estimates are as precise or imprecise, and therefore, treats all assets equally. Some practitioners of mean-variance optimization incorporate their beliefs on the precision of the estimates by imposing constraints on the maximum exposure of some asset classes in a portfolio.[5] The asset classes on which these constraints are imposed are generally those whose expected performances are either harder to estimate, or those whose performances are estimated less precisely. A different approach taken by other practitioners is to increase the volatility of the asset classes so as to reflect their uncertainty in the expected return estimates of those asset classes. The end result is the same: the higher volatility makes those asset classes less attractive in a mean-variance framework and therefore those asset classes receive smaller allocations in optimal portfolios.

The extent to which we can use personal judgment to subjectively alter estimates obtained from historical data depends on our understanding of what factors influence the returns on assets, and what is their impact. The political environment within and across countries, monetary and fiscal policies, consumer confidence, and the business cycles of sectors and regions are some of the key factors that can assist in forming future expectations of the performance of asset classes.

To summarize, it would be fair to say that using historical returns to estimate parameters that can be used as inputs to obtain the set of efficient portfolios depends on whether the underlying economies giving rise to the observed outcomes of returns are strong and stable. Strength and stability of economies comes from political stability and consistency in economic policies. It is only after an economy has a lengthy and proven record of a healthy and consistent performance under varying (political and economic) forces

---

[4] It is quite common that the optimal strategic bond/equity mix within a portfolio differs significantly across portfolio managers.
[5] For a further discussion of the benefits and costs of constraining the allocation to an asset class, see Gupta and Eichorn (1998).

that impact free markets that historical performance of its markets can be seen as a fair indicator of their future performance.

APPLICATION OF PORTFOLIO THEORY TO ASSET ALLOCATION

Now that we are familiar with the theoretical concepts and various building blocks of modern portfolio theory, we use an example to illustrate how portfolio managers use this theory to build optimal portfolios for their clients. In this example we construct an efficient frontier made up of U.S. bonds and U.S. and international equity, and shed some light into the selection of an optimal portfolio.

Asset Classes and Inputs

By now we know that the first decision to be made is the assets we would like to include in the portfolio and their corresponding returns, risks (standard deviations), and correlations to be used as inputs in the mean-variance optimization. For our purposes, we are going to build a portfolio made up of four asset classes—three domestic and one international. As discussed earlier, these asset classes have associated indexes and those indexes can be used when implementing the optimal portfolio. Table 3.3 presents the forward-looking assumptions for the four asset classes.

These inputs are an example of estimates that are not totally based on historical performance of these asset classes. The risk and correlation figures are mainly historical.

TABLE 3.3 Forward Looking Inputs (Expected Returns, Standard Deviations, and Correlations)

				Correlations			
$E(R)$	$SD(R)$	Asset Classes	Asset	1	2	3	4
6.4%	4.7%	U.S. Bonds	1	1.00			
10.8	14.9	U.S. Large-Cap Equity	2	0.32	1.00		
11.9	19.6	U.S. Small-Cap Equity	3	0.06	0.76	1.00	
11.5	17.2	EAFE International Equity	4	0.17	0.44	0.38	1.00

The Efficient Frontier

The next step is to use a software package to perform the optimization that results in the efficient frontier. For purposes of exposition, Figure 3.3 presents the efficient frontier using only two of the four asset classes from Table 3.3—U.S. bonds and large-cap equity. (This efficient frontier is very similar to the efficient frontier presented in the previous chapter which was made up of assets C and D.) Starting with only two asset classes will enable us to understand how the addition of more asset classes may be desirable to the building of an optimal portfolio. Because it is efficient, the corresponding portfolio on the efficient frontier for any given level of risk will result in the highest possible expected return. We show two such portfolios: A and B corresponding to standard deviations of 9% and 12%, respectively. Portfolio B has the higher risk, but it also has the higher expected return.

In addition to the trade-off between return and risk among the efficient portfolios, the other factor that determines an entity's optimal portfolio is the entity's risk aversion, or appetite for risk. Therefore, depending on the entity's risk aversion, any one of the portfolios on the efficient frontier could be a candidate optimal portfolio. However, for purposes of exposition, we concentrate on portfolios A and B.

Table 3.4 presents the compositions of portfolios A and B, and some important characteristics that may assist us in understanding how risk averse individuals choose an optimal portfolio from the set of efficient portfolios.

FIGURE 3.3 The Efficient Frontier Using Only U.S. Bonds and U.S. Large-Cap Equity from Table 3.3

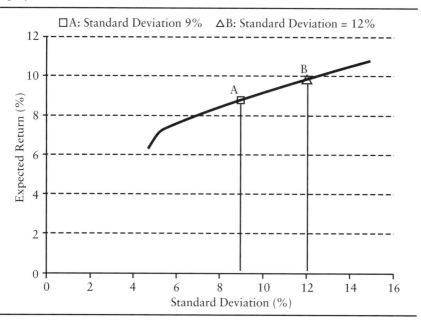

TABLE 3.4 Growth of $100 Illustrates the Risk-Return Trade-Off of Portfolios A and B

Characteristic	Portfolio A			Portfolio B		
U.S. Fixed Income	45.8%			22.0%		
U.S. Large-Cap Equity	54.2			78.0		
Expected return	8.79%			9.83%		
Standard deviation (risk)	9.00%			12.00%		
Return per unit of risk	98 basis points (bps)			82 basis points (bps)		
Growth of $100	1 Year	5 Years	10 Years	1 Year	5 Years	10 Years
95th percentile (upside)	$124	$203	$345	$131	$232	$424
Average (expected)	109	152	232	110	160	255
5th percentile (downside)	95	111	146	91	104	137

As one would expect, the more conservative portfolio (A), allocates more to the more conservative asset class. Portfolio A allocated a little more than 45% of the portfolio to fixed income, while portfolio B only allocates 22% to that asset class. This results in a significantly higher standard deviation for portfolio B (12% versus 9%). In exchange for the 3% (or 300 basis points) of higher risk, portfolio B results in 104 basis points of higher expected return (9.83% versus 8.79%). This is the risk-return trade-off that we discussed earlier. The question that a risk averse individual faces when choosing an optimal portfolio is this: Does the increase in the expected return compensate me for the increased risk that I will be bearing? If it does, then the individual will choose portfolio B.

Though we know that the standard deviation is a measure of risk, in reality it is a difficult concept to comprehend. We can get around this by expressing risk in terms of the distribution of wealth over time. The higher the risk, the wider the spread of the distribution. A wider spread implies a greater upside and a greater downside. The key to translating risk into something more comprehensible is to quantify the upside and downside.[6]

Table 3.4 also presents the 95th percentile, expected, and 5th percentiles for every $100 invested in portfolios A and B over 1, 5, and 10 years, respectively. Over a one-year period, there is a 1 in 20 chance that the $100 invested in portfolio A will grow to $124, but there is also a 1 in 20 chance that the portfolio will lose $5 (i.e., it will it shrink to $95). In comparison,

---

[6]Though easier to understand, the computation of the wealth distribution over multiple periods entails simulations, and is also best left to an off-the-shelf software package.

for portfolio B there is a 1 in 20 chance that $100 will grow to $131 (the upside is $6 more than if invested in portfolio A). But there is also a 1 in 20 chance that the portfolio will shrink to $91 (the downside is $4 more than if invested in portfolio A). If the investment horizon is one year, is this investor willing to accept a 1 in 20 chance of losing $9 instead of $4 for a 1 in 20 chance of gaining $31 instead of $24?[7] The answer depends on the investor's risk aversion.

As the investment horizon becomes longer, the chances that a portfolio will lose its principal keep declining. Over 10 years, there is a 1 in 20 chance that portfolio A will grow to $345, but there is also a 1 in 20 chance that the portfolio will only grow to $146 (the chances that the portfolio results in a balance less than $100 are much smaller). In comparison, over 10 years, there is a 1 in 20 chance that portfolio B will grow to $424 (the upside is $79 more than if invested in portfolio A)! And even though there is a 1 in 20 chance that the portfolio will only grow to $137—that is only $7 less than if invested in portfolio A! Also portfolio B's average (expected) balance over 10 years is $23 more than portfolio A's ($255 versus $232). Somehow, compounding makes the more risky portfolio seems more attractive over the longer run. In other words, a portfolio that may not be acceptable to the investor over a short run may be acceptable over a longer investment horizon. In summary, it is sufficient to say that the optimal portfolio depends not only on risk aversion, but also on the investment horizon.

Expanding the Efficient Frontier

Figure 3.4 compares the efficient frontier using two asset classes, namely, U.S. bonds and large-cap equity with one obtained from using all four asset classes from Table 3.3 in the optimization. The inclusion of U.S. small-cap and EAFE international equity into the mix makes the opportunity set bigger (i.e., the frontier covers a larger risk-return spectrum). It also moves the efficient frontier outwards (i.e., the frontier results in a larger expected return at any given level of risk, or conversely, results in a lower risk for any given level of expected return). The frontier also highlights portfolios A′ and B′—the portfolios with the same standard deviation as portfolios A and B, respectively.

Figure 3.5 shows the composition of the underlying portfolios that make up the frontier. Interestingly, U.S. small-cap and EAFE international equity—the more aggressive asset classes—are included in all the portfo-

---

[7]It may be useful to mention here that more recently researchers in behavioral finance have found some evidence to suggest that investors view the upside and downside differently. In particular, they equate each downside dollar to more than one upside dollar.

FIGURE 3.4 Expanding the Efficient Frontier Using All Asset Classes from Table 3.3

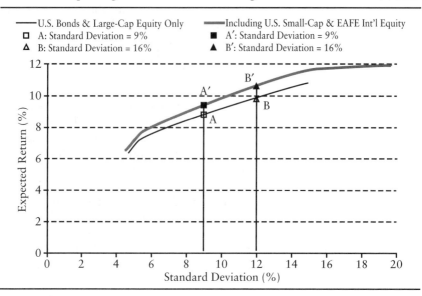

FIGURE 3.5 Composition of the Efficient Frontier

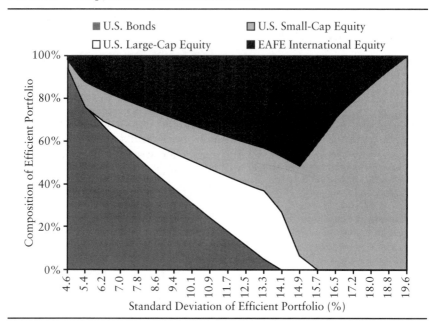

lios. Even the least risky portfolio has a small allocation to these two asset classes. On the other hand, U.S. large-cap equity—an asset class that is thought of as the backbone of a domestic portfolio—gets excluded from the more aggressive portfolios.

Table 3.6 compares the composition and expected performance of portfolios A and B to A' and B', respectively. Both the new portfolios, A' and B', find U.S. small-cap and EAFE international equity very attractive and replace a significant proportion of U.S. large-cap equity with those asset classes. In B', the more aggressive mix, the allocation to U.S. bonds also declines (15.1% versus 22%).

Inclusion of U.S. small-cap and EAFE international equity results in sizable increases in the expected return and return per unit of risk. In particular, the conservative portfolio A', has an expected return of 9.39% (60 basis points over portfolio A) and the aggressive portfolio B' has an expected return of 10.61% (78 basis points over portfolio B). Note also the increases in the returns per unit of risk.

It is conceivable that the huge allocations to U.S. small-cap and EAFE international equity in A' and B' may be uncomfortable for some investors. U.S. small-cap equity is the most risky asset class and EAFE international equity is the second most aggressive asset class. The conservative portfolio allocates more than 40% of the portfolio to these two assets, while the aggressive allocates more than 50%. As explained in the section when we discussed inputs based on historical returns, these two would also be the asset classes whose expected returns, because of the large volatilities, would

TABLE 3.6 Composition of Equally Risky Efficient Portfolios in the Expanded Frontier

Asset Class	Standard Deviation = 9.0%		Standard Deviation = 12.0%	
	A	A'	B	B'
U.S. Fixed Income	34.3%	40.4%	22.0%	15.1%
U.S. Large-Cap Equity	18.7	15.8	78.0	27.8
U.S. Small-Cap Equity	—	16.1	—	18.6
EAFE International Equity	—	27.7	—	38.5
Expected return	8.79%	9.39%	9.83%	10.61%
Standard deviation (risk)	9.00%	9.00%	12.00%	12.00%
Return per unit of risk	98 bps	104 bps	82 bps	88 bps

be harder to estimate. Consequently, investors may not want to allocate more than a certain amount of their portfolios to these two asset classes.[8]

Figure 3.6 presents the composition of the efficient frontier when the maximum allocation to EAFE is constrained at 10% of the portfolio, implying a 90% allocation to domestic asset classes. As a result of this constraint, all the portfolios now receive an allocation of U.S. large-cap equity.

Figure 3.7 compares the composition A′ and B′ to A″ and B″ the respective equally risky portfolios that lie on the constrained efficient frontier. In the conservative portfolio A″, the combined allocation to U.S. small-cap and EAFE international equity has declined to 30% (from 43.8%) and in B″ it has fallen to 34.8% (from 57.1%). Also, now the bond allocation increases for both of the portfolios.

The decline in the expected return can be used to quantify the cost of this constraint. The conservative portfolio's expected return fell from 9.39% to 9.20%—a decline of 19 basis points—a cost that may be well

FIGURE 3.6 Composition of the Constrained Efficient Frontier Maximum Allocation to EAFE International Equity = 10%

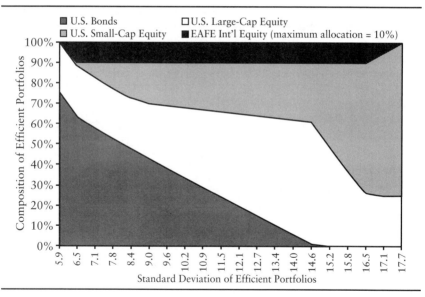

---

[8]For example, investors in the United States may also want to limit their exposure to EAFE international equity because of psychological reasons. Familiarity to domestic asset classes leads them to believe that those asset classes are "less" risky. Similarly, investors in Europe may believe that EAFE equity is "less" risky than U.S. equity and may want to limit their exposure to U.S. asset classes. This is often referred to as the "domestic asset class bias."

Applying Mean-Variance Analysis

FIGURE 3.7 The Benefits and Costs of Constraining an Efficient Frontier

Asset Class	Unconstrained		Maximum Allocation to EAFE International Equity = 10.0%	
	A′	B′	A″	B″
U.S. Fixed Income	40.4%	15.1%	43.1%	20.1%
U.S. Large-Cap Equity	15.8	27.8	26.9	45.1
U.S. Small-Cap Equity	16.1	18.6	20.0	24.8
EAFE International Equity	27.7	38.5	10.0	10.0
Expected return	9.39%	10.61%	9.20%	10.26%
Standard deviation	9.00%	12.00%	9.00%	12.00%
Cost of constraint	—	—	19 bps	35 bps

worth it for an investor whose optimal appetite for risk is 9%. The more aggressive portfolio pays more for the constraint (10.61% − 10.26% = 35 basis points).

IMPLEMENTING THE OPTIMAL PORTFOLIO

Now that we understand the process of obtaining the optimal portfolio, the next step in portfolio management deals with implementing the optimal portfolio. The optimal portfolio that we derived was made up of asset classes, but asset classes by themselves cannot be invested in. To implement the optimal portfolio, the investor has to purchase either market indexes (that the asset classes represent), or mutual funds or exchange-traded funds (that are supposed to represent those asset classes and are discussed in Chapter 25), or if an investor is more sophisticated, she can buy individual securities that broadly represent the asset classes that comprise the optimal portfolio. Here, we will limit ourselves to implementing the optimal portfolio using market indexes.

Passive Implementation of the Optimal Portfolio

For purposes of exposition, let's assume that B″ (from Figure 3.6) is the optimal portfolio. As stated earlier, one easy way to implement this portfolio is to buy the index funds that represent the respective asset classes that make up the optimal portfolio. This is equivalent to purchasing the index. Since none of these index funds are actively managed (i.e., they perfectly track the index), gaining exposure to the asset classes using index funds is referred to as *passive implementation of the optimal portfolio*. Table 3.7 shows the indexes used to gain exposure to the various asset classes in the optimal portfolio, passively.

Since there are many indexes for each asset class, it is important to note that the choice of the index used to gain exposure to an asset class is a matter of personal taste. Each index has its pros and cons as to how well it replicates the asset class it is supposed to represent.

Another aspect of portfolio implementation has to do with rebalancing the portfolio back to its strategic weights (i.e., the weights in the optimal portfolio). Due to the differences in returns of the various holdings over time, weights of the various asset classes within the portfolio may start to differ markedly from those in the optimal portfolio. This not only changes the risk profile of the portfolio,[9] but at any given time the "current" portfolio may not even be efficient. To rebalance, the asset classes that are overweight are sold and the asset classes that are underweight are bought. Thus rebalancing generally incurs trading costs.

Figure 3.7 shows the growth of a $100 investment in the optimal portfolio B″ for three different rebalancing frequencies over the 10-year period, 1991–2000.[10] Notice, that no clear relationship exists between the frequency of rebalancing and the performance of a portfolio. In our example the quarterly rebalanced portfolio outperforms the one that is

TABLE 3.7 Passive Implementation of the Optimal Portfolio B″ from Figure 3.7

Asset Class	Index	Allocation to B″
U.S. Fixed Income	Lehman Aggregate	20.1%
U.S. Large-Cap Equity	S&P 500	45.1%
U.S. Small-Cap Equity	FR 2000	24.8%
EAFE International Equity	MSCI EAFE	10.0%

---

[9]Remember, the optimal portfolio was dependent on the investor's appetite for risk. A portfolio with different weights from the optimal may have a risk that is very different from what the investor is willing to tolerate.

[10]This means that in the beginning of 1991, $100 was allocated among the indexes shown in Table 3.7. As already discussed, these indexes represent the asset classes that make up the optimal portfolio. The allocation to each index is meant to reflect the weight of its respective asset class in the optimal portfolio. Therefore, of the $100 invested in the portfolio, $20.1 was invested in the Lehman Brothers Aggregate Bond Index, $45.1 was invested in the S&P 500 stock index, $24.8 in the Frank Russell 2000, and $10 in the MSCI EAFE index.

FIGURE 3.7 Growth of $100 Differs by the Frequency of Rebalancing

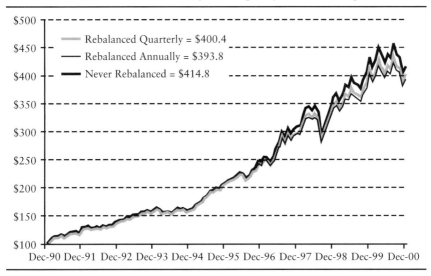

Frequency of Rebalancing	Annual Return	Annual Standard Deviation
Quarterly	14.88%	10.56%
Annually	14.69	10.75
Never	15.29	11.54

Note: Uses monthly returns for the indexes.

rebalanced annually, implying that the higher the frequency of rebalancing, the better the return. But then the portfolio that is never rebalanced over the 10 years results in the biggest ending balance. Also notice that the quarterly rebalanced portfolio has the least risk as measured by the standard deviation, whereas the portfolio that is never rebalanced is the most risky, indicating some relationship between the frequency of rebalancing and the volatility. For our purposes, it would not be an understatement to say that all individuals who are serious about practicing portfolio management should understand that the issue of rebalancing is an important component of portfolio implementation and is worth giving some serious thought.[11]

---

[11]Instead of using a time frequency for rebalancing, some investors use rules based on asset class weights. For example, a simple rule would be one which rebalances the portfolio whenever any asset classes' weight differs by more than 10% from its optimal weight.

Implementation Using Active Strategies

Gaining exposure to the optimal portfolio using passive strategies is relatively easy. Investors first decide which indexes best represent the asset classes that comprise the optimal portfolio and allocate their total portfolio among the indexes so as to replicate the asset class weights. Then all they need to worry about is rebalancing. In terms of performance they know what to expect. Since their entire portfolio is invested in indexes, the return on the portfolio is a weighted average of the return on the indexes, where the weights are the relative dollar amounts invested in the respective indexes. But some investors may believe that their portfolios can outperform the broad market. Therefore, they may implement their optimal portfolios by picking individual securities that they feel will outperform the market. Or, they may invest in strategies that actively focus on picking a group of stocks with the hope that the manager of the strategy (i.e., the portfolio manager) will be able to generate some excess return over and above the market. These strategies are marketed to investors as *active mutual funds* and are described in Chapter 25. The tools for implementing optimal portfolios using active strategies are discussed in later chapters of this book.

SUMMARY

It is a major step moving from the theory of portfolio selection as set forth in the mean-variance model and the implementation of that model in order to generate the efficient frontier. Implementing the theory requires estimating the required inputs from historical returns. When estimating these inputs from historical data, the assumption is that the estimated values are reasonable estimates for the expected returns, standard deviations, and correlations in the future or that the time period chosen to obtain the estimates best represents the beliefs of the future performance of the asset classes in an asset allocation problem or the securities when a portfolio of one asset class is being selected.

In this chapter, we illustrate the drawbacks of using historical performance to obtain estimates and the issues faced in implementation. Using historical returns to estimate parameters that can be used as inputs to obtain the set of efficient portfolios depends on whether the underlying economies giving rise to the observed outcomes of returns are strong and stable. The extent to which a portfolio manager can use personal judgment to subjectively alter estimates obtained from historical data depends on his or her understanding of what factors influence the returns on assets, and what is their impact.

REFERENCES

Chan, L. K. C., J. Karceski, and J. Lakonishok. 1999. On portfolio optimization: Forecasting covariances and choosing the risk model. *Review of Financial Studies* 12, no. 5: 80-90.

Fabozzi, F. J., F. Gupta, and H. M. Markowitz. 2002. The legacy of modern portfolio theory. *Journal of Investing* 11, no. 3: 7–22.

Fabozzi, F. J., P. N. Kolm, D. Pachamanova, and S. M. Focardi. 2007. *Robust portfolio optimization and management*. Hoboken, NJ: John Wiley & Sons.

Gupta, F., and D. Eichorn. 1998. Mean-variance optimization for practitioners of asset allocation. In *Handbook of portfolio management*, edited by F. J. Fabozzi (pp. 57–74). Hoboken, NJ: John Wiley & Sons.

CHAPTER 4
Issues in the Theory of Portfolio Selection

As explained in Chapter 2, the goal of portfolio selection is the construction of portfolios that maximize expected returns consistent with individually acceptable levels of risk. Using both historical data and investor expectations of future returns, portfolio selection uses modeling techniques to quantify "expected portfolio returns" and "acceptable levels of portfolio risk" and provides methods to select an optimal portfolio. Prior to the development of mean-variance analysis by Markowitz (1952, 1959) for the selection of portfolios, the focus of portfolio management was the risk of individual assets. Markowitz's portfolio selection theory shifted the focus to the risk of the entire portfolio. This theory shows that it is possible to combine risky assets and produce a portfolio whose expected return reflects its components, but with considerably lower risk. In other words, it is possible to construct a portfolio whose risk is smaller than the sum of all its individual parts.

Though practitioners realized that the risks of individual assets were related, prior to modern portfolio theory they were unable to formalize how combining them into a portfolio impacted the risk at the portfolio level or how the addition of a new asset would change the return/risk characteristics of the portfolio. This is because practitioners did not attempt to quantify the returns and risks of their investments. Furthermore, in the context of the entire portfolio, they did not realize how to formalize the interaction of the returns and risks across asset classes and individual assets. The failure to quantify these important measures and formalize these important relationships made the goal of constructing an optimal portfolio highly subjective and provided no insight into the return investors could expect and the risk they were undertaking. The other drawback

---

This chapter draws from my joint writings with Sergio Focardi, Petter N. Kolm, Christian Menn, and Svetlozar T. Rachev.

before the advent of the theory of portfolio selection was that there was no measurement tool available to investors for judging the performance of the asset managers that they engaged.

The theory of portfolio selection set forth by Markowitz was based on some modeling assumptions regarding the behavior of investors when making investment decisions and about the probability distribution of the return on assets that made it acceptable to use the variance or standard deviation as a measure of risk. Moreover, in terms of implementation of the portfolio selection model that relied on the estimation of inputs from historical data, no consideration was given to the implications of the misestimation of the inputs on the optimal portfolio.

In this chapter, we look at the issues surrounding the theory of portfolio selection and the implementation of the model. We begin with a brief review of probability theory and then focus on the normal probability distribution. This probability distribution is important not only to the theory of portfolio selection but other theories in finance. We discuss the empirical evidence and the theoretical evidence that challenges the widely accepted notion in traditional finance that return distributions are normally distribution. We also identify a distribution that has been proposed as an alternative to the normal distribution because it better characterizes the behavior of real-world asset returns. We then discuss alternative risk measures. In the last section of the chapter, we discuss an attack on portfolio selection theory by those who are advocates of a branch of finance known as behavioral finance.

QUICK REVIEW OF PROBABILITY THEORY

A probability measures the decision maker's degree of belief in the likelihood of a given outcome. A decision maker may formulate a probability based on empirical evidence. For example, if a portfolio manager wants to estimate the probability that the return on the S&P 500 will increase by more than 5% in a given month, she can look at historical returns on the S&P 500 and base her probability on the percentage of times that a return greater than 5% occurred. In some instances, however, empirical evidence may not be available. The manager, then, draws on a variety of information and her experience to formulate a probability.

A *random variable* is a variable for which a probability can be assigned to each possible value that can be taken by the variable. A *probability distribution* or *probability function* is a function that describes all the values that the random variable can take on, and the probability associated with each. A *cumulative probability distribution* is a function that shows the probability that the random variable will attain a value less than or equal to each value that the random variable can take.

Describing a Probability Distribution

In describing a probability distribution function, it is common to summarize it by using various measures. The four most commonly used measures are:

- Location
- Dispersion
- Asymmetry
- Concentration in tails

The first way to describe a probability distribution function is by some measure of *central value* or *location*. The various measures that can be used are the mean or average value, the median, or the mode. The relationship among these three measures of location depends on the skewness of a probability distribution function that we will describe later. The most commonly used measure of location is the *mean*.

Another measure that can help us to describe a probability distribution function is the dispersion or how spread out the values of the random variable can realize. Various measures of dispersion are the range, variance, and mean absolute deviation. The most commonly used measure is the *variance*. It measures the dispersion of the values that the random variable can realize relative to the mean. It is the average of the squared deviations from the mean. The variance is in squared units. Taking the square root of the variance one obtains the *standard deviation*. In contrast to the variance, the *mean absolute deviation* takes the average of the absolute deviations from the mean.

We discussed and illustrated the mean and variance concepts in Chapter 2 when we explained their role in the theory of portfolio selection based on mean-variance analysis. However, there are other measures that may be critical for assessing a portfolio's risk depending on the probability distribution of the return of the assets. The use of only the mean and variance assumes that the return distribution of assets is a normal distribution as explained later in this chapter.

A probability distribution may be symmetric or asymmetric around its mean. A popular measure for the asymmetry of a distribution is called its *skewness*. A negative skewness measure indicates that the distribution is skewed to the left; that is, compared to the right tail, the left tail is elongated (see Figure 4.1A). A positive skewness measure indicates that the distribu-

FIGURE 4.1 Skewed Distributions
A. Distribution Skewed to the Left

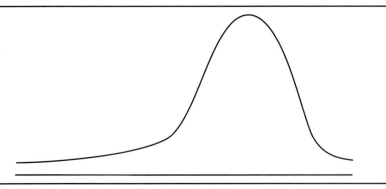

B. Distribution Skewed to the Right

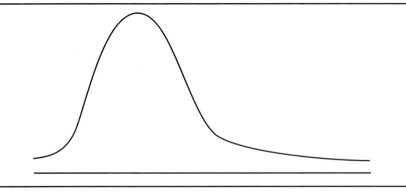

tion is skewed to the right; that is, compared to the left tail, the right tail is elongated (see Figure 4.1B).

Additional information about a probability distribution function is provided by measuring the concentration (mass) of potential outcomes in its tails. The tails of a probability distribution function contain the extreme values. In financial applications, it is the tails that provide information about the potential for a financial fiasco or financial ruin. The fatness of the tails of the distribution is related to the peakedness of the distribution around its mean or center. The joint measure of peakedness and tail fatness is called *kurtosis*.

In the parlance of the statistician, the four measures described above are called *statistical moments* or simply *moments*. The mean is the *first central moment* and is also referred to as the *expected value*. The variance is the *second central moment*, skewness is a rescaled *third central moment*, and kurtosis is a rescaled *fourth central moment*.[1]

Normal Probability Distribution

In mean-variance analysis, the assumption is that probability distribution of asset returns follows a *normal distribution* (also referred to as a *Gaussian distribution*). The normal distribution is depicted in Figure 4.2.

The area under the normal distribution or normal curve between any two points on the horizontal axis is the probability of obtaining a value between those two values. For example, the probability of realizing a value for the random variable X that is between X_1 and X_2 in Figure 4.2 is shown by the shaded area. Mathematically, the probability of realizing a value for X between these two variables can be written as follows:

$$P(X_1 < X < X_2)$$

The entire area under the normal curve is equal to 1.

The normal distribution has the following properties:

1. The point in the middle of the normal curve is the expected value for the distribution.

FIGURE 4.2 Example of a Normal Distribution (or normal curve)

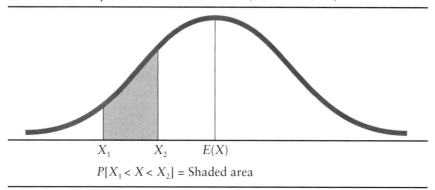

$P[X_1 < X < X_2]$ = Shaded area

---

[1]The definition of skewness and kurtosis is not as unified as for the mean and the variance. The various skewness calculations are the so-called Fishers' skewness and the Pearson's skewness, which equals the square of the Fisher's skewness. The same holds true for kurtosis: there is the Pearson's kurtosis and Fishers' kurtosis (sometimes denoted as excess kurtosis), which can be obtained by subtracting three from Pearson's kurtosis.

2. The distribution is symmetric around the expected value. That is, half the distribution is to the left of the expected value, and the other half is to the right. Thus, the probability of obtaining a value less than the expected value is 50%. The probability of obtaining a value greater than the expected value is also 50%.
3. The probability that the actual outcome will be within a range of one standard deviation above the expected value and one standard deviation below the expected value is 68.26%, rounded off to 68.3%.
4. The probability that the actual outcome will be within a range of two standard deviations above the expected value and two standard deviations below the expected value is 95.46%, rounded off to 95.5%.
5. The probability that the actual outcome will be within a range of three standard deviations above the expected value and three standard deviations below the expected value is 99.74%, rounded off to 99.7%.

For example, suppose that the one-year rate of return for a portfolio has an expected value of 7% and a standard deviation of 4%, and that the probability distribution is a normal distribution. The probability is 68.3% that the one-year rate of return will be between 3% (the expected value of 7% minus one standard deviation of 4%) and 11% (the expected value of 7% plus one standard deviation of 4%). The probability is 95.5% that the one-year rate of return will be between –1% (the expected value minus two standard deviations) and 15% (the expected value plus two standard deviations).

Suppose that the standard deviation for the one-year rate of return in the previous illustration is 2% rather than 4%. Then the probability is 68.3% that the one-year rate of return will be between 5% and 9%; the probability is 95.5% that the one-year rate of return will be between 3% and 11%. Notice that the smaller the standard deviation, the smaller the range of the possible outcome for a given probability.

Empirically it has been demonstrated that returns are better described as following a *lognormal distribution* rather than a normal distribution. A distribution is said to be lognormal if the logarithm of the variable follows a normal distribution.

LIMITATIONS OF THE VARIANCE AS A RISK MEASURE

If the return distribution is normally distributed, then the variance is a useful measure of risk. The distribution is symmetric so outcomes (area under the normal distribution curve) above and below the expected value are equally likely. However, there are both empirical studies of real-world financial markets as well as theoretical arguments that would suggest that the normal distribution assumption should be rejected.

The Empirical Evidence against the Normal Distribution

The original empirical evidence that refuted the assumption that return distributions are not normally distributed was first presented in the 1960s by Benoit Mandelbrot (Mandelbrot 1963), and further supported by Fama (1963).[2] Mandelbrot argued that return distributions follow a non-normal probability distribution called a *stable Paretian distribution*. Although a discussion of the stable Paretian distribution is beyond the scope of this chapter, the important point here is that it has only been in recent years that more attention has been paid to this distribution in asset management.[3]

To appreciate the importance of the Mandelbrot study, shortly after the publication of the study a leading financial economist, Paul Cootner, expressed his concern regarding the implications of those findings for the statistical tests that had been published in prominent scholarly journals in economics and finance. Cootner warned the finance profession that:

> Almost without exception, past econometric work is meaningless. Surely, before consigning centuries of work to the ash pile, we should like to have some assurance that all our work is truly useless. If we have permitted ourselves to be fooled for as long as this into believing that the Gaussian assumption is a workable one, is it not possible that the Paretian revolution is similarly illusory? (Cootner 1964, 337).

Over the 45 years following that statement by Cootner, the preponderance of the empirical evidence fails to support the normality assumption. In fact, the following three properties have been reported in numerous studies of asset returns. First, real-world return distributions have "fatter" or "heavier" tails than the normal distribution. The "tails" of the return distribution are where the extreme outcomes occur. Figure 4.3 shows the tail of a normal distribution and another symmetric distribution that has fatter tails.

---

[2] For a discussion of these empirical studies, see Rachev, Menn, and Fabozzi (2005).
[3] There are many other types of probability distributions that can describe a non-normal distribution. The technical reason supporting the stable Paretian distribution is that it is the only member of a large and flexible class of probability distributions that allows for the skewness and fat tails that we will explain what has been observed for real-world asset returns. For a further discussion, see Rachev, Menn, and Fabozzi (2005). A more technical treatment of this topic is provided in Rachev and Mittnik (2000).

If a probability distribution for the return of assets exhibits fat tails, extreme outcomes are more likely than would be predicted by the normal distribution. As a result, between periods when the market exhibits relatively modest changes in returns, there will be periods when there are changes that are much higher than the normal distribution predicts. Such extreme outcomes are referred to as crashes and booms. Second, a normal distribution assumes symmetry of asset returns. In many markets, return distributions have been found to be asymmetric. If an asset return distribution is one such as in Figure 4.3, asset returns have greater downside risk than suggested by a normal distribution.

Let's look at some empirical evidence using stock market returns. Figure 4.4 shows the daily returns on a popular stock market index, the Standard & Poor's 500 (S&P 500), from 1928 to April 2006. Imposed on the figure is the normal distribution. In our earlier explanation of the properties of the normal distribution, recall that if stock returns do in fact follow a normal distribution, returns that are three standard deviations from the expected value or mean (the mean is zero) are highly unlikely to occur. This is not an attribute of the S&P 500 as can be seen in Figure 4.4. A considerable

FIGURE 4.3 Illustration of Kurtosis: Difference between a Standard Normal Distribution and a Distribution with High Excess Kurtosis

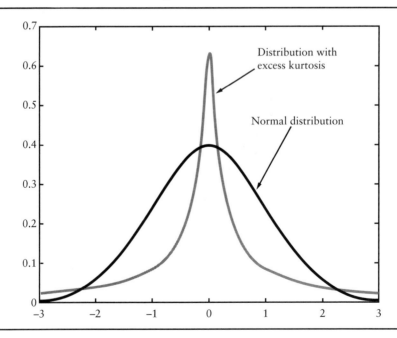

FIGURE 4.4 Distribution of Daily S&P 500 Returns (1928–April 2006)

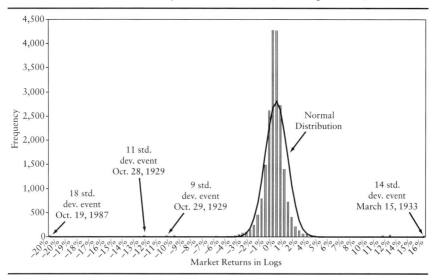

Source: Exhibit 4 in Jeremy Grantham, "Risk Management in Investing (Part Two): Risk and the Passage of Time," *Letters to the Investment Committee VII* (April 2006), ©2006 GMO LLC. The data to construct the figure was obtained from S&P. Permission to reprint only the exhibit granted by GMO.

number of outliers (i.e., extreme values) have occurred. The four noteworthy events shown in the figure are the market crashes of October 19, 1987, October 28, 1929, and October 29, 1929 and the market boom on March 15, 1933. The number of standard deviations from the mean is reported for these events. The likelihood of an event with the number of standard deviations shown for these four events if daily returns follow a normal distribution is very close to zero. The time period covered in the figure stops at April 2006. If the stock market events for several days in October and November 2008 were included, they would provide further support for rejecting the normal distribution.

Theoretical Arguments against the Normal Distribution

Mathematical models of the stock market developed through the joint efforts of economists and physicists have provided support for price and return distributions with heavy tails. This has been done by modeling the interaction of market agents. Probably the most well-known model is the Santa Fe Stock Market Model.[4]

---

[4] See Arthur et al. (1997).

There are other such studies. Bak, Paczuski, and Shubik (1996) and Lux (1999) analyze the interaction between two categories of market agents: "rational investors" and "noise traders." *Rational investors* act on fundamental information in order to analyze risk-return opportunities and then act to optimize their utility function. *Noise traders* are market agents whose behavior is governed only by their analysis of market dynamics. Their choice at which to transact (buy or sell) may imitate the choice of other market agents. Cont and Bouchaud (2000) develop a model based on herding or crowd behavior that has been observed in financial markets.

While these mathematical models by their nature are a gross simplification of real-world financial markets, they provide sufficient structure to analyze return distributions. Computer simulations of these models have been found to generate fat tails and other statistical characteristics that have been observed in real-world financial markets.

DESIRABLE FEATURES OF INVESTMENT RISK MEASURES

The failure of asset return distributions to follow a normal distribution leads to the question of how risk should be measured. There is a growing literature in finance that has proposed alternative risk measures. However, the measures proposed are highly technical and we can only provide the very basics here. We begin with a discussion of the desirable features of investment risk measures.

Although in portfolio theory the variance of a portfolio's return has been the most commonly used measure of investment risk, different investors adopt different investment strategies in seeking to realize their investment objectives. Consequently, intuitively, it is difficult to believe that investors have come to accept only one definition of risk. Regulators of financial institutions and commentators to risk measures proposed by regulators have proffered alternative definitions of risk. As noted by Dowd (2002, 1):

> The theory and practice of risk management—and, included with that, risk measurement—have developed enormously since the pioneering work of Harry Markowitz in the 1950s. The theory has developed to the point where risk management/measurement is now regarded as a distinct sub-field of the theory of finance, . . .

Szegö (2004) categorizes risk measures as one of the three major revolutions in finance and places the start of that revolution in 1997. He notes that alternative risk measures have been accepted by practitioners but "rejected by the academic establishment and, so far discarded by regulators!" (p. 4).

Basic Features of Investment Risk Measures

Balzer (2001) argues that a risk measure is investor specific and, therefore, there is "no single universally acceptable risk measure." He suggests the following three features that an investment risk measure should capture:[5]

- Relativity of risk
- Multidimensionalility of risk
- Asymmetry of risk

The *relativity of risk* means that risk should be related to performing worse than some alternative investment or benchmark. Balzer (1994, 2001) and Sortino and Satchell (2001), among others, have proposed that investment risk might be measured by the probability of the investment return falling below a specified risk benchmark. The risk benchmark might itself be a random variable, such as a liability benchmark (for example an insurance product), the inflation rate or possibly inflation plus some safety margin, the risk-free rate of return, the bottom percentile of return, a sector index return, a budgeted return or other alternative investments. Each benchmark can be justified in relation to the goal of the portfolio manager. Should performance fall below the benchmark, the consequences could have major adverse consequences for the portfolio manager.

In addition, the same investor could have multiple objectives and hence multiple risk benchmarks. Thus, risk is also a *multidimensional* phenomenon. However, an appropriate choice of the benchmarks is necessary in order to avoid an incorrect evaluation of opportunities available to investors. For example, historically too often little recognition is given to liability targets by some institutional investors. This is the major factor contributing to the underfunding of U.S. corporate pension sponsors of defined benefit plans.[6]

Intuition suggests that risk is an asymmetric concept related to the downside outcomes, and any realistic risk measure has to value and consider upside and downside differently. The standard deviation considers the positive and the negative deviations from the mean as a potential risk. Thus, in this case, over-performance relative to the mean is penalized just as much as underperformance.

Intertemporal Dependence and Correlation with Other Sources of Risk

The standard deviation is a measure of dispersion and it cannot always be used as a measure of risk. The preferred investment does not always pres-

---

[5] There are other features he suggests but they are not discussed here.
[6] See Ryan and Fabozzi (2002).

ent better returns than the other. It could happen that the worst investment presents the greatest return in some periods. Hence, time could influence the investor's choices. We will illustrate this feature of investment risk with a realistic example.

Figure 4.5 shows the S&P 500 daily return series from January 4, 1995 to January 30, 1998. The dispersion around the mean changes sensibly, in particular during the last period of our observations when the Asian market crisis began (i.e., the spike in the series). Hence, in some periods there are big oscillations around zero and in other periods the oscillations are reduced.

Clearly, if the degree of uncertainty changes over time, the risk too has to change during the time. In this case, the investment return process is not stationary; that is, we cannot assume that returns maintain their distribution unvaried in the course of time. In much of finance theory, stationary and independent realizations are assumed. The latter assumption implies that history has no impact on the future. More concrete, the distribution of tomorrow's return is the same independent of the fact whether yesterday the biggest stock market crash ever recorded took place or whether yesterday's return equaled 10%.

As a result, the oldest observations are assumed to have the same weight in an investor's decisions as the most recent ones. Is this assumption realistic? Recent studies on investment return processes have shown that historical realizations are not independent and present a clustering of the volatility effect (time-varying volatility). That phenomena lead to the fundamental

FIGURE 4.5 S&P 500 Return Time Series from 1/4/1995 to 1/30/1998

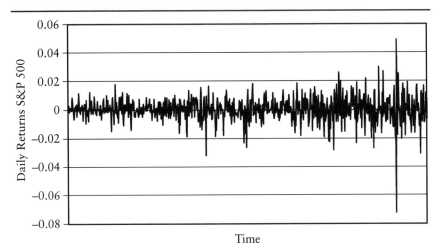

Source: Figure 12.1 in Rachev, Menn, and Fabozzi (2005, 183).

time-series model *autoregressive conditional heteroscedasticity* (ARCH). In particular, the last observations have a greater impact in investment decisions than the oldest ones. Thus, any realistic measure of risk changes and evolves over time, taking into consideration the heteroscedastic (time-varying volatility) behavior of the historical return series.

Figure 4.6 shows the S&P 500 daily return series from September 8, 1997 to January 30, 1998. The wavy behavior of returns also has a *propagation effect* on the other markets. This can be seen in Figure 4.7 which describes the German stock market index, the DAX 30, daily return series valued in U.S. dollars during the same period as the S&P 500 series. When we observe the highest peaks in the S&P 500 returns, there is an analogous peak in the German stock market index, the DAX 30. This propagation effect is known as cointegration of the return series.[7] The propagation effect in this case is a consequence of the globalization of financial markets—the risk of a country/sector is linked to the risk of the other countries/sectors. Therefore, it could be important to limit the propagation effect by diversifying the risk. As a matter of fact, it is largely proven that the diversification, opportunely modeled, diminishes the probability of big losses. Hence, an

FIGURE 4.6 S&P 500 Return Time Series from 9/8/1997 to 1/30/1998

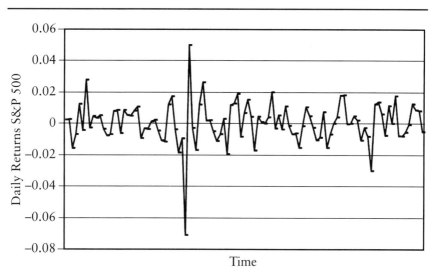

Source: Figure 12.2 in Rachev, Menn, and Fabozzi (2005, 184).

---

[7]Cointegration was introduced by the fundamental work of Granger (1981) and elaborated upon further by Engle and Granger (1987).

FIGURE 4.7 DAX 30 Return Time Series from 9/8/1997 to 1/30/1998

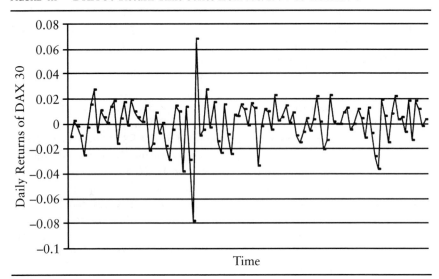

Source: Figure 12.3 in Rachev, Menn, and Fabozzi (2005, 185).

adequate risk measure values and models correctly the correlation among different investments, sectors, and markets.

Axiomatic Properties of a Coherent Risk Measure

The issue in not only investment management but in risk management and the establishment of capital requirements for banks and insurance companies is whether one can establish a set of desirable properties that a risk measure should satisfy. Such properties were formulated by Artzner et al. (1998) who provide an axiomatic definition that they call a *coherent risk measure*. The four properties are (1) monotonicity, (2) positive homogeneity, (3) subadditivity, and (4) invariance. These properties that a proposed risk measure should satisfy are too technical to present here. Instead, we provide alternative interpretations of these properties for a proposed investment risk measure to be a coherent risk measure for the return on a security and a portfolio.[8]

To explain these risk measures, we will consider the case of two securities X and Y. Let the random return of these two securities be denoted by r_X and r_Y. We will denote a proposed risk measure by M. Thus, $M(r_X)$ and $M(r_Y)$ would be the proposed risk measure for the random return for

---
[8] For a further discussion, see Rachev, Stoyanov, and Fabozzi (2007).

security X and Y, respectively. For example, if the proposed risk measure is the variance, then $M(r_X)$ and $M(r_Y)$ would be the variance of the return for security X and Y, respectively.

Now let's look at the properties of a coherent risk measure.

The monotonicity property requires that if security Y has a random return which is not less than the return of security X at the end of a given investment horizon in all states of the world, then for a proposed risk measure to be a coherent risk measure, the risk of security Y should not be greater than the risk of security X. In terms of our notation, this can be expressed as[9]

$$M(r_Y) \leq M(r_X), \text{ if } r_Y \geq r_X$$

The positive homogeneity property states that scaling the return of the portfolio by a positive factor scales the risk by the same factor. That is, for a proposed risk measure to be a coherent risk measures, if a position in a security triples, for example, so does the risk of that position. The positive homogeneity property implies that if the risk of the securities in a portfolio of all risky assets increases by a factor of h, the new portfolio will be the risk of the original portfolio (without the cash) but scaled by h. That is, for a risk measure M to be a coherent risk measure, it must satisfy the following property:

$$M(h\, r_x) = h\, M(r_X)$$

The subadditivity property states if X and Y describe random returns, then the risk of the portfolio is not greater than the sum of the risks of the two random returns. To understand this for the two security case, let w be the percentage of the portfolio invested in security X and $(1 - w)$ the percentage of the portfolio invested in security Y. Then

Security X return: $w\, r_x$
Security Y return: $(1 - w)\, r_Y$
Portfolio return: $w\, r_x + (1 - w)\, r_Y$

The risk of the two securities and the portfolio is denoted by

Risk of security X: $M\,[w\, r_x]$
Risk of security Y: $M\,[(1 - w)\, r_Y]$
Risk of portfolio: $M\,[w\, r_x + (1 - w)\, r_Y]$

---

[9] There is a qualifier here. This property holds in what probability theorists refer to as an "almost surely" sense and denote by "a.s." In probability theory, an event happens almost surely (a.s.) if it happens with probability equal to 1.

For a proposed risk measure M to be a coherent risk measure, it must satisfy the following property:

$$M[wr_X + (1 - w)r_Y] \leq M[wr_X] + M[(1 - w)r_Y]$$

Look at the right-hand side of the above inequality. If we apply the positive homogeneity property that must be satisfied by a coherent risk measure, instead of h we have w and $(1 - w)$. Therefore,

$$M[wr_X] = wM[r_X]$$

$$M[(1 - w)r_Y] = (1 - w)M[r_Y]$$

Therefore,

$$M[wr_X] + M[(1 - w)r_Y] = wM[r_X] + (1 - w)M[r_Y]$$

Substituting the right-hand side of the above equation into the inequality for the subadditivity property implies that the proposed risk measure satisfy

$$M[wr_X + (1 - w)r_Y] \leq wM[r_X] + (1 - w)M[r_Y]$$

This property, by combining the positive homogeneity property with the subadditivity property, is called the *convexity property*, which requires that the risk of a portfolio is not greater than the sum of the risks of the securities comprising the portfolio.

We have seen the convexity property before. Recall that when we described mean-variance analysis in Chapter 2, we saw the diversification effect: if securities are combined into a portfolio, the variance of the portfolio will be less than or equal to the sum of the variance of the individual securities. How much less in the case of securities X and Y depends on the correlation between the returns of the two securities.

In the context of security returns, the invariance property (sometimes referred to as the *translation invariance* or *cash invariance property*) says that if a risk-free security is added to a portfolio, then for a proposed risk measure, the risk of the portfolio should be reduced.

ALTERNATIVE RISK MEASURES FOR PORTFOLIO SELECTION

It would be wrong to think that Markowitz (1952) did not carefully consider the problems associated with using the variance of returns as a measure of investment risk. In fact, Markowitz recognized that an alternative to the variance is the semivariance. The *semivariance* is similar to the variance except that in the calculation no consideration is given to returns above the expected return. Portfolio selection could be recast in terms of mean-semivariance. However, if the return distribution is symmetric, Markowitz (1959, 190) notes that "an analysis based on (expected return) and (standard deviation) would consider these . . . (assets) as equally desirable." He rejected the semivariance noting that the variance "is superior with respect to cost, convenience, and familiarity" and when the asset return distribution is symmetric, either measure "will produce the same set of efficient portfolios." (Markowitz 1959, 193–194).[10]

There is a heated debate on risk measures used for valuing and optimizing the investor's portfolio. In this section and the one to follow, we will describe the various portfolio risk measures proposed in the literature. However, we do not include the mathematical formulation here for each of these measures.

According to the literature on portfolio theory, two disjointed categories of risk measures can be defined: dispersion measures and safety-risk measures. We describe some of the most well-known dispersion measures and safety-first measures next.

Dispersion Measures

The variance or standard deviation (more technically referred to as the *mean-standard deivation*) is a dispersion measure. Several alternative portfolio mean dispersion approaches have been proposed in the last few decades. The most commonly used measure (and easiest to understand) is the mean-absolute deviation.[11]

The *mean-absolute deviation* (MAD) dispersion measure is based on the absolute value of the deviations from the mean rather than the squared deviations as in the case of the mean-standard deviation. The MAD is more robust with respect to outliers (i.e., observations in the tail of the return distribution).

Safety-First Risk Measures

Many researchers have suggested the *safety-first rules* as a criterion for decision making under uncertainty.[12] In these models, a subsistence, a bench-

---

[10]The mean-semivariance approach was revisited by Stefani and Szegö (1976).
[11]Other such measures are the mean-absolute moment, the Gini index of dissimilarity, and mean entropy.
[12]See, among others, Roy (1952), Tesler (1955/6), and Bawa (1976, 1978).

mark, or a disaster level of returns is identified. The objective is the maximization of the probability that the returns are above the benchmark. Thus, most of the safety-first risk measures proposed in the literature are linked to the benchmark-based approach.

Even if there are not apparent connections between the expected utility approach and a more appealing benchmark-based approach, Castagnoli and LiCalzi (1996) have proven that the expected utility can be reinterpreted in terms of the probability that the return is above a given benchmark. Hence, when it is assumed that investors maximize their expected utility, it is implicitly assumed that investors minimize the probability of the investment return falling below a specified risk benchmark.

Although in practice it is not always simple to identify the underlying benchmark, expected utility theory partially justifies the use of the benchmark-based approach. Moreover, it is possible to prove that the two approaches are in many cases equivalent even if the economic reasons and justifications are different.[13]

Some of the most well-known safety-first risk measures proposed in the literature are

- Classical safety-first
- Value at risk
- Conditional value at risk/expected tail loss
- Lower partial moment

In the *classical safety-first* portfolio choice problem as formulated by Roy (1952), the risk measure is the probability of loss or, more generally, the probability of portfolio return less than some specified value. In terms of implementation, generally, this approach involves optimization that requires solving a much more complex optimization problem to find the optimal portfolios in contrast to the mean-variance model.[14]

Probably the most well-known downside risk measure is *value at risk* (VaR). This measure is related to the percentiles of loss distributions, and measures the predicted maximum loss at a specified probability level (for example, 95%) over a certain time horizon (for example, 10 days). The main characteristic of VaR is that of synthesizing in a single value the possible losses which could occur with a given probability in a given temporal horizon. This feature, together with the (very intuitive) concept of maximum probable loss, allows investors to figure out how risky a portfolio or

---

[13]See Castagnoli and LiCalzi (1996, 1999), Bordley and LiCalzi (2000), Ortobelli and Rachev (2001), Rachev and Mittnik (2000), and Rachev, Ortobelli, and Schwartz (2004).

[14]More specifically, it involves a complex mixed integer linear programming problem.

trading position is. There are various ways to calculate the VaR of a security or a portfolio but a discussion of these methodologies are beyond the scope of this chapter.

Despite the advantages cited for VaR as a measure of risk, it does have several theoretical limitations. Specifically, it is not a coherent risk measure and therefore cannot offer an exhaustive representation of an investor's preferences. Moreover, it ignores returns beyond the VaR (i.e., it does not consider the concentration of returns in the tails beyond VaR). To overcome these limitations and problems, Artzner et al. (1999) propose the *conditional value at risk* (CVaR) as an alternative risk measure. CVaR, also called *expected shortfall* or *expected tail loss*, measures the expected value of portfolio returns, given that the VaR has been exceeded. CVaR is a coherent risk measure, and portfolio selection using this risk measure can be reduced to a linear optimization problem.

A natural extension of semivariance is the lower *partial moment* risk measure.[15] This measure, also called *downside risk* or *probability-weighted function of deviations below a specified target return*, depends on two parameters: (1) a power index that is a proxy for the investor's degree of risk aversion and (2) the target rate of return that is the minimum return that must be earned.

EXTENSIONS OF THE THEORY OF PORTFOLIO SELECTION

In addition to the alternative risk measures, other advances in the theory of portfolio selection are (1) the inclusion of higher moments and (2) robust portfolio optimization.

Portfolio Selection with Higher Moments

Markowitz's mean-variance framework is a special case of general utility maximization that arises when investors have a special type of utility function (i.e., quadratic utility) or when asset returns are normally distributed. However, as discussed earlier, return distributions in the financial markets exhibit fat tails and asymmetry, and therefore cannot be described by their means and variances alone. Recall from our earlier discussion, the mean and the variance are the first two moments of a probability distribution. The third moment is a measure of skewness and the fourth moment is a measure of kurtosis.

A generalization of the mean-variance framework that incorporates higher moments such as skewness and kurtosis had been developed. The first

---
[15] See Bawa (1976) and Fishburn (1977).

attempt to extend the mean-variance optimization to higher moments was done almost 40 years ago by Jean (1971). At the turn of the century, more general and rigorous treatments have been presented by several researchers.[16] Because of the technical complexity of these models, we do not discuss them here.

Robust Portfolio Optimization

Despite the great influence and theoretical impact of modern portfolio theory, today—more than 50 years after Markowitz's seminal work—full risk-return optimization at the asset level is primarily done only at the more quantitatively oriented asset management firms. The availability of quantitative tools is not the issue—today's optimization technology is mature and much more user-friendly than it was at the time Markowitz first proposed the theory of portfolio selection—yet many asset managers avoid using the quantitative portfolio allocation framework altogether.

A major reason for the reluctance of portfolio managers to apply quantitative risk-return optimization is that they have observed that it may be unreliable in practice. Specifically, mean-variance optimization (or any measure of risk for that matter) is very sensitive to changes in the inputs (in the case of mean-variance optimization, such inputs include the expected return and variance of each asset and the asset covariance between each pair of assets). While it can be difficult to make accurate estimates of these inputs, estimation errors in the forecasts significantly impact the resulting portfolio weights. As a result, the optimal portfolios generated by the mean-variance analysis generally have extreme or counterintuitive weights for some assets.[17] Such examples, however, are not necessarily a sign that the theory of portfolio selection is flawed; rather, that when used in practice, the mean-variance analysis as presented by Markowitz has to be modified in order to achieve reliability, stability, and robustness with respect to model and estimation errors.

It goes without saying that advances in the mathematical and physical sciences have had a major impact upon finance. In particular, mathematical areas such as probability theory, statistics, econometrics, operations research, and mathematical analysis have provided the necessary tools and discipline for the development of modern financial economics. Substantial advances in the areas of robust estimation and robust optimization were made during the 1990s, and have proven to be of great importance for the practical applicability and reliability of portfolio management and optimization.

---

[16]See, for example, Athayde and Flôres (2002, 2004), Harvey et al. (2003), and Fabozzi, Focardi, and Kolm (2006).

[17]See Best and Grauer (1991), Broadie (1993), and Chopra and Ziemba (1993).

Any statistical estimate is subject to error—estimation error. A *robust estimator* is a statistical estimation technique that is less sensitive to outliers in the data. For example, in practice, it is undesirable that one or a few extreme returns have a large impact on the estimation of the average return of a stock. Nowadays, statistical techniques such as Bayesian analysis and robust statistics are more commonplace in asset management. Taking it one step further, practitioners are starting to incorporate the uncertainty introduced by estimation errors directly into the optimization process. This is very different from traditional mean-variance analysis, where one solves the portfolio optimization problem as a problem with deterministic inputs (i.e., inputs that are assumed to be known with certainty), without taking the estimation errors into account. In particular, the statistical precision of individual estimates is explicitly incorporated into the portfolio allocation process. Providing this benefit is the underlying goal of *robust portfolio optimization*.[18]

First introduced by El Ghaoui and Lebret (1997) and by Ben-Tal and Nemirovski (1998, 1999), modern robust optimization techniques allow a portfolio manager to solve the robust version of the portfolio optimization problem in about the same time as needed for the traditional mean-variance portfolio optimization problem. The robust approach explicitly uses the distribution from the estimation process to find a robust portfolio in a single optimization, thereby directly incorporating uncertainty about inputs in the optimization process. As a result, robust portfolios are less sensitive to estimation errors than other portfolios, and often perform better than optimal portfolios determined by traditional mean-variance portfolios. Moreover, the robust optimization framework offers great flexibility and many new interesting applications. For instance, robust portfolio optimization can exploit the notion of statistically equivalent portfolios. This concept is important in large-scale portfolio management involving many complex constraints such as transaction costs, turnover, or market impact that we discuss in Chapter 12. Specifically, with robust optimization, a portfolio manager can find the best portfolio that (1) minimizes trading costs with respect to the current holdings and (2) has an expected portfolio return and variance that are statistically equivalent to those of the classical mean-variance portfolio.

Once again, we do not present the mathematical models involved because of their reliance on advanced mathematical and statistical concept. For a discussion of these models see Fabozzi et al. (2007a, 2007b, and 2009).

---

[18] Another way of dealing with estimation is by using a statistical technique known as Bayesian analysis. See Rachev et al (2008).

BEHAVIORAL FINANCE ATTACK ON THE THEORY OF PORTFOLIO

In building economic models, financial economists make assumptions about the behavior of those who make investment decisions in financial markets. They refer to these entities as "economic agents." More specifically, they make assumptions about how economic agents make investment choices in selecting assets to include in their portfolio. This was clear when we described the theory of portfolio selection in Chapter 2.

The underlying economic theory that financial economists draw upon in formulating various theories of choice is utility theory. There are concerns with the reliance on such theories. In the selection of investments, prominent economists such as John Maynard Keynes have argued that investor psychology affects security prices. Support for this view came in the late 1970 when two psychologists, Daniel Kahneman and Amos Tversky, demonstrated that the actions of economic agents in making investment decisions under uncertainty are inconsistent with the assumptions made by financial economists in formulating financial theories.[19] Based on numerous experiments, Kahneman and Tversky attacked utility theory and presented their own view as to how investors made choices under uncertainty that they called "prospect theory." Other attacks on the assumptions of traditional financial theory drawing from the field of psychology lead to the specialized field in finance known as *behavioral finance*.[20] Behavioral finance looks at how psychology affects investor decisions and the implications not only for the theory of portfolio selection that has been the focus of attention in this chapter, but in deriving a theory about asset pricing that we describe in the next chapter (the capital asset pricing model) and the pricing of options in Chapter 15.

The foundations of behavioral finance draw from the research by Kahneman, Slovic, and Tversky (1982) and has the following three themes:[21]

> *Behavioral Finance Theme 1.* When making investment decisions, investors make errors because they rely on rules of thumb.
> *Behavioral Finance Theme 2.* Investors are influenced by form as well as substance in making investment decisions.
> *Behavioral Finance Theme 3.* Prices in the financial market are affected by errors and decision frames.

---

[19]See Kahneman and Tversky (1979).
[20]For a further discussion of behavioral finance, see Statman (2008), Wilcox (2008), and Ricciardi (2008a, 2008b).
[21]These themes are from Shefrin (2002).

Behavioral Finance Theme 1 involves the concept of *heuristics*. This term means a rule of thumb strategy or good guide to pursue so as to reduce the time required to make a decision. For example, in planning for retirement, a rule of thumb that has been suggested for having sufficient funds to retire is to invest 10% of annual pretax income. As for what to invest in to reach that retirement goal (that is, the allocation among asset classes), a rule of thumb that has been suggested is that the percentage that an investor should allocate to bonds should be determined by subtracting from 100 the investor's age. So, for example, a 45-year old individual should invest 55% of his or her retirement funds in bonds.

Although there are circumstances where heuristics can work fairly well, studies in the field of psychology suggest that heuristics can lead to systematic biases in decision making. This systematic bias is referred to by psychologists as *cognitive biases*. In the context of finance, these biases lead to errors in making investment decisions, what Shefrin (2002) refers to as *heuristic-driven biases*. Contrast this with the assumption made in the theory of portfolio selection that all investors estimate the mean and variance of every asset return and based on those estimates construct an optimal portfolio for each level of risk (i.e., the efficient frontier).

Behavioral Finance Theme 2 involves the concept of *framing*. This term deals with the way in which a situation or choice is presented to an investor. Behavioral finance theorists argue that the framing of investment choices can result in significantly different assessments by an investor as to the risk and return of each choice and, therefore, the ultimate decision made.[22]

Shefrin and Statman (1985) provide an example of faulty framing coupled with a cognitive bias. Individual investors often fail to treat the value of their stock portfolio at market value. Instead, investors maintain a "mental account," where they continue to market the value of each stock in their portfolio at the purchase price despite the change in the market value. The psychological reason for investor reluctance to acknowledge any losses on stocks in their portfolio is that it keeps alive the prospect that those stocks that have realized losses will subsequently recover and produce a gain. When investors ultimately dispose of their stocks, they close the mental account and only at that time acknowledge the loss that had occurred on paper. Hence, investment decisions are affected by this mental accounting treatment rather than being based on the true economic impact that an investment decision would have on the investor.

Hence, the second theme of behavioral finance is many times referred to as "frame dependence" because theorists argue that investment decisions are affected by framing. Traditional finance theorists, in contrast, assume believe that "frame independence." This means, according to Shefrin (2001,

---
[22]See Tversky and Kahneman (1961 and 1986).

4), that investors "view all decisions through the transparent, objective lens of risk and return."

How errors caused by heuristics and framing dependence affect the pricing of assets is Behavioral Finance Theme 3. In Chapter 7, we will discuss the efficiency of markets. Behavioral finance theorists argue that markets will be inefficient because asset prices will not reflect their fundamental value due to the way investors make decisions. For this reason, Shefrin (2001) labels this theme of behavioral finance as "inefficient markets."

We have tossed out quite a bit of theory so far in this book and will have more in the next chapter. In traditional finance, we have a cornerstone theory in finance—Markowitz's theory of portfolio selection—as well see in the next chapter asset pricing theory formulated by William Sharpe and others that rests on the theory of portfolio selection. In the other camp is the behavioral finance theory lead by the various theories and studies by Kahneman. These are not minor theories. They all lead to the awarding of the Nobel Prize in Economic Sciences for their contribution—Markowitz and Sharpe in 1990 "for their pioneering work in the theory of financial economics" and Kahneman in 2002 "for having integrated insights from psychological research into economic science, especially concerning human judgment and decision-making under uncertainty." That leaves us with two theories: traditional finance theory or behavioral finance theory. Which theory is correct?

In fairness, we have not provided the responses of the supporters of traditional finance theory to the criticisms of those who support behavioral finance theory. Nor have we presented the attacks on behavioral finance. Fortunately, Hirshleifer (2001) provided that analysis by describing the common objections to both theories. He refers to the traditional finance theory as the "fully rational approach" and behavioral finance theory as the "psychological approach." A criticism of both approaches is that they can go "theory fishing" to find theories in market data to support their respective position. Objections to the fully rational approach are that (1) the calculations required for the implementation of this approach are extremely difficult to do, and (2) there is ample empirical evidence that fails to support rational behavior by investors. Objections to the psychological approach according to Hirshleifer are that (1) "alleged psychology biases are arbitrary" and (2) the experiments performed by researchers that find alleged psychological biases are arbitrary.

SUMMARY

Mean-variance analysis for portfolio selection as set forth by Markowitz is based on several assumptions regarding investor behavior when making investment decisions and about the probability distribution of the return on assets that make it acceptable to use the variance or standard deviation as a measure of risk. In this chapter, we discussed these attacks on mean-variance analysis. We first reviewed probability theory and then explained the normal distribution. Given that the empirical evidence from real-world financial markets did not support the assumption that asset returns are normally distributed, we discussed an alternative distribution that is consistent with the empirical evidence on returns: fat tails and asymmetry. This distribution is the stable Paretian distribution.

We then discussed desirable features of investment risk measures. These features include relativity of risk, multidimensionalility of risk, and asymmetry of risk. In addition, there are axiomatic properties that a risk measure should satisfy to be a coherent risk measures.

There is a heated debate on risk measures used for valuing and optimizing the investor's risk portfolio. The two disjointed categories of risk measures that have been suggested are classified as dispersion measures and safety-risk measures. The variance and mean-absolute deviation are the most commonly discussed dispersion measures. Safety-first measures require the identification of a subsistence, a benchmark, or a disaster level of returns. The objective is the maximization of the probability that the returns are above the benchmark. Some of the most well-known safety-first risk measures proposed in the literature are classical safety-first, value at risk, conditional value at risk/expected tail loss, and lower partial moment.

In addition to alternative risk measures, we discussed two advances in the theory of portfolio selection. The first is generalization of the mean-variance framework that incorporates higher moments such as skewness and kurtosis. The second involves dealing with the problem associated with the sensitivity of the portfolio weights in the optimal solution of the mean-variance optimization to the estimated inputs (i.e., expected returns, variances, and covariances). Robust portfolio optimization is now used to allow the statistical precision of individual estimates of the inputs to be explicitly incorporated in the portfolio allocation process.

Another attack on the traditional mean-variance framework is from a branch of finance known as behavioral finance. This branch of finance, which draws from the field of psychology, asserts that investor behavior is far different from that postulated in standard finance theory. The foundations of behavioral finance are based on three themes: (1) when making investment decisions, investors make errors because they rely on rules of thumb (heuristics); (2) investors are influenced by form as well as substance in making investment decisions (framing); and (3) prices in the financial market are affected by errors and decision frames.

REFERENCES

Arthur, W. B., J. H. Hollan, B. LeBaron, R. Palmer, and P. Tayler. 1997. Asset pricing under endogenous expectations in an artificial stock market. In *The economy as an evolving complex system, II*, edited by W. B. Arthur, S. Durlauf, and D. Lane, SFI Studies in the Sciences of Complexity. Redwood, CA: Addison-Wesley.

Artzner, P., F. Delbaen, J. M. Eber, and D. Heath. 1999. Coherent measures of risk *Mathematical Finance* 9: 203–228.

Athayde, G. M. and R. G. Flôres. 2002. The portfolio frontier with higher moments: The undiscovered country. *Computing in Economics and Finance 2002*, Society for Computational Economics.

Athayde, G. M. and R. G. Flôres. 2004. Finding a maximum skewness portfolio—A general solution to three-moments portfolio choice. *Journal of Economic Dynamics and Control* 28: 1335–1352.

Bak, P., M. Paczuski, and M. Shubik. 1996. Price variations in a stock market with many agents. Cowles Foundation Discussion Papers No. 1132, Cowles Foundation, Yale University.

Balzer, L. A. 1994. Measuring investment risk: A review. *Journal of Investing* 3, no. 3: 47–58.

———. 2001. Investment risk: A unified approach to upside and downside returns. In *Managing Downside Risk in Financial Markets: Theory Practice and Implementation*, edited by F. A. Sortino and S. E. Satchell (pp. 103–155). Oxford: Butterworth-Heinemann.

Bawa, V. S. 1976. Admissible portfolio for all individuals. *Journal of Finance* 31: 1169–1183.

———. 1978. Safety-first stochastic dominance and optimal portfolio choice. *Journal of Financial and Quantitative Analysis* 13: 255–271.

Ben-Tal, A., and A. S. Nemirovski. 1998. Robust convex optimization. *Mathematics of Operations Research* 23: 769–805.

Ben-Tal, A., and A. S. Nemirovski. 1999. Robust solutions to uncertain linear programs. *Operations Research Letters* 25: 1–13.

Best, M. J., and R. R. Grauer. 1991. On the sensitivity of mean-variance efficient portfolios to changes in asset means: Some analytical and computational results. *Review of Financial Studies*, 4, no. 2: 315–342.

Bordley, R., and M. LiCalzi. 2000. Decision analysis using targets instead of utility functions. *Decision in Economics and Finance* 23: 53–74.

Broadie, M. 1993. Computing efficient frontiers using estimated parameters. *Annals of Operations Research*, 45: 21–58.

Castagnoli, E., and M. LiCalzi. 1996. Expected utility without utility. *Theory and Decision* 41: 281–301.

Castagnoli, E., and M. LiCalzi. 1999. Nonexpected utility theories and benchmarking under risk. *SZIGMA* 29: 199–211.

Chopra, V. K., and W. T. Ziemba. 1993. The effects of errors in means, variances, and covariances on optimal portfolio choice. *Journal of Portfolio Management* 19, no. 2: 6–11.

Cont, R., and J. P. Bouchaud. 2000. Herd behavior and aggregate fluctuations in financial markets. *Macroeconomic Dynamics* 4: 170–196.
Cootner, P. H. 1964. *The random character of stock market prices.* Cambridge, MA: MIT Press.
Dowd, K. 2002. *Measuring market risk.* Chichester, UK: John Wiley & Sons.
El Ghaoui, L., and H. Lebret. 1997. Robust solutions to least-squares problems with uncertain data. *SIAM Journal on Matrix Analysis and Applications* 18: 1035–1064.
Fabozzi, F. J., S. M. Focardi, and P. N. Kolm. 2006. *Financial modeling of the equity market.* Hoboken, NJ: John Wiley & Sons.
Fabozzi, F. J., D. Huang, and G. Zhou. 2009. Robust portfolios: Some recent contributions from operations research and finance. Forthcoming *Annals of Operations Research*.
Fabozzi, F. J., P. N. Kolm, D. Pachamanova, and S. M. Focardi. 2007a. *Robust portfolio optimization and management.* Hoboken, NJ: John Wiley & Sons.
Fabozzi, F. J., P. N. Kolm, D. Pachamanova, and S. M. Focardi. 2007b. Robust portfolio optimization. *Journal of Portfolio Management* 33 (Spring): 40–48.
Fama, E. F. 1963. Mandelbrot and the stable Paretian hypothesis. *Journal of Business* 36: 420–429.
Fishburn, P. C. 1977. Mean-risk analysis with risk associated with below-target returns. *American Economic Review* 67: 116–126.
Harvey, C. R., J. C. Liechty, M. W. Liechty, and P. Mueller. 2003. Portfolio selection with higher moments. Working paper, Duke University.
Hirshleifer, D. 2001. Investor psychology and asset pricing. *Journal of Finance* 56: 1533–1597.
Jean, W. H. 1971. The extension of portfolio analysis to three or more parameters. *Journal of Financial and Quantitative Analysis* 6: 505–515.
———. 1973. More on multidimensional portfolio analysis. *Journal of Financial and Quantitative Analysis* 8: 475–490.
Kahneman, D. and A. Tversky. 1979. Prospect theory: An analysis of decision under risk. *Econometrica* 47 (March): 236–291.
Kahneman, D. and A. Tversky. 1992. Advances in prospect theory: Cumulative representation of uncertainty. *Journal of Risk and Uncertainty* 5: 297–323.
Kahneman, D., P. Slovic, and A. Tversky. 1982. *Judgment under uncertainty: Heuristics and biases.* New York: Cambridge University Press.
Lux, T. 1998. The socio-economic dynamics of speculative markets. *Journal of Economic Behavior and Organization* 33: 143–165.
Mandelbrot, B. B. 1963. The variation of certain speculative prices. *Journal of Business* 36: 394–419.
Markowitz, H. M. 1952. Portfolio selection. *Journal of Finance* 7, no. 1: 77–91.
———. 1959. *Portfolio selection: Efficient diversification of investment.* New York: John Wiley & Sons.
Ortobelli, S., and S. T. Rachev. 2001. Safety first analysis and stable Paretian approach. *Mathematical and Computer Modelling* 34: 1037–1072.

Ortobelli, S., S. T. Rachev, S. Stoyanov, F. J. Fabozzi, and A. Biglova. 2005. The proper use of risk measures in portfolio theory. *International Journal of Theoretical and Applied Finance* 8: 1–27.
Rachev, R. T., J. Hsu, B. Bagasheva, and F. J. Fabozzi. 2008. *Bayesian methods in finance*. Hoboken, NJ: John Wiley & Sons.
Rachev, S. T., C. Menn, and F. J. Fabozzi. 2005. *Fat-tailed and skewed asset return distributions: Implications for risk management, portfolio selection, and option pricing*. Hoboken, NJ: John Wiley & Sons.
Rachev, S. T., and S. Mittnik. 2000. *Stable paretian models in finance*. Chichester: John Wiley & Sons.
Rachev, S. T., S. Ortobelli, and E. Schwartz. 2004. The problem of optimal asset allocation with stable distributed returns. In *Stochastic Processes and Functional Analysis*, edited by A. Krinik and R. J. Swift (pp. 295–261). Dekker Series of Lecture Notes in Pure and Applied Mathematics. New York: Marcel Dekker.
Rachev, S. T., S. Ortobelli, S. Stoyanov, F. J. Fabozzi, and A. Biglova. 2008. Desirable properties of an ideal risk measure in portfolio theory. *International Journal of Theoretical and Applied Finance* 11: 19–54.
Rachev, S. T., S. Stoyanov, and F. J. Fabozzi. 2008. *Advanced stochastic models, risk assessment, and portfolio optimization: The ideal risk, uncertainty, and performance measures*. Hoboken, NJ: John Wiley & Sons.
Ricciardi, V. 2008a. The psychology of risk: The behavioral finance perspective. In *Handbook of Finance, vol. 2*, edited by F. J. Fabozzi (pp. 85–112). Hoboken, NJ: John Wiley & Sons.
Ricciardi, V. 2008b. Risk: Traditional finance versus behavioral finance. In *Handbook of Finance, vol. 3*, edited by F. J. Fabozzi (pp. 11–38). Hoboken, NJ: John Wiley & Sons.
Roy, A. D. 1952. Safety-first and the holding of assets. *Econometrica* 20: 431–449.
Shefrin, H. 2002. *Beyond greed and fear: Understanding behavioral finance and the psychology of investing*. New York: Oxford University Press.
Shefrin, H., and M. Statman. 1985. The disposition to sell winners too early and ride losers too long: Theory and evidence. *Journal of Finance* 40: 777–790.
Statman, M. 2008. What is behavioral finance. In *Handbook of Finance, vol. 2*, edited by F. J. Fabozzi (pp. 79–84). Hoboken, NJ: John Wiley & Sons.
Stefani, S., and G. Szegö. 1976. Formulazione analitica della funzione utilità dipendente da media e semivarianza mediante il principio dell'utilità attesa. *Bollettino UMI* 13A: 157–162.
Szegö, G. 2004. On the (non)acceptance of innovations. In *Risk Measures for the 21st Century*, edited by G. Szegö (pp. 1–6). Chichester, UK: John Wiley & Sons.
Tesler, L. G. 1955/6. Safety first and hedging. *Review of Economic Studies* 23: 1–16.
Treynor, J. L. 1961. Toward a theory of market value of risky assets. Unpublished paper, Arthur D. Little, Cambridge, MA.

Tversky, A., and D. Kahneman. 1961. The framing of decisions and the psychology of choice. *Science* 211: 453–458.
Tversky, A., and D. Kahneman. 1986. Rational choice and the framing of decisions. *Journal of Business* 59, no. 4 (pt. 2): S251–S278.
Wilcox, J. W. 2008. Behavioral finance. In *Handbook of Finance, vol. 2*, edited by F. J. Fabozzi (pp. 71–78). Hoboken, NJ: John Wiley & Sons.

CHAPTER 5

Asset Pricing Theories

As explained in previous chapters, a key input in portfolio selection is the expected return for an asset. Asset pricing models describe the relationship between risk and expected return. So while we refer to asset pricing models in this chapter, we mean the expected return investors require given the risk associated with an investment.

The two most well-known equilibrium pricing models are the *capital asset pricing model* (CAPM) developed in the 1960s and the *arbitrage pricing theory* (APT) model developed in the mid-1970s. In this chapter, we describe these two models and we present their applications in later chapters. More specifically, while in this chapter we provide the theory, we apply one of these models to common stock portfolio construction in Chapter 11 and bond portfolio management construction in Chapter 23.

When reading this chapter, keep in mind the discussion in the previous chapter regarding the assumptions of the underlying model the theory of portfolio selection which one particularly with respect to the CAPM. Specifically, if an asset pricing model assumes that investors construct portfolios according to the mean-variance (Markowitz) model, the criticisms of the Markowitz framework apply. Consequently, the issues regarding the appropriate risk measure and the criticisms leveled by behavioral finance theory apply. It is also important to realize that the theory of portfolio selection is a normative theory. A normative theory is one that describes a standard or norm of behavior that investors should pursue in constructing a portfolio, in contrast to a theory that is actually followed. The CAPM goes on to formalize the relationship that should exist between asset returns and risk if investors behave in a hypothesized manner. Therefore, in contrast to a normative theory, CAPM is a positive theory—a theory that hypothesizes how investors behave rather than how investors should behave.

CHARACTERISTICS OF AN ASSET PRICING MODEL

In well-functioning capital markets, an investor should be rewarded for accepting the various risks associated with investing in an asset. Risks are also referred to as "risk factors" or "factors." We can express an *asset pricing model* in general terms based on risk factors as follows:

$$E(R_i) = f(F_1, F_2, F_3, ..., F_N) \qquad (5.1)$$

where

$E(R_i)$ = expected return for asset i
F_k = risk factor k
N = number of risk factors

Equation (5.1) says that the expected return is a function of N risk factors. The trick is to figure out what the risk factors are and to specify the precise relationship between expected return and the risk factors.

We can fine-tune the asset pricing model given by equation (5.1) by thinking about the minimum expected return we would want from investing in an asset. There are securities issued by the U.S. Department of the Treasury that offer a known return if held over some period of time. The expected return offered on such securities is called the risk-free return or the risk-free rate because there is believed to be no default risk. By investing in an asset other than such securities, investors will demand a premium over the risk-free rate. That is, the expected return that an investor will require is

$$E(R_i) = R_f + \text{Risk premium}$$

where R_f is the risk-free rate.

The "risk premium" or additional return expected over the risk-free rate depends on the risk factors associated with investing in the asset. Thus, we can rewrite the general form of the asset pricing model given by equation (5.1) as follows:

$$E(R_i) = R_f + f(F_1, F_2, F_3, ..., F_N) \qquad (5.2)$$

Risk factors can be divided into two general categories. The first category is risk factors that cannot be diversified away. That is, no matter what the investor does, the investor cannot eliminate these risk factors. These risk factors are referred to as *systematic risk factors* or *nondiversifiable risk factors*. The second category is risk factors that can be eliminated via diversification. These risk factors are unique to the asset and are referred to as *unsystematic risk factors* or *diversifiable risk factors*.

CAPITAL ASSET PRICING MODEL

The first asset pricing model derived from economic theory was formulated by Sharpe (1964), Lintner (1965), Treynor (1961), and Mossin (1966) and is called the *capital asset pricing model* (CAPM). The CAPM has only one systematic risk factor—the risk of the overall movement of the market. This risk factor is referred to as "market risk." So, in the CAPM, the terms "market risk" and "systematic risk" are used interchangeably. By "market risk" it is meant the risk associated with holding a portfolio consisting of all assets, called the "market portfolio." As will be explained later, in the market portfolio an asset is held in proportion to its market value. So, for example, if the total market value of all assets is \$X and the market value of asset *j* is \$Y, then asset *j* will comprise \$Y/\$X of the market portfolio.

The CAPM is given by the following formula:

$$E(R_i) = R_f + \beta_i[E(R_M) - R_f] \quad (5.3)$$

where

$E(R_M)$ = expected return on the "market portfolio"
β_i = measure of systematic risk of asset *i* relative to the "market portfolio"

We will derive the CAPM later. For now, let's look at what this asset pricing model says.

The expected return for an asset *i* according to the CAPM is equal to the risk-free rate plus a risk premium. The risk premium is

$$\text{Risk premium in the CAPM} = \beta_i[E(R_M) - R_f]$$

First look at *beta* (β_i) in the risk premium component of the CAPM. Beta is a measure of the sensitivity of the return of asset *i* to the return of the market portfolio. A beta of 1 means that the asset or a portfolio has the same quantity of risk as the market portfolio. A beta greater than 1 means that the asset or portfolio has more market risk than the market portfolio, and a beta less than 1 means that the asset or portfolio has less market risk than the market portfolio.

The second component of the risk premium in the CAPM is the difference between the expected return on the market portfolio, $E(R_M)$, and the risk-free rate. It measures the potential reward for taking on the risk of the market above what can earned by investing in an asset that offers a risk-free rate.

Taken together, the risk premium is a product of the quantity of market risk (as measured by beta) and the potential compensation of taking on market risk (as measured by $[E(R_M) - R_f]$).

Let's use some values for beta to see if all of this makes sense. Suppose that a portfolio has a beta of zero. That is, the return for this portfolio has no market risk. Substituting zero for β in the CAPM given by equation (5.3), we would find that the expected return is just the risk-free rate. This makes sense since a portfolio that has no market risk should have an expected return equal to the risk-free rate.

Consider a portfolio that has a beta of 1. This portfolio has the same market risk as the market portfolio. Substituting 1 for β in the CAPM given by equation (5.3) results in an expected return equal to that of the market portfolio. Again, this is what one should expect for the return of this portfolio since it has the same market risk exposure as the market portfolio.

If a portfolio has greater market risk than the market portfolio, beta will be greater than 1 and the expected return will be greater than that of the market portfolio. If a portfolio has less market risk than the market portfolio, beta will be less than 1 and the expected return will be less than that of the market portfolio.

Derivation of the CAPM

The CAPM is an equilibrium asset pricing model derived from a set of assumptions. Here, we demonstrate how the CAPM is derived.

Assumptions

The CAPM is an abstraction of the real world capital markets and, as such, is based on some assumptions. These assumptions simplify matters a great deal, and some of them may even seem unrealistic. However, these assumptions make the CAPM more tractable from a mathematical standpoint. The CAPM assumptions are as follows:

Assumption 1. Investors make investment decisions based on the expected return and variance of returns and subscribe to the Markowitz method of portfolio diversification.
Assumption 2. Investors are rational and risk averse.
Assumption 3. Investors all invest for the same period of time.

Asset Pricing Theories

Assumption 4. Investors have the same expectations about the expected return and variance of all assets.

Assumption 5. There is a risk-free asset and investors can borrow and lend any amount at the risk-free rate.

Assumption 6. Capital markets are completely competitive and frictionless.

The first four assumptions deal with the way investors make decisions. The last two assumptions relate to characteristics of the capital market. These assumptions require further explanation. Many of these assumptions have been challenged resulting in modifications of the CAPM. As explained in the previous chapter, there is a branch of financial theory called behavioral finance which is highly critical of these assumptions.

With respect to Assumption 1, we devoted the previous chapter to issues associated with mean-variance analysis. We need not repeat those criticisms here.

Assumption 2 indicates that in order to accept greater risk, investors must be compensated by the opportunity of realizing a higher return. We refer to the behavior of such investors as being *risk averse*.[1] What this means is that if an investor faces a choice between two portfolios with the same expected return, the investor will select the portfolio with the lower risk. Certainly, this is a reasonable assumption.

By Assumption 3, all investors are assumed to make investment decisions over some single-period investment horizon. The theory does not specify how long that period is (i.e., six months, one year, two years, and so on). In reality, the investment decision process is more complex than that, with many investors having more than one investment horizon. Nonetheless, the assumption of a one-period investment horizon is necessary to simplify the mathematics of the theory.

To obtain the efficient frontier (i.e., the set of efficient portfolios) which we will be used in developing the CAPM, it will be assumed that investors have the same expectations with respect to the inputs that are used to derive the efficient portfolios: asset returns, variances, and correlations/covariances. This is Assumption 4 and is referred to as the "homogeneous expectations assumption."

As we will see, the existence of a risk-free asset and unlimited borrowing and lending at the risk-free rate, Assumption 5, is important in deriving the CAPM. This is because efficient portfolios are created for portfolios consisting of risky assets. No consideration is given to how to create efficient port-

---

[1] This is an oversimplified definition. Actually, a more rigorous definition of risk aversion is described by a mathematical specification of an investor's utility function. However, this complexity need not be of concern here.

folios when a risk-free asset is available. In the CAPM, it is assumed not only that there is a risk-free asset but that an investor can borrow funds at the same interest rate paid on a risk-free asset. This is a common assumption in many economic models developed in financed despite the fact it is well that that there is a different rate at which investors can borrow and lend funds.

Finally, Assumption 6 specifies that the capital market is perfectly competitive. In general, this means the number of buyers and sellers is sufficiently large, and all investors are small enough relative to the market so that no individual investor can influence an asset's price. Consequently, all investors are price takers, and the market price is determined where there is equality of supply and demand. In addition, according to this assumption, there are no transactions costs or impediments that interfere with the supply of and demand for an asset. Economists refer to these various costs and impediments as "frictions." The costs associated with frictions generally result in buyers paying more than in the absence of frictions and sellers receiving less.

In economic modeling, the model is modified by relaxing one or more of the assumptions. There are several extensions and modifications of the CAPM and we will review two of them in the appendix to this chapter. No matter the extension or modification, however, the basic implications are unchanged: Investors are only rewarded for taking on systematic risk and the only systematic risk is market risk.

Capital Market Line

To derive the CAPM, we begin with the efficient frontier from the theory of portfolio selection, which is shown in Figure 5.1. Every point on the efficient frontier is derived as explained earlier and is the maximum portfolio return for a given level of risk. In the figure, risk is measured on the horizontal axis by the standard deviation of the portfolio's return, which is the square root of the variance.

In creating an efficient frontier, there is no consideration of a risk-free asset. In the absence of a risk-free rate, efficient portfolios can be constructed based on expected return and variance, with the optimal portfolio being the one portfolio that is tangent to the investor's indifference curve. The efficient frontier changes, however, once a risk-free asset is introduced and assuming that investors can borrow and lend at the risk-free rate (Assumption 6). This is illustrated in Figure 5.1.

Every combination of the risk-free asset and the efficient portfolio denoted by point M is shown on the line drawn from the vertical axis at the risk-free rate tangent to the efficient frontier. The point of tangency is denoted by M, which represents portfolio M. All the portfolios on the line

FIGURE 5.1 The Capital Market Line

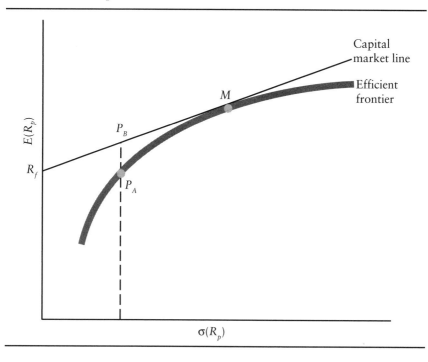

are feasible for the investor to construct. Portfolios to the left of portfolio M represent combinations of risky assets and the risk-free asset. Portfolios to the right of M include purchases of risky assets made with funds borrowed at the risk-free rate. Such a portfolio is called a *leveraged portfolio* because it involves the use of borrowed funds. The line from the risk-free rate that is tangent to portfolio M is called the *capital market line* (CML).

Let's compare a portfolio on the CML to a portfolio on the efficient frontier with the same risk. For example, compare portfolio P_A, which is on the efficient frontier, with portfolio P_B, which is on the CML and therefore is comprised of some combination of the risk-free asset and the efficient portfolio M. Notice that for the same risk, the expected return is greater for P_B than for P_A. By Assumption 2, a risk-averse investor will prefer P_B to P_A. That is, P_B will dominate P_A. In fact, this is true for all but one portfolio on the CML: portfolio M, which is on the efficient frontier.

With the introduction of the risk-free asset, we can now say that an investor will select a portfolio on the CML that represents a combination of borrowing or lending at the risk-free rate and the efficient portfolio M. The particular efficient portfolio on the CML that the investor will select will depend on the investor's risk preference. This can be seen in Figure 5.2, which is the same as Figure 5.1 but has the investor's indifference curves included. The investor will select the portfolio on the CML that is tangent to the highest indifference curve, u_3 in the exhibit. Notice that without the risk-free asset, an investor could only get to u_2, which is the indifference curve that is tangent to the efficient frontier. Thus, the opportunity to borrow or lend at the risk-free rate results in a capital market where risk-averse investors will prefer to hold portfolios consisting of combinations of the risk-free asset and some portfolio M on the efficient frontier.

We can derive a formula for the CML algebraically. Based on the assumption of homogeneous expectations (Assumption 4), all investors can create an efficient portfolio consisting of w_f placed in the risk-free asset and w_M in the market portfolio, where w represents the corresponding percentage (weight) of the portfolio allocated to each asset. Thus,

FIGURE 5.2 Optimal Portfolio and the Capital Market Line

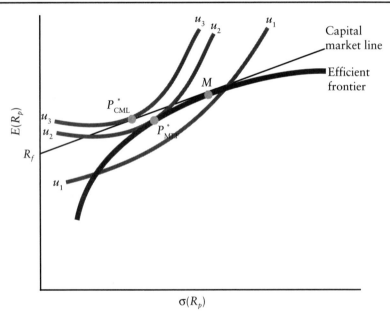

u_1, u_2, u_3 = indifference curves with $u_1 < u_2 < u_3$
M = market portfolio
R_f = risk-free rate
P^*_{CML} = optimal portfolio on capital market line
P^*_{MEF} = optimal portfolio on efficient frontier

Asset Pricing Theories

$$w_f + w_M = 1 \quad \text{or} \quad w_f = 1 - w_M$$

The expected return is equal to the weighted average of the expected return of the two assets. Therefore, the expected portfolio return, $E(R_p)$, is equal to

$$E(R_p) = w_f R_f + w_M E(R_M)$$

Since we know that $w_f = 1 - w_M$, we can rewrite $E(R_p)$ as follows:

$$E(R_p) = (1 - w_M)R_f + w_M E(R_M)$$

This can be simplified as follows:

$$E(R_p) = R_f + w_M[E(R_M) - R_f] \tag{5.4}$$

The variance of the portfolio consisting of the risk-free asset and portfolio M can be found using the formula for the variance of a two-asset portfolio. It is

$$\text{var}(R_p) = w_f^2 \text{var}(R_f) + w_M^2 \text{var}(R_M) + 2w_f w_M \text{cov}(R_f, R_M)$$

The variance of the risk-free asset, $\text{var}(R_f)$, is equal to zero. This is because there is no possible variation in the return since the future return is known. The covariance between the risk-free asset and portfolio M, $\text{cov}(R_f, R_M)$, is zero. This is because the risk-free asset has no variability and therefore does not move at all with the return on portfolio M, a risky portfolio. Substituting these two values into the formula for the portfolio's variance, we get

$$\text{var}(R_p) = w_M^2 \text{var}(R_M)$$

In other words, the variance of the portfolio is represented by the weighted variance of portfolio M.

We can solve for the weight of portfolio M by substituting standard deviations for variances. Since the standard deviation (σ) is the square root of the variance, we can write

$$\sigma(R_p) = w_M \sigma(R_M)$$

and, therefore,

$$w_m = \frac{\sigma(R_p)}{\sigma(R_M)}$$

If we substitute the above result for w_M in equation (5.4) and rearrange terms we get the CML:

$$E(R_p) = R_f + \left[\frac{E(R_M) - R_f}{\sigma(R_M)}\right]\sigma(R_p) \qquad (5.5)$$

What Is Portfolio M? Now that we know that portfolio M is pivotal to the CML, we need to know what portfolio M is. That is, how does an investor construct portfolio M? Fama (1970) demonstrated that portfolio M must consist of all assets available to investors, and each asset must be held in proportion to its market value relative to the total market value of all assets. That is, portfolio M is the "market portfolio" described earlier. So, rather than referring to the market portfolio, we can simply refer to the "market."

Risk Premium in the CML With homogeneous expectations, $\sigma(R_M)$ and $\sigma(R_p)$ are the market's consensus for the expected return distributions for portfolio M and portfolio p. The risk premium for the CML is

$$\left[\frac{E(R_M) - R_f}{\sigma(R_M)}\right]\sigma(R_p)$$

Let's examine the economic meaning of the risk premium.

The numerator of the first term is the expected return from investing in the market beyond the risk-free return. It is a measure of the reward for holding the risky market portfolio rather than the risk-free asset. The denominator is the market risk of the market portfolio. Thus, the first term measures the reward per unit of market risk. Since the CML represents the return offered to compensate for a perceived level of risk, each point on the CML is a balanced market condition, or equilibrium. The slope of the CML (that is, the first term) determines the additional return needed to compensate for a unit change in risk. That is why the slope of the CML is also referred to as the equilibrium market price of risk.

The CML says that the expected return on a portfolio is equal to the risk-free rate, plus a risk premium equal to the market price of risk (as measured by the reward per unit of market risk), multiplied by the quantity of risk for the portfolio (as measured by the standard deviation of the portfolio). That is,

$$E(R)_p = R_f + (\text{Market price of risk} \times \text{Quantity of risk})$$

Systematic and Unsystematic Risk

Now we know that a risk-averse investor who makes decisions based on expected return and variance should construct an efficient portfolio using a combination of the market portfolio and the risk-free rate. The combinations are identified by the CML. Based on this result, Sharpe (1964) derived an asset pricing model that shows how a risky asset should be priced. In the process of doing so, we can fine-tune our thinking about the risk associated with an asset. Specifically, we can show that the appropriate risk that investors should be compensated for accepting is not the variance of an asset's return but some other quantity. In order to do this, let's take a closer look at risk.

We can do this by looking at the variance of the portfolio. It can be demonstrated that the variance of the market portfolio containing N assets can be shown to be equal to:

$$\text{var}(R_M) = w_{1M} \text{cov}(R_1, R_M) + w_{2M} \text{cov}(R_2, R_M) + \cdots + w_{NM} \text{cov}(R_N, R_M) \quad (5.6)$$

where w_{iM} is equal to the proportion invested in asset i in the market portfolio.

Notice that the portfolio variance does not depend on the variance of the assets comprising the market portfolio, but rather their covariance with the market portfolio. Sharpe defined the degree to which an asset co-varies with the market portfolio as the asset's systematic risk. More specifically, he defined systematic risk as the portion of an asset's variability that can be attributed to a common factor. Systematic risk is the minimum level of risk that can be obtained for a portfolio by means of diversification across a large number of randomly chosen assets. As such, systematic risk is that which results from general market and economic conditions that cannot be diversified away.

Sharpe defined the portion of an asset's variability that can be diversified away as nonsystematic risk. It is also sometimes called unsystematic risk, diversifiable risk, unique risk, residual risk, and company-specific risk. This is the risk that is unique to an asset.

Consequently, total risk (as measured by the variance) can be partitioned into systematic risk as measured by the covariance of asset i's return with the market portfolio's return and nonsystematic risk. The relevant risk for decision-making purposes is the systematic risk. We will see how to measure the systematic risk later.

How diversification reduces nonsystematic risk for portfolios is illustrated in Figure 5.3. The vertical axis shows the variance of the portfolio

FIGURE 5.3 Systematic and Unsystematic Portfolio Risk

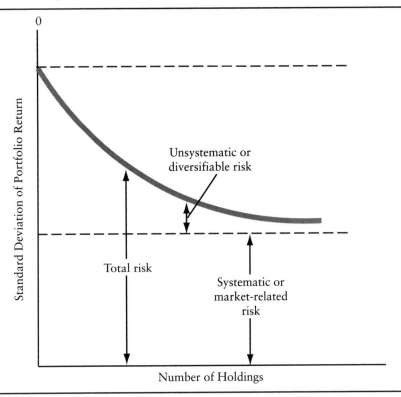

return. The variance of the portfolio return represents the total risk for the portfolio (systematic plus nonsystematic). The horizontal axis shows the number of holdings of different assets (e.g., the number of common stock held of different issuers). As can be seen, as the number of asset holdings increases, the level of nonsystematic risk is almost completely eliminated (that is, diversified away). Studies of different asset classes support this. For example, for common stock, several studies suggest that a portfolio size of about 20 randomly selected companies will completely eliminate nonsystematic risk leaving only systematic risk (see Wagner and Lau 1971).

Security Market Line

The CML represents an equilibrium condition in which the expected return on a portfolio of assets is a linear function of the expected return of the market portfolio. Individual assets do not fall on the CML. Instead, Sharpe (1970) demonstrated that the following relationship holds for individual assets:

$$E(R_i) = R_f + \left[\frac{E(R_i) - R_f}{\text{var}(R_M)}\right]\text{cov}(R_i, R_M) \qquad (5.7)$$

Equation (5.7) is called the *security market line* (SML).

In equilibrium, the expected return of individual securities will lie on the SML and not on the CML. This is true because of the high degree of nonsystematic risk that remains in individual assets that can be diversified out of portfolios. In equilibrium, only efficient portfolios will lie on both the CML and the SML.

The SML also can be expressed as

$$E(R_i) = R_f + [E(R_i) - R_f]\left[\frac{\text{cov}(R_i, R_M)}{\text{var}(R_M)}\right]$$

How can the ratio in equation (5.8) be estimated for each asset? It can be estimated empirically using return data for the market portfolio and the return on the asset. The empirical analogue for equation (5.8) is:

$$r_{it} - R_{ft} = \alpha_i + \beta_i[r_{Mt} - r_{ft}] + e_{it} \qquad (5.9)$$

where e_{it} is the error term. Equation (5.9) is called the *characteristic line*.

β_i, beta, in equation (5.9) is the estimate of the ratio in equation (5.8); that is,

$$\beta_i = \frac{\text{cov}(R_i, R_M)}{\text{var}(R_M)} \qquad (5.10)$$

Substituting β_i into the SML given by equation (5.8) gives the beta version of the SML:

$$E(R_i) = R_f + b_i[E(R_M) - R_f] \qquad (5.11)$$

This is the CAPM form given by equation (5.3). This equation states that, given the assumptions of the CAPM, the expected return on an individual asset is a positive linear function of its index of systematic risk as measured by beta. The higher the beta, the higher the expected return.

An investor pursuing an active strategy will search for underpriced securities to purchase or retain and overpriced securities to sell or avoid (if held in the current portfolio, or sold short if permitted). If an investor believes that the CAPM is the correct asset pricing model, then the SML can be used to identify mispriced securities. A security is perceived to be underpriced (that is, undervalued) if the "expected" return projected by the investor is greater than the "required" return stipulated by the SML. A security is perceived to be overpriced (that is, overvalued), if the "expected" return projected by the investor is less than the "required" return stipulated by the SML. Said another way, if the expected return plots above (over) the SML, the security is "underpriced;" if it plots below the SML, it is "overpriced."

Tests of the CAPM

Now that's the theory. The question is whether or not the theory is supported by empirical evidence. There has been probably more than 1,000 academic papers written on the subject. (Almost all studies use common stock to test the theory.) These papers cover not only the empirical evidence but the difficulties of testing the theory.

Let's start with the empirical evidence. There are two important results of the empirical tests of the CAPM that question its validity. First, it has been found that stocks with low betas have exhibited higher returns than the CAPM predicts and stocks with high betas have been found to have lower returns than the CAPM predicts. Second, market risk is not the only risk factor priced by the market. Several studies have discovered other factors that explain stock returns.

While on the empirical level there are serious questions raised about the CAPM, there is an important paper challenging the validity of these empirical studies. Roll (1977) demonstrates that the CAPM is not testable until the exact composition of the "true" market portfolio is known, and the only valid test of the CAPM is to observe whether the ex ante true market portfolio is mean-variance efficient. As a result of his findings, Roll states that he does not believe there ever will be an unambiguous test of the CAPM. He does not say that the CAPM is invalid. Rather, Roll says that there is likely to be no unambiguous way to test the CAPM and its implications due to the nonobservability of the true market portfolio and its characteristics.

ARBITRAGE PRICING THEORY MODEL

An alternative to the equilibrium asset pricing model just discussed, an asset pricing model based purely on arbitrage arguments was derived by Ross (1976). The model, called the *arbitrage pricing theory* (APT) *model*, postulates that an asset's expected return is influenced by a variety of risk factors, as opposed to just market risk as suggested by the CAPM. The APT model states that the return on a security is linearly related to H risk factors. However, the APT model does not specify what these risk factors are, but it is assumed that the relationship between asset returns and the risk factors is

Arbitrage Principle

Since the model relies on arbitrage arguments, we will digress at this point to define what is meant by arbitrage. In its simple form, arbitrage is the simultaneous buying and selling of an asset at two different prices in two different markets. The arbitrageur profits without risk by buying cheap in one market and simultaneously selling at the higher price in the other market. Investors don't hold their breath waiting for such situations to occur because they are rare. In fact, a single arbitrageur with unlimited ability to sell short could correct a mispricing condition by financing purchases in the underpriced market with proceeds of short sales in the overpriced market. (Short-selling means selling an asset that is not owned, in anticipation of a price decline.) This means that riskless arbitrage opportunities are short-lived.

Less obvious arbitrage opportunities exist in situations where a package of assets can produce a payoff (expected return) identical to an asset that is priced differently. This arbitrage relies on a fundamental principle of finance called the *law of one price*, which states that a given asset must have the same price regardless of the means by which one goes about creating that asset. The law of one price implies that if the payoff of an asset can be synthetically created by a package of assets, the price of the package and the price of the asset whose payoff it replicates must be equal.

When a situation is discovered whereby the price of the package of assets differs from that of an asset with the same payoff, rational investors will trade these assets in such a way so as to restore price equilibrium. This market mechanism is assumed by the APT model, and is founded on the fact that an arbitrage transaction does not expose the investor to any adverse movement in the market price of the assets in the transaction.

For example, let us consider how we can produce an arbitrage opportunity involving the three assets A, B, and C. These assets can be purchased today at the prices shown below, and can each produce only one of two payoffs (referred to as State 1 and State 2) a year from now:

Asset	Price	Payoff in State 1	Payoff in State 2
A	$70	$50	$100
B	60	30	120
C	80	38	112

While it is not obvious from the data presented above, an investor can construct a portfolio of assets A and B that will have the identical return as asset C in both State 1 and State 2. Let w_A and w_B be the proportion of assets A and B, respectively, in the portfolio. Then the payoff (that is, the terminal value of the portfolio) under the two states can be expressed mathematically as follows:

If State 1 occurs: $\$50w_A + \$30w_B$
If State 2 occurs: $\$100w_A + \$120w_B$

We create a portfolio consisting of assets A and B that will reproduce the payoff of C regardless of the state that occurs one year from now. Here is how: For either condition (State 1 and State 2) we set the expected payoff of the portfolio equal to the expected payoff for C as follows:

State 1: $\$50w_A + \$30w_B = \$38$
State 2: $\$100w_A + \$120w_B = \$112$

We also know that $w_A + w_B = 1$.

If we solved for the weights for w_A and w_B that would simultaneously satisfy the above equations, we would find that the portfolio should have 40% in asset A (that is, $w_A = 0.4$) and 60% in asset B (that is, $w_B = 0.6$). The cost of that portfolio will be equal to

$$(0.4)(\$70) + (0.6)(\$60) = \$64$$

Our portfolio (that is, package of assets) comprised of assets A and B has the same payoff in State 1 and State 2 as the payoff of asset C. The cost of asset C is $80 while the cost of the portfolio is only $64. This is an arbitrage opportunity that can be exploited by buying assets A and B in the proportions given above and shorting (selling) asset C.

For example, suppose that $1 million is invested to create the portfolio with assets A and B. The $1 million is obtained by selling short asset C. The proceeds from the short sale of asset C provide the funds to purchase assets A and B. Thus, there would be no cash outlay by the investor. The payoffs for States 1 and 2 are shown below:

Asset	Investment	Payoff in State 1	Payoff in State 2
A	$400,000	$285,715	$571,429
B	600,000	300,000	1,200,000
C	–1,000,000	–475,000	–1,400,000
Total	0	$110,715	$371,429

In either State 1 or 2, the investor profits without risk. The APT model assumes that such an opportunity would be quickly eliminated by the marketplace.

APT Model Formulation

The APT model postulates that an asset's expected return is influenced by a variety of risk factors, as opposed to just market risk of the CAPM. That is, the APT model asserts that the return on an asset is linearly related to H "factors." The APT does not specify what these factors are, but it is assumed that the relationship between asset returns and the factors is linear. Specifically, the APT model asserts that the rate of return on asset i is given by the following relationship:

$$R_i = E(R_i) + \beta_{i,1} F_1 + \beta_{i,2} F_2 + \cdots + \beta_{i,H} F_H + e_i$$

where

R_i = the rate of return on asset i
$E(R_i)$ = the expected return on asset i
F_h = the hth factor that is common to the returns of all assets ($h = 1, ..., H$)
$\beta_{i,h}$ = the sensitivity of the ith asset to the hth factor
e_i = the unsystematic return for asset i

For an equilibrium to exist, the following conditions must be satisfied: Using no additional funds (wealth) and without increasing risk, it should not be possible, on average, to create a portfolio to increase return. In essence, this condition states that there is no "money machine" available in the market.

Ross (1976) derived the following relationship, which is what is referred to as the APT model:

$$E(R_i) = R_f + \beta_{i,F1}[E(R_{F1}) - R_F] + \beta_{i,F2}[E(R_{F2}) - R_F] \\ + \cdots + \beta_{i,FH}[E(R_{FH}) - R_F] \quad (5.12)$$

where $[E(R_{Fj}) - R_f]$ is the excess return of the jth systematic risk factor over the risk-free rate, and can be thought of as the price (or risk premium) for the jth systematic risk factor. The appendix to this chapter presents a derivation of the APT.

The APT model as given by equation (5.12) asserts that investors want to be compensated for all the risk factors that systematically affect the return of a security. The compensation is the sum of the products of each risk factor's systematic risk ($\beta_{i,FH}$), and the risk premium assigned to it by the financial market $[E(R_{Fh}) - R_f]$. As in the case of the CAPM, an investor is not compensated for accepting unsystematic risk.

It turns out that the CAPM is actually a special case of the APT model. If the only risk factor in the APT model as given by equation (5.12) is market risk, the APT model reduces to the CAPM. Now contrast the APT model given by equation (5.3). They look similar. Both say that investors are compensated for accepting all systematic risk and no nonsystematic risk. The CAPM states that systematic risk is market risk, while the APT model does not specify the systematic risk.

Supporters of the APT model argue that it has several major advantages over the CAPM or multifactor CAPM. First, it makes less restrictive assumptions about investor preferences toward risk and return. As explained earlier, the CAPM theory assumes investors trade off between risk and return solely on the basis of the expected returns and standard deviations of prospective investments. The APT model, in contrast, simply requires some rather unobtrusive bounds be placed on potential investor utility functions. Second, no assumptions are made about the distribution of asset returns. Finally, since the APT model does not rely on the identification of the true market portfolio, the theory is potentially testable.

Multifactor Risk Models In Practice

The APT model provides theoretical support for an asset pricing model where there is more than one risk factor. Consequently, models of this type are referred to as *multifactor risk models*. These models provide the tools for quantifying the risk profile of a portfolio relative to a benchmark, for constructing a portfolio relative to a benchmark, and controlling risk. Below we provide a brief review of the two types of multifactor risk models used in both equity and bond portfolio management: statistical models and fundamental factor models.[2]

In a *statistical factor model*, historical and cross-sectional data on stock returns are tossed into a statistical model. The goal of the statistical model is to best explain the observed stock returns with "factors" that are linear return combinations and uncorrelated with each other. For example, suppose that monthly returns for 5,000 companies for 10 years are computed. The goal of the statistical analysis is to produce "factors" that best explain the variance of the observed stock returns. For example, suppose that there are six "factors" that do this. These "factors" are statistical artifacts. The

---

[2] For a discussion of the econometric issues associated with estimating these models, see Chapter 13 in Rachev et. al. (2007).

objective in a statistical factor model then becomes to determine the economic meaning of each of these statistically derived factors. Because of the problem of interpretation, it is difficult to use the factors from a statistical factor model for valuation, portfolio construction, and risk control. Instead, practitioners prefer the next model described, which allows an asset manager to prespecify meaningful factors, and thus produce a more intuitive model.

Fundamental factor models use company and industry attributes and market data as raw descriptors. Examples of raw descriptors in equity factor models are price/earnings ratios, book/price ratios, estimated economic growth, and trading activity. The inputs into a fundamental factor model are stock returns and the raw descriptors about a company. Those fundamental variables about a company that are pervasive in explaining stock returns are then the raw descriptors retained in the model. Using cross-sectional analysis, the sensitivity of a stock's return to a raw descriptor is estimated. There are several fundamental factor models available from vendors.

SOME PRINCIPLES TO TAKE AWAY

Thus far in Part One, we have covered the heart of what is popularly called *modern portfolio theory* and *asset pricing theory*. We have emphasized the assumptions and their critical role in the development of these theories and summarized the empirical findings. While you may understand the topics covered, you may still be uncomfortable about where we have progressed in asset management, given the lack of theoretical and empirical support for the CAPM or the difficulty of identifying the factors in the multifactor CAPM and APT model. You're not alone. A good number of practitioners and academics feel uncomfortable with these models, particularly the CAPM.

Nevertheless, what is comforting is that there are several general principles of investing and evaluating the performance of asset managers that are derived from these theories that very few would question. All these principles are used in later chapters:

1. Investing has two dimensions, risk and return. Therefore, focusing only on the actual return that an asset manager has achieved without looking at the risk that had to be accepted to achieve that return is inappropriate.
2. It is also inappropriate to look at the risk of an individual asset when deciding whether it should be included in a portfolio. What is important is how the inclusion of an asset into a portfolio will affect the risk of the portfolio.

3. Whether investors consider one risk or a thousand risks, risk can be divided into two general categories: systematic risks that cannot be eliminated by diversification, and unsystematic risk that can be diversified away.
4. Investors should be compensated only for accepting systematic risks. Thus, it is critical in formulating an investment strategy to identify the systematic risks.

SUMMARY

Asset pricing involves determining the expected return required by investors in order to invest in financial assets. The output of asset pricing models are used by financial managers in estimating a firm's cost of capital and by investors as the interest rate used in calculating the present value of an asset's cash flows in order to estimate the asset's fair value. The two most well-known equilibrium pricing models are the capital asset pricing model developed in the 1960s and the arbitrage pricing theory model developed in the mid-1970s.

In deriving the CAPM, assumptions are made. A key assumption is that investors make investment decisions in according with the theory of portfolio selection as formulated by Markowitz. The goal of portfolio selection is the construction of portfolios that maximize expected returns consistent with individually acceptable levels of risk. In the theory of portfolio selection risk is measured by the variance (or standard deviation) of historical returns and the expected return as the mean of historical returns. Hence, this theory is popularly referred to as mean-variance analysis. The CAPM goes on to formalize the relationship that should exist between asset returns and risk if investors behave in a hypothesized manner. Together, the theory of portfolio selection and CAPM Provide a framework to specify and measure investment risk and to develop relationships between expected asset return and risk (and hence between risk and required return on an investment).

The CAPM asserts that the only risk that is priced by rational investors is systematic risk, because that risk cannot be eliminated by diversification. Essentially, the CAPM says that the expected return of a security or a portfolio is equal to the rate on a risk-free security plus a risk premium. The risk premium in the CAPM is the product of the quantity of risk times the market price of risk.

The beta of a security or portfolio is an index of the systematic risk of the asset and is estimated statistically. Historical beta is calculated from a time series of observations on both the asset's return and the market portfolio's return. This assumed relationship is called the characteristic line and is not an equilibrium model for predicting expected return, but rather a description of historical data.

There have been numerous empirical tests of the CAPM, and, in general, these have failed to fully support the theory. Roll (1977) criticized these studies because of the difficulty of identifying the true market portfolio. Furthermore, Roll asserts that such tests are not likely to appear soon, if at all.

The arbitrage pricing theory is developed purely from arbitrage arguments. It postulates that the expected return on a security or a portfolio is influenced by several factors. Proponents of the APT model cite its less restrictive assumptions as a feature that makes it more appealing than the CAPM. Moreover, testing the APT model does not require identification of the "true" market portfolio. It does, however, require empirical determination of the factors because they are not specified by the theory. Consequently, the APT model replaces the problem of identifying the market portfolio in the CAPM with the problem of choosing and measuring the underlying factors.

Despite the fact that the theories presented are controversial or may be difficult to implement in practice, there are several principles of investing that are not controversial and can be used in developing investment strategies. First, investing has two dimensions, risk and return. Therefore, focusing only on the actual return of an asset or portfolio without looking at the risk that had to be accepted to achieve that return is inappropriate. Second, it is also inappropriate to look at the risk of an individual asset when deciding whether it should be included in a portfolio. What is important is how the inclusion of an asset into a portfolio will affect the risk of the portfolio. Third, whether investors consider one risk or a thousand risks, risk can be divided into two general categories: systematic risks that cannot be eliminated by diversification, and unsystematic risk that can be diversified away. Finally, investors should be compensated only for accepting systematic risks. Thus, it is critical in formulating an investment strategy to identify the systematic risks.

APPENDIX

In this appendix, we will discuss extensions of the CAPM derived by modifying its assumptions: Black's zero-beta version of the CAPM and Merton's multifactor CAPM. We will also show the derivation of the APT.

Black's Zero-Beta Version of the CAPM Model

As we discussed in the chapter, in a world without a risk-free asset, an investor will select some portfolio on the Markowitz efficient frontier. When a risk-free asset is assumed, the capital market line can be generated. The CML dominates the Markowitz efficient frontier. From the CML, the CAPM is derived.

Not only is the existence of a risk-free asset important in developing the CAPM, but there are two related assumptions. First, it is assumed that investors can borrow or lend at the risk-free rate. The risk-free asset is one in which there is no uncertainty about the return that will be realized over some investment horizon. To realize that return, it is assumed the borrower will not default on its obligation. In the United States, the short-term obligations of the federal government are viewed as default-free and therefore risk-free assets. As we will explain in Chapter 19, there is not just one interest rate in an economy but a structure of interest rates. The U.S. government pays the lowest interest rate, and individual borrowers pay a higher rate. The greater the perceived risk that the borrower will default, the higher the interest rate. Thus, while the U.S. government may be able to borrow at the risk-free rate, an individual investor must pay a higher rate. Consequently, this assumption does not reflect the situation facing investors in the real world.

The second related assumption is that investors can borrow and lend at the same risk-free rate. In real-world markets, investors typically lend and borrow money at different rates, the former being less than the latter. Again, the assumption does not reflect the economic situation facing investors in real-world capital markets.

Black (1972) examined the results for the original CAPM, when there is no risk-free asset in which the investor can borrow and lend. He demonstrated that neither the existence of a risk-free asset nor the requirement that investors can borrow and lend at the risk-free rate is necessary for the theory to hold. However, without the risk-free asset, a different form of the CAPM will result.

Black's argument is as follows. The beta of a risk-free asset is zero. That is, since there is no variability of the return on a risk-free asset, it cannot covary with the market. Suppose that a portfolio can be created such that it is uncorrelated with the market. This portfolio would have a beta of zero. We shall refer to any portfolio with a beta of zero as a *zero-beta portfolio*. The assumptions necessary to create such a portfolio will be discussed later. For now, let's assume that such portfolios can be created.

Figure 5.A1 shows the situation graphically. This figure includes the Markowitz efficient frontier. A tangent is drawn from the expected return axis (i.e., the vertical axis) starting at the expected return for the zero-beta portfolio to the Markowitz efficient frontier. This line will dominate the Markowitz efficient frontier and can be viewed as the capital market line when there is no risk-free asset.

Asset Pricing Theories

Black demonstrated that if zero-beta portfolios can be constructed, then the CAPM should be modified as follows:

$$E(R_p) = E(R_Z) + \beta_p[E(R_M) - E(R_Z)] \tag{5.A1}$$

where $E(R_Z)$ is the expected return on the zero-beta portfolio and $[E(R_M) - E(R_Z)]$ is the risk premium.

This version of the CAPM is the same as equation (5.3) in the chapter, except that the expected return for the zero-beta portfolio is substituted for the risk-free rate. Black's zero-beta version of the CAPM is called the *two-factor model*. Empirical tests of the two-factor model suggest that it does a better job in explaining historical returns than does the pure CAPM.[3]

Selecting the Zero-Beta Portfolio

Assuming that many zero-beta portfolios can be created, which zero-beta portfolio should be selected? The situation is depicted in Figure 5.A1. Two zero-beta portfolios, P_1 and P_2, are shown. Neither portfolio is on the Mar-

FIGURE 5.A1 The Capital Market Line with No Risk-Free Asset but Zero-Beta Portfolios

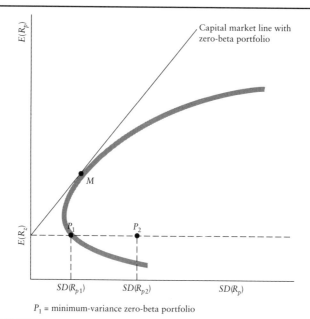

P_1 = minimum-variance zero-beta portfolio

---

[3] See Black, Jensen, and Scholes (1972).

kowitz efficient frontier, but both are feasible portfolios. (Recall from Chapter 2 that the feasible set includes all the portfolios that are achievable and that have the maximum expected return for a given risk. Note that P_1 is an achievable portfolio but not an efficient one.)

Given the choice of the zero-beta portfolios P_1 and P_2, which one will the investor select? Since both have the same expected return, we said that an investor will select the one with the minimum risk. That is P_1. In general, of all the possible zero-beta portfolios, an investor will select the one with the minimum risk. The portfolio is called the *minimum-variance zero-beta portfolio*.

Assumptions Needed to Construct Zero-Beta Portfolios

A natural question, of course, is how does an investor obtain a portfolio that has a zero beta? The basic principle is that by means of short selling, a zero-beta portfolio can be created from a combination of securities. As explained in Chapter 6, short selling involves selling an asset that is not owned in order to benefit from an anticipated decline in the asset's price. Since the asset has been presold at a price today, a decline in the asset's price means that an investor can buy the asset in the future at a lower price.

The reason why short selling is a necessary assumption is that since assets such as stocks are positively correlated—as we noted in the previous chapter—the only way to get a portfolio that is uncorrelated with the market portfolio is to create a portfolio in which stocks are owned and stocks are shorted. Thus, when the price of stocks increases, there will be a gain on the stocks owned in the portfolio, giving a positive return; however, there will be a loss on the stocks that have been shorted and therefore a negative return. The zero-beta portfolio is created such that this combination of stocks owned and stocks shorted will have a beta of zero.

Unfortunately, not all investors are permitted to sell short. Many institutional investors are prohibited or constrained from selling short.

Thus, the two-factor version of the CAPM avoids relying on the myth of "borrowing and lending at a risk-free rate." It still cannot reflect the real world for all investors, however, because it does require unrestricted short selling, which is not available to everyone.

Merton's Multifactor CAPM

In Markowitz portfolio theory and in the CAPM, it is assumed that the only risk that an investor is concerned with is the uncertainty about the future price of a security. Investors, however, usually are concerned with other risks that will affect their ability to consume goods and services in the future. Three examples would be the risks associated with future labor income, the future relative prices of consumer goods, and future investment opportunities. Consequently, using the variance of expected returns as the sole measure of risk is inappropriate.

Recognizing these other risks that investors face, Merton (1973) extended the CAPM based on consumers deriving their optimal lifetime consumption when they face these *extra-market* sources of risk.[4] These extra-market sources of risk are also referred to as *factors*, hence the model derived by Merton is called a *multifactor CAPM* and is given below:

$$E(R_p) = R_F + \beta_{p,M}[E(R_M) - R_F] \\ + \{\beta_{p,F1}[E(R_{F1}) - R_F] + \beta_{p,F2}[E(R_{F2})R_F] + \ldots + \beta_{p,FK}[E(R_{FK}) - R_F]\} \quad (5.A2)$$

where

R_F = the risk-free return
$F1, F2, \ldots, FK$ = factors or extra-market sources of risk, 1 to K
K = number of factors or extra-market sources of risk
$\beta_{p,M}$ = the sensitivity of the portfolio to the market
$\beta_{p,FK}$ = the sensitivity of the portfolio to the kth factor
$E(R_{FK})$ = the expected return of factor k

The total extra-market sources of risk are equal to

$$\beta_{p,F1}[E(R_{F1}) - R_F] + \beta_{p,F2}[E(R_{F2}) - R_F] + \ldots + \beta_{p,FK}[E(R_{FK}) - R_F] \quad (5.A3)$$

This expression says that investors want to be compensated for the risk associated with each source of extra-market risk, in addition to market risk. Note that if there are no extra-market sources of risk, then equation (5.A2) reduces to the expected return for the portfolio as predicted by the CAPM:

$$E(R_p) = R_F + \beta_p[E(R_M) - R_F] \quad (5.A4)$$

In the case of the CAPM, investors hedge the uncertainty associated with future security prices by diversification. This is done by holding the market portfolio, which can be thought of as a mutual fund[5] that invests in all securities based on their relative capitalizations. In the multifactor

---
[4] Other papers on multifactor CAPMs include Cox, Ingersoll, and Ross (1985) and Breeden (1979).
[5] As explained in Chapter 25, a mutual fund is an investment vehicle that invests in a portfolio of assets. Investors in a mutual fund own a pro rata share of the assets less the liabilities.

CAPM, in addition to investing in the market portfolio, investors will also allocate funds to something equivalent to a mutual fund that hedges a particular extra-market risk (see Figure 5.A2). While not all investors are concerned with the same sources of extra-market risk, those that are concerned with a specific extra-market risk will basically hedge them in the same way.

We have just described the multifactor model for a portfolio. How can this model be used to obtain the expected return for an individual security? Since individual securities are nothing more than portfolios consisting of only one security, equation (5.A2) must hold for each security i. That is,

$$E(R_i) = R_F + \beta_{i,M}[E(R_M) - R_F] + \beta_{i,F1}[E(R_{F1}) - R_F] \\ + \beta_{i,F2}[E(R_{F2}) - R_F] + \ldots + \beta_{i,FK}[E(R_{FK}) - R_F] \quad (5.A5)$$

The multifactor CAPM is an attractive model because it recognizes nonmarket risks. The pricing of an asset by the marketplace, then, must reflect risk premiums to compensate for these extra-market risks. Unfortunately, it may be difficult to identify all the extra-market risks and to value each of these risks empirically. Furthermore, when these risks are taken together, the multifactor CAPM begins to resemble the APT model.

Derivation of the APT Model

In the chapter, we explained the APT model. We explained that for equilibrium to exist among assets, the following arbitrage condition must be satisfied: Using no additional funds (wealth) and without increasing risk, it should not be possible, on average, to create a portfolio to increase return. In essence, this condition states that there is no "money machine" available in the market.

To see how this principle works, let

V_i = The *change* in the dollar amount invested in the ith security as a percentage of the investor's wealth

For example, using the three securities in the chapter, suppose that the market value of the investor's portfolio is initially $100,000, comprised as follows: (1) $20,000 in security 1, (2) $30,000 in security 2, and (3) $50,000 in security 3. Suppose an investor changes the initial portfolio as follows: (1) $35,000 in security 1, (2) $25,000 in security 2, and (3) $40,000 in security 3. Then the V_i's would be as follows:

$$V_1 = \frac{\$35,000 - \$20,000}{\$100,000} = 0.15$$

$$V_2 = \frac{\$25,000 - \$30,000}{\$100,000} = -0.05$$

$$V_3 = \frac{\$40,000 - \$50,000}{\$100,000} = -0.10$$

Note that the sum of the V_i's is equal to zero since no additional funds were invested. That is, rebalancing the portfolio does not change the market value of the initial portfolio. Rebalancing does do two things. First, it changes the future return of the portfolio. Second, it changes the total risk of the portfolio, both the systematic risk associated with the two factors and the unsystematic risk. Let's consider the first consequence.

Mathematically, the *change* in the portfolio's future return ($\Delta \tilde{R}_p$) can be shown to be as follows:

$$\Delta \tilde{R}_p = [V_1 E(R_1) + V_2 E(R_2) + V_3 E(R_3)] + [V_1 \beta_{1,1} + V_2 \beta_{2,1} + V_3 \beta_{3,1}]\tilde{F}_1 \\ + [V_1 \beta_{1,2} + V_2 \beta_{2,2} + V_3 \beta_{3,2}]\tilde{F}_2 + [V_1 \tilde{e}_2 + V_2 \tilde{e}_2 + V_3 \tilde{e}_2] \quad (5.A6)$$

Equation (5.A6) indicates that the change in the portfolio return will have a component that depends on systematic risk as well as unsystematic risk. While in our example we have assumed only three securities, when there are a large number of securities, the unsystematic risk can be eliminated by diversification. Thus, equation (5.A6) would reduce to

$$\Delta \tilde{R}_p = [V_1 E(R_1) + V_2 E(R_2) + V_3 E(R_3)] + [V_1 \beta_{1,1} + V_2 \beta_{2,1} + V_3 \beta_{3,1}]\tilde{F}_1 \\ + [V_1 \beta_{1,2} + V_2 \beta_{2,2} + V_3 \beta_{3,2}]\tilde{F}_2 \quad (5.A7)$$

Now let's look at the systematic risk with respect to each factor. The *change* in the portfolio risk with respect to factor 1 is just the betas of each security multiplied by their respective V_i's. Consequently, the change in the portfolio's sensitivity to systematic risk from factor 1 is

$$V_1 \beta_{1,1} + V_2 \beta_{2,1} + V_3 \beta_{3,1} \quad (5.A8)$$

For factor 2, it is

$$V_1 \beta_{1,2} + V_2 \beta_{2,2} + V_3 \beta_{3,2} \quad (5.A9)$$

One of the conditions that is imposed for no arbitrage is that the change in systematic risk with respect to each factor will be zero. That is, equations (5.A8) and (5.A9) should satisfy the following:

$$V_1\beta_{1,1} + V_2\beta_{2,1} + V_3\beta_{3,1} = 0 \qquad (5.A10)$$

$$V_1\beta_{1,2} + V_2\beta_{2,2} + V_3\beta_{3,2} = 0 \qquad (5.A11)$$

If equations (5.A10) and (5.A11) are satisfied, then equation (5.A7) reduces to

$$\Delta E(R_p) = V_1 E(R_1) + V_2 E(R_2) + V_3 E(R_3) \qquad (5.A12)$$

Now let's put all the conditions for no arbitrage together in terms of the equations above. As stated earlier, using no additional funds (wealth) and without increasing risk, it should not be possible, on average, to create a portfolio to increase return. By no additional funds (wealth), this means the following condition: $V_1 + V_2 + V_3 = 0$.

The condition that there be no change in the portfolio's sensitivity to each systematic risk is set forth in equations (5.A10) and (5.A11).

Finally, the expected additional portfolio return from reshuffling the portfolio must be zero. This can be expressed by setting equation (5.A12) equal to zero:

$$V_1 E(R_1) + V_2 E(R_2) + V_3 E(R_3) = 0$$

Taken together, these equations, as well as the condition that there be a sufficiently large number of securities so that unsystematic risk can be eliminated, describe mathematically the conditions for equilibrium pricing. These conditions can be solved mathematically, since the number of securities is greater than the number of factors, to determine the equilibrium value for the portfolio as well as the equilibrium value for each of the three securities. Ross (1976) has shown that the following risk and return relationship will result for each security i:

$$E(R_i) = R_F + \beta_{i,F1}[E(R_{F1}) - R_F] + \beta_{i,F2}[E(R_{F2}) - R_F] \qquad (5.A13)$$

where

$\beta_{i,Fj}$ = the sensitivity of security i to the jth factor
$E(R_{Fj}) - R_F$ = the excess return of the jth systematic factor over the risk-free rate, and can be thought of as the price (or risk premium) for the jth systematic risk

Equation (5.A13) can be generalized to the case where there are H factors as follows:

$$E(R_i) = R_F + \beta_{i,F1}[E(R_{F1}) - R_F] + \beta_{i,F2}[E(R_{F2}) - R_F] + \cdots$$
$$+ \beta_{i,FH}[E(R_{FH}) - R_F] \quad (5.A14)$$

Equation (5.A14) is the APT model. It states that investors want to be compensated for all the factors that *systematically* affect the return of a security. The compensation is the sum of the products of each factor's systematic risk ($\beta_{i,FH}$) and the risk premium assigned to it by the financial market [$E(R_{FH}) - R_F$]. As in the case of the other risk and return models described, an investor is not compensated for accepting unsystematic risk.

REFERENCES

Black, F. 1972. Capital market equilibrium with restricted borrowing. *Journal of Business* 45, no. 3: 444–455.

Black, F., M. C. Jensen, and M. Scholes. 1972. The capital asset pricing model. In *Studies in the Theory of Capital Markets*, edited by M. C. Jensen. New York: Praeger.

Breeden, D. 1979. An intertemporal asset pricing model with stochastic consumption and investment opportunities. *Journal of Financial Economics* 7: 265–296.

Cox, J. C., J. E. Ingersoll, and S. A. Ross. 1985. An intertemporal asset pricing model with rational expectations. *Econometrica* 53 (February): 363–384.

Fama, E. F. 1970. Efficient capital markets: A review of theory and empirical work. *Journal of Finance* 25, no. 2: 383–417.

Lintner, J. 1965. The valuation of risk assets and the selection of risky investments in stock portfolio and capital budgets. *Review of Economics and Statistics* 47, no. 1: 13–37.

Markowitz, H. M. 1952. Portfolio selection. *Journal of Finance* 7, no. 1: 77–91.

Merton, R. C. 1973. An intertemporal capital asset pricing model. *Econometrica* 41 (September): 867–888.

Mossin, J. 1966. Equilibrium in a capital asset market. *Econometrica* 34 (October): 768–783.

Rachev, S. T., S. Mittnik, F. J. Fabozzi, S. M. Focardi, and T. Jasic. 2007. *Financial econometrics: From basics to advanced modeling techniques*. Hoboken, NJ: John Wiley & Sons.

Roll, R. 1977. A critique of the asset pricing theory's tests. *Journal of Financial Economics* 4 (March): 129–176.

Ross, R. A. 1976. The arbitrage theory of capital asset pricing. *Journal of Economic Theory* 13 (December): 343–362.

Sharpe, W. F. 1964. Capital asset prices. *Journal of Finance* 19, no. 3: 425–442.

———. 1970. *Portfolio Theory and Capital Markets*. New York: McGraw-Hill.

Treynor, J. L. 1961. Toward a theory of market value of risky assets. Unpublished paper, Arthur D. Little, Cambridge, MA.

Wagner, W. H., and S. Lau. 1971. The effect of diversification on risks. *Financial Analysts Journal* 27, no. 3: 48–53.

Part Two

Common Stock Analysis and Portfolio Management

CHAPTER 6

The U.S. Equity Markets

This chapter describes the structure of the stock markets and the different venues and practices for trading in the United States.

EXCHANGE MARKET STRUCTURES

An *exchange* is often defined as a market where intermediaries meet to deliver and execute customer orders. This description, however, also applies to many dealer networks. In the United States, an exchange is an institution that performs this function and is registered with the Securities and Exchange Commission (SEC) as an exchange. There are also some off-exchange markets which perform this function.

There are two overall market models for trading stocks. The first model is *order driven*, in which buy and sell orders of public participants who are the holders of the stocks establish the prices at which other public participants can trade. These orders can be either *market orders* or *limit orders*. The second model is *quote driven*, in which intermediaries, that is market makers or dealers, quote the prices at which the public participants trade. Market makers provide a *bid quote* (to buy) and an *offer quote* (to sell) and realize revenues from the spread between these two quotes. Thus, market makers derive a profit from the spread and the turnover of their stocks.

Order-Driven Markets

Participants in a *pure order-driven market* are referred to as "naturals" (the natural buyers and sellers). No intermediary participates as a trader in a pure order-driven market. Rather, the investors supply the liquidity themselves. That is, the *natural buyers* are the source of liquidity for the *natural sellers*, and vice versa. The naturals can be either buyers or sellers, each using market or limit orders.

This chapter is coauthored with Frank Jones.

Order-driven markets can be structured in two very different ways: a continuous market and a call auction at a specific point in time. In a *continuous market*, a trade can be made at any moment in continuous time during which a buy order and a sell order meet at a specific time. In this case, trading is a series of bilateral matches. In the *call auction*, orders are batched together for simultaneous execution in a multilateral trade at a specific point in time. At the time of the call auction, a market-clearing price is determined; buy orders at this price and higher, and sell orders at this price and lower are executed.

Continuous trading is better for customers who need immediacy. On the other hand, for markets with very low trading volume, an intraday call auction may focus liquidity at one (or a few) times of the trading day and permit the trades to occur. In addition, very large orders—block trades that will be described later—may be advantaged by the feasibility of continuous trading.

Nonintermediated markets involve only naturals, that is, such markets do not require a third party. A market may not, however, have sufficient liquidity to function without the participation of intermediaries, who are third parties in addition to the natural buyers and natural sellers. This leads to the need for intermediaries and quote-driven markets.

Quote-Driven Markets

Quote-driven markets permit intermediaries to provide liquidity. Intermediaries may be *brokers* (who are *agents* for the naturals); *dealers* or *market makers* (who are *principals* in the trade); and *specialist*, as on the New York Stock Exchange (who act as both agents and principals). Dealers are independent, profit-making participants in the process.

Dealers operate as principals, not agents. Dealers continually provide bid and offer quotes to buy for or sell from their own accounts and profit from the spread between their bid and offer quotes.

Dealers compete with each other in their bids and offers. Obviously, from the customer's perspective, the "best" market is highest bid and lowest offer among the dealers. This highest bid/lowest offer combination is referred to as the "inside market" or the "top of the book." For example, assume that dealers A, B, and C have the bids and offers (also called *asking prices*) for stock Alpha as shown in Figure 6.1

The best (highest) bid is by dealer A of 40.50; the best (lowest) offer is by dealer C of 41.00. Thus, the inside market is 40.50 bid (by dealer A) and 41.00 offer (by dealer C). Note that dealer A's spread is 40.50 bid and 41.20 offer for a spread (or profit margin) of 0.70. Dealer A has the highest bid but not the lowest offer. Dealer C has the lowest offer but not the highest bid. Dealer B has neither the highest bid nor the lowest offer.

FIGURE 6.1 Quote-Driven Dealer Market

Stock Alpha				
Bids		Offers		
Dealer	Bid	Dealer	Offer	
A	40.50	C	41.00	← Top of the book: 40.50/41.00
B	40.35	B	41.10	
C	40.20	A	41.20	

For a stock in the U.S. market, the highest bid and lowest offer across all markets is called the *national best bid and offer* (NBBO).

Dealers provide value to the transaction process by providing capital for trading and facilitating order handling. With respect to providing capital for trading, they buy and sell for their own accounts at their bid and offer prices, respectively, thereby providing liquidity. With respect to order handling, they provide value in two ways. First, they assist in the price improvement of customer orders, that is, the order is executed within the bid-offer spread. Second, they facilitate the market timing of customer orders to achieve price discovery. Price discovery is a dynamic process which involves customer orders being translated into trades and transaction prices. Because price discovery is not instantaneous, individual participants have an incentive to "market-time" the placement of their orders. Intermediaries may understand the order flow and may assist the customer in this regard. The intermediary may be a person or an electronic system.

The over-the-counter markets (OTC markets) are quote-driven markets. The OTC markets began during a time when stocks were bought and sold in banks and the physical certificates were passed over the counter.

A customer may choose to buy or sell to a specific market maker to whom they wish to direct an order. Directing an order to a specific market maker is referred to as "preferencing."

Order-Driven vs. Quote-Driven Markets

Overall, nonintermediated, order-driven markets may be less costly due to the absence of profit-seeking dealers. But the markets for many stocks are not inherently sufficiently liquid to operate in this way. For this reason, intermediated, dealer markets are often necessary for inherently less liquid markets. The dealers provide dealer capital, participate in price discovery, and facilitate market timing, as discussed above.

Because of the different advantages of these two market structures, many equity markets are now *hybrid markets*. For example, the New York

Stock Exchange (NYSE) is primarily a continuous auction order-driven system based on customer orders but the specialists enhance the liquidity by their market making to maintain a fair and orderly market. Overall, the NYSE is primarily an auction, order-driven market which has specialists (who often engage in market making), other floor traders, call markets at the open and close, and upstairs dealers who provide proprietary capital to facilitate block transactions. Thus, the NYSE is a hybrid combination of these two models. Another hybrid aspect of the NYSE is that it opens and closes trading with a call auction. The continuous market and call auction market are combined. Thus, the NYSE is a continuous market during the trading day and a call auction market to open and close the market and to reopen after a stop in trading. Thus, the NYSE is a hybrid market.

The National Association of Securities Dealers Quotations (Nasdaq) began as a descendent of the OTC dealer network, and is a dealer quote-driven market. It remains primarily a quote-driven market, but has added some order-driven aspects such as its limit order book called SuperMontage, which is discussed below, which made it a hybrid market.

An overview of the nonintermediated, auction, order-driven market and the intermediated, dealer, quote driven markets is provided in Figure 6.2.

Another structural change that has occurred in exchanges is their evolution from membership-owned, floor-traded, organizations to publicly owned electronically traded (that is, no trading floor) organizations. The nature of this evolution (or revolution) is discussed in the next section.

FIGURE 6.2 Structure of Stock Markets

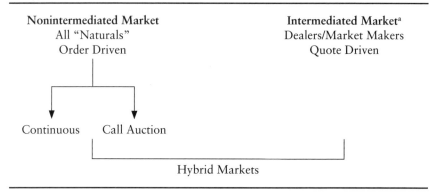

[a]Intermediaries include:

- Dealers/Market Makers(principals)
- Brokers(agents)
- Specialists (operate as both principals and agents)

THE U.S STOCK MARKETS: EXCHANGES AND OTC MARKETS

The U.S. stock market is now composed of the stock exchanges and OTC markets and also, more recently, the off-exchange markets. Although the exchanges have been the main component of the U.S. stock market, the OTC markets and the off-exchange markets have become important parts of the U.S. stock market.

This section covers the exchanges and the OTC markets; the next section considers the off-exchange markets. Given the pace and extent of recent changes in the U.S. stock markets, there is a high likelihood that the stock markets will be much different during the next decade than it is now. The international stock exchanges have also changed and, in fact, in some cases, have become integrated with the U.S. exchanges.

Figure 6.3 provides a general overview, or the "big picture," of the current construct of the U.S. stock markets. The components of the current U.S. stock market are discussed individually in following sections. This section treats the components of the U.S. stock market, including the national exchanges, the NYSE and the American Stock Exchange (Amex); the regional stock exchanges; Nasdaq, technically an OTC market not an exchange (until June 2006); other OTC markets; and other stock exchange markets.

National Exchanges

As of early 2009, the U.S. stock markets are dominated by the NYSE and Nasdaq, the two largest exchanges, both of which are discussed next.

New York Stock Exchange

The NYSE lists stocks throughout the United States (as well as some international stocks) and, thus, is a "national exchange." The NYSE trading mechanism has been based on the specialist system. This system, as previously mentioned, is a hybrid of primarily an order-driven market with some quote-driven features. According to this mechanism, each stock is assigned to an individual specialist. Each specialist "specializes" in many stocks but each stock is assigned to only one specialist. Each specialist is located at a "booth" or "post." All orders for a stock are received at this post and the specialist conducts an auction based on these orders to determine the execution price. The orders arrive at the specialists' posts either physically (delivered via firm brokers) or electronically (via the Designated Order Turnaround (DOT) system or its successors). In conducting the auction, typically the specialist is an agent, simply matching orders. At times, how-

FIGURE 6.3 The "Big Picture" of the U.S Stock Market

I. Stock Exchanges
  A. National Exchanges
    1. New York Stock Exchange Euronext
      a. NYSE Hybrid Market
      b. Arcapelago ("Arca")
    2. American Stock Exchange

  B. Regional Exchanges
    1. Chicago Stock Exchange (CHX)
    2. Philadelphia Stock Exchange (PHLX)
    3. Boston Stock Exchange (BSE)
    4. National Stock Exchange (formerly the Cincinnati Stock Exchange) (NSX)
    5. Pacific Stock Exchange (owned by Archipelago; in turn owned by the NYSE)

  C. Nasdaq-the OTC Market (technically became an exchange during June 2006)
    1. Nasdaq National Market (NNM)
    2. Small Cap Market

  D. Other OTC Markets
    1. Bulletin Board ("Bullies")
    2. Pink Sheets

  E. Off Exchange Markets /Alternative Electronic Markets
    1. Electronic Communication Networks (ECNs)
    2. Alternative Trading Systems (ATS)
      a. Crossing Networks
      b. Dark Pools

ever, the specialist becomes a principal and trades for itself in the interest of maintaining an "orderly market."

A market order is an order to be executed at the best price available in the market. A limit order is an order that designates a price threshold for the execution of the trade. Limit orders, as opposed to market orders, are kept by the specialist in their "book," originally a physical paper book but now an electronic book. These limit orders are executed by the specialist when the market price moves to the limit specified by the order. At one time, the book of limited orders (simply referred to as the "book") could be seen only by the specialist. This was viewed to be a significant advantage for the specialist. Today the book is open to all the traders on the exchange floor. Overall, the NYSE trading mechanism is an auction-based, order-driven market. This type of mechanism is often judged to provide the best price but, on a time basis, often a less rapid execution. There is, therefore, a tradeoff between price and speed.

As indicated earlier, the traditional trading mechanism for the NYSE is the specialist system. However, the volume of trading that has occurred electronically has increased continually over time. Here we discuss the traditional NYSE specialist system in more detail.

Trading in stocks listed on the NYSE is conducted as a centralized continuous auction market at a designated physical location on the trading floor, the post, with brokers representing their customers' buy and sell orders. The NYSE SuperDOT is an electronic order routing and reporting system which links member firms worldwide electronically directly to the specialist's post on the trading floor of the NYSE rather than through a broker. The specialist then executes the orders. The SuperDOT system is used for small market orders, limit orders, basket (or portfolio) trades, and program trades that we describe in Chapter 12. The system can be used for under 100,000 shares with priority given to orders of 2,100 shares or less. After the order has been executed, the report of the transaction is sent back through the SuperDOT system. According to the NYSE, as of 2007, over 99% of the orders executed through the NYSE were done through SuperDOT.

In addition to the single specialist market maker on the exchange, other firms that are members of an exchange can trade for themselves or on behalf of their customers. NYSE member firms, which are broker-dealer organizations that serve the investing public, are represented on the trading floor by brokers who serve as fiduciaries in the execution of customer orders.

The largest membership category on the NYSE is that of the *commission broker*. A commission broker is an employee of one of the securities houses (stock brokers or wire houses) devoted to handling business on the exchange. Commission brokers execute orders for their firm on behalf of their customers at agreed commission rates. These houses may deal for their own account as well as on behalf of their clients.

Other transactors on the exchange floor include the following categories. Independent *floor brokers* (nicknamed "$2 brokers") work on the exchange floor and execute orders for other exchange members who have more orders than they can handle alone or who require assistance in carrying out large orders. Floor brokers take a share in the commission received by the firm they are assisting. Another category, *registered traders*, are individual members who buy and sell for their own account. Alternatively, they may be trustees who maintain memberships for the convenience of dealing and to save fees.

NYSE Specialist   The major type of exchange participant is the specialist. As indicated, specialists are dealers or market makers assigned by the NYSE to conduct the auction process and maintain an orderly market in one or more designated stocks. Specialists may act as both a broker (agent) and a dealer (principal). In their role as a broker or agent, specialists represent customer orders in their assigned stocks, which arrive at their post electronically or are entrusted to them by a floor broker to be executed if and when a stock reaches a price specified by a customer (e.g., limit order). As a dealer or principal, specialists buy and sell shares in their assigned stocks for their own account as necessary to maintain an "orderly market." Specialists must always give precedence to public orders over trading for their own account.

In general, public orders for stocks traded on the NYSE, if they are not sent to the specialist's post via SuperDOT, are sent from the member firm's office to its representative on the exchange floor, who attempts to execute the order in the trading crowd. There are certain types of orders where the order will not be executed immediately on the trading floors. These are limit orders and stop orders. Another type of conditional order is the *stop order*, which specifies that we previously discussed a limit order. A stop order is an order that is not to be executed until the market moves to a designated price, at which time it becomes a market order. If the order is at a limit order or a stop order and the member firm's floor broker cannot transact the order immediately, the floor broker can wait in the trading crowd or give the order to the specialist in the stock, who will enter the order in that specialist's limit order book for later execution based on the relationship between the market price and the price specified in the limit or stop order. The book is the list on which specialists keep the limit and stop orders that are given to them, arranged with size, from near the current market price to further away from it. Whereas the limit order book used to be an actual physical paper book, it is now electronic. Although for many years only the specialist could see the orders in the limit order book, with the NYSE's introduction of OpenBook in January 2002, the limit order book was electronically made available to the traders on the exchange floor.

NYSE-assigned specialists have four major roles:

1. As agents, they execute market orders entrusted to them by brokers, as well as orders awaiting a specific market price.
2. As catalysts, they help to bring buyers and sellers together.
3. As dealers, they trade for their own accounts when there is a temporary absence of public buyers or sellers, and only after the public orders in their possession have been satisfied at a specified price.

4. As auctioneers, they quote current bid-ask prices that reflect total supply and demand for each of the stocks assigned to them.

In carrying out their duties, specialists may, as indicated, act as either an agent or a principal. When acting as an agent, the specialists simply fill customer market orders or limit or stop orders (either new orders or orders from their limit order book) by opposite orders (buy or sell). While acting as a principal, the specialists are charged with the responsibility of maintaining a "fair and orderly market." Specialists are prohibited from engaging in transactions in securities in which they are registered unless such transactions are necessary to maintain a fair and orderly market. Specialists profit only from those trades in which they are involved; that is, they realize no revenue for trades in which they are an agent.

The term "fair and orderly market" means a market in which there is price continuity and reasonable depth. Thus specialists are required to maintain a reasonable spread between bids and offers and small changes in price between transactions. Specialists are expected to bid and offer for their own account if necessary to promote such a fair and orderly market. They cannot put their own interests ahead of public orders and are obliged to trade on their own accounts against the market trend to help maintain liquidity and continuity as the price of a stock goes up or down. They may purchase stock for their investment account only if such purchases are necessary to create a fair and orderly market.

Specialists are also responsible for balancing buy and sell orders at the opening of the trading day in order to arrange an equitable opening price for the stock. Specialists are expected to participate in the opening of the market only to the extent necessary to balance supply and demand for the stock to affect a reasonable opening price. While trading throughout the day is via a continuous auction-based system, as explained earlier, the opening is conducted via a single-priced call auction system. The specialists conduct the call and determine the single price.

If there is an imbalance between buy and sell orders either at the opening of or during the trading day, and the specialists cannot maintain a fair and orderly market, then they may, under restricted conditions, close the market in that stock (that is, discontinue trading) until they are able to determine a price at which there is a balance of buy and sell orders. Such closes of trading can occur either during the trading day or at the opening, which is more common, and can last for minutes or days. Closings of a day or more may occur when, for example, there is an acquisition of one corporation by another or when there is an extreme announcement by the corporation. For this reason, many announcements are made after the close of trading.

Amercian Stock Exchange

The American Stock Exchange (Amex) is a national exchange. Amex is also an auction-type market based on orders. Its specialist system is similar to that of the NYSE. The number of listings on and the trading volume of stocks on the Amex have continued to decline in recent years and as of early 2008 the Amex was regarded as a minor market in U.S. stocks, although it continues to trade some small to mid-sized capitalization stocks.

Regional Exchanges

Regional exchanges developed to trade stocks of local firms which listed their shares on the regional exchanges and also to provide alternatives to the national stock exchanges for their listed stocks. Regional stock exchanges now exist in Chicago, Philadelphia, and Boston and have existed in many other U.S. cities. These exchanges have also been specialist-type, auction-based systems. Some of the regional stock exchanges, including Philadelphia and Boston, as well as the Amex have been driven by trading in stock options and index options rather than stock in recent years.

Nasdaq Stock Market: The OTC Market

A significant change in the U.S. stock market occurred in 1971 when NASDAQ (for National Association of Securities Dealers Automated Quotations System and often referred to as Nasdaq) was founded. When it began trading on February 8, 1971, Nasdaq was the world's first electronic stock market. Nasdaq was founded by the NASD (the National Association of Securities Dealers). Fundamentally, Nasdaq is a dealer-type system based on quotes (quote-driven market). NASD divested itself of Nasdaq in a series of sales to form a publicly traded company, the Nasdaq Stock Market, Inc.

The Nasdaq, as an electronic exchange, has no physical trading floor, but makes all its trades through a computer and telecommunications system. The exchange is a dealers' market, meaning brokers buy and sell stocks through a market maker rather than from each other. A market maker deals in a particular stock and holds a certain number of stocks on its own books so that when a broker wants to purchase shares, the broker can purchase them directly from the market maker.

Nasdaq is a dealer system or OTC system where multiple dealers provide quotes (bids and offers) and make trades. There is no specialist system and therefore there is no single place where an auction takes place. Nasdaq is essentially a telecommunication network that links thousands of geographically dispersed, market-making participants. Nasdaq is an electronic quotation system that provides price quotations to market participants on Nasdaq listed stocks. Nasdaq is essentially an *electronic communication network* (ECN) structure which allows multiple market participants to trade through it, as discussed below. Nasdaq allows multiple market participants to trade through its ECN structure, increasing competition for the market making of stocks.

Since Nasdaq dealers provide their quotes independently, the market has been called "fragmented." So, while the NYSE market is an auction agency, order-based market, the Nasdaq is a *competitive dealer, quote-based system*.

Nasdaq operates a Small Order Execution System (SOES) that provides an electronic method for dealers to enter their trades. The Nasdaq requires that the market makers honor their trades over SOES. The purpose of SOES is to ensure that during turbulent market conditions, small market orders are not forgotten but are automatically processed.

Over the years, the Nasdaq became more of a stock market by adding trade and volume reporting and automated trading systems. In October 2002, the Nasdaq started a system, called SuperMontage, which has led to a change in the Nasdaq from a quote-driven market to a market which provides both quote-driven and order-driven aspects; that is, it became a hybrid market. This system permits dealers to enter quotes and orders at multiple prices and then displays these aggregate submissions at five different prices on both the bid and offer sides of the market. SuperMontage also provides full anonymity, permits dealers to specify a reserve size (i.e., they do not have to display their full order), offers price and time priority, allows market makers to internalize orders, and includes preferenced orders. In effect, SuperMontage is the Nasdaq's order display and execution system.

The advent of SuperMontage continues completing Nasdaq's transformation from a quote-driven market to a hybrid market that contains both quote- and order-driven features. The Nasdaq added a third component to the hybrid, which is a call auction that both opens and closes the market.

The two sections of the Nasdaq stock market are the Nasdaq National Market (NNM) and the Small Cap Market (also known as the Nasdaq Capital Market Issues). For a stock to be listed on the NNM, the company must meet certain financial criteria. To qualify for listing on the exchange, a company must be registered with the U.S. Securities and Exchange Commission (SEC) and have at least three market makers. However the Nasdaq also has a market for smaller companies unable to meet its listing requirements: the Nasdaq Small Cap Market. Nasdaq will move companies from one market to the other as their eligibility changes.

In December 2005, Nasdaq acquired Instinet, the largest ECN and a large trader of Nasdaq-listed stocks. On June 30, 2006, the SEC approved

Nasdaq to begin operating as an exchange in Nasdaq-listed securities. Prior to this, as indicated above, Nasdaq had been an OTC stock market but not formally an exchange. This change is more technical then substantive.

The NYSE vs. Nasdaq

Fundamentally, the NYSE has been an auction-type market based on orders (order-driven) while Nasdaq has been a dealer-type market based on quotes (quote-driven). For years, debates continued about which system—the NYSE or Nasdaq system—was most competitive and efficient. Those who think the Nasdaq OTC market is superior to the specialist-based NYSE often cite the greater competition from numerous dealers and the greater amount of capital they bring to the trading system. They also argue that specialists are conflicted in balancing their obligation to conduct a fair and orderly market and their need to make a profit.

Proponents of the specialist NYSE market structure argue that the commitment of the dealers in the OTC market to provide a market for shares is weaker than the obligation of the specialists on the exchanges. On the NYSE, specialists are obligated to maintain fair and orderly markets. Failure to fulfill this obligation may result in a loss of specialist status. A dealer in the OTC market is under no such obligation to continue its market-making activity during volatile and uncertain market conditions. Supporters of the specialist system also assert that without a single location for an auction, the OTC markets are fragmented and do not achieve the best trade price.

Another difference of opinion comes from traders who say that the specialist system may arrive at the better price, but take a longer period of time, during which the market price may move against the trader, or at least expose the trader to the risk that it will do so. The OTC market may, on the other hand, lead to a faster execution but not arrive at a better, market-clearing price. Professional traders, in this case, often prefer faster speed over better pricing. Retail investors on the other hand may prefer a better price.

While the NYSE has been an auction-type, order-driven market, it has adopted many dealer-type features. Similarly, while the Nasdaq has been a dealer-type, quote-driven market, it has adopted many auction-type features. Thus, while distinct differences continue between these two markets, they have converged considerably and are both currently hybrid markets, although with different mixes of order-driven and quote-driven features.

Other OTC Markets

The OTC market is often called a market for "unlisted" stocks. As described previously, there are listing requirements for exchanges. And while technically the Nasdaq has not been an exchange—it was an OTC market—there are also listing requirements for the Nasdaq National Market and Small Cap systems. Nevertheless, exchange-traded stocks are called "listed," and stocks traded on the OTC markets, including Nasdaq, are commonly referred to as "unlisted."

There are three parts to the OTC market: the two under Nasdaq and a third market for truly unlisted stocks which are therefore non-Nasdaq OTC markets. The third non-Nasdaq OTC Market is composed of two parts, the OTC Bulletin Board (OTCBB) and the Pink Sheets. Thus, technically, both exchanges and the Nasdaq have listing requirements and only the non-Nasdaq OTC markets are non-listed. However, as just noted, in common parlance, the exchanges are often called the "listed market," and Nasdaq, by default, referred to as the "unlisted market." As a result, a more useful and practical categorization of the U.S. stock trading mechanisms is as follows.

1. Exchange listed stocks
   a. National Exchanges
   b. Regional Exchanges
2. Nasdaq listed OTC stocks
   a. Nasdaq National Market (NNM)
   b. Nasdaq Small Cap Market (Capital Market Issues)
3. Non-Nasdaq OTC stocks-unlisted
   a. OTC Bulletin Board (OTCBB)
   b. Pink Sheets

There are two categories of non-Nasdaq stocks. The first is the OTC Bulletin Board (OTCBB), also called simply the Bulletin Board or Bulletin (often just the "Bullies"). The OTCBB is a regulated electronic quotation service that displays real time quotes, last sale prices, and volume information on OTC equity securities. These equity securities are generally securities which are not listed or traded on the Nasdaq or the national stock exchanges. The OTCBB is not part of, nor related to the Nasdaq Stock Market. The OTCBB provides access to more than 3,300 securities and includes more than 230 participating market makers.

The second non-Nasdaq OTC market is the Pink Sheets. The Pink Sheets[1] is an electronic quotation system that displays quotes from broker dealers for many OTC securities. Market markers and other brokers who buy and sell OTC securities can use the Pink Sheets to publish their bid and ask quotation prices.

---

[1] "Pink Sheets" comes from the color of the paper on which the quotes were historically printed prior to the electronic system.

OFF-EXCHANGE MARKETS AND ALTERNATIVE ELECTRONIC MARKETS

The national and regional exchanges have continued to evolve and, in particular, have become much more electronically oriented. As of early 2008, however, a large volume of U.S. stock trading was done off any of the regulated stock exchanges. There has been significant growth and innovation in this sector of the U.S. stock markets in recent years. The *off-exchange markets* (also called *alternative electronic markets*) have continued to grow rapidly and become much more diverse.

Innovation in nonexchange (or off-exchange) trading began even before Nasdaq began. For example, Instinet (an acronym for Institutional Network) began trading in 1969 and was essentially the first electronic communications network (although it was not called an ECN until the late 1990s when the SEC introduced the term as part of the development of its order handling rules). In general, these off-exchange markets are divided into two categories: electronic communication networks and alternative trading systems.

Electronic Communication Networks

Electronic communication networks (ECNs) are essentially off-exchange exchanges. They are direct descendants of (and part of) Nasdaq, not the NYSE. ECNs are privately owned broker-dealers that operate as market participants, initially within the Nasdaq system. They display bids and offers; that is, they provide an open display. They provide institutions and market makers with an anonymous way to enter orders. Essentially, an ECN is a limit order book that is widely disseminated and open for continuous trading to subscribers who may enter and access orders displayed on the ECN. ECNs offer transparency, anonymity, automated service, and reduced costs, and are therefore effective for handling small orders. ECNs may also be linked into the Nasdaq marketplace via a quotation representing the ECN's best buy and sell quote. In general, ECNs use the Internet to link buyers and sellers, bypassing brokers and trading floors. ECNs are informationally linked, even though they are distinct businesses.

Instinet, the first ECN, began operating in 1969. It was designed to be a trading system for institutional investors (and hence the acronym for its name which stands for "Institutional Network"). Instinet was intended to be a trading system for institutional investors which allowed them to meet in an anonymous, disintermediated market.

Alternative Trading Systems

It is not necessary in order for two natural parties to conduct a transaction to use an intermediary. That is, the services of a broker or a dealer are not required to execute a trade. The direct trading of stocks between two customers without the use of a broker or an exchange is called an *alternative trading systems* (ATS).

A number of proprietary ATS have been developed. These ATSs are for-profit "broker's brokers" that match investor orders and report trading activity to the marketplace via the Nasdaq or the NYSE. More recently, such trades have been reported through Trade Reporting Facilities. In a sense, ATSs are similar to exchanges because they are designed to allow two participants to meet directly on the system and are maintained by a third party who also serves a limited regulatory function by imposing requirements on each subscriber.

Broadly, there are two types of ATS, crossing networks (which have functioned since the 1980s), and dark pools (which are much more recent).

Crossing Networks

Crossing networks are electronic venues that do not display quotes but anonymously match large orders. Crossing networks are systems developed to allow institutional investors to cross trades—that is, match buyers and sellers directly—typically via computer. These networks are batch processors that aggregate orders for execution at prespecified times. Crossing networks provide anonymity and reduce cost, and are specifically designed to minimize market impact trading costs. They vary considerably in their approach, including the type of order information that can be entered by the subscriber and the amount of pretrade transparency that is available to participants.

A crossing network matches buy and sell orders in a multinational trade at a price that is set elsewhere. The price used at the cross can be the midpoint of a bid-ask spread (such as the national best bid and offer, as discussed earlier) or the last transaction price at a major market (such as the NYSE or Nasdaq) or linkage of markets. Thus no price discovery results from a crossing network.

The two major drawbacks of the crossing networks are (1) that their execution rates tend to be low and (2) that if they draw too much order flow away from the main market, they can, to their own detriment, undermine the quality of the very prices on which they are basing their trades. These limitations can be overcome in a call auction environment that includes price discovery.

ATS began developing in October 1987 with the start of Investment Technologies Group's (ITG) Posit, a crossing network that matches customer buy and sell orders as they meet or cross each other in price (hence the name *crossing networks*) at a price established by the NYSE, the Nasdaq markets, or the overall national market.

Another crossing network, LiquidNet, started operation in 2001. LiquidNet is an ATS that enables institutional customers to meet anonymously, negotiate a price, and trade in large sizes (average trade size is nearly 50,000 shares). Part of LiquidNet's ability to attract order flow is attributable to its customers being able to negotiate their trades with reference to quotes prevailing in the major market centers. In other words, LiquidNet's customers do not have to participate in significant price discovery. Further, LiquidNet customers' anonymity and knowledge that counterparties in the system also wish to trade in size offers them some assurance that their orders will not have undue market impact (a cost of transacting that we discuss in Chapter 12). A key feature of the LiquidNet system is that customer matches are found electronically, and negotiations are also conducted electronically by the natural buyer and seller.

Instinet, in addition to its continuous ECN, also developed an after-hours crossing, the Instinet Crossing Network. The Burlington Capital Markets, Burlington Large Order Cross (BLOX) also provides crossing systems. These systems enable institutions to trade with no price impact in a batched environment; the crosses are made at prices set in other stock market places. In addition, Harborside, which started operations in 2002, provides crossing services. These systems assist institutional customers to meet anonymously and negotiate their trades in an anonymous manner in an electronic environment that uses current quotes from external stock markets as benchmarks.

These crossing system are designed exclusively for institutional order flow. Among the major current crossing networks and their area of specializations are:

LiquidNet. For the buy-side to buy-side only.
Pipeline. For buy-side to buy-side block business only.
ITG Posit. Provides timed crossings 5-10 times per day for buy-side to buy-side only.
BIDS. Unlike the first three is an agency broker, that is, it does not engage in proprietary trading and, thus, compete with its customers.

Crossing networks have provided attractive alternatives to institutions to trade without their orders having any impact on the prices. However, due to lack of liquidity, their execution rates tend to be low and if they draw too much order flow from the established markets, they could undermine the quality of the prices which are the bases for the trades.

Crossing markets are offered by some of the major broker-dealers who may also use such systems to "internalize" their order flow, that is match or cross bids and offers "upstairs" that is in their own organization. These orders may both be customer orders or one may be a customer order which they cross with their own proprietary orders. Some firms involved in internalization include Citigroup, Credit Suisse, Goldman Sachs, Merrill Lynch, Morgan Stanley, and UBS.

Dark Pools

Another step in the evolution of nonexchange trading is the use of *dark pools*. Dark pools fulfill the need for a neutral gathering place and fulfill the traditional role of an exchange in the new paradigm. Dark pools are private crossing networks in which participants submit orders to cross trades at externally specified prices and, thus, provide anonymous sources of liquidity (hence the name "dark"). No quotes are involved, only orders at the externally determined price. Therefore, there is no price discovery.

Dark pools are electronic execution systems which do not display quotes but provide transactions at externally provided prices. Both the buyer and seller must submit a willingness to transact at this externally provided price—often the midpoint of the NBBO—to complete a trade. Dark pools are designed to prevent information leakage and offer access to undisclosed liquidity. Unlike open or displayed quotes, dark pools are anonymous and leave no "footprints."

Dark pools, as well as crossing networks, are creating very fragmented markets for large trades and block trades. Customers are also using algorithmic trading (discussed in Chapter 12) to respond to such hidden liquidity.

Among the advantages of dark pools are:

- Nondisplayed liquidity
- Prevent information leakage (anonymous trading)
- Volume discovery
- Reduced market impact

Among the disadvantages are:

- Less or no visibility
- Difficulty to interact with order flow
- No price discovery

EVOLVING STOCK MARKET PRACTICES

In this section, we describe evolving stock market practices: SEC Reg. NMS, internalization, alternative display facility, and direct market access. Other practices such as algorithmic trading are described in Chapter 12.

SEC Reg. NMS

The Securities Act amendments of 1975 mandated a U.S. national market system (NMS). The core of this national market was the Intermarket Trading System (ITS) which began operating in 1978. The ITS electronically linked nine markets at the time via ITS computers. The ITS permitted traders at any of these exchanges to go to the best available price at the other exchanges on which the security could trade. The NMS also included a consolidated electronic tape, which combined the last-sale prices from all the markets onto a single continuous tape. The use of the ITS, however, was voluntary.

Even though ITS evolved, by 2007 it was based on obsolete technology. During 2007, the ITS system was replaced by the new NMS. Reg. NMS (National Market System) was designed by the SEC for electronic exchanges. Reg. NMS requires that orders be executed at the market (exchanges or other execution venues), which offers the best price for customers. Thus exchanges must compete with each other on a level playing field. The Reg. NMS's impact is attributable to two of its component rules.

The first rule is the Order Protection Rule—or Trade-Through Rule. This rule requires that trades be executed at the best displayed prices provided by an electronic trading system and accessible under one second. This means that markets will have to route out their orders to other markets if the other markets have better prices (bids or offers). That is, a market cannot "trade through" a better price from another market and trade on their own market. As a result of NMS, each exchange has to send its orders to other exchanges if the other exchange has a better price.

The Trade-Through Rule provides price protection to top-of-book orders (best bids or best offers) placed on exchanges which are electronically accessible. Reserve and hidden orders are not protected. Only electronic quotes are protected. All exchanges are required to have capabilities to route orders to the market with the best bid or offer if they are not able to match the price to execute an order on their own exchange. Only the BBO (or top-of-book) is displayed. In this environment, competitive pricing and low-latency systems are essential in attracting order flow.

The second rule is the Access Rule, which requires the use of private linkages among exchanges to facilitate access to quotes and sets a limit on the access fees by the markets. These private linkages replaced the ITS.

Exchanges had to go to electronic trading to offer protection under Reg. NMS. ECNs and broker-dealers are also covered by Reg. NMS.

Internalization

Internalization refers to off-the-exchange ("upstairs") trades, mainly of retail trades. As opposed to block trading, internalization involves keeping retail orders within the firm ("internalized") with the broker-dealer buying from its sell orders and selling from its buy orders, generally at the published best bid-offer or a penny better. This practice results in proprietary trading revenue for the broker-dealer. A broker-dealer with a large number of customer orders thereby has a trading opportunity to make a "dealer spread" (buying at the bid and selling at the offer) without interference and will lay off any unwanted positions in the primary market. Brokerage firms internalize through proprietary ATSs.

The equity markets permit broker-dealers to internalize retail order flow upstairs. The trades are reported on the TRF (trade reporting facility), a mechanism for reporting transactions not transacted on an exchange Off-exchange (internalized) trades as of the end of 2007 accounted for about 30% of volume in Nasdaq's listed stocks and 16% of the consolidated volume in listed NYSE stocks. Brokers that internalize are reporting 500,000 trades a day in the Nasdaq world and about 350,000 trades a day in NYSE-listed stocks. This volume comes from broker-dealers interacting with their customers' order flow in their upstairs environment and then printing those trades on Nasdaq, as discussed next.[2]

Alternative Display Facility

An *alternative display facility* (ADF) is an entity independent of a registered securities exchange that collects and disseminates securities quotes and trades. It is a display-only facility. The ADF is an alternative to exchanges for publishing quotations and for comparing and reporting trades. This differs from a trading facility with execution capabilities (a stock exchange) in that the exchange would simply send back to the owner of the displayed order a notice of execution. The National Association of Securities Dealers (NASD) has operated an ADF since July 2002. It is now operated by FINRA, as discussed below.

The ADF provides members with a facility for the display of quotations, the reporting of trades, and the comparison of trades. As of March 2007, Consolidated Tape Association (CTA)-listed securities (NYSE, Amex, and the regional exchanges), as well as Nasdaq-listed securities, are eligible

---

[2]Schmerken (2007).

for posting quotations through the ADF. ADF best bid and offer and trade reports are included in the consolidated data stream for CTA and Nasdaq-listed securities. The ADF competes with Nasdaq's Super Montage system.

These organizations exist to capture some of the values of this information (which has historically been captured by exchanges) for the ADF's information suppliers, usually ECNs.

Direct Market Access

In general, buy-side firms have been taking more control over the way their transactions are executed. Direct Market Access (DMA) refers to the use of electronic systems to access various liquidity pools and execution venues directly, without the intervention of a sell-side firm trading desk or broker. There are several advantages of DMA to a sell-side firm:

- It is faster, allowing traders to benefit from short-term market opportunities.
- It has lower transactions costs.
- It provides anonymous transactions.
- It is not handled by brokers, so there is less chance for error.

With respect to cost, it is estimated that DMA commissions are about one cent per share; program trades are two cents per share; and block trades cost four to five cents per share. Hedge funds are aggressive users of DMA.[3]

Initially, the providers of DMA electronic services were independent firms. But increasingly, traditional sell-side firms have either acquired the independent firms or developed their own DMA systems to provide DMA services to sell-side firms. Among the major providers of this type are Goldman Sachs, Morgan Stanley, CSFB, Citigroup, and Bank of New York.

DMA has become commoditized and its providers now often provide a comprehensive set of services including program trading, block trading, and the more sophisticated technique, algorithmic trading, which is discussed in Chapter 12.

BASIC FUNCTIONING OF STOCK MARKETS

In this section, we describe the basic functioning of stock markets which includes price reporting, regulation, clearance and settlement, tick size, short-selling rules, block trade, and commissions.

---

[3]Schmerken (2005).

Price Reporting

Price reporting in the U.S. stock markets is conducted by the Consolidated Tape Association (CTA). The CTA oversees the dissemination of real-time trade and quote information (market data) from the NYSE- and Amex-listed securities (stocks and bonds). The CTA is an independent, industrywide organization. CTA manages two systems to govern the collection, processing, and dissemination of trade and quote data. The two systems are (1) the Consolidated Tape System (CTS), which governs trades, and the (2) Consolidated Quotation System (CQS), which governs quotes. All SEC-registered exchanges and market centers that trade NYSE or Amex-listed securities send their trades and quotes to a central consolidator where the CTS and CQS data streams are produced and distributed worldwide.

The data collected by the CTA are provided on two networks, Network A (or Tape A) for NYSE-listed securities which is administered by the NYSE and Network B (or Tape B) for Amex and regional exchange-listed securities which is administered by the Amex. Nasdaq operates a similar tape for its listed securities, which is called Network C (or Tape C).

CTS is the electronic service that provides last sale and trade data for issues listed on the NYSE, Amex, and U.S. regional stock exchanges. CTS is the basis for the trade reports from the consolidated tape that run across television screens on financial news programs or on Internet sites. The "consolidated tape" is a high-speed, electronic system that constantly reports the latest price and volume data on sales of exchange-listed stocks.

CQS is the electronic service that provides quotation information for issues listed on the NYSE, Amex, and U.S. regional stock exchanges. For every quote message received from a market center, CQS calculates a NBBO based on a price, size, and time priority schema. If the quote is a Nasdaq market maker quote, CQS also calculates a Nasdaq BBO. CQS disseminates the market center's root quote with an appendage that includes the NBBO and Nasdaq BBOs.

In general, Tapes A and B are referred to as the "CTS Tapes" and Tape C as the "Nasdaq Tapes."

Regulation

The basis for the federal government regulation of the stock market resides with the SEC. The SEC's authority is primarily based on two important pieces of federal legislation. The first is the Securities Act of 1933 (the "Securities Act") which covers the primary markets, that is, new issues of securities. The second is the Securities Act of 1934 (the "Exchange Act") which covers the secondary markets. The SEC was created by the Exchange Act.

In addition to the SEC regulations, the exchanges also play a role in their own regulation through self-regulating organizations (SROs). The SRO of the NYSE has been responsible for member regulation, enforcement, and arbitration functions of the NYSE. In addition, the NASD has had the SEC authority to set standards for its member firms and standards of conduct for issuing securities and selling securities to the public. The NASD has also monitored the Nasdaq stock market. There have, however, been some overlapping responsibilities of these two SROs and, thus, some competition between them.

As a result, these two SROs merged and in July 2007 were replaced by a single organization, the Financial Industry Regulation Authority (FINRA), which consolidated the NASD and the member regulation, enforcement, and arbitration functions of NYSE. This consolidation resulted in all firms dealing with only one rulebook, one set of examiners, and one enforcement staff, thereby reducing costs and inconsistencies. Thus, FINRA is the single remaining SRO.

Clearance and Settlement

After a stock trade is completed, the delivery of the shares by the seller and the payment of cash by the buyer must occur quickly and efficiently. The efficiency of the trade settlement affects the total speed and the overall cost of the transaction. In the United States, there are several execution mechanisms (exchanges and other) for stocks. There is, however, only a single clearance and settlement mechanism for securities, the Depository Trust and Clearing Corporation (DTTC).

All clearance and settlement services for U.S equities market (as well as corporate bonds, municipal bonds, exchange-traded funds, and unit investment trusts trades) are provided by the National Securities Clearance Corporation (NSCC). NSCC is a wholly owned subsidiary of the DTCC. NSCC generally clears and settles trades on a T+3 basis (that is, three business days after the trade date). DTCC is essentially a utility organization for the exchanges.

Other subsidiaries of DTCC provide clearance and settlement for other products and also trust services.

Tick Size

The minimum price variation for a security is referred to as its *tick size*. The U.S. stock market historically had a tick size of one-eighth of 1 point. The SEC wanted to reduce the bid-offer spread to increase competition and lower costs. As a result, the NYSE and Nasdaq reduced the tick size first to one-sixteenth and then in 2001 to pennies (1 cent).

This reduction in the tick size narrowed the bid-offer spread considerably, which reduced the costs to customers and the profits of the market makers. In addition, as an unintended consequence, it adversely affected the liquidity of the market. With pennies, there are 100 pricing points per dollar, while with eighths there are only eight. So with pennies, there is less liquidity at each pricing point and so there is less depth at the inside market (the best bid and best offer or the top of the book). Since only the top of the book is displayed, the advent of pennies reduced transparency and was one of the reasons for the development of dark pools, as discussed above.

In addition, with pennies, quotes (bids or offers) are changed more frequently, and so the technology must have lower latency. Low latency, that is a small amount of time necessary to complete a trade instruction, means high speed. Latency below 1 millisecond is now common. As indicated above, the advent of pennies is one reason for the development and growth of algorithmic trading.[4]

Short-Selling Rules

During and after the 1929 stock market crash, part of the blame for the crash was attributed to "short selling." In short selling, an investor borrows stock and sells the borrowed stock to profit from an expected subsequent decline in the price when the investor buys the stock back at a lower price to repay the borrowed stock. In the short run at least, short selling the stock causes a decline in the market. In the longer run, the stock must be bought back to "cover the short" and causes the stock price to increase.

As a result of the stock market crash, Rule 10A-1 was adopted a decade after the 1929 stock market crash to prevent short sellers from adding to the downward pressure on a stock whose price is already declining. This short-selling rule permitted short sales only when the last sales price was higher than the previous price (an *uptick trade*) or if there was no change in the last sales price but the previous sales price was higher than the sales price that proceeded it (a *zero uptick trade*). Short sales were not permitted on a downtick.

In June 2007, the SEC eliminated the short-selling rule. The SEC stated that this rule was obsolete due to decimalization, changes in trading strategies, and increased market transparency. However, in the market turbulence of 2008, the SEC became concerned with what it viewed as "abusive" or "fraudulent" naked short selling that it believed allowed investors to manipulate the price of the stock of some companies. The SEC refers to abusive or fraudulent naked short selling as one in which the short seller does not actually borrow the stock, thereby failing to deliver it to the

---

[4]Sub-penny pricing is prohibited except for stocks that trade for less than a dollar.

buyer in the transaction. As a result, short selling in the manner can allow manipulators to force prices lower than would be possible if legitimate short selling is followed. As a result, the SEC took the following actions in September 2008. First, it adopted, on an interim basis, a rule mandating that short sellers and their broker-dealers deliver securities by the close of business on the settlement date. As indicated earlier, this is three days after the trade date (T+3). Failure to do so results in the imposition of penalties on the short seller, and the broker-dealer acting on the short seller's behalf is prohibited from further short sales in the same security. Second, the SEC adopted an anti-fraud rule (Rule 10b-21) that clearly sets forth that short sellers who deceive broker-dealers or any other market participants about their intention to deliver are in violation of the law.

Block Trades

A *block* is a large holding or transaction of stock, generally 10,000 or more shares or any amount over $200,000. In a *block trade* (also known as a "block facilitation trade"), a broker-dealer commits capital to accommodate a large trade for an institutional customer. These trades are conducted "upstairs" (off the exchange) and "shown to" the market, for potential price improvement. Block trades are reported through the standard price reporting systems. With the growth in algorithmic trading, however, blocks which have traditionally been accomplished "upstairs" via internalization are now accomplished via algorithmic trading as described in Chapter 12.

Commissions

Before 1975, stock exchanges were allowed to set minimum commissions on transactions. The fixed commission structure did not allow the commission rate to decline as the number of shares in the order increased, thereby ignoring the economies of scale in executing transactions.

Pressure from institutional investors, who transacted large trades, led the SEC to eliminate fixed commission rates in 1975. Since May 1, 1975, popularly referred to as Black Thursday, commissions have been fully negotiable between investors and their brokers. Black Thursday began a period of severe price competition among brokers, with many brokerage firms failing, and a consolidation of brokerage firms taking place in the securities industry.

Since the introduction of negotiated commissions, the opportunity has arisen for the development of discount brokers. These brokers charge commissions at rates much less than those charged by full-service brokers, but offer little or no advice or any other service apart from the execution of the transaction.

SUMMARY

In this chapter, we describe the structure of the stock markets and the different venues and practices for trading equities. There are two overall market models for trading stocks: order driven and quote driven. Because of the different advantages of these two market structures, many equity markets are now hybrid markets, sharing attributes of both types of structures. The off-exchange markets (also called alternative electronic markets) are divided into two categories: electronic communication networks and alternative trading systems. There are two types of alternative trading systems: crossing networks and dark pools.

We also described several evolving stock market practices: SEC Reg. NMS, internalization, alternative display facility, and direct market access. Internalization refers to off-the-exchange ("upstairs") trades, mainly of retail trades. As opposed to block trading, internalization involves keeping retail orders within the firm ("internalized") with the broker-dealer buying from its sell orders and selling from its buy orders, generally at the published best bid-offer or a penny better. An alternative display facility is an entity independent of a registered securities exchange that collects and disseminates securities quotes and trades. That is, it is a display-only facility that is an alternative to exchanges for publishing quotations and for comparing and reporting trades.

The basic function of the stock markets that we described in this chapter are reporting, regulation, clearance and settlement, tick size, short-selling rules, block trade, and commissions. Price reporting in the U.S. stock markets is conducted by the Consolidated Tape Association. The basis for the federal government regulation of the stock market resides with the SEC. In addition to SEC regulations, the exchanges also play a role in their own regulation through self-regulating organizations. The single remaining SRO is the Financial Industry Regulation Authority (FINRA).

REFERENCES

Lucchetti, A. 2008. CME fires back on clearing proposal. *Wall Street Journal*, February 7: C3.

Schmerken, I. 2005. Direct-market-access trading. *Wall Street & Technology*, February 4.

———. 2006. NYSE explores point trade reporting facility with NASD. *Wall Street & Technology*, October 17.

CHAPTER 7
Common Stock Strategies and Performance Evaluation

There are numerous strategies about how to "beat the market." At one time, these strategies were debated, and casual observations regarding performance would confirm or dispute a strategy. Today, the statistical tool kit of the modern portfolio manager allows a manager to better test whether or not a strategy can consistently outperform the stock market. In this chapter, we provide an overview of several popular strategies. We begin with a discussion of an important concept about markets that affects the type of strategy that an investor may wish to pursue: market efficiency. We then discuss the various common stock strategies. We conclude the chapter with a discussion of how to measure and evaluate performance.

MARKET EFFICIENCY

Investors do not like risk and they must be compensated for taking on risk—the larger the risk, the more the compensation. An important question about financial markets, which has implication for the different strategies that investors can pursue (as explained in this chapter), is: Can investors earn a return in financial markets beyond that necessary to compensate them for the risk? Economists refer to this excess compensation as an *abnormal return*. Whether this can be done in the stock market is an empirical question. If a strategy is identified that can generate abnormal returns, the attributes that lead one to implement such a strategy is referred to as a *market anomaly*.

This issue of how efficiently a financial market prices the assets traded in that market is referred to as *market efficiency*. An *efficient market* is defined as a financial market where asset prices rapidly reflect all available information. This means that all available information is already impounded in an asset's price, so that investors should expect to earn a return necessary to compensate them for their opportunity cost, anticipated inflation, and risk. That would seem to preclude abnormal returns. But according to Fama (1970), there are the following three levels of efficiency:

1. Weak form efficient
2. Semistrong form efficient
3. Strong form efficient

In the *weak form of market efficiency*, current asset prices reflect all past prices and price movements. In other words, all worthwhile information about previous prices of the stock has been used to determine today's price; the investor cannot use that same information to predict tomorrow's price and still earn abnormal profits. Empirical evidence from the U.S. stock market suggests that in this market there is weak-form efficient. In other words, you cannot outperform ("beat") the market by using information on past stock prices.

In the *semistrong form of market efficiency*, the current asset prices reflect all publicly available information. The implication is that if investors employ investment strategies based on the use of publicly available information, they cannot earn abnormal profits. This does not mean that prices change instantaneously to reflect new information, but rather that information is impounded rapidly into asset prices. Empirical evidence supports the idea that U.S. stock market is for the most part semistrong form efficient. This, in turn, implies that careful analysis of companies that issue stocks cannot consistently produce abnormal returns.

In the *strong form of market efficiency*, asset prices reflect all public and private information. In other words, the market (which includes all investors) knows everything about all financial assets, including information that has not been released to the public. The strong form implies that you cannot make abnormal returns from trading on inside information, where inside information is information that is not yet public.[1] In the U.S. stock market, this form of market efficiency is not supported by empirical studies. In fact, we know from recent events that the opposite is true; gains are available from inside information. Thus, the U.S. stock market, the empirical evidence suggests, is essentially semistrong efficient but not in the strong form.

---

[1] There is no exact definition of "inside information" in law. Laws pertaining to insider trading remain a gray area, subject to clarification mainly through judicial interpretation.

STOCK MARKET INDICATORS

Stock market indicators perform a variety of functions, from serving as benchmarks for evaluating the performance of professional money managers to answering the question "How did the market do today?" Thus stock market indicators (indexes or averages) are a part of everyday life. Even though many of the stock market indicators are used interchangeably, it is important to realize that each indicator applies to, and measures, a different facet of the stock market.

Tables 7.1 and 7.2 provides a list of the various stock indexes in the United States. In general, stock market indexes rise and fall in fairly similar patterns. The indexes do not move in exactly the same ways at all times. The differences in movement reflect the different ways in which the indexes are constructed. Three factors enter into that construction:

- The universe of stocks represented by the sample underlying the index.
- The relative weights assigned to the stocks included in the index.
- The method of averaging across all the stocks in the index.

The stocks included in a stock market index must be combined in certain proportions, and each stock must be given a weight. The three main approaches to weighting are (1) weighting by the market capitalization of the stock's company, which is the value of the number of shares multiplied by the price per share; (2) weighting by the price of the stock; and (3) equal weighting for each stock, regardless of its price or its firm's market value. With the exception of the Dow Jones averages and the Value Line Composite Index, all the most widely used indexes are market-value weighted and the Value Line Composite Index is a value-weighted index. The Dow Jones Industrial Average (DJIA) is a price-weighted average.

Stock market indicators can be classified into three groups:

1. Those produced by stock exchanges based on all stocks traded on the exchanges.
2. Those produced by organizations that subjectively select the stocks to be included in indexes.
3. Those where stock selection is based on an objective measure, such as the market capitalization of the company.

The first group, exchange-provided indexes, are shown in Table 7.1. The more popular indexes include the New York Stock Exchange Composite Index and, although it is not an exchange, the Nasdaq Composite Index,

TABLE 7.1 U.S. Stock Market Indexes

Exchange-Provided Indexes	
New York Stock Exchange	
NYSE Composite Index	NYSE World Leaders Index
NYSE U.S. 100 Index	NYSE TMT Index
The American Stock Exchange	
Amex Composite	Amex Gold Bugs
Amex 20 Stock Index	Amex Industrial Sector Index
Amex Airline Index	Amex LT 20 Index
Amex Basic Industries Sector Index	Amex MS Consumer Index
Amex Biotech Index	Amex MS Cyclical Index
Amex Broker/Dealer Index	Amex MS Healthcare Payer Index
Amex Composite Index	Amex MS Healthcare Products Index
Amex Computer Technology Index	Amex MS Healthcare Providers Index
Amex Consumer Service Sector Index	Amex MS Hi-Tech 35 Index
Amex Consumer Staples Sector Index	Amex MS REIT Index
Amex CSFB Technology Index	Amex Natural Gas Index
Amex Cyclical/Transport Sector Index	Amex Networking Index
Amex Defense Index I	Amex Oil & Gas Index
Amex Disk Drive Index	Amex Stockcar Stocks
Amex Drug Index	Amex Technology Sector Index
Amex Electric Power & Natural Gas	Amex Telecomm Index
Amex Energy Sector Index	Amex Utility Sector Index
Amex Financial Sector Index	Amex Institutional Index
Nasdaq	
Nasdaq Composite Index	Nasdaq Bank Index
Nasdaq National Market Composite Index	Nasdaq Computer Index
Nasdaq-100 Index	Nasdaq Health Care Index
Nasdaq-100 Equal Weighted Index	Nasdaq Industrial Index
Nasdaq-100 Technology Sector Index	Nasdaq National Market Industrial Index
Nasdaq-100 Ex-Tech Sector Index	
Nasdaq Financial-100 Index	Nasdaq Insurance Index
Nasdaq Biotechnology Index	Nasdaq Other Finance Index
Nasdaq Biotechnology Equal Weighted Index	Nasdaq Telecommunications Index
	Nasdaq Transportation Index

falls into this category because the index represents all stocks tracked by the Nasdaq system.

Indexes that fall into the second group are shown in Table 7.2. The two most popular stock market indicators in the second group are the Dow Jones Industry Average (DJIA) and the Standard & Poor's 500 (S&P 500). The DJIA is constructed from 30 of the largest and most widely held U.S. industrial companies. The companies included in the average are those

Common Stock Strategies and Performance Evaluation

TABLE 7.2 Nonexchange Indexes

Dow Jones & Co.	
Dow Jones Average–30 Industrial	Dow Jones Average–15 Utilities
Dow Jones Average–20 Transportation	

Dow Jones & Co./Wilshire Associates	
Dow Jones Wilshire 5000 Total Market Index	Dow Jones Wilshire U.S. Small-Cap Growth Index
The Dow Jones Wilshire 4500 Completion Index	Dow Jones Wilshire U.S. 2500 Index
Dow Jones Wilshire U.S. Large-Cap Index	The Wilshire Large Cap 750 Index
Dow Jones Wilshire U.S. Mid-Cap Index	The Wilshire Mid-Cap 500 Index
Dow Jones Wilshire U.S. Small-Cap Index	The Wilshire Small Cap 1750 Index
Dow Jones Wilshire U.S. Micro-Cap Index	The Wilshire Micro-Cap Index
Dow Jones Wilshire U.S. Large-Cap Value Index	The Wilshire Large Value Index
	The Wilshire Large Growth Index
Dow Jones Wilshire U.S. Large-Cap Growth Index	The Wilshire Mid-Cap Value Index
	The Wilshire Mid-Cap Growth Index
Dow Jones Wilshire U.S. Mid-Cap Value Index	The Wilshire Small Value Index
	The Wilshire Small Growth Index
	The Wilshire All Value Index
Dow Jones Wilshire U.S. Mid-Cap Growth Index	The Wilshire All Growth Index
	The Wilshire Small Cap 250
Dow Jones Wilshire U.S. Small-Cap Value Index	

Standard & Poor's	
S&P Composite 1500 Index	S&P MidCap 400 Index
S&P 100 Index	S&P SmallCap 600 Index
S&P 500 Index	

Frank Russell	
Russell–3000 Index	Russell 2000 Value
Russell–2000 Index	Russell 1000 Growth
Russell–1000 Index	Russell 1000 Value
Russell 2000 Growth	Frank Russell–Midcap Index

Value Line	
Value Line Composite Index	

selected by Dow Jones & Company, publisher of the *Wall Street Journal*. The S&P 500 represents stocks chosen from the two major national stock exchanges and the over-the-counter market. The stocks in the index at any given time are determined by a committee of the Standard & Poor's Corporation, which may occasionally add or delete individual stocks or the stocks of entire industry groups. The aim of the committee is to capture present overall stock market conditions as reflected in a broad range of economic indicators. The Value Line Composite Index, produced by Value Line Inc., covers a broad range of widely held and actively traded NYSE, the American Stock Exchange (AMEX), and over-the-counter (OTC) issues selected by Value Line.

Some indexes represent a broad segment of the stock market while others represent a particular sector such as technology, oil and gas, and financial. In addition, because the notion of an equity investment style (which we discuss later in this chapter) is widely accepted in the investment community, early acceptance of equity style investing (in the form of growth versus value and small market capitalization versus large capitalization) has led to the creation and proliferation of published *style indexes*. Both the broad and the style indexes are shown in Table 7.2.

In the third group, also shown in Table 7.2, we have the Wilshire indexes produced by Wilshire Associates (Santa Monica, California) and published jointly with Dow Jones and Russell indexes produced by the Frank Russell Company (Tacoma, Washington), a consultant to pension funds and other institutional investors. The criterion for inclusion in each of these indexes is solely a firm's market capitalization. The most comprehensive index is the Wilshire 5000, which actually includes more than 6,700 stocks now, up from 5,000 at its inception. The Wilshire 4500 includes all stocks in the Wilshire 5000 except for those in the S&P 500. Thus, the shares in the Wilshire 4500 have smaller capitalization than those in the Wilshire 5000. The Russell 3000 encompasses the 3,000 largest companies in terms of their market capitalization. The Russell 1000 is limited to the largest 1,000 of those, and the Russell 2000 has the remaining smaller firms.

TOP-DOWN VS. BOTTOM-UP APPROACHES

An equity manager who pursues an active strategy may follow either a *top-down approach* or *bottom-up approach*. With the top-down approach, an equity manager begins by assessing the macroeconomic environment and forecasting its near-term outlook. Based on this assessment and forecast, an equity manager decides on how much of the portfolio's funds to allocate among the different sectors of the equity market and how much to allocate to cash equivalents (i.e., short-term money market instruments).

The sectors of the equity market can be classified as follows: basic materials, communications, consumer staples, financials, technology, utilities, capital goods, consumer cyclicals, energy, healthcare, transportation.[2] Industry classifications give a finer breakdown and include, for example,

---

[2] These are the categories used by Standard & Poor's. There is another sector labeled "miscellaneous" that includes stocks that do not fall into any of the other sectors.

aluminum, paper, international oil, beverages, electric utilities, telephone and telegraph, and so on.

In making the allocation decision, a manager who follows a top-down approach relies on an analysis of the equity market to identify those sectors and industries that will benefit the most on a relative basis from the anticipated economic forecast. Once the amount to be allocated to each sector and industry is made, the manager then looks for the individual stocks to include in the portfolio.

In contrast to the top-down approach, an equity manager who follows a bottom-up approach focuses on the analysis of individual stocks and gives little weight to the significance of economic and market cycles. The primary tool of the manager who pursues a bottom-up approach is fundamental security analysis. We will discuss this tool below. The product of the analysis is a set of potential stocks to purchase that have certain characteristics that the manager views as being attractive. For example, these characteristics can be low price/earnings ratios or small market capitalizations. Three well-known managers who follow a bottom-up approach are Warren Buffett (Berkshire Hathaway, Inc.), Dean LeBaron (Batterymarch Financial Management), and Peter Lynch (formerly of Fidelity Magellan Fund).

Within the top-down and bottom-up approaches, there are different strategies pursued by active equity managers. These strategies are often referred to as *equity styles* and will be discussed later in this chapter.

FUNDAMENTAL VS. TECHNICAL ANALYSIS

Also within top-down and bottom-up approaches to active management are two camps as to what information is useful in the selection of stocks and the timing of the purchase of stocks. These two camps are the fundamental analysis camp and the technical analysis camp.

Traditional fundamental analysis involves the analysis of a company's operations to assess its economic prospects. The analysis begins with the financial statements of the company in order to investigate the earnings, cash flow, profitability, and debt burden. The fundamental analyst will look at the major product lines, the economic outlook for the products (including existing and potential competitors), and the industries in which the company operates. The results of this analysis will be the growth prospects of earnings. Based on the growth prospects of earnings, a fundamental analyst attempts to determine the fair value of the stock using one or more of the equity valuation models discussed in Chapter 9. The estimated fair value is then compared to the market price to determine if the stock is fairly priced in the market, cheap (a market price below the estimated fair value), or rich (a market price above the estimated fair value). The father of traditional fundamental analysis is Benjamin Graham, who espoused this analysis in his classic book, *Security Analysis*.[3]

The limitation of traditional fundamental analysis is that it does not quantify the risk factors associated with a stock and how those risk factors affect its valuation. In Chapter 11, we described how risk can be quantified within an asset pricing framework.

Technical analysis ignores company information regarding the economics of the firm. Instead, technical analysis focuses on price or trading volume of individual stocks, groups of stocks, and the overall market resulting from shifting supply and demand. This type of analysis is not only used for the analysis of common stock, but it is also a tool used in the trading of commodities, bonds, and futures contracts. This analysis can be traced back to the seventeenth century, where it was applied in Japan to analyze the trend in the price of rice.[4] The father of modern technical analysis is Charles Dow, a founder of the *Wall Street Journal* and its first editor from July 1889 to December 1902.

In a later section in this chapter, we will discuss some of the strategies that are employed by active managers who follow fundamental analysis and technical analysis. We'll also look at the evidence regarding the performance of these strategies. It is critical to understand, however, that fundamental analysis and technical analysis can be integrated within a strategy. Specifically, a manager can use fundamental analysis to identify stocks that are candidates for purchase or sale, and the manager can employ technical analysis to time the purchase or sale.

STRATEGIES BASED ON TECHNICAL ANALYSIS

Various common stock strategies that involve only historical price movement, trading volume, and other technical indicators have been suggested since the beginning of stock trading in the United States, as well as in commodity markets throughout the world. Many of these strategies involve investigating patterns based on historical trading data (past price data and trading volume) to identify the future movement of individual stocks or the market as a whole. Based on the observed patterns, mechanical trading rules indicating when a stock should be bought, sold, or sold short are developed. Thus, no consideration is given to any factor other than the specified tech-

---

[3]There have been several editions of this book. The first edition was printed in 1934 and coauthored with Sidney Cottle. A more readily available edition is a coauthored version with David Dodd (Graham, Dodd, and Cottle 1962).
[4]See Shaw (1998, 313).

nical indicators. As we explained earlier, this approach to active management is called technical analysis. Because some of these strategies involve the analysis of charts that plot price and volume movements, investors who follow a technical analysis approach are sometimes called *chartists*. The overlying principle of these strategies is to detect changes in the supply of and demand for a stock and capitalize on the expected changes. The book by Edwards and Magee (1948) is widely acknowledged as the bible of technical analysis.

There is considerable debate on the value of technical analysis. Consider the following quotes from well-know market observers and practitioners:

> The central proposition of charting is absolutely false, and investors who follow its precepts will accomplish nothing but increasing substantially the brokerage charges they pay. There has been a remarkable uniformity in the conclusions of studies done on all forms of technical analysis. Not one has consistently outperformed the placebo of a buy-and-hold strategy. (Malkiel 1996)

> The one principal that applies to nearly all these so-called 'technical approaches' is that one should buy *because* a stock or the market has gone up and one should sell *because* it has declined. This is the exact opposite of sound business sense everywhere else, and it is most unlikely that it can lead to lasting success in Wall Street. In our own stock-market experience and observation, extending over 50 years, we have not known a single person who has consistently or lastingly made money by thus "following the market." We do not hesitate to declare that this approach is as fallacious as it is popular. (Graham 1973)

> Technical analysts are the witch doctors of our business. By deciphering stock price movement patterns and volume changes, these Merlins believe they can forecast the future. (Gross 1997)

On the other side of the debate is Mark Hulbert, a columnist for *Forbes* magazine. He takes issue with the statement that there is no support for technical analysis. As evidence, he cites a study by Brock, Lakonishok, and LeBaron (1992). In their empirical tests, they find support for some of the trading strategies based on technical analysis discussed below and conclude that earlier conclusions that technical analysis had no merit were premature. However, several years latter, Sullivan, Timmermann, and White (1999) found that for the best technical analysis strategies reported by Brock, Lakonishok and LeBaron, "there is scant evidence that technical trading rules were of any economic value." More recently, Hsu and Kuan (2005) examined the profitability of almost 40,000 technical trading strategies for the period 1989 to 1992 for four stock indexes that we describe later in this chapter. They found that the performance of trading strategies depended on the maturity of the indexes (i.e., how long the indexes were outstanding). Basically they found that technical trading strategies were significantly profitable when applied to the two relatively immature stock indexes they studied but not when applied to the two mature stock indexes studied.

A comprehensive discussion of all of the empirical studies of technical analysis strategies is beyond the scope of this chapter. In the next subsection, we provide a brief description of four technical-analysis based strategies: Dow Theory strategies, simple filter rules strategies, momentum strategies, and market overreaction strategies. But before doing so, let's review such strategies in the context of pricing efficiency. Recall that the weak form of pricing efficiency asserts that an investor cannot generate abnormal returns by merely looking at historical price and volume movements. Thus, if technical analysis strategies can outperform the market, then the market is price-inefficient in the weak form. Another way of viewing this is that if a manager or client believes that the stock market is price-efficient in the weak form, then pursuing a strategy based on technical analysis will not consistently outperform the market after consideration of transaction costs and risk.

It is important to note that some market observers believe that the patterns of stock price behavior are so complex that simple mathematical models are insufficient for detecting historical price patterns and developing models for forecasting future price movements. Thus, while stock prices may appear to change randomly, there may be a pattern, but simple mathematical tools are insufficient for that purpose. Scientists have developed complex mathematical models for detecting patterns from observations of some phenomena that appear to be. Generically, these models are called *nonlinear dynamic models* because the mathematical equations used to detect if there is any structure in a pattern are nonlinear equations and there is a system of such equations. The particular form of nonlinear dynamic models that has been suggested is *chaos theory*. At this stage, the major insight provided by chaos theory is that stock price movements that may appear to be random may, in fact, have a structure that can be used to generate abnormal returns. However, the actual application seems to have fallen far short of the mark.[5]

Dow Theory Strategies

The grandfather of the technical analysis school is Charles Dow. During his tenure as editor of the *Wall Street Journal*, his editorials theorized about the

---
[5] See Scheinkman and LeBaron (1989) and Peters (1991).

future direction of the stock market. The ideas presented by Dow, which were refined by Hamilton (1922) after Dow's death in 1902, are what we now refer to as the *Dow Theory*. This theory rests on two basic assumptions. First, according to Charles Dow, "The averages in their day-to-day fluctuations discount everything known, everything foreseeable, and every condition which can affect the supply of or the demand for corporate securities." This assumption sounds very much like the efficient market theory. But there's more. The second basic assumption is that the stock market moves in trends—up and down—over periods of time. According to Charles Dow, it is possible to identify these stock price trends and predict their future movement. If this is so and an investor can realize abnormal returns, then the stock market is not price-efficient in the weak form.

According to the Dow Theory, there are three types of trends, or market cycles. The primary trend is the long-term movement in the market. These are basically four-year trends in the market. From the primary trend, a trend line showing where the market is heading can be derived. The secondary trend represents short-run departures of stock prices from the trend line. The third trend is short-term fluctuations in the stock prices. Charles Dow believed that upward movements in the stock market were tempered by fallbacks that lost a portion of the previous gain. A *market turn* occurs when the upward movement was not greater than the last gain. In assessing whether or not a gain did in fact occur, he suggested examining the comovements in different stock market indexes such as the Dow Jones Industrial Average and the Dow Jones Transportation Average. One of the averages is selected as the primary index, and the other as the confirming index. If the primary index reaches a high above its previous high, the increase is expected to continue if it is confirmed by the other index also reaching a high above its previous high.

The theory formulated by Dow focused on the longer-term trends of business activity and its impact on the relationship between stock prices of stock averages. While employed as the financial editor of *Forbes* magazine in the early 1930, Schabacker modified the Dow theory to bar charts of individual securities on a short to intermediate time frame, and is the principal architect of many of the chart patterns used by technical analysts today (see Schabacker 1930, 1932, 1934).

Empirically, it is difficult to test the Dow Theory because it is dependent upon identifying turning points. Several studies have attempted to test this theory as formulated by Hamilton. The first was by Cowles (1934) who found that that it simply did not work. However, a study by Glickstein and Wubbels (1983) found support for the Dow Theory, the authors concluding that "successful market timing is by no means impossible." Brown, Goetzmann, and Kumar (1998) revisited the Cowles study by taking into account risk. More specifically, they used the Sharpe ratio that we describe later in this chapter. In contrast to the findings of Cowles, they found support for the Dow Theory.

Simple Filter Rules Strategy

The simplest type of technical strategy is to buy and sell on the basis of a predetermined movement in the price of a stock. The rule is basically that if the stock increases by a certain percentage, the stock is purchased and held until the price declines by a certain percentage, at which time the stock is sold. The percentage by which the price must change is called the "filter." Every investor pursuing this technical strategy makes up their own filter.

The original study of the profitability of simple filter rules was performed by more than 40 years ago by Alexander (1961). Adjustments for methodological deficiencies of the Alexander study by Fama and Blume (1966) found that price changes do show persistent trends; however, the trends were too small to exploit after considering transaction costs and other factors that must be taken into account in assessing the strategy. Two subsequent studies by Sweeney (1988, 1990), however, suggest that a short-term technical trading strategy based on past price movements can produce statistically significant risk-adjusted returns after adjusting for the types of transaction costs faced by floor traders and professional equity managers.

Momentum Strategies

Practitioners and researchers alike have identified several ways to successfully predict security returns based on the historical returns. Among these findings, perhaps the most popular ones are those of price momentum and price reversal strategies. The basic idea of a *price momentum strategy* is to buy stocks that have performed well (referred to as "winners") and to sell the stocks that have performed poorly (referred to as "losers") with the hope that the same trend will continue in the near future. In contrast, in a *price reversal strategy* stocks that have historically poor performance are purchased (i.e., losers are purchased) with the hope that they will eventually reverse and outperform in the future or short stocks that that have historically poor performance (i.e., winners are shorted) hoping that they will underperform in the future. Because a price reversal strategy is one in which the performance in the future is expected to be contrary to the historical performance, it is also referred to as a *contrarian strategy*. Basically, the price reversal strategy is the inverse of the price momentum strategy.

Some asset managers are only permitted to buy and not short stocks; these asset managers are referred to as "long-only" managers. As a result, they can only pursue a price momentum strategy in which they buy winners and one in which they sell losers. Asset managers, such as hedge funds manager, that are free to take on both long and short positions can pursue any of the price momentum or reversal strategies. In fact, to create leverage, these asset managers can employ a price momentum strategy such that the value of the portfolio of winners is funded by shorting a portfolio of losers. That is, the net investment to the fund is close to zero. Similarly, in price reversal strategy the shorting of the winner portfolio is used to fund the purchase of the loser portfolio.

There is ample evidence supporting price momentum and price reversal strategies. The effect was first documented in the academic literature by Jegadeesh and Titman (1993) for the U.S. stock market and has thereafter been shown to be present in many other international equity markets by Rouwenhorst. The empirical findings show that stocks that outperformed (underperformed) over a horizon of 6 to 12 months will continue to perform well (poorly) on a horizon of 3 to 12 months to follow. Jegadeesh (1990) was the first to identify a short-term (one month) reversal effect and De Bondt and Thaler (1985) a long-term reversal effect. Typical backtests of these strategies have historically earned about 1% per month over the following 12 months. However, there is an empirical question regarding the changing nature of markets that suggests price momentum strategies will not longer produce superior returns. This has been documented by Hwang and Rubesam (2007) who, using data from 1927 to 2005, argued that momentum phenomena disappeared during the 2000–2005 period. Figelman (2007), however, analyzing the S&P 500 Index over the 1970–2004 period, found new evidence of momentum and reversal phenomena previously not described.

Today, many practitioners rely on momentum strategies—both on shorter as well as longer horizons. Short-term strategies tend to capitalize on intraday buy and sell pressures, whereas more intermediate and long-term strategies can be attributed to over- and underreaction of prices relative to their fundamental value as new information becomes available.[6]

Momentum portfolios tend to have high turnover, so transaction and trading costs become an issue. Most studies show that the resulting profits of momentum strategies decrease if transaction costs are taken into account. For example, Korajczyk and Sadka,[7] taking into account the different costs of buying and short-selling stocks, report that depending on the method of measurement and the particular strategy, profits between 17 and 35 basis points per month (after transaction costs) are achievable.

While researchers seem to be in somewhat of an agreement on the robustness and pervasiveness of the momentum phenomenon, the debate is

---

[6]See Daniel, Hirshleifer and Subrahmanyam (1998).
[7]See Korajczyk and Sadka (2004).

still ongoing on whether the empirical evidence indicates market inefficiency or if it can be explained by rational asset pricing theories.

Let's briefly look at an explanation from behavioral finance theory that provides a foundation for price momentum and reversal strategies. To benefit from favorable news or to reduce the adverse effect of unfavorable news, investors must react quickly to new information. Cognitive psychologists have shed some light on how people react to extreme events. In general, people tend to overreact to extreme events. People tend to react more strongly to recent information; and they tend to heavily discount older information.

The question is, do investors follow the same pattern? That is, do investors overreact to extreme events? The *overreaction hypothesis* in finance suggests that when investors react to unanticipated news that will benefit a company's stock, the price rise will be greater than it should be, given that information, resulting in a subsequent decline in the price of the stock. In contrast, the overreaction to unanticipated news that is expected to adversely affect the economic well-being of a company will force the price down too much, followed by a subsequent correction that will increase the price.

If, in fact, the market does overreact, investors may be able to exploit this to realize positive abnormal returns if they can (1) identify an extreme event and (2) determine when the effect of the overreaction has been impounded in the market price and is ready to reverse. We refer to this theory as the market overreaction hypothesis. Investors who are capable of doing this will pursue the following strategies. When positive news is identified, investors will buy the stock and sell it before the correction to the overreaction. In the case of negative news, investors will short the stock and then buy it back to cover the short position before the correction to the overreaction.

As originally formulated by DeBondt and Thaler (1985) the overreaction hypothesis can be described by two propositions. First, the extreme movement of a stock price will be followed by a movement in the stock price in the opposite direction. This is called the *directional effect*. Second, the more extreme the initial price change (i.e., the greater the overreaction), the more extreme the offsetting reaction (i.e., the greater the price correction). This is called the *magnitude effect*. However, as Bernstein (1985) pointed out, the directional effect and the magnitude effect may simply mean that investors overweight short-term sources of information. To rectify this, Brown and Harlow (1988) added a third proposition, called the *intensity effect*, which states that the shorter the duration of the initial price change, the more extreme the subsequent response will be.

Several empirical studies support the directional effect and the magnitude effect.[8] Brown and Harlow tested for all three effects (directional,

---

[8] See DeBondt and Thaler (1985, 1987), Howe (1986), and Brown and Harlow (1988).

magnitude, and intensity) and found that for intermediate and long-term responses to *positive* events, there is only mild evidence that market pricing is inefficient; however, evidence on short-term trading responses to *negative* events is strongly consistent with all three effects. They conclude that "the tendency for the stock market to correct is best regarded as an asymmetric, short-run phenomenon." It is asymmetric because investors appear to overreact to negative, not positive, extreme events.

STRATEGIES BASED ON FUNDAMENTAL ANALYSIS

As explained earlier, fundamental analysis involves an economic analysis of a firm with respect to its earnings growth prospects, ability to meet debt obligations, its competitive environment, and so on. Proponents of semistrong market efficiency argue that strategies based on fundamental analysis will not produce abnormal returns. The reason is simply that there are many analysts undertaking basically the same sort of analysis, with the same publicly available data, so that the price of the stock reflects all the relevant factors that determine value.

The focus of strategies based on fundamental analysis is on the earnings of a company and the expected change in earnings. In fact, a study by Chugh and Meador (1994) found that two of the most important measures used by analysts are short-term and long-term changes in earnings.

In the rest of this section, we will describe several popular fundamental analysis–related strategies.

Earnings Surprise Strategies

Studies have found that it is not merely the change in earnings that is important to investors. The reason is that analysts have a consensus forecast of a company's earnings. What might be expected to generate abnormal returns is the extent to which the market's forecast of future earnings differs from actual earnings that are subsequently announced. The divergence between the forecasted earnings by the market and the actual earnings announced is called an *earnings surprise*. When the actual earnings exceed the market's forecast, then this is a *positive earnings surprise;* a *negative earnings surprise* arises when the actual earnings are less than the market's forecast.

There have been numerous studies of earnings surprises.[9] These studies seem to suggest that identifying stocks that may have positive earnings surprises and purchasing them may generate abnormal returns. Of course, the difficulty is identifying such stocks.

---

[9]The first of these tests was by Joy, Lizenberger, and McEnally (1977).

Low Price/Earnings (P/E) Ratio Strategies

The legendary Benjamin Graham proposed a classic investment model in 1949 for the "defensive investor"—one without the time, expertise, or temperament for aggressive investment. The model was updated in each subsequent edition of his book, *The Intelligent Investor*.[10] Some of the basic investment criteria outlined in the 1973 edition are representative of the approach:

1. A company must have paid a dividend in each of the past 20 years.
2. Minimum size of a company is $100 million in annual sales for an industrial company and $50 million for a public utility.
3. Positive earnings must have been achieved in each of the past 10 years.
4. Current price should not be more than 1.5 times the latest book value.
5. Market price should not exceed 15 times the average earnings for the past 3 years.

Graham considered the P/E ratio as a measure of the price paid for value received. He viewed high P/Es with skepticism and as representing a large premium for difficult-to-forecast future earnings growth. Hence, lower-P/E, higher-quality companies were viewed favorably as having less potential for earnings disappointments and the resulting downward revision in price.

A study by Oppenheimer and Schlarbaum (1981) reveals that over the period 1956–1975, significant abnormal returns were obtained by following Graham's strategy, even after allowing for transaction costs. While originally intended for the defensive investor, numerous variations of Graham's low-P/E approach are currently followed by a number of professional investment advisers.[11]

Market-Neutral Long-Short Strategy

An active strategy that seeks to capitalize on the ability of a manager to select stocks is a market-neutral long-short strategy. The basic idea of this strategy is as follows. First, using the models described in Chapter 11, a manager analyzes the expected returns of individual stocks within a universe of stocks. Based on this analysis, the manager can classify those stocks as either "high-expected-return stocks" or "low-expected-return stocks." A manager could then do one of the following: (1) purchase only high-expected-return

---

[10]This model is fully described in Chapter 14 in Graham (1973).
[11]For a thorough presentation of the low P/E investment strategy, see Dreman (1982).

stocks, (2) short low-expected-return stocks, or (3) simultaneously purchase high-expected return stocks and short low-expected-return stocks.

The problem with the first two strategies is that movements in the market in general can have an adverse affect. For example, suppose that a manager selects high-expected-return stocks and that the market declines. Because of the positive correlation between the return on all stocks and the market, the drop in the market will produce a negative return even though the manager may have indeed been able to identify high-expected-return stocks. Similarly, if a manager shorts low-expected return stocks and the market rallies, the portfolio will realize a negative return. This is because a rise in the market means that the manager must cover the short position of each stock at a price higher than the price at which a stock was sold.

Let's look at the third alternative—simultaneously purchasing stocks with high expected returns and shorting those stocks with low expected returns. Consider what happens to the long and the short positions when the general market in moves. A drop in the market will hurt the long position but benefit the short position. A market rally will hurt the short position but benefit the long position. Consequently, the long and short positions provide a hedge against each other.

Although the long-short positions provide a hedge against general market movements, the degree to which one position moves relative to the other is not controlled by simply going long the high-expected-return stocks and going short the low-expected-return stocks. That is, the two positions do not neutralize the risk against general market movements. However, the long and short positions can be created with a market exposure that neutralizes any market movement. Specifically, long and short positions can be constructed to have the same beta, and, as a result, the beta of the long-short position is zero. For this reason, this strategy is called a *market-neutral long-short strategy*. If, indeed, a manager is capable of identifying high- and low-expected-return stocks, then neutralizing the portfolio against market movements will produce a positive return whether the market rises or falls.

Here is how a market-neutral long-short portfolio is created. It begins with a list of stocks that fall into the high-expected-return stocks and low-expected-return stocks. One or a combination of the models described is used. (In fact, we classify this strategy as a fundamental analysis strategy because fundamental analysis is used to identify the stocks that fall into the high- and low-expected return stock categories.) The high-expected-return stocks are referred to as "winners" and are those that are candidates to be included in the long portfolio; the low-expected-return stocks are referred to as "losers" and are those that are candidates to be included in the short portfolio.

Suppose a client allocates $10 million to a manager to implement a market-neutral long-short strategy.[12] Suppose that the manager (with the approval of the client) uses the $10 million to buy stocks on margin. As explained later in this chapter, the investor can borrow up to a specified percentage of the market value of the margined stocks, with the percentage determined by the Federal Reserve. Let's assume that the margin requirement is 50%. This means that the manager has $20 million to invest—$10 million in the long position and $10 million in the short position.

When buying securities on margin, the manager must be prepared for a margin call. Thus, a prudent policy with respect to managing the risk of a margin call is not to invest the entire amount. Instead, a liquidity buffer of about 10% of the equity capital is typically maintained. This amount is invested in a high-quality short-term money market instrument. The portion held in this instrument is said to be held in "cash." In our illustration, since the equity capital is $10 million, $1 million is held in cash, leaving $9 million to be invested in the long position; therefore, $9 million is shorted. The portfolio then looks as follows: $1 million cash, $9 million long, and $9 million short.

Market Anomaly Strategies

While there are managers who are skeptical about technical analysis and fundamental analysis, some managers believe that there are pockets of pricing inefficiency in the stock market. That is, there are some investment strategies that have historically produced statistically significant positive abnormal returns. These market anomalies are referred to as the *small-firm effect*, the *low-price/earnings-ratio effect*, the *neglected-firm effect*, and various *calendar effects*. There is also a strategy that involves following the trading transactions of insiders of a company.

Some of these anomalies are a challenge to the semistrong form of pricing efficiency because they use the financial data of a company. These would include the small-firm effect and the low-price/earnings-ratio effect. The calendar effects are a challenge to the weak form of pricing efficiency. Following insider activities with regard to buying and selling the stock of their company is a challenge to both the weak and strong forms of pricing efficiency. The challenge to the former is that, as will be explained below, information on insider activity is publicly available and, in fact, has been suggested as a technical indicator in popular television programs such as *Wall Street Week*. Thus, the question is whether "outsiders" can use information about trading activity by insiders to generate abnormal returns. The challenge to the strong form of pricing efficiency is that insiders are viewed as having special

---

[12] This illustration is from is Jacobs and Levy (1997).

information, and, therefore, they may be able to generate abnormal returns using information acquired from their special relationship with the firm.

Small-Firm Effect Strategy

The small-firm effect emerges in several studies that have shown that portfolios of small firms (in terms of total market capitalization) have outperformed the stock market (consisting of both large and small firms).[13] Because of these findings, there has been increased interest in stock market indicators that monitor small-capitalization firms. We will describe this more fully when we discuss equity style management later.

Low-P/E Effect Strategy

Earlier, we discussed Benjamin Graham's strategy for defensive investors based on low price/earnings ratios. The low-price/earnings-ratio effect is supported by several studies showing that portfolios consisting of stocks with a low price/earnings ratio have outperformed portfolios consisting of stocks with a high price/earnings ratio.[14] However, there have been studies that found that after adjusting for transaction costs necessary to rebalance a portfolio as prices and earnings change over time, the superior performance of portfolios of low-price/earnings-ratio stocks no longer holds.[15] An explanation for the presumably superior performance is that stocks trade at low price/earnings ratios because they are temporarily out of favor with market participants. Because fads do change, companies not currently in vogue will rebound at some indeterminate time in the future.[16]

Neglected-Firm Effect

Not all firms receive the same degree of attention from security analysts, and one school of thought is that firms that are neglected by security analysts will outperform firms that are the subject of considerable attention. One study has found that an investment strategy based on changes in the level of attention devoted by security analysts to different stocks may lead to positive abnormal returns.[17] This market anomaly is referred to as the *neglected-firm effect*.

---

[13]See Reinganum (1981) and Banz (1981).
[14]See Basu (1977).
[15]See Levy and Lerman (1985).
[16]See Dreman (1979).
[17]See Arbel and Stebel (1983).

Calendar Effects

While some empirical work focuses on selected firms according to some criteria such as market capitalization, price/earnings ratio, or degree of analysts' attention, the calendar effect looks at the best time to implement strategies. Examples of anomalies are the January effect, month-of-the-year effect, day-of-the-week effect, and holiday effect. It seems from the empirical evidence that there are times when the implementation of a strategy will, on average, provide a superior performance relative to other calendar time periods. However, since it is not possible to predict when such a strategy will work, this again supports the idea that the market is at least weak-form efficient.

EQUITY STYLE INVESTING[18]

As explained earlier in this chapter, the notion of an equity investment style is widely accepted in the profession today. We mentioned the various style indices. In this section, we will look at the important aspects of style investing.[19]

Evolution of Specific Equity Styles

Sorensen et al. (2000, 23) define style investing

> as the implementation of investment strategies that are designed to earn abnormal average returns from the mispriced securities that result from the empirically observed market anomalies.

Specifically, a *growth stock manager* seeks to perform better than the broad market by buying companies with high-earnings-growth expectations. The current price of the shares is less important than the future fundamentals. That is, the stock will appreciate as the firm continues to generate future cash flow increments. In contrast, a *value manager* seeks to perform with cheap stocks that the market has somehow incorrectly priced. It is notable that the growth manager terminology emanates from the term "growth company." There is no analog for the value manager—as in "value company." That is, dictionaries and finance textbooks all have formal definitions of a growth company such as, higher than average corporate

---

[18]This section is coauthored with Eric H. Sorensen.
[19]Empirical evidence on the performance of style investing is provided in Sorensen (2000), Hogue and Loughran (2006), Miller et al. (2006), and Qian, Hua, and Sorensen (2007).

growth rates, able to earn economic returns in excess of the cost of capital, high return on equity (ROE) firms, and so on.

Clearly there are dramatically differing philosophies between the practitioner cohorts of these two style camps. Growth managers believe they can identify firms' relative earnings growth rates into the future. They presume that the market is underestimating what is their proprietary forecast of future fundamental corporate potential. As such, they are willing to pay higher prices—price-to-earnings (P/E) or price-to-book-value (P/B)—for these great companies. Active growth portfolios are generally characterized by consistent and high earnings growth, longer duration (that is, highly sensitive to changes in interest rates), more susceptible to adverse earnings events, have higher market beta, and are in more exciting industries, other things equal. Basically, the market has under reacted to the positive growth and underestimated this growth.

In contrast, value managers seeks to find bargains—cheapskates. They seek stocks that have been sold off for any number of reasons, and for which the market has temporarily given up on. Active value managers hold portfolios of stocks with recent unfavorable news, higher dividend yields, lower P/E ratios, and within boring industries with lower general growth prospects, other things equal. Basically, the market has overreacted to the dull or weak fundamentals and underestimated the potential for improvement or turnaround.

In addition to many generalizations between these two philosophies, the portfolio implementation between the two can also be quite different. Growth managers will often use positive earnings momentum and buy into a rising price scenario. If they are in a hurry, they may be demanders of liquidity as they build positions—driving the price up. In addition, in the event of adverse earnings events, they sometimes unload and are in-part responsible for downward price pressure. In contrast, value managers are often buying stocks that are already depressed, and thus suppliers of liquidity. Often, they might buy early before the stock hits some bottom, and sell early as it rises above one's notion of fair value.

Value Manager Techniques and Factors

In the world of value managers, there are many criteria or factors to assess in security selection. Some measure(s) of cheapness are at the top of the list. A so-called *contrarian investor* is often considered a buyer of deep discount securities. These stocks might have extremely low P/E ratios and/or nominally high-dividend yields.[20] Low P/B is also a criterion for certain types of companies. The contrarian manager looks at the book value of a company

---

[20]Christopherson and Williams (1997) and Schlarbaum (1997).

and focuses on those companies that are selling at low valuation relative to book value. The companies that fall into this category may be depressed cyclical stocks or companies that have little or no future earnings growth prospects. The expectation is that the stock is on a cyclical rebound or that the company's earnings will turn around. Both these occurrences are expected to lead to substantial price appreciation.

Many of such oversold stocks in a portfolio may take quarters and even years to realize the hoped for appreciation. This requires patience, and is not typically a good approach for managers that seek consistency in outperforming a benchmark on a regular basis.

Other value managers are more moderate in their selection processes. Many focus on relative value, meaning that cheapness is only one, albeit important, consideration. (We discuss relative valuation tools in Chapter 9.) "Relative" sometimes pertains to comparable stocks, like those in the same industry. Therefore, a relative value portfolio may be sector neutral or industry neutral compared to a broad index like the S&P 500. In this instance, the percentages allocated to industries mimic the broad benchmark, but the specific holdings are cheap relative to other stocks in the same industry. This is in sharp contrast to deep value investing that often may results in major industry concentrations (overweights and underweights) relative to the percent of the industry comprising the broad index. Such contrarian portfolios will typically not track the chosen index as consistently as a relative value portfolio.

Another conditioning the value manager may invoke is growth as a key consideration. Growth is good, but don't overpay. GARP (growth at a reasonable price) is a common label for this approach. Here the manager will compare the cheapness metric, say P/E or P/B, with the firm's growth potential, such as dividing the P/E ratio by the projected growth rate. High P/E stocks may be "good value" if the price is supported by expected earnings growth.

Growth Manager Techniques and Factors

Growth managers seek companies with above average growth prospects. In the growth manager style category, there tends to be two major substyles.[21] The first is a growth manager who focuses on high-quality companies with consistent growth. A manager who follows this substyle is referred to as a *consistent growth manager*. These are commonly large-cap growth managers. The second growth substyle is followed by an *earnings momentum growth manager*. In contrast to a growth manager, an earnings momentum growth manager prefers companies with more volatile, above-average

---

[21]Christopherson and Williams (1997).

growth. They often seek companies with accelerating growth. These are commonly mid-cap or small-cap managers.

There are studies that identify factors that work the best in the selection of stocks in varying universes and across various styles. In Sorensen, Hua, and Qian (2005), for example, "good factors" are observed to vary across relevant "contexts." This work utilizes modern portfolio theory to empirically determine the optimal weights ascribed to factors. These factors come from five common categories used by quantitative portfolio managers: valuation, operating efficiency, accounting accruals, external financing, and momentum. The approach uses historical returns to estimate the ex post optimal combination of these factor categories that deliver the highest return per unit of risk.

PASSIVE STRATEGIES[22]

Investors who believe that the market is efficient should pursue a passive investment strategy. There are two types of passive strategies. The first is a *buy-and-hold strategy*. This strategy is quite simple: Buy a portfolio of stocks based on some criterion and hold those stocks over some investment horizon. There is no active buying and selling of stocks once the portfolio is created.

The second approach, and the more commonly followed one, is index fund management, popularly referred to as simply *indexing*. With this approach, the money manager does not attempt to identify undervalued or overvalued stock issues based on fundamental security analysis. Nor does the money manager attempt to forecast general movements in the stock market and then structure the portfolio so as to take advantage of those movements. Instead, an indexing strategy involves designing a portfolio to track the total return performance of an index of stocks.

While indexing may be a passive form of investing, there are still many issues that the money manager must address. In this section, we explain how an indexed portfolio is constructed and maintained.

Motivation for Equity Indexing

Both theoretical and empirical reasons underlie the increased use of common stock indexing. If a market is sufficiently price-efficient so that superior risk-adjusted return cannot be consistently earned after adjusting for transaction costs, then the appropriate strategy to pursue is a passive strategy. While both buy-and-hold and indexing are passive strategies, there is theoretical

---
[22] This section is coauthored with Bruce Collins.

justification for indexing. The theoretical underpinning for this strategy is capital market theory. According to this theory, in an efficient market, the "market portfolio" offers the highest level of return per unit of risk because it captures the efficiency of the market. The theoretical market portfolio is a capitalization-weighted portfolio of all risky assets. As a proxy for the theoretical market portfolio, an index that is representative of the market should be used. With a buy-and-hold strategy, the selected stock may not capture the efficiency of the market.

This, then, is the question: Is the market efficient? Although there is evidence of pockets of pricing inefficiency, there is ample evidence that it is difficult to consistently outperform the stock market on a risk-adjusted basis after accounting for transaction costs. Moreover, a pension sponsor must pay a management fee to an external money manager. From the sponsor's perspective, even if a money manager can outperform the market after adjusting for risk and transaction costs, the amount by which it outperforms may not be greater than the management fee. So, for example, if on a risk-adjusted basis and after transaction costs, the money manager outperforms the index by 20 basis points, but the management fee is greater than 20 basis points, the manager has not added any value. Empirical studies of the performance of mutual funds (which take into consideration management fees) and money managers of pension funds indicate that professional money managers have underperformed popular indexes.

If these findings are accepted, then the costs associated with active equity portfolio management may not purchase an enhanced return on a portfolio. These costs, which we describe in Chapter 12, consist of the research costs associated with uncovering mispriced stocks, the transaction costs of buying and selling stocks to take advantage of mispricing, and the transaction costs incurred in trying to time the market. Consequently, a passive approach to equity portfolio management may be more appropriate for the typical sponsor of a pension fund.

Due to the transaction costs of managing an indexed portfolio, however, indexing has also fallen short of matching the benchmark. In the case of a mutual fund, other operating expenses are associated with managing the fund.

Selecting the Benchmark

The first step in index fund management is the selection of the index or benchmark. We described the various stock market indexes in the United States at the beginning of this chapter. There are broad-based indexes and special indexes, or subindexes. A *pure index fund* is a portfolio that is managed so as to perfectly replicate the performance of the market portfolio.

The market portfolio in reality is not known with certainty. Nonetheless, the S&P 500 has served as the consensus representative of the market portfolio. Recently, the Wilshire indexes and the Russell indexes have served as benchmarks for some index funds.

The major problem with the use of the S&P 500 as the benchmark is that the stocks are arbitrarily selected by a committee of the Standard & Poor's Corporation. This committee's selection criterion has nothing to do with the growth and earnings potential of a company. Nor is a selection based on whether an issue is undervalued. Thus, money managers who have a quarrel with indexing do not argue that an active strategy is better than a passive strategy, but rather that the selection of the S&P 500, or any broad-based index, is simply an arbitrary benchmark.

Considerations for Constructing a Replicating Portfolio

Once a portfolio manager has decided to pursue an indexing strategy and has selected a benchmark, the next step is to construct a portfolio that will track the index. We refer to the portfolio constructed to match an index or benchmark as the *replicating portfolio*. The objective in constructing the replicating portfolio is to minimize the difference in performance between it and the benchmark.

Transaction Costs and Tracking Error Risk

Transaction costs may be particularly high for some of the smaller capitalized issues in the benchmark. In formulating an indexing strategy, the portfolio manager seeks to minimize the costs incurred when trading in some of the smaller-capitalized issues while retaining the replicating portfolio's ability to track the index.

Designing the optimal replicating portfolio may involve holding all the stock issues in the benchmark or a subset of those issues. The number of stock issues in the replicating portfolio affects transaction costs, but holding fewer stock issues than contained in the benchmark means that the portfolio is exposed to the risk that the replicating portfolio will underperform the benchmark. This risk is referred to as *tracking error risk*. There is a trade-off between the number of issues in the replicating portfolio and tracking error risk that is illustrated in Chapter 11 where the concept of tracking error is covered. The trade-off between tracking error risk and number of issues held must also be considered in terms of transaction costs, which increase with the number of issues traded.

It is next to impossible for a portfolio's returns to exactly match the return on the benchmark. Even if a replicating portfolio is designed to exactly replicate a benchmark by buying all the stock issues, tracking error risk will result.[23] There are several reasons for this.

First, because odd-lot purchases are cumbersome, replicating portfolios usually comprise round lots, and as such the number of shares of each stock in the portfolio is rounded off to the nearest hundred from the exact number of shares indicated by the computer programs that have been developed to build the optimal replicating portfolio. This rounding may affect the ability of smaller replicating portfolios (less than $25 million) to accurately track the index.

Second, and more important, the maintenance of a replicating portfolio is a dynamic process. Since, as explained later in this chapter, most indexes are capitalization-weighted, the relative weights of individual issues are constantly changing. In addition, the stocks that compose the index often change. Thus, the cost of continually adjusting the portfolio, as well as timing differences, hinders an indexer's ability to accurately track a benchmark. The former problem is eliminated by holding all stocks in the benchmark. The portfolio is then self-replicating, which simply means the weights are self-adjusting. If, however, the replicating portfolio contains fewer stocks than the benchmark, the weights are not self-adjusting and may require periodic rebalancing.

Benchmark Construction and the Replicating Portfolio

The method used to construct a replicating portfolio is to formulate a procedure to determine the weight of each issue. There are three basic ways to look at weighting: (1) capitalization or market value, (2) price, and (3) equal dollar weighting. The market value weighting for a single stock in an index is determined by the proportion of its value to the total market value of all stocks in the index. The typical priceweighting scheme assumes equal shares invested in each stock, and the price serves as the weight. Equal dollar weighting requires investing the same dollar amount in each stock. With capitalization weighting, the largest companies naturally have the greatest influence over the index value. Consequently, underweighting or overweighting in a large-capitalization stock can lead to substantial tracking error risk. Also, these stocks tend to be the most liquid. Price weighting endows the highest-priced stock with the greatest influence on the index value. Equal dollar weighting does the opposite. In this case, the lowest-priced stocks have the greatest potential to move the index for a given change in

---

[23]Through the use of relatively inexpensive forms of financing, institutional investors have access to derivative instruments (the subject of Chapters 13 and 14) that can achieve zero-tracking error risk.

stock price. It is important to understand these properties when constructing a replicating portfolio.

There are two methods of constructing a replicating portfolio: arithmetic and geometric. The currently used stock market indexes use arithmetic averaging. Consequently, we focus only on arithmetic averaging. An arithmetic index is simply the weighted average of all stocks that make up the index where the weights are determined by one of the weighting schemes mentioned; that is,

$$\text{Index} = \text{Constant} \times \sum_{i=1}^{N} (\text{Weight}_i \times \text{Price}_i)$$

where N is the number of stock issues in the index, and the constant represents an arbitrary number used to initialize the value of the index.

Indexes based on arithmetic averages can be easily replicated regardless of the weighting scheme. Over time, however, if there are no changes in the composition of the index, as the price of a stock changes, the weights adjust automatically for consistency with the share amounts. This is true only for an arithmetic index where the share amounts do not change. Consequently, no rebalancing is necessary. However, this is not true for equally weighted indexes because share amounts must change to maintain equal dollar amounts for each stock.

The implication for the management of the replicating portfolio is that holding all the issues in the index reduces the need for rebalancing. But even if the entire index is held, rebalancing may be necessary because changes in the weighting may occur for any of the following reasons:

- Some issues may cease to exist due to merger activity.
- A company may be added to or deleted from the index should it meet or fail to meet capitalization or liquidity requirements for inclusion in an index or listing on an exchange.
- A company may split its stock or issue a stock dividend.
- New stock may be issued.
- Current stock may be repurchased.

Should any of these events occur, the constant term in the index valuation expression may require adjustment to avoid a discontinuous jump in the index value.

Methods of Constructing a Representative Replicating Portfolio

As we discussed, one way to replicate an index is by purchasing all stock issues in the index in proportion to their weightings. Constructing a replicating portfolio with fewer stock issues than the index involves one of three methods.

Capitalization Method

Using the *capitalization method*, the manager purchases a number of the largestcapitalized names in the index stock issues and equally distributes the residual stock weighting across the index. For example, if the top 200 highest-capitalization stock issues are selected for the replicating portfolio and these issues account for 85% of the total capitalization of the index, the remaining 15% is evenly proportioned among the other stock issues.

Stratified Method

The second method for replicating an index is the *stratified method*. The first step in using this method is to define a factor by which the stocks that make up an index can be categorized. A typical factor is industry sector. Other factors might include risk characteristics such as beta or capitalization levels. The use of two characteristics would add a second dimension to the stratification. In the case of industry sectors, each company in the index is assigned to an industry. This means that the companies in the index have been stratified by industry. The objective of this method is then to reduce residual risk by diversifying across industry sectors in the same proportion as the benchmark. Stock issues within each stratum, or, in this case, industry sector, can then be selected randomly or by some other method such as capitalization ranking, valuation, or optimization.

Quadratic Optimization Method

The final method uses a quadratic optimization procedure to generate an efficient set of portfolios, and hence is called the *quadratic optimization method*. This is the same procedure that we described in Chapter 2 to generate the Markowitz efficient set. The efficient set includes minimum-variance portfolios for different levels of expected returns. The investor can select a portfolio among the set that satisfies the money manager's risk tolerance.

Transaction Costs

The costs of initiating and maintaining an S&P 500 index fund involve commissions, market impact costs, and rebalancing costs. These costs are discussed in more detail in Chapter 12.

Passive strategies, such as index fund investments, usually incur less turnover than active strategies when the benchmark is dominated by large-capitalization issues. Small-capitalization stock index funds incur larger transaction costs because the stocks tend to be lower priced and less liquid. Historically, the average cost for small-capitalization portfolios is 25 basis points in commissions, 75 to 125 basis points in market impact, and, due to higher turnover, 10 basis points in annual rebalancing costs.

The Link with Active Equity Strategies

Index fund management can be extended into active management by designing well-diversified portfolios that take advantage of superior estimates of expected returns and control market risk. Such a strategy is referred to as enhanced indexing. Two methods are intended to improve risk-adjusted portfolio return. The first involves creating a "tilted" portfolio, while the second utilizes the futures market.

The *tilted portfolio* can be constructed to emphasize a particular industry sector or performance factor—for example, fundamental measures such as earnings momentum, dividend yield, and price/earnings ratio. Or it can be constructed to emphasize economic factors such as interest rates and inflation. The portfolio can be designed to maintain a strong relationship with a benchmark by minimizing the variance of the tracking error. An illustration is presented in Chapter 11.

The second method involves the use of stock index futures. The introduction of index-derivative products has provided managers with the tools that, when used correctly, may be able to enhance the returns to an index fund. As explained in Chapter 13, the replacement of stocks with undervalued futures contracts can add value to an indexed portfolio's annualized return without incurring any significant additional risk.

The distinction between active strategies and enhanced indexing is the degree of risk control. In enhanced indexing, the focus is on risk control. The bets that are made by an enhanced indexer do not cause the portfolio's characteristics to depart materially from the benchmark. An active manager's portfolio can deviate materially from the characteristics of the benchmark. John Loftus of Pacific Investment Management Company, a firm that sells an enhanced indexing product, notes that "risk-controlled active management" would be a more appropriate description of enhanced indexing.[24] The analytical tool for controlling risk is a factor model that we will describe in Chapter 11.

---

[24]See Loftus (2000).

MEASURING AND EVALUATING PERFORMANCE

We conclude this chapter with how to evaluate the investment performance of a portfolio manager. In doing so, we must distinguish between performance measurement and performance evaluation. *Performance measurement* involves the calculation of the return realized by a portfolio manager over some time interval that we call the *evaluation period*. There are several important issues must be addressed in developing a methodology for calculating a portfolio's return.

Performance evaluation is concerned with two issues: (1) determining whether the portfolio manager added value by outperforming the established benchmark; and (2) determining how the portfolio manager achieved the calculated return. For example, as explained earlier in this chapter, there are several strategies the manager of a stock portfolio can employ. Did the portfolio manager achieve the return by market timing, buying undervalued stocks, buying low-capitalization stocks, overweighting specific industries, and so on? The decomposition of the performance results to explain the reasons why those results were achieved is called *performance attribution analysis*. Moreover, performance evaluation requires the determination of whether the portfolio manager achieved superior performance (i.e., added value) by skill or by luck.

Measuring Performance

The starting point for evaluating the performance of a portfolio manager is measuring return. This might seem quite simple, but several practical issues make the task complex because one must take into account any cash distributions made from a portfolio during the evaluation period.

Alternative Return Measures

The dollar return realized on a portfolio for any evaluation period (i.e., a year, month, or week) is equal to the sum of:

1. The difference between the market value of the portfolio at the end of the evaluation period and the market value at the beginning of the evaluation period.
2. Any distributions made from the portfolio.

It is important that any capital or income distributions from the portfolio to a client or beneficiary of the portfolio be taken into account.

The rate of return, or simply return, expresses the dollar return in terms of the amount of the market value at the beginning of the evaluation period. Thus, the return can be viewed as the amount (expressed as a fraction of the initial portfolio value) that can be withdrawn at the end of the evaluation period while maintaining the initial market value of the portfolio intact.

In equation form, the portfolio's *return* can be expressed as follows:

$$R_P = \frac{MV_1 - MV_0 + D}{MV_0} \quad (7.1)$$

where

R_P = the return on the portfolio
MV_1 = the portfolio market value at the end of the evaluation period
MV_0 = the portfolio market value at the beginning of the evaluation period
D = the cash distributions from the portfolio to the client during the evaluation period

To illustrate the calculation of a return, assume the following information for the portfolio manager of a common stock portfolio: The portfolio's market value at the beginning and end of the evaluation period is $25 million and $28 million, respectively, and, during the evaluation period, $1 million is distributed to the client from investment income. Therefore,

MV_1 = $28,000,000 MV_0 = $25,000,000 D = $1,000,000

Then

$$R_P = \frac{\$28,000,000 - \$25,000,000 + \$1,000,000}{\$25,000,000} = 0.16 = 16\%$$

There are three assumptions in measuring return as given by equation (7.1). The first assumption is that cash inflows into the portfolio from dividends that occur during the evaluation period but are not distributed are reinvested in the portfolio. For example, suppose that during the evaluation period, $2 million is received from dividends. This amount is reflected in the market value of the portfolio at the end of the period.

The second assumption is that if there are distributions from the portfolio, they either occur at the end of the evaluation period or are held in the form of cash until the end of the evaluation period. In our example, $1 million is distributed to the client. But when did that distribution actually occur? To understand why the timing of the distribution is important, consider two extreme cases: (1) the distribution is made at the end of the evaluation period, as assumed by equation (7.1); and (2) the distribution is made at the beginning of the evaluation period. In the first case, the money manager had the use of the $1 million to invest for the entire evaluation period. By contrast, in the second case, the portfolio manager loses the opportunity to invest the funds until the end of the evaluation period. Consequently, the timing of the distribution will affect the return, but this is not considered in equation (7.1).

The third assumption is that there is no cash paid into the portfolio by the client. For example, suppose that sometime during the evaluation period, the client gives an additional $1.5 million to the portfolio manager to invest. Consequently, the market value of the portfolio at the end of the evaluation period, $28 million in our example, would reflect the contribution of $1.5 million. Equation (7.1) does not reflect that the ending market value of the portfolio is affected by the cash paid in by the client. Moreover, the timing of this cash inflow will affect the calculated return.

Thus, while the return calculation for a portfolio using equation (7.1) can be evaluated for any length of time—such as one day, one month, five years—from a practical point of view, the assumptions of this approach limit its application. The longer the evaluation period, the more likely the assumptions will be violated. For example, it is highly likely that there may be more than one distribution to the client and more than one contribution from the client if the evaluation period is five years. Therefore, a return calculation made over a long period of time, if longer than a few months, would not be very reliable because of the assumption underlying the calculations that all cash payments and inflows are made and received at the end of the period.

Not only does the violation of the assumptions make it difficult to compare the returns of two portfolio managers over some evaluation period, but it is also not useful for evaluating performance over different periods. For example, equation (7.1) will not give reliable information to compare the performance of a one-month evaluation period and a three-year evaluation period. To make such a comparison, the return must be expressed per unit of time, for example, per year.

The way to handle these practical issues is to calculate the return for a short unit of time such as a month or a quarter. We call the return so calculated the *subperiod return*. To get the return for the evaluation period, the subperiod returns are then averaged. So, for example, if the evaluation period is one year, and 12 monthly returns are calculated, the monthly returns are the subperiod returns, and they are averaged to get the one-year return. If a three-year return is sought, and 12 quarterly returns can be calculated, quarterly returns are the subperiod returns, and they are averaged to get

TABLE 7.3 Three Methods for Averaging Subperiod Returns

Method	Interpretation	Limitations
Arithmetic average (mean) rate of return	Average value of the withdrawals (expressed as a fraction of the initial portfolio market value) that can be made at the end of each subperiod while keeping the initial portfolio market value intact	Overvalues total return when subperiod returns vary greatly. Assumes the maintenance of initial market value
Time-weighted (geometric) rate of return	The compounded rate of growth of the initial portfolio market value during the evaluation period	Assumes all proceeds are reinvested
Dollar-weighted rate of return (internal rate of return)	The interest rate that will make the present value of the sum of the subperiod cash flows (plus the terminal market value) equal to the initial market value of the portfolio	Is affected by client contributions and withdrawals beyond the control of the money manager

the three-year return. The three-year return can then be converted into an annual return by the straightforward procedure described later.

Three methodologies have been used in practice to calculate the average of the subperiod returns:

1. The arithmetic average rate of return.
2. The time-weighted rate of return (also called the *geometric rate of return*).
3. The dollar-weighted return.

Table 7.3 compares these methods side by side.

Arithmetic Average (Mean) Rate of Return

The *arithmetic average (mean) rate of return* is an unweighted average of the subperiod returns. The general formula is

$$R_A = \frac{R_{P1} + R_{P2} + \cdots + R_{PN}}{N} \tag{7.2}$$

where

R_A = the arithmetic average rate of return

R_{Pk} = the portfolio return for subperiod k as measured by equation (17.1), where $k = 1, \ldots, N$

N = the number of subperiods in the evaluation period

For example, if the portfolio returns [as measured by equation (7.2)] were −10%, 20%, and 5% in months July, August, and September, respectively, the arithmetic average monthly return is 5%, as shown:

$$N = 3 \quad R_{P1} = -0.10 \quad R_{P2} = 0.20 \quad \text{and} \quad R_{P3} = 0.05$$

$$R_A = \frac{-0.10 + 0.20 + 0.05}{3} = 0.05 = 5\%$$

There is a major problem with using the arithmetic average rate of return. To see this problem, suppose the initial market value of a portfolio is $28 million, and the market values at the end of the next two months are $56 million and $28 million, respectively, and assume that there are no distributions or cash inflows from the client for either month. Then, using equation (7.1), we find the subperiod return for the first month (R_{P1}) is 100%, and the subperiod return for the second month (R_{P2}) is −50%. The arithmetic average rate of return using equation (7.2) is then 25%. Not a bad return! But think about this number. The portfolio's initial market value was $28 million. Its market value at the end of two months is $28 million. The return over this two-month evaluation period is zero. Yet equation (7.2) says it is a whopping 25%.

Thus it is improper to interpret the arithmetic average rate of return as a measure of the average return over an evaluation period. The proper interpretation is as follows: It is the average value of the withdrawals (expressed as a fraction of the initial portfolio market value) that can be made at the end of each subperiod while keeping the initial portfolio market value intact. In our first example, in which the average monthly return is 5%, the investor must add 10% of the initial portfolio market value at the end of the first month, can withdraw 20% of the initial portfolio market value at the end of the second month, and can withdraw 5% of the initial portfolio market value at the end of the third month. In our second example, the average monthly return of 25% means that 100% of the initial portfolio market value ($28 million) can be withdrawn at the end of the first month, and 50% must be added at the end of the second month.

Time-Weighted Rate of Return

The *time-weighted rate of return* measures the compounded rate of growth of the initial portfolio market value during the evaluation period, assuming that all cash distributions are reinvested in the portfolio. This return is also

Common Stock Strategies and Performance Evaluation 181

commonly referred to as the *geometric mean return* because it is computed by taking the geometric average of the portfolio subperiod returns calculated from equation (7.1). The general formula is

$$R_T = [(1 + R_{P1})(1 + R_{P2}) \cdots (1 + R_{PN})]^{1/N} - 1 \qquad (7.3)$$

where R_T is the time-weighted rate of return, and R_{Pk} and N are as defined earlier.

For example, let us assume the portfolio returns were −10%, 20%, and 5% in July, August, and September, as in the first example above. Then the time-weighted rate of return as given by equation (7.3) is

$$R_T = \{[1 + (-0.10)](1 + 0.20)(1 + 0.05)\}^{1/3} - 1$$
$$= [(0.90)(1.20)(1.05)]^{1/3} - 1 = 0.043$$

Because the time-weighted rate of return is 4.3% per month, $1 invested in the portfolio at the beginning of July would have grown at a rate of 4.3% per month during the three-month evaluation period.

The time-weighted rate of return in the second example is 0%, as expected, shown here:

$$R_T = \{(1 + 1.00)[1 + (-0.50)]\}^{1/2} - 1 = [(2.00)(0.50)]^{1/2} - 1 = 0\%$$

In general, the arithmetic and time-weighted average returns will give different values for the portfolio return over some evaluation period. This is because, in computing the arithmetic average rate of return, the amount invested is assumed to be maintained (through additions or withdrawals) at its initial portfolio market value. The time-weighted return, on the other hand, is the return on a portfolio that varies in size because of the assumption that all proceeds are reinvested.

In general, the arithmetic average rate of return will exceed the time-weighted average rate of return. The exception is in the special situation where all the subperiod returns are the same, in which case the averages are identical. The magnitude of the difference between the two averages is smaller the less the variation in the subperiod returns over the evaluation period. For example, suppose that the evaluation period is four months, and that the four monthly returns are as follows:

$$R_{P1} = 0.04 \qquad R_{P2} = 0.06 \qquad R_{P3} = 0.02 \qquad R_{P4} = -0.02$$

The arithmetic average rate of return is 2.5%, and the time-weighted average rate of return is 2.46%. Not much of a difference. In our earlier example, in which we calculated an average rate of return of 25% but a time-weighted average rate of return of 0%, the large discrepancy is due to the substantial variation in the two monthly returns.

Dollar-Weighted Rate of Return

The *dollar-weighted rate of return* is computed by finding the interest rate that will make the present value of the cash flows from all the subperiods in the evaluation period plus the terminal market value of the portfolio equal to the initial market value of the portfolio. The cash flow for each subperiod reflects the difference between the cash inflows due to investment income (i.e., dividends and interest) and to contributions made by the client to the portfolio and the cash outflows reflecting distributions to the client. Notice that it is not necessary to know the market value of the portfolio for each subperiod to determine the dollar-weighted rate of return.

The dollar-weighted rate of return is simply an internal rate of return calculation, and, hence, it is also called the *internal rate of return*. The general formula for the dollar-weighted return is

$$V_0 = \frac{C_1}{(1+R_D)} + \frac{C_2}{(1+R_D)^2} + \cdots + \frac{C_N + V_N}{(1+R_D)^n} \tag{7.4}$$

where

R_D = the dollar-weighted rate of return
V_0 = the initial market value of the portfolio
V_N = the terminal market value of the portfolio
C_k = the cash flow for the portfolio (cash inflows minus cash outflows) for subperiod k, where $k = 1, 2, \ldots, N$

For example, consider a portfolio with a market value of $100,000 at the beginning of July, capital withdrawals of $5,000 at the end of months July, August, and September, no cash inflows from the client in any month, and a market value at the end of September of $110,000. Then

$$V_0 = \$100{,}000 \quad N = 3 \quad C_1 = C_2 = C_3 = \$5{,}000 \quad V_3 = \$110{,}000$$

and R_D is the interest rate that satisfies the following equation:

$$\$100{,}000 = \frac{\$5{,}000}{(1+R_D)} + \frac{\$5{,}000}{(1+R_D)^2} + \frac{\$5{,}000 + \$110{,}000}{(1+R_D)^3}$$

It can be verified that the interest rate that satisfies the above expression is 8.1%. This, then, is the dollar-weighted return.

The dollar-weighted rate of return and the time-weighted rate of return will produce the same result if no withdrawals or contributions occur over the evaluation period and if all investment income is reinvested. The problem with the dollar-weighted rate of return is that it is affected by factors that are beyond the control of the money manager. Specifically, any contributions made by the client or withdrawals that the client requires will affect the calculated return. This may make it difficult to compare the performance of two money managers. Despite this limitation, the dollar-weighted rate of return does provide information. It indicates information about the growth of the fund that a client will find useful. This growth, however, is not attributable to the performance of the portfolio manager because of contributions and withdrawals.

Annualizing Returns

The evaluation period may be less than or greater than one year. Typically, return measures are reported as an average annual return. This requires the annualization of the subperiod returns. The subperiod returns are usually calculated for a period of less than one year for the reasons described earlier. The subperiod returns are then annualized using the following formula:

$$\text{Annual return} = (1 + \text{Average period return})^{\text{Number of periods in year}} - 1$$

So, for example, suppose the evaluation period is three years, and a monthly period return is calculated. Suppose further that the average monthly return is 2%. Then the annual return would be

$$\text{Annual return} = (1.02)^{12} - 1 = 26.8\%$$

Suppose, instead, that the period used to calculate returns is quarterly, and the average quarterly return is 3%. Then the annual return is

$$\text{Annual return} = (1.03)^4 - 1 = 12.6\%$$

Evaluating Performance

A performance measure does not answer two questions: (1) How did the portfolio manager perform after adjusting for the risk associated with the active strategy employed? And (2) how did the asset manager achieve the reported return?

The answers to these two questions are critical in assessing how well or how poorly the portfolio manager performed relative to some benchmark. In answering the first question, we must draw upon the various measures of risk that we described earlier. We can then judge whether the performance was acceptable in the face of the risk.

The answer to the second question tells us whether the portfolio manager, in fact, achieved a return by following the anticipated strategy. While a client would expect that any superior return accomplished is a result of a stated strategy, that may not always be the case. For example, suppose a manager solicits funds from a client by claiming he can achieve superior common stock performance by selecting underpriced stocks. Suppose also that this manager does generate a superior return compared with the S&P 500 Index. The client should not be satisfied with this performance until the return realized by the manager is segregated into the various components that generated the return. A client may find that the superior performance is the result of the manager's timing of the market, rather than of his selecting underpriced stocks. In such an instance, the portfolio manager may have outperformed the S&P 500 (even after adjusting for risk), but not by following the strategy the asset manager told the client he intended to pursue.

Below we briefly describe methodologies for adjusting returns for risk so as (1) to determine whether a superior return was realized and (2) to analyze the actual return of a portfolio to uncover the reasons why a return was realized. We refer to this analysis as performance evaluation. We begin with a discussion of the various benchmarks that can be used to evaluate the performance of an asset manager.

Benchmark Portfolios

To evaluate the performance of a portfolio manager, a client must specify a market index to be used as a benchmark against which the portfolio manager will be measured when there are nonliability driven objectives specified by a client.

Single-Index Performance Evaluation Measures

Several single-index measures have been used to evaluate the relative performance of portfolio managers. These measures of performance evaluation do not specify how or why a manager may have outperformed or underperformed a benchmark. The most popular measure is the Sharpe ratio or index.[25]

---

[25] Other single index performance measures include the Treynor index (Treynor, 1965), the Jensen measure (Jensen, 1968), and the information ratio (discussed in Chapter 11).

The *Sharpe ratio* is a measure of the reward-risk ratio. Introduced by William Sharpe (1966), the numerator of this ratio is spread between the return on the portfolio and the risk-free interest rate. The risk of the portfolio is measured by the standard deviation of the portfolio's return. Therefore,

$$\text{Sharpe ratio} = \frac{\text{Portfolio return} - \text{Risk-free rate}}{\text{Standard deviation of the portfolio's return}}$$

That is, the Sharpe ratio is a measure of the excess return relative to the total variability of the portfolio.

More recently, there have been several single-index measures that have been proposed based on the risk measures described in Chapter 4.

Performance Attribution Models

In broad terms, the return performance of a portfolio can be explained by three actions followed by a portfolio manager. The first is actively managing a portfolio to capitalize on factors that are expected to perform better than other factors. The second is actively managing a portfolio to take advantage of anticipated movements in the market. For example, the manager of a common stock portfolio can increase the portfolio's beta when the market is expected to increase, and decrease it when the market is expected to decline. The third is actively managing the portfolio by buying securities that are believed to be undervalued, and selling (or shorting) securities that are believed to be overvalued.

The methodology for answering these questions is called *performance attribution analysis*. Single index measures do not help answer these questions. However, there are commercially available models that can be used to do this analysis. We will not describe these models here. These models employ the factor model approach described in Chapter 11. Instead, we provide an illustration of how these models are used.

Rennie and Cowhey (1989) report the performance of three external money managers for Bell Atlantic (now Verizon Communications).[26] Table 7.4 shows the results for the three money managers since they began managing funds for Bell Atlantic. The values shown in parentheses in Table 7.4 are statistical measures that indicate the probability that the estimated value is statistically different from zero. The value in parentheses is referred to as a *confidence level*. The higher the confidence level, the more likely the estimated value is different from zero and, therefore, performance can be attributed to skill rather than luck.

---

[26] Bell Atlantic merged with GTE to form Verizon Communications, Inc.

TABLE 7.4 Performance Attribution Analysis for Three Money Managers

	Manager A		Manager B		Manager C	
Actual return	19.1%		17.0%		12.6%	
Benchmark portfolio	14.9		15.2		12.6	
Active management return	4.2%	(99)	1.8%	(53)	0.0%	(3)
Components of return:						
Market timing	−0.2%	(40)	−0.6%	(64)	−0.5%	(73)
Industry exposure	0.2	(20)	−2.0	(89)	0.3	(34)
Sector emphasis	2.2	(99)	3.9	(99)	0.3	(51)
Security selection	1.9	(84)	0.6	(43)	0.1	(7)
Unreconciled return[a]	0.1		−0.1		−0.2	

Note: Numbers set in parentheses denote confidence level.
[a]Difference between actual management return and sum of components of return.
Source: Adapted from Rennie and Cowhey (1989, 37).

The active management return represents the difference between the actual portfolio return and the benchmark return. Manager A's active management return is 420 basis points and, therefore, seems to have outperformed the benchmark. But was this by investment skill or luck? The confidence level of 99% suggests that it was through investment skill. The lower panel of the table shows how this was achieved. Of the four components of return, two are statistically significant—sector emphasis and security selection. The other two components—market timing and industry exposure—are not statistically significant. This means that either manager A's skills in these two areas did not significantly impact the portfolio's return, or the manager did not emphasize these skills. In fact, this manager's stated investment style is to add value through sector emphasis and security selection and neutralize market timing and industry exposure. The results of the performance attribution analysis are consistent with this investment style.

An analysis of the results of manager B indicates that the manager outperformed the benchmark by 180 basis points. The confidence level, however, is 53%. In most statistical tests, this confidence level would suggest that the 180 basis points is not statistically different from zero. That is, the 180-basis-point active management return can be attributed to luck rather than skill. However, Rennie and Cowhey state that this is an acceptable level of confidence for Bell Atlantic, but that it does provide a warning to the company to carefully monitor this manager's performance for improvement or deterioration. The stated investment style of this manager is to identify undervalued securities. The component return of 60 basis points from security selection with a confidence level of only 43% suggests that this manager is not adding value in this way. This is another warning sign that this manager must be more carefully monitored.

Manager C has to be carefully monitored because this manager did not outperform the benchmark, and none of the component returns are statistically significant. This manager is a candidate for termination. What is the minimum active management return that Bell Atlantic expects from its active equity managers? According to Rennie and Cowhey, it is 1% per year over a 2.5-year investment horizon with a confidence level of at least 70%. Moreover, the component analysis should corroborate what the manager states is the manager's investment style.

SUMMARY

Markets are classified according to their pricing efficiency, referred to as market efficiency. A financial market where asset prices rapidly reflect all available information is said to be an efficient market and such markets abnormal returns are precluded. There are the levels of market efficiency. Weak form of market efficiency means that current asset prices reflect all past prices and price movements. Semistrong form of market efficiency means that current asset prices reflect all publicly available information. Strong form of market efficiency means that current asset prices reflect all public and private information. The form of market efficiency has implications for investment management strategies.

Stock market indicators can be classified into three groups: (1) those produced by stock exchanges that include all stocks traded on the exchange; (2) those in which a committee subjectively selects the stocks to be included in the index; and (3) those in which the stocks selected are based solely on the stocks' market capitalizations.

We outlined a number of active portfolio management strategies. These strategies are characterized by the emphasis on the stock selection process. Traditionally speaking, there are two major types of stock selection approaches, those based on fundamental analysis and those based on technical analysis. Fundamental analysis tries to assess the viability of a company from a business point of view, looking at financial statements as well as operations. The objective is to identify companies that will produce a solid future stream of cash flows. Technical analysis looks at patterns in prices and returns and is based on the assumption that prices and returns follow discernable patterns.

The underpinning of active portfolio management is the belief that there are market inefficiencies, that is, that there are situations where a stock's price does not fully reflect all available information. Both fundamental and technical analysis attempt to identify situations where the market somehow makes mistakes in processing information, leading to pricing anomalies.

There are a myriad of investment "styles." We have focused on one of the more important alternatives—growth investing versus value investing.

Indexing is one form of passive equity management. This approach is supported by the findings that the stock market appears to be sufficiently price-efficient that it is difficult to consistently outperform the market after adjusting for risk and transaction costs. Moreover, pension sponsors have found that external money managers have not consistently outperformed their benchmark after taking management fees into consideration. Index fund management involves creating a portfolio to replicate an index.

The index is selected by the client, the most popular index being the S&P 500. Once an index is selected, the money manager must decide how to construct the replicating portfolio so as to minimize tracking error risk. In doing so, the money manager must consider the trade-off between the number of stock issues in the index to include in the replicating portfolio and the transaction costs.

Constructing a replicating portfolio with fewer stock issues than are included in the index involves one of three methods: the capitalization method, stratified method, or quadratic optimization method.

Some managers utilize active strategies within an index fund management framework in an attempt to enhance returns but still control market risk. The two most popular methods are creating a tilted portfolio and utilizing the stock index futures market.

Performance measurement involves the calculation of the return realized by a portfolio manager over some evaluation period. Performance evaluation is concerned with determining whether the money manager added value by outperforming the established benchmark, and with how the portfolio manager achieved the calculated return.

The rate of return expresses the dollar return in terms of the amount of the initial investment (i.e., the initial market value of the portfolio). Three methodologies have been used in practice to calculate the average of the subperiod returns: (1) the arithmetic average rate of return, (2) the time-weighted (or geometric) rate of return, and (3) the dollar-weighted return. Several return-risk measures have been used to evaluate the relative performance of portfolio managers, the most commonly used one being the Sharpe ratio. However, such single-index measures fail to identify how or why a portfolio manager may have outperformed or underperformed a benchmark.

In contrast to single-index measures, performance attribution models identify the sources of return. In the equity area, multifactor models are the foundation for performance attribution models, and these models can be used to determine whether active added value provided by a portfolio manager comes from the various risk sources identified to drive returns.

REFERENCES

Alexander, S. S. 1961. Price movements in speculative markets: Trends or random walks. *Industrial Management Review* 2 (May): 7–26.

Banz, R. W. 1981. The relationship between return and market value of stocks. *Journal of Financial Economics* 9, no. 1: 103–126.

Bernstein, P. L. 1985. Does the market overreact?: Discussion. *Journal of Finance* 40, no. 3: 806–808.

Birinyi, L., and K. Miller. 1987. Market breadth: An analysis. Salomon Brothers, September.

Brock, W., J. Lakonishok, and B. LeBaron. 1992. Simple technical trading rules and the stochastic properties of stock returns. *Journal of Finance* 47, no. 5: 1731–1764.

Brown, K. C., and W. van Harlow. 1988. Market overreaction: Magnitude and intensity. *Journal of Portfolio Management* 14 (Winter): 6–13.

Brown, S. J., W. A. Goetzmann, and A. Kumar. 1998. The Dow theory: William Peter Hamilton's track record reconsidered. *Journal of Finance* 53, no. 4: 1311–1333.

Christopherson, J. A., and C. N. Williams. 1997. Equity style: What it is and why it matters. In *The handbook of equity style management*, 2nd ed., edited by D. Coggin, F. J. Fabozzi, and R. D. Arnott (pp. 1–20). Hoboken, NJ: John Wiley & Sons.

Cootner, P. H. 1962. Stock prices: Random vs. systematic risk. *Industrial Management Review* 3 (Spring): 24–45.

Daniel, K. D., D. Hirshleifer, and A. Subrahmanyam. 1998. Investor psychology and security market under- and overreactions. *Journal of Finance* 53, no. 4: 1839–1885.

DeBondt, W., and R. Thaler. 1985. Does the market overreact? *Journal of Finance* 40, no. 3: 793–805.

DeBondt, W., and R. Thaler. 1987. Further evidence on investor overreaction and stock market seasonality. *Journal of Finance* 42, no. 3: 557–581.

Dreman, D. 1982. *The new contrarian investment strategy*. New York: Random House.

Edwards, R. D., and J. Magee. 1992. *Technical analysis of stock trends*. Boston: John Magee Inc.

Fabozzi, F. J., and F. J. Jones. 2008. The U.S. equity markets. In *The handbook of finance*, vol. 1, edited by Frank J. Fabozzi (pp. 125–150). Hoboken, NJ: John Wiley & Sons.

Fama, E. F. 1970. Efficient capital markets: A review of theory and empirical work. *Journal of Finance* 25, no. 2: 383–417.

Fama, E. F., and M. Blume. 1966. Filter rules and stock-market trading. *Journal of Business* 39 (October): 226–241.

Fama, E. F., and K. R. French. 1993. Common risk factors on stocks and bonds. *Journal of Financial Economics* 33, no. 1: 3–56.

Farrell, J. L., Jr. 1975. Homogenous stock groupings: Implications for portfolio management. *Financial Analysts Journal* 31 (May–June): 50–62.

Figelman, I. 2007. Stock return momentum and reversal. *Journal of Portfolio Management* 34 (Fall): 51–69.

Glickstein, D., and R. Wubbels. 1983. Dow theory is alive and well! *Journal of Portfolio Management* 9 (Spring): 28–32.

Graham, B. 1973. *The intelligent investor,* 4th rev. ed. New York: Harper & Row.

Graham, B., D. L. Dodd, and S. Cottle. 1962. *Security analysis*, 4th ed. New York: McGraw-Hill.

Gross, W. 1997. *Everything you've heard about investing is wrong!* New York: Crown Business.

Hamilton, W. P. 1922. *The stock market barometer.* New York: Harper & Brothers.

Houge, T., and T. Loughran. 2006. Do investors capture the value premium? *Financial Management* 35, no. 2: 5–19.

Hwang, S. and A. Rubesam. 2007. The disappearance of momentum. Working paper, Cass Business School, City University London.

Jacobs, Bruce I., and Kenneth N. Levy. 1997. The long and short on long-short. *Journal of Investing* 6 (Spring): 78–88.

James, F. E. 1969. Monthly moving averages—An effective investment tool? *Journal of Financial and Quantitative Analysis* 3 (September): 315–326.

Jegadeesh, N. 1990. Evidence of predictable behavior of security returns. *Journal of Finance* 45, no. 3: 881–898.

Jegadeesh, N. and S. Titman. 1993. Returns to buying winners and selling losers: Implications for stock market efficiency. *Journal of Finance* 48, no. 1: 65–91.

Jensen, M. C. 1967. Random walks: A comment. *Financial Analysts Journal* 23 (November–December): 77–78.

Jensen, M. C. 1968. The performance of mutual funds in the period 1945–1964. *Journal of Finance* 23, no. 2: 389–416.

Jensen, M. C., and G. Bennington. 1970. Random walks and technical theories: Some additional evidence. *Journal of Finance* 25, no. 2: 469–482.

Korajczyk, R. A., and R. Sadka. 2004. Are momentum profits robust to trading costs? *Journal of Finance* 59, no. 2: 1039–1082.

Levy, R. 1966. Conceptual foundations of technical analysis. *Financial Analysts Journal* 22 (July–August): 83–89.

Loftus, J. S. 2000. Enhanced equity indexing. In *Professional Perspectives on Indexing,* edited by F. J. Fabozzi (pp. 78–97). Hoboken, NJ: John Wiley & Sons.

Malkiel, B. G. 1996. *A random walk down street,* 6th ed. New York: W. W. Norton.

Miller, K. L, H. Li, and D. E. Cox. 2006. *Quantitative strategy: In style.* Citicorp Research, October 2.

O'Higgins, M. 1992. *Beating the Dow.* New York: Harper Perennial.

Oppenheimer, H. R., and G. G. Schlarbaum. 1981. Investing with Ben Graham: An ex ante test of the efficient market hypothesis. *Journal of Financial and Quantitative Analysis* 16, no. 3: 341–360.

Peters, E. E. 1991. *Chaos and order in the capital markets: A new view of cycles, prices, and market volatility.* New York: John Wiley & Sons.

Qian, E., R. Hua, and E. H. Sorensen. 2007. *Quantitative equity portfolio management: Modern techniques and applications.* London: CRC Press.

Reinganum, M. R. 1981. Misspecification of capital asset pricing: Empirical anomalies based on earnings yields and market values. *Journal of Financial Economics* 9, no. 1: 19–46.

Rennie, E. P., and T. J. Cowhey. 1989. The successful use of benchmark portfolios. In *Improving Portfolio Performance with Quantitative Models*, edited by Darwin M. Bayston and H. Russell Fogler (pp. 32–44). Charlottesville, VA: Institute of Chartered Financial Analysts.

Rouwenhorst, K. G. 1998. International momentum strategies. *Journal of Finance* 53, no. 1: 267–283.

Schabacker, R. W. 1930. *Stock market theory and practice.* New York: B. C. Forbes Publishing Company.

Schabacker, R. W. [1932] 1997. *Technical Analysis and Stock Market Profits.* New York: Pitman Publishing.

Schabacker, R. W. 1934. *Stock market profits.* New York: B. C. Forbes Publishing Company.

Sharpe, W. F. 1966. Mutual fund performance. *Journal of Business* 34, no. 1 (Part I): 119–38.

Scheinkman, J., and B. LeBaron. 1989. Nonlinear dynamics and stock returns. *Journal of Business* 62 (July): 311–337.

Schlarbaum, G. G. 1997. Value-based equity strategies. *The handbook of equity style management*, 2nd ed. (pp. 133–150). New York: John Wiley & Sons.

Shaw, A. R. 1988. Market timing and technical analysis. In *The Financial Analyst's Handbook*, edited by Summer N. Levine (pp. 944–988). Homewood, IL: Dow Jones–Irwin.

Sorensen, E. H., D. E. Cox, J. P. Ginty, H. Li, K. L. Miller, T. S. Nadbielny, J. Rowe, R. W. Schlatter, Sullivan, and D. Xiao. 2000. *Equity style investing and the Salomon Smith Barney World Equity Style Indices.* New York: Salomon Smith Barney.

Sorensen, E. H., R. Hua, and E. Qian. 2005. Contextual fundamentals, models and active management. *Journal of Portfolio Management* 31, no. 1: 23–36.

Sweeney, R. J. 1988. Some new filter rule tests: Methods and results. *Journal of Financial and Quantitative Analysis* 23, no. 3: 285–300.

Sweeney, R. J. 1990. Evidence on short-term trading strategies. *Journal of Portfolio Management* 17 (Fall): 20–26.

Treynor, J. 1965. How to rate management of investment funds. *Harvard Business Review* 44, no. 1: 63–75.

Van Horne, J. C., and G. Parker. 1967. The random walk theory: An empirical test. *Financial Analysts Journal* 23 (November–December): 87–92.

CHAPTER 8

Financial Analysis

Financial analysis involves the selection, evaluation, and interpretation of financial data and other pertinent information to assist in evaluating the operating performance and financial condition of a company. The information that is available for analysis includes economic, market, and financial information. But some of the most important financial data are provided by the company in its annual and quarterly financial statements.

The operating performance of a company is a measure of how well a company has used its resources to produce a return on its investment. The financial condition of a company is a measure of its ability to satisfy its obligations, such as the payment of interest on its debt in a timely manner. An investor has many tools available in the analysis of financial information. These tools include:

- Financial ratio analysis
- Cash flow analysis
- Quantitative analysis

Cash flows provide a way of transforming net income based on an accrual system to a more comparable basis. Additionally, cash flows are essential ingredients in valuation: The value of a company today is the present value of its expected future cash flows. Therefore, understanding past and current cash flows may help in forecasting future cash flows and, hence, determine the value of the company. Moreover, understanding cash flow allows the assessment of the ability of a firm to maintain current dividends and its current capital expenditure policy without relying on external financing.

In this chapter, we describe and illustrate the basic tools of financial analysis: financial ratio analysis and cash flow analysis.

This chapter is coauthored with Pamela Peterson Drake.

FINANCIAL RATIO ANALYSIS

In financial ratio analysis, we select the relevant information—primarily the financial statement data—and evaluate it. We show how to incorporate market data and economic data in the analysis of financial ratios. Finally, we show how to interpret financial ratio analysis, identifying the pitfalls that occur when it's not done properly.

Ratios and Their Classification

A financial ratio is a comparison between one bit of financial information and another. Consider the ratio of current assets to current liabilities, which we refer to as the current ratio. This ratio is a comparison between assets that can be readily turned into cash—current assets—and the obligations that are due in the near future—current liabilities. A current ratio of 2 or 2:1 means that we have twice as much in current assets as we need to satisfy obligations due in the near future.

Ratios can be classified according to the way they are constructed and the financial characteristic they are describing. For example, we will see that the current ratio is constructed as a coverage ratio (the ratio of current assets—available funds—to current liabilities—the obligation) that we use to describe a firm's liquidity (its ability to meet its immediate needs).

There are as many different financial ratios as there are possible combinations of items appearing on the income statement, balance sheet, and statement of cash flows. We can classify ratios according to the financial characteristic that they capture.

When we assess a firm's operating performance, a concern is whether the company is applying its assets in an efficient and profitable manner. When an investor assesses a firm's financial condition, a concern is whether the company is able to meet its financial obligations. The investor can use financial ratios to evaluate five aspects of operating performance and financial condition:

1. Return on investment
2. Liquidity
3. Profitability
4. Activity
5. Financial leverage

There are several ratios reflecting each of the five aspects of a firm's operating performance and financial condition. We apply these ratios to the Fictitious Corporation, whose balance sheets, income statements, and statement of cash flows for two years are shown in Tables 8.1, 8.2, and 8.3, respectively. We refer to the most recent fiscal year for which financial statements are available as the "current year." The "prior year" is the fiscal year prior to the current year.

The ratios we introduce here are by no means the only ones that can be formed using financial data, though they are some of the more commonly used. After becoming comfortable with the tools of financial analysis, an investor will be able to create ratios that serve a particular evaluation objective.

TABLE 8.1 Fictitious Corporation Balance Sheets for Years Ending December 31, in Thousands

	Current Year	Prior Year
Assets		
Cash	$400	$200
Marketable securities	200	0
Accounts receivable	600	800
Inventories	1,800	1,000
Total current assets	$3,000	$2,000
Gross plant and equipment	$11,000	$10,000
Accumulated depreciation	(4,000)	(3,000)
Net plant and equipment	7,000	7,000
Intangible assets	1,000	1,000
Total assets	$11,000	$10,000
Liabilities and Shareholders' Equity		
Accounts payable	$500	$400
Other current liabilities	500	200
Long-term debt	4,000	5,000
Total liabilities	$5,000	$5,600
Common stock, $1 par value;		
Authorized 2,000,000 shares		
Issued 1,500,000 and 1,200,000 shares	1,500	1,200
Additional paid-in capital	1,500	800
Retained earnings	3,000	2,400
Total shareholders' equity	6,000	4,400
Total liabilities and shareholders' equity	$11,000	$10,000

TABLE 8.2 Fictitious Corporation Income Statements for Years Ending December 31, in Thousands

	Current Year	Prior Year
Sales	$10,000	$9,000
Cost of goods sold	(6,500)	(6,000)
Gross profit	$3,500	$3,000
Lease expense	(1,000)	1,000)
Administrative expense	(500)	(500)
Earnings before interest and taxes (EBIT)	$2,000	$2,000
Interest	(400)	(500)
Earnings before taxes	$1,600	$1,500
Taxes	(400)	(500)
Net income	$1,200	$1,000
Preferred dividends	(100)	(100)
Earnings available to common shareholders	$1,100	$900
Common dividends	(500)	(400)
Retained earnings	$600	$500

Return-on-Investment Ratios

Return-on-investment ratios compare measures of benefits, such as earnings or net income, with measures of investment. For example, if an investor wants to evaluate how well the firm uses its assets in its operations, he could calculate the return on assets—sometimes called the *basic earning power ratio*—as the ratio of *earnings before interest and taxes* (EBIT) (also known as *operating earnings*) to total assets:

$$\text{Basic earning power} = \frac{\text{Earnings before interest and taxes}}{\text{Total assets}}$$

For Fictitious Corporation, for the current year:

$$\text{Basic earning power} = \frac{\$2,000,000}{\$11,000,000} = 0.1818 \text{ or } 18.18\%$$

For every dollar invested in assets, Fictitious earned about 18 cents in the current year. This measure deals with earnings from operations; it does not consider how these operations are financed.

Another return-on-assets ratio uses net income—operating earnings less interest and taxes—instead of earnings before interest and taxes:

Financial Analysis

TABLE 8.3 Fictitious Company Statement of Cash Flows, Years Ended December 31, in Thousands

	Current Year	Prior Year
Cash flow from (used for) operating activities		
Net income	$1,200	$1,000
Add or deduct adjustments to cash basis:		
Change in accounts receivables	$200	$(200)
Change in accounts payable	100	400
Change in marketable securities	(200)	200
Change in inventories	(800)	(600)
Change in other current liabilities	300	0
Depreciation	1,000	1,000
Cash flow from operations	$1,800	$1,800
Cash flow from (used for) investing activities		
Purchase of plant and equipment	$(1,000)	$0
Cash flow from (used for) investing activities	$(1,000)	$0
Cash flow from (used for) financing activities		
Sale of common stock	$1,000	$0
Repayment of long-term debt	(1,000)	(1,500)
Payment of preferred dividends	(100)	(100)
Payment of common dividends	(500)	(400)
Cash flow from (used for) financing activities	(600)	(1,900)
Increase (decrease) in cash flow	$200	$(100)
Cash at the beginning of the year	200	300
Cash at the end of the year	$400	$200

$$\text{Return on assets} = \frac{\text{Net income}}{\text{Total assets}}$$

(In actual application the same term, return on assets, is often used to describe both ratios. It is only in the actual context or through an examination of the numbers themselves that we know which return ratio is presented. We use two different terms to describe these two return-on-asset ratios in this chapter simply to avoid any confusion.)

For Fictitious in the current year:

$$\text{Return on assets} = \frac{\$1,200,000}{\$11,000,000} = 0.1091 \text{ or } 10.91\%$$

Thus, without taking into consideration how assets are financed, the return on assets for Fictitious is 18%. Taking into consideration how assets are financed, the return on assets is 11%. The difference is due to Fictitious financing part of its total assets with debt, incurring interest of $400,000 in the current year; hence, the return-on-assets ratio excludes taxes of $400,000 in the current year from earnings in the numerator.

If we look at Fictitious's liabilities and equities, we see that the assets are financed in part by liabilities ($1 million short term, $4 million long term) and in part by equity ($800,000 preferred stock, $5.2 million common stock). Investors may not be interested in the return the firm gets from its total investment (debt plus equity), but rather shareholders are interested in the return the firm can generate on their investment. The *return on equity* is the ratio of the net income shareholders receive to their equity in the stock:

$$\text{Return on equity} = \frac{\text{Net income}}{\text{Book value of shareholders' equity}}$$

For Fictitious Corporation, there is only one type of shareholder: common. For the current year:

$$\text{Return on equity} = \frac{\$1,200,000}{\$6,000,000} = 0.2000 \text{ or } 20.00\%$$

Recap: Return-on-Investment Ratios The return-on-investment ratios for Fictitious Corporation for the current year are:

Basic earning power = 18.18%
Return on assets   = 10.91%
Return on equity   = 20.00%

These return-on-investment ratios indicate:

- Fictitious earns over 18% from operations, or about 11% overall, from its assets.
- Shareholders earn 20% from their investment (measured in book value terms).

These ratios do not provide information on:

Financial Analysis

- Whether this return is due to the profit margins (that is, due to costs and revenues) or to how efficiently Fictitious uses its assets.
- The return shareholders earn on their actual investment in the firm, that is, what shareholders earn relative to their actual investment, not the book value of their investment. For example, $100 may be invested in the stock, but its value according to the balance sheet may be greater than or, more likely, less than $100.

DuPont System The returns on investment ratios provides a "bottom line" on the performance of a company, but do not tell us anything about the "why" behind this performance. For an understanding of the "why," an investor must dig a bit deeper into the financial statements. A method that is useful in examining the source of performance is the DuPont system. The *DuPont system* is a method of breaking down return ratios into their components to determine which areas are responsible for a firm's performance. This method of analyzing return ratios in terms of profit margin and turnover ratios is credited to the E. I. Du Pont Corporation, whose management developed a system of breaking down return ratios into their components.

To see how the DuPont system is used, let us take a closer look at the first definition of the return on assets:

$$\text{Basic earning power} = \frac{\text{Earnings before interest and taxes}}{\text{Total assets}}$$

Suppose the return on assets changes from 20% in one period to 10% the next period. We do not know whether this decreased return is due to a less efficient use of the firm's assets—that is, lower activity—or to less effective management of expenses (i.e., lower profit margins). A lower return on assets could be due to lower activity, lower margins, or both. Because an investor is interested in evaluating past operating performance to evaluate different aspects of the management of the firm and to predict future performance, knowing the source of these returns is valuable.

Let us take a closer look at the return on assets and break it down into its components: measures of activity and profit margin. We do this by relating both the numerator and the denominator to sales activity. Divide both the numerator and the denominator of the basic earning power by revenues:

$$\text{Basic earning power} = \frac{\text{Earnings before interest and taxes}/\text{Revenues}}{\text{Revenues total assets}/\text{Revenues}}$$

which is equivalent to

Basic earning power
$$= \left(\frac{\text{Earnings before interest and taxes}}{\text{Revenues}}\right)\left(\frac{\text{Revenues}}{\text{Revenues total assets}}\right)$$

This says that the earning power of the company is related to profitability (in this case, operating profit) and a measure of activity (total asset turnover).

Basic earning power = (Operating profit margin)(Total asset turnover)

When analyzing a change in the company's basic earning power, an investor could look at this breakdown to see the change in its components: operating profit margin and total asset turnover.

Let's look at the return on assets of Fictitious for the two years. Its returns on assets were 20% in the prior year and 18.18% in the current year. We can decompose the firm's returns on assets for the two years to obtain:

Year	Basic Earning Power	Operating Profit Margin	Total Asset Turnover
Prior	20.00%	22.22%	0.9000 times
Current	18.18	20.00	0.9091 times

We see that operating profit margin declined over the two years, yet asset turnover improved slightly, from 0.9000 to 0.9091. Therefore, the return-on-assets decline is attributable to lower profit margins.

The return on assets can be broken down into its components in a similar manner:

$$\text{Return on assets} = \left(\frac{\text{Net income}}{\text{Revenues}}\right)\left(\frac{\text{Revenues}}{\text{Revenues total assets}}\right)$$

or

Return on assets = (Net profit margin)(Total asset turnover)

The basic earning power ratio relates to the return on assets. Recognizing that

Net income = Earnings before tax(1 − Tax rate)

then

Financial Analysis

$$\text{Net income} = \text{Earnings before interest and taxes}$$
$$\times \left(\frac{\text{Earnings before taxes}}{\text{Earnings before interest and taxes}}\right)(1 - \text{Tax rate})$$

$$\underset{\text{Equity's share of earnings}}{\uparrow} \quad \underset{\text{Tax retention \%}}{\uparrow}$$

The ratio of earnings before taxes to earnings before interest and taxes reflects the interest burden of the company, where as the term (1 − Tax rate) reflects the company's tax burden. Therefore,

$$\text{Return on assets} = \left(\frac{\text{Earnings before interest and taxes}}{\text{Revenues}}\right)$$
$$\times \left(\frac{\text{Revenues}}{\text{Revenues total assets}}\right)$$
$$\times \left(\frac{\text{Earnings before taxes}}{\text{Earnings before interest and taxes}}\right)(1 - \text{Tax rate})$$

or

$$\text{Return on assets} = (\text{Operating profit margin})(\text{Total asset turnover})$$
$$\times (\text{Equity's share of earnings})(\text{Tax retention \%})$$

The breakdown of a return-on-equity ratio requires a bit more decomposition because instead of total assets as the denominator, the denominator in the return is shareholders' equity. Because activity ratios reflect the use of all of the assets, not just the proportion financed by equity, we need to adjust the activity ratio by the proportion that assets are financed by equity (i.e., the ratio of the book value of shareholders' equity to total assets):

$$\text{Return on equity} = (\text{Return on assets})\left(\frac{\text{Total assets}}{\text{Shareholders' equity}}\right)$$

$$\text{Return on equity} = \left(\frac{\text{Net income}}{\text{Revenues}}\right)\left(\frac{\text{Revenues}}{\text{Total assets}}\right)\left(\frac{\text{Total assets}}{\text{Shareholders' equity}}\right)$$

$$\underset{\text{Equity multiplier}}{\uparrow}$$

The ratio of total assets to shareholders' equity is referred to as the *equity multiplier*. The equity multiplier, therefore, captures the effects of how a company finances its assets, that is, its financial leverage. Multiplying the total asset turnover ratio by the equity multiplier allows us to break down the return-on-equity ratios into three components: profit margin, asset turnover, and financial leverage. For example, the return on equity can be broken down into three parts:

Return on equity = (Net profit margin)(Total asset turnover)(Equity multiplier)

Applying this breakdown to Fictitious for the two years:

Year	Return on Equity	Net Profit Margin	Total Asset Turnover	Total Debt to Assets	Equity Multiplier
Prior	22.73%	11.11%	0.9000 times	56.00%	2.2727
Current	20.00	12.00	0.9091	45.45%	1.8332

The return on equity decreased over the two years because of a lower operating profit margin and less use of financial leverage.

The investor can decompose the return on equity further by breaking out the equity's share of before-tax earnings (represented by the ratio of earnings before and after interest) and tax retention percentage. Consider the example in Figure 8.1A, in which we provide a DuPont breakdown of the return on equity for Microsoft Corporation for the fiscal year ending June 30, 2006. The return on equity of 31.486% can be broken down into three and then five components, as shown in this figure. We can also use this breakdown to compare the return on equity for the 2005 and 2006 fiscal years, as shown in Figure 8.1B. As you can see, the return on equity improved from 2005 to 2006 and, using this breakdown, we can see that this was due primarily to the improvement in the asset turnover and the increased financial leverage.

This decomposition allows the investor to take a closer look at the factors that are controllable by a company's management (e.g., asset turnover) and those that are not controllable (e.g., tax retention). The breakdowns lead the investor to information on both the balance sheet and the income statement. And this is not the only breakdown of the return ratios—further decomposition is possible.

Liquidity

Liquidity reflects the ability of a firm to meet its short-term obligations using those assets that are most readily converted into cash. Assets that may be converted into cash in a short period of time are referred to as liquid assets; they are listed in financial statements as current assets. Current assets

Financial Analysis **203**

FIGURE 8.1 The DuPont System Applied to Microsoft Corporation

A. For the fiscal year ending June 30, 2006.

$$\text{Return on equity} = \frac{\text{Net income}}{\text{Total assets}} = \frac{\$12.599}{\$40.014} = 0.31486 \text{ or } 31.486\%$$

Breaking return on equity into three components:

$$\text{Return on equity} = \frac{\text{Net income}}{\text{Revenues}} \times \frac{\text{Revenues}}{\text{Total assets}} \times \frac{\text{Total assets}}{\text{Shareholders' equity}}$$

$$= \frac{\$12.599}{\$44.282} \times \frac{\$44.282}{\$69.597} \times \frac{\$69.597}{\$40.014} = 0.31486 \text{ or } 31.486\%$$

Breaking the return on equity into five components:

$$\text{Return on equity} = \left(\frac{\text{Earnings before interest and taxes}}{\text{Revenues}}\right) \times \left(\frac{\text{Earnings before taxes}}{\text{Earnings before interest and taxes}}\right) \times (1 - \text{Tax rate})$$

$$\times \left(\frac{\text{Revenues}}{\text{Total assets}}\right) \times \left(\frac{\text{Total assets}}{\text{Shareholders' equity}}\right)$$

$$\text{Return on equity} = \left(\frac{\$18.262}{\$44.282}\right) \times \left(\frac{\$18.262}{\$18.262}\right) \times (1 - 0.31010) \times \left(\frac{\$44.282}{\$69.597}\right) \times \left(\frac{\$69.597}{\$40.014}\right)$$

$$= 0.41240 \times 1.0 \times 0.68990 \times 0.63626 \times 1.73932$$

$$= 0.31486 \text{ or } 31.486\%$$

B. Comparing the components between the June 30, 2006 fiscal year and the June 30, 2005 fiscal year.

$$\text{Return on equity} = \left(\frac{\text{Earnings before interest and taxes}}{\text{Revenues}}\right) \times \left(\frac{\text{Earnings before taxes}}{\text{Earnings before interest and taxes}}\right) \times (1 - \text{Tax rate})$$

$$\times \left(\frac{\text{Revenues}}{\text{Total assets}}\right) \times \left(\frac{\text{Total assets}}{\text{Shareholders' equity}}\right)$$

$$\frac{\text{Return on equity}}{\text{June 30, 2006}} = 0.41240 \times 1.0 \times 0.68990 \times 0.63626 \times 1.73932 = 31.486\%$$

$$\frac{\text{Return on equity}}{\text{June 30, 2006}} = 0.41791 \times 1.0 \times 0.73695 \times 0.56186 \times 1.47179 = 25.468\%$$

are often referred to as working capital, since they represent the resources needed for the day-to-day operations of the firm's long-term capital investments. Current assets are used to satisfy short-term obligations, or current liabilities. The amount by which current assets exceed current liabilities is referred to as the net working capital.

Operating Cycle How much liquidity a firm needs depends on its operating cycle. The *operating cycle* is the duration from the time cash is invested in goods and services to the time that investment produces cash. For example, a firm that produces and sells goods has an operating cycle comprising four phases:

1. Purchase raw materials and produce goods, investing in inventory.
2. Sell goods, generating sales, which may or may not be for cash.
3. Extend credit, creating accounts receivable.
4. Collect accounts receivable, generating cash.

The four phases make up the cycle of cash use and generation. The operating cycle would be somewhat different for companies that produce services rather than goods, but the idea is the same—the operating cycle is the length of time it takes to generate cash through the investment of cash.

What does the operating cycle have to do with liquidity? The longer the operating cycle, the more current assets are needed (relative to current liabilities) since it takes longer to convert inventories and receivables into cash. In other words, the longer the operating cycle, the greater the amount of net working capital required.

To measure the length of an operating cycle we need to know:

- The time it takes to convert the investment in inventory into sales (that is, cash → inventory → sales → accounts receivable).
- The time it takes to collect sales on credit (that is, accounts receivable → cash).

We can estimate the operating cycle for Fictitious Corporation for the current year, using the balance sheet and income statement data. The number of days Fictitious ties up funds in inventory is determined by the total amount of money represented in inventory and the average day's cost of goods sold. The current investment in inventory—that is, the money "tied up" in inventory—is the ending balance of inventory on the balance sheet. The *average day's cost of goods sold* is the cost of goods sold on an average day in the year, which can be estimated by dividing the cost of goods sold (which is found on the income statement) by the number of days in the year. The average day's cost of goods sold for the current year is

$$\text{Average day's cost of goods sold} = \frac{\text{Cost of goods sold}}{365 \text{ days}}$$

$$= \frac{\$6,500,000}{365 \text{ days}} = \$17,808 \text{ per day}$$

In other words, Fictitious incurs, on average, a cost of producing goods sold of $17,808 per day.

Fictitious has $1.8 million of inventory on hand at the end of the year. How many days' worth of goods sold is this? One way to look at this is to imagine that Fictitious stopped buying more raw materials and just finished producing whatever was on hand in inventory, using available raw materials and work-in-process. How long would it take Fictitious to run out of inventory?

We compute the *days sales in inventory* (DSI), also known as the *number of days of inventory*, by calculating the ratio of the amount of inventory on hand (in dollars) to the average day's cost of goods sold (in dollars per day):

$$\text{Days sales in inventory} = \frac{\text{Amount of inventory on hand}}{\text{Average day's cost of goods sold}}$$

$$= \frac{\$1,800,000}{\$17,808 \text{ day}} = 101 \text{ days}$$

In other words, Fictitious has approximately 101 days of goods on hand at the end of the current year. If sales continued at the same price, it would take Fictitious 101 days to run out of inventory.

If the ending inventory is representative of the inventory throughout the year, then it takes about 101 days to convert the investment in inventory into sold goods. Why worry about whether the year-end inventory is representative of inventory at any day throughout the year? Well, if inventory at the end of the fiscal year-end is lower than on any other day of the year, we have understated the DSI. Indeed, in practice most companies try to choose fiscal year-ends that coincide with the slow period of their business. That means the ending balance of inventory would be lower than the typical daily inventory of the year. To get a better picture of the firm, we could, for example, look at quarterly financial statements and take averages of quarterly inventory balances. However, here for simplicity we make a note of the problem of representatives and deal with it later in the discussion of financial ratios.

It should be noted that as an attempt to make the inventory figure more representative, some suggest taking the average of the beginning and ending inventory amounts. This does nothing to remedy the representativeness problem because the beginning inventory is simply the ending inventory from the previous year and, like the ending value from the current year, is measured at the low point of the operating cycle. A preferred method, if data is available, is to calculate the average inventory for the four quarters of the fiscal year.

We can extend the same logic for calculating the number of days between a sale—when an account receivable is created—and the time it is collected in cash. If we assume that Fictitious sells all goods on credit, we can first calculate the average credit sales per day and then figure out how many days' worth of credit sales are represented by the ending balance of receivables.

The *average credit sales per day* are:

$$\text{Credit sales per day} = \frac{\text{Credit sales}}{365 \text{ days}} = \frac{\$10,000,000}{365 \text{ days}} = \$27,397 \text{ per day}$$

Therefore, Fictitious generates $27,397 of credit sales per day. With an ending balance of accounts receivable of $600,000, the *days sales outstanding* (DSO), also known as the number of days of credit, in this ending balance is calculated by taking the ratio of the balance in the accounts receivable account to the credit sales per day:

$$\text{Number of days of credit} = \frac{\text{Accounts receivable}}{\text{Credit sales per day}}$$

$$= \frac{\$600,000}{\$27,297 \text{ per day}} = 22 \text{ days}$$

If the ending balance of receivables at the end of the year is representative of the receivables on any day throughout the year, then it takes, on average, approximately 22 days to collect the accounts receivable. In other words, it takes 22 days for a sale to become cash.

Using what we have determined for the inventory cycle and cash cycle, we see that for Fictitious,

$$\text{Operating cycle} = \text{DSI} + \text{DSO} = 101 \text{ days} + 22 \text{ days} = 123 \text{ days}$$

We also need to look at the liabilities on the balance sheet to see how long it takes a firm to pay its short-term obligations. We can apply the same logic to accounts payable as we did to accounts receivable and inventories. How long does it take a firm, on average, to go from creating a payable (buying on credit) to paying for it in cash?

First, we need to determine the amount of an average day's purchases on credit. If we assume all the Fictitious purchases are made on credit, then the total purchases for the year would be the cost of goods sold less any amounts included in cost of goods sold that are not purchases. For example, depreciation is included in the cost of goods sold yet is not a purchase. Since we do not have a breakdown on the company's cost of goods sold showing how much was paid for in cash and how much was on credit, let us assume for simplicity that purchases are equal to cost of goods sold less depreciation. The average day's purchases then become

$$\text{Average day's purchases} = \frac{\text{Cost of goods sold} - \text{Depreciation}}{365 \text{ days}}$$

$$= \frac{\$6,500,000 - \$1,000,000}{365 \text{ days}} = \$15,068 \text{ per day}$$

The *days payables outstanding* (DPO), also known as the *number of days of purchases*, represented in the ending balance in accounts payable is calculated as the ratio of the balance in the accounts payable account to the average day's purchases:

$$\text{Days payables outstanding} = \frac{\text{Accounts payable}}{\text{Average day's purchases}}$$

For Fictitious in the current year:

$$\text{Days payables outstanding} = \frac{\$500,000}{\$15,065 \text{ per day}} = 33 \text{ days}$$

This means that on average Fictitious takes 33 days to pay out cash for a purchase.

The operating cycle tells us how long it takes to convert an investment in cash back into cash (by way of inventory and accounts receivable). The number of days of payables tells us how long it takes to pay on purchases made to create the inventory. If we put these two pieces of information together, we can see how long, on net, we tie up cash. The difference between the operating cycle and the number of days of purchases is the *cash conversion cycle* (CCC), also known as the *net operating cycle*:

Cash conversion cycle = Operating cycle − Number of days of payables

Or, substituting for the operating cycle,

CCC = DSI + DSO + DPO

The cash conversion cycle for Fictitious in the current year is:

CCC = 101 + 22 − 33 = 90 days

The CCC is how long it takes for the firm to get cash back from its investments in inventory and accounts receivable, considering that purchases may be made on credit. By not paying for purchases immediately (that is, using trade credit), the firm reduces its liquidity needs. Therefore, the longer the net operating cycle, the greater the required liquidity.

Measures of Liquidity The investor can describe a firm's ability to meet its current obligations in several ways. The *current ratio* indicates the firm's ability to meet or cover its current liabilities using its current assets:

$$\text{Current ratio} = \frac{\text{Current assets}}{\text{Current liabilities}}$$

For the Fictitious Corporation, the current ratio for the current year is the ratio of current assets, $3 million, to current liabilities, the sum of accounts payable and other current liabilities, or $1 million.

$$\text{Current ratio} = \frac{\$3,000,000}{\$1,000,000} = 3.0 \text{ times}$$

The current ratio of 3.0 indicates that Fictitious has three times as much as it needs to cover its current obligations during the year. However, the current ratio groups all current asset accounts together, assuming they are all as easily converted to cash. Even though, by definition, current assets can be transformed into cash within a year, not all current assets can be transformed into cash in a short period of time.

An alternative to the current ratio is the *quick ratio*, also called the *acid-test ratio*, which uses a slightly different set of current accounts to cover the same current liabilities as in the current ratio. In the quick ratio, the least liquid of the current asset accounts, inventory, is excluded. Hence,

$$\text{Quick ratio} = \frac{\text{Current assets} - \text{Inventory}}{\text{Current liabilities}}$$

We typically leave out inventories in the quick ratio because inventories are generally perceived as the least liquid of the current assets. By leaving out the least liquid asset, the quick ratio provides a more conservative view of liquidity.

For Fictitious in the current year,

$$\text{Quick ratio} = \frac{\$3,000,000 - 1,800,000}{\$1,000,000} = \frac{\$1,200,000}{\$1,000,000} = 1.2 \text{ times}$$

Still another way to measure the firm's ability to satisfy short-term obligations is the *net working capital-to-sales ratio*, which compares net working capital (current assets less current liabilities) with sales:

$$\text{Net working capital-to-sales ratio} = \frac{\text{Net working capital}}{\text{Sales}}$$

This ratio tells us the "cushion" available to meet short-term obligations relative to sales. Consider two firms with identical working capital of

$100,000, but one has sales of $500,000 and the other sales of $1,000,000. If they have identical operating cycles, this means that the firm with the greater sales has more funds flowing in and out of its current asset investments (inventories and receivables). The company with more funds flowing in and out needs a larger cushion to protect itself in case of a disruption in the cycle, such as a labor strike or unexpected delays in customer payments. The longer the operating cycle, the more of a cushion (net working capital) a firm needs for a given level of sales.

For Fictitious Corporation,

$$\text{Net working capital-to-sales ratio} = \frac{\$3,000,000 - 1,000,000}{\$10,000,000}$$
$$= 0.2000 \text{ or } 20\%$$

The ratio of 0.20 tells us that for every dollar of sales, Fictitious has 20 cents of net working capital to support it.

Recap: Liquidity Ratios Operating cycle and liquidity ratio information for Fictitious using data for the current year, in summary, is:

Days sales in inventory	= 101 days
Days sales outstanding	= 22 days
Operating cycle	= 123 days
Days payables outstanding	= 33 days
Cash conversion cycle	= 90 days
Current ratio	= 3.0
Quick ratio	= 1.2
Net working capital–to-sales ratio	= 20%

Given the measures of time related to the current accounts—the operating cycle and the cash conversion cycle—and the three measures of liquidity—current ratio, quick ratio, and net working capital–to-sales ratio—we know the following about Fictitious Corporation's ability to meet its short-term obligations:

- Inventory is less liquid than accounts receivable (comparing days of inventory with days of credit).
- Current assets are greater than needed to satisfy current liabilities in a year (from the current ratio).
- The quick ratio tells us that Fictitious can meet its short-term obligations even without resorting to selling inventory.

- The net working capital "cushion" is 20 cents for every dollar of sales (from the net working capital–to-sales ratio).

What don't ratios tells us about liquidity? They don't provide us with answers to the following questions:

- How liquid are the accounts receivable? How much of the accounts receivable will be collectible? Whereas we know it takes, on average, 22 days to collect, we do not know how much will never be collected.
- What is the nature of the current liabilities? How much of current liabilities consists of items that recur (such as accounts payable and wages payable) each period and how much consists of occasional items (such as income taxes payable)?
- Are there any unrecorded liabilities (such as operating leases) that are not included in current liabilities?

Profitability Ratios

Liquidity ratios indicate a firm's ability to meet its immediate obligations. Now we extend the analysis by adding *profitability ratios*, which help the investor gauge how well a firm is managing its expenses. *Profit margin ratios* compare components of income with sales. They give the investor an idea of which factors make up a firm's income and are usually expressed as a portion of each dollar of sales. For example, the profit margin ratios we discuss here differ only in the numerator. It is in the numerator that we can evaluate performance for different aspects of the business.

For example, suppose the investor wants to evaluate how well production facilities are managed. The investor would focus on gross profit (sales less cost of goods sold), a measure of income that is the direct result of production management. Comparing gross profit with sales produces the *gross profit margin*:

$$\text{Gross profit margin} = \frac{\text{Revenues} - \text{Cost of goods sold}}{\text{Revenues}}$$

This ratio tells us the portion of each dollar of sales that remains after deducting production expenses. For Fictitious Corporation for the current year:

$$\text{Gross profit margin} = \frac{\$10,000,000 - \$6,500,000}{\$10,000,000} = \frac{\$3,500,000}{\$10,000,000}$$
$$= 0.3500 \text{ or } 35\%$$

Financial Analysis

For each dollar of revenues, the firm's gross profit is 35 cents. Looking at sales and cost of goods sold, we can see that the gross profit margin is affected by:

- Changes in sales volume, which affect cost of goods sold and sales.
- Changes in sales price, which affect revenues.
- Changes in the cost of production, which affect cost of goods sold.

Any change in gross profit margin from one period to the next is caused by one or more of those three factors. Similarly, differences in gross margin ratios among firms are the result of differences in those factors.

To evaluate operating performance, we need to consider operating expenses in addition to the cost of goods sold. To do this, remove operating expenses (e.g., selling and general administrative expenses) from gross profit, leaving operating profit, also referred to as earnings before interest and taxes (EBIT). The *operating profit margin* is therefore

$$\text{Operating profit margin} = \frac{\text{Revenues} - \text{Cost of goods sold} - \text{Operating expenses}}{\text{Revenues}}$$

$$= \frac{\text{Revenues earnings before interest and taxes}}{\text{Revenues}}$$

For Fictitious in the current year,

$$\text{Operating profit margin} = \frac{\$2,000,000}{\$10,000,000} = 0.20 \text{ or } 20\%$$

Therefore, for each dollar of revenues, Fictitious has 20 cents of operating income. The operating profit margin is affected by the same factors as gross profit margin, plus operating expenses such as:

- Office rent and lease expenses.
- Miscellaneous income (for example, income from investments).
- Advertising expenditures.
- Bad debt expense.

Most of these expenses are related in some way to revenues, though they are not included directly in the cost of goods sold. Therefore, the difference between the gross profit margin and the operating profit margin is due to these indirect items that are included in computing the operating profit margin.

Both the gross profit margin and the operating profit margin reflect a company's operating performance. But they do not consider how these operations have been financed. To evaluate both operating and financing decisions, the investor must compare net income (that is, earnings after deducting interest and taxes) with revenues. The result is the *net profit margin*:

$$\text{Net profit margin} = \frac{\text{Net income}}{\text{Revenues}}$$

The net profit margin tells the investor the net income generated from each dollar of revenues; it considers financing costs that the operating profit margin does not consider. For Fictitious for the current year,

$$\text{Net profit margin} = \frac{\$1,200,000}{\$10,000,000} = 0.12 \text{ or } 12\%$$

For every dollar of revenues, Fictitious generates 12 cents in profits.

Recap: Profitability Ratios The profitability ratios for Fictitious in the current year are:

Gross profit margin = 35%
Operating profit margin = 20%
Net profit margin = 12%

They indicate the following about the operating performance of Fictitious:

- Each dollar of revenues contributes 35 cents to gross profit and 20 cents to operating profit.
- Every dollar of revenues contributes 12 cents to owners' earnings.
- By comparing the 20-cent operating profit margin with the 12-cent net profit margin, we see that Fictitious has 8 cents of financing costs for every dollar of revenues.

What these ratios do not indicate about profitability is the sensitivity of gross, operating, and net profit margins to:

- Changes in the sales price.
- Changes in the volume of sales.

Looking at the profitability ratios for one firm for one period gives the investor very little information that can be used to make judgments regarding future profitability. Nor do these ratios provide the investor any information about why current profitability is what it is. We need more information to make these kinds of judgments, particularly regarding the future profitability of the firm. For that, turn to activity ratios, which are measures of how well assets are being used.

Activity Ratios

Activity ratios—for the most part, turnover ratios—can be used to evaluate the benefits produced by specific assets, such as inventory or accounts receivable, or to evaluate the benefits produced by the totality of the firm's assets.

Inventory Management The *inventory turnover ratio* indicates how quickly a firm has used inventory to generate the goods and services that are sold. The inventory turnover is the ratio of the cost of goods sold to inventory:

$$\text{Inventory turnover ratio} = \frac{\text{Cost of goods sold}}{\text{Inventory}}$$

For Fictitious for the current year,

$$\text{Inventory turnover ratio} = \frac{\$6,500,000}{\$1,800,000} = 3.61 \text{ times}$$

This ratio indicates that Fictitious turns over its inventory 3.61 times per year. On average, cash is invested in inventory, goods and services are produced, and these goods and services are sold 3.6 times a year. Looking back to the number of days of inventory, we see that this turnover measure is consistent with the results of that calculation: There are 101 calendar days of inventory on hand at the end of the year; dividing 365 days by 101 days, or 365/101 days, we find that inventory cycles through (from cash to sales) 3.61 times a year.

Accounts Receivable Management In much the same way inventory turnover can be evaluated, an investor can evaluate a firm's management of its accounts receivable and its credit policy. The *accounts receivable turnover ratio* is a measure of how effectively a firm is using credit extended to customers. The reason for extending credit is to increase sales. The downside to extending credit is the possibility of default—customers not paying when promised. The benefit obtained from extending credit is referred to as net credit sales—sales on credit less returns and refunds.

$$\text{Accounts receivable turnover} = \frac{\text{Net credit sales}}{\text{Accounts receivable}}$$

Looking at the Fictitious Corporation income statement, we see an entry for sales, but we do not know how much of the amount stated is on credit. In the case of evaluating a firm, an investor would have an estimate of the amount of credit sales. Let us assume that the entire sales amount represents net credit sales. For Fictitious for the current year,

$$\text{Accounts receivable turnover} = \frac{\$10,000,000}{\$600,000} = 16.67 \text{ times}$$

Therefore, almost 17 times in the year there is, on average, a cycle that begins with a sale on credit and finishes with the receipt of cash for that sale. In other words, there are 17 cycles of sales to credit to cash during the year.

The number of times accounts receivable cycle through the year is consistent with the days sales outstanding (22) that we calculated earlier—accounts receivable turn over 17 times during the year, and the average number of days of sales in the accounts receivable balance is 365 days/16.67 times = 22 days.

Overall Asset Management The inventory and accounts receivable turnover ratios reflect the benefits obtained from the use of specific assets (inventory and accounts receivable). For a more general picture of the productivity of the firm, an investor can compare the sales during a period with the total assets that generated these revenues.

One way is with the *total asset turnover ratio*, which indicates how many times during the year the value of a firm's total assets is generated in revenues:

$$\text{Total assets turnover} = \frac{\text{Revenues}}{\text{Total assets}}$$

For Fictitious in the current year,

$$\text{Total assets turnover} = \frac{\$10,000,000}{\$11,000,000} = 0.91 \text{ times}$$

The turnover ratio of 0.91 indicated that in the current year, every dollar invested in total assets generates 91 cents of sales. Or, stated differently, the total assets of Fictitious turn over almost once during the year. Because total assets include both tangible and intangible assets, this turnover indicates how efficiently all assets were used.

An alternative is to focus only on fixed assets, the long-term, tangible assets of the firm. The *fixed asset turnover* is the ratio of revenues to fixed assets:

Financial Analysis

$$\text{Fixed asset turnover ratio} = \frac{\text{Revenues}}{\text{Fixed assets}}$$

For Fictitious in the current year,

$$\text{Fixed asset turnover ratio} = \frac{\$10,000,000}{\$7,000,000} = 1.43 \text{ times}$$

Therefore, for every dollar of fixed assets, Fictitious is able to generate $1.43 of revenues.

Recap: Activity Ratios   The activity ratios for Fictitious Corporation are:

Inventory turnover ratio	= 3.61 times
Accounts receivable turnover ratio	= 16.67 times
Total asset turnover ratio	= 0.91 times
Fixed asset turnover ratio	= 1.43 times

From these ratios, the investor can determine that:

- Inventory flows in and out almost four times a year (from the inventory turnover ratio).
- Accounts receivable are collected in cash, on average, 22 days after a sale (from the number of days of credit). In other words, accounts receivable flow in and out almost 17 times during the year (from the accounts receivable turnover ratio).

Here is what these ratios do not indicate about the firm's use of its assets:

- The sales not made because credit policies are too stringent.
- How much of credit sales is not collectible.
- Which assets contribute most to the turnover.

Financial Leverage Ratios

A firm can finance its assets with equity or with debt. Financing with debt legally obligates the firm to pay interest and to repay the principal as promised. Equity financing does not obligate the firm to pay anything because dividends are paid at the discretion of the board of directors. There is always some risk, which we refer to as *business risk*, inherent in any business enterprise. But how a firm chooses to finance its operations—the particular mix of debt and equity—may add financial risk on top of business risk. *Financial risk* is risk associated with a firm's ability to satisfy its debt obligations, and is often measured using the extent to which debt financing is used relative to equity.

Financial leverage ratios are used to assess how much financial risk the firm has taken on. There are two types of financial leverage ratios: component percentages and coverage ratios. Component percentages compare a firm's debt with either its total capital (debt plus equity) or its equity capital. Coverage ratios reflect a firm's ability to satisfy fixed financing obligations, such as interest, principal repayment, or lease payments.

Component Percentage Ratios A ratio that indicates the proportion of assets financed with debt is the *debt-to-assets ratio*, which compares total liabilities (short-term + long-term debt) with total assets:

$$\text{Total debt-to-assets ratio} = \frac{\text{Debt}}{\text{Total assets}}$$

For Fictitious in the current year,

$$\text{Total debt-to-assets ratio} = \frac{\$5,000,000}{\$11,000,000} = 0.4546 \text{ or } 45.46\%$$

This ratio indicates that 45% of the firm's assets are financed with debt (both short term and long term).

Another way to look at the financial risk is in terms of the use of debt relative to the use of equity. The *debt-to-equity ratio* indicates how the firm finances its operations with debt relative to the book value of its shareholders' equity:

$$\text{Debt-to-equity ratio} = \frac{\text{Debt}}{\text{Book value of shareholders' equity}}$$

For Fictitious for the current year, using the book-value definition,

$$\text{Debt-to-equity ratio} = \frac{\$5,000,000}{\$6,000,000} = 0.8333 \text{ or } 83.33\%$$

For every one dollar of book value of shareholders' equity, Fictitious uses 83 cents of debt.

Both of these ratios can be stated in terms of total debt, as above, or in terms of long-term debt or even simply interest-bearing debt. And it is not always clear in which form—total, long-term debt, or interest-bearing—the ratio is calculated. Additionally, it is often the case that the current portion of long-term debt is excluded in the calculation of the long-term versions of these debt ratios.

One problem with using a financial ratio based on the book value of equity to analyze financial risk is that there is seldom a strong relationship between the book value and market value of a stock. The distortion in values on the balance sheet is obvious by looking at the book value of equity and comparing it with the market value of equity. The book value of equity consists of:

- The proceeds to the firm of all the stock issues since it was first incorporated, less any stock repurchased by the firm.
- The accumulative earnings of the firm, less any dividends, since it was first incorporated.

Let's look at an example of the book value versus the market value of equity. IBM was incorporated in 1911, so the book value of its equity represents the sum of all its stock issued and all its earnings, less any dividends paid since 1911. As of the end of 2006, IBM's book value of equity was approximately $28.5 billion, yet its market value was $142.8 billion.

Book value generally does not give a true picture of the investment of shareholders in the firm because:

- Earnings are recorded according to accounting principles, which may not reflect the true economics of transactions.
- Due to inflation, the earnings and proceeds from stock issued in the past do not reflect today's values.

Market value, on the other hand, is the value of equity as perceived by investors. It is what investors are willing to pay. So why bother with book value? For two reasons: First, it is easier to obtain the book value than the market value of a firm's securities, and second, many financial services report ratios using book value rather than market value.

However, any of the ratios presented in this chapter that use the book value of equity can be restated using the market value of equity. For example, instead of using the book value of equity in the debt-to-equity ratio, the market value of equity to measure the firm's financial leverage can be used.

Coverage Ratios The ratios that compare debt to equity or debt to assets indicate the amount of financial leverage, which enables an investor to assess the financial condition of a firm. Another way of looking at the financial condition and the amount of financial leverage used by the firm is to see how well it can handle the financial burdens associated with its debt or other fixed commitments.

One measure of a firm's ability to handle financial burdens is the *interest coverage ratio*, also referred to as the *times interest–covered ratio*. This ratio tells us how well the firm can cover or meet the interest payments associated with debt. The ratio compares the funds available to pay interest (that is, earnings before interest and taxes) with the interest expense:

$$\text{Interest coverage ratio} = \frac{\text{EBIT}}{\text{Interest expense}}$$

The greater the interest coverage ratio, the better able the firm is to pay its interest expense. For Fictitious for the current year,

$$\text{Interest coverage ratio} = \frac{\$2,000,000}{\$400,000} = 5 \text{ times}$$

An interest coverage ratio of 5 means that the firm's earnings before interest and taxes are five times greater than its interest payments.

The interest coverage ratio provides information about a firm's ability to cover the interest related to its debt financing. However, there are other costs that do not arise from debt but that nevertheless must be considered in the same way we consider the cost of debt in a firm's financial obligations. For example, lease payments are fixed costs incurred in financing operations. Like interest payments, they represent legal obligations.

What funds are available to pay debt and debt-like expenses? Start with EBIT and add back expenses that were deducted to arrive at EBIT. The ability of a firm to satisfy its fixed financial costs—its fixed charges—is referred to as the *fixed charge coverage ratio*. One definition of the fixed charge coverage considers only the lease payments:

$$\text{Fixed charge coverage ratio} = \frac{\text{EBIT} + \text{Lease expense}}{\text{Interest} + \text{Lease expense}}$$

For Fictitious for the current year,

$$\text{Fixed charge coverage ratio} = \frac{\$2,000,000 + \$1,000,000}{\$400,000 + \$1,000,000} = 2.14 \text{ times}$$

This ratio tells us that Fictitious's earnings can cover its fixed charges (interest and lease payments) more than two times over.

What fixed charges to consider is not entirely clear-cut. For example, if the firm is required to set aside funds to eventually or periodically retire debt—referred to as sinking funds—is the amount set aside a fixed charge? As another example, since preferred dividends represent a fixed financing charge, should they be included as a fixed charge? From the perspective of the common shareholder, the preferred dividends must be covered either to enable the payment of common dividends or to retain earnings for future growth. Because debt principal repayment and preferred stock dividends are paid on an after-tax basis—paid out of dollars remaining after taxes are paid—this fixed charge must be converted to before-tax dollars. The fixed charge coverage ratio can be expanded to accommodate the sinking funds and preferred stock dividends as fixed charges.

Up to now we considered earnings before interest and taxes as funds available to meet fixed financial charges. EBIT includes noncash items such as depreciation and amortization. If an investor is trying to compare funds available to meet obligations, a better measure of available funds is cash flow from operations, as reported in the statement of cash flows. A ratio that considers cash flows from operations as funds available to cover interest payments is referred to as the *cash flow interest coverage ratio.*

$$\text{Cash flow interest coverage ratio} = \frac{\text{Cash flow from operations} + \text{Interest} + \text{Taxes}}{\text{Interest}}$$

The amount of cash flow from operations that is in the statement of cash flows is net of interest and taxes. So we have to add back interest and taxes to cash flow from operations to arrive at the cash flow amount before interest and taxes in order to determine the cash flow available to cover interest payments.

For Fictitious for the current year,

$$\text{Cash flow interest coverage ratio} = \frac{\$1,800,000 + \$400,000 + \$400,000}{\$400,000}$$

$$= \frac{\$2,600,000}{\$400,000} = 6.5 \text{ times}$$

This coverage ratio indicates that, in terms of cash flows, Fictitious has 6.5 times more cash than is needed to pay its interest. This is a better picture of interest coverage than the five times reflected by EBIT. Why the difference? Because cash flow considers not just the accounting income, but noncash items as well. In the case of Fictitious, depreciation is a noncash charge that reduced EBIT but not cash flow from operations—it is added back to net income to arrive at cash flow from operations.

Recap: Financial Leverage Ratios Summarizing, the financial leverage ratios for Fictitious Corporation for the current year are:

Debt-to-assets ratio	= 45.45%
Debt-to-equity ratio	= 83.33%
Interest coverage ratio	= 5.00 times
Fixed charge coverage ratio	= 2.14 times
Cash flow interest coverage ratio	= 6.50 times

These ratios indicate that Fictitious uses its financial leverage as follows:

- Assets are 45% financed with debt, measured using book values.
- Long-term debt is approximately two-thirds of equity. When equity is measured in market value terms, long-term debt is approximately one-sixth of equity.

These ratios do not indicate:

- What other fixed, legal commitments the firm has that are not included on the balance sheet (for example, operating leases).
- What the intentions of management are regarding taking on more debt as the existing debt matures.

Common-Size Analysis

An investor can evaluate a company's operating performance and financial condition through ratios that relate various items of information contained in the financial statements. Another way to analyze a firm is to look at its financial data more comprehensively.

Common-size analysis is a method of analysis in which the components of a financial statement are compared with each other. The first step in common-size analysis is to break down a financial statement—either the balance sheet or the income statement—into its parts. The next step is to calculate the proportion that each item represents relative to some benchmark. This form of common-size analysis is sometimes referred to as vertical common-size analysis. Another form of common-size analysis is horizontal common-size analysis, which uses either an income statement or a balance sheet in a fiscal year and compares accounts to the corresponding items in another year. In common-size analysis of the balance sheet, the benchmark is total assets. For the income statement, the benchmark is sales.

Let us see how it works by doing some common-size financial analysis for the Fictitious Corporation. The company's balance sheet is restated in Table 8.4. This statement does not look precisely like the balance sheet we have seen before. Nevertheless, the data are the same but reorganized. Each item in the original balance sheet has been restated as a proportion of total assets for the purpose of common size analysis. Hence, we refer to this as the common-size balance sheet.

In this balance sheet, we see, for example, that in the current year cash is 3.6% of total assets, or $400,000/$11,000,000 = 0.036. The largest investment is in plant and equipment, which comprises 63.6% of total assets.

TABLE 8.4 Fictitious Corporation Common-Size Balance Sheets for Years Ending December 31

	Current Year	Prior Year
Asset Components		
Cash	3.6%	2.0%
Marketable securities	1.8%	0.0%
Accounts receivable	5.5%	8.0%
Inventory	16.4%	10.0%
Current assets	27.3%	20.0%
Net plant and equipment	63.5%	70.0%
Intangible assets	9.2%	10.0%
Total assets	100.0%	100.0%
Liability and Shareholders' Equity Components		
Accounts payable	4.6%	4.0%
Other current liabilities	4.6%	1.0%
Long-term debt	36.4%	50.0%
Total liabilities	45.4%	56.0%
Shareholders' equity	54.6%	44.0%
Total liabilities and shareholders' equity	100.0%	100.0%

On the liabilities side, that current liabilities are a small portion (9.1%) of liabilities and equity.

The common-size balance sheet indicates in very general terms how Fictitious has raised capital and where this capital has been invested. As with financial ratios, however, the picture is not complete until trends are examined and compared with those of other firms in the same industry.

In the income statement, as with the balance sheet, the items may be restated as a proportion of sales; this statement is referred to as the common-size income statement. The common-size income statements for Fictitious for the two years are shown in Table 8.5. For the current year, the major costs are associated with goods sold (65%); lease expense, other expenses, interest, taxes, and dividends make up smaller portions of sales. Looking at gross profit, EBIT, and net income, these proportions are the profit margins we calculated earlier. The common-size income statement provides information on the profitability of different aspects of the firm's business. Again, the picture is not yet complete. For a more complete picture, the investor must look at trends over time and make comparisons with other companies in the same industry.

TABLE 8.5 Fictitious Corporation Common-Size Income Statement for Years Ending December 31

	Current Year	Prior Year
Sales	100.0%	100.0%
Cost of goods sold	65.0%	66.7%
Gross profit	35.0%	33.3%
Lease and administrative expenses	15.0%	16.7%
Earnings before interest and taxes	20.0%	16.7%
Interest expense	4.0%	5.6%
Earnings before taxes	16.0%	16.7%
Taxes	4.0%	5.7%
Net income	12.0%	11.1%
Common dividends	6.0%	5.6%
Retained earnings	6.0%	5.5%

Using Financial Ratio Analysis

Financial analysis provides information concerning a firm's operating performance and financial condition. This information is useful for an investor in evaluating the performance of the company as a whole, as well as of divisions, products, and subsidiaries. An investor must also be aware that financial analysis is also used by investors and investors to gauge the financial performance of the company.

But financial ratio analysis cannot tell the whole story and must be interpreted and used with care. Financial ratios are useful but, as noted in the discussion of each ratio, there is information that the ratios do not reveal. For example, in calculating inventory turnover we need to assume that the inventory shown on the balance sheet is representative of inventory throughout the year. Another example is in the calculation of accounts receivable turnover. We assumed that all sales were on credit. If we are on the outside looking in—that is, evaluating a firm based on its financial statements only, such as the case of a financial investor or investor—and therefore do not have data on credit sales, assumptions must be made that may or may not be correct.

In addition, there are other areas of concern that an investor should be aware of in using financial ratios:

- Limitations in the accounting data used to construct the ratios.

Financial Analysis

- Selection of an appropriate benchmark firm or firms for comparison purposes.
- Interpretation of the ratios.
- Pitfalls in forecasting future operating performance and financial condition based on past trends.

CASH FLOW ANALYSIS

One of the key financial measures that an analyst should understand is the company's cash flow. This is because the cash flow aids the analyst in assessing the ability of the company to satisfy its contractual obligations and maintain current dividends and current capital expenditure policy without relying on external financing. Moreover, an analyst must understand why this measure is important for external parties, specifically stock analysts covering the company. The reason is that the basic valuation principle followed by stock analysts is that the value of a company today is the present value of its expected future cash flows. In this section, we discuss cash flow analysis.

Difficulties with Measuring Cash Flow

The primary difficulty with measuring a cash flow is that it is a flow: Cash flows into the company (i.e., cash inflows) and cash flows out of the company (i.e., cash outflows). At any point in time there is a stock of cash on hand, but the stock of cash on hand varies among companies because of the size of the company, the cash demands of the business, and a company's management of working capital. So what is cash flow? Is it the total amount of cash flowing into the company during a period? Is it the total amount of cash flowing out of the company during a period? Is it the net of the cash inflows and outflows for a period? Well, there is no specific definition of cash flow—and that's probably why there is so much confusion regarding the measurement of cash flow. Ideally, a measure of the company's operating performance that is comparable among companies is needed—something other than net income.

A simple, yet crude method of calculating cash flow requires simply adding noncash expenses (e.g., depreciation and amortization) to the reported net income amount to arrive at cash flow. For example, the estimated cash flow for Procter & Gamble (P&G) for 2002, is:

Estimated cash flow = Net income + Depreciation and amortization
= $4,352 million + 1,693 million
= $6,045 million

This amount is not really a cash flow, but simply earnings before depreciation and amortization. Is this a cash flow that stock analysts should use in valuing a company? Though not a cash flow, this estimated cash flow does allow a quick comparison of income across firms that may use different depreciation methods and depreciable lives. (As an example of the use of this estimate of cash flow, *The Value Line Investment Survey*, published by Value Line, Inc., reports a cash flow per share amount, calculated as reported earnings plus depreciation, minus any preferred dividends, stated per share of common stock.)

The problem with this measure is that it ignores the many other sources and uses of cash during the period. Consider the sale of goods for credit. This transaction generates sales for the period. Sales and the accompanying cost of goods sold are reflected in the period's net income and the estimated cash flow amount. However, until the account receivable is collected, there is no cash from this transaction. If collection does not occur until the next period, there is a misalignment of the income and cash flow arising from this transaction. Therefore, the simple estimated cash flow ignores some cash flows that, for many companies, are significant.

Another estimate of cash flow that is simple to calculate is *earnings before interest, taxes, depreciation, and amortization* (EBITDA). However, this measure suffers from the same accrual-accounting bias as the previous measure, which may result in the omission of significant cash flows. Additionally, EBITDA does not consider interest and taxes, which may also be substantial cash outflows for some companies.[1]

These two rough estimates of cash flows are used in practice not only for their simplicity, but because they experienced widespread use prior to the disclosure of more detailed information in the statement of cash flows. Currently, the measures of cash flow are wide-ranging, including the simplistic cash flow measures, measures developed from the statement of cash flows, and measures that seek to capture the theoretical concept of *free cash flow*.

Cash Flows and the Statement of Cash Flows

Prior to the adoption of the statement of cash flows, the information regarding cash flows was quite limited. The first statement that addressed the issue of cash flows was the statement of financial position, which was required starting in 1971 (*APB Opinion No. 19*, "Reporting Changes in Financial Position"). This statement was quite limited, requiring an analysis of the sources and uses of funds in a variety of formats. In its earlier years of adoption, most companies provided this information using what is referred to as

---

[1] For a more detailed discussion of the EBITDA measure, see Eastman (1997).

the *working capital concept*—a presentation of working capital provided and applied during the period. Over time, many companies began presenting this information using the *cash concept*, which is a most detailed presentation of the cash flows provided by operations, investing, and financing activities.

Consistent with the cash concept format of the funds flow statement, the statement of cash flows is now a required financial statement. The requirement that companies provide a statement of cash flows applies to fiscal years after 1987 (*Statement of Financial Accounting Standards No. 95*, "Statement of Cash Flows"). This statement requires the company to classify cash flows into three categories, based on the activity: operating, investing, and financing. Cash flows are summarized by activity and within activity by type (e.g., asset dispositions are reported separately from asset acquisitions).

The reporting company may report the cash flows from operating activities on the statement of cash flows using either the *direct method*—reporting all cash inflows and outflows—or the *indirect method*—starting with net income and making adjustments for depreciation and other noncash expenses and for changes in working capital accounts. Though the direct method is recommended, it is also the most burdensome for the reporting company to prepare. Most companies report cash flows from operations using the indirect method. The indirect method has the advantage of providing the financial statement user with a reconciliation of the company's net income with the change in cash. The indirect method produces a cash flow from operations that is similar to the estimated cash flow measure discussed previously, yet it encompasses the changes in working capital accounts that the simple measure does not. For example, Procter & Gamble's cash flow from operating activities (taken from their 2002 statement of cash flows) is $7,742 million, which is over $1 billion more than the cash flow that we estimated earlier. (Procter & Gamble's fiscal year ends June 30, 2002.)

The classification of cash flows into the three types of activities provides useful information that can be used by an analyst to see, for example, whether the company is generating sufficient cash flows from operations to sustain its current rate of growth. However, the classification of particular items is not necessarily as useful as it could be. Consider some of the classifications:

- Cash flows related to interest expense are classified in operations, though they are clearly financing cash flows.
- Income taxes are classified as operating cash flows, though taxes are affected by financing (e.g., deduction for interest expense paid on debt) and investment activities (e.g., the reduction of taxes from tax credits on investment activities).
- Interest income and dividends received are classified as operating cash flows, though these flows are a result of investment activities.

Whether these items have a significant effect on the analysis depends on the particular company's situation. Procter & Gamble, for example, has very little interest and dividend income, and its interest expense of $603 million is not large relative to its earnings before interest and taxes ($6,986 million). Table 8.6 shows that by adjusting P&G's cash flows for the interest expense only (and related taxes) changes the complexion of its cash flows slightly to reflect greater cash flow generation from operations and less cash flow reliance on financing activities.

The adjustment is for $603 million of interest and other financing costs, less its tax shield (the amount that the tax bill is reduced by the interest deduction) of $211 (estimated from the average tax rate of 35% of $603): adjustment = $603 (1 − 0.35) = $392.

For other companies, however, this adjustment may provide a less flattering view of cash flows. Consider Amazon.com's 2001 fiscal year results. Moving interest expense to financing, along with their respective estimated tax effects, results in a more accurate picture of the company's reliance on cash flow from financing as can be seen in Table 8.7.

Looking at the relation among the three cash flows in the statement provides a sense of the activities of the company. A young, fast-growing company may have negative cash flows from operations, yet positive cash flows from financing activities (i.e., operations may be financed in large part with external financing). As a company grows, it may rely to a lesser extent on external financing. The typical, mature company generates cash from operations and reinvests part or all of it back into the company. Therefore,

TABLE 8.6 Adjusted Cash Flow for P&G (2002)

(In millions)	As Reported	As Adjusted
Cash flow from operations	$7,741	$8,134
Cash flow for investing activities	(6,835)	(6,835)
Cash flow from (for) financing activities	197	(195)

Source: Procter & Gamble 2002 Annual Report.

TABLE 8.7 Adjusted Cash Flow Amazon.com (2001)

(In millions)	As Reported	As Adjusted
Cash flow from operations	$(120)	$(30)
Cash flow for investing activities	(253)	(253)
Cash flow from financing activities	(107)	17

Note: The adjustment is based on interest expense of $139 million, and a tax rate of 35%.
Source: Amazon.com 2001 10-K.

cash flow related to operations is positive (i.e., a source of cash) and cash flow related to investing activities is negative (i.e., a use of cash). As a company matures, it may seek less financing externally and may even use cash to reduce its reliance on external financing (e.g., repay debts). We can classify companies on the basis of the pattern of their sources of cash flows, as shown in Table 8.8. Though additional information is required to assess a company's financial performance and condition, examination of the sources of cash flows, especially over time, gives us a general idea of the company's operations. P&G's cash flow pattern is consistent with that of a mature company, whereas Amazon.com's cash flows are consistent with those of a fast-growing company that relies on outside funds for growth.

Fridson (1995) suggests reformatting the statement of cash flows as shown in Table 8.9. From the basic cash flow, the nondiscretionary cash needs are subtracted resulting in a cash flow referred to as *discretionary cash flow*. By restructuring the statement of cash flows in this way, it can be seen how much flexibility the company has when it must make business decisions that may adversely impact the long-run financial health of the enterprise.

For example, consider a company with a basic cash flow of $800 million and operating cash flow of $500 million. Suppose that this company pays dividends of $130 million and that its capital expenditure is $300 million. Then the discretionary cash flow for this company is $200 million found by subtracting the $300 million capital expenditure from the operating cash flow of $500 million. This means that even after maintaining a dividend payment of $130 million, its cash flow is positive. Notice that asset sales and other investing activity are not needed to generate cash to meet the dividend payments because in Table 8.9 these items are subtracted after accounting for the dividend payments. In fact, if this company planned to increase its capital expenditures, the format in Table 8.9 can be used to assess how much that expansion can be before affecting dividends and/or increasing financing needs.

TABLE 8.8 Patterns of Sources of Cash Flows

Cash Flow	Financing Growth Externally and Internally	Financing Growth Internally	Mature	Temporary Financial Downturn	Financial Distress	Downsizing
Operations	+	+	+	–	–	+
Investing activities	–	–	–	+	–	+
Financing activities	+	–	+ or –	+	–	–

TABLE 8.9 Suggested Reformatting of Cash Flow Statement to Analyze a Company's Flexibility

	Basic cash flow
Less:	Increase in adjusted working capital
	Operating cash flow
Less:	Capital expenditures
	Discretionary cash flow
Less:	Dividends
Less:	Asset sales and other investing activities
	Cash flow before financing
Less:	Net (increase) in long-term debt
Less:	Net (increase) in notes payable
Less:	Net purchase of company's common stock
Less:	Miscellaneous
	Cash flow

Notes:
1. The basic cash flow includes net earnings, depreciation, and deferred income taxes, less items in net income not providing cash.
2. The increase in adjusted working capital excludes cash and payables.
Source: This format was suggested by Fridson (1995).

Though we can classify a company based on the sources and uses of cash flows, more data is needed to put this information in perspective. What is the trend in the sources and uses of cash flows? What market, industry, or company-specific events affect the company's cash flows? How does the company being analyzed compare with other companies in the same industry in terms of the sources and uses of funds?

Let's take a closer look at the incremental information provided by cash flows. Consider Wal-Mart Stores, Inc., which had growing sales and net income from 1990 to 2005, as summarized in Figure 8.2. We see that net income grew each year, with the exception of 1995, and that sales grew each year.

We get additional information by looking at the cash flows and their sources, as graphed in Figure 8.3. We see that the growth in Wal-Mart was supported both by internally generated funds and, to a lesser extent, through external financing. Wal-Mart's pattern of cash flows suggests that Wal-Mart is a mature company that has become less reliant on external financing, funding most of its growth in recent years (with the exception of 1999) with internally generated funds.

Financial Analysis

FIGURE 8.2 Wal-Mart Stores, Inc., Revenues, Operating Profit, and Net Income, 1990–2005

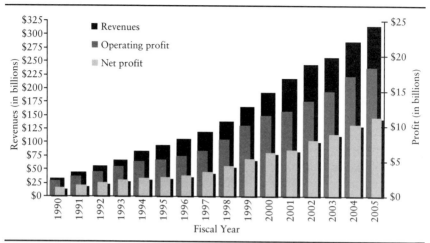

Source: Wal-Mart Stores, Inc., Annual Report, various years.

FIGURE 8.3 Wal-Mart Stores, Inc., Cash Flows, 1990–2005

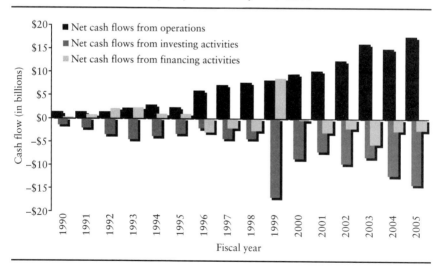

Source: Wal-Mart Stores, Inc., Annual Report, various years.

Free Cash Flow

Cash flows without any adjustment may be misleading because they do not reflect the cash outflows that are necessary for the future existence of a firm. An alternative measure, free cash flow, was developed by Jensen (1986) in his theoretical analysis of agency costs and corporate takeovers. In theory, *free cash flow* is the cash flow left over after the company funds all positive net present value projects. Positive net present value projects are those capital investment projects for which the present value of expected future cash flows exceeds the present value of project outlays, all discounted at the cost of capital. (The cost of capital is the cost to the company of funds from creditors and shareholders. The cost of capital is basically a hurdle: If a project returns more than its cost of capital, it is a profitable project.) In other words, free cash flow is the cash flow of the firm, less capital expenditures necessary to stay in business (i.e., replacing facilities as necessary) and grow at the expected rate (which requires increases in working capital).

The theory of free cash flow was developed by Jensen to explain behaviors of companies that could not be explained by existing economic theories. Jensen observed that companies that generate free cash flow should disgorge that cash rather than invest the funds in less profitable investments. There are many ways in which companies can disgorge this excess cash flow, including the payment of cash dividends, the repurchase of stock, and debt issuance in exchange for stock. The debt-for-stock exchange, for example, increases the company's leverage and future debt obligations, obligating the future use of excess cash flow. If a company does not disgorge this free cash flow, there is the possibility that another company—a company whose cash flows are less than its profitable investment opportunities or a company that is willing to purchase and lever-up the company—will attempt to acquire the free-cash-flow-laden company.

As a case in point, Jensen observed that the oil industry illustrates the case of wasting resources: The free cash flows generated in the 1980s were spent on low-return exploration and development and on poor diversification attempts through acquisitions. He argues that these companies would have been better off paying these excess cash flows to shareholders through share repurchases or exchanges with debt.

By itself, the fact that a company generates free cash flow is neither good nor bad. What the company does with this free cash flow is what is important. And this is where it is important to measure the free cash flow as that cash flow in excess of profitable investment opportunities. Consider the simple numerical exercise with the Winner Company and the Loser Company:

	Winner Company	Loser Company
Cash flow before capital expenditures	$1,000	$1,000
Capital expenditures, positive net present value projects	(750)	(250)
Capital expenditures, negative net present value projects	0	(500)
Cash flow	$250	$250
Free cash flow	$250	$750

These two companies have identical cash flows and the same total capital expenditures. However, the Winner Company spends only on profitable projects (in terms of positive net present value projects), whereas the Loser Company spends on both profitable projects and wasteful projects. The Winner Company has a lower free cash flow than the Loser Company, indicating that they are using the generated cash flows in a more profitable manner. The lesson is that the existence of a high level of free cash flow is not necessarily good—it may simply suggest that the company is either a very good takeover target or the company has the potential for investing in unprofitable investments.

Positive free cash flow may be good or bad news; likewise, negative free cash flow may be good or bad news:

	Good News	Bad News
Positive free cash flow	The company is generating substantial operating cash flows, beyond those necessary for profitable projects.	The company is generating more cash flows than it needs for profitable projects and may waste these cash flows on unprofitable projects.
Negative free cash flow	The company has more profitable projects than it has operating cash flows and must rely on external financing to fund these projects.	The company is unable to generate sufficient operating cash flows to satisfy its investment needs for future growth.

Therefore, once the free cash flow is calculated, other information (e.g., trends in profitability) must be considered to evaluate the operating performance and financial condition of the firm.

Calculating Free Cash Flow

There is some confusion when this theoretical concept is applied to actual companies. The primary difficulty is that the amount of capital expenditures necessary to maintain the business at its current rate of growth is generally not known; companies do not report this item and may not even be able to determine how much of a period's capital expenditures are attributed to maintenance and how much are attributed to expansion.

Consider Procter & Gamble's property, plant, and equipment for 2002, which comprise some, but not all, of P&G's capital investment:[2]

Additions to property, plant, and equipment	$1,679 million
Dispositions of property, plant, and equipment	(227 million)
Net change before depreciation	$1,452 million

How much of the $1,679 million is for maintaining P&G's current rate of growth and how much is for expansion? Though there is a positive net change of $1,452 million, does it mean that P&G is expanding? Not necessarily: The additions are at current costs, whereas the dispositions are at historical costs. The additions of $1,679 are less than P&G's depreciation and amortization expense for 2001 of $1,693 million, yet it is not disclosed in the financial reports how much of this latter amount reflects amortization. (P&G's depreciation and amortization are reported together as $1,693 million on the statement of cash flows.) The amount of necessary capital expenditures is therefore elusive.

Some estimate free cash flow by assuming that all capital expenditures are necessary for the maintenance of the current growth of the company. Though there is little justification in using all expenditures, this is a practical solution to an impractical calculation. This assumption allows us to estimate free cash flows using published financial statements.

Another issue in the calculation is defining what is truly "free" cash flow. Generally we think of "free" cash flow as that being left over after all necessary financing expenditures are paid; this means that free cash flow is after interest on debt is paid. Some calculate free cash flow before such financing expenditures, others calculate free cash flow after interest, and still others calculate free cash flow after both interest and dividends (assuming that dividends are a commitment, though not a legal commitment).

There is no one correct method of calculating free cash flow and different analysts may arrive at different estimates of free cash flow for a company. The problem is that it is impossible to measure free cash flow as dictated by the theory, so many methods have arisen to calculate this cash flow. A simple method is to start with the cash flow from operations and then deduct capital expenditures. For P&G in 2002,

---

[2] In addition to the traditional capital expenditures (i.e., changes in property, plant, and equipment), P&G also has cash flows related to investment securities and acquisitions. These investments are long-term and are hence part of P&G's investment activities cash outflow of $6,835 million.

Financial Analysis

Cash flow from operations $7,742 million
Deduct capital expenditures (1,692 million)
Free cash flow $6,050 million

Though this approach is rather simple, the cash flow from the operations amount includes a deduction for interest and other financing expenses. Making an adjustment for the after-tax interest and financing expenses, as we did earlier for Procter & Gamble,

Cash flow from operations (as reported) $7,742 million
Adjustment 392 million
Cash flow from operations (as adjusted) $8,134 million
Deduct capital expenditures (1,692 million)
Free cash flow $6,442 million

We can relate free cash flow directly to a company's income. Starting with net income, we can estimate free cash flow using four steps:

Step 1: Determine earnings before interest and taxes (EBIT).
Step 2: Calculate earnings before interest but after taxes.
Step 3: Adjust for noncash expenses (e.g., depreciation).
Step 4: Adjust for capital expenditures and changes in working capital.

Using these four steps, we can calculate the free cash flow for Procter & Gamble for 2002, as shown in Table 8.10.

Net Free Cash Flow

There are many variations in the calculation of cash flows that are used in analyses of companies' financial condition and operating performance. As an example of these variations, consider the alternative to free cash flow developed by Fitch, a company that rates corporate debt instruments. This cash flow measure, referred to as *net free cash flow* (NFCF), is free cash flow less interest and other financing costs and taxes. In this approach, free cash flow is defined as earnings before depreciation, interest, and taxes, less capital expenditures. Capital expenditures encompass all capital spending, whether for maintenance or expansion, and no changes in working capital are considered.

The basic difference between NFCF and free cash flow is that the financing expenses—interest and, in some cases, dividends—are deducted to arrive at NFCF. If preferred dividends are perceived as nondiscretionary—that is, investors come to expect the dividends—dividends may be included with the interest commitment to arrive at net free cash flow. Otherwise, dividends are

TABLE 8.10 Calculation of Procter & Gamble's Free Cash Flow for 2002 (in millions)[a]

Step 1:	
Net income	$4,352
Add taxes	2,031
Add interest	603
Earnings before interest and taxes	$6,986
Step 2:	
Earnings before interest and taxes	$6,986
Deduct taxes (@35%)	(2,445)
Earnings before interest	$4,541
Step 3:	
Earnings before interest	$4,541
Add depreciation and amortization	1,693
Add increase in deferred taxes	389
Earnings before noncash expenses	$6,623

Step 4:		
Earnings before noncash expenses		$6,623
Deduct capital expenditures		(1,679)
Add decrease in receivables	$96	
Add decrease in inventories	159	
Add cash flows from changes in accounts payable, accrued expenses, and other liabilities	684	
Deduct cash flow from changes in other operating assets and liabilities	(98)	
Cash flow from change in working capital accounts		841
Free cash flow		$5,785

[a] Procter & Gamble's fiscal year ended June 30, 2002. Charges in operating accounts are taken from Procter & Gamble's Statement of Cash Flows.

deducted from net free cash flow to produce cash flow. Another difference is that NFCF does not consider changes in working capital in the analysis.

Further, cash taxes are deducted to arrive at net free cash flow. Cash taxes are the income tax expense restated to reflect the actual cash flow related to this obligation, rather than the accrued expense for the period.

Cash taxes are the income tax expense (from the income statement) adjusted for the change in deferred income taxes (from the balance sheets). For Procter & Gamble in 2002,[3]

Income tax expense	$2,031
Deduct increase in deferred income tax	(389)
Cash taxes	$1,642

In the case of Procter & Gamble for 2002,

EBIT	$6,986
Add depreciation and amortization	1,693
Earnings before interest, taxes, depreciation, and amortization	$8,679
Deduct capital expenditures	(1,679)
Free cash flow	$7,000
Deduct interest	(603)
Deduct cash taxes	(1,642)
Net free cash flow	$4,755
Deduct cash common dividends	(2,095)
Net cash flow	$2,660

The free cash flow amount per this calculation differs from the $5,785 that we calculated earlier for two reasons: Changes in working capital and the deduction of taxes on operating earnings were not considered.

Net cash flow gives an idea of the unconstrained cash flow of the company. This cash flow measure may be useful from a creditor's perspective in terms of evaluating the company's ability to fund additional debt. From a shareholder's perspective, net cash flow (i.e., net free cash flow net of dividends) may be an appropriate measure because this represents the cash flow that is reinvested in the company.

USEFULNESS OF CASH FLOWS IN FINANCIAL ANALYSIS

The usefulness of cash flows for financial analysis depends on whether cash flows provide unique information or provide information in a manner that is more accessible or convenient for the analyst. The cash flow information provided in the statement of cash flows, for example, is not necessarily unique because most, if not all, of the information is available through

---

[3] Note that cash taxes require taking the tax expense and either increasing this to reflect any decrease in deferred taxes (that is, the payment this period of tax expense recorded in a prior period) or decreasing this amount to reflect any increase in deferred taxes (that is, the deferment of some of the tax expense).

analysis of the balance sheet and income statement. What the statement does provide is a classification scheme that presents information in a manner that is easier to use and, perhaps, more illustrative of the company's financial position.

An analysis of cash flows and the sources of cash flows can reveal the following information:

- *The sources of financing the company's capital spending.* Does the company generate internally (i.e., from operations) a portion or all of the funds needed for its investment activities? If a company cannot generate cash flow from operations, this may indicate problems up ahead. Reliance on external financing (e.g., equity or debt issuance) may indicate a company's inability to sustain itself over time.
- *The company's dependence on borrowing.* Does the company rely heavily on borrowing that may result in difficulty in satisfying future debt service?
- *The quality of earnings.* Large and growing differences between income and cash flows suggest a low quality of earnings.

Consider the financial results of Krispy Kreme Doughnuts, Inc., a wholesaler and retailer of donuts. Krispy Kreme grew from having fewer than 200 stores before its initial public offering (IPO) in 2000 to over 400 stores at the end of its 2005 fiscal year. Accompanying this growth in stores is the growth in operating and net income, as we show in Figure 8.4. The growth in income continued after the IPO as the number of stores increased, but the tide in income turned in the 2004 fiscal year and losses continued into the 2005 fiscal year as well.

Krispy Kreme's growth just after its IPO was financed by both operating activities and external financing, as we show in Figure 8.5. However, approximately half of the funds to support its rapid growth and to purchase some of its franchised stores in the 2000–2003 fiscal years came from long-term financing. This resulted in problems as the company's debt burden became almost three times its equity as revenue growth slowed by the 2005 fiscal year. Krispy Kreme demonstrated some ability to turn itself around in the 2006 fiscal year, partly by slowing its expansion through new stores.

Ratio Analysis

One use of cash flow information is in ratio analysis, primarily with the balance sheet and income statement information. Once such ratio is the cash flow-based ratio, the *cash flow interest coverage ratio*, which is a measure of financial risk. There are a number of other cash flow-based ratios that an

Financial Analysis

FIGURE 8.4 Krispy Kreme Doughnuts, Inc. Income, 1997–2006

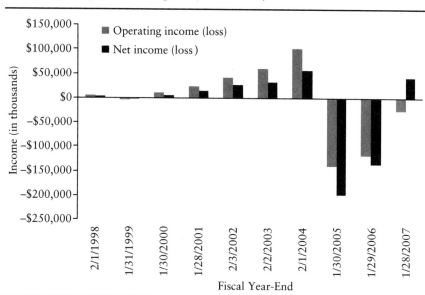

Source: Krispy Kreme Doughnuts, Inc., 10-K filings, various years.

FIGURE 8.5 Krispy Kreme Doughnuts, Inc.'s Cash Flows, 1997–2006

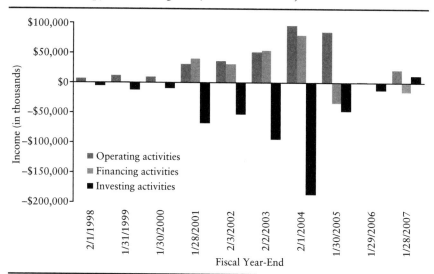

Source: Krispy Kreme Doughnuts, Inc., 10-K filings, various years.

analyst may find useful in evaluating the operating performance and financial condition of a company.

A useful ratio to help further assess a company's cash flow is the *cash flow to capital expenditures ratio*, or *capital expenditures coverage ratio*:

$$\text{Cash flow to capital expenditures} = \frac{\text{Cash flow}}{\text{Capital expenditures}}$$

The cash flow measure in the numerator should be one that has not already removed capital expenditures; for example, including free cash flow in the numerator would be inappropriate.

This ratio provides information about the financial flexibility of the company and is particularly useful for capital-intensive firms and utilities (see Fridson, 1995, p. 173). The larger the ratio, the greater the financial flexibility. However, one must carefully examine the reasons why this ratio may be changing over time and why it might be out of line with comparable firms in the industry. For example, a declining ratio can be interpreted in two ways. First, the firm may eventually have difficulty adding to capacity via capital expenditures without the need to borrow funds. The second interpretation is that the firm may have gone through a period of major capital expansion and therefore it will take time for revenues to be generated that will increase the cash flow from operations to bring the ratio to some normal long-run level.

Another useful cash flow ratio is the *cash flow to debt ratio*:

$$\text{Cash flow to debt} = \frac{\text{Cash flow}}{\text{Debt}}$$

where debt can be represented as total debt, long-term debt, or a debt measure that captures a specific range of maturity (e.g., debt maturing in five years). This ratio gives a measure of a company's ability to meet maturing debt obligations. A more specific formulation of this ratio is Fitch's *CFAR* ratio, which compares a company's three-year average net free cash flow to its maturing debt over the next five years.[4] By comparing the company's average net free cash flow to the expected obligations in the near term (i.e., five years), this ratio provides information on the company's credit quality.

Using Cash Flow Information

The analysis of cash flows provides information that can be used along with other financial data to help assess the financial condition of a company. Consider the cash flow to debt ratio calculated using three different mea-

---

[4] See McConville (1996).

sures of cash flow—EBITDA, free cash flow, and cash flow from operations (from the statement of cash flows)—each compared with long-term debt, as shown in Figure 8.6 for Weirton Steel.

This example illustrates the need to understand the differences among the cash flow measures. The effect of capital expenditures in the 1988–1991 period can be seen by the difference between the free cash flow measure and the other two measures of cash flow; both EBITDA and cash flow from operations ignore capital expenditures, which were substantial outflows for this company in the earlier period.

Cash flow information may help identify companies that are more likely to encounter financial difficulties. Consider the study by Largay and Stickney (1980) that analyzed the financial statements of W. T. Grant during the 1966–1974 period preceding its bankruptcy in 1975 and ultimate liquidation. They noted that financial indicators such as profitability ratios, turnover ratios, and liquidity ratios showed some downward trends, but provided no definite clues to the company's impending bankruptcy. A study of cash flows from operations, however, revealed that company operations

FIGURE 8.6 Cash Flow to Debt Using Alternative Estimates of Cash Flow for Weirton Steel, 1988–1996

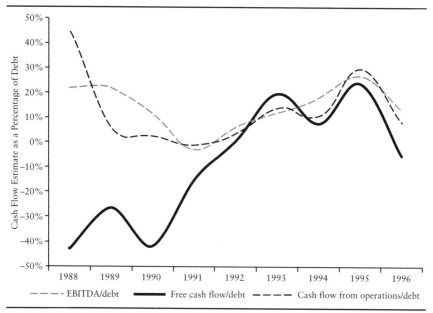

Source: Weirton Steel's 10-K reports, various years.

were causing an increasing drain on cash, rather than providing cash.[5] This necessitated an increased use of external financing, the required interest payments on which exacerbated the cash flow drain. Cash flow analysis clearly was a valuable tool in this case since W. T. Grant had been running a negative cash flow from operations for years. Yet none of the traditional ratios discussed above take into account the cash flow from operations. Use of the cash flow to capital expenditures ratio and the cash flow to debt ratio would have highlighted the company's difficulties.

Dugan and Samson (1996) examined the use of operating cash flow as an early warning signal of a company's potential financial problems. The subject of the study was Allied Products Corporation because for a decade this company exhibited a significant divergence between cash flow from operations and net income. For parts of the period, net income was positive while cash flow from operations was a large negative value. In contrast to W. T. Grant, which went into bankruptcy, the auditor's report in the 1991 Annual Report of Allied Products Corporation did issue a going-concern warning. Moreover, the stock traded in the range of $2 to $3 per share. There was then a turnaround of the company by 1995. In its 1995 annual report, net income increased dramatically from prior periods (to $34 million) and there was a positive cash flow from operations ($29 million). The stock traded in the $25 range by the Spring of 1996. As with the W. T. Grant study, Dugan and Samson found that the economic realities of a firm are better reflected in its cash flow from operations.

The importance of cash flow analysis in bankruptcy prediction is supported by the study by Foster and Ward (1997), who compared trends in the statement of cash flows components—cash flow from operations, cash flow for investment, and cash flow for financing—between healthy companies and companies that subsequently sought bankruptcy. They observe that healthy companies tend to have relatively stable relations among the cash flows for the three sources, correcting any given year's deviation from their norm within one year. They also observe that unhealthy companies exhibit declining cash flows from operations and financing and declining cash flows for investment one and two years prior to the bankruptcy. Further, unhealthy companies tend to expend more cash flows to financing sources than they bring in during the year prior to bankruptcy. These studies illustrate the importance of examining cash flow information in assessing the financial condition of a company.

---

[5]For the period investigated, a statement of changes of financial position (on a working capital basis) was required to be reported prior to 1988.

SUMMARY

The basic data for financial analysis is the financial statement data. We use this data to analyze relationships between different elements of a firm's financial statements. Through this analysis, we develop a picture of the operating performance and financial condition of a firm. Looking at the calculated financial ratios, in conjunction with industry and economic data, we can make judgments about past and future financial performance and condition.

We can classify ratios by the financial characteristic that we wish to measure—liquidity, profitability, activity, financial leverage, or return. Liquidity ratios tell us about a firm's ability to satisfy short-term obligations. These ratios are closely related to a firm's operating cycle, which tells us how long it takes a firm to turn its investment in current assets back into cash. Profitability ratios tell us how well a firm manages its assets, typically in terms of the proportion of revenues that are left over after expenses. Activity ratios tell us how efficiently a firm manages its assets, that is, how effectively a firm uses its assets to generate sales. Financial leverage ratios tell us (1) to what extent a firm uses debt to finance its operations and (2) its ability to satisfy debt and debt-like obligations. Return-on-investment ratios tell us how much of each dollar of an investment is generated in a period. The DuPont system breaks down return ratios into their profit margin and activity ratios, allowing us to analyze changes in return on investments.

Common-size analysis expresses financial statement data relative to some benchmark item—usually total assets for the balance sheet and sales for the income statement. Representing financial data in this way allows an investor to spot trends in investments and profitability.

Interpretation of financial ratios requires an investor to put the trends and comparisons in perspective with the company's significant events. In addition to company-specific events, issues that can cause the analysis of financial ratios to become more challenging include the use of historical accounting values, changes in accounting principles, and accounts that are difficult to classify.

Comparison of financial ratios across time and with competitors is useful in gauging performance. In comparing ratios over time, an investor should consider changes in accounting and significant company events. In comparing ratios with a benchmark, an investor must take care in the selection of the companies that constitute the benchmark and the method of calculation.

The term cash flow has many meanings and the challenge is to determine the cash flow definition and calculation that is appropriate. The simplest calculation of cash flow is the sum of net income and noncash expenses.

This measure, however, does not consider other sources and uses of cash during the period.

The statement of cash flows provides a useful breakdown of the sources of cash flows: operating activities, investing activities, and financing activities. Though attention is generally focused on the cash flows from operations, what the company does with the cash flows (i.e., investing or paying off financing obligations) and what are the sources of invested funds (i.e., operations versus external financing) must be investigated. Minor adjustments can be made to the items classified in the statement of cash flows to improve the classification.

Examination of the different patterns of cash flows is necessary to get a general idea of the activities of the company. For example, a company whose only source of cash flow is from investing activities, suggesting the sale of property or equipment, may be experiencing financial distress.

Free cash flow is a company's cash flow that remains after making capital investments that maintain the company's current rate of growth. It is not possible to calculate free cash flow precisely, resulting in many different variations in calculations of this measure. A company that generates free cash flow is not necessarily performing well or poorly; the existence of free cash flow must be taken in context with other financial data and information on the company.

One of the variations in the calculation of a cash flow measure is net free cash flow, which is, essentially, free cash flow less any financing obligations. This is a measure of the funds available to service additional obligations to suppliers of capital.

REFERENCES

Bernstein, L. A. 1999. *Analysis of financial statements,* 5th ed. New York: McGraw-Hill.

Dugan, M. T., and W. D. Samson, 1996. Operating cash flow: Early indicators of financial difficulty and recovery. *Journal of Financial Statement Analysis* 1, no. 4: 41–50.

Eastman, K. 1997. EBITDA: An overrated tool for cash flow analysis. *Commercial Lending Review* 12 (January–February): 64–69.

Fabozzi, F. J., P. P. Drake, and R. S. Polimeni. 2007. *The complete CFO handbook: From accounting to accountability.* Hoboken, NJ: John Wiley & Sons.

Fridson, M. 1995. *Financial statement analysis: A practitioner's guide.* New York: John Wiley & Sons.

Fridson, M., and F. Alvarez. 2002. *Financial statement analysis: A practitioner's guide,* 3rd ed. Hoboken, NJ: John Wiley & Sons.

Jensen, M. C. 1986. Agency costs of free cash flow, corporate finance, and takeovers. *American Economic Review* 76, no. 2: 323–329.

Largay, J. A., and C. P. Stickney. 1980. Cash flows, ratio analysis and the W. T. Grant Company bankruptcy. *Financial Analysts Journal* 36 (July–August): 51–54.

McConville, D. J. 1996. Cash flow ratios gains respect as useful tool for credit rating. *Corporate Cashflow Magazine*, January p. 18.

Peterson, P. P., and F. J. Fabozzi. 2006. *Analysis of financial statements,* 2nd ed. Hoboken, NJ: John Wiley & Sons.

Stumpp, P. M. 2001. Critical failings of EBITDA as a cash flow measure. In *Bond Credit Analysis: Framework and Case Studies,* edited by F. J. Fabozzi (pp. 139–170), Hoboken, NJ: John Wiley & Sons.

CHAPTER 9
Applied Equity Valuation

In this chapter, we discuss practical methods of valuing a firm's equity based on *discounted cash flow models* and *relative valuation models*. The individual in an asset management firm or on a portfolio management team responsible for valuation is the *security analyst*, which we refer to simply as the *analyst* in this chapter. The recommendations are passed on to the senior portfolio manager who then considers those stocks that are favorably recommended for inclusion in the portfolio.

Although stock and firm valuation is very strongly tilted toward the use of discounted cash flow models, it is impossible to ignore the fact that many analysts use other methods to value equity and entire firms. These two models are the subject of this chapter. The primary alternative valuation method is relative valuation. Both the discounted cash flow model and the relative valuation methods require strong assumptions and expectations about the future. No one single valuation model or method is perfect. All valuation estimates are subject to model error and estimation error. Nevertheless, investors use these models to help form their expectations about a fair market price. Markets then generate an observable market-clearing price based on investor expectations, and this market-clearing price constantly changes along with investor expectations.

DISCOUNTED CASH FLOW MODELS

There are various *discounted cash flow* (DCF) models that are used to value common stock. We will not describe all of the models. Rather our primary focus is on models that are referred to as dividend discount models.

This chapter is coauthored with Pamela Peterson Drake and Glen Larsen, Jr.

Dividend Discount Models

Most dividend discount models use current dividends, some measure of historical or projected dividend growth, and an estimate of the required rate of return. Popular models include the basic dividend discount model that assumes a constant dividend growth, and the multiple-phase models (which include the two-stage dividend growth and three-stage dividend growth models), and stochastic dividend discount models.

We now discuss these dividend discount models and their limitations, beginning with a review of the various ways to measure dividends. Then we look at how dividends and stock prices are related.

Dividend Measures

Dividends are measured using three different metrics:

- Dividends per share
- Dividend yield
- Dividend payout

The value of a share of stock today is the investors' assessment of today's worth of future cash flows for each share. Because future cash flows to shareholders are dividends, we need a measure of dividends for each share of stock to estimate future cash flows per share. The *dividends per share* is the dollar amount of dividends paid out during the period per share of common stock:

$$\text{Dividends per share} = \frac{\text{Dividends}}{\text{Number of shares outstanding}}$$

If a company has paid $600,000 in dividends during the period and there are 1.5 million shares of common stock outstanding, then

$$\text{Dividends per share} = \frac{\$600,000}{1,500,000 \text{ shares}} = \$0.40 \text{ per share}$$

The company paid out 40 cents in dividends per common share during this period.

The *dividend yield*, the ratio of dividends to price, is

$$\text{Dividend yield} = \frac{\text{Annual cash dividends per share}}{\text{Market price per share}}$$

The dividend yield is also referred to as the *dividend-price ratio*. Historically, the dividend yield for U.S. stocks has been a little less than 5% according to a study by Campbell and Shiller (1998). In an exhaustive study of the relation between dividend yield and stock prices, Campbell and Shiller find that:

- There is a weak relation between the dividend yield and subsequent 10-year dividend growth.
- The dividend yield does not forecast future dividend growth.
- The dividend yield predicts future price changes.

The weak relation between the dividend yield and future dividends may be attributed to the effects of the business cycle on dividend growth. The tendency for the dividend yield to revert to its historical mean has been observed by researchers.

Another way of describing dividends paid out during a period is to state the dividends as a portion of earnings for the period. This is referred to as the *dividend payout ratio*:

$$\text{Dividend payout ratio} = \frac{\text{Dividends}}{\text{Earnings available to common shareholders}}$$

If a company pays $360,000 in dividends and has earnings available to common shareholders of $1.2 million, the payout ratio is 30%:

$$\text{Dividend payout ratio} = \frac{\$360,000}{\$1,200,000} = 0.30 \text{ or } 30\%$$

This means that the company paid out 30% of its earnings to shareholders.

The proportion of earnings paid out in dividends varies by company and industry. For example, companies in the steel industry typically pay out 25% of their earnings in dividends, whereas electric utility companies pay out approximately 75% of their earnings in dividends.

If companies focus on dividends per share in establishing their dividends (e.g., a constant dividends per share), the dividend payout will fluctuate along with earnings. We generally observe that companies set the dividend policy such that dividends per share grow at a relatively constant rate, resulting in dividend payouts that fluctuate.

Dividends and Stock Prices

If an investor buys a common stock, he or she has bought shares that represent an ownership interest in the corporation. Shares of common stock are a perpetual security—that is, there is no maturity. The investor who owns shares of common stock has the right to receive a certain portion of any dividends—but dividends are not a sure thing. Whether or not a corporation pays dividends is up to its board of directors—the representatives of the common shareholders. Typically, we see some pattern in the dividends companies pay: Dividends are either constant or grow at a constant rate. But there is no guarantee that dividends will be paid in the future.

Preferred shareholders are in a similar situation as the common shareholders. They expect to receive cash dividends in the future, but the payment of these dividends is up to the board of directors. There are, however, three major differences between the dividends of preferred and common shares. First, the dividends on preferred stock usually are specified at a fixed rate or dollar amount, whereas the amount of dividends is not specified for common shares. Second, preferred shareholders are given preference: Their dividends must be paid before any dividends are paid on common stock. Third, if the preferred stock has a cumulative feature, dividends not paid in one period accumulate and are carried over to the next period. Therefore, the dividends on preferred stock are more certain than those on common shares.

It is reasonable to figure that what an investor pays for a share of stock should reflect what he or she expects to receive from it—a return on the investor's investment. What an investor receives are cash dividends in the future. How can we relate that return to what a share of common stock is worth? Well, the value of a share of stock should be equal to the present value of all the future cash flows an investor expects to receive from that share. To value stock, therefore, an analyst must project future cash flows, which, in turn, means projecting future dividends. This approach to the valuation of common stock is referred to the discounted cash flow approach and the models used are what we referred to earlier as dividend discount models.

Basic Dividend Discount Models

As discussed, the basis for the *dividend discount model* (DDM) is simply the application of present value analysis, which asserts that the fair price of an asset is the present value of the expected cash flows. This model was first suggested by Williams (1938). In the case of common stock, the cash flows are the expected dividend payouts. The basic DDM model can be expressed mathematically as

$$P = \frac{D_1}{(1+r_1)^1} + \frac{D_2}{(1+r_2)^2} + \cdots \quad (9.1)$$

Applied Equity Valuation

where

P = the fair value or theoretical value of the common stock
D_t = the expected dividend for period t
r_t = the appropriate discount or capitalization rate for period t

The dividends are expected to be received forever.

If investors never expected a dividend to be paid, then this model implies that the stock would have no value. To reconcile the fact that stocks not paying a current dividend do have a positive market value with this model, one must assume that investors expect that someday, at some time N, the firm must pay out some cash, even if only a liquidating dividend.

Practitioners rarely use the dividend discount model given by equation (9.1). Instead, one of the DDMs discussed next is typically used.

The Finite Life General Dividend Discount Model

The DDM given by equation (9.1) can be modified by assuming a finite life for the expected cash flows. In this case, the expected cash flows are the expected dividend payouts and the expected sale price of the stock at some future date. The expected sale price is also called the terminal price and is intended to capture the future value of all subsequent dividend payouts. This model is called the *finite life general DDM* and is expressed mathematically as

$$P = \frac{D_1}{(1+r_1)^1} + \frac{D_2}{(1+r_2)^2} + \cdots + \frac{D_N}{(1+r_N)^N} + \frac{P_N}{(1+r_N)^N} \quad (9.2)$$

where

P_N = the expected sale price (or terminal price) at the horizon period N
N = the number of periods in the horizon

and P, D_t, and r_t are the same as defined for equation (9.1).

Assuming a Constant Discount Rate A special case of the finite life general DDM that is more commonly used in practice is one in which it is assumed that the discount rate is constant. That is, it is assumed each r_t is the same for all t. Denoting this constant discount rate by r, equation (9.2) becomes

$$P = \frac{D_1}{(1+r)^1} + \frac{D_2}{(1+r)^2} + \cdots + \frac{D_N}{(1+r)^N} + \frac{P_N}{(1+r)^N} \quad (9.3)$$

Equation (9.3) is referred to as the *constant discount rate version of the finite life general DDM.* When practitioners use any of the DDM models presented in this section, typically the constant discount rate version form is used.

Let's illustrate the finite life general DDM based on a constant discount rate assuming each period is a year. Suppose that the following data are determined for stock XYZ by a security analyst:

$D_1 = \$2.00 \quad D_2 = \$2.20 \quad D_3 = \$2.30 \quad D_4 = \$2.55 \quad D_5 = \$2.65$
$P_5 = \$26 \quad\quad N = 5 \quad\quad r = 0.10$

Based on these data, the fair price of stock XYZ is

$$P = \frac{\$2.00}{(1.10)^1} + \frac{\$2.20}{(1.10)^2} + \frac{\$2.30}{(1.10)^3} + \frac{\$2.55}{(1.10)^4} + \frac{\$2.65}{(1.10)^5} + \frac{\$26.00}{(1.10)^5} = \$24.895$$

Required Inputs The finite life general DDM requires three forecasts as inputs to calculate the fair value of a stock:

1. Expected terminal price (P_N).
2. Dividends up to the assumed horizon (D_1 to D_N).
3. Discount rates (r_1 to r_N) or r (in the case of the constant discount rate version).

Thus, the relevant issue is how accurately these inputs can be forecasted.

The terminal price is the most difficult of the three forecasts. According to theory, P_N is the present value of all future dividends after N; that is, $D_{N+1}, D_{N+2}, \ldots, D_\infty$. Also, the future discount rate (r_t) must be forecasted. In practice, forecasts are made of either dividends (D_N) or earnings (E_N) first, and then the price P_N is estimated by assigning an "appropriate" requirement for yield, price/earnings ratio, or capitalization rate. Note that the present value of the expected terminal price $P_N/(1 + r)^N$ becomes very small if N is very large.

The forecasting of dividends is "somewhat" easier. Usually, past history is available, management can be queried, and cash flows can be projected for a given scenario. The discount rate r is the required rate of return. Forecasting r is more complex than forecasting dividends, although not nearly as difficult as forecasting the terminal price (which requires a forecast of future discount rates as well). As noted before, in practice for a given company, r is assumed to be constant for all periods and typically generated from the capital asset pricing model (CAPM). As explained in Chapter 5, the CAPM provides the expected return for a company based on its systematic risk (beta).

Assessing Relative Value Given the fair price derived from a DDM, the assessment of the stock proceeds along the following lines. If the market price is below the fair price derived from the model, the stock is undervalued or cheap. The opposite holds for a stock whose market price is greater than the model-derived price. In this case, the stock is said to be overvalued or expensive. A stock trading equal to or close to its fair price is said to be fairly valued.

The DDM tells us the relative value but does not tell us when the price of the stock should be expected to move to its fair price. That is, the model says that based on the inputs generated by the analyst, the stock may be cheap, expensive, or fair. However, it does not tell us that if it is mispriced how long it will take before the market recognizes the mispricing and corrects it. As a result, an investor may hold on to a stock perceived to be cheap for an extended period of time and may underperform a benchmark during that period.

While a stock may be mispriced, an analyst and portfolio manager must also consider how mispriced it is in order to take the appropriate action (buy a cheap stock and sell or sell short an expensive stock). This will depend on by how much the stock is trading from its fair value and transaction costs. An analyst and portfolio manager should also consider that a stock may look as if it is mispriced (based on the estimates and the model), but this may be the result of estimates and the use of these estimates in the model may introduce error in the valuation.

Constant Growth Dividend Discount Model

If future dividends are assumed to grow at a constant rate (g) and a single discount rate (r) is used, then the finite life general DDM assuming a constant growth rate given by equation (9.3) becomes

$$P = \frac{D_0(1+g)^1}{(1+r)^1} + \frac{D_0(1+g)^2}{(1+r)^2} + \frac{D_0(1+g)^3}{(1+r)^3} + \cdots + \frac{D_0(1+g)^N}{(1+r)^N} + \frac{P_N}{(1+r)^N} \quad (9.4)$$

and it can be shown that if N is assumed to approach infinity, equation (9.4) is equal to

$$P = \frac{D_0(1+g)}{r-g} \quad (9.5)$$

Equation (9.5) is called the *constant growth dividend discount model* (Gordon and Shapiro 1956). An equivalent formulation for the constant growth DDM is

$$P = \frac{D_1}{r-g} \tag{9.6}$$

where D_1 is equal to $D_0(1 + g)$.

Consider a company that currently pays annual dividends of $3.00 per share. If the dividend is expected to grow at a rate of 3% per year and the discount rate is 12%, the estimated value of a share of stock of this company using equation (9.5) is

$$P = \frac{\$3.00(1+0.03)}{0.12-0.03} = \frac{\$3.09}{0.09} = \$34.33$$

If the growth rate for this company's dividends is 5%, instead of 3%, the estimated value is $45.00 as shown below:

$$P = \frac{\$3.00(1+0.05)}{0.12-0.05} = \frac{\$3.15}{0.07} = \$45.00$$

Therefore, the greater the expected growth rate of dividends, the greater the estimated value of a share of stock.

In this last example, if the discount rate is 14% instead of 12% and the growth rate of dividends is 3%, the estimated value of a share of this stock is

$$P = \frac{\$3.00(1+0.03)}{0.14-0.03} = \frac{\$3.09}{0.11} = \$28.09$$

Therefore, the greater the discount rate, the lower the estimated value of a share of stock.

Let's apply the model as given by equation (9.5) to estimate the price at the end of 2006 of three companies: Eli Lilly, Schering-Plough, and Wyeth Laboratories. The discount rate for each company was estimated using the capital asset pricing model assuming (1) a market risk premium of 5% and (2) a risk-free rate of 4.63%. The market risk premium is based on the historical spread between the return on the market (often proxied with the return on the S&P 500 Index) and the risk-free rate. Historically, this spread has been approximately 5%. The risk-free rate is often estimated by the yield on U.S. Treasury securities. At the end of 2006, 10-year Treasury securities were yielding approximately 4.625%. We use 4.63% as an estimate for the purposes of this illustration. The beta estimate for each company was obtained from the Value Line Investment Survey: 0.9 for Eli Lilly and 1.0 for both Schering-Plough and Wyeth. The discount rate, r, for each company based on the CAPM is

Eli-Lilly $r = 0.0463 + 0.9(0.05) = 9.125\%$
Schering-Plough $r = 0.0463 + 1.0(0.05) = 9.625\%$
Wyeth $r = 0.0463 + 1.0(0.05) = 9.625\%$

The dividend growth rate can be estimated by using the compounded rate of growth of historical dividends.

The compound growth rate, g, is found using the following formula:

$$g = \left(\frac{\text{Last dividend}}{\text{Starting dividend}}\right)^{1/\text{no. of years}} - 1$$

This formula is equivalent to calculating the geometric mean of 1 plus the percentage change over the number of years. Using time value of money mathematics, the 2006 dividend is the future value, the starting dividend is the present value, the number of years is the number of periods; solving for the interest rate produces the growth rate.

Substituting the values for the starting and ending dividend amounts and the number of periods into the formula, we get:

Company	1991 Dividend	2006 Dividend	Estimated Annual Growth Rate
Eli-Lilly	$0.50	$1.60	8.063%
Schering-Plough	$0.16	$0.22	2.146%
Wyeth	$0.60	$1.01	3.533%

The value of D_0, the estimate for g, and the discount rate r for each company are summarized next:

Company	Current Dividend D_0	Estimated Annual Growth Rate g	Required Rate of Return r
Eli-Lilly	$1.60	8.063%	9.125%
Schering-Plough	$0.22	2.146%	9.625%
Wyeth	$1.01	3.533%	9.625%

Substituting these values into equation (9.5), we obtain

$$\text{Eli Lilly estimated price} = \frac{\$1.60(1+0.08063)}{0.09125 - 0.08063} = \frac{\$1.729}{0.0162} = \$162.79$$

$$\text{Schering-Plough estimated price} = \frac{\$0.022(1+0.02146)}{0.09625 - 0.02146} = \frac{\$0.225}{0.07479} = \$3.00$$

$$\text{Wyeth estimated price} = \frac{\$1.01(1+0.03533)}{0.09625-0.03533} = \frac{\$1.046}{0.06092} = \$17.16$$

Comparing the estimated price with the actual price, we see that this model does not do a good job of pricing these stocks:

Company	Estimated Price at the End of 2006	Actual Price at the End of 2006
Eli Lilly	$162.79	$49.87
Schering-Plough	$3.00	$23.44
Wyeth	$17.16	$50.52

Notice that the constant growth DDM is considerably off the mark for all three companies. The reasons include: (1) the dividend growth pattern for none of the three companies appears to suggest a constant growth rate; and (2) the growth rate of dividends in recent years has been much slower than earlier years (and, in fact, negative for Schering-Plough after 2003), causing growth rates estimated from the long time periods to overstate future growth. And this pattern is not unique to these companies.

Another problem that arises in using the constant growth rate model is that the growth rate of dividends may exceed the discount rate, r. Consider the following three companies and their dividend growth over the 16-year period from 1991 through 2006, with the estimated required rates of return:

Company	1991 Dividend	2006 Dividend	Estimated Growth Rate g	Estimated Required Rate of Return
Coca Cola	$0.24	$1.24	11.70%	7.625%
Hershey	$0.24	$1.03	10.198%	7.875%
Tootsie Roll	$0.04	$0.31	14.627%	8.625%

For these three companies, the growth rate of dividends over the prior 16 years is greater than the discount rate. If we substitute the D_0 (the 2006 dividends), the g, and the r into equation (9.5), the estimated price at the end of 2006 is negative, which doesn't make sense. Therefore, there are some cases in which it is inappropriate to use the constant rate DDM.

The potential for misvaluation using the constant rate DDM is highlighted by Fogler (1988) in his illustration using ABC prior to its being taken over by Capital Cities in 1985. He estimated the value of ABC stock to be $53.88, which was less than its market price at the time (of $64) and less than the $121 paid per share by Capital Cities.

Multiphase Dividend Discount Models

The assumption of constant growth is unrealistic and can even be misleading. Instead, most practitioners modify the constant growth DDM by assuming that companies will go through different growth phases. Within a given phase, dividends are assumed to growth at a constant rate. Molodovsky, May, and Chattiner (1965) were some of the pioneers in modifying the DDM to accommodate different growth rates.

Two-Stage Growth Model The simplest form of a multiphase DDM is the two-stage growth model. A simple extension of equation (9.4) uses two different values of g. Referring to the first growth rate as g_1 and the second growth rate as g_2 and assuming that the first growth rate pertains to the next four years and the second growth rate refers to all years following, equation (9.4) can be modified as

$$P = \frac{D_0(1+g_1)^1}{(1+r)^1} + \frac{D_0(1+g_1)^2}{(1+r)^2} + \frac{D_0(1+g_1)^3}{(1+r)^3} + \frac{D_0(1+g_1)^4}{(1+r)^4}$$
$$+ \frac{D_0(1+g_2)^5}{(1+r)^5} + \frac{D_0(1+g_2)^6}{(1+r)^6} + \cdots$$

which simplifies to

$$P = \frac{D_0(1+g_1)^1}{(1+r)^1} + \frac{D_0(1+g_1)^2}{(1+r)^2} + \frac{D_0(1+g_1)^3}{(1+r)^3} + \frac{D_0(1+g_1)^4}{(1+r)^4} + P_4$$

Because dividends following the fourth year are presumed to grow at a constant rate g_2 forever, the value of a share at the end of the fourth year (that is, P_4) is determined by using equation (9.5), substituting $D_0(1+g_1)^4$ for D_0 (because period 4 is the base period for the value at end of the fourth year) and g_2 for the constant rate g:

$$P = \frac{D_0(1+g_1)^1}{(1+r)^1} + \frac{D_0(1+g_1)^2}{(1+r)^2} + \frac{D_0(1+g_1)^3}{(1+r)^3} + \frac{D_0(1+g_1)^4}{(1+r)^4}$$
$$+ \left[\frac{1}{(1+r)^4}\left(\frac{D_0(1+g_1)^4(1+g_2)}{r-g_2}\right)\right] \quad (9.7)$$

Suppose a company's dividends are expected to grow at a 4% for the next four years and then 8% thereafter. If the current dividend is $2.00 and the discount rate is 12%,

$$P = \frac{\$2.08}{(1+0.12)^1} + \frac{\$2.16}{(1+0.12)^2} + \frac{\$2.25}{(1+0.12)^3} + \frac{\$2.34}{(1+0.12)^4}$$
$$+ \left[\frac{1}{(1+0.12)^4} \left(\frac{\$2.53}{0.12-0.08} \right) \right] = \$46.87$$

If this company's dividends are expected to grow at the rate of 4% forever, the value of a share is $26.00; if this company's dividends are expected to grow at the rate of 8% forever, the value of a share is $52.00. But because the growth rate of dividends is expected to increase from 4% to 8% in four years, the value of a share is between those two values, or $46.87.

As can be seen from this example, the basic valuation model can be modified to accommodate different patterns of expected dividend growth.

Three-Stage Growth Model The most popular multiphase model employed by practitioners appears to be the *three-stage DDM*.[1] This model assumes that all companies go through three phases, analogous to the concept of the product life cycle. In the growth phase, a company experiences rapid earnings growth as it produces new products and expands market share. In the transition phase the company's earnings begin to mature and decelerate to the rate of growth of the economy as a whole. At this point, the company is in the maturity phase in which earnings continue to grow at the rate of the general economy.

Different companies are assumed to be at different phases in the three-phase model. An emerging growth company would have a longer growth phase than a more mature company. Some companies are considered to have higher initial growth rates and hence longer growth and transition phases. Other companies may be considered to have lower current growth rates and hence shorter growth and transition phases.

In the typical investment management organization, analysts supply the projected earnings, dividends, growth rates for earnings, and dividend and payout ratios using the fundamental security analysis. The basis for the three-stage model is that the current information on growth rates and the like are useful in determining the phase of the company and then the valuation model—whether one, two, or three stages—is applied to value the company's stock. Generally, the growth in the mature stage of a company's life cycle is assumed to be equal to the long-run growth rate for the economy. As a generalization, approximately 25% of the expected return from a company (projected by the DDM) comes from the growth phase, 25% from the transition phase, and 50% from the maturity phase. However, a company with high growth and low dividend payouts shifts the relative

---

[1] The formula for this model can be found in Sorensen and Williamson (1985).

contribution toward the maturity phase, while a company with low growth and a high payout shifts the relative contribution toward the growth and transition phases.

Stochastic Dividend Discount Models

As we noted in our discussion and illustration of the constant growth DDM, an erratic dividend pattern such as that of Wyeth can lead to quite a difference between the estimated price and the actual price. In the case of the pharmaceutical companies, the estimated price overstated the actual price for Eli Lilly, but understated the price of Schering-Plough and Wyeth.

Hurley and Johnson (1998a, 1998b) suggested a new family of valuation models. Their models allow for a more realistic pattern of dividend payments. The basic model generates dividend payments based on a model that assumes that either the firm will increase dividends for the period by a constant amount or keep dividends the same. The model is referred to as a *stochastic DDM* because the dividend can increase or be constant based on some estimated probability of each possibility occurring. The dividend stream used in the stochastic DDM is called the stochastic dividend stream.

There are two versions of the stochastic DDM. One assumes that dividends either increase or decrease at a constant growth rate. This version is referred to as a *binomial stochastic DDM* because there are two possibilities for dividends. The second version is called a *trinomial stochastic DDM* because it allows for an increase in dividends, no change in dividends, and a cut in dividends. We discuss each version next.

Binomial Stochastic Model For both the binomial and trinomial stochastic DDM, there are two versions of the model—the *additive growth model* and the *geometric growth model*. The former model assumes that dividend growth is additive rather than geometric. This means that dividends are assumed to grow by a constant dollar amount. So, for example, if dividends are $2.00 today and the additive growth rate is assumed to be $0.25 per year, then next year dividends will grow to $2.25, in two years dividends will grow to $2.50, and so on. The second model assumes a geometric rate of dividend growth. This is the same growth rate assumption used in the earlier DDMs presented in this chapter.

This formulation of the model is expressed as follows:

$$D_{t+1} = \begin{cases} D_t + C & \text{with probability } p \\ D_t & \text{with probability } 1-p \end{cases} \text{ for } t = 1, 2, \ldots$$

where

D_t = dividend in period t
D_{t+1} = dividend in period $t + 1$
C = dollar amount of the dividend increase
p = probability that the dividend will increase

Hurley and Johnson (1998a) have shown that the theoretical value of the stock based on the additive stochastic DDM assuming a constant discount rate is equal to

$$P = \frac{D_0}{r} + \left[\frac{1}{r} + \frac{1}{r^2}\right]C_p \qquad (9.8)$$

For example, consider once again Wyeth. In the illustration of the constant growth model, we used D_0 of $1.01 and a g of 3.533%. We estimate C by calculating the dollar increase in dividends for each year that had a dividend increase and then taking the average dollar dividend increase. The average of the increases is $0.0373.

In the 15 year span 1991 through 2006, dividends increased 11 of the 14 year-to-year differences. Therefore, $p = 11/15 = 73.3333\%$. Substituting these values into equation (9.8), we find the estimated price to be:

$$P = \frac{\$1.01}{0.09625} + \left[\left(\frac{1}{0.09125} + \frac{1}{0.09125^2}\right)(\$0.03727)\left(\frac{11}{15}\right)\right]$$
$$= \$10.49351 + [(1118.33361)(\$0.3727)(0.73333)]$$
$$= \$10.49351 + \$323445 = \$13.72796$$

Applying this model to the other two pharmaceutical companies, we see that the model produces an estimated price that is closer to the actual price for Eli Lilly and Schering-Plough, but farther for Wyeth:

Company	Actual Price at the End of 2006	Estimated Price at the End of 2006 Using a Constant Growth Model	Estimated Price at the End of 2006 Using the Binomial Additive Stochastic Model
Eli Lilly	$49.87	$162.79	$23.82
Schering-Plough	$23.44	$3.00	$5.36
Wyeth	$50.52	$17.16	$13.73

Letting g be the growth rate of dividends, the geometric dividend stream is

$$D_{t+1} = \begin{cases} D_t(1+g) & \text{with probability } p \\ D_t & \text{with probability } 1-p \end{cases} \quad \text{for } t = 1, 2, \ldots$$

Hurley and Johnson (1998b) show that the price of the stock in this case is

$$P = \frac{D_0(1+pg)}{r-pg} \quad (9.9)$$

Equation (9.9) is the binomial stochastic DDM assuming a geometric growth rate and a constant discount rate.

Trinomial Stochastic Models The trinomial stochastic DDM allows for dividend cuts. Within the Hurley-Johnson stochastic DDM framework, Yao (1997) derived this model that allows for a cut in dividends. He notes that is not uncommon for a firm to cut dividends temporarily.

The additive stochastic DDM can be extended to allow for dividend cuts as follow:

$$D_{t+1} = \begin{cases} D_t + C & \text{with probability } p_U \\ D_t - C & \text{with probability } p_D \\ D_t & \text{with probability } 1 - p_C = 1 - p_U - p_D \end{cases} \quad \text{for } t = 1, 2, \ldots$$

where

p_U = probability that the dividend will increase
p_D = probability that the dividend will decrease
p_C = probability that the dividend will be unchanged

The theoretical value of the stock based on the trinomial additive stochastic DDM then becomes

$$P = \frac{D_0}{r} + \left[\frac{1}{r} + \frac{1}{r^2}\right] C(p_U - p_D) \quad (9.10)$$

Notice that when p_D is zero (that is, when it is highly unlikely that there will be a cut in dividends), equation (9.10) reduces to equation (9.8).

For the trinomial geometric stochastic DDM allowing for a possibility of cuts, we have

$$D_{t+1} = \begin{cases} D_t(1+g) & \text{with probability } p_U \\ D_t(1-g) & \text{with probability } p_D \\ D_t & \text{with probability } 1 - p_C = 1 - p_U - p_D \end{cases} \quad \text{for } t = 1, 2, \ldots$$

and the theoretical price is:

$$p = \frac{D_0[1+(p_U+p_D)]}{r-(p_U-p_D)g} \qquad (9.11)$$

Once again, substituting zero for p_D, equation (9.11) reduces to equation (9.9)—the binomial geometric stochastic DDM.

Applications of the Stochastic DDM Yao (1997) applied the stochastic DDMs to five electric utility stocks that had regular dividends from 1979 to 1994 and found that the models fit the various utility stocks differently.

We see similar results in an updated example using five electric utilities, as shown in Table 9.1. For three of the five utilities, the binomial model provides an estimate closest to the actual stock price, whereas for the other two utilities, the trinomial model offers the closest estimate. In none of the cases, however, did the constant dividend growth model offer the closest approximation to the actual stock price.

Advantages of the Stochastic DDM The stochastic DDM developed by Hurley and Johnson is a powerful tool for the analyst because it allows the analyst to generate a probability distribution for a stock's value. The probability distribution can be used by an analyst to assess whether a stock is sufficiently mispriced to justify a buy or sell recommendation. For example, suppose that a three-phase DDM indicates that the value of a stock trading at $35 is $42. According to the model, the stock is underpriced and the analyst would recommend the purchase of this stock. However, the analyst cannot express his confidence as to the degree to which the stock is undervalued.

TABLE 9.1 Fit of the Different Dividend Models Applied to Five Electric Utilities

Company	Consolidated Edison	Dominion Resources	FPL Group	PPL	TECO Energy
Actual stock price, end of 2006	$45.82	$40.73	$52.98	$34.89	$16.46
Estimated stock price given the . . .					
Constant dividend growth model	$33.57	$19.36	$22.14	$16.54	$7.46
Binomial stochastic dividend model	$43.59	$30.51	$36.12	$28.30	$23.02
Trinomial stochastic dividend model	$63.12	$25.84	$41.23	$23.71	$14.45

Hurley and Johnson show how the stochastic DDM can be used to overcome this limitation of traditional DDMs. An analyst can use the derived probability distribution from the stochastic DDM to assess the probability that the stock is undervalued. For example, an analyst may find from a probability distribution that the probability that the stock is greater than $35 (the market price) is 90%.

To employ a stochastic DDM, an analyst must be prepared to make subjective assumptions about the uncertain nature of future dividends. Monte Carlo simulation can then be used to generate the probability distribution.

Expected Returns and Dividend Discount Models Thus far, we have seen how to calculate the fair price of a stock given the estimates of dividends, discount rates, terminal prices, and growth rates. The model-derived price is then compared to the actual price and the appropriate action is taken.

The analysis can be recast in terms of expected return. This is found by calculating the return that will make the present value of the expected cash flows equal to the actual price. Mathematically, this is expressed as follows:

$$P_A = \frac{D_1}{(1+ER)^1} + \frac{D_2}{(1+ER)^2} + \cdots + \frac{D_N}{(1+ER)^N} + \frac{P_N}{(1+ER)^N} \quad (9.12)$$

where

P_A = actual price of the stock
ER = expected return

For example, consider the following inputs used at the outset of this chapter to illustrate the finite life general DDM as given by equation (9.3). For stock XYZ, the inputs assumed are

D_1 = $2.00 D_2 = $2.20 D_3 = $2.30 D_4 = $2.55
D_5 = $2.65 P_5 = $26 N = 5

We calculated a fair price based on equation (9.12) to be $24.90. Suppose that the actual price is $25.89. Then the expected return is found by solving the following equation for ER:

$$\$25.89 = \frac{\$2.00}{(1+ER)} + \frac{\$2.20}{(1+ER)^2} + \frac{\$2.30}{(1+ER)^3} + \frac{\$2.55}{(1+ER)^4} + \frac{\$2.65}{(1+ER)^5} + \frac{\$26.00}{(1+ER)^5}$$

the expected return is 9%.

The expected return is the discount rate that equates the present value of the expected future cash flows with the present value of the stock. The higher the expected return—for a given set of future cash flows—the lower the current value. The relation between the fair value of a stock and the expected return of a stock is shown in Figure 9.1.

Given the expected return and the required return (that is, the value for r), any mispricing can be identified. If the expected return exceeds the required return, then the stock is undervalued; if it is less than the required return then the stock is overvalued. A stock is fairly valued if the expected return is equal to the required return. In our illustration, the expected return (9%) is less than the required return (10%); therefore, stock XYZ is overvalued.

With the same set of inputs, the identification of a stock being mispriced or fairly valued will be the same regardless of whether the fair value is determined and compared to the market price or the expected return is calculated and compared to the required return. In the case of XYZ stock, the fair value is $24.90. If the stock is trading at $25.89, it is overvalued. The expected return if the stock is trading at $25.89 is 9%, which is less

FIGURE 9.1 The Relation between the Fair Value of a Stock and the Stock's Expected Return

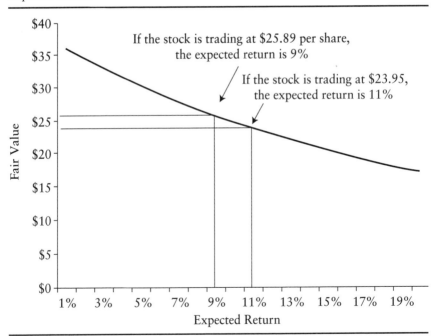

than the required return of 10%. If, instead, the stock price is $24.90, it is fairly valued. The expected return can be shown to be 10%, which is the same as the required return. At a price of $23.95, it can be shown that the expected return is 11%. Since the required return is 10%, stock XYZ would be undervalued.

While the illustration above uses the basic DDM, the expected return can be computed for any of the models. In some cases, the calculation of the expected return is simple since a formula can be derived that specifies the expected return in terms of the other variables. For example for the constant growth DDM given by equation (9.5), the expected return can be easily solved to give

$$ER = \frac{D_1}{p} + g$$

Rearranging the constant growth model to solve for the expected return, we see that the required rate of return can be specified as the sum of the dividend yield and the expected growth rate of dividends.

Adapting to the Complications: The Earnings per Share Approach

In the real world, it is difficult to compute a fair price through the basic dividend formulas presented. One solution involves substituting earnings per share (EPS) for dividends. This doesn't really work in a theoretical DDM sense, but it does work within the context of a growth culture. Shareholders have so thoroughly accepted and adopted growth that they act as if all corporate EPS (whether paid as dividends or reinvested back into the business) is in their hands. So, instead of working with a dividend yield as presented earlier, we can substitute an earnings (E) yield, which is computed as follows:

$$\text{Earnings yield} = E/P$$

Turn the above formula upside down and we get something investors see reported all the time: the P/E (price/earnings) ratio.

It is important to emphasize that P/E ratios are not just one of those things we use for the heck of it. They have a serious and solid intellectual underpinning. They are equivalent to earnings yields, which are the modern-day substitute for dividend yields—the true basis for valuing ownership of corporate stock. Buying any stock without addressing the P/E ratio is not sensible.

When we flip P/E back over and think of earnings yield, we can understand, from the prior discussion of dividend yield, that a bad company's stock will have to offer a higher yield to attract buyers. Similarly, the yield for a great company will be low (otherwise, there would be too many would-be buyers). Let's see how this works when we flip the earnings yields back to P/Es.

If EPS equals $3.00 and the earnings yield is 5%, the price will be $60. If it's a bad company and the yield is higher, at 8%, the stock price will be $37.50. If it is a good company and the yield is lower, say 3%, the stock price will be $100. The starting number translates to a P/E as follows: a $60 price divided by $3.00 EPS gives us a P/E of 20. A bad-company stock price of $37.50 divided by EPS of $3.00 produces a P/E of 12.5. A good-company stock price of $100 divided by EPS of $3.00 produces a P/E of 33.3.

That is the basis for the generally recognized phenomenon of good stocks having higher P/Es and bad stocks generally having lower P/Es. When evaluating companies, good or bad is usually determined based on growth prospects and risk.

We handled the complicating factors by treating EPS as if it were the same as a dividend. But notwithstanding, we still have a reasonably rational basis for stock prices. We can argue over what the growth prospects are and what the market return ought to be (based on differing assessments of market conditions and company-quality issues). So there will always be disagreement on what, exactly, a fair stock price ought to be. But all rational investors should be somewhere in the same ballpark. We may have a big ballpark and debate if a stock that commands $25 today is worth $15 or $35. But we are unlikely to seriously consider a price of, say, $350. More is said about the P/E ratio and other P/X ratios later, where "X" can be any measure of performance that is highly correlated with expected future cash flow to the investor when we discuss relative valuation later in this chapter.

Free Cash Flow DCF Model—Total Firm Valuation

While estimating future cash flows to an individual share of stock can seem daunting, some analysts prefer to estimate the free cash flow to the entire firm. Doing this allows analysts to estimate the value of the entire firm and then "back out" an estimated value of a share of stock. This is called the *free cash flow* (FCF) *model*. While legitimate accounting rules do enable managers and auditors some range of choices, at the end of the day, good companies wind up looking good and bad companies wind up looking bad. In short, there is no one number in an income report that truly gives an investor the necessary information to value a firm from a discounted expected future cash flow viewpoint. An investor still has to select which type of cash flow he or she is going to look at. But the choice becomes very easy once an investor answers the following question: What is my specific purpose for wanting to know how a company is doing?

There are many different types of users of financial information, and each is best served by concentrating on the information most relevant to him or her. Let's look at various kinds of numbers and consider what they say, and what types of investors will find them most useful.

Generally accepted accounting principles (GAAP) is a set of formal rules that produces what most of us have come to accept as the most official, or standard, version of income that a public corporation can report. Novices often believe this is the only valid number and are perplexed to learn otherwise. Essentially, GAAP is simple: revenues minus costs equal profits. But the world is a complex place. For our convenience, we divide our activities into time periods. In a simple world, all costs would be incurred in the same period as the revenues with which they are associated. But that is often not the case, so accountants have to find ways to identify which expenses should be matched against which revenues. One example is depreciation, a concept used to allocate multiperiod costs of a given expense to all the periods in which the expense generates revenue (e.g., if a factory can produce revenue for 20 years, charge one-fifth of the cost to build it against revenue in each year).

Observers correctly note that depreciation rules are artificial, and advocate use of other performance measures that are supposedly more "real." But for now, it's important to understand that depreciation rules are motivated by good purpose. They, and other GAAP rules, are designed to paint a picture of the "economic" performance of the business, something that is not necessarily the same as a running tally of physical dollars coming in and going out within a specific period of time.

If an analyst is looking to see how a company is doing because he wants to form an opinion as to whether or not it has a track record of "success" (defined however the analyst wishes), GAAP income is very important in that respect.

As noted, many analysts do not like GAAP because of the artificial nature of depreciation. Their objection is valid. GAAP is, indeed, imperfect. Companies have latitude to determine how to calculate it. They do not always use an equal allocation for each year. It's difficult, if not impossible, to reliably estimate useful life, especially since assets are usually enhanced (that is, factories modernized) as time passes, thereby giving rise to extended life and additional depreciable expenses tacked on. An assumption that at the end of the depreciation period the asset will be worth zero, or some predetermined salvage value, is often untrue in the real world. And besides, there are other kinds of "artificial" revenue-expense matching formulations to cover other situations. But depreciation is usually the biggest objection.

Difference between Cash Flow and Free Cash Flow

The response is often to add depreciation back to net income to calculate cash flow. This can be a trap for the unwary. The phrase "cash flow" sounds comforting. After all, how much more reliable a gauge of performance can an investor seek than cash in minus cash out? Read the warning label closely. Is the reported cash flow truly computed by adding depreciation back to net income? If that is what is happening, be very careful. Companies spend money to enhance their assets every year. Because it is understood that the benefits of these expenditures will span many years, they are not put on the income statement in any single year. So, in truth, simple cash flow understates a company's true cash-in minus cash-out situation. The solution lies in the firm's *free cash flow* (FCF). To arrive at a firm's FCF, we start with net income, add back the noncash depreciation charge, and then subtract the year's capital-spending outlays.[2]

Once an analyst hones in on FCF, he is not likely to be misled regarding liquidity. But that does not mean the analyst is learning about general corporate success or failure. Capital spending programs are not "smooth." In some years, expenditures are very large as major programs ramp up. In other years, capital spending shrinks as these programs wind down toward completion. If the company is in a heavy spending year, FCF could be negative, even though the company may be having a great year.

DCF valuation depends on the construction of pro forma financial statements in order to estimate a firm's future cash flows. *Pro forma* is Latin for "as if." This measure shows how a company might perform in the future "as if" it performs as it has in the past and other assumptions that are made by the analyst. In any event, it is necessary to construct pro forma financial statements in order to estimate future free cash flows that are the basis for total firm valuation.

RELATIVE VALUATION METHODS

Although stock and firm valuation is very strongly tilted toward the use of DCF methods, it is impossible to ignore the fact that many analysts use other methods to value equity and entire firms. The primary alternative valuation method is the use of multiples (ratios) that have "price" as the numerator and a "cash flow generating performance measure" for the denominator and that are observable for other "similar" or like-kind firms. These multiples are sometimes called "price/X ratios," where the denominator "X" is the

---

[2]There are other adjustments, such as those relating to dividends and changes in net working capital; but for now, these simple adjustments will suffice.

appropriate cash flow generating performance measure. For example, the price/earnings (P/E) ratio is a popular multiple used for relative valuation (RV) where an earnings estimate is the cash flow generating performance measure. Keep in mind that the terms RV and *valuation by multiples* are used interchangeably here as are the terms price and value.

The essence of valuation by multiples assumes that "similar" firms are fairly valued in the market. As a result, the "scaled" price or value (the present value of expected future cash flows) of similar firms should be much the same. That is, "similar" firms should have "similar" price/X ratios. The key is to find "similar" firms that can be used for valuing a "target" using valuation by multiples.

Valuation by multiples, or simply RV, is quick and convenient. The simplicity and convenience of valuation by multiples, however, constitute both the appeal of this valuation method and the problems associated with its use. Simplicity means that too many facts are swept under the carpet and too many questions remain unasked. Multiples should never be an analyst's only valuation method and preferably not even the primary focus because no two firms, or even groups of firms, are exactly the same. The term *similar* entails just as much uncertainty as the concept of "expected future cash flows" in DCF valuation methods. Actually, when an analyst has more than five minutes to value a firm, the DCF method, which forces an analyst to consider the many aspects of an ongoing concern, is the preferred valuation method and the use of multiples should be secondary.

Having said this, valuation by multiples can provide a valuable "sanity check." If an analyst has done a thorough valuation, he can compare his predicted multiples, such as the P/E ratio and market value to book value (MV/BV) ratio, to representative multiples of similar firms. In the MV/BV ratio, the book value of assets is the cash flow generating performance measure. That is, each dollar of book value of assets is assumed to generate cash flow for the firm. If an analyst's predicted multiples are comparable, he can, perhaps, feel more assured of the validity of his analysis. On the other hand, if an analyst's predicted multiples are out of line with the representative multiples of the market, then an analyst has some explaining to do—first to himself, to convince himself that his model is reasonable, and then to the firm's clients.

When using RV, an analyst does not attempt to explain observed prices of companies. Instead, an analyst uses the appropriately scaled average price of similar firms to estimate values without specifying why prices are what they are. That is, the average price of similar firms is scaled by the appropriate "price/X" ratio. In addition, there is nothing to say that multiple price/X ratios can be used and that each one will generally provide a different estimate of price (value). Hence, the trick in valuing with multiples is selecting truly comparable firms and choosing the appropriate scaling bases—the appropriate "X" measure.

The Basic Principles of Relative Valuation

To use the word "multiples" is to use a fancy name for market prices divided (or "scaled") by some measure of performance, a "price/X" ratio where "X" is the measure of performance that is highly correlated with cash flow. In a typical valuation with multiples, the average multiple—the average price scaled (divided) by some measure of performance—is applied to a performance measure of the target firm that an analyst is attempting to value.

For example, suppose an analyst chooses earnings as the scaling measure; that is, the analyst chooses earnings to be the performance measure by which prices of similar firms will be scaled. To scale the observed prices of firms by their earnings, the analyst computes for each firm the ratio of its price to its earnings—its P/E ratio or its earnings multiple. He then averages the individual P/E ratios to estimate a "representative" P/E ratio, or a representative earnings multiple. To value a firm, the analyst multiplies the projected profits of the firm being valued by the representative earnings multiple, the average P/E.

When valuing with multiples, the analyst is being agnostic about what determines prices. This means that there is no theory to guide the analyst on how best to scale observed market prices by:

- Net earnings
- Earnings before interest and taxes (EBIT)
- Sales, or
- Book value of assets

In practice, this means that valuation with multiples requires the use of several scaling factors or, in other words, several multiples. Often the best multiples for one industry may not be the preferred multiples in another industry. This implies, for example, that the practice of comparing P/E ratios of firms in different industries is problematic (and in many cases inappropriate altogether). This further implies that when the analyst performs a multiple-based valuation, it is important first to find what the industry considers as the best measure of relative values.

Although valuation by multiples differs from valuation by discounting cash flows, its application entails a similar procedure—first projecting performance, and then converting projected performance to values using market prices. This is done as follows:

- Project performance for the firm being valued, for example, by using pro forma financial statements (the analyst must forecast the future and this involves estimation risk or forecast error).
- Compute the average price per performance-measure dollar (i.e., the average multiple) by dividing observed prices of similar firms by the same performance measures projected.
- Convert the projected performance to values by multiplying each projected performance measure by the relevant average multiple.

Specifically, if the analyst believes that an appropriate forward-looking P/E (or any price/X ratio) for a target firm is 17 and expects earnings to be $3.00 per share in the next period, then an estimate of a fair market price based on RV assumptions is

Appropriate P/E ratio × Expected earnings = 17 × $3.00 = $51.00 per share

Steps in Relative Valuation

The steps in relative valuation are:

- Choose similar (comparable or like-kind) firms
- Choose bases for multiples
- Determine an appropriate multiple
- Project bases for the valued firm
- Value the firm

Choose Similar (Comparable or Like-Kind) Firms

Since prices of other firms are scaled to value the firm being analyzed, the analyst would like to use data of firms that are as similar as possible to the firm being valued. The flip side of this argument, however, is that by specifying too stringent criteria for similarity, the analyst ends up with too few firms to compare. With a small sample of comparable firms, the idiosyncrasies of individual firms affect the average multiples too much so that the average multiple is no longer a representative multiple. In selecting the sample of comparable firms, the analyst has to balance these two conflicting considerations. The idea is to obtain as large a sample as possible so that the idiosyncrasies of a single firm do not affect the valuation by much, yet not to choose so large a sample that the "comparable firms" are not comparable to the one being valued. Financial theory states that assets that are of equivalent risk should be priced the same, all else equal. The key idea here is that comparable firms are "assumed" to be of equivalent risk. Thus, the concept of being able to find comparable firms is the foundation for valuation by multiples. If there are no comparable firms, then valuation by multiples is not an option.

Choose Bases for Multiples

To convert market prices of comparable firms to a value for the firm being analyzed, an analyst has to scale the valued firm relative to the comparable firms. This is typically done by using several bases of comparison. Some generic measures of relative size often used in valuation by multiples are sales, gross profits, earnings, and book values. Often, however, industry-specific multiples are more suitable than generic multiples. Examples of industry-specific multiples are price per restaurant for fast-food chains, paid miles flown for airlines, and price per square foot of floor space for retailers. In general, the higher-up that the scaling basis is in the income statement, the less it is subject to the vagaries of accounting principles. Thus, sales is a scaling basis that is much less dependent on accounting methods than *earnings per share* (EPS). Depreciation or treatment of convertible securities critically affect EPS calculations but hardly affect sales. On the other hand, the higher-up that the scaling basis is in the income statement, the less it reflects differences in operating efficiency across firms—differences that critically affect the values of the comparable firms as well as the value of the firm being analyzed.

Determine an Appropriate Multiple

Once the analyst has a sample of firms that he is considering similar to the firm being valued, an average of the multiples provides a measure of what investors are willing to pay for comparable firms in order to estimate a "fair" price for the target firm. For example, after dividing each comparable firm's share price by its EPS to get individual P/E ratios, the analyst can average the P/E ratios of all comparable firms to estimate the earnings multiple that investors think is fair for firms with these characteristics. The same thing can be done for all the scaling bases chosen, calculating a "fair price" per dollar of sales, per restaurant, per square foot of retail space, per dollar of book value of equity, and so on.

Note that we put "fair price" in quotation marks: Since there is no market for either EPS or sales or any other scaling measure, the computation of average multiples is merely a scaling exercise and not an exercise in finding "how much the market is willing to pay for a dollar of earnings." Investors do not want to buy earnings; they only want cash flows (in the form of either dividends or capital gains). Earnings (or sales) are paid for only to the extent that they generate cash. In computing average ratios for various bases, we implicitly assume that the ability of firms to convert each basis (e.g., sales, book value, and earnings) to cash is the same. Keep in mind that this assumption is more tenable in some cases than in others and for some scaling factors than for others.

Realize that the term "average" is used here to mean the "appropriate" value that is determined by the average firm in the comparable group. It may not be the strict average. It may be a mean, median, or mode. The analyst is also free to throw out outliers that do not seem to conform to the majority of firms in the group. Outliers are most likely "outliers" because the markets has determined that they are different for any number of reasons.

Project Bases for the Valued Firm

The average "prices per (Selected base – X measure)" of comparable firms are applied to the projected performance of the firm being valued. Therefore, the analyst needs to project the same measures of the relative size used in scaling the prices of the comparable firms for the firm being valued. For example:

1. To value a firm, we use earnings as a scaling basis to determine the average earnings multiple (i.e., the average P/E ratio). Thus, the earnings of the firm being valued must be projected.
2. To use the average "price per restaurant" to value a fast-food chain, the number of restaurants the chain will have must be projected. Realize the assumption here is that each restaurant in all fast-food chains generates the same cash flow.
3. To use the average "price per dollar of book value" (the market to book or MB ratio), the book value of equity must be projected.

The simplest application of valuation with multiples is by projecting the scaling bases one year forward and applying the average multiple of comparable firms to these projections. For example, the comparable firms' average P/E ratio to the projected next year's earnings of the firm being valued is applied. Clearly, by applying the average multiple to the next year's projections, an analyst overemphasizes the immediate prospects of the firm and gives no weight to more distant prospects.

To overcome this weakness of the one-step-ahead projections, a more sophisticated approach can be used, that is, apply the average multiples to "representative" projections—projections that better represent the long-term prospects of the firm. For example, instead of applying the average P/E ratio to next year's earnings, the comparable P/E ratio to the projected average EPS over the next five years can be projected. In this way, the representative earnings' projections can also capture some of the long-term prospects of the firm, while next year's figures (with their idiosyncrasies) do not dominate valuations.

Value the Firm

In the final step, an analyst combines the average multiples of comparable firms to the projected parameters of the target firm (the firm to be valued) in order to obtain an estimated value. On the face of it, this is merely a simple technical step. Yet often it is not. The values that we obtain from various multiples (i.e., by using several scaling bases) are typically not the same; in fact, frequently they are quite different. This means that this step requires some analysis of its own—explaining why valuation by the average P/E ratio yields a lower value than the valuation by the sales multiple (e.g., the valued firm has higher than normal selling, general, and administrative expenses) or why the MB ratio yields a relatively low value. The combination of several values into a final estimate of value, therefore, requires an economic analysis of both "appropriate" multiples and how multiple-based values should be adjusted to yield values that are economically reasonable.

DCF VS. RV METHODS

We conclude this chapter by looking at when the DCF works best and when the RV method works best.

When DCF Valuation Works Best

Hopefully, it is somewhat intuitive at this point to realize that the DCF approach is easiest to use for assets (firms) whose cash flows are currently positive and can be estimated with some reliability for future periods, and where a proxy for risk that can be used to obtain discount rates is available.

DCF works best for analysts who either have a long time horizon, allowing the market time to correct its valuation mistakes and for price to revert to "true" value, or are capable of providing the catalyst needed to move price to value, as would be the case if one was an activist investor or a potential acquirer of the whole firm.

As will be explained in Chapter 20, U.S. Treasury securities can be priced so easily, relative to common stocks, using present value methods because their future cash flow streams and discount rates (at any point in time) are known with more certainty. This is why it is very important to perform sensitivity analysis on valuation estimates. Realize that a "single value" estimates for the "price/X" ratios (P/E, P/Sales, P/BV, etc.) to use in relative valuation and for the growth rate and discount rate used in discounted cash flow valuation are just "estimates." Do not just use dividend discount models for stock valuation without considering other models and how the model inputs can differ. Does an analyst really believe the estimates are that accurate and that the assumptions of any model hold perfectly for the firms analyzed?

When Relative Valuation Works Best

Relative valuation estimates the value of an asset by looking at the pricing of "comparable" assets relative to a common variable like earnings, cash flows, book value or sales. Remember, RV assumes that the value of any asset can be estimated by looking at how the market prices "similar" or 'comparable" assets, that comparable firms are "exactly" like the firm being valued (same industry, same products, same management ability, same risks, etc.), and that all comparable firms are selling at a "fair price."

Think about this. All firms cannot be valued based on the RV approach. There must be "fair price" benchmark firms. This is why RV is a useful tool for new firms; that is, firms without a cash flow history on which to base future cash flow expectations.

In essence, RV is a method for estimating a firm's current fair value per share relative to other like-kind firms by assuming that the "price per share/X" ratios for the like-kind firms are the same as for the target firm. Relative valuation is much more likely to reflect market perceptions and moods than discounted cash flow valuation. This can be an advantage when it is important that the price reflect these perceptions as is the case when the objective is to sell a security at that price today (as in the case of an initial public offering) and investing on momentum-based strategies explained in Chapter 7.

With relative valuation, there will always be a significant proportion of securities that are undervalued and overvalued. Since portfolio managers are judged based upon how they perform on a relative basis (to the market and other portfolio managers), relative valuation is more tailored to their needs. A popular belief is that relative valuation generally requires less information than discounted cash flow valuation (especially when multiples are used as screens). The reality is that the assumptions are just as strong as those used in DCF and are subject to just as much, if not more, estimation risk error.

A portfolio that is composed of stocks which are undervalued on a relative basis may still be overvalued, even if the judgments of analysts are right. It is just less overvalued than other securities in the market. Relative valuation is built on the assumption that markets are correct in the aggregate, but make mistakes on individual securities. To the degree that markets can be overvalued or undervalued in the aggregate, relative valuation will fail. Relative valuation may require less information in the way in which most analysts and portfolio managers use it. However, this is because implicit assumptions are made about other variables (that would have been required in a discounted cash flow valuation). To the extent that these implicit assumptions are wrong, the relative valuation will also be wrong.

The RV approach is easiest to use when there are a large number of comparable assets to the one being valued, these assets are priced in a market, and there exists some common variable that can be used to standardize the price.

The Need for Sensitivity Analysis in Both DCF and RV—"What If" and Simulation

It is very important to understand the assumptions involved with each type of valuation technique. Using all of the techniques on any one firm gets as many different value estimates as techniques. If an analyst performs "sensitivity analysis" (change the input variables), he will obtain another set of value estimates. Consider the stochastic DDM described earlier in this chapter. Given the development of easy to use computer software, Monte Carlo simulation is being used more and more today.

In the end, an analyst's worth comes from making a "value judgment" based on all of his work. If a computer program could make the best value estimate, an analyst would not be needed. When performing security valuation, always remember that no single valuation model can provide a precise or true estimate of value. All valuations are biased. The only questions are how much and in which direction. The payoff to valuation from the investor's viewpoint, however, is the greatest when the market's valuation is least precise.

Here is the moral of the story. In his own mind, an analyst should always be able to construct some sort of logical connection between today's stock price and a stream of expected future cash flow. The logical chain might be long: The analyst might assume years of startup losses will be followed by more years of all profits being reinvested. But the analyst should be able to envision some connection between today's stock prices and a stream of dividends that will commence someday in the future. The analyst does not actually have to do the calculations. But the analyst should feel comfortable that the numbers are such that if he wanted to take the time to do it as an interesting exercise, he could come up with some plausible set of assumptions that make the present-day price seem somewhere in the ballpark.

A portfolio manager who believes that there are market inefficiencies must decide, given her investment philosophy, time horizon, and beliefs about markets (that she will be investing in), which of the approaches to valuation obtained from a security analyst are appropriate:

- Discounted cash flow valuation (DDM or FCF Models)
- Relative valuation
- All available methods, both RV and DCF

One of the world's foremost investors is Warren Buffett, chairman of Berkshire Hathaway. At the firm's annual meeting, May 4, 2002, he told the more than 13,000 faithful attendees there is no sure-fire investing technique, no formula.

Rather, the only way to value a stock or a company, is to estimate what cash business will throw off over the course of its life, work out the value of that cash now, and buy it for less. A great IQ is not needed to do well, what is needed is the ability to detach yourself from the crowd.

SUMMARY

In this chapter, practical methods that can be used by a security analyst for valuing a firm's equity are explained. The two approaches are based on discounted cash flow models and relative valuation models.

The discounted cash flow approach to valuing common stock requires projecting future dividends. Hence, the model used to value common stock is called a dividend discount model. The simplest dividend discount model is the constant growth model. More complex models include the multi-stage phase model and stochastic models. Stock valuation using a dividend discount model is highly dependent on the inputs used.

A dividend discount model does not indicate when the current market price will reach its fair value. The output of a dividend discount model is the fair price. However, the model can be used to generate the expected return. The expected return is the interest rate that will make the present value of the expected dividends plus terminal price equal to the stock's market price. The expected return is then compared to the required return to assess whether a stock is fairly priced in the market.

It cannot be overemphasized that there are uncertainties (estimation risks or forecast errors) always present in discounted cash flow models, as well as relative valuation models. The basic sources of estimation risk when using DCF models in calculating the value of any financial asset is that the present value depends on expected future cash flows and the appropriate discount rates that reflect the risk of the future cash flows. Cash flow valuation models, therefore, rely on assumptions (often extreme). With cash flow valuation, the main problem is "estimation risk." No human being can correctly and consistently forecast the future.

Relative valuation is also subject to estimation risk. Valuation with multiples requires the use of several scaling factors or, in other words, several multiples. Often the best multiples for one industry may not be the preferred multiples in another industry. This implies, for example, that the practice of comparing P/E ratios of firms in different industries is problematic and in many cases inappropriate altogether. This further implies that when an analyst uses a multiple-based valuation, it is important first to find what the industry considers as the best measure of relative values.

REFERENCES

Campbell, John Y., and Robert J. Shiller. 1998. Valuation ratios and the long-run stock market outlook. *Journal of Portfolio Management* 24, no. 2: 11–26.

Fogler, Russell H. 1988. Security analysis, DDMs, and probability. In *Equity markets and valuation methods* (pp. 51–52). Charlottesville, VA: Institute of Chartered Financial Analysts.

Gordon, Myron, and Eli Shapiro. 1956. Capital equipment analysis: The required rate of profit. *Management Science* 3, no. 1 (October): 102–110.

Hurley, William J., and Lewis Johnson. 1994. A realistic dividend valuation model. *Financial Analysts Journal* 50 (July–August): 50–54.

Hurley, William J., and Lewis Johnson. 1998a. Generalized Markov dividend discount models. *Journal of Portfolio Management* 25 (Fall): 27–31.

Hurley, William J., and Lewis Johnson. 1998b. *The theory and application of stochastic dividend models.* Monograph 7, Clarica Financial Services Research Centre, School of Business and Economics, Wilfrid Laurier University.

Molodovsky, Nicholas, Catherine May, and Sherman Chattiner. 1965. Common stock valuation: Principles, tables, and applications. *Financial Analysts Journal* 21 (November–December): 111–117.

Sorensen, Eric, and David Williamson. 1985. Some evidence on the value of dividend discount models. *Financial Analysts Journal* 41 (November–December): 60–69.

Williams, John B. 1938. *The theory of investment value.* Cambridge, MA: Harvard University Press.

Yao, Y. 1997. A trinomial dividend valuation model. *Journal of Portfolio Management* 21 (Summer): 99–103.

CHAPTER 10
Forecasting Stock Returns

As explained in Chapter 1, one of the key tasks in seeking to generate attractive returns is producing realistic and reasonable return expectations and forecasts. In the Markowitz mean-variance framework, an investor's objective is to choose a portfolio of securities that has the largest expected return for a given level of risk (as measured by the portfolio's variance). In the case of common stock, by return (or expected return) of a stock, we mean the change (or expected change) in the stock price over the period, plus any dividends paid, divided by the starting price. Of course, since we do not know the true values of the securities' expected returns and covariances, these must be estimated or forecasted. In our description of common stock strategies in Chapter 7, we described strategies that assume that it is reasonable to expect that stock prices and returns can be forecasted so as to generate excess risk-adjusted returns. However, we also described the efficient market theory that takes quite a different view about the ability to forecast stock prices and returns

In contrast to forecasting events such as the weather, forecasting stock prices and returns is difficult to predict because the predictions themselves will produce market movements that in turn provoke immediate changes in prices, thereby invalidating the predictions themselves. This leads to the concept of market efficiency: An efficient market is a market where all new information about the future behavior of prices is immediately impounded in the prices themselves and therefore exploits all information.

Actually the debate about the predictability of stock prices and returns has a long history.[1] More than 75 years ago, Cowles (1933) asked the question: "Can stock market forecasters forecast?" Armed with the state-of-the-art econometric tools at the time, Cowles analyzed the recommendations of stock market forecasters and concluded, "It is doubtful." Subsequent academic studies support Cowles' conclusion. However, the history goes fur-

---

[1] See Bernstein (2008).

This chapter is coauthored with Sergio Focardi and Petter N. Kolm.

ther back. In 1900, a French mathematician, Louis Bachelier, in his doctoral dissertation in mathematical statistics entitled *Théorie de la Spéculation* (*The Theory of Speculation*), showed using mathematical techniques why the stock market behaves as it does.[2] He also provided empirical evidence based on the French capital markets at the turn of the century. He wrote:

> Past, present, and even discounted future events are reflected in market price, but often show no apparent relation to price changes.... [A]rtificial causes also intervene: the Exchange reacts on itself, and the current fluctuation is a function, not only of the previous fluctuations, but also of the current state. The determination of these fluctuations depends on an infinite number of factors; it is, therefore, impossible to aspire to mathematical predictions of it.... [T]he dynamics of the Exchange will never be an exact science. (Bachelier, 1900).

In other words, according to Bachelier, stock price movements are difficult to forecast and even explain after the fact.

Despite this conclusion, the adoption of modeling techniques by asset management firms has greatly increased since the turn of the century. Models to predict expected returns are routinely used at asset management firms. In most cases, it is a question of relatively simple models based on factors or predictor variables. However, more statistical or econometric-oriented models are also being experimented with and adopted by some asset management firms, as well as what are referred to as *nonlinear models* based on specialized areas of statistics such as neural networks and genetic algorithms are being tried.

Historical data are often used for forecasting future returns as well as estimating risk. For example, a portfolio manager might proceed in the following way: observing weekly or monthly returns, the portfolio manager might use the past five years of historical data to estimate the expected return and the covariances by the sample mean and sample covariances. The portfolio manager would then use these as inputs for mean-variance optimization, along with any ad hoc adjustments to reflect any views about expected returns on future performance. Unfortunately this historical approach most often leads to counterintuitive, unstable, or merely "wrong" portfolios generated by the mean-variance optimization model. Better forecasts are nec-

---

[2] A detailed description of the contributions of Bachelier are too exhaustive (and technical) to describe here. In addition to his study of the behavior of prices, his work in the area of random walks predated Albert Einstein's study of Brownian motion in physics by five years. His work in option pricing theory predated the well-known Black-Scholes option pricing model that we describe in Chapter 15 by 73 years.

essary. Statistical estimates can be very noisy and typically depend on the quality of the data and the particular statistical techniques used to estimate the inputs. In general, it is desirable that an estimator of expected return and risk have the following properties:

- It provides a forward-looking forecast with some predictive power, not just a backward-looking historical summary of past performance.
- The estimate can be produced at a reasonable computational cost.
- The technique used does not amplify errors already present in the inputs used in the process of estimation.
- The forecast should be intuitive, that is, the portfolio manager should be able to explain and justify them in a comprehensible manner.

In this chapter, we look at the issue of whether forecasting stock returns can be done so as to generate trading profits and excess returns. Unfortunately, the issue about predictability of stock returns or prices cannot be discussed without some understanding of statistical concepts that are typically not covered in most introductory statistics books. Consequently, we will provide a brief description of the relevant concepts in probability theory and statistics. We then discuss the different types of predictive return models that are used by portfolio managers.

THE CONCEPT OF PREDICTABILITY

To predict (or forecast) involves forming an expectation of a future event or future events. Since ancient times it has been understood that the notion of predicting the future is subject to potential inconsistencies. Consider what might happen if one receives a highly reliable prediction that tomorrow one will have a car accident driving to work. This might alter one's behavior such that a decision is made not to go to work. Hence, one's behavior will be influenced by the prediction, thus potentially invalidating the prediction. It is because of inconsistencies of this type that two economists in the mid 1960s, Paul Samuelson and Eugene Fama, arrived at the apparently paradoxical conclusion that "properly anticipated prices fluctuate randomly."[3]

The concept of forecastability rests on how one can forecast the future given the current state of knowledge. In probability theory, the state of knowledge on a given date is referred to as the *information set* known at that date. Forecasting is the relationship between the information set today and future events. By altering the information set, the forecast changes. However, the relationship between the information set and the future is fixed and

---
[3] See Samuelson (1965) and Fama (1965).

immutable. Academicians and market practitioners adopt in finance theories this concept of forecastability. Prices or returns are said to be forecastable if the knowledge of the past influences our forecast of the future. For example, if the future returns of a firm's stock depend on the value of key financial ratios, such as those described in Chapter 8 that can be computed from a firm's financial statements, then those returns are predictable. If the future returns of that stock do not depend on any variable known today, then returns are unpredictable.

As explained in the introduction to this chapter, the merits of stock return forecasting is an ongoing debate. There are two beliefs that seem to be held in the investment community. First, predictable processes allow investors to earn excess returns. Second, unpredictable processes do not allow investors to earn excess returns. Neither belief is necessarily true. Understanding why will shed some light on the crucial issues in the debate regarding return modeling. The reasons can be summed up as follows. First, predictable processes do not necessarily produce excess returns if they are associated with unfavorable risk. Second, unpredictable expectations can be profitable if the expected value is favorable.

Because most of our knowledge is uncertain, our forecasts are also uncertain. Probability theory provides the conceptual tools to represent and measure the level of uncertainty.[4] Probability theory assigns a number—referred to as the "probability"—to every possible event. This number, the probability, might be interpreted in one of two ways. The first is that a probability is the "intensity of belief" that an event will occur, where a probability of 1 means certainty.[5] The second interpretation is the one normally used in statistics: Probability is the percentage of times (i.e., frequency) that a particular event is observed in a large number of observations (or trials).[6] This interpretation of probability is the *frequentist interpretation*, also referred to as the *relative frequency concept of probability*. Although it is this interpretation that is used in finance and the one adopted in this book, there are attempts to apply the subjective interpretation to financial decision making using of an approach called the *Bayesian approach*.[7]

With this background, let's consider again the returns of some stock. Suppose that returns are unpredictable in the sense that future returns do not depend on the current information set. This does not mean that future returns are completely uncertain in the same sense in which the outcome of

---

[4] See Bernstein (1998) for an account of the development of the concepts of risk and uncertainty from the beginning of civilization to modern risk management.
[5] The idea of probability as intensity of belief was introduced by Keynes (1921).
[6] The idea of probability as a relative frequency was introduced by von Mises (1921).
[7] See Rachev et al. (2007).

throwing a die is uncertain. Clearly, we cannot believe that every possible return on the stock is equally likely: There are upper and lower bounds for real returns in an economy. More important, if we collect a series of historical returns for a stock, a distribution of returns would be observed.

It is therefore reasonable to assume that our uncertainty is embodied in a probability distribution of returns. The absence of predictability means that the distribution of future returns does not change as a function of the current information set. More specifically, the distribution of future returns does not change as a function of the present and past values of prices and returns. This entails that the distribution of returns does not change with time. We can therefore state that (1) a price or return process is predictable if its probability distributions depends on the current information set and (2) a price or return process is unpredictable if its probability distributions are time-invariant.

Given the concept of predictability as we have just defined it, we can now discuss why prices and returns are difficult (or perhaps impossible) to predict. The key is that any prediction that might lead to an opportunity to generate a trading profit or an excess return tends to make that opportunity disappear. For example, suppose that the price of a stock is predicted to increase significantly in the next five trading days. A large price increase is a source of trading profit or excess return. As a consequence, if that prediction is widely shared by the investment community, investors will rush to purchase that stock. But the demand thus induced will make the stock's price rise immediately, thus eliminating the source of trading profit or excess return and invalidating the forecast.

Suppose that the predictions of stock returns were certain rather than uncertain. By a certain prediction it is meant a prediction that leaves no doubt about what will happen. For example, as explained in Chapter 17, U.S. Treasury zero-coupon securities if held to maturity offer a known or certain prediction of returns because the maturity value is guaranteed by the full faith and credit of the U.S. government. Any forecast that leaves open the possibility that market forces will alter the forecast cannot be considered a certain forecast. If stock return predictions are certain, then simple arbitrage arguments would dictate that all stocks should have the same return. In fact, if stock returns could be predicted with certainty and if there were different returns, then investors would choose only those stocks with the highest returns.

Stock return forecasts are not certain; as we have seen, uncertain predictions are embodied in probability distributions. Suppose that we have a joint probability distribution of the returns of the universe of investable stocks. Investors will decide the rebalancing of their portfolios depending on their probabilistic predictions and their risk-return preferences. The problem we are discussing here is whether general considerations of market efficiency are able to determine the mathematical form of price or return processes. In particular, we are interested in understanding if stock prices or returns are necessarily unpredictable.

The problem discussed in the literature is expressed roughly as follows. Suppose that returns are a series of random variables. These series will be fully characterized by the joint distributions of returns at any given time t and at any given set of different times. Suppose that investors know these distributions and that they select their portfolios according to specific rules that depend on these distributions. Can we determine the form of admissible processes, that is, of admissible distributions?

Ultimately, the objective in solving this problem is to avoid models that allow unreasonable inferences. Historically, three solutions have been proposed:

1. Returns fluctuate randomly around a given mean.
2. Returns are a fair game.
3. Returns are a fair game after adjusting for risk.

In statistical terminology, returns fluctuating randomly around a given mean refers to returns following *multivariate random walks*. By a fair game it meant that returns are *martingales*. These concepts and their differences will be explained below. The first two proposed solutions are incorrect; the third is too general to be useful for asset management. Before we discuss the above models of prices, we digress to briefly explain some statistical concepts.

Statistical Concepts of Predictability and Unpredictability

Because we have stressed how we must we rely on probability to understand the concepts of predictability and unpredictability, we will first explain the concepts of conditional probability, conditional expectation, independent and identically distributed random variables, strict white noise, martingale difference sequence, and white noise. In addition, we have to understand the concept of an error term and an innovation.

Conditional probability and conditional expectation are fundamental in the probabilistic description of financial markets. In Chapter 4, we explained what is meant by a probability distribution for a random variable. A *conditional probability* of some random variable X is the probability for X given a particular value for another random variable Y is known. Similarly, a *conditional probability distribution* can be determined. For the conditional probability distribution, an expected value can be computed and is referred to as a *conditional expected value* or *conditional mean* or, more commonly, a *conditional expectation.*

The statistical concept *independent and identically distributed variables* (denoted by IID variables) means two conditions about probability distributions for random variables. First consider "independent." This means if we have a time series for some random variable, then at each time the random variable has a probability distribution. By independently distributed, it is meant that the probability distributions remain the same regardless of the history of past values for the random variable. "Identically" distributed means that all returns have the same distribution in every time period. These two conditions entail that, over time, the mean and the variance do not change from period to period. In the parlance of the statistician, we have a *stationary time-series process.*

A *strict white noise* is a sequence of IID variables that have a mean equal to zero and a finite variance. Hence, a strict white noise is unpredictable in the sense that the conditional probability distribution of the random variables is fixed and independent from the past. Because a strict white noise is unpredictable, expectations and higher moments are unpredictable. In Chapter 4, we explained that the moments are measures to summarize the probability distribution. The first four moments are expected value or mean (location), variance (dispersion), skewness (asymmetry), and kurtosis (concentration in the tails). The higher moments of a probability distribution are those beyond the mean and variance, that is skewness and kurtosis.

A *martingale difference sequence* is a sequence of random variables that have a mean of zero that are uncorrelated such that their conditional expectations given the past values of the series is always zero. Because expectations and conditional expectations are both zero, in a martingale difference sequence, expectations are unpredictable. However, if higher moments exist, they might be predictable.

A *white noise* is a sequence of uncorrelated random variables with a mean of zero and a finite variance. Since the random variables are uncorrelated, in a white noise expectations are linearly unpredictable. Higher moments, if they exist, might be predictable. The key here is that they are unpredictable using a linear model. However, they may be predicted as nonlinear functions of past values. It is for this reason that certain statistical techniques that involve nonlinear functions such as neutral networks have been used by some quantitative asset management firms to try to predict expectations.

Random Walks and Martingales

In Chapter 4, we discussed the normal distribution of a random variable. In the special case where the random variables are normally distributed, it can be proven that strict white noise, martingale difference sequence, and white noise coincide. In fact, two uncorrelated, normally distributed random variables are also independent.

We can now define what is mean by an arithmetic random walk, a martingale, and a strict arithmetic random walk that are used to describe the stochastic process for returns and prices as follows:

- An *arithmetic random walk* is the sum of white-noise terms. The mean of an arithmetic random walk is linearly unpredictable but might be predictable with nonlinear predictors. Higher moments might be predictable.
- A *martingale* is the sum of martingale difference sequence terms. The mean of a martingale is unpredictable (linearly and nonlinearly); that is, the expectation of a martingale coincides with its present value. Higher moments might be predictable.
- A *strict random walk* is the sum of strict white-noise terms. A strict random walk is unpredictable: Its mean, variance, and higher moments are all unpredictable.

Error Terms and Innovations

Any statistical process can be broken down into a predictable and an unpredictable component. The first component is that which can be predicted from the past values of the process. The second component is that which cannot be predicted. The component that cannot be predicted is called the *innovation process*. Innovation is not specifically related to a model, it is a characteristic of the process. Innovations are therefore unpredictable processes.

Now consider a model that is supposed to explain empirical data such as predicting future returns or prices. For a given observation, the difference between the value predicted by the model and the observation is called the *residual*. In econometrics, the residual is referred to as an *error term* or, simply, *error* of the model. It is not necessarily true that errors are innovations; that is, it is not necessarily true that errors are unpredictable. If errors are innovations, then the model offers the best possible explanation of data. If not, errors contain residual forecastability. The previous discussion is relevant because it makes a difference if errors are strict white noise, martingale difference sequences, or simply white noise.

More specifically, a random walk whose changes (referred to as *increments*) are nonnormal white noise contains a residual structure not explained by the model both at the level of expectations and higher moments. If data follow a martingale model, then expectations are completely explained by the model but higher moments are not.

The Importance of the Statistical Concepts

We have covered a good number of complex statistical concepts. What's more, many of these statistical concepts are not discussed in basic statistics courses offered in business schools. So, why are these apparently arcane statistical considerations of practical significance to investors? The reason is that the properties of models that are used in attempting to forecast returns and prices depend on the assumptions made about "noise" in the data. For example, a linear model makes linear predictions of expectations and cannot capture nonlinear events such as the clustering of volatility that we noted in Chapter 4 have been observed in real-world stock markets. It is therefore natural to assume that errors are white noise. In other models attempting to forecast returns and prices, however, different assumptions about noise need to be made; otherwise the properties of the model conflict with the properties of the noise term.

Now, the above considerations have important practical consequences when testing error terms to examine how well the models that will be described later in this chapter perform. When testing a model, one has to make sure that the residuals have the properties that we assume they have. Thus, if we use a linear model, say a linear regression, we will have to make sure that residuals from time-series data are white noise; that is, that the residuals are uncorrelated over time. The correlation between the residuals from a model based on time-series data is referred to as *autocorrelation*. In a linear regression using time-series data, the presence of autocorrelation violates the ordinary least squares assumption when estimating the parameters of the statistical model.[8] In general, it will suffice to add lags to the set of predictor variables to remove the existence of autocorrelation of the residuals.[9] However, if we have to check that residuals are martingale difference sequences or strict white noise, we will have to use more powerful tests. In addition, adding lags will not be sufficient to remove undesired properties of

---

[8]More specifically, the presence of autocorrelation does not bias the estimated parameters of the model but results in biases in the standard errors of the estimated parameters which are used in testing the goodness of fit of the model.

[9]Statements like this are intended as exemplifications but do not strictly embody sound econometric procedures. Adding lags has side effects, such as making estimations noisier, and cannot be used indiscriminately.

residuals. Models will have to be redesigned. These effects are not marginal: They can have a significant impact on the profitability and performance of investment strategies.

A CLOSER LOOK AT PRICING MODELS

Armed with these concepts from statistics, let's now return to a discussion of pricing models. The first hypothesis on equity price processes that was advanced as a solution to the problem of forecastability was the *random walk hypothesis*. The strongest formulation assumes that returns are a sequence of IID variables, that is, a strict random walk. This means that, over time, the mean and the variance do not change from period to period. If returns are IID variables, it can be shown that the logarithms of prices follow a random walk and the prices themselves follow what is called a *geometric random walk*. The IID model is clearly a model without forecastability as the distribution of future returns does not depend on any information set known at the present moment. It does however allow stock prices to have a *fixed drift*.

There is a weaker form of the random walk hypothesis that only requires that returns at any two different times be uncorrelated. According to this weaker definition, returns are a sequence formed by a constant drift plus white noise. If returns are a white noise, however, they are not unpredictable. In fact, a white noise, although uncorrelated at every lag, might be predictable in the sense that its expectation might depend on the present information set.

At one time, it was believed that if one assumes investors make perfect forecasts, then the strict random walk model was the only possible model. However, this conclusion was later demonstrated to be incorrect by LeRoy (1973). He showed that the class of admissible models is actually much broader. That is, the strict random walk model is too restricted to be the only possible model and proposed the use of the martingale model (i.e., the fair game model) that we explain next.

The idea of a martingale has a long history in gambling. Actually the word "martingale" originally meant a gambling strategy in which the gambler continually doubles his or her bets. In modern statistics, a martingale embodies the idea of a fair game where, at every bet, the gambler has exactly the same probability of winning or losing. In fact, as explained earlier in this chapter, the martingale is a process where the expected value of the process at any future date is the actual value of the process. If a price process or a game is represented by a martingale, then the expectation of gains or losses is zero. As from our discussion, a random walk with uncorrelated increments is not necessarily a martingale as its expectations are only linearly unpredictable.

Technically, the martingale model applies to the logarithms of prices. Returns are the differences of the logarithms of prices. The martingale model requires that the expected value of returns is not predictable because it is zero or a fixed constant. However, there can be subtle patterns of forecastability for higher moments of the return distribution. Higher moments, to repeat, are those moments of a probability distribution beyond the expected value (mean) and variance, for example, skewness and kurtosis. In other words, the distribution of returns can depend on the present information set provided that the expected value of the distribution remains constant.

The martingale model does not fully take into consideration risk premiums because it allows higher moments of returns to vary while expected values remain constant. It cannot be a general solution to the problem of what processes are compatible with the assumptions that investors can make perfect probabilistic forecasts.

The definitive answer is due to Harrison and Kreps (1979) and Harrison and Pliska (1981, 1985). They demonstrated that stock prices must indeed be martingales but after multiplication for a factor that takes into account risk. The conclusion of their work (which involves a very complicated mathematical model), however, is that a broad variety of predictable processes are compatible with the assumption that the market is populated by market agents capable of making perfect forecasts. Predictability is due to the interplay of risk and return.

However, it is precisely due to the market being populated by market agents capable of making perfect forecasts, it is not necessarily true that successful predictions will lead to excess returns. For example, it is generally accepted that predicting volatility is easier than predicting returns. The usual explanation of this fact is that investors and portfolio managers are more interested in returns than in volatility. With the maturing of the quantitative methods employed by asset managers coupled with the increased emphasis placed on risk-return, risk and returns have become equally important. However, this does not entail that both risk and returns have become unpredictable. It is now admitted that it is possible to predict combinations of the two.

PREDICTIVE RETURN MODELS

Equity portfolio managers have used various statistical models for forecasting returns and risk. These models, referred to as *predictive return models*, make conditional forecasts of expected returns using the current information set. That information set could include past prices, company information, and financial market information such as economic growth or the level of interest rates.

Most predictive return models employed in practice are statistical models. More specifically, they use tools from the field of econometrics. We will provide a nontechnical review of econometric-based predictive return models below.

Predictive return models can be classified into four general types:[10]

1. *Regressive model.* This model involves the use of regression analysis where the variables used to predict returns (also referred to as *predictors* or *explanatory variables*) are the factors that are believed to impact returns.
2. *Linear autoregressive model.* In this model, the variables used to predict returns are the lagged returns (i.e., past returns).
3. *Dynamic factor model.* Models of this type use a mix of prices and returns.
4. *Hidden-variable model.* This type of model seeks to capture regime change.

Although these models use traditional econometric techniques, and are the most commonly used in practice, in recent years other models based on the specialized area of *machine learning* have been proposed. The machine-learning approach in forecasting returns involves finding a model without any theoretical assumptions. This is done through a process of what is referred to as *progressive adaptation*. Machine-learning approaches, rooted in the fields of statistics and *artificial intelligence* (AI), include neural networks, decision trees, clustering, genetic algorithms, support vector machines, and text mining.[11] We will not describe machine-learning based predictive return models in this book. However, in the 1990s, there were many exaggerated claims and hype about their potential value for forecasting stock returns that could completely revolutionize portfolio management. Consequently, they received considerable attention by the investment community and the media. It seems these claims never panned out.[12]

---

[10] Fabozzi, Focardi, and Kolm (2006a, 66).
[11] For a non-technical discussion of these models, see Chapter 6 in Fabozzi, Focardi, and Kolm (2006a). For a more technical discussion see Fabozzi, Focardi, and Kolm (2006b).
[12] For discussion of the merits and limits of AI from a practical perspective, see Leinweber and Beinart (1996).

As a prerequisite for the adoption of a predictive return model, there are a number of key questions that a portfolio manager must address. These include:[13]

- What are the statistical properties of the model?
- How many predictor (explanatory) variables should be used in the model?
- What is the best statistical approach to estimate the model and is commercial software available for the task?
- How does one statistically test whether the model is valid?
- How can the consequences of errors in the choice of a model be mitigated?

The first and last questions rely on the statistical concepts that we described earlier. These questions are addressed in more technical-oriented equity investment management books.[14] Consequently, we will limit our discussion in this chapter to only the first question, describing the statistical properties of the four types of predictive return models. That is, we describe the fundamental statistical concepts behind these models and their economic meaning, but we omit the mathematical details.

Regressive Models

Regressive models of returns are generally based on linear regressions on *factors*. Factors are also referred to as *predictors*. Linear regression models are used in several aspects of portfolio management beyond that of return forecasting. For example, an equity analyst may use such models to forecast future sales of a company being analyzed.

Regressive models can be categorized as one of two fundamental kinds. The first is *static regressive models*. These models do not make predictions about the future but regress present returns on present factors. The second type is *predictive regressive models*. In such models future returns are regressed on present and past factors to make predictions. For both types of models, the statistical concepts and principles are the same. What differs is the economic meaning of each type of model.

Static Regressive Models

Static regressive models for predicting returns should be viewed as timeless relationships that are valid at any moment. They are not useful for predictive purposes because there is no time lag between the return and the factor.

---
[13]Fabozzi, Focardi, and Kolm (2006a, 66).
[14]See, for example, Fabozzi, Focardi, and Kolm (2006b).

For example, consider the empirical analogue of the CAPM as represented by the characteristic line given by the regression model of equation (5.9) of Chapter 5, which is reproduced below dropping the subscript i to denote stock i:

$$r_t - r_{ft} = \alpha_i + \beta_i[r_{Mt} - r_{ft}] + e_{it} \qquad (10.1)$$

where

r_t = return on the stock in month t
r_{ft} = the risk-free rate in month t
r_{Mt} = the return on the market index (say S&P 500) in month t
e_t = the error term for the stock in month t
α and β = parameters for the stock to be estimated by the regression model
t = month ($t = 1, 2, \ldots, T$)

The above model says that the conditional expectation of a stock's return at time t is proportional to the excess return of the market index at time t. This means that to predict the stock return at time $T + 1$, the portfolio manager must know the excess return of the market index at time $T + 1$, which is, of course, unknown at time $T + 1$. Predictions would be possible only if a portfolio manager could predict the excess return of the market index at time $T + 1$ (i.e., $r_{MT+1} - r_{fT+1}$).

There are also static multifactor models of return where the return at time t is based on the factor returns at time t. For example, suppose that there are N factors. Letting F_{nt} ($n = 1, 2, \ldots, N; t = 1, 2, \ldots, T$), then a regression model for a multifactor model for stock i (again dropping the subscript i for stock i) would be

$$r_t - r_{ft} = \alpha + \beta_{F1}[r_{F1,t} - r_{ft}] + \beta_{F2}[r_{F2,t} - r_{ft}] + \ldots + \beta_{FN}[r_{FN,,t} - r_{ft}] + e_t \qquad (10.2)$$

where

r_t = return on the stock in month t
r_{ft} = the risk-free rate in month t
$r_{FN,t}$ = the return on factor N in month t
e_t = the error term for the stock in month t
α and β_{FN}'s = parameters for the stock to be estimated by the regression model
t = month ($t = 1, 2, \ldots, T$)

Thus, in order for a portfolio manager to build a portfolio or to compute portfolio risk measures using the above multifactor model for month $T + 1$, just as in the case of the characteristic line, some assumption about how to forecast the excess returns (i.e., $r_{FN,T+1} - r_{f,T+1}$) for each factor is required.

Predictive Regressive Models

In the search for models to predict returns, predictive regressive models have been developed. To explain predictive regressive models, consider some stock return and an assumed number of predictors. These predicators could be financial measures and market measures. A predictive linear regressive model assumes that the stock return at any given time t is a weighted average of its predictors at an earlier time plus a constant and some error. Hence, the information needed for predicting a stock's return does not require the forecasting of the predictor used in the regression model.

Predictive regressive models can also be defined by estimating a regression model where there are factors used as predictors at different lags. Such models, referred to as *distributed lag models,* have the advantage that they can capture the eventual dependence of returns not only on factors but also on the rate of change of factors. Here is the economic significance of such models. Suppose that a portfolio manager wants to create a predictive model based on, among other factors, "market sentiment." In practice, market sentiment is typically measured as a weighted average of analysts' forecasts. A reasonable assumption is that stock returns will be sensitive to the value of market sentiment but will be even more sensitive to changes in market sentiment. Hence, distributed lag models will be useful in this setting.

Linear Autoregressive Models

In a linear autoregressive model, a variable is regressed on its own past values. Past values are referred to as *lagged values* and when they are used as predictors in the model they are referred to as *lagged variables*. In the case of predictive return models, one of the lagged variables would be the past values of the return of the stock. If the model involves only the lagged variable of the stock return, it is called an *autoregressive model* (AR model). An AR model prescribes that the value of a variable at time t be a weighted average of the values of the same variable at times $t - 1, t - 2, \ldots$, and so on (depending on number of lags) plus an error term. The weighting coefficients are the model parameters that must be estimated. If the model includes p lags, then p parameters must be estimated.

If there are other lagged variables in addition to the lagged variable representing the past values of the return on the stock included in the regression model, the model is referred to as a *vector autoregressive model* (VAR model). The model expresses each variable as a weighted average of its own lagged values plus the lagged values of the other variables. A VAR model with p lags is denoted by VAR(p) model. The benefit of a VAR model is that it can capture cross-autocorrelations; that is, a VAR model can model how values of a variable at time t are linked to the values of another variable at some other time. An important question is whether these links are causal or simply correlations.[15]

For a model to be useful, the number of parameters to be estimated needs to be small. In practice, the implementation of a VAR is complicated by the fact that such models can only deal with a small number of series. This is because when there is a large number of series—for example, the return processes for the individual stocks making up such aggregates as the S&P 500 Index—this would require a large number of parameters to be estimated. For example, if one wanted to model the daily returns of the S&P 500 with a VAR model that included two lags, the number of parameters to estimate would be 500,000. To have at least as many data points as parameters, one would need at least four years of data, or 1,000 trading days, for each stock return process, which is $1,000 \times 500 = 500,000$ data points. Under these conditions, estimates would be extremely noisy and the estimated model would be meaningless.

Dynamic Factor Models

Unlike a VAR model which involves regressing returns on factors but does not model the factors, a dynamic factor model assumes factors follow a VAR model and returns (or prices) are regressed on these factors. The advantage of such models is that unlike the large amount of data needed to estimate the large number of parameters in a VAR model, a dynamic factor model can significantly reduce the number of parameters to be estimated and therefore the amount of data needed.

Hidden-Variable Models

Hidden-variable models attempt to represent states of the market using hidden variables. Probably the best known hidden-variable model is the *autoregressive conditional heteroscedasticity* (ARCH) and *generalized autoregressive conditional heteroscedasticity* (GARCH) family. ARCH/GARCH models use an autoregressive process to model the volatility of another process. The result is a rich representation of the behavior of the model volatility.

---

[15] For a discussion of the analysis of causality in VAR models, see Fabozzi, Focardi, and Kolm (2006b).

Another category of hidden-variable models is the *Markov switching–vector autoregressive* (MS–VAR) family. These models do allow forecasting of expected returns. The simplest MS–VAR model is the Hamilton model.[16] In economics, this model is based on two random walk models—one with a drift for periods of economic expansion and the other with a smaller drift for periods of economic recession. The switch between the two models is governed by a probability transition table that prescribes the probability of switching from recession to expansion, and vice versa, and the probability of remaining in the same state.

IS FORECASTING MARKETS WORTH THE EFFORT?

In the end, all of this discussion leads to the question: What are the implications for portfolio managers and investors who are attempting or contemplating attempting building predictive return models? That is, how does this help portfolio managers and investors to decide if there is potentially sufficient benefit (i.e., trading profits and/or excess returns) in trying to extract information from market price data through quantitative modeling? There are three important points regarding this potential benefit.

The first, as stated by Fabozzi, Focardi, and Kolm (2006a, 11), is the following:

> It is not true that progress in our ability to forecast will necessarily lead to a simplification in price and return processes. Even if investors were to become perfect forecasters, price and return processes might still exhibit complex patterns of forecastability in both expected values and higher moments, insofar as they might be martingales after dynamically adjusting for risk. No simple conclusion can be reached simply by assuming that investors are perfect forecasters: in fact, it is not true that the ability to forecast prices implies that prices are unpredictable random walks.

It is noteworthy that when the random walk hypothesis was first proposed in the academic community, it was the belief that the task of price forecasting efforts was a worthless exercise because prices were random walks. However, it seems reasonable to conclude that price processes will always be structured processes simply because investors are trying to forecast them. Modeling and sophisticated forecasting techniques will be needed to understand the risk-return trade-offs offered by the market.

---

[16] Hamilton (1989).

The second point is that the idealized behavior of perfect forecasters does not have much to do with the actual behavior of real-world investors. The behavior of markets is the result, not of perfectly rational market agents, but of the action of market agents with limited intelligence, limited resources, and subject to unpredictable exogenous events. Consequently, the action of market agents is a source of uncertainty in itself. As a result, there is no theoretical reason to maintain that the multivariate random walk is the most robust model.

This criticism was noted in Chapter 4 when we discussed the attack on the assumed investor behavior made in asset pricing theory and mean-variance framework of portfolio selection by those in the behavioral finance camp. Real-world investors use relatively simple forecasting techniques such as linear regressions. It is reasonable to believe that when real-world investors employ judgment, there is the possibility of making large forecasting errors. As the behavioral finance camp argues, the preoccupation with the idealized behavior of markets populated by perfect forecasters seems to be misguided. Theorists who defend the assumption that investors in the real world are perfect forecasters, believe that it is unreasonable to assume that investors make systematic mistakes. Proponents of this assumption claim that, on average, investors make correct forecasts.

However, the evidence suggests that this claim is not true. Investors can make systematic mistakes and then hit some boundary, the consequences of which can be extremely painful in terms of wealth accumulation as we saw in the late 1990s with the bursting of the technology, media, and telecommunications bubble. As Fabozzi, Focardi, and Kolm (2006a, 11) conclude:

> A pragmatic attitude prevails. Markets are considered to be difficult to predict but to exhibit rather complex structures that can be (and indeed are) predicted, either qualitatively or quantitatively.

Finally, an important point is that predictability is not the only path to profitability/excess returns. Citing once again from Fabozzi, Focardi, and Kolm (2006a, 11–12):

> If prices behaved as simple models such as the random walk model or the martingale, they could nevertheless exhibit high levels of persistent profitability. This is because these models are characterized by a fixed structure of expected returns. Actually, it is the time-invariance of expected returns coupled with the existence of risk premiums that makes these models unsuitable as long-term models. . . . A model such as the geometric random walk model of prices leads to exponentially diverging expected returns. This is unrealistic in the

long run, as it would lead to the concentration of all market capitalization in one asset. As a consequence, models such as the random walk model can only be *approximate* models over *limited* periods of time. This fact, in turn, calls attention to robust estimation methods. A random walk model is not an idealization that represents the final benchmark model: It is only a short-term approximation of what a model able to capture the dynamic feedbacks present in financial markets should be.

Hence, whether the random walk assumption is in fact the benchmark model of price processes must be addressed empirically. Yet, the view of portfolio managers is that markets offer patterns of predictability in returns, volatility (variance), and, possibly, higher moments. Because any such patterns might offer opportunities for realizing excess returns, a portfolio manager who ignores these patterns will be risking lost opportunities to enhance performance. As Fabozzi, Focardi, and Kolm (2006a, 24) state:

> [S]imple random walk models with risk premiums are not necessarily the safest models. The joint assumptions that markets are unforecastable and that there are risk premiums is not necessarily the safest assumption.

SUMMARY

Despite the ongoing debate about the predictability of stock prices and returns, asset management firms have adopted statistical models of various levels of complexity for forecasting these values. The concept of forecastability rests on how one can forecast the future given the current *information set* known at that date. Prices or returns are said to be forecastable if the knowledge of the past influences our forecast of the future.

The two beliefs that seem to be held in the investment community are (1) predictable processes allow investors to earn excess returns and (2) unpredictable processes do not allow investors to earn excess returns. In the chapter, we argued that neither belief is necessarily true. That is predictable processes do not necessarily produce excess returns if they are associated with unfavorable risk and unpredictable expectations can be profitable if the expected value is favorable.

Probability theory is used in decision making to represent and measure the level of uncertainty. The frequentist interpretation of a probability is used in finance: Probability is the percentage of times (i.e., frequency) that a particular event is observed in a large number of observations (or trials). It is assumed that our uncertainty is embodied in a probability distribution of returns. The absence of predictability means that the distribution of future returns does not change as a function of the present and past values of prices and returns. From this perspective, a price or return process is said to be predictable if its probability distributions depend on the current information set and a price or return process is said to be unpredictable if its probability distributions are do not vary over time. Using this concept of predictability, we explained why prices and returns are difficult, perhaps even impossible, to predict. The key is that any prediction that might lead to an opportunity to generate a trading profit or an excess return tends to make that opportunity disappear. If stock return predictions are certain, then simple arbitrage arguments would dictate that all stocks should have the same return. In fact, if stock returns could be predicted with certainty and if there were different returns, then investors would choose only those stocks with the highest returns. Because stock return forecasts are not certain, uncertain predictions are embodied in probability distributions. The problem faced by investors is whether general considerations of market efficiency are capable of determining the mathematical form of price or return processes. In particular, investors are interested in understanding if stock prices or returns are necessarily unpredictable.

In solving this problem, the investor's objective is to shun models that permit unreasonable inferences. The following solutions have been proposed: (1) returns fluctuate randomly around a given mean (i.e., return follow multivariate random walks); (2) returns are a fair game (i.e., returns are martingales); and (3) returns are a fair game after adjusting for risk.

Concepts from probability theory and statistics that are relevant in understanding return forecasting models are conditional probability, conditional expectation, independent and identically distributed random variables, strict white noise, martingale difference sequence, white noise, error terms, and innovations. Given an understanding of these concepts, we explained what is meant by an arithmetic random walk, a martingale, and a strict arithmetic random walk to describe the stochastic process for returns and prices. If stock prices or returns follow an arithmetic random walk, the mean is linearly unpredictable but higher moments might be predictable. In the case of a martingale, the mean is unpredictable (linearly and nonlinearly), although higher moments might be predictable. If stock prices or returns follow a strict random walk, the mean, variance, and higher moments are all unpredictable.

The statistical-based predictive return models used by portfolio managers make conditional forecasts of expected returns using the current information set: past prices, company information, and financial market information. These models are classified as regressive models, linear autoregressive models, dynamic factor models, and hidden-variable models. We briefly explained each type of model, as well as identifying the key questions a portfolio model must answer before adopting a predictive return model.

We concluded the chapter with the implications for portfolio managers and investors who are attempting, or contemplating attempting, building predictive return models.

REFERENCES

Bachelier, L. 1900. Théorie de la spéculation. *Annales Scientifiques de l' École Normale Supérieure* 3, no. 17: 21–86.

Bernstein, P. L. 1996. *Against the gods: The remarkable story of risk*. New York: John Wiley & Sons.

Bernstein, P. L. 2008. Are stock prices predictable? In *Handbook of Finance*, vol. 3, edited by F. J. Fabozzi (pp. 273–380). Hoboken, NJ: John Wiley & Sons.

Fabozzi, F. J., S. M. Focardi, and P. N. Kolm. 2006a. *Trends in quantitative finance*. Charlottesville, Va.: Research Foundation of the CFA Institute.

Fabozzi, F. J., S. M. Focardi, and P. N. Kolm. 2006b. *Financial modeling of the equity market: From CAPM to cointegration*. Hoboken, NJ: John Wiley & Sons.

Fama, E. F. 1965. The behavior of stock market prices. *Journal of Business* 38 (January): 34–105.

Hamilton, J. D. 1989. A new approach to the economic analysis of nonstationary time series and the business cycle. *Econometrica* 57, no. 2: 357–384.

Harrison, J. M., and D. M. Kreps. 1979. Martingales and arbitrage in multiperiod securities markets. *Journal of Economic Theory* 20: 381–408.

Harrison, J. M., and S. R. Pliska. 1981. Martingales and stochastic integrals in the theory of continuous trading. *Stochastic Process Application* 11: 215–260.

Harrison, J. M., and S. R. Pliska. 1985. A stochastic calculus model of continuous trading: complete markets. *Stochastic Process Application* 15: 313–316.

Keynes, J. M. 1921. *Treatise on probability*. London: Macmillan.

Leinweber, D. J., and Y. Beinart. 1996. Little AI goes a long way on Wall Street. *Journal of Portfolio Management* 27, no. 2: 95–106.

LeRoy, S. F. 1973. Risk aversion and the martingale property of stock prices. *International Economic Review* 14: 436–446.

Rachev, S. T., J. Hsu, B. Bagasheva, and F. J. Fabozzi. 2008. *Bayesian methods in finance*. Hoboken, NJ: John Wiley & Sons.

Samuelson, P. A. 1965. Proof that properly anticipated prices fluctuate randomly. *Industrial Management Review* 6, no. 2: 41–50.

von Mises, R. 1928. *Wahrscheinlichkeitsrechnung, Statisik and Wahrheit*. Vienna: Julius Spring. (English edition translated in 1939 by J. Neyman, D. Scholl, and E. Rabinowitsch, *Probability, statistics and truth*. New York: Macmillan, 1939.)

CHAPTER 11

Managing a Common Stock Portfolio with Fundamental Factor Models

Equity portfolio managers who pursue a quantitative-oriented common strategy typically employ a multifactor equity risk model to construct and rebalance a portfolio and then evaluate performance. Such models are commonly referred to as *factor risk models* or simply *factor models*. In equity portfolio management, factor models fall into three types: statistical, macroeconomic, and fundamental models. We briefly reviewed these models in Chapter 5.[1] The most popular type of factor model used in practice is a fundamental factor model. While some asset management firms develop their own model, most use commercially available models. In this chapter, we use one commercially available model to illustrate the general features of fundamental factor models and how they are used to construct portfolios.[2]

We begin this chapter with an explanation of tracking error which is a key concept in understanding the potential performance of a portfolio relative to a benchmark index and the actual performance of a portfolio relative to a benchmark index. In Chapter 23, the use of a factor model in managing a bond portfolio is explained and illustrated.

---

[1] For more details about the different models, see Connor (1995). A description of macroeconomic factors models is provided by Burmeister, Roll, and Ross (2003). A popular factor model based on style is provided by French and French (1993). Their three-factor model adds to the capital asset pricing model two style factors: (1) small market capitalization minus large market capitalization excess return and (2) a proxy for value as measured by the excess return of high book/price ratio versus low book/price ratio stocks.
[2] For other applications, see Fabozzi, Jones, and Vardharaj (2002).

This chapter is coauthored with Frank J. Jones and Raman Vardharaj.

TRACKING ERROR

The risk of a portfolio can be measured by the standard deviation of portfolio returns. This statistical measure provides a range around the average return of a portfolio within which the actual return over a period is likely to fall with some specific probability. The mean return and standard deviation (or volatility) of a portfolio can be calculated over a period of time.

The standard deviation or volatility of a portfolio or a market index is an absolute number. A portfolio manager or client can also ask what the variation of the return of a portfolio is relative to a specified benchmark. Such variation is called the portfolio's *tracking error*.

Specifically, tracking error measures the dispersion of a portfolio's returns relative to the returns of its benchmark. That is, tracking error is the standard deviation of the portfolio's *active return* where active return is defined as:

Active return = Portfolios actual return − Benchmarks actual return

A portfolio created to match the benchmark index (that is, an index fund) that regularly has zero active returns (that is, always matches its benchmark's actual return) would have a tracking error of zero. But a portfolio that is actively managed that takes positions substantially different from the benchmark would likely have large active returns, both positive and negative, and thus would have an annual tracking error of, say, 5% to 10%.

To find the tracking error of a portfolio, it is first necessary to specify the benchmark. The tracking error of a portfolio, as indicated, is its standard deviation relative to the benchmark, *not* its total standard deviation. Table 11.1 presents the information used to calculate the tracking error for a hypothetical portfolio and benchmark using 30 weekly observations. The fourth column in the table shows the active return for the week. It is from the data in this column that the tracking error is computed. As reported in the table, the standard deviation of the weekly active returns is 0.54%. This value is then annualized by multiplying by the square root of 52—52 representing the number of weeks in a year. This gives a value of 3.89%. If the observations were monthly rather than weekly, the monthly tracking error would be annualized by multiplying by the square root of 12.

Given the tracking error, a range for the possible portfolio active return and corresponding range for the portfolio can be estimated assuming that the active returns are normally distributed. For example, assume the following:

Benchmark = S&P 500

TABLE 11.1 Data and Calculation for Active Return, Alpha, and Information Ratio

Week	Weekly Returns (%)		
	Portfolio	Benchmark	Active
1	3.69	3.72	−0.02
2	−0.56	−1.09	0.53
3	−1.41	−1.35	−0.06
4	0.96	0.34	0.62
5	−4.07	−4.00	−0.07
6	1.27	0.91	0.37
7	−0.39	−0.08	−0.31
8	−3.31	−2.76	−0.55
9	2.19	2.11	0.09
10	−0.02	−0.40	0.37
11	−0.46	−0.42	−0.05
12	0.09	0.71	−0.62
13	−1.93	−1.99	0.06
14	−1.91	−2.37	0.46
15	1.89	1.98	−0.09
16	−3.75	−4.33	0.58
17	−3.38	−4.22	0.84
18	0.60	0.62	−0.02
19	−10.81	−11.60	0.79
20	6.63	7.78	−1.15
21	3.52	2.92	0.59
22	1.24	1.89	−0.66
23	−0.63	−1.66	1.03
24	3.04	2.90	0.14
25	−1.73	−1.58	−0.15
26	2.81	3.05	−0.23
27	0.40	1.64	−1.23
28	1.03	1.03	0.01
29	−0.94	−0.95	0.00
30	1.45	1.66	−0.21

Average of active returns = 0.04%; Standard deviation of active returns = 0.54%
Annualizing
Annual average = Weekly average × 52
Annual variance = Weekly variance × 52
Annual std dev = Weekly std dev × $(52^{0.5})$

Expected return on S&P 500 = 20%
Tracking error relative to S&P 500 = 2%

then to simplify the analysis, assuming that the tracking error is normally distributed:

Number of Standard Deviations	Range for Portfolio Active Return	Corresponding Range for Portfolio Return	Probability
1	±2%	18%–22%	67%
2	±4%	16%–24%	95%
3	±6%	14%–26%	99%

As explained in Chapter 7, a manager can pursue a blend of an active and passive (e.g., indexing) strategy. That is, a manager can construct a portfolio such that a certain percentage of the portfolio is indexed to some benchmark index and the balance actively managed. Assume that the passively managed portion (that is, the indexed portion) has a zero tracking error relative to the index. For such a strategy, we can show (after some algebraic manipulation) that the tracking error for the overall portfolio would be as follows:

Portfolio tracking error relative to index
= (Percent of portfolio actively managed)
× (Tracking error of the actively managed portion relative to index)

An enhanced index fund differs from an index fund in that it deviates from the index holdings in small amounts and hopes to slightly outperform the index through those small deviations. In terms of an active/passive strategy, the manager allocates a small percentage of the portfolio to be actively managed. The reason is that in case the bets prove detrimental, then the underperformance would be small. Thus, realized returns would always deviate from index returns only by small amounts. There are many enhancing strategies. Suppose that a manager whose benchmark is the S&P 500 pursues an enhanced indexing strategy allocating only 5% of the portfolio to be actively managed and 95% indexed. Assume further that the tracking error of the actively managed portion is 15% with respect to the S&P 500. The portfolio would then have a tracking error calculated as follows:

Percent of portfolio actively managed relative to S&P 500 = 5%

Tracking error relative to S&P 500 = 15%

Portfolios tracking error relative to S&P 500 = 5% × 15% = 0.75%

Forward-Looking vs. Backward-Looking Tracking Error

In Table 11.1 the tracking error of the hypothetical portfolio is shown based on the active returns reported. However, the performance shown is the result of the portfolio manager's decisions during those 30 weeks with respect to portfolio positioning issues such as beta, sector allocations, style tilt (that is, value versus growth), stock selections, etc. Hence, we can call the tracking error calculated from these trailing active returns a *backward-looking tracking error*. It is also called the *ex post tracking error*.

One problem with a backward-looking tracking error is that it does not reflect the effect of current decisions by the portfolio manager on the future active returns and hence the future tracking error that may be realized. If, for example, the manager significantly changes the portfolio beta or sector allocations today, then the backward-looking tracking error that is calculated using data from prior periods would not accurately reflect the current portfolio risks going forward. That is, the backward-looking tracking error will have little predictive value and can be misleading regarding portfolio risks going forward.

The portfolio manager needs a forward-looking estimate of tracking error to accurately reflect the portfolio risk going forward. This is done in practice by using the services of a commercial vendor that has a model, called a *multifactor risk model*, that has defined the risks associated with a benchmark index. Statistical analysis of the historical return data of the stocks in the benchmark index are used to obtain the factors and quantify their risks. (This involves the use of variances and correlations.) Using the portfolio manager's current portfolio holdings, the portfolio's current exposure to the various factors can be calculated and compared to the benchmark's exposures to the factors. Using the differential factor exposures and the risks of the factors, a *forward-looking tracking error* for the portfolio can be computed. This tracking error is also referred to as the *predicted tracking error* or *ex ante tracking error*.

There is no guarantee that the forward-looking tracking error at the start of, say, a year would exactly match the backward-looking tracking error calculated at the end of the year. There are two reasons for this. The first is that as the year progresses and changes are made to the portfolio, the forward-looking tracking error estimate would change to reflect the new exposures. The second is that the accuracy of the forward-looking tracking error depends on the extent of the stability in the variances and correlations that were used in the analysis. These problems notwithstanding, the average of forward-looking tracking error estimates obtained at different times during the year will be reasonably close to the backward-looking tracking error estimate obtained at the end of the year.

Each of these estimates has its use. The forward-looking tracking error is useful in risk control and portfolio construction. The portfolio manager can immediately see the likely effect on tracking error of any intended change in the portfolio. Thus, she can do a what-if analysis of various portfolio strategies and eliminate those that would result in tracking errors beyond her tolerance for risk. The backward-looking tracking error can be useful for assessing actual performance analysis, such as the information ratio discussed next.

Information Ratio

Alpha is the average active return over a time period. Since backward-looking tracking error measures the standard deviation of a portfolio's active return, it is different from alpha. A portfolio does not have backward-looking tracking error simply because of outperformance or underperformance. For instance, consider a portfolio that outperforms (or underperforms) its benchmark by exactly 10 basis points every month. This portfolio would have a backward-looking tracking error of zero and a positive (negative) alpha of 10 basis points. In contrast, consider a portfolio that outperforms its benchmark by 10 basis points during half the months and underperforms by 10 bp during the other months. This portfolio would have a backward-looking tracking error that is positive but an alpha equal to zero.

The *information ratio* combines alpha and tracking error as follows:

$$\text{Information ratio} = \frac{\text{Alpha}}{\text{Backward-looking tracking error}}$$

The *information ratio* is essentially a reward-risk ratio. The reward is the average of the active return, that is, alpha. The risk is the standard deviation of the active return, the tracking error, and, more specifically, backward-looking tracking error. The higher the information ratio, the better the manager performed relative to the risk assumed.

To illustrate the calculation of the information ratio, consider the active returns for the hypothetical portfolio shown in Table 11.1. The weekly average active return is 0.04%. Annualizing the weekly average active return by multiplying by 52 gives an alpha of 1.83%. Since the backward-looking tracking error is 3.89%, the information ratio is 0.47 (1.83%/3.89%).

Determinants of Tracking Error

Several factors affect the level of tracking error. The major factors include:

- Number of stocks in the portfolio
- Portfolio market capitalization and style difference relative to the benchmark
- Sector deviation from the benchmark
- Market volatility
- Portfolio beta

The impact of each of these factors is investigated in Vardharaj, Fabozzi, and Jones (2004).

Number of Stocks in Portfolio

Tracking error decreases as the portfolio progressively includes more of the stocks that are in the benchmark index. This general effect is illustrated in Figure 11.1 which shows the effect of portfolio size for a large-cap portfolio benchmarked to the S&P 500. Notice that an optimally chosen portfolio of just 50 stocks can track the S&P 500 within 2.3%. For mid-cap and small-cap stocks, Vardharaj, Fabozzi, and Jones (2004) found that the tracking errors are 3.5% and 4.3%, respectively. In contrast, tracking error increases as the portfolio progressively includes more stocks that are not in the benchmark. This effect is illustrated in Figure 11.2. In this case, the benchmark index is the S&P 100 and the portfolio progressively includes more and more stocks from the S&P 500 that are not in the S&P 100. The result is that the tracking error with respect to the S&P 100 rises.

FIGURE 11.1 Typical Tracking Error vs. Number of Benchmark Stocks in Portfolio for S&P 500

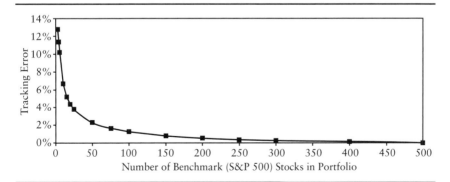

FIGURE 11.2 Tracking Error vs. Number of Nonbenchmark Stocks in Portfolio

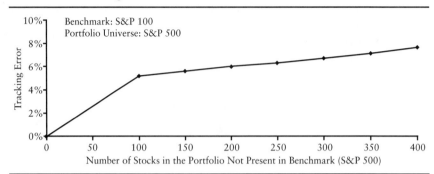

Portfolio Market Cap and Style Difference Relative to Benchmark

Vardharaj, Fabozzi, and Jones (2004) found tracking error increases as the average market cap of the portfolio deviates from that of the benchmark index. Tracking error also increases as the overall style (growth/value) of the portfolio deviates from that of the benchmark index. First, holding style constant, they find that tracking error rises when the cap size difference increases. For example, a mid-cap blend portfolio has a tracking error of 7.07% while a small-cap blend portfolio has a tracking error of 8.55% with respect to the S&P 500, which is a large-cap blend portfolio. Second, for a given cap size, tracking error is greater when the style is either growth or value than when it is the blend.

Sector Deviation from Benchmark

When a portfolio's allocations to various economic sectors differ from those of its benchmark, it results in tracking error. In general, when the differences in sector allocation increase, the tracking error increases. Vardharaj, Fabozzi, and Jones (2004) found that in general, the tracking error increased as the level of sector bets increased.

Market Volatility

Managed portfolios generally hold only a fraction of the assets in their benchmark. Given this, a highly volatile benchmark index (as measured in terms of standard deviation) would be harder to track closely than a generally less volatile benchmark index. As market volatility rises, the portfolio tracking error increases. This correspondingly increases the probability of "dramatic underperformance," by which we mean an underperformance of

FIGURE 11.3 Tracking Error and Dramatic Shortfall

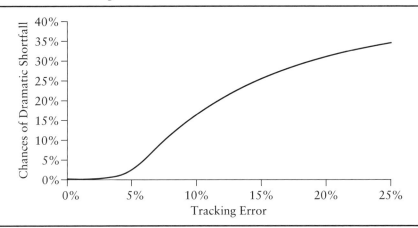

10% or more. This can be seen in Figure 11.3. On the horizontal axis of the figure is the tracking error and on the vertical axis is the probability of a shortfall of 10% or more from the benchmark index. (In this calculation, we assumed normal distribution of active returns and an alpha of –0.26%, which is the average alpha for domestic stock mutual funds.)

As the tracking error rises, the probability of dramatic outperformance increases just as much as the probability of dramatic underperformance. But, the portfolio management consequences of these two types of extreme relative performances are not symmetric—dramatic underperformance can cause a manager to be terminated. Another implication is that since an increase in market volatility increases tracking error and thereby the chances of dramatic underperformance, there is an increased need for managers to monitor the portfolio tracking error more frequently and closely during periods of high market volatility.

Portfolio Beta

The beta for the market portfolio is 1 and beta for the risk-free portfolio (cash) is zero. Suppose an investor holds a combination of cash and the market portfolio. Then, the portfolio beta falls below 1. The managed portfolio is less sensitive to systematic risk than the market, and is therefore less risky than the market. Conversely, when the investor holds a leveraged market portfolio, by borrowing at the risk-free rate and investing in the market portfolio, the beta is above 1, and the portfolio is more risky than the market.

FIGURE 11.4 Tracking Error and Beta

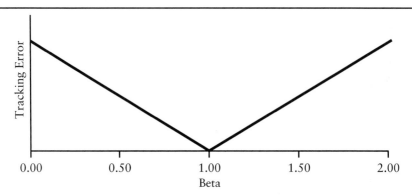

It can be demonstrated that the portfolio tracking error with respect to the market portfolio, increases both when the beta falls below 1 and when the beta rises above 1. So, as the portfolio increases the proportion of cash held, even though its absolute risk falls, its tracking error risk rises. As shown in Figure 11.4, tracking error rises linearly as the beta deviates from 1.

In the above example, we make the simplistic assumption that the manager only chooses between holding the market portfolio and cash when making changes to its beta. In the more general case where the fund can hold any number of stocks in any proportion, its beta can differ from 1 due to other reasons. But, even in this general case, the tracking error increases when the portfolio beta deviates from the market beta.

Marginal Contribution to Tracking Error

Since tracking error arises from various bets (some intentional and some unintentional) placed by the manager through overweights and underweights relative to the benchmark index, it would be useful to understand how sensitive the tracking error is to small changes in each of these bets.

Suppose, for example, a portfolio initially has an overweight of 3% in the semiconductor industry relative to its benchmark index, and that the tracking error is 6%. Suppose that the tracking error subsequently increases to 6.1% due to the semiconductor industry weight in the portfolio increasing by 1% (and hence the overweight goes to 4%). Then, it can be said that this industry adds 0.1% to tracking error for every 1% increase in its weight. That is, its *marginal contribution to tracking error* is 0.1%. This would hold only at the margin, that is, for a small change, and not for large changes.

Marginal contributions can be also calculated for individual stocks. If the risk analysis employs a multifactor risk model, then similar marginal contribution estimates can be obtained for the risk factors also.

Generally, marginal contributions would be positive for overweighted industries (or stocks) and negative for underweighted ones. The reason is as follows. If a portfolio already holds an excess weight in an industry, then increasing this weight would cause the portfolio to diverge further from the benchmark index. This increased divergence adds to tracking error, leading to a positive marginal contribution for this industry. Suppose, however, the portfolio has an underweight in an industry. Then, increasing the portfolio weight in this industry would make the portfolio converge towards the benchmark, thus reducing tracking error. This leads to a negative marginal contribution for this industry.

An analysis of the marginal contributions can be useful for a manager who seeks to alter the portfolio tracking error. Suppose a manager wishes to reduce the tracking error, then she should reduce portfolio overweights in industries (or stocks) with the highest positive marginal contributions. Alternatively, she can reduce the underweights (that is, increase the overall weights) in industries (or stocks) with the most negative marginal contributions. Such changes would be most effective in reducing the tracking error while minimizing the necessary turnover and the associated expenses.

FUNDAMENTAL FACTOR MODEL DESCRIPTION AND ESTIMATION[3]

The basic relationship to be estimated in a fundamental factor model is

$$R_i - R_f = \beta_{i,F1} R_{F1} + \beta_{i,F2} R_{F2} + \cdots + \beta_{i,FH} R_{FH} + e_i$$

where

R_i = rate of return on stock i
R_f = risk-free rate of return
$\beta_{i,Fj}$ = sensitivity of stock i to risk factor j
R_{Fj} = rate of return on risk factor j
e_i = nonfactor (specific) return on security i

---

[3] In our illustration, we will use an old version of a model developed by Barra (now MSCI Barra). While that model has been updated, the discussion and illustrations provide the essential points for appreciating the value of using fundamental factor models.

The above function is referred to as a *return generating function*.

Fundamental factor models use company and industry attributes and market data as "descriptors." Examples are earnings/price ratios, book/price ratios, estimated earnings growth, and trading activity. The estimation of a fundamental factor model begins with an analysis of historical stock returns and descriptors about a company. In the MSCI Barra model, for example, the process of identifying the risk factors begins with monthly returns for hundreds of stocks that the descriptors must explain. Descriptors are not the "risk factors." They are the candidates for risk factors. The descriptors are selected in terms of their ability to explain stock returns. That is, all of the descriptors are potential risk factors but only those that appear to be important in explaining stock returns are used in constructing risk factors.

Once the descriptors that are statistically significant in explaining stock returns are identified, they are grouped into "risk indexes" or "factors" to capture related company attributes. For example, descriptors such as market leverage, book leverage, debt-to-equity ratio, and company's debt rating are combined to obtain a risk index or factor referred to as "leverage." Thus, a risk index is a combination of descriptors that captures a particular attribute of a company.

For example, the Barra fundamental factor model, the "E3 model" used for illustration purposes only in this chapter, has 13 risk indexes and 55 industry groups.[4] Table 11.2 lists the 13 risk indexes in the Barra model. Also shown in the table are the descriptors used to construct each risk index. The 55 industry classifications are further classified into sectors. For example, the following three industries comprise the energy sector: energy reserves and production, oil refining, and oil services. The consumer noncyclicals sector consists of the following five industries: food and beverages, alcohol, tobacco, home products, and grocery stores. The 13 sectors in the Barra model are basic materials, energy, consumer noncylicals, consumer cyclicals, consumer services, industrials, utility, transport, health care, technology, telecommunications, commercial services, and financial.

Given the risk factors, information about the exposure of every stock to each risk factor ($\beta_{i,Fj}$) is estimated using statistical analysis. For a given time period, the rate of return for each risk factor (R_{Fj}) also can be estimated using statistical analysis. The prediction for the expected return can be obtained from equation (1) for any stock. The nonfactor return (e_i) is found by subtracting the actual return for the period for a stock from the return as predicted by the risk factors.

---

[4]See Appendix A in Barra (1998).

TABLE 11.2 Barra E3 Model Risk Definitions

Descriptors in Risk Index	Risk Index
Beta times sigma Daily standard deviation High-low price Log of stock price Cumulative range Volume beta Serial dependence Option-implied standard deviation	Volatility
Relative strength Historical alpha	Momentum
Log of market capitalization	Size
Cube of log of market capitalization	Size Nonlinearity
Share turnover rate (annual) Share turnover rate (quarterly) Share turnover rate (monthly) Share turnover rate (five years) Indicator for forward split Volume to variance	Trading Activity
Payout ratio over five years Variability in capital structure Growth rate in total assets Earnings growth rate over the last five years Analyst-predicted earnings growth Recent earnings change	Growth
Analyst-predicted earnings-to-price Trailing annual earnings-to-price Historical earnings-to-price	Earnings Yield
Book-to-price ratio	Value
Variability in earnings Variability in cash flows Extraordinary items in earnings Standard deviation of analyst-predicted earnings-to-price	Earnings Variability
Market leverage Book leverage Debt to total assets Senior debt rating	Leverage
Exposure to foreign currencies	Currency Sensitivity
Predicted dividend yield	Dividend Yield
Indicator for firms outside US-E3 estimation universe	Nonestimation Universe Indicator

Adapted from Table 8-1 in Barra (1998, 71–73). Adapted with permission.

Moving from individual stocks to portfolios, the predicted return for a portfolio can be computed. The exposure to a given risk factor of a portfolio is simply the weighted average of the exposure of each stock in the portfolio to that risk factor. For example, suppose a portfolio has 42 stocks. Suppose further that stocks 1 through 40 are equally weighted in the portfolio at 2.2%, stock 41 is 5% of the portfolio, and stock 42 is 7% of the portfolio. Then the exposure of the portfolio to risk factor j is

$$0.022\beta_{1,Fj} + 0.022\beta_{2,Fj} + \cdots + 0.022\beta_{40,Fj} + 0.050\beta_{41,Fj} + 0.007\beta_{42,Fj}$$

The nonfactor error term is measured in the same way as in the case of an individual stock. However, in a well-diversified portfolio, the nonfactor error term will be considerably less for the portfolio than for the individual stocks in the portfolio.

The same analysis can be applied to a stock market index because an index is nothing more than a portfolio of stocks.

RISK DECOMPOSITION

The real usefulness of a fundamental factor model lies in the ease with which the risk of a portfolio with several assets can be estimated. Consider a portfolio with 100 assets. Risk is commonly defined as the variance of the portfolio's returns. So, in this case, we need to find the variance-covariance matrix of the 100 assets. That would require us to estimate 100 variances (one for each of the 100 assets) and 4,950 covariances among the 100 assets. That is, in all we need to estimate 5,050 values, a very difficult undertaking. Suppose, instead, that we use a three-factor model to estimate risk. Then, we need to estimate (1) the three factor loadings for each of the 100 assets (that is, 300 values), (2) the six values of the factor variance-covariance matrix, and (3) the 100 residual variances (one for each asset). That is, in all, we need to estimate only 406 values. This represents a nearly 90% reduction from having to estimate 5,050 values, a huge improvement. Thus, with well-chosen factors, we can substantially reduce the work involved in estimating a portfolio's risk.

A fundamental factor model allows a portfolio manager and a client to decompose risk in order to assess the potential performance of a portfolio to the factors and to assess the potential performance of a portfolio relative to a benchmark. This is the portfolio construction and risk control application of the model. Also, the actual performance of a portfolio relative to a benchmark can be assessed.

MSCI Barra (1998) suggests that there are various ways that a portfolio's total risk can be decomposed when employing a fundamental factor model.[5] Each decomposition approach can be useful to managers depending on the equity portfolio management that they pursue. The four approaches are (1) total risk decomposition, (2) systematic-residual risk decomposition, (3) active risk decomposition, and (4) active systematic-active residual risk decomposition. We describe each below and explain how managers pursuing different strategies will find the decomposition helpful in portfolio construction and evaluation.

In all of these approaches to risk decomposition, the total return is first divided into the risk-free return and the total excess return. The *total excess return* is the difference between the actual return realized by the portfolio and the risk-free return. The risk associated with the total excess return, called *total excess risk*, is what is further partitioned in the four approaches.

Total Risk Decomposition

There are managers who seek to minimize total risk. For example, a manager pursuing a long-short or market neutral strategy, seeks to construct a portfolio that minimizes total risk. For such managers, total risk decomposition which breaks down the total excess risk into two components—*common factor risks* (e.g., capitalization and industry exposures) and *specific risk*—is useful. This decomposition is shown in Figure 11.5. There is no provision for market risk, only risk attributed to the common factor risks and company-specific influences (that is, risk unique to a particular company and therefore

FIGURE 11.5 Total Risk Decomposition

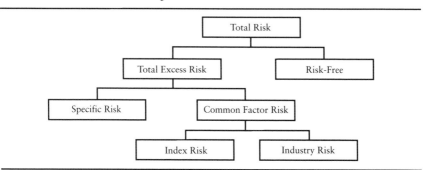

Source: Figure 4.2 in Barra (1998, 34). Reprinted with permission.

---

[5]The discussion to follow in this section follows that in the 1998 handbook of Barra (1998) in describing the firm's model.

uncorrelated with the specific risk of other companies). Thus, the market portfolio is not a risk factor considered in this decomposition.

Systematic-Residual Risk Decomposition

There are managers who seek to time the market or who intentionally make bets to create a different exposure than that of a market portfolio. Such managers would find it useful to decompose total excess risk into systematic risk and residual risk as shown in Figure 11.6. Unlike in the total risk decomposition approach just described, this view brings market risk into the analysis.

Residual risk in the systematic-residual risk decomposition is defined in a different way than residual risk is in the total risk decomposition. In the systematic-residual risk decomposition, residual risk is risk that is uncorrelated with the market portfolio. In turn, residual risk is partitioned into specific risk and common factor risk. Notice that the partitioning of risk described here is different from that in the Arbitrage Pricing Model Theory model developed by Ross (1976) and described in Chapter 5. In that model, all risk factors that could not be diversified away were referred to as "systematic risks." In our discussion here, risk factors that cannot be diversified away are classified as market risk and common factor risk. Residual risk can be diversified to a negligible level.

Active Risk Decomposition

In previous chapters, the need to assess a portfolio's risk exposure and actual performance relative to a benchmark index is explained. The active risk

FIGURE 11.6 Systematic-Residual Risk Decomposition

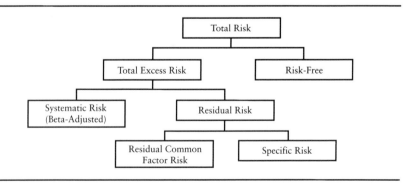

Source: Figure 4.3 in Barra (1998, 34). Reprinted with permission.

FIGURE 11.7 Active Risk Decomposition

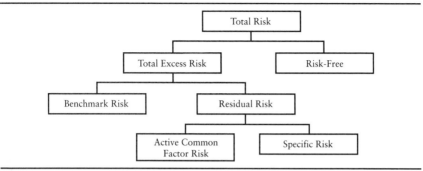

Source: Figure 4.4 in Barra (1998, 34). Reprinted with permission.

decomposition approach is useful for that purpose. In this type of decomposition, shown in Figure 11.7, the total excess return is divided into benchmark risk and active risk. Benchmark risk is defined as the risk associated with the benchmark portfolio.

Active risk is the risk that results from the manager's attempt to generate a return that will outperform the benchmark. Another name for active risk is tracking error. The active risk is further partitioned into common factor risk and specific risk.

Active Systematic-Active Residual Risk Decomposition

There are managers who overlay a market-timing strategy on their stock selection. That is, they not only try to select stocks they believe will outperform but also try to time the purchase of the acquisition. For a manager who pursues such a strategy, it will be important in evaluating performance to separate market risk from common factor risks. In the active risk decomposition approach just discussed, there is no market risk identified as one of the risk factors.

Since market risk (that is, systematic risk) is an element of active risk, its inclusion as a source of risk is preferred by managers. When market risk is included, we have the active systematic-active residual risk decomposition approach shown in Figure 11.8. Total excess risk is again divided into benchmark risk and active risk. However, active risk is further divided into active systematic risk (that is, active market risk) and active residual risk. Then active residual risk is divided into common factor risks and specific risk.

FIGURE 11.8 Active Systematic-Active Residual Risk Decomposition

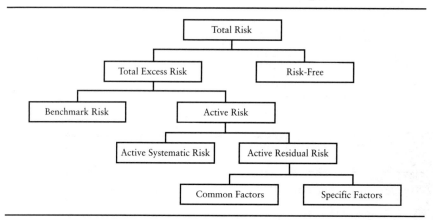

Source: Figure 4.5 in Barra (1998, 37). Reprinted with permission.

Summary of Risk Decomposition

The four approaches to risk decomposition are just different ways of slicing up risk to help a portfolio manager in constructing and controlling the risk of a portfolio and for a client to understand how the portfolio manager performed. Figure 11.9 provides an overview of the four approaches to carving up risk into specific and common factor, systematic and residual, and benchmark and active risks.

APPLICATIONS IN PORTFOLIO CONSTRUCTION AND RISK CONTROL

The power of a fundamental factor model is that given the risk factors and the risk factor sensitivities, a portfolio's risk exposure profile can be quantified and controlled. The three examples below show how this can be done so that the a portfolio manager can avoid making unintended bets by (1) assessing the exposure of a portfolio, (2) controlling risk against a stock market index, and (3) tilting a portfolio. In the examples, we use the Barra E3 factor model.[6]

Assessing the Exposure of a Portfolio

A fundamental factor model can be used to assess whether the current portfolio is consistent with a manager's strengths. Table 11.3 is a list of the top

---
[6]The illustrations were created based on applications suggested by Barra (1998).

FIGURE 11.9 Risk Decomposition Overview

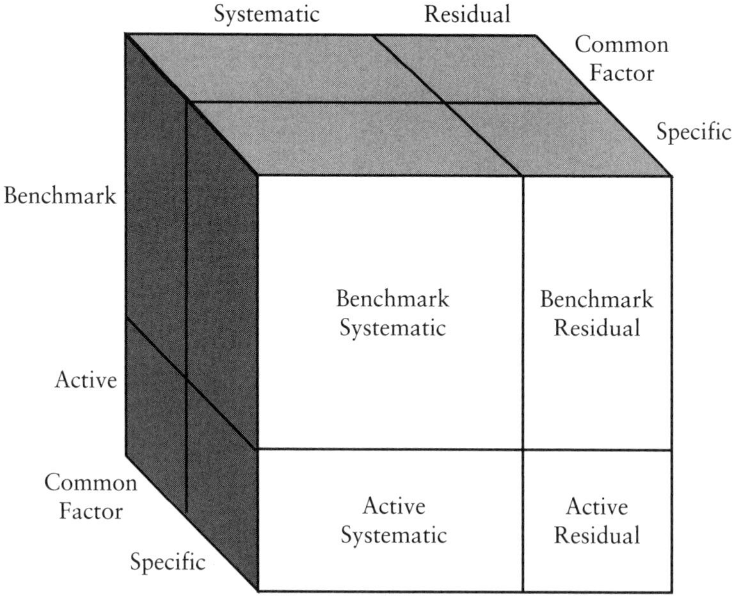

```
                    Systematic          Residual
                                                      Common
                                                      Factor
                                                         Specific
       Benchmark

                                      Benchmark     Benchmark
                                      Systematic    Residual
       Active

       Common
       Factor                         Active        Active
                                      Systematic    Residual
               Specific
```

Source: Figure 4.6 in Barra (1998, 38). Reprinted with permission.

15 holdings of Portfolio ABC as of September 30, 2000. Table 11.4 is a risk-return report for the same portfolio. The portfolio had a total market value of over $3.7 billion, 202 holdings, and a predicted beta of 1.20. The risk report also shows that the portfolio had an active risk of 9.83%. This is its tracking error with respect to the benchmark, the S&P 500. Notice that over 80% of the active risk variance (which is 96.67) comes from the common factor risk variance (which is 81.34), and only a small proportion comes from the stock-specific risk variance (which is 15.33). Clearly, the manager of this portfolio has placed fairly large factor bets.

Table 11.5A assesses the factor risk exposures of Portfolio ABC relative to those of the S&P 500, its benchmark. The first column shows the exposures of the portfolio (Mgd), and the second column shows the exposures for the benchmark (Bmk). The last column shows the active exposure (Act), which is the difference between the portfolio exposure and the benchmark exposure. The exposures to the risk index factors are measured in units of standard deviation, while the exposures to the industry factors are measured in percentages. The portfolio has a high active exposure to the momentum risk index factor. That is, the stocks held in the portfolio have significant

TABLE 11.3 Portfolio ABC's Holdings (Only the Top 15 Holdings Shown)

Portfolio:	ABC Fund	Benchmark:	S&P500	Model date:	2000-10-02
Report date:	2000-10-15	Price date:	2000-09-29	Model:	U.S. Equity 3

Name	Shares	Price ($)	Weight (%)	Beta	Main Industry Name	Sector
General Elec. Co.	2,751,200	57.81	4.28	0.89	Financial Services	Financial
Citigroup, Inc.	2,554,666	54.06	3.72	0.98	Banks	Financial
Cisco Sys., Inc.	2,164,000	55.25	3.22	1.45	Computer Hardware	Technology
EMC Corp. Mass.	1,053,600	99.50	2.82	1.19	Computer Hardware	Technology
Intel Corp.	2,285,600	41.56	2.56	1.65	Semiconductors	Technology
Nortel Networks Corp. N	1,548,600	60.38	2.52	1.40	Electronic Equipment	Technology
Corning, Inc.	293,200	297.50	2.35	1.31	Electronic Equipment	Technology
International Business	739,000	112.50	2.24	1.05	Computer Software	Technology
Oracle Corp.	955,600	78.75	2.03	1.40	Computer Software	Technology
Sun Microsystems, Inc.	624,700	116.75	1.96	1.30	Computer Hardware	Technology
Lehman Bros. Hldgs. Inc.	394,700	148.63	1.58	1.51	Sec. & Asset Management	Financial
Morgan Stanley Dean Wi.	615,400	91.44	1.52	1.29	Sec. & Asset Management	Financial
Disney Walt Co.	1,276,700	38.25	1.32	0.85	Entertainment	Cnsmr. Services
Coca-Cola Co.	873,900	55.13	1.30	0.68	Food & Beverage	Cnsmr. (non-cyc.)
Microsoft Corp.	762,245	60.31	1.24	1.35	Computer Software	Technology

Managing a Common Stock Portfolio with Fundamental Factor Models

TABLE 11.4 Portfolio ABC's Risk-Return Decomposition

		Risk-Return	
Number of assets	202	Total shares	62,648,570
		Average share price	$59.27
Portfolio beta	1.20	Portfolio value	$3,713,372,229.96

Risk Decomposition	Variance	Standard Deviation (%)
Active specific risk	15.33	3.92
Active common factor		
Risk indexes	44.25	6.65
Industries	17.82	4.22
Covariance	19.27	
Total active common factor risk[a]	81.34	9.02
Total active[b]	96.67	9.83
Benchmark	247.65	15.74
Total risk	441.63	21.02

[a] Equal to risk indexes + Industries + Covariances.
[b] Equal to active specific risk + Total active common factor risk.

momentum. The portfolio's stocks were smaller than the benchmark average in terms of market cap. The industry factor exposures reveal that the portfolio had an exceptionally high active exposure to the semiconductor industry and electronic equipment industry. Table 11.5B combines the industry exposures to obtain sector exposures. It shows that Portfolio ABC had a very high active exposure to the technology sector. Such large bets can expose the portfolio to large swings in returns.

An important use of such risk reports is the identification of portfolio bets, both explicit and implicit. If, for example, the manager of Portfolio ABC did not want to place such a large technology sector bet or momentum risk index bet, then she can rebalance the portfolio to minimize any such bets.

Controlling Risk Against a Stock Market Index

The objective of equity indexing is to match the performance of some specified stock market index with little tracking error. To do this, the risk profile of the indexed portfolio must match the risk profile of the designated stock market index. Put in other terms, the factor risk exposure of the indexed portfolio must match as closely as possible the exposure of the designated stock market index to the same factors. Any differences in the factor

TABLE 11.5 Analysis of Portfolio ABC's Exposures
A. Analysis of Risk Exposures to S&P 500

Factor Exposures			
Risk Index Exposures (std. dev.)			
	Mgd	Bmk	Act
Volatility	0.220	−0.171	0.391
Momentum	0.665	−0.163	0.828
Size	−0.086	0.399	−0.485
Size Nonlinearity	0.031	0.097	−0.067
Trading Activity	0.552	−0.083	0.635
Growth	0.227	−0.167	0.395
Earnings Yield	−0.051	0.081	−0.132
Value	−0.1.69	−0.034	−0.136
Earnings Variation	0.058	−0.146	0.204
Leverage	0.178	−0.149	0.327
Currency Sensitivity	0.028	−0.049	−0.077
Yield	−0.279	0.059	−0.338
Non-EST Universe	0.032	0.000	0.032

Industry Weights (percent)			
	Mgd	Bmk	Act
Mining and Metals	0.013	0.375	−0.362
Gold	0.000	0.119	−0.119
Forestry and Paper	0.198	0.647	−0.449
Chemicals	0.439	2.386	−1.947
Energy Reserves	2.212	4.589	−2.377
Oil Refining	0.582	0.808	−0.226
Oil Services	2.996	0.592	2.404
Food & Beverages	2.475	3.073	−0.597
Alcohol	0.000	0.467	−0.467
Tobacco	0.000	0.403	−0.403
Home Products	0.000	1.821	−1.821
Grocery Stores	0.000	0.407	−0.407
Consumer Durables	0.165	0.125	0.039
Motor Vehicles and Parts	0.000	0.714	−0.714
Apparel and Textiles	0.000	0.191	−0.191
Clothing Stores	0.177	0.308	−0.131
Specialty Retail	0.445	2.127	−1.681
Department Stores	0.000	2.346	−2.346
Construction Real Property	0.569	0.204	0.364

TABLE 11.5 (Continued)

Industry Weights (percent)			
	Mgd	Bmk	Act
Publishing	0.014	0.508	−0.494
Media	1.460	2.077	−0.617
Hotels	0.090	0.112	−0.022
Restaurants	0.146	0.465	−0.319
Entertainment	1.179	1.277	−0.098
Leisure	0.000	0.247	−0.247
Environmental Services	0.000	0.117	−0.117
Heavy Electrical Equipment	1.438	1.922	−0.483
Heavy Machinery	0.000	0.062	−0.062
Industrial Parts	0.234	1.086	−0.852
Electric Utility	1.852	1.967	−0.115
Gas Utilities	0.370	0.272	0.098
Railroads	0.000	0.211	−0.211
Airlines	0.143	0.194	−0.051
Truck/Sea/Air Freight	0.000	0.130	−0.130
Medical Services	1.294	0.354	0.940
Medical Products	0.469	2.840	−2.370
Drugs	6.547	8.039	−1.492
Electronic Equipment	11.052	5.192	5.860
Semiconductors	17.622	6.058	11.564
Computer Hardware	12.057	9.417	2.640
Computer Software	9.374	6.766	2.608
Defense and Aerospace	0.014	0.923	−0.909
Telephone	0.907	4.635	−3.728
Wireless Telecom.	0.000	1.277	−1.277
Information Services	0.372	1.970	−1.598
Industrial Services	0.000	0.511	−0.511
Life/Health Insurance	0.062	1.105	−1.044
Property/Casualty Ins.	1.069	2.187	−1.118
Banks	5.633	6.262	−0.630
Thrifts	1.804	0.237	1.567
Securities and Asst. Mgmt.	6.132	2.243	3.888
Financial Services	5.050	5.907	−0.857
Internet	3.348	1.729	1.618
Equity SEIT	0.000	0.000	0.000

Note: Mgd = Managed; Bmk = S&P 500 (the benchmark); Act = Active, which is Managed − Benchmark.

TABLE 11.5 (Continued)
B. Analysis of Sector Exposures Relative to S&P 500 Sector Weights (percent)

	Mgd	Bmk	Act
Basic Materials	0.65	3.53	−2.88
Mining	0.01	0.38	−0.36
Gold	0.00	0.12	−0.12
Forest	0.20	0.65	−0.45
Chemical	0.44	2.39	−1.95
Energy	5.79	5.99	−0.20
Energy Reserves	2.21	4.59	−2.38
Oil Refining	0.58	0.81	−0.23
Oil Services	3.00	0.59	2.40
Consumer (noncyclical)	2.48	6.17	−3.70
Food/Beverage	2.48	3.07	−0.60
Alcohol	0.00	0.47	−0.47
Tobacco	0.00	0.40	−0.40
Home Prod.	0.00	1.82	−1.82
Grocery	0.00	0.41	−0.41
Consumer (cyclical)	1.36	6.01	−4.66
Consumer Durables	0.17	0.13	0.04
Motor Vehicles	0.00	0.71	−0.71
Apparel	0.00	0.19	−0.19
Clothing	0.18	0.31	−0.13
Specialty Retail	0.45	2.13	−1.68
Dept. Store	0.00	2.35	−2.35
Construction	0.57	0.20	0.36
Consumer Services	2.89	4.69	−1.80
Publishing	0.01	0.51	−0.49
Media	1.46	2.08	−0.62
Hotels	0.09	0.11	−0.02
Restaurants	0.15	0.47	−0.32
Entertainment	1.18	1.28	−0.10
Leisure	0.00	0.25	−0.25
Industrials	1.67	3.19	−1.51
Env. Services	0.00	0.12	−0.12
Heavy Electrical	1.44	1.92	−0.48
Heavy Machinery	0.00	0.06	−0.06
Industrial Parts	0.23	1.09	−0.85

TABLE 11.5 (Continued)
B. Analysis of Sector Exposures Relative to S&P 500

	Mgd	Bmk	Act
Utility	2.22	2.24	−0.02
Electric Utility	1.85	1.97	−0.12
Gas Utility	0.37	0.27	0.10
Transport	0.14	0.54	−0.39
Railroad	0.00	0.21	−0.21
Airlines	0.14	0.19	−0.05
Truck Freight	0.00	0.13	−0.13
Health Care	8.31	11.23	−2.92
Medical Provider	1.29	0.35	0.94
Medical Products	0.47	2.84	−2.37
Drugs	6.55	8.04	−1.49
Technology	53.47	30.09	23.38
Electronic Equipment	11.05	5.19	5.86
Semiconductors	17.62	6.06	11.56
Computer Hardware	12.06	9.42	2.64
Computer Software	9.37	6.77	2.61
Defense & Aerospace	0.01	0.92	−0.91
Internet	3.35	1.73	1.62
Telecommunications	0.91	5.91	−5.00
Telephone	0.91	4.63	−3.73
Wireless	0.00	1.28	−1.28
Commercial Services	0.37	2.48	−2.11
Information Services	0.37	1.97	−1.60
Industrial Services	0.00	0.51	−0.51
Financial	19.75	17.94	1.81
Life Insurance	0.06	1.11	−1.04
Property Insurance	1.07	2.19	−1.12
Banks	5.63	6.26	−0.63
Thrifts	1.80	0.24	1.57
Securities/Asst. Mgmt.	6.23	2.24	3.89
Financial Services	5.05	5.91	−0.86
Equity REIT	0.00	0.00	0.00

Note: Mgd = Managed; Bmk = Benchmark; Act = Active, which is Managed − Benchmark.

risk exposures result in tracking error. Identification of any differences allows the indexer to rebalance the portfolio to reduce tracking error.

To illustrate this, suppose that an index manager has constructed a portfolio of 50 stocks to match the S&P 500. Table 11.6 shows output of the exposure to the Barra risk indexes and industry groups of the 50-stock portfolio and the S&P 500. The last column in the exhibit shows the difference in the exposure. The differences are very small except for the exposures to the size factor and one industry (equity REIT). That is, the 50-stock portfolio has more exposure to the size risk index and equity REIT industry.

The illustration in Table 11.6 uses price data as of December 31, 2001. It demonstrates how a fundamental factor model can be combined with an optimization model to construct an indexed portfolio when a given number of holdings is sought. Specifically, the portfolio analyzed in Table 11.5 is the result of an application in which the manager wants a portfolio constructed that matches the S&P 500 with only 50 stocks and that minimizes tracking error. Not only is the 50-stock portfolio constructed, but the optimization model combined with the factor model indicates that the tracking error is only 2.19%. Since this is the optimal 50-stock portfolio to replicate the S&P 500 that minimizes tracking error risk, this tells the index manager that if he or she seeks a lower tracking error, more stocks must be held. Note, however, that the optimal portfolio changes as time passes and prices move.

TABLE 11.6 Factor Exposures of a 50-Stock Portfolio that Optimally Matches the S&P 500

Risk Index Exposures (std. dev.)			
	Mgd	Bmk	Act
Volatility	−0.141	−0.084	−0.057
Momentum	−0.057	−0.064	0.007
Size	0.588	0.370	0.217
Size Nonlinearity	0.118	0.106	0.013
Trading Activity	−0.101	−0.005	−0.097
Growth	−0.008	−0.045	0.037
Earnings Yield	0.103	0.034	0.069
Value	−0.072	−0.070	−0.003
Earnings Variation	−0.058	−0.088	0.029
Leverage	−0.206	−0.106	−0.100
Currency Sensitivity	−0.001	−0.012	0.012
Yield	0.114	0.034	0.080
Non-EST Universe	0.000	0.000	0.000

TABLE 11.6 (Continued)

Industry Weights (percent)

	Mgd	Bmk	Act
Mining and Metals	0.000	0.606	−0.606
Gold	0.000	0.161	−0.161
Forestry and Paper	1.818	0.871	0.947
Chemicals	2.360	2.046	0.314
Energy Reserves	5.068	4.297	0.771
Oil Refining	1.985	1.417	0.568
Oil Services	1.164	0.620	0.544
Food and Beverages	2.518	3.780	−1.261
Alcohol	0.193	0.515	−0.322
Tobacco	1.372	0.732	0.641
Home Products	0.899	2.435	−1.536
Grocery Stores	0.000	0.511	−0.511
Consumer Durables	0.000	0.166	−0.166
Motor Vehicles and Parts	0.000	0.621	−0.621
Apparel and Textiles	0.000	0.373	−0.373
Clothing Stores	0.149	0.341	−0.191
Specialty Retail	1.965	2.721	−0.756
Department Stores	4.684	3.606	1.078
Construction and Real Property	0.542	0.288	0.254
Publishing	2.492	0.778	1.713
Media	1.822	1.498	0.323
Hotels	1.244	0.209	1.035
Restaurants	0.371	0.542	−0.171
Entertainment	2.540	1.630	0.910
Leisure	0.000	0.409	−0.409
Environmental Services	0.000	0.220	−0.220
Heavy Electrical Equipment	1.966	1.949	0.017
Heavy Machinery	0.000	0.141	−0.141
Industrial Parts	1.124	1.469	−0.345
Electric Utility	0.000	1.956	−1.956
Gas Utilities	0.000	0.456	−0.456
Railroads	0.000	0.373	−0.373

TABLE 11.6 (Continued)

	Mgd	Bmk	Act
Airlines	0.000	0.206	−0.206
Truck/Sea/Air Freight	0.061	0.162	−0.102
Medical Services	1.280	0.789	0.491
Medical Products	3.540	3.599	−0.059
Drugs	9.861	10.000	−0.140
Electronic Equipment	0.581	1.985	−1.404
Semiconductors	4.981	4.509	0.472
Computer Hardware	4.635	4.129	0.506
Computer Software	6.893	6.256	0.637
Defense and Aerospace	1.634	1.336	0.297
Telephone	3.859	3.680	0.180
Wireless Telecom	1.976	1.565	0.411
Information Services	0.802	2.698	−1.896
Industrial Services	0.806	0.670	0.136
Life/Health Insurance	0.403	0.938	−0.535
Property/Casualty Ins.	2.134	2.541	−0.407
Banks	8.369	7.580	0.788
Thrifts	0.000	0.362	−0.362
Securities and Asset Mgmt.	2.595	2.017	0.577
Financial Services	6.380	6.321	0.059
Internet	0.736	0.725	0.011
Equity REIT	2.199	0.193	2.006

Note: Mgd = Managed; Bmk = S&P 500 (the benchmark); Act = Active, which is Managed − Benchmark.

Tilting a Portfolio

Now let's look at how an active manager can construct a portfolio to make intentional bets. Suppose that a portfolio manager seeks to construct a portfolio that generates superior returns relative to the S&P 500 by tilting it toward low P/E stocks. At the same time, the manager does not want to increase tracking error significantly. An obvious approach may seem to be to identify all the stocks in the universe that have a lower than average P/E. The problem with this approach is that it introduces unintentional bets with respect to the other risk indexes.

Instead, an optimization method combined with a fundamental factor model can be used to construct the desired portfolio. The necessary inputs to this process are the tilt exposure sought and the benchmark stock market index. Additional constraints can be placed, for example, on the number of stocks to be included in the portfolio. The Barra optimization model can also handle additional specifications such as forecasts of expected returns or alphas on the individual stocks.

In our illustration, the tilt exposure sought is towards low P/E stocks, that is, towards high earnings yield stocks (since earnings yield is the inverse of P/E). The benchmark is the S&P 500. We seek a portfolio that has an average earnings yield that is at least 0.5 standard deviations more than that of the earnings yield of the benchmark. We do not place any limit on the number of stocks to be included in the portfolio. We also do not want the active exposure to any other risk index factor (other than earnings yield) to be more than 0.1 standard deviations in magnitude. This way we avoid placing unintended bets. While we do not report the holdings of the optimal portfolio here, Table 11.7 provides an analysis of that portfolio by comparing the risk exposure to that of the S&P 500.

TABLE 11.7 Factor Exposures of a Portfolio Tilted towards Earnings Yield

Risk Index Exposure (std. dev.)			
	Mgd	Bmk	Act
Volatility	−0.126	−0.084	−0.042
Momentum	0.013	−0.064	0.077
Size	0.270	0.370	−0.100
Size Nonlinearity	0.067	0.106	−0.038
Trading Activity	0.095	−0.005	0.100
Growth	−0.023	−0.045	0.022
Earnings Yield	0.534	0.034	0.500
Value	0.030	−0.070	0.100
Earnings Variation	−0.028	−0.088	0.060
Leverage	−0.006	−0.106	0.100
Currency Sensitivity	−0.105	−0.012	−0.093
Yield	0.134	0.034	0.100
Non-EST Universe	0.000	0.000	0.000

TABLE 11.7 (Continued)

Industry Weights (percent)	Mgd	Bmk	Act
Mining and Metals	0.022	0.606	−0.585
Gold	0.000	0.161	−0.161
Forestry and Paper	0.000	0.871	−0.871
Chemicals	1.717	2.046	−0.329
Energy Reserves	4.490	4.297	0.193
Oil Refining	3.770	1.417	2.353
Oil Services	0.977	0.620	0.357
Food and Beverages	0.823	3.780	−2.956
Alcohol	0.365	0.515	−0.151
Tobacco	3.197	0.732	2.465
Home Products	0.648	2.435	−1.787
Grocery Stores	0.636	0.511	0.125
Consumer Durables	0.000	0.166	−0.166
Motor Vehicles and Parts	0.454	0.621	−0.167
Apparel and Textiles	0.141	0.373	−0.232
Clothing Stores	0.374	0.341	0.033
Specialty Retail	0.025	2.721	−2.696
Department Stores	3.375	3.606	−0.231
Construction and Real Property	9.813	0.288	9.526
Publishing	0.326	0.778	−0.452
Media	0.358	1.498	−1.140
Hotels	0.067	0.209	−0.141
Restaurants	0.000	0.542	−0.542
Entertainment	0.675	1.630	−0.955
Leisure	0.000	0.409	−0.409
Environmental Services	0.000	0.220	−0.220
Heavy Electrical Equipment	1.303	1.949	−0.647
Heavy Machinery	0.000	0.141	−0.141
Industrial Parts	1.366	1.469	−0.103
Electric Utility	4.221	1.956	2.265
Gas Utilities	0.204	0.456	−0.252
Railroads	0.185	0.373	−0.189

TABLE 11.7 (Continued)

	Mgd	Bmk	Act
Airlines	0.000	0.206	−0.206
Truck/Sea/Air Freight	0.000	0.162	−0.162
Medical Services	0.000	0.789	−0.789
Medical Products	1.522	3.599	−2.077
Drugs	7.301	10.000	−2.699
Electronic Equipment	0.525	1.985	−1.460
Semiconductors	3.227	4.509	−1.282
Computer Hardware	2.904	4.129	−1.224
Computer Software	7.304	6.256	1.048
Defense and Aerospace	1.836	1.336	0.499
Telephone	6.290	3.680	2.610
Wireless Telecom	2.144	1.565	0.580
Information Services	0.921	2.698	−1.777
Industrial Services	0.230	0.670	−0.440
Life/Health Insurance	1.987	0.938	1.048
Property/Casualty Ins.	4.844	2.541	2.304
Banks	8.724	7.580	1.144
Thrifts	0.775	0.362	0.413
Securities and Asset Mgmt	3.988	2.017	1.971
Financial Services	5.510	6.321	−0.811
Internet	0.434	0.725	−0.291
Equity REIT	0.000	0.193	−0.193

Note: Mgd = Managed; Bmk = S&P 500 (the benchmark); Act = Active, which is Managed − Benchmark.

SUMMARY

In quantitative-oriented equity portfolio management, factor models are typically used to construct, rebalance, and evaluate the performance of a portfolio. While there are different types of factor models, in this chapter we discussed the most commonly used model, a fundamental factor model. In a fundamental factor model, company and industry attributes and market data are used as "descriptors" to identify which are statistically significant in explaining stock returns. Examples of descriptors are earnings/price ratios, book/price ratios, estimated earnings growth, and trading activity. The descriptors that are found to be statistically significant are then grouped into "factors" or "risk indexes" so as to capture related company attributes. For example, descriptors such as market leverage, book leverage, debt-to-equity ratio, and company's debt rating are combined to obtain a factor referred to as "leverage." In this chapter, we illustrate how a fundamental factor model can be used to assess the exposure of a portfolio, control risk against a stock market index, and tilt a portfolio.

A key measure used in factor models is tracking error. This measure quantifies the variation of a portfolio's actual return (i.e., the difference between the return on the portfolio and the return on the benchmark index). There are two types of tracking error: backward looking and forward looking. The former is calculated from the actual returns realized from a portfolio. A major drawback of backward-looking tracking error is that it does not reflect the effect of current decisions by the portfolio manager on the future active returns and hence may be misleading if the portfolio manager has significantly rebalanced the portfolio. In contrast, forward-looking tracking error is the estimated future tracking error of the current portfolio.

A fundamental factor model can be used in portfolio construction and risk control by decomposing a portfolio's risk in order to assess the potential performance of a portfolio to the factors and to assess the potential performance of a portfolio relative to a benchmark. Moreover, this decomposition of risk can be use to assess the actual performance of a portfolio relative to a benchmark. As explained in this chapter, there are four approaches that can be used to decompose a portfolio's risk: total risk decomposition, systematic-residual risk decomposition, active risk decomposition, and active systematic-active residual risk decomposition.

REFERENCES

Barra. 1998. *Risk model handbook for United States equity: Version 3.* Berkeley, CA.
Burmeister, E., R. R. Roll, and S. A. Ross. 2003. Using macroeconomic factors to control portfolio risk. Working paper.
Connor, G. 1995. The three types of factor models. *Financial Analysts Journal* 51 (May–June): 42–57.
Fabozzi, F. J., F. J. Jones, and R. Vardharaj. 2002. Multifactor equity risk models. In *Theory and Practice of Investment Management*, edited by F. J. Fabozzi and H. M. Markowitz (pp. 343–372). New York: John Wiley & Sons.
Fama, E. F., and K. R. French. 1993. Common risk factors in the returns on stocks and bonds. *Journal of Financial Economics* 33, no. 1: 3–56.
Vardharaj, R., F. J. Fabozzi, and F. J. Jones. 2004. Determinants of tracking error for equity portfolios. *Journal of Investing* 13, no. 2: 37–47.

CHAPTER 12

Transaction Costs and Trade Execution in Common Stock Portfolio Management

Trading is an integral component of the investment process. A poorly executed trade can eat directly into portfolio returns. This is because financial markets are not frictionless and transactions have a cost associated to them. Costs are incurred when buying or selling securities in the form of, brokerage commissions, bid-ask spreads, taxes, and market impact costs.

One way of describing transaction costs is to categorize them in terms of (1) *explicit costs* such as brokerage commissions and taxes, and (2) implicit costs, which include market impact costs, price movement risk, and opportunity cost. *Market impact cost* is, broadly speaking, the price an investor has to pay for obtaining liquidity in the market, whereas *price movement risk* is the risk that the price of a stock increases or decreases from the time the investor decides to transact in the stock until the transaction actually takes place. *Opportunity cost* is the cost suffered when a trade is not executed. Another way of categorizing transaction costs is in terms of *fixed costs* versus *variable costs*. Whereas commissions and trading fees are fixed, bid-ask spreads, taxes, and all implicit transaction costs are variable.

In this chapter, we will first present a simple taxonomy of trading costs. and the linkage between transaction costs and liquidity, as well as the measurement of these quantities. Portfolio managers and traders need to be able to effectively model the impact of trading costs on their portfolios and trades. In particular, if possible, they would like to minimize total transaction costs. To address these issues, several approaches for the modeling of transaction costs have been proposed and we will identify them. We then provide a brief introduction to optimal execution strategies. We begin the

---

This chapter is coauthored with Sergio Focardi and Petter N. Kolm.

chapter with a description of trading mechanics and trading arrangements used by institutional investors.

TRADING MECHANICS

In this section, we describe the key features involved in trading stocks. In the next section, we discuss trading arrangements that developed specifically for coping with the trading needs of institutional investors.

Types of Orders and Trading Priority Rules

When an investor wants to buy or sell a share of common stock, the price and conditions under which the order is to be executed must be communicated to a broker. The simplest type of order is the *market order*, an order to be executed at the best price available in the market. If the stock is listed and traded on an organized exchange, the best price is assured by the exchange rule that when more than one order on the same side of the buy/sell transaction reaches the market at the same time, the order with the best price is given priority. Thus, buyers offering a higher price are given priority over those offering a lower price; sellers asking a lower price are given priority over those asking a higher price.

Another priority rule of exchange trading is needed to handle receipt of more than one order at the same price. Most often, the priority in executing such orders is based on the time of arrival of the order—the first orders in are the first orders executed—although there may be a rule that gives higher priority to certain types of market participants over other types of market participants who are seeking to transact at the same price. For example, on exchanges, orders can be classified as either *public orders* or orders of those member firms dealing for their own account (both nonspecialists and specialists). Exchange rules require that public orders be given priority over orders of member firms dealing for their own account.

The danger of a market order is that an adverse move may take place between the time the investor places the order and the time the order is executed. To avoid this danger, the investor can place a *limit order* that designates a price threshold for the execution of the trade.[1] A *buy limit order* indicates that the stock may be purchased only at the designated

---

[1]There are many different limit order types available such as pegging orders, discretionary limit orders, IOC orders, and fleeting orders. For example, fleeting orders are those limit orders that are cancelled within two seconds of submission. Hasbrouck and Saar (2008) find that fleeting limit orders are much closer substitutes for market orders than for traditional limit orders.

price or lower. A *sell limit order* indicates that the stock may be sold at the designated price or higher. The key disadvantage of a limit order is that there is no guarantee that it will be executed at all; the designated price may simply not be obtainable. A limit order that is not executable at the time it reaches the market is recorded in the limit order book that we mentioned in Chapter 6.

The limit order is a *conditional order* that is executed only if the limit price or a better price can be obtained. Another type of conditional order is the *stop order*, which specifies that the order is not to be executed until the market moves to a designated price, at which time it becomes a market order. A *buy stop order* specifies that the order is not to be executed until the market rises to a designated price, that is, until it trades at or above, or is bid at or above, the designated price. A *sell stop order* specifies that the order is not to be executed until the market price falls below a designated price—that is, until it trades at or below, or is offered at or below, the designated price. A stop order is useful when an investor cannot watch the market constantly. Profits can be preserved or losses minimized on a stock position by allowing market movements to trigger a trade. In a sell (buy) stop order, the designated price is lower (higher) than the current market price of the stock. In a sell (buy) limit order, the designated price is higher (lower) than the current market price of the stock.

There are two dangers associated with stop orders. Stock prices sometimes exhibit abrupt price changes, so the direction of a change in a stock price may be quite temporary, resulting in the premature trading of a stock. Also, once the designated price is reached, the stop order becomes a market order and is subject to the uncertainty of the execution price noted earlier for market orders.

A *stop-limit order*, a hybrid of a stop order and a limit order, is a stop order that designates a price limit. In contrast to the stop order, which becomes a market order if the stop is reached, the stop-limit order becomes a limit order if the stop is reached. The stop-limit order can be used to cushion the market impact of a stop order. The investor may limit the possible execution price after the activation of the stop. As with a limit order, the limit price may never be reached after the order is activated, which therefore defeats one purpose of the stop order—to protect a profit or limit a loss.

An investor may also enter a *market-if-touched order*. This order becomes a market order if a designated price is reached. A market if touched order to buy becomes a market order if the market falls to a given price, while a stop order to buy becomes a market order if the market rises to a given price. Similarly, a market if touched order to sell becomes a market order if the market rises to a specified price, while the stop order to sell becomes a market order if the market falls to a given price. We can think of the stop order as an order designed to get out of an existing position at an acceptable price (without specifying the exact price), and the market if touched order as an order designed to get into a position at an acceptable price (also without specifying the exact price).

Orders may be placed to buy or sell at the open or the close of trading for the day. An opening order indicates a trade to be executed only in the opening range for the day, and a closing order indicates a trade is to be executed only within the closing range for the day.

An investor may enter orders that contain order cancellation provisions. A *fill-or-kill order* must be executed as soon as it reaches the trading floor or it is immediately canceled. Orders may designate the time period for which the order is effective—a day, week, or month, or perhaps by a given time within the day. An *open order*, or *good-till-canceled order*, is good until the investor specifically terminates the order.

Orders are also classified by their size. A *round lot* is typically 100 shares of a stock. An *odd lot* is defined as less than a round lot.

Margin Transactions

Investors can borrow cash to buy securities and use the securities themselves as collateral. A transaction in which an investor borrows to buy shares using the shares themselves as collateral is referred to as *buying on margin*. By borrowing funds, an investor creates leverage. The funds borrowed to buy the additional stock will be provided by the broker, and the broker gets the money from a bank. The interest rate that banks charge brokers for these funds is the *call money rate* (also referred to as the *broker loan rate*). The broker charges the borrowing investor the call money rate plus a service charge.

The brokerage firm is not free to lend as much as it wishes to the investor to buy securities. The Securities Exchange Act of 1934 prohibits brokers from lending more than a specified percentage of the market value of the securities. The *initial margin requirement* is the proportion of the total market value of the securities that the investor must pay as an equity share, and the remainder is borrowed from the broker. The 1934 Act gives the Board of Governors of the Federal Reserve (the Fed) the responsibility to set initial margin requirements.

The Fed also establishes a maintenance margin requirement. This is the minimum proportion of (1) the equity in the investor's margin account to (2) the total market value. If the investor's margin account falls below the minimum maintenance margin (which would happen if the share price fell), the investor is required to put up additional cash. The investor receives a margin call from the broker specifying the additional cash to be put into the investor's margin account. If the investor fails to put up the additional cash, the broker has the authority to sell the securities in the investor's account.

TRADING ARRANGEMENTS FOR INSTITUTIONAL INVESTORS

With the increase in trading by institutional investors, trading arrangements more suitable to these investors were developed. Institutional investor needs include trading in large size and trading groups of stocks, both at a low commission and with low market impact. This has resulted in the evolution of special arrangements for the execution of certain types of orders commonly sought by institutional investors: (1) orders requiring the execution of a trade of a large number of shares of a given stock and (2) orders requiring the execution of trades in a large number of different stocks at as near the same time as possible. The former types of trades are called *block trades*; the latter are called *program trades*. An example of a block trade would be a mutual fund seeking to buy 15,000 shares of IBM stock. An example of a program trade would be a pension fund wanting to buy shares of 100 names (companies) at the end of a trading day ("at the close").

The institutional arrangement that has evolved to accommodate these two types of institutional trades is a network of trading desks of the major securities firms and other institutional investors that communicate with each other by means of electronic display systems and telephones. As explained in Chapter 6, this network is referred to as the upstairs market. Participants in the upstairs market play a key role by providing liquidity to the market so that such institutional trades can be executed, and by arbitrage activities that help to integrate the fragmented stock market.

Block Trades

On the New York Stock Exchange (NYSE), block trades are defined as trades of at least 10,000 shares of a given stock. Since the execution of large numbers of block orders places strains on the specialist system in the NYSE, special procedures have been developed to handle them. Typically, an institutional customer contacts its salesperson at a brokerage firm, indicating that it wishes to place a block order. The salesperson then gives the order to the block execution department of the brokerage firm. Note that the salesperson does not submit the order to be executed to the exchange where the stock might be traded or, in the case of an unlisted stock, try to execute the order on the Nasdaq system. The sales traders in the block execution department contact other institutions to attempt to find one or more institutions that would be willing to take the other side of the order. That is, they use the upstairs market in their search to fill the block trade order. If this can be accomplished, the execution of the order is completed.

If the sales traders cannot find enough institutions to take the entire block, then the balance of the block trade order is given to the firm's market maker. The market maker must then make a decision as to how to handle the balance of the block trade order. There are two choices. First, the brokerage firm may take a position in the stock and buy the shares for its own account. Second, the unfilled order may be executed by using the services of competing market makers. In the former case, the brokerage firm is committing its own capital.

NYSE Rule 127 states that if a member firm receives an order for a large block of stock that might not be readily absorbed by the market, the member firm should nevertheless explore the market on the NYSE floor, including, where appropriate, consulting with the specialist as to his interest in the security. If a member firm intends to cross a large block of stock for a public account at a price that is outside of the current quote, it should inform the specialist of its intention.

Program Trades

Program trades involve the buying and selling of a large number of names simultaneously. Such trades are also called *basket trades* because effectively a "basket" of stocks is being traded. The NYSE defines a program trade as any trade involving the purchase or sale of a basket of at least 15 stocks with a total value of $1 million or more. Some examples of why an institutional investor may want to use a program trade are deployment of new cash into the stock market; implementation of a decision to move funds invested in the bond market to the stock market (or vice versa); and rebalancing the composition of a stock portfolio because of a change in investment strategy. A mutual fund portfolio manager can, for example, move funds quickly into or out of the stock market for an entire portfolio of stocks through a single program trade. All these strategies are related to asset allocation.

The growth of mutual fund sales and massive equity investments by pension funds and insurance companies during the 1990s have all given an impetus to such methods to trade baskets or bundles of stocks efficiently. Other reasons for which an institutional investor may have a need to execute a program trade is in implementing an indexing strategy.

There are several commission arrangements available to an institution for a program trade and each arrangement has numerous variants. Considerations in selecting one (in addition to commission costs) are the risk of failing to realize the best execution price; and the risk that the brokerage firms to be solicited about executing the program trade will use their knowledge of the program trade to benefit from the anticipated price movement that might result—in other words, that they will *front-run* the transaction (for example, buying a stock for their own account before filling the customer buy order). From a dealer's perspective, program trades can be conducted in two ways, namely on an agency basis and on a principal basis. An intermediate type of program trade, the agency incentive arrangement, is an additional alternative. A program trade executed on an agency basis involves the selection by the investor of a brokerage firm solely on the basis of commission bids (cents per share) submitted by various brokerage firms.

The brokerage firm selected uses its best efforts as an agent of the institution to obtain the best price. Such trades have low explicit commissions. To the investor, the disadvantage of the agency program trade is that, while commissions may be the lowest, the execution price may not be the best because of impact costs and the potential front-running by the brokerage firms solicited to submit a commission bid. The investor knows in advance the commission paid, but does not know the price at which the trades will be executed.

Related to the agency basis is an *agency incentive arrangement*, in which a benchmark portfolio value is established for the group of stocks in the program trade. The price for each "name" (i.e., specific stock) in the program trade is determined as either the price at the end of the previous day or the average price of the previous day. If the brokerage firm can execute the trade on the next trading day such that a better-than benchmark portfolio value results—a higher value in the case of a program trade involving selling, or a lower value in the case of a program trade involving buying—then the brokerage firm receives the specified commission plus some predetermined additional compensation. In this case, the investor does not know in advance the commission or the execution price precisely, but has a reasonable expectation that the price will be better than a threshold level.

If the brokerage firm does not achieve the benchmark portfolio value, the program variants come into play. One arrangement may call for the brokerage firm to receive only the previously agreed-upon commission. Other arrangements may involve sharing the risk of not realizing the benchmark portfolio value with the brokerage firm. That is, if the brokerage firm falls short of the benchmark portfolio value, it must absorb a portion of the shortfall. In these risk-sharing arrangements, the brokerage firm is risking its own capital. The greater the risk sharing the brokerage firm must accept, the higher the commission it will charge.

The brokerage firm can also choose to execute the trade on a principal basis. In this case, the dealer would commit its own capital to buy or sell the portfolio and complete the investor's transaction immediately. Since the dealer incurs market risk, it would also charge higher commissions. The key factors in pricing principal trades are liquidity characteristics, absolute dollar value, nature of the trade, customer profile, and market volatility. In this case, the investor knows the trade execution price in advance, but pays a higher commission.

To minimize front-running, institutions often use other types of program trade arrangements. They call for brokerage firms to receive, not specific names and quantities of stocks, but only aggregate statistical information about key portfolio parameters. Several brokerage firms then bid on a cents per share basis on the entire portfolio (also called *blind baskets*), guaranteeing execution at either the closing price (termed *market-at-close*) or a particular intraday price to the customer. Note that this is a principal trade. Since mutual fund net asset values are calculated using closing prices, a mutual fund that follows an indexing strategy (i.e., an index fund), for instance, would want guaranteed market-at-close execution to minimize the risk of not performing as well as the benchmark stock index. When the winning bidder has been selected, it receives the details of the portfolio. While the commission in this type of transaction is higher, this procedure increases the risk to the brokerage firm of successfully executing the program trade. However, the brokerage firm can use stock index futures to protect itself from market-wide movements if the characteristics of the portfolio in the program trade are similar to the index underlying the stock index futures contract.

Algorithmic Trading

Traditionally, orders for stock executions have been conducted by traders who execute the trades on a trading desk for a portfolio manager or whomever determines what trades should be executed. Traders are judged to have "market information and savy" which permits them to conduct the trades at a lower cost and with less market impact than the portfolio manager conducting the trades on a less formal basis themselves.

The effectiveness of these traders is often measured by execution evaluation services, and traders are often compensated partially on the basis of their effectiveness. But some observers believe that the traders, in the interest of maximizing their compensation, may have different incentives than the portfolio managers and do not optimize the portfolio manager's objectives—this is referred to as an agency effect. In addition, some think that trades could be conducted more efficiently by electronic systems than by human traders.

As a result, due to improved technology and quantitative techniques, and also regulatory changes, electronic trading systems have been developed to supplement or replace human traders and their trading desks. Such trading is called *algorithmic trading* or *algo*.

Algorithmic trading is a relatively recent type of trading technique whereby an overall trade (either buy or sell) is conducted electronically in a series of small transactions instead of one large transaction. Such trades are conducted via computers, which make the decision to trade or not trade depending on whether recent price movements indicate whether the market will be receptive to the intended trade at the moment or, instead, will cause the price to move significantly against the intended price. Algorithmic trading also permits the traders to hide their intentions. Trading may involve small trades on a continuous basis rather than a large trade at a point in time. The algo is often said to leave no "footprint" and is a "soft touch" way of trading.

Algos, like dark pools, provide anonymity, which the "visible markets," like exchanges and electronic communication networks (ECNs), do not. Algos are often described as "hiding in plain view."

The advent and wide use of algos is due primarily to both technology and regulation. The technology element is based on faster and cheaper technological systems to execute via improved quantitative methods. The regulatory element is the adoption of pennies and the approval of the order handling rules which provided for the growth of ECNs. The adoption of "pennies," which provides for smaller pricing increments, and technological advancements which provide for low-latency trading have made algorithmic trading more necessary and feasible (*low latency* refers to a short period of time to execute an instruction, i.e., high speed).

One important result of pennies in conjunction with algorithmic trading has been that the average trade size has decreased significantly, again increasing the requirements for reporting and systems.

The use of algorithmic trading is significant by large traders such as hedge funds and mutual funds. Some traders maintain their own algorithmic trading facilities and others use the systems provided by another organization. Overall, algorithmic trading has the advantages of being scalable, anonymous, transparent, and very fast.

Soft Dollars Arrangements

Investors often choose their broker-dealer based on who will give them the best execution at the lowest transaction cost on a specific transaction, and also based on who will provide complementary services (such as research) over a period of time. Order flow can also be "purchased" by a broker-dealer from an investor with "soft dollars." In this case, the broker-dealer provides the investor, without explicit charge, services such as research or electronic services, typically from a third party for which the investor would otherwise have had to pay "hard dollars" to the third party, in exchange for the investor's order flow. Of course, the investor pays the broker-dealer for the execution service.

According to such a relationship, the investor preferentially routes their order to the broker-dealer specified in the soft dollar relationship and does not have to pay "hard dollars," or real money, for the research or other services. This practice is called paying "soft dollars" (i.e., directing their order flow) for the ancillary research. For example, client A preferentially directs his order flow to broker-dealer B (often a specified amount of order flow over a specified period, such as a month or year) and pays the broker-dealer for these execution services. In turn, broker-dealer B pays for some research services provided to client A. Very often the research provider is a separate firm, say, firm C. Thus, soft dollars refer to money paid by an investor to a broker-dealer or a third party through commission revenue rather than by direct payments.

The disadvantage to the broker-dealer is that they have to pay hard dollars (to the research provider) for the client's order flow. The disadvantage to the client is that they are not free to "shop around" for the best bid or best offer, net of commissions, for all their transactions, but have to do an agreed amount of transaction volume with the specific broker-dealer. In addition, the research provider may give a preferential price to the broker-dealer. Thus, each of these participants in the soft dollar relationship experiences some advantage, but also an offsetting disadvantage.

The SEC has imposed formal and informal limitations on the type and amount of soft dollar business institutional investors can conduct. For example, while an institutional investor can accept research in a soft dollar relationship, they cannot accept furniture or vacations. SEC disclosure rules, passed in 1995, require investment advisors to disclose, among other things, the details on any product or services received through soft dollars. The CFA Institute has published standards that provide guidance as to how investment professionals should utilize soft dollars in a manner that benefits clients.

A TAXONOMY OF TRANSACTION COSTS

Probably the easiest way to describe transaction costs is to categorize them in terms of fixed versus variable transaction costs, and explicit versus implicit transaction costs as shown below as suggested by Kissell and Glantz (2003):

	Fixed	Variable
Explicit	Commissions	Bid-ask spreads
	Fees	Taxes
Implicit		Delay cost
		Price movement risk
		Market impact costs
		Timing risk
		Opportunity cost

Fixed transaction costs are independent of factors such as trade size and market conditions.[2] In contrast, variable transaction costs depend on some or all of these factors. In other words, although fixed transaction costs are "what they are," portfolio managers and traders can seek to reduce, optimize, and efficiently manage variable transaction costs.

Explicit transaction costs are those costs that are observable and known upfront such as commissions, fees, and taxes. Implicit transaction costs, in contrast, are nonobservable and not known in advance. Examples of transaction costs that fall into this category are market impact and opportunity cost. In general, the implicit costs make up the dominant part of the total transaction costs.

Explicit Transaction Costs

Trading commissions and fees, taxes, and bid-ask spreads are explicit transaction costs. Explicit transaction costs are also referred to as observable transaction costs.

Commissions and Fees

Commissions are paid to brokers to execute trades. Normally, commissions on trades are negotiable. Fees charged by an institution that holds the securities in safekeeping for an investor are referred to as *custodial fees*. When the ownership over a stock is transferred, the investor is charged a *transfer fee*.

Taxes

The most common taxes are *capital gains tax* and *tax on dividends*. The tax law distinguishes between two types of capital gains taxes: *short term* and

---

[2]Different exchanges and trading networks may have different fixed costs. Furthermore, the fixed costs may also be different depending upon whether a trade is an agency trade or a principal trade.

long term.[3] In the United States, the tax law as of this writing requires that an asset must be held for more than one year to qualify for the lower long-term capital gains rate. Although tax planning is an important component of many investment strategies, this topic is outside the scope of this book.

Bid-Ask Spreads

The difference between the quoted sell and buy order is called the *bid-ask spread*. The bid-ask spread is the immediate transaction cost that the market charges anyone for the privilege of trading. High immediate liquidity is synonymous with small spreads. We can think about the bid-ask spread as the price charged by dealers for supplying immediacy and short-term price stability in the presence of short-term order imbalances. Dealers act as a buffer between the investors that want to buy and sell, and thereby provide stability in the market by making sure a certain order is maintained. In negotiated markets such as the New York Stock Exchange, market makers and dealers maintain a certain minimum inventory on their books. If the dealer is unable to match a buyer with a seller (or vice versa), he or she has the capability to take on the exposure on his book.

However, the bid-ask spread does not necessarily represent the best prices available, and the "half spread" is therefore not always the minimal cost for immediate buy or sell executions. Certain price improvements are possible and occur, for example, because:

- NYSE specialists fill the incoming market orders at improved prices.[4]
- The market may have moved in the investor's favor during the time it took to route the order to the trading venue (a so-called "lucky saving").
- The presence of hidden liquidity.[5]
- Buy and sell orders can be "crossed."[6]

The bid-ask spread is misleading as a true liquidity measure because it only conveys the price for small trades. For large trades, due to price impact,

---

[3] In 2003, the long-term tax was reduced to 15% in general, and to 5% for individuals in the lowest two income tax brackets. In late 2008, there were proposals to raise this rate to 20%.
[4] See for example, Harris and Panchapagesan (2005).
[5] For example, on ECNs and on the Nasdaq, although it is possible to view the limit order book, a significant portion of the book cannot be seen. This is referred to as *hidden* or *discretionary orders*.
[6] A *cross order* is an offsetting or noncompetitive matching of the buy order of one investor against the sell order of another investor. This practice is permissible only when executed in accordance with the Commodity Exchange Act, U.S. Commodity Futures Trading Commission (CFTC) regulations, and the rules of the particular market.

Implicit Transaction Costs

Investment delay, market impact cost, price movement risk, market timing, and opportunity cost are implicit transaction costs. Implicit transaction costs are also referred to as nonobservable transaction costs.

Investment Delay

Normally, there is a delay between the time when the portfolio manager makes a buy/sell decision of a security and when the actual trade is brought to the market by a trader. If the price of the security changes during this time, the price change (possibly adjusted for general market moves) represents the *investment delay cost*, or the cost of not being able to execute immediately. This cost depends on the investment strategy. For example, modern quantitative trading systems that automatically submit an electronic order after generating a trading decision are exposed to smaller delay costs. More traditional approaches where investment decisions first have to be approved by, for example, an investment committee, exhibit higher delay costs. Some practitioners view the investment delay cost as part of the opportunity cost discussed below.

Market Impact Costs

The *market impact cost* of a transaction, also referred to as *price impact cost*, is the deviation of the transaction price from the market (mid) price[7] that would have prevailed had the trade not occurred. The price movement is the cost, the market impact cost, of liquidity. The price impact of a trade can be negative if, for example, a trader buys at a price below the no-trade price (i.e., the price that would have prevailed had the trade not taken place).

We distinguish between two kinds of market impact costs, temporary and permanent. Total market impact cost is computed as the sum of the two. Figure 12.1 illustrates the different components of the market impact costs of a sell order. The temporary price impact cost is of transitory nature and can be seen as the additional *liquidity concession* necessary for the liquidity provider (for example, the market maker) to take the order, *inventory effects* (price effects due to broker-dealer inventory imbalances), or *imperfect substitution* (for example, price incentives to induce market participants to absorb the additional shares).

---

[7]Since the buyer buys at the ask and the seller sells at the bid, this definition of market impact cost ignores the bid/ask spread which is an explicit cost.

FIGURE 12.1 Market Impact Costs: Sell Order

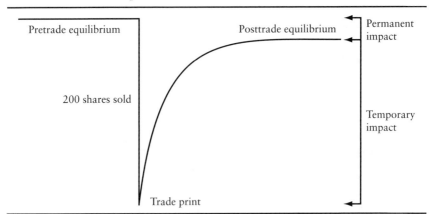

Source: Kolm and Machlin (2008).

The permanent price impact cost, however, reflects the persistent price change that results as the market adjusts to the information content of the trade. Intuitively, a sell transaction reveals to the market that the security may be overvalued, whereas a buy transaction signals that the security may be undervalued. Security prices change when market participants adjust their views and perceptions as they observe news and the information contained in new trades during the trading day.

Traders can decrease the temporary market impact by extending the trading horizon of an order. For example, a trader executing a less urgent order can buy/sell his position in smaller portions over a period and make sure that each portion only constitutes a small percentage of the average volume. However, this comes at the price of increased opportunity costs, delay costs, and price movement risk. We discuss this issue in more detail later in this chapter when we cover optimal execution models.

Several studies have found that market impact costs are often asymmetric; that is, market impact costs are different for buy and sell orders.[8] More specifically, empirical studies suggest that market impact costs are generally higher for buy orders. Nevertheless, while buying costs might be higher than

---

[8] For instance, Bikker and Spierdijk (2007) estimated the market impact costs from a data sample consisting of 3,728 worldwide equity trades executed during the first quarter of 2002 at the Dutch pension fund Algemeen Burgerlijk Pensioenfonds (ABP). The trades, of which 1,963 were buys and 1,765 sales, had a total transaction value of €5.7 billion. They concluded that the temporary and persistent price effects of buy orders were 7.2 basis points and 12.4 basis points, respectively. For sell orders, on the other hand, these price effects were –14.5 basis points and –16.5 basis points.

sell costs, this empirical fact is most likely due to observations during rising and falling markets, rather than any true market microstructure effects.[9]

Despite the enormous global size of equity markets, the impact of trading is important even for relatively small funds. In fact, a sizable fraction of the stocks that compose an index might have to be excluded or their trading severely limited. For example, as reported in Fabozzi et al. (2009), RAS Asset Management, which is the asset manager arm of the large Italian insurance company RAS, has determined that single trades exceeding 10% of the daily trading volume of a stock cause an excessive price impact and have to be excluded, while trades between 5% and 10% need execution strategies distributed over several days.

Price Movement Risk

In general, the stock market exhibits a positive drift that gives rise to price movement risk. Similarly, individual stocks, at least temporarily, trend up or down. A trade that goes in the same direction as the general market or an individual security is exposed to price risk. For example, when a trader is buying in a rising market, he might pay more than he initially anticipated to fully satisfy the order. In practice, it can be difficult to separate price movement risk from market impact costs. Typically, the price movement risk for a buy order is defined as the price increase during the time of the trade that is attributed to the general trend of a security, whereas the remaining part is market impact costs.

Market Timing Costs

The market timing costs are due to the movement in the price of a security at the time of the transaction that can be attributed to other market participants or general market volatility. Market timing costs are higher for larger trades, in particular when they are divided into smaller blocks and traded over a period of time. Practitioners often define market timing costs to be proportional to the standard deviation of the security returns times the square root of the time anticipated in order to complete the transaction.

---

[9]For example, a study by Hu (2003) shows that the difference in market impact costs between buys and sells is an artifact of the trade benchmark. (We discuss trade benchmarks later in this chapter.) When a pretrade measure is used, buys (sells) have higher implicit trading costs during rising (falling) markets. Conversely, if a posttrade measure is used, sells (buys) have higher implicit trading costs during rising (falling) markets. In fact, both pretrade and posttrade measures are highly influenced by market movement, whereas during- or average-trade measures are neutral to market movement.

Opportunity Costs

The cost of not transacting represents an opportunity cost. For example, when a certain trade fails to execute, the portfolio manager misses an opportunity. Commonly, this cost is defined as the difference in performance between a portfolio manager's desired investment and his actual investment after transaction costs. Opportunity costs are in general driven by price risk or market volatility. As a result, the longer the trading horizon, the greater the exposure to opportunity costs.

Identifying Transaction Costs: An Example[10]

We will use an example to highlight the key cost components of an equity trade. Following the completion of an institutional trade, suppose that the ticker tape for XYZ stock reveals that 6,000 shares of XYZ stock were purchased at $82.00. Although 6,000 XYZ shares were bought, the following indicates what may have happened behind the scenes—beginning with the initial security selection decision by the manager (the investment idea), to the release of the buy order by the equity trader, to the subsequent trade execution by the broker (the essential elements of trading implementation):

- Equity manager wants to buy 10,000 shares of XYZ at the current price of $80.
- Trade desk releases 8,000 shares to broker when price is $81.
- Broker purchases 6,000 shares of XYZ stock at $82 plus $0.045 (per share) commission.
- XYZ stock jumps to $85, and remainder of order is canceled.
- 15 days later the price of XYZ stock is $88.

We can assess the cost of trading XYZ stock as follows. The commission charge is the easiest to identify—namely, $0.045 per share, or $270 on the purchase of 6,000 shares of XYZ stock.

Since the trade desk did not release the order to buy XYZ stock until it was selling for $81, the assessed trader timing cost is $1 per share. Also, the market impact costs is $1 per XYZ share traded, as the stock was selling for $81 when the order was received by the broker—just prior to execution of the 6,000 XYZ shares at $82.

The opportunity cost—resulting from unexecuted shares—of the equity trade is more difficult to estimate. Assuming that the movement of XYZ stock's price from $80 to $88 can be largely attributed to information used by the equity manager in his security selection decision, it appears that the

---

[10]This illustration is similar to the example provided in Wagner and Edwards (1998). The example used here is taken from Fabozzi and Grant (1999).

value of the investment idea to purchase XYZ stock was 10% ($88/$80 − 1) over a 15-day trading interval. Since 40% of the initial buy order on XYZ stock was "left on the table," the opportunity cost of not purchasing 4,000 shares of XYZ stock is 4% (10% × 40%).

The basic trading cost illustration suggests that without efficient management of the equity trading process, it is possible that the value of the manager's investment ideas is impacted negatively by sizable trading costs in addition to commission charges, including trader timing, market impact cost, and opportunity cost. Moreover, trading cost management is especially important in a world where active equity managers are hard pressed to outperform a simple buy-and-hold approach such as that employed in a market index fund.

LIQUIDITY AND TRANSACTION COSTS

Liquidity is created by agents transacting in the financial markets when they buy and sell securities. Market makers, brokers, and dealers do not create liquidity. They are intermediaries who facilitate trade execution and maintain an orderly market.

Liquidity and transaction costs are interrelated. A highly liquid market is one were large transactions can be immediately executed without incurring high transaction costs. In an indefinitely liquid market, traders would be able to perform very large transactions directly at the quoted bid-ask prices. In reality, particularly for larger orders, the market requires traders to pay more than the ask when buying, and to pay less than the bid when selling. As we discussed above, this percentage degradation of the bid-ask prices experienced when executing trades is the market impact cost.

The market impact cost varies with transaction size: the larger the trade size the larger the impact cost. Impact costs are not constant in time, but vary throughout the day as traders change the limit orders that they have in the limit order book. As explained earlier, a limit order is a conditional order; it is executed only if the limit price or a better price can be obtained. Therefore, a limit order is very different from a market order, which is an unconditional order to execute at the current best price available in the market (guarantees execution, not price). With a limit order a trader can improve the execution price relative to the market order price, but the execution is neither certain nor immediate (guarantees price, not execution).

At any given instant, the list of orders sitting in the limit order book embodies the liquidity that exists at a particular point in time. By observing the entire limit order book, impact costs can be calculated for different transaction sizes. The limit order book reveals the prevailing supply and demand in the market.[11] Therefore, in a pure limit order market, we can obtain a measure of liquidity by aggregating limit buy orders (representing the demand) and limit sell orders (representing the supply).[12]

We start by sorting the bid and ask prices, $p_1^{bid},\ldots,p_k^{bid}$ and $p_1^{ask},\ldots,p_l^{ask}$, (from the most to the least competitive) and the corresponding order quantities $q_1^{bid},\ldots,q_k^{bid}$ and $q_1^{ask},\ldots,q_l^{ask}$. We then combine the sorted bid and ask prices into a supply and demand schedule according to Figure 12.2. For example, the block (p_2^{bid},q_2^{bid}) represents the second best sell limit order with price p_2^{bid} and quantity q_2^{bid}.

Note that unless there is a gap between the bid (demand) and the ask (supply) sides, there will be a match between a seller and buyer, and a trade would occur. The larger the gap, the lower the liquidity and the market participants' desire to trade. For a trade of size Q, we can define its liquidity as the reciprocal of the area between the supply and demand curves up to Q (i.e., the "dotted" area in Figure 12.2).

FIGURE 12.2 The Supply and Demand Schedule of a Security

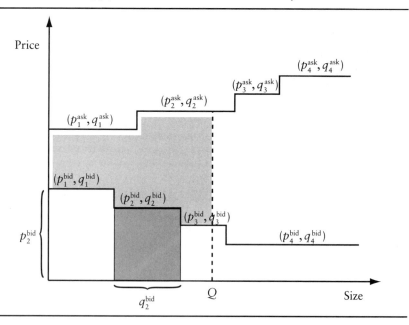

Source: Figure 1A of Domowitz and Wang (2002, 38).

[11]Even if it is possible to view the entire limit order book, it does not give a *complete* picture of the liquidity in the market. This is because hidden and discretionary orders are not included. For a discussion of this topic, see Tuttle (2002).
[12]See Domowitz and Wang (2002) and Foucault, Kadan, and Kandel (2005).

However, few order books are publicly available and not all markets are pure limit order markets. In 2004, the NYSE started selling information on its limit order book through its new system called the *NYSE OpenBook®*. The system provides an aggregated real-time view of the exchange's limit-order book for all NYSE-traded securities.

In the absence of a fully transparent limit order book, expected market impact cost is the most practical and realistic measure of market liquidity. It is closer to the true cost of transacting faced by market participants as compared to other measures such as those based upon the bid-ask spread.

MARKET IMPACT MEASUREMENTS AND EMPIRICAL FINDINGS

The problem with measuring implicit transaction costs is that the true measure, which is the difference between the price of the stock in the absence of a portfolio manager's trade and the execution price, is not observable. Furthermore, the execution price is dependent on supply and demand conditions at the margin. Thus, the execution price may be influenced by competitive traders who demand immediate execution or by other investors with similar motives for trading. This means that the execution price realized by an investor is the consequence of the structure of the market mechanism, the demand for liquidity by the marginal investor, and the competitive forces of investors with similar motivations for trading.

There are many ways to measure transaction costs. However, in general this cost is the difference between the execution price and some appropriate benchmark, a so-called *fair market benchmark*. The fair market benchmark of a security is the price that would have prevailed had the trade not taken place, referred to as the *no-trade price*. Since the no-trade price is not observable, it has to be estimated. Practitioners have identified three different basic approaches to measure the market impact:[13]

- *Pretrade measures* use prices occurring before or at the decision to trade as the benchmark, such as the opening price on the same day or the closing price on the previous day.
- *Posttrade measures* use prices occurring after the decision to trade as the benchmark, such as the closing price of the trading day or the opening price on the next day.
- *Same-day* or *average measures* use average prices of a large number of trades during the day of the decision to trade, such as the *volume-*

---

[13] Collins and Fabozzi (1991) and Chan and Lakonishok (1993).

weighted average price (VWAP) calculated over all transactions in the security on the trade day.[14]

The volume-weighted average price is calculated as follows. Suppose that it was a trader's objective to purchase 10,000 shares of XYZ stock. After completion of the trade, the trade sheet showed that 4,000 shares were purchased at $80, another 4,000 at $81, and finally 2,000 at $82. In this case, the resulting VWAP is (4,000 × 80 + 4,000 × 81 + 2,000 × 82)/10,000 = $80.80.

We denote by χ the indicator function that takes on the value 1 or –1 if an order is a buy or sell order, respectively. Formally, we now express the three types of measures of *market impact* (MI) as follows:

$$\mathrm{MI}_{\mathrm{pre}} = \left(\frac{p^{\mathrm{ex}}}{p^{\mathrm{pre}}} - 1 \right) \chi$$

$$\mathrm{MI}_{\mathrm{post}} = \left(\frac{p^{\mathrm{ex}}}{p^{\mathrm{post}}} - 1 \right) \chi$$

$$\mathrm{MI}_{\mathrm{VWAP}} = \left(\frac{\sum_{i=1}^{k} V_i \cdot p_i^{\mathrm{ex}}}{\sum_{i=1}^{k} V_i} \bigg/ p^{\mathrm{pre}} - 1 \right) \chi$$

where p^{ex}, p^{pre}, and p^{post} denote the execution price, pretrade price, and post-trade price of the stock, and k denotes the number of transactions in a particular security on the trade date. Using this definition, for a stock with market impact MI the resulting *market impact cost* for a trade of size V, MIC, is given by

$$\mathrm{MIC} = \mathrm{MI} \times V$$

It is also common to adjust market impact for general market movements. For example, the pretrade market impact with market adjustment would take the form

$$\mathrm{MI}_{\mathrm{pre}} = \left(\frac{p^{\mathrm{ex}}}{p^{\mathrm{pre}}} - \frac{p_M^{\mathrm{ex}}}{p_M^{\mathrm{pre}}} \right) \chi$$

---

[14] Strictly speaking, VWAP is not the benchmark here but rather the transaction type.

where p_M^{ex} represent the value of the index at the time of the execution, and p_M^{pre} the price of the index at the time before the trade. Market-adjusted market impact for the posttrade and same-day trade benchmarks are calculated in an analogous fashion.

The previous three approaches to measure market impact are based upon measuring the fair market benchmark of a stock at a point in time. Clearly, different definitions of market impact lead to different results. Which one should be used is a matter of preference and is dependent on the application at hand. For example, Elkins/McSherry, a financial consulting firm that provides customized trading costs and execution analysis, calculates a same-day benchmark price for each stock by taking the mean of the day's open, close, high, and low prices. The market impact is then computed as the percentage difference between the transaction price and this benchmark. However, in most cases VWAP and the Elkins/McSherry approach lead to similar measurements.[15]

As we analyze a portfolio's return over time, an important question to ask is whether we can attribute good/bad performance to investment profits/losses or to trading profits/losses. In other words, in order to better understand a portfolio's performance, it can be useful to decompose investment decisions from order execution. This is the basic idea behind the *implementation shortfall approach* suggested by Perold (1998).

In the implementation shortfall approach we assume that there is a separation between investment and trading decisions. The portfolio manager makes decisions with respect to the investment strategy (i.e., what should be bought, sold, and held). Subsequently, these decisions are implemented by the traders.

By comparing the actual portfolio profit/loss (P/L) with the performance of a hypothetical "paper" portfolio in which all trades are made at hypothetical market prices, we can get an estimate of the implementation shortfall. For example, with a paper portfolio return of 6% and an actual portfolio return of 5%, the implementation shortfall is 1%.

There is considerable practical and academic interest in the measurement and analysis of international trading costs. Domowitz, Glen, and Madhavan (1999) examine international equity trading costs across a broad sample of 42 countries using quarterly data from 1995 to 1998. They find that the mean total one-way trading cost is 69.81 basis points. However, there is an enormous variation in trading costs across countries. For example, in their study the highest was Korea with 196.85 basis points whereas the lowest was France with 29.85 basis points. Explicit costs are roughly two-thirds of total costs. However, one exception to this is the United States where the implicit costs are about 60% of the total costs.

---

[15] See Willoughby (1998) and McSherry (1998).

Transaction costs in emerging markets are significantly higher than those in more developed markets. Domowitz, Glen, and Madhavan (1999) argue that this fact limits the gains of international diversification in these countries, explaining in part the documented "home bias" of domestic investors. In general, they find that transaction costs declined from the middle of 1997 to the end of 1998, with the exception of Eastern Europe. It is interesting to notice that this reduction in transaction costs happened despite the turmoil in the financial markets during this period. A few explanations that Domowitz, Glen, and Madhavan suggest are that (1) the increased institutional presence has resulted in a more competitive environment for brokers/dealers and other trading services; (2) technological innovation has led to a growth in the use of low-cost ECNs by institutional traders; and (3) soft dollar payments are now more common.

FORECASTING AND MODELING MARKET IMPACT

As discussed in the previous section, the explicit transaction costs are relatively straightforward to estimate and forecast. With respect to market impact cost, there have been several models that are used in practice for forecasting and modeling this cost. These models are very useful in predicting the resulting trading costs of specific trading strategies and in devising optimal trading approaches.

We emphasize that in the modeling of transaction costs, it is important to factor in the objective of the trader or investor. For example, one market participant might trade just to take advantage of price movement and hence will only trade during favorable periods. His trading cost is different from an investor who has to rebalance a portfolio within a fixed time period and can therefore only partially use an opportunistic or liquidity searching strategy. In particular, this investor has to take into account the risk of not completing the transaction within a specified time period. Consequently, even if the market is not favorable, he may decide to transact a portion of the trade. The market impact models described above assume that orders will be fully completed and ignore this point.

Although a complete description of these statistical models is beyond the scope of this chapter, we discuss the variables that are considered in these models.[16] The variables or forecasting factors used in modeling market impact costs are grouped in terms of trade-based and asset-based variables. We discuss each in this section.

---

[16] For a general methodology for constructing forecasting models for market impact, see Fabozzi et al. (2009).

Trade-Based Factors

Some examples of trade-based factors include:

- Trade size
- Relative trade size
- Price of market liquidity
- Type of trade (information or noninformation trade)
- Efficiency and trading style of the investor
- Specific characteristics of the market or the exchange
- Time of trade submission and trade timing
- Order type

Probably the most important market impact forecasting variables are based on absolute or relative trade size. Absolute trade size is often measured in terms of the number of shares traded, or the dollar value of the trade. Relative trade size, on the other hand, can be calculated as the number of shares traded divided by average daily volume, or number of shares traded divided by the total number of shares outstanding. The former can be seen as an explanatory variable for the temporary market impact and the latter for the permanent market impact. In particular, we expect the temporary market impact to increase as the trade size to the average daily volume increases because a larger trade demands more liquidity.

Each type of investment style requires a different need for immediacy.[17] Technical trades often have to be traded at a faster pace in order to capitalize on some short-term signal and therefore exhibits higher market impact costs. In contrast, more traditional long-term value strategies can be traded more slowly. These type of strategies can in many cases even be liquidity providing, which might result in negative market impact costs.

Several studies show that there is a wide variation in equity transaction costs across different countries.[18] Markets and exchanges in each country are different, and so are the resulting market microstructures. Forecasting variables can be used to capture specific market characteristics such as liquidity, efficiency, and institutional features.

The particular timing of a trade can affect the market impact costs. For example, it appears that market impact costs are generally higher at the beginning of the month as compared to the end of it.[19] One of the reasons for this phenomenon is that many institutional investors tend to rebalance

---

[17] See, for example, Keim and Madhavan (1997).
[18] See, for example, Domowitz, Glen, and Madhavan (1999), and Chiyachantana, et al. (2004).
[19] See Foster and Viswanathan (1990).

their portfolios at the beginning of the month. Because it is likely that many of these trades will be executed in the same stocks, this rebalancing pattern will induce an increase in market impact costs. The particular time of the day a trade takes place also has an effect. Many informed institutional traders tend to trade at the market open as they want to capitalize on new information that appeared after the market close the day before.

As we discussed earlier in this chapter, market impact costs are asymmetric. In other words, buy and sell orders have significantly different market impact costs. Separate models for buy and sell orders can therefore be estimated.

Asset-Based Factors

Some examples of asset-based factors are:

- Price momentum
- Price volatility
- Market capitalization
- Growth versus value
- Specific industry or sector characteristics

For a stock that is exhibiting positive price momentum, a buy order is liquidity demanding and it is therefore likely that it will have higher price impact cost than a sell order.

Generally, trades in high volatility stocks result in higher permanent price effects. It has been suggested by Chan and Lakonishok (1997) and Smith et al. (2001) that this is because trades have a tendency to contain more information when volatility is high. Another possibility is that higher volatility increases the probability of hitting and being able to execute at the liquidity providers' price. Consequently, liquidity suppliers display fewer shares at the best prices to mitigate adverse selection costs.

Large-cap stocks are more actively traded and therefore more liquid in comparison to small-cap stocks. As a result, market impact cost is normally lower for large-cap stocks.[20] However, if we measure market impact costs with respect to relative trade size (normalized by average daily volume, for instance), they are generally higher. Similarly, growth and value stocks have different market impact cost. One reason for that is related to the trading style. Growth stocks commonly exhibit momentum and high volatility. This attracts technical traders that are interested in capitalizing on short-term price swings. Value stocks are traded at a slower pace and holding periods tend to be slightly longer.

---

[20] See Keim and Madhavan (1997) and Spierdijk, Nijman, and van Soest (2003).

Different market sectors show different trading behaviors. For instance, Bikker and Spierdijk (2007) show that equity trades in the energy sector exhibit higher market impact costs than other comparable equities in non-energy sectors.

INCORPORATING TRANSACTION COSTS IN ASSET-ALLOCATION MODELS

Standard asset-allocation models generally ignore transaction costs and other costs related to portfolio and allocation revisions. However, the effect of transaction costs is far from insignificant. On the contrary, if transaction costs are not taken into consideration, they can eat into a significant part of the returns. Whether transaction costs are handled efficiently or not by the portfolio manager can therefore make all the difference in attempting to outperform the peer group or a particular benchmark.

The typical asset-allocation model consists of one or several forecasting models for expected returns and risk. Small changes in these forecasts can result in reallocations which would not occur if transaction costs had been taken into account. Therefore, it is to be expected that the inclusion of transaction costs in asset-allocation models will result in a reduced amount of trading and rebalancing.

Given the complexity of the mathematical models that have been proposed for incorporating transaction costs into asset-allocation models such as the Markowitz mean-variance model, we cannot present them here. Instead, we provide some general remarks about these models.

Pogue (1970) gave one of the first descriptions of an extension of the mean-variance framework that included transaction costs. The formulation of more sophisticated modeling of portfolio rebalancing with transaction costs within the mean-variance framework was first proposed by Chen, Jen, and Zionts (1971). Their model assumes that transaction costs are a constant proportion of the transaction's dollar value. Several other models were subsequently proposed. For example:

- Adcock and Meade (1994) add a linear term for the transaction costs to the mean-variance risk term and minimize this quantity.
- Yoshimoto (1996) proposes a nonlinear programming algorithm to solve the problem of portfolio revision with transaction costs.
- Best and Hlouskova (2005) give an efficient solution procedure for the case of proportional transfer costs where the transfer costs are paid at the end of the period, impacting both the risk and the return.

- Lobo et al. (2007) provide a model for the case of linear and fixed transaction costs that maximizes the expected return subject to the variance constraint.
- Chen, Fabozzi, and Huang (2009) demonstrate how the impact of transaction costs can be integrated into the mean-variance framework and show that even some analytical solutions under mild assumptions can be obtained via optimization techniques.

Transaction costs models can involve complicated nonlinear functions. Although there exists software for general nonlinear optimization problems, the computational time required for solving such problems is often too long for realistic investment management applications, and the quality of the solution is frequently not guaranteed. Very efficient and reliable software is available, however, for linear and quadratic optimization problems. It is therefore common in practice to approximate a complicated nonlinear optimization problem by simpler problems that can be solved quickly. In particular, portfolio managers frequently employ approximations of some function that represents the penalty due to transaction costs in the mean-variance framework.

OPTIMAL TRADING

The decisions of the portfolio manager and the trader are based upon different objectives. The portfolio manager constructs the optimal portfolio to reflect the best trade-off between expected returns and risk, given his assessment of the prevailing trading costs. The trader decides on the timing of the execution of the trades based upon the trade-off between opportunity costs and market impact costs.

One way of reducing market impact cost is to delay the trade until the price is right. However, this process will also lead to missed investment opportunities. This trade-off between market impact and opportunity costs is illustrated in Figure 12.3. The vertical axis represents unit cost, where the units could be cents per share, basis points, or dollars. The horizontal axis represents the time periods, which could be ticks, minutes, hours, days and so on. First, we observe that market impact cost declines over time as it is positively related to the immediacy of execution. In other words, if a trader can "work an order" over time, the resulting transaction costs are expected to be lower. Second, opportunity cost increases over time as it is positively related to the delay in execution. This means that if a trader waits too long, a part of the extra return of the investment opportunity might disappear. Taken together, these two basic mechanisms give a total cost that is shaped like a parabola. As Figure 12.3 suggests, the total cost can be minimized by appropriately trading off market impact and opportunity costs.

FIGURE 12.3 Cost Trade-Offs: Market Impact Versus Opportunity Cost

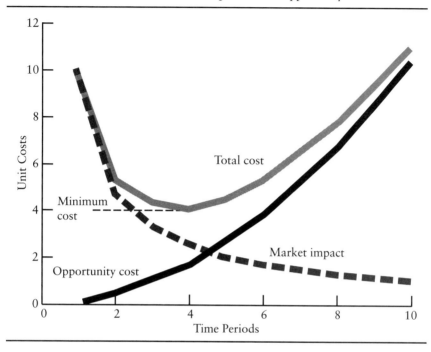

Source: Exhibit 2 in Fabozzi and Grant (1999).

Schematically, we can formulate this idea as an optimization problem where we attempt to minimize the expected total transaction costs. In general, this problem is a complicated stochastic and dynamic optimization problem. For example, Bertsimas, Hummel, and Lo (1999), Almgren and Chriss (2000/2001), and Almgren (2003) develop continuous-time models for optimal execution that minimize average transaction costs over a specific time horizon. In particular, Almgren and Chriss (2000/2001) assume that securities prices evolve according to a random-walk process as described in Chapter 10. Their model is an important contribution as it is one of the first of its kind that considers a dynamic model with market impact costs in which transactions occur over time.

As these techniques are rather involved mathematically, we describe only the basic ideas behind them. Realized transaction costs can deviate substantially from expected or average transaction costs. Therefore, it is convenient to use an objective function that takes this risk into account. Price volatility creates uncertainty in the realized trading costs in the same way it creates uncertainty in the realized return for an investment strategy.

Therefore, we can think about opportunity costs as represented by the variance of the total transaction costs.

The models of optimal execution that have been proposed are designed to get the best execution of a single trade, or sometimes a sequence of trades. They achieve this objective by optimizing the trade-off between the risk and the mean cost of execution. Note that the risk considered here is the variance of execution costs. Intuitively, we can think of this as the risk of not getting having a trade executed at a certain cost.

Depending on the size of the trade, it may take anything from a few minutes, a few hours, or even a few days to fully execute an order. The cost of trading is a random variable as some portions of the trade will be executed after prices have moved. Importantly, the delay in trading introduces price risk due to price movements beyond that which can be anticipated as a natural response to the trade itself. Now, if we think about the trade as part of a larger portfolio, then this price risk due to trading clearly affects the overall portfolio risk. However, often the models discussed in the literature ignore the effect of other stocks in the portfolio, including those whose positions are not changing during a trade.

In contrast, Engle and Ferstenberg (2007) developed a model that combines portfolio risk with execution risk in a single framework. Moreover, they studied characteristics of the joint optimization of positions and trades under different assumptions on the stock price processes and market impact of trades. While their results are rather technical to be presented here in detail, they provide several important insights. First, Engle and Ferstenberg show conditions under which the optimal execution of trades does not depend upon the holdings of the portfolio. That means that the generalized problem under these conditions reduces to two separate problems that are more familiar: the optimal allocation problem and the optimal execution problem. Second, they show that, in order to hedge trading risks, sometimes it may be optimal to execute trades in stocks that may not have been in the trading order. Finally, they point out that taking trade execution risk into account leads to a natural measure of liquidity risk. Namely, typically the value of a portfolio is marked to market. Instead, they suggest looking at the portfolio liquidation value because it represents correctly the fact that the stocks in the portfolio cannot necessarily be liquidated at their current market prices. The portfolio liquidity risk can be estimated by computing a percentile of the possible distribution of portfolio liquidation values. There is, in fact, a range of possible distributions for future portfolio liquidation values. This range depends on how the trade execution is accomplished, but the specific liquidity risk measure can be defined relative to the distribution of portfolio values obtained with the optimal execution policy according to the integrated asset allocation and trading model Engle and Ferstenberg suggest. This risk measure will incorporate both market and liquidity risk.

INTEGRATED PORTFOLIO MANAGEMENT: BEYOND EXPECTED RETURN AND PORTFOLIO RISK

As we mentioned at the outset of this chapter, equity trading should not be viewed separately from equity portfolio management. On the contrary, the management of equity trading costs is an integral part of any successful investment management strategy. In this context, the firm of MSCI Barra points out that superior investment performance is based on careful consideration of four key elements:[21]

- Forming realistic return expectations
- Controlling portfolio risk
- Efficient control of trading costs
- Monitoring total investment performance

Unfortunately, most discussions of equity portfolio management focus solely on the relationship between expected return and portfolio risk—with little if any emphasis on whether the selected stocks in the "optimal" or target portfolio can be acquired in a cost efficient manner.

To illustrate the seriousness of the problem that can arise with suboptimal portfolio decisions, Figure 12.4 highlights the "typical" versus "ideal" approach to (equity) portfolio management. In the typical approach (top portion of Figure 12.4), portfolio managers engage in fundamental and/or quantitative research to identify investment opportunities—albeit with a measure of investment prudence (risk control) in mind. Upon completion, the portfolio manager reveals the list of stocks that form the basis of the target portfolio to the senior trader. At this point, the senior trader informs the portfolio manager of certain nontradable positions—which causes the portfolio manager to adjust the list of stocks either by hand or some other ad hoc procedure. This, in turn, causes the investor's portfolio to be suboptimal.

Figure 12.4 also shows that as the trader begins to fill the portfolio with the now suboptimal set of stocks, an additional portfolio imbalance may occur as market impact costs cause the prices of some stocks to "run away" during trade implementation. It should be clear that any ad hoc adjustments by the trader at this point will in turn build a systematic imbalance in the

---

[21]The trading cost factor model described in this section is based on MSCI Barra's Market Impact Model™. A basic description of the model is covered in a three-part newsletter series. See Torre (1998).

FIGURE 12.4 Typical Versus Ideal Portfolio Management

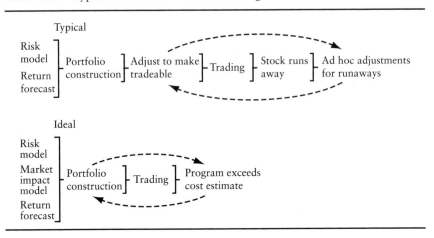

Source: Figure 4 in Torre (1998).

investor's portfolio—such that the portfolio manager's actual portfolio will depart permanently from that which would be efficient from a return-risk and trading cost perspective.

A better approach to equity portfolio management (lower portion of Figure 12.4) requires a systematic integration of portfolio management and trading processes. In this context, the returns forecast, risk estimates, and trading cost program are jointly combined in determining the optimal investment portfolio. In this way, the portfolio manager knows up front if (complete) portfolio implementation is either not feasible or is too expensive when accounting for trading costs.

Accordingly, the portfolio manager can incorporate the appropriate trading cost information into the portfolio construction and risk control process—before the trading program begins. The portfolio manager can then build a portfolio of securities whereby actual security positions are consistent with those deemed to be optimal from an integrated portfolio context.

SUMMARY

Trading and execution are integral components of the investment process. A poorly executed trade can eat directly into portfolio returns because of transaction costs. In this chapter, we described the types of orders that can be executed, special trading arrangements for institutional investors, the different components of transaction costs, and how transaction costs can be estimated and integrated into a portfolio management strategy.

The types of orders that can be executed are market orders and conditional orders. A market order is an order to execute a trade at the current best price available in the market. Conditional orders include limit orders and stop orders. A limit order is an order to execute a trade only if the limit price or a better price can be obtained. A stop order specifies that the order is not to be executed until the market moves to a designated price. For institutional investors, there are special types of trading arrangements. These include block trades, program trades, and algorithmic trading. Order flow can be purchased by a broker-dealer from an institutional investor with soft dollars.

Transaction costs are typically categorized in two dimensions: fixed costs versus variable costs, and explicit costs versus implicit costs. In the first dimension, fixed costs include commissions and fees. Bid-ask spreads, taxes, delay cost, price movement risk, market impact costs, timing risk, and opportunity cost are variable trading costs. In the second dimension, explicit costs include commissions, fees, bid-ask spreads, and taxes. Delay cost, price movement risk, market impact cost, timing risk, and opportunity cost are implicit transaction costs.

Implicit costs make up the larger part of the total transaction costs. These costs are not observable and have to be estimated. Liquidity is created by agents transacting in the financial markets by buying and selling securities. Liquidity and transaction costs are interrelated: In a highly liquid market, large transactions can be executed immediately without incurring high transaction costs.

In general, trading costs are measured as the difference between the execution price and some appropriate fair market benchmark. The fair market benchmark of a security is the price that would have prevailed had the trade not taken place.

Typical forecasting models for market impact costs are based on a statistical factor approach. Some common trade-based factors are trade size, relative trade size, price of market liquidity, type of trade, efficiency and trading style of the investor, specific characteristics of the market or the exchange, time of trade submission, trade timing, and order type. Some common asset-based factors are price momentum, price volatility, market capitalization, growth versus value, and specific industry and sector characteristics.

Transaction costs models can be incorporated into standard asset-allocation models such as the mean-variance framework. Optimal trading and execution systems rely on mathematical models that determine the timing of the execution of the trades by balancing the trade-off between opportunity costs and market impact costs.

Efficient equity portfolio management requires a systematic integration of trading costs management, trading execution, and portfolio management.

REFERENCES

Adcock, C. J., and N. Meade. 1994. A simple algorithm to incorporate transaction costs in quadratic optimization. *European Journal of Operational Research*, 79: 85–94.

Almgren, R. 2003. Optimal execution with nonlinear impact functions and trading-enhanced risk. *Applied Mathematical Finance* 10, no. 1: 1–18.

Almgren, R. and N. Chriss. 2000/2001. Optimal execution of portfolio transactions. *Journal of Risk* 3: 5–39.

Bertsimas, D., P. Hummel, and A. W. Lo. 1999. Optimal control of execution costs for portfolios. Working Paper, MIT Sloan School of Management.

Best, M. J., and R. R. Grauer. 1991. On the sensitivity of mean-variance efficient portfolios to changes in asset means: Some analytical and computational results. *Review of Financial Studies* 4, no. 2: 315–342.

Bikker, J. A., L. Spierdijk, and P. J. van der Sluis, (2007). Market impact costs of institutional equity trades. *Journal of International Money and Finance* 26, no. 6: 974–1000.

Chan, L., and J. Lakonishok. 1993. Institutional trades and intraday stock price behavior. *Journal of Financial Economics* 33: 173–199.

Chan, L., and J. Lakonishok. 1993. Institutional equity trading costs: NYSE versus Nasdaq. *Journal of Finance* 52, no. 1: 71–75.

Chen, A. H., F. J. Fabozzi, and D. Huang. 2009. Models for portfolio revision with transaction costs in the mean-variance framework. Forthcoming in *The Handbook of Portfolio Construction: Contemporary Applications of Markowitz Techniques*, edited by J. Geurard. New York: Springer.

Chen, A. H., F. C. Jen, and S. Zionts. 1971. The optimal portfolio revision policy. *Journal of Business* 44: 51–61.

Chiyachantana, C. N., P. K. Jain, C. Jian, and R. A. Wood. 2004. International evidence on institutional trading behavior and price impact. *Journal of Finance* 59: 869–895.

Collins, B. C., and F. J. Fabozzi, (1991). A methodology for measuring transaction costs. *Financial Analysts Journal* 47: 27–36.

Domowitz, I., J. Glen, and A. Madhavan. 1999. International equity trading costs: A cross-sectional and time-series analysis. Technical Report, Pennsylvania State University, International Finance Corp., University of Southern California.

Domowitz, I., and X. Wang. 2002. Liquidity, liquidity commonality and its impact on portfolio theory. Working Paper, Smeal College of Business Administration, Pennsylvania State University.

Engle, R. F., and R. Ferstenberg. 2007. Execution risk. *Journal of Portfolio Management* 33 (Winter): 34–44.

Fabozzi, F. J., S. Focardi, P. N. Kolm, and M. Anson. 2009. *Quantitative equity portfolio management*. Hoboken, NJ: John Wiley & Sons.

Fabozzi, F. J., and J. L. Grant. 1999. *Equity portfolio management*. Hoboken, NJ: John Wiley & Sons.

Foster, F. D., and S. Viswanathan. 1990. A theory of the interday variations in volume, variance, and trading costs in securities markets. *Review of Financial Studies* 4: 593–624.

Foucault, T., O. Kadan, and E. Kandel. 2005. Limit order book as a market for liquidity. *Review of Financial Studies* 18, no. 2: 1171–1271.

Harris, L. E., and V. Panchapagesan. 2005. The information content of the limit order book: Evidence from NYSE specialist trading decisions. *Journal of Financial Markets* 8: 25–67.

Hasbrouck, J., and G. Saar. 2009. Technology and liquidity provision: The blurring of traditional definitions. *Journal of Financial Markets* 12, no. 2: 143–172.

Hu, G. 2005. Measures of implicit trading costs and buy-sell asymmetry. Working Paper, Babson College.

Keim, D. B., and A. Madhavan. 1997. Transaction costs and investment style: An inter-exchange analysis of institutional equity trades. *Journal of Financial Economics* 46: 265–292.

Kissell, R., and M. Glantz. 2003. *Optimal trading strategies*. New York: AMACOM.

Kolm, P. N., and L. Maclin. 2008. Algorithmic trading: Where are we headed? Working Paper, Courant Institute, New York University.

Lobo, M. S., M. Fazel, and S. Boyd. 2007. Portfolio optimization with linear and fixed transaction costs. *Annals of Operatons Research* 152, no. 1: 341-365.

Perold, A. F. 1998. The implementation shortfall: Paper versus reality. *Journal of Portfolio Management* 14: 4–9.

Pogue, G. A. 1970. An extension of the Markowitz portfolio selection model to include variable transactions costs, short sales, leverage policies and taxes. *Journal of Finance* 25, no. 5: 1005–1027.

McSherry, R. 1998. Global trading cost analysis. Elkins/McSherry Co., Inc.

Smith, B. F., D. Alasdair, S. Turnbull, and R. W. White. 2001. Upstairs market for principal and agency trades: Analysis of adverse information and price effects. *Journal of Finance* 56: 1723–1746.

Spierdijk, L., T. Nijman, and A. van Soest. 2003. Temporary and persistent price effects of trades in infrequently traded stocks. Working Paper, Tilburg University and Center.

Torre, N. 1998. The Market Impact Model™. Three-part series in *Barra Newsletters* NL165–NL167.

Tuttle, L. A. 2002. Hidden orders, trading costs and information. Working Paper, Ohio State University.

Wagner, W. H., and M. Edwards. 1998. Implementing investment strategies: The art and science of investing. In *Active equity portfolio management*, edited by F. J. Fabozzi (pp. 179–194), Hoboken, NJ: John Wiley & Sons.

Willoughby, J. 1998. Executions song. *Institutional Investor* 32, no. 11: 51–56.

Yoshimoto, A. 1996. The mean-variance approach to portfolio optimization subject to transaction costs. *Journal of Operations Research Society of Japan* 39, no. 1: 99–117.

CHAPTER 13

Using Stock Index Futures and Equity Swaps in Equity Portfolio Management

Derivative instruments, or simply derivatives, are contracts that essentially derive their value from the behavior of cash market instruments such as stocks, stock indexes, bonds, currencies, and commodities that underlie the contract. There are three general categories of derivatives: (1) futures and forwards, (2) options, and (3) swaps. When the underlying for a derivative is a stock or stock index, the contract is called an *equity derivative*.

Derivatives are either traded on an exchange or in the *over-the-counter* (OTC) market. That is, there are exchange-traded derivatives (also referred to as *listed derivatives*) and OTC derivatives. Exchange-traded derivatives are standardized contracts. An advantage of OTC derivatives over exchange-traded derivatives is that they offer portfolio managers customized solutions to deal with an investment strategy. In fact, one of the keys to the success of OTC derivatives is the flexibility of the structures that can be created. A key difference between exchange-traded and OTC derivatives, is that the former are guaranteed by the exchange, while the latter are the obligation of a non-exchange entity that is the counterparty. Thus, the user of an OTC derivative is subject to credit risk or counterparty risk.

In this chapter and the one to follow, we explain how equity derivatives can be used in the management of equity portfolios. Our goal in this chapter is to provide the basics of stock index futures, how they are priced, and how they are used in equity portfolio management. At the end of the chapter we discuss the use of equity swaps in portfolio management.

This chapter is coauthored with Bruce Collins.

DERIVATIVES PROCESS

Regardless of the portfolio manager's orientation or portfolio composition, the decision to use derivatives is not unlike any other business decision. It requires careful attention and must be explicitly incorporated into the investment process described in Chapter 1. Derivatives represent an investment opportunity for investment managers. For any business, whenever a new technology or a new methodology emerges, managers must do their homework to prepare for the use of the technology or method. The same holds true for the use of derivatives. Before derivatives are used as part of the investment process, investment managers must do their homework. Nonetheless, derivatives must be regarded as an investment opportunity and not an obligation or a curiosity.

Sanford and Borge discuss a "derivatives process" that they recommend that those interested in utilizing derivatives go through.[1] If we apply this process to investment management, we come up with a set of guidelines for asset management firms on the use of derivatives. A list of some important aspects of this process are:

- Define the investment process in terms of risk management.
- Establish clear investment objectives and acceptable risk tolerance level.
- Create a set of boundary conditions for the level of risk.
- Assess the full range of possible outcomes from using derivatives.
- Assess the impact of using derivatives on the portfolio's risk profile.
- Establish monitoring protocol to measure risk.
- Develop an adjustment response mechanism.

The process of using derivatives requires the portfolio manager to manage the investment process in terms of a risk management process. What this means is that the portfolio manager views the portfolio as a mechanism to capture the benefits of taking prudent risks. The reallocation of risk incorporates asset exposure, return enhancement, and cost management into a single theme of risk management. For portfolio managers, this means designing a portfolio that assumes a level of risk consistent with the investment objectives of the client. Derivatives provide portfolio managers with a quick and efficient method to realize the desired portfolio profile emanating from the manager's style. The combination of asset selection and establishing the optimal level of portfolio risks is the key to consistent portfolio performance. In order to accomplish this, however, portfolio managers

---

[1] See Charles Sanford and Dan Borge, "The Risk Management Revolution," available at http://www.libs.uga.edu/hargrett/manuscrip/sanford/charles.html.

must be clear about their objectives and tolerance for risk. Once the process is established, the portfolio manager can actively manage the portfolio in terms of risk and make the necessary adjustments when the benefits are no longer expected to accrue.

BASIC FEATURES OF FUTURES CONTRACTS

A *futures contract* is a legal agreement between a buyer and a seller in which:

1. The buyer agrees to take delivery of something at a specified price at the end of a designated period of time.
2. The seller agrees to make delivery of something at a specified price at the end of a designated period of time.

Of course, no one buys or sells anything when entering into a futures contract. Rather, those who enter into a contract agree to buy or sell a specific amount of a specific item at a specified future date. When we speak of the "buyer" or the "seller" of a contract, we are simply adopting the jargon of the futures market, which refers to parties of the contract in terms of their future obligation.

Let's look closely at the key elements of a futures contract. The price at which the parties agree to transact in the future is called the *futures price*. The designated date at which the parties must transact is called the *settlement date* or *delivery date*. The "something" that the parties agree to exchange is called the *underlying*.

To illustrate, suppose a futures contract is traded on an exchange where the underlying to be bought or sold is asset XYZ, and the settlement is 3 months from now. Assume further that Bob buys this futures contract, and Sally sells this futures contract, and the price at which they agree to transact in the future is $100. Then $100 is the futures price. At the settlement date, Sally will deliver asset XYZ to Bob. Bob will give Sally $100, the futures price.

When an investor takes a position in the market by buying a futures contract, the investor is said to be in a *long position* or to be *long futures*. If, instead, the investor's opening position is the sale of a futures contract, the investor is said to be in a *short position* or *short futures*.

The buyer of a futures contract will realize a profit if the futures price increases; the seller of a futures contract will realize a profit if the futures price decreases. For example, suppose that one month after Bob and Sally take their positions in the futures contract, the futures price of asset XYZ increases to $120. Bob, the buyer of the futures contract, could then sell the futures contract and realize a profit of $20. Effectively, at the settlement date, he has agreed to buy asset XYZ for $100 and has agreed to sell asset XYZ for $120. Sally, the seller of the futures contract, will realize a loss of $20. If the futures price falls to $40 and Sally buys back the contract at $40, she realizes a profit of $60 because she agreed to sell asset XYZ for $100 and now can buy it for $40. Bob would realize a loss of $60. Thus, if the futures price decreases, the buyer of the futures contract realizes a loss while the seller of the futures contract realizes a profit.

Liquidating a Position

Most financial futures contracts have settlement dates in the months of March, June, September, or December. This means that at a predetermined time in the contract settlement month, the contract stops trading, and a price is determined by the exchange for settlement of the contract. For example, on January 4, 201X, suppose Bob buys and Sally sells a futures contract that settles on the third Friday of March of 201X. Then, on that date, Bob and Sally must perform—Bob agreeing to buy asset XYZ at $100, and Sally agreeing to sell asset XYZ at $100. The exchange will determine a settlement price for the futures contract for that specific date. For example, if the exchange determines a settlement price of $130, then Bob has agreed to buy asset XYZ for $100 but can settle the position for $130, thereby realizing a profit of $30. Sally would realize a loss of $30.

Instead of Bob or Sally entering into a futures contract on January 4, 201X, that settles in March, they could have selected a settlement in June, September, or December. The contract with the closest settlement date is called the *nearby futures contract*. The *next futures contract* is the one that settles just after the nearby contract. The contract farthest away in time from settlement is called the *most distant futures contract*.

A party to a futures contract has two choices regarding the liquidation of the position. First, the position can be liquidated prior to the settlement date. For this purpose, the party must take an offsetting position in the same contract. For the buyer of a futures contract, this means selling the same number of identical futures contracts; for the seller of a futures contract, this means buying the same number of identical futures contracts. An identical contract means the contract for the same underlying and the same settlement date. So, for example, if Bob buys one futures contract for asset XYZ with settlement in March 201X on January 4, 201X, and wants to liquidate a position on February 14, 201X, he can sell one futures contract for asset XYZ with settlement in March 201X. Similarly, if Sally sells one futures contract for asset XYZ with settlement in March 201X on January 4, 201X, and wants to liquidate a position on February 22, 201X, she can buy one futures contract for asset XYZ with settlement in March 201X. A futures contract on asset XYZ that settles in June 201X is not the same contract as a futures contract on asset XYZ that settles in March 201X.

The alternative is to wait until the settlement date. At that time, the party purchasing a futures contract accepts delivery of the underlying; the party that sells a futures contract settles the position by delivering the underlying at the agreed upon price. For some futures contracts that we shall describe later in this chapter, settlement is made in cash only. Such contracts are referred to as *cash settlement contracts*.

A useful statistic for measuring the liquidity of a contract is the number of contracts that have been entered into but not yet liquidated. This figure is called the contract's *open interest*. An open interest figure is reported by an exchange for every futures contracts traded on that exchange.

The Role of the Clearinghouse

Associated with every futures exchange is a clearinghouse which performs several functions. One of these functions is to guarantee that the two parties to the transaction will perform. Because of the clearinghouse, the two parties need not worry about the financial strength and integrity of the other party taking the opposite side of the trade. After initial execution of an order, the relationship between the two parties ends. The clearinghouse interposes itself as the buyer for every sale and as the seller for every purchase. Thus, the two parties are free to liquidate their positions without involving the other party in the original trade, and without worry that the other party may default.

Margin Requirements

When a position is first taken in a futures contract, the investor must deposit a minimum dollar amount per contract as specified by the exchange. This amount, called *initial margin*, is required as a deposit for the contract. The initial margin may be in the form of an interest-bearing security such as a Treasury bill. The initial margin is placed in an account, and the amount in this account is referred to as the *investor's equity*. As the price of the futures contract changes at the end of each trading day, the value of the investor's equity in the position changes.

At the end of each trading day, the exchange determines the "settlement price" for the futures contract. The settlement price is different from the closing price, which is the price of the security for the final trade of the day (whenever that trade occurred during the day). By contrast, the settlement price is that value which the exchange considers to be representative of trading at the end of the trading day. The exchange uses the settlement price to mark to market the investor's position, so that any gain or loss from the position is quickly reflected in the investor's equity account at the end of the trading day.

Maintenance margin is the minimum level by which an investor's equity position may fall as a result of unfavorable price movements before the investor is required to deposit additional margin. The maintenance margin requirement is a dollar amount that is less than the initial margin requirement. It sets the floor that the investor's equity account can fall to before the investor is required to furnish additional margin. The additional margin deposited, called *variation margin,* is an amount necessary to bring the equity in the account back to its initial margin level. Unlike initial margin, variation margin must be in cash, not interest-bearing instruments. Any excess margin in the account may be withdrawn by the investor. If a party to a futures contract who is required to deposit variation margin fails to do so within 24 hours, the futures position is liquidated by the clearinghouse.[2]

To illustrate the mark-to-market procedure, let's assume the following margin requirements for asset XYZ initial and maintenance margin of $7 and $4 per contract, respectively. Suppose that Bob buys 500 contracts at a futures price of $100, and Sally sells the same number of contracts at the same futures price. The initial margin for both Bob and Sally is $3,500, which is determined by multiplying the initial margin of $7 by the number of contracts, 500. Bob and Sally must put up $3,500 in cash or Treasury bills or other acceptable collateral. At this time, $3,500 is the equity in the account.

The maintenance margin for the two positions is $2,000 (the maintenance margin per contract of $4 multiplied by 500 contracts). That means the equity in the account may not fall below $2,000. If it does, the party whose equity falls below the maintenance margin must put up additional margin, which is the variation margin.

Regarding the variation margin, note two things: First, the variation margin must be cash. Second, the amount of variation margin required is the amount to bring the equity up to the initial margin, not the maintenance margin.

---

[2] Although there are initial and maintenance margin requirements for buying securities on margin, the concept of margin differs for securities and futures. When securities are acquired on margin, the difference between the price of the security and the initial margin is borrowed from the broker. The security purchased serves as collateral for the loan, and the investor pays interest. For futures contracts, the initial margin, in effect, serves as "good-faith" money, an indication that the investor will satisfy the obligation of the contract. Normally, no money is borrowed by the investor.

Now, to illustrate the mark-to-market procedure, we will assume the following settlement prices at the end of four consecutive trading days after the transaction was entered into:

Trading Day	Settlement Price
1	$99
2	97
3	98
4	95

First consider Bob's position. At the end of trading day 1, Bob realizes a loss of $1 per contract, or $500 for the 500 contracts he bought. Bob's initial equity of $3,500 is reduced by $500 to $3,000. No action is taken by the clearinghouse because Bob's equity is still above the maintenance margin of $2,000. At the end of the second day, Bob realizes a further loss as the price of the futures contract declines $2 to $97, resulting in an additional reduction in his equity position by $1,000. Bob's equity is then $2,000. Despite the loss, no action is taken by the clearinghouse since the equity is not less than the $2,000 maintenance margin requirement. At the end of trading day 3, Bob realizes a profit from the previous trading day of $1 per contract, or $500. Bob's equity increases to $2,500. The drop in price from 98 to 95 at the end of trading day 4 results in a loss for the 500 contracts of $1,500 and a reduction of Bob's equity to $1,000. Since Bob's equity is now below the $2,000 maintenance margin, Bob is required to put up additional margin of $2,500 (variation margin) to bring the equity up to the initial margin of $3,500. If Bob cannot put up the variation margin, his position will be liquidated. That is, his contracts will be sold by the clearinghouse.

Now let's look at Sally's position. Since Sally sold the futures contract, she benefits if the price of the futures contract declines. As a result, her equity increases at the end of the first two trading days. In fact, at the end of trading day 1, she realizes a profit of $500, which increases her equity to $4,000. She is entitled to remove the $500 profit and utilize these funds elsewhere. Suppose she does, and, as a result, her equity remains at $3,500 at the end of trading day 1. At the end of trading day 2, she realizes an additional profit of $1,000 that she can withdraw. At the end of trading day 3, she realizes a loss of $500, because the price increased from $97 to $98. This results in a reduction of her equity to $3,000. Finally, on trading day 4, she realizes a profit of $1,500, making her equity $4,500. She can withdraw $1,000.

Leveraging Aspect of Futures

When taking a position in a futures contract, a party need not put up the entire amount of the investment. Instead, the exchange requires that only the initial margin be invested. To see the implications, suppose Bob has $100 and wants to invest in asset XYZ because he believes its price will appreciate. If asset XYZ is selling for $100, he can buy one unit of the asset in the cash market (i.e., the market where goods are delivered upon purchase). His payoff will then be based on the price action of one unit of asset XYZ.

Suppose that the exchange where the futures contract for asset XYZ is traded requires an initial margin of only 5%, which in this case would be $5. Then Bob can purchase 20 contracts with his $100 investment. (This example ignores the fact that Bob may need funds for variation margin.) His payoff will then depend on the price action of 20 units of asset XYZ. Thus, he can leverage the use of his funds. The degree of leverage equals 1/margin rate. In this case, the degree of leverage equals 1/0.05, or 20. While the degree of leverage available in the futures market varies from contract to contract, as the initial margin requirement varies, the leverage attainable is considerably greater than in the cash market.

At first, the leverage available in the futures market may suggest that the market benefits only those who want to speculate on price movements. This is not true. As we shall see, futures markets can be used to reduce price risk. Without the leverage possible in futures transactions, the cost of reducing price risk using futures would be too high for many market participants.

Basic Features of Forward Contracts

A *forward contract*, just like a futures contract, is an agreement for the future delivery of the underlying at a specified price at the end of a designated period of time. Futures contracts are standardized agreements as to the delivery date (or month) and quality of the deliverable, and are traded on organized exchanges. A forward contract differs in that it is usually nonstandardized (that is, the terms of each contract are negotiated individually between buyer and seller), there is no clearinghouse, and secondary markets are often nonexistent or extremely thin. Unlike a futures contract, which is an exchange-traded derivative, a forward contract is an OTC derivative.

Because there is no clearinghouse that guarantees the performance of a counterparty in a forward contract, the parties to a forward contract are exposed to *counterparty risk,* the risk that the other party to the transaction will fail to perform. Futures contracts are marked to market at the end of each trading day. Consequently, futures contracts are subject to interim cash flows because additional margin may be required in the case of adverse price movements or because cash may be withdrawn in the case of favorable price movements. A forward contract may or may not be marked to market. Where the counterparties are two high-credit-quality entities, the two parties may agree not to mark positions to market. However, if one or both of the parties are concerned with the counterparty risk of the other, then positions may be marked to market. Thus, when a forward contract is marked to market, there are interim cash flows just as with a futures contract. When a forward contract is not marked to market, then there are no interim cash flows.

Other than these differences, what we said about futures contracts applies to forward contracts too.

BASIC FEATURES OF STOCK INDEX FUTURES

The underlying for a stock index futures contract can be a broad-based stock market index or a narrow-based stock market index. Examples of broad-based stock market indexes that are the underlying for a futures contract are the S&P 500, S&P Midcap 400, Dow Jones Industrial Average, Nasdaq 100 Index, NYSE Composite Index, and the Russell 2000 Index.

A narrow-based stock index futures contract is one based on a subsector or components of a broad-based stock index containing groups of stocks or a specialized sector developed by a bank. For example, the Dow Jones Micro-Sector Indexes are traded on OneChicago. There are 15 sectors in the index.

The dollar value of a stock index futures contract is the product of the futures price and a "multiple" that is specified for the futures contract. That is,

Dollar value of a stock index futures contract = Futures price × Multiple

For example, suppose that the futures price for the S&P500 is 1,410. The multiple for the S&P 500 futures contract is $250. Therefore, the dollar value of the S&P 500 futures contract would be $352,500 (= 1,410 × $250). If an investor buys an S&P 500 futures contract at 1,410 and sells it at 1,430, the investor realizes a profit of 20 times $250, or $5,000. If the futures contract is sold instead for 1,360, the investor will realize a loss of 50 times $250, or $12,500.

Stock index futures contracts are cash settlement contracts. This means that at the settlement date, cash will be exchanged to settle the contract. For example, if an investor buys an S&P 500 futures contract at 1,410 and the futures settlement price is 1,430, settlement would be as follows. The investor has agreed to buy the S&P 500 for 1,410 times $250, or $352,500. The S&P 500 value at the settlement date is 1,430 times $250, or $357,500.

The seller of this futures contract must pay the investor $5,000 ($357,500 − $352,500). Had the futures price at the settlement date been 1360 instead of 1,430, the dollar value of the S&P 500 futures contract would be $340,000. In this case, the investor must pay the seller of the contract $12,500 ($352,500 − $340,000). (Of course, in practice, the parties would be realizing any gains or losses at the end of each trading day as their positions are marked to market.)

Clearly, an investor who wants to short the entire market or a sector will use stock index futures contracts. The costs of a transaction are small relative to shorting the individuals stocks comprising the stock index or attempting to construct a portfolio that replicates the stock index with minimal tracking error.

Pricing of Futures and Forward Contracts

When using derivatives, a market participant should understand the basic principles of how they are valued. While there are many models that have been proposed for valuing financial instruments that trade in the cash (spot) market, the valuation of all derivative models are based on arbitrage arguments. Basically, this involves developing a strategy or a trade wherein a package consisting of a position in the underlying (that is, the underlying asset or instrument for the derivative contract) and borrowing or lending so as to generate the same cash flow profile of the derivative. The value of the package is then equal to the theoretical price of the derivative. If the market price of the derivative deviates from the theoretical price, then the actions of arbitrageurs will drive the market price of the derivative toward its theoretical price until the arbitrage opportunity is eliminated.

In developing a strategy to capture any mispricing, certain assumptions are made. When these assumptions are not satisfied in the real world, the theoretical price can only be approximated. Moreover, a close examination of the underlying assumptions necessary to derive the theoretical price indicates how a pricing formula must be modified to value specific contracts.

Here we describe how futures and forward contracts are valued. The pricing of these contracts is similar. If the underlying asset for both contracts is the same, the difference in pricing is due to differences in features of the contract that must be dealt with by the pricing model.

We will illustrate the basic model for pricing futures contract. By "basic" we mean that we are extrapolating from the nuisances of the underlying for a specific contract. The issues associated with applying the basic pricing model to some of the more popular futures contracts are described later in this chapter for stock index futures contract and for Treasury futures in Chapter 24. Moreover, while the model described here is said to be a model for pricing futures, technically, it is a model for pricing forward contracts with no mark-to-market requirements.

Rather than deriving the formula algebraically, we demonstrate the basic pricing model using an example. We make the following six assumptions for a futures contract that has no initial and variation margin and the underlying is asset U:

1. The price of asset U in the cash market is $100.
2. There is a known cash flow for asset U over the life of the futures contract.
3. The cash flow for asset U is $8 per year paid quarterly ($2 per quarter).
4. The next quarterly payment is exactly three months from now.
5. The futures contract requires delivery three months from now.
6. The current three-month interest rate at which funds can be lent or borrowed is 4% per year.

The objective is to determine what the futures price of this contract should be. To do so, suppose that the futures price in the market is $105. Let's see if that is the correct price. We can check this by implementing the following simple strategy:

- Sell the futures contract at $105.
- Purchase asset U in the cash market for $100.
- Borrow $100 for three months at 4% per year ($1 per quarter).

The purchase of asset U is accomplished with the borrowed funds. Hence, this strategy does not involve any initial cash outlay. At the end of three months, the following occurs

- $2 is received from holding asset U.
- Asset U is delivered to settle the futures contract.
- The loan is repaid.

This strategy results in the following outcome:

From settlement of the futures contract:

Proceeds from sale of asset U to settle the futures contract	= $105
Payment received from investing in asset U for three months	= 2
Total proceeds	= $107

From the loan:

Repayment of principal of loan	= $100
Interest on loan (1% for three months)	= 1
Total outlay	= $101
Profit from the strategy	= $6

The profit of $6 from this strategy is guaranteed regardless of what the cash price of asset U is three months from now. This is because in the preceding analysis of the outcome of the strategy, the cash price of asset U three months from now never enters the analysis. Moreover, this profit is generated with no investment outlay; the funds needed to acquire asset U are borrowed when the strategy is executed. In financial terms, the profit in the strategy we have just illustrated arises from a riskless arbitrage between the price of asset U in the cash market and the price of asset U in the futures market.

In a well-functioning market, arbitrageurs who could realize this riskless profit for a zero investment would implement the strategy described above. By selling the futures and buying asset U in order to implement the strategy, this would force the futures price down so that at some price for the futures contract, the arbitrage profit is eliminated.

This strategy that resulted in the capturing of the arbitrage profit is referred to as a *cash-and-carry trade*. The reason for this name is that implementation of the strategy involves borrowing cash to purchase the underlying and "carrying" that underlying to the settlement date of the futures contract.

From the cash-and-carry trade we see that the futures price cannot be $105. Suppose instead that the futures price is $95 rather than $105. Let's try the following strategy to see if that price can be sustained in the market:

- Buy the futures contract at $95.
- Sell (short) asset U for $100.
- Invest (lend) $100 for three months at 1% per year.

We assume once again that in this strategy that there is no initial margin and variation margin for the futures contract. In addition, we assume that there is no cost to selling the asset short and lending the money. Given these assumptions, there is no initial cash outlay for the strategy just as with the cash-and-carry trade. Three months from now,

- Asset U is purchased to settle the long position in the futures contract.
- Asset U is accepted for delivery.
- Asset U is used to cover the short position in the cash market.
- Payment is made of $2 to the lender of asset U as compensation for the quarterly payment.

- Payment is received from the borrower of the loan of $101 for principal and interest.

More specifically, the strategy produces the following at the end of three months:

From settlement of the futures contract:

Price paid for purchase of asset U to settle futures contract	=	$95
Proceeds to lender of asset U to borrow the asset	=	2
Total outlay	=	$97

From the loan:

Principal from loan	=	$100
Interest earned on loan ($1 for three months)	=	1
Total proceeds	=	$101
Profit from the strategy	=	$4

As with the cash and trade, the $4 profit from this strategy is a riskless arbitrage profit. This strategy requires no initial cash outlay, but it will generate a profit whatever the price of asset U is in the cash market at the settlement date. In real-world markets, this opportunity would lead arbitrageurs to buy the futures contract and short asset U. The implementation of this strategy would be to raise the futures price until the arbitrage profit disappeared.

This strategy that is implemented to capture the arbitrage profit is known as a *reverse cash-and-carry trade*. That is, with this strategy, the underlying is sold short and the proceeds received from the short sale are invested.

We can see that the futures price cannot be $95 or $105. What is the theoretical futures price given the assumptions in our illustration? It can be shown that if the futures price is $99, there is no opportunity for an arbitrage profit. That is, neither the cash-and-carry trade nor the reverse cash-and-carry trade will generate an arbitrage profit.

In general, the formula for determining the theoretical futures price given the assumptions of the model is

$$\text{Theoretical futures price} = \text{Cash market price} + (\text{Cash market price}) \times (\text{Financing cost} - \text{Cash yield}) \quad (13.1)$$

In the formula given by (13.1), "Financing cost" is the interest rate to borrow funds and "Cash yield" is the payment received from investing in the asset as a percentage of the cash price. In our illustration, the financing cost is 1% and the cash yield is 2%.

In our illustration, since the cash price of asset U is $100, the theoretical futures price is

$$\$100 + [\$100 \times (1\% - 2\%)] = \$99$$

The future price can be above or below the cash price depending on the difference between the financing cost and cash yield. The difference between these rates is called the *net financing cost*. A more commonly used term for the net financing cost is the *cost of carry*, or simply, *carry*. *Positive carry* means that the cash yield exceeds the financing cost. (Note that while the difference between the financing cost and the cash yield is a negative value, carry is said to be positive.) *Negative carry* means that the financing cost exceeds the cash yield. Below is a summary of the effect of carry on the difference between the futures price and the cash market price:

Positive carry	Futures price will sell at a discount to cash price.
Negative carry	Futures price will sell at a premium to cash price.
Zero	Futures price will be equal to the cash price.

Note that at the settlement date of the futures contract, the futures price must equal the cash market price. The reason is that a futures contract with no time left until delivery is equivalent to a cash market transaction. Thus, as the delivery date approaches, the futures price will converge to the cash market price. This fact is evident from the formula for the theoretical futures price given by (13.1). The financing cost approaches zero as the delivery date approaches. Similarly, the yield that can be earned by holding the underlying approaches zero. Hence, the cost of carry approaches zero, and the futures price approaches the cash market price.

A Closer Look at the Theoretical Futures Price

In deriving the theoretical futures price using the arbitrage argument, several assumptions had to be made. These assumptions, as well as the differences in contract specifications, will result in the futures price in the market deviating from the theoretical futures price as given by (13.1). It may be possible to incorporate these institutional and contract specification differences into the formula for the theoretical futures price. In general, however, because it is oftentimes too difficult to allow for these differences in building a model for the theoretical futures price, the end result is that one can develop bands or boundaries for the theoretical futures price. So long as the futures price in the market remains within the band, no arbitrage opportunity is possible.

Interim Cash Flows

In the derivation of a basic pricing model, it is assumed that no interim cash flows arise because of changes in futures prices (that is, there is no variation margin). For a stock index, there are interim cash flows. In fact, there are many cash flows that are dependent upon the dividend dates of the component companies. To correctly price a stock index future contract, it is necessary to incorporate the interim dividend payments. Yet, the dividend rate and the pattern of dividend payments are not known with certainty. Consequently, they must be projected from the historical dividend payments of the companies in the index. Once the dividend payments are projected, they can be incorporated into the pricing model. The only problem is that the value of the dividend payments at the settlement date will depend on the interest rate at which the dividend payments can be reinvested from the time they are projected to be received until the settlement date. The lower the dividend, and the closer the dividend payments to the settlement date of the futures contract, the less important the reinvestment income is in determining the futures price.

Differences in Borrowing and Lending Rates

In the formula for the theoretical futures price given by equation (13.1), it is assumed in the cash-and-carry trade and the reverse cash-and-carry trade that the borrowing rate and lending rate are equal. In real-world financial markets, however, the borrowing rate is higher than the lending rate. The impact of this inequality in rates is important and easy to quantify.

In the cash-and-carry trade, the theoretical futures price as given by equation (13.1) becomes

$$\begin{aligned}&\text{Theoretical futures price based on borrowing rate}\\&= \text{Cash market price} + (\text{Cash market price}) \\&\quad \times (\text{Borrowing rate} - \text{Cash yield})\end{aligned} \quad (13.2)$$

For the reverse cash-and-carry trade, it becomes

$$\begin{aligned}&\text{Theoretical futures price based on lending rate}\\&= \text{Cash market price} + (\text{Cash market price}) \\&\quad \times (\text{Lending rate} - \text{Cash yield})\end{aligned} \quad (13.2)$$

Equations (13.2) and (13.3) together provide a band between which the actual futures price can exist without allowing for an arbitrage profit. Equation (13.2) establishes the upper value for the band while equation (13.3) provides the lower value for the band. For example, assume that the borrowing rate is 6% per year, or 1.5% for three months, while the lending rate is 4% per year, or 1% for three months. Using equation (13.2), the upper value for the theoretical futures price is $99.5 and using equation (13.3) the lower value for the theoretical futures price is $99.

Transaction Costs

The two strategies to exploit any price discrepancies between the cash market and theoretical futures price requires the arbitrageur to incur transaction costs. In financial markets, the costs of entering into and closing the cash position as well as round-trip transaction costs for the futures contract affect the futures price. As in the case of differential borrowing and lending rates, transaction costs widen the bands for the theoretical futures price.

Short Selling

The reverse cash-and-strategy trade requires the short selling of the underlying. It is assumed in this strategy that the proceeds from the short sale are received and reinvested. In practice, for individual investors, the proceeds are not received, and, in fact, the individual investor is required to deposit margin (securities margin and not futures margin) to short sell. For institutional investors, the underlying may be borrowed, but there is a cost to borrowing. This cost of borrowing can be incorporated into the model by reducing the cash yield on the underlying. For strategies applied to stock index futures, a short sale of the components stocks in the index means that all stocks in the index must be sold simultaneously. This may be difficult to do and therefore would widen the band for the theoretical futures price.

Deliverable Is a Basket of Securities

The problem in arbitraging stock index futures contracts is that it may be too expensive to buy or sell every stock included in the stock index. Instead, a portfolio containing a smaller number of stocks may be constructed to track the index which means having price movements that are very similar to changes in the stock index. Nonetheless, the two arbitrage strategies involve a tracking portfolio rather than a single asset for the underlying, and the strategies are no longer riskless because of the risk that the tracking portfolio will not precisely replicate the performance of the stock index.

For this reason, the market price of stock index futures contracts is likely to diverge from the theoretical futures price and have wider bands (i.e., lower and upper theoretical futures prices) that cannot be exploited.

APPLICATIONS FOR STOCK INDEX FUTURES

Now that we know what stock index futures are and how they are priced, we can look at how they can be used by institutional investors. Prior to the development of stock index futures, an investor who wanted to speculate on the future course of stock prices had to buy or short individual stocks. Now, however, the stock index can be bought or sold in the futures market. But making speculation easier for investors is not the main function of stock index futures contracts. The other strategies discussed below show how institutional investors can effectively use stock index futures to meet various investment objectives.

Controlling the Risk of a Stock Portfolio

An asset manager who wishes to alter exposure to the market can do so by revising the portfolio's beta. This can be done by rebalancing the portfolio with stocks that will produce the target beta, but there are transaction costs associated with rebalancing a portfolio. Because of the leverage inherent in futures contracts, asset managers can use stock index futures to achieve a target beta at a considerably lower cost. Buying stock index futures will increase a portfolio's beta, and selling will reduce it.

Hedging against Adverse Stock Price Movements

The major economic function of futures markets is to transfer price risk from hedgers to speculators. *Hedging* is the employment of futures contracts as a substitute for a transaction to be made in the cash market. If the cash and futures markets move together, any loss realized by the hedger on one position (whether cash or futures) will be offset by a profit on the other position. When the profit and loss are equal, the hedge is called a *perfect hedge*.

Short Hedge and Long Hedge

A *short hedge* is used to protect against a decline in the future cash price of the underlying. To execute a short hedge, the hedger sells a futures contract. Consequently, a short hedge is also referred to as a *sell hedge*. By establishing a short hedge, the hedger has fixed the future cash price and transferred the price risk of ownership to the buyer of the contract.

As an example of an asset manager who would use a short hedge, consider a pension fund manager who knows that the beneficiaries of the fund must be paid a total of $30 million four months from now. This will necessitate liquidating a portion of the fund's common stock portfolio. If the value of the shares that she intends to liquidate in order to satisfy the payments to be made decline in value four months from now, a larger portion of the portfolio will have to be liquidated. The easiest way to handle this situation is for the asset manager to sell the needed amount of stocks and invest the proceeds in a Treasury bill that matures in four months. However, suppose that for some reason, the asset manager is constrained from making the sale today. She can use a short hedge to lock in the value of the stocks that will be liquidated.

A *long hedge* is undertaken to protect against rising prices of future intended purchases. In a long hedge, the hedger buys a futures contract, so this hedge is also referred to as a *buy hedge*. As an example, consider once again a pension fund manager. This time, suppose that the manager expects a substantial contribution from the plan sponsor four months from now, and that the contributions will be invested in common stock of various companies. The pension fund manager expects the market price of the stocks in which he will invest the contributions to be higher in four months and, therefore, takes the risk that she will have to pay a higher price for the stocks. The manager can use a long hedge to effectively lock in a future price for these stocks now.

Return on a Hedged Position

Hedging is a special case of controlling a stock portfolio's exposure to adverse price changes. In a hedge, the objective is to alter a current or anticipated stock portfolio position so that its beta is zero. A portfolio with a beta of zero should generate a risk-free interest rate. This is consistent with the capital asset pricing model discussed in Chapter 5. Thus, in a perfect hedge, the return will be equal to the risk-free interest rate. More specifically, it will be the risk-free interest rate corresponding to a maturity equal to the number of days until settlement of the futures contract.

Therefore, a portfolio that is identical to the S&P 500 (i.e., an S&P 500 index fund) is fully hedged by selling an S&P 500 futures contract with 60 days to settlement that is priced at its theoretical futures price. The return on this hedged position will be the 60-day, risk-free return. Notice what has been done. If a portfolio manager wanted to temporarily eliminate all exposure to the S&P 500, she could sell all the stocks and, with the funds received, invest in a Treasury bill. By using a stock index futures contract, the manager can eliminate exposure to the S&P 500 by hedging, and the hedged position will earn the same return as that on a Treasury bill. The manager thereby saves on the transaction costs associated with selling a stock portfolio. Moreover, when the manager wants to get back into the stock market, rather than having to incur the transaction costs associated with buying stocks, she simply removes the hedge by buying an identical number of stock index futures contracts.

Cross Hedging

In practice, hedging is not a simple exercise. When hedging with stock index futures, a perfect hedge can be obtained only if the return on the portfolio being hedged is identical to the return on the futures contract.

The effectiveness of a hedged stock portfolio is determined by:

1. The relationship between the cash portfolio and the index underlying the futures contract.
2. The relationship between the cash price and futures price when a hedge is placed and when it is lifted (liquidated).

The difference between the cash price and the futures price is called the *basis*. It is only at the settlement that the basis is known with certainty. As explained earlier, at the settlement date, the basis is zero. If a hedge is lifted at the settlement date, the basis is therefore known. However, if the hedge is lifted at any other time, the basis is not known in advance. The uncertainty about the basis at the time a hedge is to be lifted is called *basis risk*. Consequently, hedging involves the substitution of basis risk for price risk.

A stock index futures contract has a stock index as its underlying. Since the portfolio that an asset manager seeks to hedge will typically have different characteristics from the underlying stock index, there will be a difference in return pattern of the portfolio being hedged and the futures contract. This practice—hedging with a futures contract that is different from the underlying being hedged—is called *cross hedging*. In the commodity futures markets, this occurs, for example, when a farmer who grows okra hedges that crop by using corn futures contracts, because there are no exchange-traded futures contracts in which okra is the underlying. In the stock market, an asset manager who wishes to hedge a stock portfolio must choose the stock index, or combination of stock indexes, that best (but imperfectly) tracks the portfolio.

Consequently, cross hedging adds another dimension to basis risk, because the portfolio does not track the return on the stock index perfectly.

Mispricing of a stock index futures contract is a major portion of basis risk and is largely random.

The foregoing points about hedging will be made clearer in the next illustrations.

Hedge Ratio

To implement a hedging strategy, it is necessary to determine not only which stock index futures contract to use, but also how many of the contracts to take a position in (i.e., how many to sell in a short hedge and buy in a long hedge). The number of contracts depends on the relative return volatility of the portfolio to be hedged and the return volatility of the futures contract. The *hedge ratio* is the ratio of volatility of the portfolio to be hedged and the return volatility of the futures contract.

It is tempting to use the portfolio's beta as a hedge ratio because it is an indicator of the sensitivity of a portfolio's return to the stock index return. It appears, then, to be an ideal way to adjust for the sensitivity of the return of the portfolio to be hedged. However, applying beta relative to a stock index as a sensitivity adjustment to a stock index futures contract assumes that the index and the futures contract have the same volatility. If futures were always to sell at their theoretical price, this would be a reasonable assumption. However, mispricing is an extra element of volatility in a stock index futures contract. Since the futures contract is more volatile than the underlying index, using a portfolio beta as a sensitivity adjustment would result in a portfolio being overhedged.

The most accurate sensitivity adjustment would be the beta of a portfolio relative to the futures contract. It can be shown that the beta of a portfolio relative to a futures contract is equivalent to the product of the portfolio relative to the underlying index and the beta of the index relative to the futures contract.[3] The beta in each case is estimated using regression analysis in which the data are historical returns for the portfolio to be hedged, the stock index, and the stock index futures contract.

The regression to be estimated is

$$r_P = a_P + B_{PI} r_I + e_P$$

where

r_P = the return on the portfolio to be hedged
r_I = the return on the stock index

---

[3]See Peters (1987).

B_{PI} = the beta of the portfolio relative to the stock index
a_P = the intercept of the relationship
e_P = the error term

and

$$r_I = a_I + B_{IF}\, r_F + e_I$$

where

r_F = the return on the stock index futures contract
B_{IF} = the beta of the stock index relative to the stock index futures contract
a_I = the intercept of the relationship
e_I = the error term

Given B_{PI} and B_{IF}, the minimum risk hedge ratio can then be expressed as

$$\text{Hedge ratio} = B_{PI} \times B_{IF}$$

The coefficient of determination of the regression (i.e., R-squared) will indicate how good the estimated relationship is, and thereby allow the asset manager to assess the likelihood of success of the proposed hedge.

The number of contracts needed can be calculated using the following three steps after B_{PI} and B_{IF} are estimated:

Step 1. Determine the equivalent market index units of the market by dividing the market value of the portfolio to be hedged by the current index price of the futures contract:

$$\text{Equivalent market index units} = \frac{\text{Market value of the portfolio to be hedged}}{\text{Current index value of the futures contract}}$$

Step 2. Multiply the equivalent market index units by the hedge ratio to obtain the beta-adjusted equivalent market index units:

Beta-adjusted equivalent market index units
= Hedge ratio × Equivalent market index units

or

Beta-adjusted equivalent market index units
$= B_{PI} \times B_{IF} \times$ Equivalent market index units

Step 3. Divide the beta-adjusted equivalent units by the multiple specified by the stock index futures contract:

$$\text{Number of contracts} = \frac{\text{Beta-adjusted equivalent market index units}}{\text{Multiple of the contract}}$$

We will use two examples to illustrate the implementation of a hedge and the risks associated with hedging.

Illustration 1 Consider a portfolio manager on January 30, 2009, who is managing a $100 million portfolio that is identical to the S&P 500. The manager wants to hedge against a possible market decline. More specifically, the manager wants to hedge the portfolio until February 27, 2009. To hedge against an adverse market move during the period January 30, 2009, to February 27, 2009, the portfolio manager decides to enter into a short hedge by selling the S&P 500 futures contracts that settled in March 2009. On January 30, 2009, the March 2009 futures contract was selling for 822.5.

Since the portfolio to be hedged is identical to the S&P 500, the beta of the portfolio relative to the index (B_{PI}) is, of course, 1. The beta relative to the futures contract (B_{IF}) was estimated to be 0.745. Therefore, the number of contracts needed to hedge the $100 million portfolio is computed as follows:

Step 1.

$$\text{Equivalent market index units} = \frac{\$100,000,000}{822.5} = \$121,581$$

Step 2.

$$\text{Beta-adjusted equivalent market index units} = 1 \times 0.745 \times \$121,581 = \$90,578$$

Step 3. The multiple for the S&P 500 contract is 250. Therefore,

$$\text{Number of contracts to be sold} = \frac{\$90,578}{\$250} = 362$$

This means that the futures position was equal to $74,500,000 (362 × $250 × 822.5). On February 27, 2009, the hedge was removed. The portfolio that mirrored the S&P 500 had lost $10,993,122. At the time the hedge was lifted, the March 2009 S&P 500 contract was selling at 734.2. Since the contract was sold on January 30, 2009 for 822.5 and bought back on February 27, 2009 for 734.2, there was a gain of 88.3 index units per contract. For the 362 contracts, the gain was $7,997,994 (88.3 × $250 × 362). This results in a smaller loss of $2,995,129 ($7,997,994 gain on the futures position and $10,993,122 loss on the portfolio). The total transaction costs for the futures position would have been less than $8,000. Remember, had the asset manager not hedged the position, the loss would have been $10,993,122.

Let's analyze this hedge to see not only why it was successful, but also why it was not a perfect hedge. As explained earlier, in hedging, basis risk is substituted for price risk. Consider the basis risk in this hedge. At the time the hedge was placed, the cash index was at 825.88, and the futures contract was selling at 822.5. The basis was equal to 3.38 index units (the cash index of 825.88 minus the futures price of 822.5). At the same time, it was calculated that, based on the cost of carry, the theoretical basis was 1.45 index units. That is, the theoretical futures price at the time the hedge was placed should have been 824.42. Thus, according to the pricing model the futures contract was mispriced by 1.92 index unit.

When the hedge was removed at the close of February 27, 2009, the cash index stood at 735.09, and the futures contract at 734.2. Thus, the basis changed from 3.38 index units at the time the hedge was initiated to 0.89 index units (735.09 − 734.2) when the hedge was lifted. The basis had changed by 2.49 index units (3.38 − 0.89) alone, or $622.5 per contract (2.49 times the multiple of $250). This means that the basis alone cost $225,538 for the 362 contracts ($622.5 × 362). The index dropped 90.79 index units, for a gain of $22,698 per contract, or $8,223,532. Thus, the futures position cost $225,538 due to the change in the basis risk, and $8,223,532 due to the change in the index. Combined, this comes out to be the $7,997,994 gain in the futures position.

Illustration 2 We examined basis risk in the first illustration. Because we were hedging a portfolio that was constructed to replicate the S&P 500 index using the S&P 500 futures contract, there was no cross-hedging risk. However, most portfolios are not matched to the S&P 500. Consequently, cross-hedging risk results because the estimated beta for the price behavior of the portfolio may not behave as predicted by B_{PI}. To illustrate this situation, suppose that an asset manager owned all the stocks in the Dow Jones Industrial Average (DJIA) on January 30, 2009. The market value of the portfolio held was $100 million. Also assume that the portfolio manager wanted to hedge the position against a decline in stock prices from January 30, 2009, to February 27, 2009, using the March 2009 S&P 500 futures contract. Since the S&P 500 futures September contract is used here to hedge a portfolio of DJIA to February 27, 2009, this is a cross hedge.

Information about the S&P 500 cash index and futures contract when the hedge was placed on January 30, 2009, and when it was removed on February 27, 2009, was given in the previous illustration. The beta of the index relative to the futures contract (B_{IF}) was 0.745. The DJIA in a regression analysis was found to have a beta relative to the S&P 500 of 1.05 (with an R-squared of 93%). We follow the three steps enumerated above to obtain the number of contracts to sell:

Step 1.

$$\text{Equivalent market index units} = \frac{\$100{,}000{,}000}{822.5} = \$121{,}581$$

Step 2.

$$\text{Beta-adjusted equivalent market index units} = 1.05 \times 0.745 \times \$121{,}581$$
$$= \$95{,}106$$

Step 3. The multiple for the S&P 500 contract is 250. Therefore,

$$\text{Number of contracts to be sold} = \frac{\$95{,}106}{250} = 380$$

During the period of the hedge, the DJIA actually lost $11,720,000. This meant a loss of 11.72% on the portfolio consisting of the component stocks of the DJIA. Since 380 S&P 500 futures contracts were sold and the gain per contract was 88.3 points, the gain from the futures position was $8,388,500 ($88.3 × 380 × 250). This means that the hedged position resulted in a loss of $3,331,500, or equivalently, a return of −3.31%.

We already analyzed why this was not a perfect hedge. In the previous illustration, we explained how changes in the basis affected the outcome. Let's look at how the relationship between the DJIA and the S&P 500 Index affected the outcome. As stated in the previous illustration, the S&P 500 over this same period declined in value by 10.99%. With the beta of the portfolio relative to the S&P 500 Index (1.05), the expected decline in the value of the portfolio based on the movement in the S&P 500 was 11.54% (1.05 × 10.99%). Had this actually occurred, the DJIA portfolio would have lost only $10,990,000 rather than $11,720,000, and the net loss from the hedge would have been $2,601,500, or −2.6%. Thus, there is a difference of a $730,000 loss due to the DJIA performing differently than predicted by beta.

Constructing an Indexed Portfolio

As we explained in Chapter 7, some institutional equity funds are indexed to some broad-based stock market index. There are management fees and transaction costs associated with creating a portfolio to replicate a stock index that has been targeted to be matched. The higher these costs, the greater the divergence between the performance of the indexed portfolio and the target index. Moreover, because an asset manager creating an indexed portfolio will not purchase all the stocks that make up a broad-based stock index, the indexed portfolio is exposed to tracking error risk. Instead of using the cash market to construct an indexed portfolio, the manager can use stock index futures.

Let's illustrate how and under what circumstances stock index futures can be used to create an indexed portfolio. If stock index futures are priced according to their theoretical price, a portfolio consisting of a long position in stock index futures and Treasury bills will produce the same portfolio return as that of the underlying cash index. To see this, suppose that an index fund manager wishes to index a $90 million portfolio using the S&P 500 as the target index. Also assume the following:

1. The S&P 500 at the time was 1200.
2. The S&P 500 futures index with six months to settlement is currently selling for 1212.
3. The expected dividend yield for the S&P 500 for the next six months is 2%.
4. Six-month Treasury bills are currently yielding 3%.

The theoretical futures price is found using the equation (13.1) is:

Cash market price + Cash market price × (Financing cost − Dividend yield)

Because the financing cost is 3% and the dividend yield is 2%, the theoretical futures price is:

$$1200 + 1200 \times (0.03 - 0.02) = 1212$$

and, therefore, the futures price in the market is equal to the theoretical futures price.

Consider two strategies that the index fund manager may choose to pursue:

Strategy 1. Purchase $90 million of stocks in such a way as to replicate the performance of the S&P 500.
Strategy 2. Buy 300 S&P 500 futures contracts with settlement six months from now at 1212, and invest $90 million in a six-month Treasury bill.[4]

How will the two strategies perform under various scenarios for the S&P 500 value when the contract settles six months from now? Let's investigate three scenarios:

Scenario 1. The S&P 500 increases to 1320 (an increase of 10%).
Scenario 2. The S&P 500 remains at 1200.
Scenario 3. The S&P 500 declines to 1080 (a decrease of 10%).

At settlement, the futures price converges to the value of the index. Table 13.1 shows the value of the portfolio for both strategies for each of the three scenarios. As can be seen, for a given scenario, the performance of the two strategies is identical.

This result should not be surprising because a futures contract can be replicated by buying the instrument underlying the futures contract with borrowed funds. In the case of indexing, we are replicating the underlying instrument by buying the futures contract and investing in Treasury bills. Therefore, if stock index futures contracts are properly priced, index fund managers can use stock index futures to create an index fund.

Several points should be noted. First, in strategy 1, the ability of the portfolio to replicate the S&P 500 depends on how well the portfolio is constructed to track the index. On the other hand, assuming that the expected dividends are realized and that the futures contract is fairly priced, the futures/Treasury bill portfolio (strategy 2) will mirror the performance of the S&P 500 exactly. Thus, tracking error is reduced.

Second, the cost of transacting is less for strategy 2. For example, if the cost of one S&P 500 futures is $15, then the transaction costs for strategy 2 would be only $4,500 for a $90 million fund. This would be considerably less than the transaction costs associated with the acquisition and maintenance of a broadly diversified stock portfolio designed to replicate the S&P

---

[4]There are two points to note here. First, this illustration ignores margin requirements. The Treasury bills can be used for initial margin. Second, 600 contracts are selected in this strategy because with the current (assumed) market index at 1200 and a multiple of 250, the cash value of 300 contracts is $90 million.

TABLE 13.1 Comparison of Portfolio Value from Purchasing Stocks to Replicate an Index and a Futures/Treasury Bill Strategy when the Futures Contract is Fairly Priced

Assumptions:
1. Amount to be invested = $90 million
2. Current value of S&P 500 = 1200
3. Current value of S&P futures contract = 1212
4. Expected dividend yield = 2%
5. Yield on Treasury bills = 3%
6. Number of S&P 500 contracts to be purchased = 300

Strategy 1. Direct Purchase of Stocks

	Index Value at Settlement		
	1320	1200	1080
Change in index value	10%	0%	−10%
Market value of portfolio that mirrors the index	$99,000,000	$90,000,000	$81,000,000
Dividends (0.02 × $90,000,000)	$1,800,000	$1,800,000	$1,800,000
Value of portfolio	$100,800,000	$91,800,000	$82,800,000
Dollar return	$1,080,000	$180,000	$(720,000)

Strategy 2. Futures/T-Bill Portfolio

	Index Value at Settlement[a]		
	1320	1200	1080
Gain/loss for 600 contracts (300 × $250 × gain/per contract)	$8,100,000	−$900,000	−$9,990,000
Value of Treasury bills ($90,000,000 × 1.03)	$92,700,000	$92,700,000	$92,700,000
Value of portfolio	$100,800,000	$91,800,000	$82,800,000
Dollar return	$1,080,000	$180,000	$(720,000)

[a]Because of convergence of cash and futures price, the S&P 500 cash index and stock index futures price will be the same.

500. In addition, for a large fund that wishes to index, the market impact cost is lessened by using stock index futures rather than using the cash market to create an index.

The third point is that custodial costs are obviously less for an index fund created using stock index futures. The fourth point is that the performance of the synthetically created index fund will depend on variation margin.

In synthetically creating an index fund, we assumed that the futures contract was fairly priced. Suppose, instead, that the stock index futures price is less than the theoretical futures price (i.e., the futures contracts are cheap). If that situation occurs, the index fund manager can enhance the indexed portfolio's return by buying the futures and buying Treasury bills. That is, the return on the futures and Treasury bill portfolio will be greater than that on the underlying index when the position is held to the settlement date.

To see this, suppose that in our previous illustration, the current futures price is 1204 instead of 1212, so that the futures contract is cheap (undervalued). The futures position for the three scenarios in Table 13.1 would be $150,000 greater (2 index units × $250 × 300 contracts). Therefore, the value of the portfolio and the dollar return for all three scenarios will be greater by $150,000 by buying the futures contract and Treasury bills rather than buying the stocks directly.

Alternatively, if the futures contract is expensive based on its theoretical price, an index fund manager who owns stock index futures and Treasury bills will swap that portfolio for the stocks in the index. An index fund manager who swaps between the futures and Treasury bills portfolio and a stock portfolio based on the value of the futures contract relative to the cash market index is attempting to enhance the portfolio's return. This strategy, referred to as a *stock replacement strategy*, is one of several strategies used in an attempt to enhance the return of an indexed portfolio.

Transaction costs can be reduced measurably by using a return enhancement strategy. Whenever the difference between the actual basis and the theoretical basis exceeds the market impact of a transaction, the aggressive manager should consider replacing stocks with futures or vice versa. Once the strategy has been put into effect, several subsequent scenarios may unfold. For example, consider an index manager who has a portfolio of stock index futures and Treasury bills. First, should the futures contract become sufficiently rich relative to stocks, the futures position is sold and the stocks repurchased, with program trading used to execute the buy orders. Second, should the futures contract remain at fair value, the position is held until expiration, when the futures settle at the cash index value and stocks are repurchased at the market at close. Should an index manager owns a portfolio of stocks and the futures contract becomes cheap relative to stocks, then the manager will sell the stocks and buy the stock index futures contracts.

EQUITY SWAPS[5]

Equity swaps are similar in concept to interest rate and currency swaps. They are contractual agreements between two counterparties which provide for the periodic exchange of a schedule of cash flows over a specified time period where at least one of the two payments is linked to the performance of an equity index, a basket of stocks, or a single stock. In a standard or plain vanilla equity swap, one counterparty agrees to pay the other the total return to an equity index in exchange for receiving either the total return of another asset or a fixed or floating interest rate. All payments are based on a notional amount and payments are made over a fixed time period.

Equity swap structures are very flexible with maturities ranging from a few months to 10 years. The returns of virtually any asset can be swapped for another without incurring the costs associated with a transaction in the cash market. Payment schedules can be denominated in any currency irrespective of the equity asset and payments can be exchanged monthly, quarterly, annually, or at maturity. The equity asset can be any equity index or portfolio of stocks, and denominated in any currency, hedged or unhedged.

Equity swaps have a wide variety of applications including asset allocation, accessing international markets, enhancing equity returns, hedging equity exposure, and synthetically shorting stocks.

An example of an equity swap is a one-year agreement where the counterparty agrees to pay the investor the total return to the S&P 500 Index in exchange for dollar-denominated LIBOR on a quarterly basis. The investor would pay LIBOR plus a spread × 91/360 × notional amount. This type of equity swap is the economic equivalent of financing a long position in the S&P 500 Index at a spread to LIBOR. The advantages of using the swap are no transaction costs, no sales or dividend withholding tax, and no tracking error or basis risk versus the index.

The basic mechanics of equity swaps are the same regardless of the structure. However, the rules governing the exchange of payments may differ. For example, a U.S. investor wanting to diversify internationally can enter into a swap and, depending on the investment objective, exchange payments on a currency-hedged basis. If the investment objective is to reduce U.S. equity exposure and increase Japanese equity exposure, for example, a swap could be structured to exchange the total returns to the S&P 500 Index for the total returns to the Nikkei 225 Index. If, however, the investment objective is to gain access to the Japanese equity market, a swap can be structured to exchange LIBOR plus a spread for the total returns to the Nikkei 225 Index. This is an example of diversifying internationally and the cash flows can be denominated in either yen or dollars. The advantages of entering into

---

[5] For a further discussion of equity swaps, see Collins and Fabozzi (1999).

an equity swap to obtain international diversification are that the investor exposure is devoid of tracking error, and the investor incurs no sales tax, custodial fees, withholding fees, or market impact associated with entering and exiting a market. This swap is the economic equivalent of being long the Nikkei 225 financed at a spread to LIBOR at a fixed exchange rate.

There are numerous applications of equity swaps, but all assume the basic structure outlined above. Investors can virtually swap any financial asset for the total returns to an equity index, a portfolio of stocks, or a single stock. There are dealers prepared to create structures that allow an investor to exchange the returns of any two assets. The schedule of cash flows exchanged is a function of the assets. For example, an investor wanting to outperform an equity benchmark may be able to accomplish this by purchasing a particular bond and swapping the cash flows for the S&P 500 total return minus a spread.

Equity swaps are a useful means of implementing an asset allocation strategy. One example is an asset swap of the S&P 500 total returns for the total returns to the German DAX index. The investor can reduce U.S. equity exposure and increase German equity exposure through an equity swap, thereby avoiding the costs associated with cash market transactions.

SUMMARY

In this chapter we explained how two types of equity derivatives—stock index futures and equity swaps—can be used in managing an equity portfolio. We explained the basic features of futures and forward contracts, what a stock index futures contract is, and how the theoretical futures price is determined via arbitrage (cash-and-carry trade and reverse cash-and-carry trade). The market price of a stock index futures contract can deviate from the theoretical futures price because the assumptions of the basic pricing model may not hold and/or due to the features of a stock index futures contract. We illustrated how a stock index futures contract can be used for hedging and for synthetically creating an index fund. In hedging using futures contracts, the hedger substitutes basis risk for price risk.

In a standard or plain vanilla equity swap, one counterparty agrees to pay the other the total return to an equity index in exchange for receiving either the total return of another asset or a fixed or floating interest rate. Equity swaps can be used for asset allocation, accessing international markets, enhancing equity returns, hedging equity exposure, and synthetically shorting stocks.

REFERENCES

Collins, B., and F. J. Fabozzi. 1999. *Derivatives and equity portfolio management*. Hoboken, NJ: John Wiley & Sons.

Peters, E. E. 1987. Hedged equity portfolios: Components of risk and return, *Advances in Futures and Options Research* 1, part B: 75–92.

CHAPTER 14

Using Equity Options in Investment Management

Options provide portfolio managers with another derivative tool to manage risk and achieve the desired investment objective. As with futures contracts described in the previous chapter, options can modify the risk characteristics of an investment portfolio, to enhance the expected return of a portfolio and reduce transaction costs associated with managing a portfolio.

In this chapter, we describe the characteristics of options and their use in portfolio management. In the next chapter, we explain and illustrate the pricing of options.

BASIC FEATURES OF OPTIONS

An *option* is a contract in which the *option seller* grants the *option buyer* the right to enter into a transaction with the seller to either buy or sell an underlying asset at a specified price on or before a specified date. The specified price is called the *strike price* or *exercise price* and the specified date is called the *expiration date*. The option seller grants this right in exchange for a certain amount of money called the *option premium* or *option price*.

The option seller is also known as the *option writer*, while the option buyer is the option holder. The asset that is the subject of the option is called the *underlying*. The underlying can be an individual stock, a stock index, a bond, or even another derivative instrument such as a futures contract. The option writer can grant the option holder one of two rights. If the right is to purchase the underlying, the option is referred to as a *call option*. If the right is to sell the underlying, the option is referred to as a *put option*.

This chapter is coauthored with Bruce Collins.

An option can also be categorized according to when it may be exercised by the buyer. This is referred to as the *exercise style*. A *European option* can only be exercised at the option's expiration date. An *American option*, in contrast, can be exercised any time on or before the expiration date. An option that can be exercised before the expiration date but only on specified dates is called a *Bermuda option* or an *Atlantic option*.

The terms of exchange are represented by the contract unit and are standardized for most contracts. Table 14.1 summarizes the obligations and rights of the parties to American call and put options.

The option holder enters into the contract with an opening transaction. Subsequently, the option holder then has the choice to exercise or to sell the option. The sale of an existing option by the holder is a closing sale.

Let's use an illustration to demonstrate the fundamental option contract. Suppose that Jack buys a call option for $3 (the option price) with the following terms:

1. The underlying is one unit of asset ABC.
2. The exercise price is $100.
3. The expiration date is three months from now, and the option can be exercised anytime up to and including the expiration date (that is, it is an American option).

TABLE 14.1 Obligations and Rights of the Parties to American[a] Option Contracts

Type of Option	Writer/Seller		Buyer	
	Obligation	Right	Obligation	Right
Call option	To sell the underlying to the buyer (at the buyer's option) at the exercise price at or before date the expiration date	Receive the option price	Pay the option price	To buy the underlying from the writer at the exercise price anytime before the expiration date
Put option	To purchase the underlying from the buyer (at the buyer's option) at the exercise price at or before the expiration date	Receive the option price	Pay the option price	To sell the underlying to the writer at the exercise price anytime before the expiration date

[a]European options may be exercised only on the expiration date.

At any time up to and including the expiration date, Jack can decide to buy from the writer of this option one unit of asset ABC, for which he will pay a price of $100. If it is not beneficial for Jack to exercise the option, he will not—how he decides when it is beneficial is explained shortly. Whether Jack exercises the option or not, the $3 he paid for it will be kept by the option writer. If Jack buys a put option rather than a call option, then he would be able to sell asset ABC to the option writer for a price of $100.

The maximum amount that an option buyer can lose is the option price. The maximum profit that the option writer can realize is the option price. The option buyer has substantial upside return potential, while the option writer has substantial downside risk. We investigate the risk-reward relationship for option positions later in this chapter.

Options, like other financial instruments, may be traded either on an organized exchange or in the over-the-counter (OTC) market. An option that is traded on an exchange is referred to as a *listed option* or an *exchange-traded option*. An option traded in the OTC market is called an *OTC option* or a *dealer option*. The advantages of a listed option are as follows. First, the exercise price and expiration date of the contract are standardized. Second, as in the case of futures contracts, the direct link between buyer and seller is severed after the trade is executed because of the interchangeability of listed options. The clearinghouse associated with the exchange where the option trades performs the same function in the options market that it does in the futures market. Finally, the transactions costs are lower for listed options than for OTC options.

The higher cost of an OTC option reflects the cost of customizing the option for the many situations where an investor seeking to use an option to manage risk needs to have a tailor-made option because the standardized listed option does not satisfy its objectives. While an OTC option is less liquid than a listed option, this is typically not of concern to the user of such an option. The explosive growth in OTC options suggests that portfolio managers find that these products serve an important investment purpose.

Differences between Options and Futures Contracts

Notice that, unlike in a futures contract, one party to an option contract is not obligated to transact—specifically, the option buyer has the right but not the obligation to transact. The option writer does have the obligation to perform. In the case of a futures contract, both buyer and seller are obligated to perform. Of course, a futures buyer does not pay the seller to accept the obligation, while an option buyer pays the seller the option price.

Consequently, the risk-reward characteristics of the these derivative contracts are also different. In the case of a futures contract, the buyer of the contract realizes a dollar-for-dollar gain when the price of the futures contract increases and suffers a dollar-for-dollar loss when the price of the futures contract decreases. The opposite occurs for the seller of a futures contract. Because of this relationship, futures contracts are said to have a "linear payoff."

Options do not provide this symmetric risk-reward relationship. The most that the buyer of an option can lose is the option price. While the buyer of an option retains all the potential benefits, the gain is always reduced by the amount of the option price. The maximum profit that the writer may realize is the option price; this is offset against substantial downside risk. Because of this characteristic, options are said to have a *nonlinear payoff*.

The difference in the type of payoff between futures and options is extremely important because market participants can use futures to protect against symmetric risk and options to protect against asymmetric risk.

BASIC FEATURES OF LISTED EQUITY OPTIONS

Listed options can be classified into four groups: (1) stock options, (2) index options, (3) Long-Term Equity Anticipation Securities™, and (4) FLexible EXchange Options™. We describe each in this section.

Stock Options

Stock options refer to listed options on individual stocks. The underlying is 100 shares of the designated stock. All listed stock options in the United States may be exercised any time before the expiration date; that is, they are American-style options. Option contracts for a given stock are based on expiration dates that fit in a cycle, typically nine months for a stock; for stock options the cycles are two near-term months plus two additional months from the January, February, or March quarterly cycles. Common cycles include January-April-July-October (JAJO) expiring options, February-May-August-November (FMAN) expiring options, and March-June-September-December (MJSD) expiring options.

Index Options

Index options are options where the underlying is a stock index rather than an individual stock. An index call option gives the option buyer the right to buy the underlying stock index, while a put index option gives the option buyer the right to sell the underlying stock index. Unlike stock options where a stock can be delivered if the option is exercised by the option holder, it would be extremely complicated to settle an index option by delivering all the stocks that constitute the index. Instead, as with stock index futures, index options are cash settlement contracts. This means that if the option is exercised by the option holder, the option writer pays cash to the option buyer. There is no delivery of any stocks.

Index options include industry options, sector options, and style options. The most liquid index options are those on the S&P 100 index (OEX) and the S&P 500 index (SPX). Both trade on the Chicago Board Options Exchange (CBOE). Index options can be American or European style. The S&P 500 index option contract is European, while the OEX is American. Both index option contracts have specific standardized features and contract terms. Moreover, both have short expiration cycles, which are the four near-term months.

The dollar value of the stock index underlying an index option is equal to the current cash index value multiplied by the contract's multiple. That is,

Dollar value of the underlying index = Cash index value × Multiple

For example, suppose the cash index value for the S&P 500 is 800. Since the contract multiple is $100, the dollar value of the SPX is $80,000 (= 800 × $100).

For a stock option, the price at which the buyer of the option can buy or sell the stock is the strike price. For an index option, the strike index is the index value at which the buyer of the option can buy or sell the underlying stock index. The strike index is converted into a dollar value by multiplying the strike index by the multiple for the contract. For example, if the strike index is 1000, the dollar value is $100,000 (= 1000 × $100). If an investor purchases a call option on the SPX with a strike index of 1000, and exercises the option when the index value is 1010, the investor has the right to purchase the index for $100,000 when the market value of the index is $101,000. The buyer of the call option would then receive $1,000 from the option writer.

Long-Term Equity Anticipation Securities™ and FLexible EXchange Options™

Long-Term Equity Anticipation Securities™ (LEAPS) and FLexible EXchange Options™ (FLEX) are options that essentially modify an existing feature of either a stock option or an index option. For example, as noted above, stock option and index option contracts have short expiration cycles. LEAPS are designed to offer options with longer maturities. These contracts are available on individual stocks and some indexes. Stock option LEAPS are comparable to standard stock options except the maturities can range up to 39 months from the origination date. Index options LEAPS differ in size compared with standard index options having a multiplier of 10 rather than 100.

FLEX options allow users to specify the terms of the option contract for either a stock option or an index option. The process for entering into a FLEX option agreement is well documented by the CBOE where these options trade. The value of FLEX options is the ability to customize the terms of the contract along four dimensions: underlying, strike price, expiration date, and settlement style. Moreover, the exchange provides a secondary market to offset or alter positions and an independent daily marking of prices. The development of the FLEX option is a response to the growing OTC market. The exchanges seek to make the FLEX option attractive by providing price discovery[1] through a competitive auction market, an active secondary market, daily price valuations, and the virtual elimination of counterparty risk. The FLEX option represents a link between listed options and OTC products.

RISK AND RETURN CHARACTERISTICS OF LISTED OPTIONS

Now we illustrate the risk and return characteristics of the four basic option positions:

- Buying a call option (long a call option)
- Selling a call option (short a call option)
- Buying a put option (long a put option)
- Selling a put option (short a put option)

More complicated positions are explained later in this chapter.

We use stock options in our example. The illustrations assume that each option position is held to the expiration date and not exercised early. Also, to simplify the illustrations, we assume that the underlying for each option is for 1 share of stock rather than 100 shares and we ignore transaction costs.

Buying Call Options

Assume that there is a call option on stock XYZ that expires in one month and has a strike price of $100. The option price is $3. Suppose that the current or spot price of stock XYZ is $100. The profit and loss will depend on the price of stock XYZ at the expiration date. Table 14.2 and Figure 14.1 show the profit and loss potential at the expiration date for buying a call option in tabular and graphical forms, respectively. The buyer of a call option benefits if the price rises above the strike price. If the price of stock XYZ is

---
[1]*Price discovery* is the valuation of an asset that reflects all currently available information, including the value of the underlying.

TABLE 14.2 Profit/Loss Profile at Expiration of a Long Call Option and a Long Stock Position

Assumptions:
Price of Stock XYZ = $100
Strike price = $100
Option price = $3
Time to expiration = 1 month

Price of Stock XYZ at Expiration Date	Profit/Loss for:	
	Long Call[a]	Long Stock XYZ[b]
$150	$47	$50
140	37	40
130	27	30
120	17	20
115	12	15
114	11	14
113	10	13
112	9	12
111	8	11
110	7	10
109	6	9
108	5	8
107	4	7
106	3	6
105	2	5
104	1	4
103	0	3
102	−1	2
101	−2	1
100	−3	0
99	−3	−1
98	−3	−2
97	−3	−3
96	−3	−4
95	−3	−5
94	−3	−6
93	−3	−7

TABLE 14.2 (Continued)

Price of Stock XYZ at Expiration Date	Profit/Loss for:	
	Long Call[a]	Long Stock XYZ[b]
$92	−$3	−$8
91	−3	−9
90	−3	−10
89	−3	−11
88	−3	−12
87	−3	−13
86	−3	−14
85	−3	−15
80	−3	−20
70	−3	−30
60	−3	−40

[a]Price at expiration − $100 − $3 Maximum loss is $3
[b]Price at expiration − $100

FIGURE 14.1 Profit/Loss Profile at Expiration of a Long Call Positions and a Long Stock Position

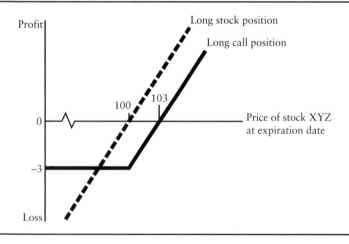

equal to $103, the buyer of a call option breaks even. The maximum loss is the option price, and there is substantial upside potential if the stock price rises above $103.

It is worthwhile to compare the profit and loss profile of the call option buyer with that of an investor taking a long position in one share of stock XYZ. The payoff from the position depends on stock XYZ's price at the expiration date. Table 14.1 and Figure 14.1 provide this comparison. This comparison clearly demonstrates the way in which an option can alter the risk-return profile for investors. An investor who takes a long position in stock XYZ realizes a profit of $1 for every $1 increase in stock XYZ's price. As stock XYZ's price falls, however, the investor loses dollar for dollar. If the price drops by more than $3, the long position in stock XYZ results in a loss of more than $3. The long call position, in contrast, limits the loss to only the option price of $3 but retains the upside potential, which will be $3 less than for the long position in stock XYZ. Which alternative is better, buying the call option or buying the stock? The answer depends on what the investor is attempting to achieve.

We can also use this hypothetical call option to demonstrate the speculative appeal of options. Suppose an investor has strong expectations that stock XYZ's price will rise in one month. At an option price of $3, the speculator can purchase 33.33 call options for each $100 invested. If stock XYZ's price rises, the investor realizes the price appreciation associated with 33.33 units of stock XYZ. With the same $100, however, the investor can purchase only one unit of stock XYZ selling at $100, thereby realizing the appreciation associated with one unit if stock XYZ's price increases. Now, suppose that in one month the price of stock XYZ rises to $120. The long call position will result in a profit of $566.50 [($20 × 33.33) – $100], or a return of 566.5% on the $100 investment in the call option. The long position in stock XYZ results in a profit of $20, only a 20% return on $100.

This greater leverage attracts investors to options when they wish to speculate on price movements. There are drawbacks to this leverage, however. Suppose that stock XYZ's price is unchanged at $100 at the expiration date. The long call position results in this case in a loss of the entire investment of $100, while the long position in stock XYZ produces neither a gain nor a loss.

Writing Call Options

To illustrate the option seller's, or writer's, position, we use the same call option we used to illustrate buying a call option. The profit/loss profile at expiration of the short call position (that is, the position of the call option writer) is the mirror image of the profit and loss profile of the long call position (the

FIGURE 14.2 Profit/Loss Profile at Expiration for a Short Call Positions and a Long Call Position

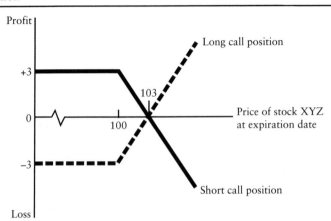

position of the call option buyer). That is, the profit of the short call position for any given price for stock XYZ at the expiration date is the same as the loss of the long call position. Consequently, the maximum profit the short call position can produce is the option price. The maximum loss is not limited because it is the highest price reached by stock XYZ on or before the expiration date, less the option price; this price can be indefinitely high. This can be seen in Figure 14.2, which shows the profit/loss profile for a short call position, as well as the profit/loss profile at expiration for a long call position.

Buying Put Options

To illustrate a long put option position, we assume a hypothetical put option on one share of stock XYZ with one month to maturity and a strike price of $100. Assume that the put option is selling for $2 and the price of stock XYZ is $100. The profit or loss for this position at the expiration date depends on the market price of stock XYZ. The buyer of a put option benefits if the price falls.

The profit/loss profile at expiration of a long put position is shown in Table 14.3 and Figure 14.3 As with all long option positions, the loss is limited to the option price. The profit potential, however, is substantial: the theoretical maximum profit is generated if stock XYZ's price falls to zero in the case of a put option. Contrast this profit potential with that of the buyer of a call option. The theoretical maximum profit for a call buyer cannot be determined beforehand because it depends on the highest price that can be reached by stock XYZ before or at the option expiration date.

To see how an option alters the risk-return profile for an investor, we again compare it with a position in stock XYZ. The long put position is compared with a short position in stock XYZ because such a position would also benefit if the price of the stock falls. A comparison of the two positions is shown in Table 14.3 and Figure 14.3. While the investor taking a short stock position faces all the downside risk as well as the upside potential, an investor taking the long put position faces limited downside risk (equal to the option price) while still maintaining upside potential reduced by an amount equal to the option price.

TABLE 14.3   Profit/Loss Profile at Expiration of a Long Put Option and a Short Stock Position

Assumptions:
Price of stock XYZ = $100   Option price = $2
Strike price = $100   Time to expiration = 1 month

Price of Stock XYZ at Expiration Date	Profit/Loss for:	
	Long Put[a]	Short Stock XYZ[b]
$150	−$2	−$50
140	−2	−40
130	−2	−30
120	−2	−20
115	−2	−15
110	−2	−10
105	−2	−5
100	−2	0
99	−1	1
98	0	2
97	1	3
96	2	4
95	3	5
94	4	6
93	5	7
92	6	8
91	7	9
90	8	10
89	9	11
88	10	12

TABLE 14.3 (Continued)

Price of Stock XYZ at Expiration Date	Profit/Loss for:	
	Long Put[a]	Short Stock XYZ[b]
$87	$11	$13
86	12	14
85	13	15
84	14	16
83	15	17
82	16	18
81	17	19
80	18	20
75	23	25
70	28	30
65	33	35
60	38	40

[a]$100 − Price at expiration − $100 − $2 Maximum loss is $2
[b]$100 − Price at expiration

FIGURE 14.3 Profit/Loss Profile at Expiration for a Long Put Position and a Short Stock Position

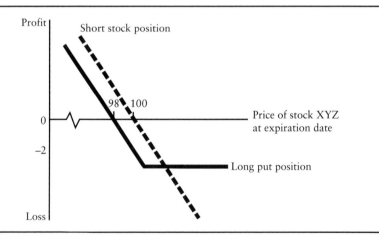

FIGURE 14.4 Profit/Loss Profile at Expiration for a Short Put Position and a Long Put Position

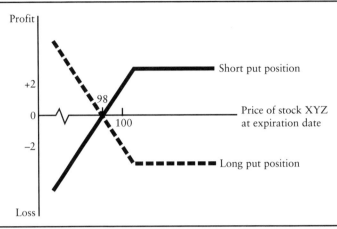

Writing Put Options

The profit and loss profile for a short put option is the mirror image of the long put option. The maximum profit to be realized from this position is the option price. The theoretical maximum loss can be substantial should the price of the underlying fall; if the price were to fall all the way to zero, the loss would be as large as the strike price less the option price. Figure 14.4 depicts this profit/loss profile at expiration for both a short put position and a long put position.

Summary of Profit/Loss from Option Positions

To summarize, buying calls or selling puts allows the investor to gain if the price of the underlying rises. Buying calls gives the investor unlimited upside potential, but limits the loss to the option price. Selling puts limits the profit to the option price, but provides no protection if the price of the underlying falls, with the maximum loss occurring if the price of the underlying falls to zero.

Buying puts and selling calls allows the investor to gain if the price of the underlying falls. Buying puts gives the investor upside potential, with the maximum profit realized if the price of the underlying declines to zero. However, the loss is limited to the option price. Selling calls limits the profit to the option price, but provides no protection if the stock price rises, with the maximum loss being theoretically unlimited.

Considering the Time Value of Money and Dividends

Our illustrations of the four option positions do not address the time value of money. Specifically, the buyer of an option must pay the seller the option price at the time the option is purchased. Thus, the buyer must finance the purchase price of the option or, assuming the option's purchase price does not have to be borrowed, the buyer loses the income that can be earned by investing the amount of the option price until the option is sold or exercised. In contrast, assuming the seller does not have to use the option price as margin for the short position or can use an interest-earning asset as security, the seller has the opportunity to earn income from the proceeds of the option sale.

The time value of money changes the profit/loss profile of the option positions. The break-even price for the buyer and the seller of an option will not be the same as in our earlier illustrations. The break-even price for the underlying stock at the expiration date is higher for the buyer of the option; for the seller, it is lower.

Our comparisons of the option position with positions in the underlying stock also ignore the time value of money. We did not consider the fact that the underlying stock may pay dividends. The buyer of a call option is not entitled to any dividends paid by the corporation. The buyer of the underlying stock, however, would receive any interim cash flows and would have the opportunity to reinvest them. A complete comparison of the long call option position and the long position in the underlying stock must take into account the additional dollars gained from reinvesting any dividends. Moreover, any effect on the price of the underlying stock as a result of the distribution of cash must also be considered. This occurs, for example, when as a result of a dividend payment, the stock declines in price.

Later in this chapter where we discuss strategies with options, we are more thorough by considering the cost of borrowing, the lending rate that reflects the opportunity to invest funds short term, and the dividends from the underlying stock or stock index.

THE OPTION PRICE

As with futures and forward contracts, the theoretical price of an option is also derived based on arbitrage arguments. However, as will be explained, the pricing of options is not as simple as the pricing of futures and forward contracts. Here we provide only the basic components and the factors that affect the value of an option. In the next chapter, we discuss option pricing models.

Basic Components of the Option Price

The theoretical price of an option is made up of two components: the intrinsic value and a premium over intrinsic value.

Intrinsic Value

The *intrinsic value* is the option's economic value if it is exercised immediately. If no positive economic value would result from exercising immediately, the intrinsic value is zero. An option's intrinsic value is easy to compute given the price of the underlying and the strike price.

For a call option, the intrinsic value is the difference between the current market price of the underlying and the strike price. If that difference is positive, then the intrinsic value equals that difference; if the difference is zero or negative, then the intrinsic value is equal to zero. For example, if the strike price for a call option is $100 and the current price of the underlying is $109, the intrinsic value is $9. That is, an option buyer exercising the option and simultaneously selling the underlying would realize $109 from the sale of the underlying, which would be covered by acquiring the underlying from the option writer for $100, thereby netting a $9 gain.

An option that has a positive intrinsic value is said to be *in-the-money*. When the strike price of a call option exceeds the underlying's market price, it has no intrinsic value and is said to be *out-of-the-money*. An option for which the strike price is equal to the underlying's market price is said to be *at-the-money*. Both at-the-money and out-of-the-money options have intrinsic values of zero because it is not profitable to exercise them. Our call option with a strike price of $100 would be (1) in the money when the market price of the underlying is more than $100; (2) out of the money when the market price of the underlying is less than $100, and (3) at the money when the market price of the underlying is equal to $100.

For a put option, the intrinsic value is equal to the amount by which the underlying's market price is below the strike price. For example, if the strike price of a put option is $100 and the market price of the underlying is $95, the intrinsic value is $5. That is, the buyer of the put option who simultaneously buys the underlying and exercises the put option will net $5 by exercising. The underlying will be sold to the writer for $100 and purchased in the market for $95. With a strike price of $100, the put option would be (1) in the money when the underlying's market price is less than $100; (2) out of the money when the underlying's market price exceeds $100; and (3) at the money when the underlying's market price is equal to $100.

We summarize the relations in Table 14.4.

TABLE 14.4 Intrinsic Value of Options

If Stock Price > Strike Price		
	Call Option	Put Option
Intrinsic value	Stock price – Strike price	Zero
Jargon	In the money	Out of the money
If Stock Price < Strike Price		
	Call Option	Put Option
Intrinsic value	Zero	Strike price – Stock price
Jargon	Out of the money	In the money
If Stock Price = Strike Price		
	Call Option	Put Option
Intrinsic value	Zero	Zero
Jargon	At the money	At the money

Time Premium

The *time premium* of an option, also referred to as the *time value of the option*, is the amount by which the option's market price exceeds its intrinsic value. The time premium consists of a volatility component and a leverage component. The volatility component is expressed as the expectation of the option buyer that at some time prior to the expiration date changes in the market price of the underlying will increase the value of the rights conveyed by the option. Because of this expectation, the option buyer is willing to pay a premium above the intrinsic value. The leverage component is the carry cost of the underlying, which is positive for calls but negative for puts. The volatility component is positive for both calls and puts. For example, if the price of a call option with a strike price of $100 is $12 when the underlying's market price is $104, the time premium of this option is $8 ($12 minus its intrinsic value of $4). Had the underlying's market price been $95 instead of $104, then the time premium of this option would be the entire $12 because the option has no intrinsic value. All other things being equal, the time premium of an option will increase with the amount of time remaining to expiration.

An option buyer has two ways to realize the value of an option position. The first way is by exercising the option. The second way is to sell the option in the market. In the first example above, selling the call for $12 is preferable to exercising, because the exercise will realize only $4 (the intrinsic value), but the sale will realize $12. As this example shows, exercise

TABLE 14.5 Summary of Factors that Affect the Price of an Option

Factor	Effect of an Increase of Factor on:	
	Call Price	Put Price
Market price of underlying	Increase	Decrease
Strike price	Decrease	Increase
Time to expiration of option	Increase	Increase
Expected stock return volatility	Increase	Increase
Short-term, risk-free interest rate	Increase	Decrease
Anticipated cash payments	Decrease	Increase

causes the immediate loss of any time premium. It is important to note that there are circumstances under which an option may be exercised prior to the expiration date. These circumstances depend on whether the total proceeds at the expiration date would be greater by holding the option or exercising and reinvesting any received cash proceeds until the expiration date.

Factors that Influence the Option Price

The factors that affect the price of an option include:

- Market price of the underlying.
- Strike price of the option.
- Time to expiration of the option.
- Expected volatility of the underlying's return over the life of the option.
- Short-term, risk-free interest rate over the life of the option.
- Anticipated cash payments on the underlying over the life of the option.

The impact of each of these factors may depend on whether (1) the option is a call or a put, and (2) the option is an American option or a European option. Table 14.5 summarizes how each of the six factors listed above affects the price of a put and call option. Here, we briefly explain why the factors have the particular effects.

Market Price of the Underlying Asset

The option price will change as the price of the underlying changes. For a call option, as the underlying's price increases (all other factors being constant), the option price increases. The opposite holds for a put option: As the price of the underlying increases, the price of a put option decreases.

Strike Price

The strike price (or exercise price) is fixed for the life of the option. All other factors being equal, the lower the strike price, the higher the price for a call option. For put options, the higher the strike price, the higher the option price.

Time to Expiration of the Option

After the expiration date, an option has no value. All other factors being equal, the longer the time to expiration of the option, the higher the option price. This is because, as the time to expiration decreases, less time remains for the underlying's price to rise (for a call buyer) or fall (for a put buyer), and therefore the probability of a favorable price movement decreases. Consequently, as the time remaining until expiration decreases, the option price approaches its intrinsic value.

Expected Volatility of the Underlying's Return over the Life of the Option

All other factors being equal, the greater the expected volatility of the underlying's return (as measured by the standard deviation), the more the option buyer would be willing to pay for the option, and the more an option writer would demand for it. This occurs because the greater the expected volatility, the greater the probability that the movement of the underlying will change so as to benefit the option buyer at some time before expiration.

Short-Term, Risk-Free Interest Rate over the Life of the Option

Buying the underlying requires an investment of funds. Buying an option on the same quantity of the underlying makes the difference between the underlying's price and the option price available for investment at an interest rate at least as high as the risk-free rate. Consequently, all other factors being constant, the higher the short-term, risk-free interest rate, the greater the cost of buying the underlying and carrying it to the expiration date of the call option. Hence, the higher the short-term, risk-free interest rate, the more attractive the call option will be relative to the direct purchase of the underlying. As a result, the higher the short-term, risk-free interest rate, the greater the price of a call option.

Anticipated Cash Payments on the Underlying over the Life of the Option

Cash payments on the underlying tend to decrease the price of a call option because the cash payments make it more attractive to hold the underlying than to hold the option. For put options, cash payments on the underlying tend to increase the price.

Option Pricing Models

Earlier in this chapter, it was explained how the theoretical price of a futures contract and forward contract can be determined on the basis of arbitrage arguments. An option pricing model uses a set of assumptions and arbitrage arguments to derive a theoretical price for an option. Deriving a theoretical option price is much more complicated than deriving a theoretical futures or forward price because the option price depends on the expected volatility of the underlying over the life of the option.

Several models have been developed to determine the theoretical price of an option. We describe these models in Chapter 15.

USE OF LISTED EQUITY OPTIONS IN PORTFOLIO MANAGEMENT

Investors can use the listed options market to address a range of investment problems. In this section, we consider the use of calls, puts, and combinations in the context of the investment process, which could involve (1) risk management, (2) cost management, or (3) return enhancement.

Recall from our earlier discussion that the distinction between options versus futures contracts is that the former have nonlinear payouts that will fundamentally alter the risk profile of an existing portfolio. The following basic strategies can be used to establish a hedged position in an individual stock or a replicating portfolio.

Risk Management Strategies

Risk management in the context of equity portfolio management focuses on price risk. Consequently, the strategies discussed in this section in some way address the risk of a price decline or a loss due to adverse price movement. Options can be used to create asymmetric risk exposures across all or part of the core equity portfolio. This allows the investor to hedge downside risk at a fixed cost with a specific limit to losses should the market turn down. The basic risk management objective is to create the optimal risk exposure and to achieve the target rate of return. Options can help accomplish this by reducing risk exposure. The various risk management strategies will also affect the expected rate of return on the position unless some form of inefficiency is involved. This may involve the current mix of risk and return or be the result of the use of options. Below we discuss two risk management strategies: protective put and collar.[2]

Protective Put Strategies

Protective put strategies are valuable to portfolio managers who currently hold a long position in the underlying security or investors who desire upside exposure and downside protection by using put options. The motivation is either to hedge some or all of the total risk. Index put options hedge mostly market risk, while equity put options hedge the total risk associated with a specific stock. This allows portfolio managers to use protective put strategies for separating tactical and strategic strategies. Consider, for example, a portfolio manager who is concerned about exogenous or nonfinancial events increasing the level of risk in the marketplace. Furthermore, assume the portfolio manager is satisfied with the core portfolio holdings and the strategic mix. Put options could be employed as a tactical risk reduction strategy designed to preserve capital and still maintain strategic targets for portfolio returns.

For this reason, a portfolio manager concerned about downside risk is a candidate for a protective put strategy. Nonetheless, protective put strategies may not be suitable for all portfolio managers. The value of protective put strategies, however, is that they provide the investor with the ability to invest in volatile stocks with a degree of desired insurance and unlimited profit potential over the life of the strategy.

The protective put involves the purchase of a put option combined with a long stock position. This is the equivalent of a position in a call option on the stock combined with the purchase of risk-free bond. In fact, the combined position yields the call option payout pattern described earlier. The put option is comparable to an insurance policy written against the long stock position. The option price is the cost of the insurance premium and the amount the option is out-of-the-money is the deductible. Just as in the case of insurance, the deductible is inversely related to the insurance premium. The deductible is reduced as the strike price increases, which makes the put option more in-the-money or less out-of-the-money. The higher strike price causes the put price to increase and makes the insurance policy more expensive.

The profitability of the strategy from inception to termination can be expressed as follows:

$$\text{Profit} = N_s(S_T - S_t) + N_p[\max(0, K - S_T) - \text{Put}]$$

---

[2] Other risk management strategies are discussed in Chapter 3 of Collins and Fabozzi (1999).

where

N_s = number of shares of the stock
N_p = number of put options
S_T = price of stock at termination date (time T)
S_t = price of stock at time t
K = strike price
Put = put price

The profitability of the protective put strategy is the sum of the profit from the long stock position and the put option. If held to expiration, the minimum payout is the strike price (K) and the maximum is the stock price (S_T). If the stock price is below the strike price of the put option, the investor exercises the option and sells the stock to the option writer for K. If we assume that the number of shares N_s = + N_p, the number of options, then the loss would amount to

$$\text{Profit} = S_T - S_t + K - S_T - \text{Put} = K - S_t - \text{Put}$$

Notice that the price of the stock at the termination date does not enter into the profit equation.

For example, if the original stock price was $100 ($S_t$), the strike price $95 ($K$), the closing stock price $80 ($S_T$), and the put premium (Put) $4, then the profit would equal the following:

$$\text{Profit} = \$95 - \$100 - \$4 = -\$9$$

The portfolio manager would have realized a loss of $20 without the hedge. If, on the other hand, the stock closed up $20, then the profit would look like this:

$$\text{Profit} = S_T - S_t - \text{Put} = \$120 - \$100 - \$4 = \$16$$

The cost of the insurance is 4% in percentage terms and is manifest as a loss of upside potential. If we add transaction costs, the shortfall is increased slightly. The maximum loss, however, is the sum of the put premium and the difference between the strike price and the original stock price, which is the amount of the deductible. The problem arises when the portfolio manager is measured against a benchmark and the cost of what amounted to an unused insurance policy causes the portfolio to underperform the benchmark. Equity managers can use stock selection, market timing, and the prudent use of options to reduce the cost of insurance. The break-even stock

FIGURE 14.5 Protective Put Strategy

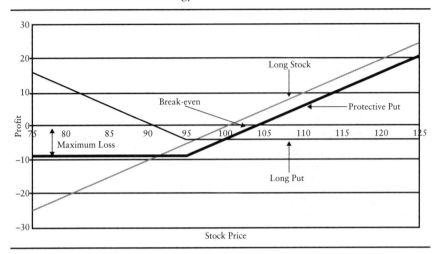

price is given by the sum of the original stock price and the put price. In this example, break-even is $104, which is the stock price necessary to recover the put premium. The put premium is never really recovered because of the performance lag. This lag falls in significance as the return increases.

A graphical depiction of the protective put strategy is provided in Figure 14.5. The figure shows the individual long stock and long put positions and the combined impact, which is essentially a long call option. The maximum loss is the put premium plus the out-of-the-money amount, which is the insurance premium plus the deductible.

Collar Strategies

An alternative to a protective put is a collar. A *collar strategy* consists of a long stock, a long put, and a short call. By varying the strike prices, a range of trade-offs among downside protection, costs, and upside potential is possible. When the long put is completely financed by the short call position, the strategy is referred to as a *zero-cost collar*.

Collars are designed for investors who currently hold a long equity position and want to achieve a level of risk reduction. The put exercise price establishes a floor and the call exercise price a ceiling. The resulting payout pattern is shown in Figure 14.6. The figure includes the components of the strategy and the combined position. This is an example of a near zero-cost collar. In order to pay for the put option, a call option was written with a strike price of $110. Selling this call option pays for the put premium,

FIGURE 14.6 Collar Strategy

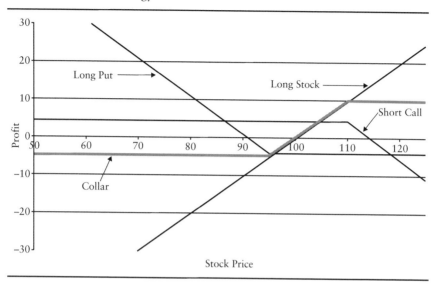

but caps the upside to 10.23%. The floor completes the collar and limits downside losses to the out-of-the money amount of the put option. In order to provide full insurance, an at-the-money put option would cost slightly above 6%, which would be paid for by limiting upside potential returns to 5%. Portfolio managers can determine the appropriate trade-offs and protection consistent with their objectives.

The profit equation for a collar is simply the sum of a long stock position, a long put, and a short call. That is,

$$\text{Profit} = N_s(S_T - S_t) + N_p[\max(0, K_p - S_T) - \text{Put}] - N_c[\max(0, S_T - K_c + \text{Call}]$$

where K_p and K_c are the strike price of the put and call, respectively, and Call is the price of the call option.

Management Strategies

Options can be used to manage the cost of maintaining an equity portfolio in a number of ways. Among the strategies are the use of short put and short call positions to serve as a substitute for a limit order in the cash market. *Cash-secured put strategies* can be used to purchase stocks at the target price, while *covered calls* or *overwrites* can be used to sell stocks at the target price. The target price is the one consistent with the portfolio manager's valuation or technical models and the price intended to produce the desired rate of return.

Choices also exist for a variety of strategies derived from put/call parity relationships. There is always an alternative method of creating a position.[3]

Return Enhancement Strategies

Options can be used for return enhancement. Here we describe the most popular return enhance strategy: covered call strategy. Other return enhancement strategies include covered combination strategy and volatility valuation strategy.[4]

Covered Call

There are many variations of what is popularly referred to as a *covered call strategy*. If the portfolio manager owns the stock and writes a call on that stock, the strategy has been referred to as an *overwrite strategy*. If the strategy is implemented all at once (i.e., buy the stock and sell the call option), it is referred to as a *buy-write strategy*. The essence of the covered call is to trade price appreciation for income. The strategy is appropriate for slightly bullish investors who don't expect much out of the stock and want to produce additional income. These are investors who are willing either to limit upside appreciation for limited downside protection or to manage the costs of selling the underlying stock. The primary motive is to generate additional income from owning the stock.

Although the call premium provides some limited downside protection, this is not an insurance strategy because it has significant downside risk. Consequently, investors should proceed with caution when considering a covered call strategy.

A covered call is less risky than buying the stock because the call premium lowers the break-even recovery price. The strategy behaves like a long stock position when the stock price is below the strike price. On the other hand, the strategy is insensitive to stock prices above the strike price and is therefore capped on the upside. The maximum profit is given by the call premium and the out-the-money amount of the call option.

The payout pattern diagram is presented in Figure 14.7, which includes the long stock, short call, and covered call positions.

---

[3]Cost management strategies are discussed in Chapter 3 of Collins and Fabozzi (1999).
[4]These strategies are described in Collins and Fabozzi (1999).

FIGURE 14.7 Covered Call Strategy

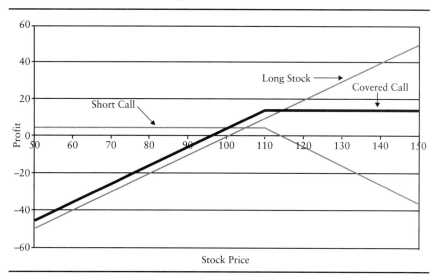

OTC EQUITY OPTIONS: THE BASICS

OTC options can be classified as first-generation and second-generation options. The latter are called *exotic options*. We survey the different types of OTC options in this section.

First-Generation OTC Options

The basic type of first-generation OTC options either relax or extend the standardized structure of an existing listed option or create an option on stocks, stock baskets, or stock indexes without listed options or futures. OTC options were therefore first used to modify one or more of the features of listed options: the strike price, maturity, size, exercise type (American or European), and delivery mechanism. The terms were tailored to the specific needs of the investor. For example, the strike price can be any level, the maturity date at any time, the contract of any size, the exercise style can be any type, the underlying can be a stock, a stock portfolio, or an equity index or a foreign equity index, and the settlement can be physical, in cash or a combination.

An example of how OTC options can differ from listed options is exemplified by an *Asian option*. Listed options are either European or American in structure relating to the timing of exercise. Flex options are listed options that go beyond standard European or American styles. One example is to provide a capped structure. Asian options are options with a payout that is dependent on the average market price over the life of the option. Due to the averaging process involved, the volatility of the market price is reduced. The lower the expected volatility for the underlying, the lower the price of the option. Therefore, Asian options are cheaper than similar European or American options.

The first generation of OTC equity options offered flexible solutions to investment situations that listed options did not. For example, hedging strategies using the OTC equity market allow portfolio managers to achieve customized total risk protection for a specific time horizon. The first generation of OTC equity options allow investors to fine-tune their traditional equity investment strategies through customizing strike prices, and maturities, and choosing any underlying equity security or portfolio of securities.

Exotics: Second-Generation OTC Options

The second generation of OTC equity options includes a set of products that have more complex payoff characteristics than standard American or European call and put options. These second-generation options are sometimes referred to as *exotic options* and are essentially options with specific rules that govern the payoff. Exotic option structures can be created on a stand-alone basis or as part of a broader financing package such as an attachment to a bond issue.

Some OTC option structures are path dependent, which means that the value of the option to some extent depends on the price pattern of the underlying asset over the life of the option. In fact, the survival of some options, such as barrier options, depends on this price pattern. Other examples of path-dependent options include Asian options, lookback options, and reset options. Another group of OTC option structures has properties similar to step functions; they have fixed singular payoffs when a particular condition is met. Examples of this include digital or binary options and contingent options. A third group of options is classified as multivariate because the payoff is related to more than one underlying asset. Examples of this group include a general category of rainbow options such as spread options and basket options.

Competitive market makers offer portfolio managers a broad range of derivative products that satisfy their specific investment needs. The fastest growing portion of this market pertaining to equities involves products with option-like characteristics on major stock indexes or stock portfolios. It is derived from investor demand for long-dated European options and for options with more complex option structures. The real attractiveness of this market is that there is virtually no limit to the types of payouts.

In this section, we review a few selective OTC product structures that can be used as management tools for equity portfolio management. (We have already reviewed one such option, Asian options.) Don't look for details here.[5]

Barrier Options

A *barrier option* is a path-dependent option whose value and survival depends on the path or price pattern of the underlying over the life of the option. Moreover, the survival of the option is dependent on whether a "barrier" or predetermined price is crossed by the price of the underlying asset. *Knock-out* and *knock-in options* are examples of barrier options. A knock-out option goes out of existence or does not survive when the barrier price is reached or exceeded. A knock-in option, however, comes into existence when a barrier is reached or exceeded. The option can be a call or a put and the barrier can be below or above the current underlying's price. In practice, when a knockout option is terminated, a rebate is given to the holder of the option. Conversely, if a knock-in option comes into existence, a rebate is paid to the option writer. Barrier options can be structured as European, American or Bermudan with regard to when they may be exercised.

Compound Options

A *compound option* is an option written against another option. In other words, the underlying asset of a compound option is an option itself. There are 16 different types of compound options based on the exercise provisions of both the option and the underlying option, and whether each is a call or a put. For that reason, a call on a put would allow the holder of the call option to purchase a put option. The call could be a European type and the underlying put could be an American type. Compound options are an alternative way of paying a premium upfront for the right to purchase an option at a later date should the need arise.

Rainbow Options

The most common *rainbow option* is the option to exchange one asset for another, which is another name for a *spread option* or an *overperformance option*. These options are structured to yield a payoff that depends on the

---

[5] A more detailed description of these options is provided in Nelken (1996) and Francis, Toy, and Whittaker (1995).

relative performance of one asset versus another. An at-the-money call structure would pay off if there is a positive return differential between the two assets. For example, a call spread option on the relative returns of two stocks, A and B, would pay off if the returns to stock A were sufficiently above the returns to stock B over the investment horizon to pay for the cost of the option. The intrinsic value of the option is the difference between the returns since inception of the contract. The usefulness of this contract is that it can pay off even when equity prices are declining.

Lookback Options

A *lookback option* is one that allows the holder to buy or sell the underlying at the most favorable price attained over the life of the contract. This is the price that maximizes the value of the option at expiration. For lookback call options with fixed strike prices, this means using the highest price over that time and for a put option it means using the lowest price. For lookback options with floating strike prices, which are the most common, the opposite holds true.

Chooser Options

A *chooser option* is also called an *as-you-like-it option* or a *pay-now-choose-later option*. It is initiated as neither a call nor a put but contains a provision that allows the holder to designate within some prescribed period whether the option will become a call or a put. There are two important types of chooser options: simple chooser and complex chooser. In the case of a simple chooser structure, the call and put alternatives have the same strike price and time to expiration. This is not the case for complex choosers, which can have call and put alternatives that vary in both strike price and expiration.

Basket Options

A *basket option* is an option structured against a portfolio or basket of assets, which may include a group of stocks or may include multiple asset classes. For equity baskets, the stocks are selected on the basis of a criterion such as industry group, risk characteristic or other factor that represents the investor's objective. This is comparable to an index option where the price of the option on an equity index is less than the average price of the options on each individual stock that makes up the index. Basket options are particularly appropriate for investors with equity portfolios that do no resemble the indexes that underlie listed index option contracts. These options are suitable for an investor wishing to use options with an underlying asset that exactly reflects their current portfolio holdings.

Binary Options

A *binary option* provides for a payoff if the price of the underlying asset is above or below a particular price at expiration of the option. Binary options are like gambles that pay something when you win and nothing when you lose. The payment can be cash or the underlying asset or nothing. Binary options are also called *digital options* or *all-or-nothing options* or *cash-or-nothing options*. These options can be structured to pay out only if the market price is higher than the strike price at expiration or if the market price exceeds the strike price at any time during the life of the option. The magnitude of the price move of the underlying is irrelevant because the payout is all or nothing.

USE OF EXOTIC EQUITY OPTIONS

Before a portfolio manager decides to use exotic options, it is important to understand the impact that a specific exotic structure will have on the risk-reward profile of the current investment and the cost of implementing the strategy. For example, a lookback option that guarantees the optimal exercise value of the option seems very attractive. However, due to the expense of such an option, the portfolio manager may not be better off than simply purchasing the underlying security. The cost therefore becomes an important consideration in evaluating the impact of using exotics.

In order to accomplish this, investors need to understand the nature of the exotic derivative in question, including the pricing dynamics, the risks, and the expected benefits. Moreover, a complete understanding of what could go wrong is necessary including the potential costs, the tax implications, and the impact on the portfolio's performance. Consider, for example, a situation where the investor chooses a put option with a barrier structure that is designed to knock out at some level above the current price. If the barrier is hit suddenly and the put option is "knocked out," the risk is that the market reverses just as suddenly leaving the investor unprotected. It is crucial, then, that the investor understand that the cost saving of a barrier option compared to a standard put option has a risk component.

Despite the potential applications, the use of exotic options brings a new element into the portfolio management process. The use of exotics ought to be carefully considered and should provide a degree of precision to satisfy the investment objective that can only be achieved with an OTC exotic structure. Investment objectives that can be met with equal efficiency, using methods that do not involve options, need not require the use of exotic options. Nonetheless, OTC options do provide investors with opportunities to fine-tune their risk-reward profiles by providing flexible product structures that meet very specific investor requirements.

Options have risk management, returns management, and cost management applications. The addition of exotics can only add to these applications. We can sum this up by saying that the value of these products is the means they provide in meeting objectives with greater flexibility and efficiency. However, it must be emphasized that exotic structures are not appropriate in all situations. On the one hand, there are some portfolio managers who are eager to use the latest derivative product whether they need to or not; on the other hand, there are portfolio managers who fear derivatives and will not use them regardless of whether it would facilitate meeting their investment objectives. It is crucial to evaluate the investor's investment objectives in terms of risk and return and how these objectives can be efficiently met. When risk management needs can be met using listed markets, it may be prudent to do so. However, for investors with specific needs that cannot be met by the listed market, a derivatives process ought to be developed and a set of criteria established that can be used as guidelines for determining whether or not an exotic structure makes sense.

SUMMARY

An option grants the buyer of the option the right either to buy from (in the case of a call option) or to sell to (in the case of a put option) the seller (writer) of the option the underlying at a stated price called the exercise (strike) price by a stated date called the expiration date. The option price or option premium is the amount that the option buyer pays to the writer. An American option allows the option buyer to exercise the option at any time up to and including the expiration date; a European option may be exercised only at the expiration date. The buyer of an option cannot realize a loss greater than the option price, and retains the upside potential. By contrast, the maximum gain that the writer (seller) of an option can realize is the option price; the writer is exposed to all the downside risk.

The risk profile of an option differs from that of a futures/forward contract. The latter has a linear payoff/symmetric payoff while the former has a nonlinear payoff/asymmetric payoff.

Options can be classified as listed or exchange-traded options and over-the-counter or dealer options. There are four types of listed options: (1) stock options, (2) index options, (3) Long-Term Equity Anticipation Securities™, and (4) FLexible EXchange Options™. OTC options can be classified as first-generation and second-generation options/exotic options. First-generation OTC options either relax or extend the standardized structure of an existing listed option or create an option on stocks, stock baskets, or stock indexes without listed options or futures. Exotic equity options include a set of products that have more complex payoff characteristics than standard American or European call and put options. Examples are barrier options, compound options, rainbow options, lookback options, chooser options, basket options, and binary options.

The two components of the price of an option are the intrinsic value and the time premium. The former is the economic value of the option if it is exercised immediately, while the latter is the amount by which the option price exceeds the intrinsic value. The option price is affected by six factors: (1) the market price of the underlying; (2) the strike price of the option; (3) the time remaining to the expiration of the option; (4) the expected volatility of underlying's return as measured by the standard deviation; (5) the short-term, risk-free interest rate over the life of the option; and (6) the anticipated cash payments on the underlying. It is the uncertainty about the expected volatility of the underlying's return that makes valuing options more complicated than valuing futures/forward contracts.

Options can be used for risk management (e.g., protective put buying and collar strategies), cost management, and return enhancement (e.g., covered call writing strategy). Care must be taken when using exotic options to assure that the exotic option is well understand and will satisfy the investor's investment objectives.

REFERENCES

Collins, B., and F. J. Fabozzi. 1999. *Derivatives and equity portfolio management.* Hoboken, NJ: John Wiley & Sons.

Francis, J. C., W. Toy, and G. Whittaker, eds. 1995. *The handbook of equity derivatives.* Burr Ridge, IL: Irwin.

Nelken, I., ed. 1996. *The handbook of exotic options.* Burr Ridge, IL: Irwin.

CHAPTER 15

Equity Option Pricing Models

In the previous chapter, we discussed the basic characteristics of stock and stock index options, strategies employing equity options, and the factors that influence the price of an equity option. In this chapter, we focus on how to determine the fair value or theoretical price of an equity option. The model for doing so is more complicated than the model for determining the fair value of a futures contract that we described in Chapter 13.

PUT-CALL PARITY RELATIONSHIP

There is a relationship between the price of a call option and the price of a put option on the same underlying instrument with the same strike price and expiration date. To see this relationship, commonly referred to as the *put-call parity relationship*, let's use an example.

Assume a put and call option on the same underlying stock (stock XYZ), with one month to expiration and with a strike price of $100. The price of the underlying stock is assumed to be $100. The call price and put price are assumed to be $3 and $2, respectively. Consider this strategy:

Buy stock XYZ at a price of $100.
Sell a call option at a price of $3.
Buy a put option at a price of $2.

This strategy involves:

Long stock XYZ.
Short the call option.
Long the put option.

Table 15.1 shows the profit and loss profile at the expiration date for this strategy for selected stock prices. For the long stock position, there is no

429

TABLE 15.1 Profit/Loss Profile for a Strategy Involving a Long Position in Stock XYZ, Short Call Option Position, and Long Put Option Position

Assumptions:
Price of stock XYZ = $100
Put option price = $2
Time to expiration = 1 month
Call option price = $3
Strike price = $100

Price of Stock XYZ at Expiration Date	Profit from Stock XYZ[a]	Price Received for Call	Price Paid for Put	Overall Profit
$150	0	3	−2	1
130	0	3	−2	1
120	0	3	−2	1
110	0	3	−2	1
100	0	3	−2	1
90	0	3	−2	1
80	0	3	−2	1
70	0	3	−2	1
60	0	3	−2	1

[a] There is no profit because at a price above $100, stock XYZ will be called from the investor at a price of $100, and at a price below $100, stock XYZ will be put by the investor at a price of $100.

profit. That is because, at a price above $100, stock XYZ will be called from the investor at a price of $100, and, at a price below $100, stock XYZ will be put by the investor at a price of $100. No matter what stock XYZ's price is at the expiration date, this strategy will produce a profit of $1 without the investor making any net investment.

Ignoring (1) the cost of financing the long position in stock XYZ and the long put position and (2) the return from investing the proceeds from the sale of the call, this situation cannot exist in an efficient market. By implementing the strategy to capture the $1 profit, the actions of market participants will have one or more of the following consequences that tend to eliminate the $1 profit: (1) the price of stock XYZ will increase, (2) the call option price will drop, or (3) the put option price will rise.

Assuming stock XYZ's price does not change, the call price and the put price will tend toward equality. However, this is true only when we ignore the time value of money (financing cost, opportunity cost, cash payments, and reinvestment income). Also, our illustration does not consider the possibility of early exercise of the option. Thus, we have been considering a put-call parity relationship applicable only for European options.

It can be shown that the put-call parity relationship for an option where the underlying stock makes cash dividends is

Put option price − Call option price
= Present value of strike price + Present value of dividends   (15.1)
− Price of underlying stock

This relationship is actually the put-call parity relationship for European options; it is approximately true for American options. If this relationship does not hold, arbitrage opportunities exist. That is, portfolios consisting of long and short positions in the stock and related options that provide an extra return with (practical) certainty will exist.

OPTION PRICING MODELS

In Chapter 13, we illustrated that the theoretical price of a futures contract can be determined on the basis of arbitrage arguments. Theoretical boundary conditions for the price of an option also can be derived using arbitrage arguments. For example, it can be shown that the minimum price for an American call option is its intrinsic value; that is,

Call option price $\geq$ Max[0, (Price of stock − Strike price)]   (15.2)

This expression says that the call option price will be greater than or equal to either the difference between the price of the underlying stock and the strike price (intrinsic value) or zero, whichever is higher.

The boundary conditions can be "tightened" by using arbitrage arguments coupled with certain assumptions about the cash distribution of the stock.[1] The extreme case is an option pricing model that uses a set of assumptions to derive a single theoretical price, rather than a range. As we shall see below, deriving a theoretical option price is much more complicated than deriving a theoretical futures price because the option price depends on the expected price volatility of the underlying stock over the life of the option.

Several models have been developed to determine the theoretical value of an option. The most popular one was developed by Black and Scholes (1973) for valuing European call options.[2] Several modifications to the

---
[1] See Chapter 4 in Cox and Rubinstein (1985).
[2] In October 1997, Myron Scholes, along with another pioneer in option pricing theory, Robert Merton, were awarded the Alfred Nobel Prize in Economic Sciences for their work. Fischer Black died in 1996 and under the rules of the Nobel Committee could not be awarded this prestigious honor. However, the Nobel Committee made it clear he would have been a corecipient.

Black-Scholes model have followed since then. Another pricing model that overcomes some of the drawbacks of the Black-Scholes option pricing model is the binomial option pricing model.

Basically, the idea behind the arbitrage argument in deriving these option pricing models is that if the payoff from owning a call option can be replicated by (1) purchasing the stock underlying the call option and (2) borrowing funds, then the price of the option will be (at most) the cost of creating the replicating strategy.

Black-Scholes Option Pricing Model

Arbitrage conditions provide boundaries for option prices; but to identify investment opportunities and construct portfolios to satisfy their investment objectives, investors want an exact price for an option. By imposing certain assumptions (to be discussed later) and using arbitrage arguments, the *Black-Scholes option pricing model* computes the fair (or theoretical) price of a European call option on a nondividend-paying stock with the following formula:

$$C = SN(d_1) - Xe^{-rt}N(d_2) \qquad (15.3)$$

where

$$d_1 = \frac{\ln(S/X) + (r + 0.5s^2)t}{s\sqrt{t}} \qquad (15.4)$$

$$d_2 = d_1 - s\sqrt{t} \qquad (15.5)$$

- ln = natural logarithm
- C = call option price
- S = current stock price
- X = strike price
- r = short-term risk-free interest rate (in decimal)
- e = 2.718 (natural antilog of 1)
- t = time remaining to the expiration date (measured as a fraction of a year)
- s = expected return volatility for the stock as measured in terms of the standard deviation (in decimal)
- $N(.)$ = the cumulative probability density. The value for $N(.)$ is obtained from a normal distribution function that is tabulated in most statistics textbooks

Equity Option Pricing Models

Notice that five of the factors that we said in the previous chapter influence the price of an option are included in the formula. However, the sixth factor, anticipated cash dividends, is not included because the model is for a nondividend-paying stock. In the Black-Scholes model, the direction of the influence of each of these factors is the same as indicated in Table 14.5 in Chapter 14. Four of the factors—strike (exercise) price, stock price, time to expiration, and risk-free interest rate—are easily observed. The standard deviation of the stock price must be estimated.

The option price derived from the Black-Scholes option pricing model is "fair" in the sense that if any other price existed, it would be possible to earn riskless arbitrage profits by taking an offsetting position in the underlying stock. That is, if the price of the call option in the market is higher than that derived from the Black-Scholes option pricing model, an investor could sell the call option and buy a certain number of shares in the underlying stock. If the reverse is true, that is, the market price of the call option is less than the "fair" price derived from the model, the investor could buy the call option and sell short a certain number of shares in the underlying stock. This process of hedging by taking a position in the underlying stock allows the investor to lock in the riskless arbitrage profit. The number of shares necessary to hedge the position changes as the factors that affect the option price change, so the hedged position must be changed constantly.

Computing a Call Option Price

To illustrate the Black-Scholes option pricing formula, assume the following values:

Strike price	= $45
Time remaining to expiration	= 183 days
Current stock price	= $47
Expected stock return volatility	= Standard deviation = 25%
Short-term risk-free interest rate	= 10%

In terms of the values in the formula:

$S = 47$
$X = 45$
$t = 0.5$ (183 *days*/365, *rounded*)
$s = 0.25$
$r = 0.10$

Substituting these values into equations (15.4) and (15.5), we get

$$d_1 = \frac{\ln(47/45) + [0.10 + 0.5(0.25)^2]0.5}{0.25\sqrt{0.5}} = 0.6172$$

$$d_2 = 0.6172 - 0.25\sqrt{0.5} = 0.4404$$

From a normal distribution table,

$$N(0.6172) = 0.7315$$

and

$$N(0.4404) = 0.6702$$

Then

$$C = 47(0.7315) - 45(e^{-(0.10)(0.5)})(0.6702) = \$5.69$$

Let's look at what happens to the theoretical option price if the expected stock return volatility is 40% rather than 25%. Then

$$d_1 = \frac{\ln(47/45) + [0.10 + 0.5(0.40)^2]0.5}{0.40\sqrt{0.5}} = 0.4719$$

$$d_2 = 0.4719 - 0.40\sqrt{0.5} = 0.1891$$

From a normal distribution table,

$$N(0.4719) = 0.6815$$

and

$$N(0.1891) = 0.5750$$

Then

$$C = 47(0.6815) - 45(e^{-(0.10)(0.5)})(0.5750) = \$7.42$$

Notice that the higher the assumed expected stock return volatility, the higher the price of a call option.

Table 15.2 shows the option value as calculated from the Black-Scholes option pricing model for different assumptions concerning (1) the expected stock return volatility, (2) the risk-free interest rate, and (3) the time remaining to expiration. Notice that the option price varies directly with three vari-

Equity Option Pricing Models

TABLE 15.2 Comparison of Black-Scholes Call Option Price Varying One Factor at a Time

Base Case
Call option:
Strike price = $45
Time remaining to expiration = 183 days
Current stock price = $47
Expected price volatility = Standard deviation = 25%
Risk-free rate = 10%

Holding All Factors Constant except Expected Stock Return Volatility

Expected Stock Return Volatility	Call Option Price
15%	4.69
20	5.17
25 (base case)	5.69
30	6.26
35	6.84
40	7.42

Holding All Factors Constant except the Risk-Free Interest Rate

Risk-Free Interest Rate	Call Option Price
7%	5.27
8	5.41
9	5.50
10 (base case)	5.69
11	5.84
12	5.99
13	6.13

Holding All Factors Constant except Time Remaining to Expiration

Time Remaining to Expiration	Call Option Price
30 days	2.85
60	3.52
91	4.15
183 (base case)	5.69
273	6.99

ables: expected stock return volatility, the risk-free rate, and the time remaining to expiration. That is, (1) the lower (higher) the expected stock return volatility, the lower (higher) the option price; (2) the lower (higher) the risk-free interest rate, the lower (higher) the option price; and (3) the shorter (longer) the time remaining to expiration, the lower (higher) the option price. All of this agrees with what we stated in the previous chapter about the effect of a change in one of the factors on the price of a call option.

Computing a Put Option Price

We have focused our attention on call options. How do we value put options? Recall that the European put-call parity relationship as given by equation (15.1) gives the relationship among the price of the common stock, the European call option price, and the European put option price. If we can calculate the fair value of a European call option, the fair value of a European put with the same strike price and expiration on the same stock can be calculated from the put-call parity relationship.

Assumptions Underlying the Black-Scholes Model and Extensions

The Black-Scholes model is based on several restrictive assumptions. These assumptions were necessary to develop the hedge to realize riskless arbitrage profits if the market price of the call option deviates from the value obtained from the model. First, we will look at these assumptions and mention some extensions of the model that make pricing more realistic. Later in the chapter, we examine these extensions of the basic model.

The Option Is a European Option

The Black-Scholes model assumes that the call option is a European call option. Because the Black-Scholes model is on a nondividend-paying stock, early exercise of an option will not be economic because by selling rather than exercising the call option, the option holder can recoup the option's time premium. The binomial option pricing model, which we describe next, can easily handle American call options.[3]

Expected Stock Return Volatility

The Black-Scholes model assumes that the expected stock return volatility is (1) constant over the life of the option and (2) known with certainty. If (1) does not hold, an option pricing model can be developed that allows the variance to change. The violation of (2), however, is more serious. Because

---
[3] See Cox, Ross, and Rubinstein (1979).

the Black-Scholes model depends on the riskless hedge argument and, in turn, the expected stock return volatility must be known to construct the proper hedge, if it is not known, the hedge will not be riskless.

Stochastic Process Generating Stock Prices

To derive an option pricing model, an assumption is needed about the way stock prices move. The Black-Scholes model is based on the assumption that stock prices are generated by one kind of stochastic (random) process called a *diffusion process*. In a diffusion process, the stock price can take on any positive value, but when it moves from one price to another, it must take on all values in between. That is, the stock price does not jump from one stock price to another, skipping over interim prices. An alternative assumption is that stock prices follow a jump process; that is, prices are not continuous and smooth, but do jump from one price across intervening values to the next. Merton (1973) and Cox and Ross (1979) have developed option-pricing models assuming a jump process.

Risk-Free Interest Rate

In deriving the Black-Scholes model, two assumptions are made about the risk-free interest rate. First, it is assumed that the interest rates for borrowing and lending are the same. Second, it is assumed that the interest rate is constant and known over the life of the option. The first assumption is unlikely to hold, because in real-world financial markets borrowing rates are higher than lending rates. The effect on the Black-Scholes model is that the option price will be between the call price derived from the model using the two interest rates. The model can handle the second assumption by replacing the risk-free interest rate over the life of the option by the geometric average of the period returns expected over the life of the option.[4]

Dividends

The original Black-Scholes model is for a nondividend-paying stock. In the case of a dividend-paying stock, it may be advantageous for the holder of the call option to exercise the option early. To understand why, suppose that a stock pays a dividend such that if the call option is exercised, dividends would be received prior to the option's expiration date. If the dividends plus the accrued interest earned from investing the dividends from the time they

---

[4] Returns on short-term Treasury bills cannot be known with certainty over the long term; only the expected return is known, and there is a variance around it. The effects of variable interest rates are considered in Merton (1973).

are received until the expiration date are greater than the time premium of the option, then it would be optimal to exercise the option.[5] In the case where dividends are not known with certainty, it will not be possible to develop a model using the riskless arbitrage argument.

In the case of known dividends, a shortcut to adjust the Black-Scholes model is to reduce the stock price by the present value of the dividends. Black (1975) suggested an approximation technique to value a call option for a dividend-paying stock.[6] A more accurate model for pricing call options in the case of known dividends was developed by Roll (1977), Geske (1979, 1981), and Whaley (1981).

Taxes and Transactions Costs

The Black-Scholes model ignores taxes and transaction costs. The model can be modified to account for taxes, but the problem is that there is not just one tax rate. Transaction costs include both commissions and the bid-ask spreads for the stock and the option, as well as other costs associated with trading options.

Binomial Option Pricing Model

To overcome some of the limitations of the Black-Scholes option pricing model, the *binomial option pricing model* was developed. To derive a one-period binomial option pricing model for a call option, we begin by constructing a portfolio consisting of (1) a long position in a certain amount of the stock and (2) a short call position in the underlying stock. The amount of the underlying stock purchased is such that the position will be hedged against any change in the price of the stock at the expiration date of the option. That is, the portfolio consisting of the long position in the stock and the short position in the call option is riskless and will produce a return that equals the risk-free interest rate. A portfolio constructed in this way is called a *hedged portfolio*.

We can show how this process works with an extended illustration. Let us first assume that there is a stock that has a current market price of $80 and that only two possible future states can occur one year from now. (Because the model assumes that there are only two possible outcomes, it is called a *binomial model*.) Each state is associated with one of only two possible values for the stock price, and they can be summarized in this way:

---

[5]Recall from the previous chapter that the time premium is the excess of the option price over its intrinsic value.

[6]The approach requires that the investor at the time of purchase of the call option and for every subsequent period specify the exact date the option will be exercised.

State	Price
1	$100
2	70

We assume further that there is a call option on this stock with a strike price of $80 (the same as the current market price) that expires in one year. Let us suppose an investor forms a hedged portfolio by acquiring two-thirds of a unit of the stock and selling one call option. The two-thirds of a unit of the stock is the so-called *hedge ratio*, the amount of the stock purchased per call option sold (how we derive the hedge ratio will be explained later). Let us consider the outcomes for this hedged portfolio corresponding to the two possible outcomes for the stock.

If the price of the stock one year from now is $100, the buyer of the call option will exercise it. This means that the investor will have to deliver one unit of the stock in exchange for the strike price, $80. As the investor has only a two-thirds unit of the stock, she has to buy one-third at a cost of $33⅓ (the market price of $100 times one-third). Consequently, the outcome will equal the strike price of $80 received, minus the $33⅓ cost to acquire the one-third unit of the stock to deliver, plus whatever price the investor initially sold the call option for. That is, the outcome will be

$$\$80 - \$33\tfrac{1}{3} + \text{Call option price} = \$46\tfrac{2}{3} + \text{Call option price}$$

If, instead, the price of the stock one year from now is $70, the buyer of the call option will not exercise it. Consequently, the investor will own two-thirds of a unit of the stock. At the price of $70, the value of ⅔ of a unit is $46⅔. The outcome in this case is the value of the stock plus whatever price the investor received when she initially sold the call option. That is, the outcome will be

$$\$46\tfrac{2}{3} + \text{Call option price}$$

It is apparent that, given the possible stock prices, the portfolio consisting of a short position in the call option and two-thirds of a unit of the stock will generate an outcome that hedges changes in the price of the stock; hence, the hedged portfolio is riskless. Furthermore, this holds regardless of the price of the call, which affects only the magnitude of the outcome.

Deriving the Hedge Ratio

To show how the hedge ratio can be calculated, we use the following notation:

S = current stock price

u = 1 plus the percentage change in the stock's price if the price goes up in the next period

d = 1 plus the percentage change in the stock's price if the price goes down in the next period

r = a risk-free one-period interest rate (the risk-free interest rate until the expiration date)

C = current price of a call option

C_u = intrinsic value of the call option if the stock price goes up

C_d = intrinsic value of the call option if the stock price goes down

E = strike price of the call option

H = hedge ratio, that is, the amount of the stock purchased per call sold

In our illustration,

u = 1.250 ($100/$80)
d = 0.875 ($70/$80)
H = ⅔

Further, state 1 in our illustration means that the stock's price goes up; state 2 means that the stock's price goes down.

The investment made in the hedged portfolio is equal to the cost of buying H amount of the stock minus the price received from selling the call option. Therefore, because

$$\text{Amount invested in the stock} = HS$$

then

$$\text{Cost of the hedged portfolio} = HS - C$$

The payoff of the hedged portfolio at the end of one period is equal to the value of the H amount of the stock purchased minus the call option price. The payoffs of the hedged portfolio for the two possible states are defined in this way:

State 1, if the stock's price goes up: $uHS - C_u$
State 2, if the stock's price goes down: $dHS - C_d$

Equity Option Pricing Models

In our illustration, we have these payoffs:

If the stock's price goes up: $1.250H\$80 - C_u$ or $\$100 H - C_u$
If the stock's price falls: $0.875H\$80 - C_d$ or $\$70 H - C_d$

If the hedge is riskless, the payoffs must be the same. Thus,

$$uHS - C_u = dHS - C_d \qquad (15.6)$$

Solving equation (15.6) for the hedge ratio H, we have

$$H = \frac{C_u - C_d}{(u-d)S} \qquad (15.7)$$

To determine the value of the hedge ratio H, we must know C_u and C_d. These two values are equal to the difference between the price of the stock and the strike price in the two possible states. Of course, the minimum value of the call option, in any state, is zero. Mathematically, the differences can be expressed as follows:

If the stock's price goes up: $C_u = \text{Max}\,[0, (uS - E)]$
If the stock's price goes down: $C_d = \text{Max}\,[0, (dS - E)]$

As the strike price in our illustration is \$80, uS is \$100, and dS is \$70, then,

If the stock's price goes up: $C_u = \text{Max}\,[0, (\$100 - \$80)] = \$20$
If the stock's price goes down: $C_d = \text{Max}\,[0, (\$70 - \$80)] = \$0$

To continue with our illustration, we substitute the values of u, d, S, C_u, and C_d into equation (15.7) to obtain the hedge ratio's value:

$$H = \frac{\$20 - \$0}{(1.25 - 0.875)\$80} = \frac{2}{3}$$

This value for H agrees with the amount of the stock purchased when we introduced this illustration.

Now we can derive a formula for the call option price. Figure 15.1 diagrams the situation. The top left half of the figure shows the price of the stock for the current period and at the expiration date. The lower left-

FIGURE 15.1 One-Period Option Pricing Model

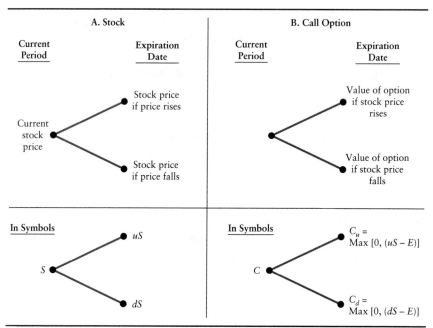

FIGURE 15.2 One-Period Option Pricing Model Illustration

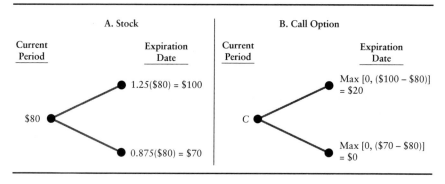

hand portion of the figure does the same thing using the notation above. The upper right-hand side of the figure gives the current price of the call option and the value of the call option at the expiration date; the lower right-hand side does the same thing using our notation. Figure 15.2 uses the values in our illustration to construct the outcomes for the stock and the call option.

Deriving the Price of a Call Option

To derive the price of a call option, we can rely on the basic principle that the hedged portfolio, being riskless, must have a return equal to the risk-free interest rate. Given that the amount invested in the hedged portfolio is $HS - C$, the amount that should be generated one period from now is

$$(1 + r)(HS - C) \tag{15.8}$$

We also know what the payoff will be for the hedged portfolio if the stock's price goes up or down. Because the payoff of the hedged portfolio will be the same whether the stock's price rises or falls, we can use the payoff if it goes up, which is

$$uHS - C_u$$

The payoff of the hedged portfolio given above should be the same as the initial cost of the portfolio given by equation (15.8). Equating the two, we have

$$(1 + r)(HS - C) = uHS - C_u \tag{15.9}$$

Substituting equation (15.7) for H in equation (15.9) and solving for the call option price C, we find

$$C = \left(\frac{1+r-d}{u-d}\right)\left(\frac{C_u}{1+r}\right) + \left(\frac{u-1-r}{u-d}\right)\left(\frac{C_d}{1+r}\right) \tag{15.10}$$

Applying equation (15.10) to our illustration, where

u = 1.250
d = 0.875
r = 0.10
C_u = $20
C_d = $0

we get

$$C = \left(\frac{1+0.10-0.875}{1.25-0.875}\right)\left(\frac{\$20}{1+0.10}\right) + \left(\frac{1.25-1-0.10}{1.25-0.875}\right)\left(\frac{\$0}{1+0.10}\right)$$
$$= \$10.90$$

Equation (15.10) is the formula for the one-period binomial option pricing model. We would have derived the same formula if we had used the payoff for a decline in the price of the underlying stock.

The approach we presented for pricing options may seem oversimplified, given that we assume only two possible future states for the price of the underlying stock. In fact, we can extend the procedure by making the periods smaller and smaller, and in that way calculate a fair value for an option. It is important to note that extended and comprehensive versions of the binomial pricing model are in wide use throughout the world of finance. Moreover, the other popular option pricing model, the Black-Scholes model mentioned earlier, is in reality the mathematical equivalent of the binomial approach as the intervals become very small. Therefore, the approach we have described in detail here provides the conceptual framework for much of the analysis of option prices that today's financial market participants regularly perform.

Extension to a Two-Period Model

By dividing the time to expiration into two periods, we can represent price changes within the time period to maturity and add more realism to our model. The extension to two intermediate periods requires that we introduce more notation. To help understand the notation, look at Figure 15.3A, which shows for the stock the initial price, the price one period from now if the price goes up or goes down, and the price at the expiration date (two periods from now) if the price in the previous period goes up or goes down. Figure 15.3B shows the value of the call option at the expiration date and the value one period prior to the expiration date.

FIGURE 15.3 Two-Period Option Pricing Model

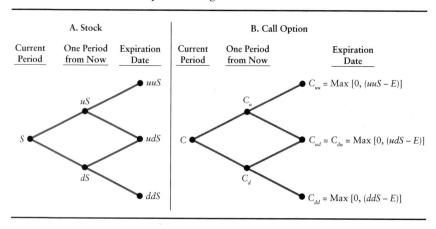

The new notation has to do with the value of the call option at the expiration date. We now use two subscripts. Specifically, C_{uu} is the call value if the stock's price went up in both periods, C_{dd} is the call value if the stock's price went down in both periods, and C_{ud} (which is equal to C_{du}) is the call value if the stock's price went down in one period and up in one period.

We solve for the call option price C by starting at the expiration date to determine the value of C_u and C_d. This can be done by using equation (15.10) because that equation gives the price of a one-period call option. Specifically,

$$C_u = \left(\frac{1+r-d}{u-d}\right)\frac{C_{uu}}{1+r} + \left(\frac{u-1-r}{u-d}\right)\frac{C_{ud}}{1+r} \tag{15.11}$$

and

$$C_d = \left(\frac{1+r-d}{u-d}\right)\frac{C_{du}}{1+r} + \left(\frac{u-1-r}{u-d}\right)\frac{C_{dd}}{1+r} \tag{15.12}$$

Once C_u and C_d are known, we can solve for C using equation (15.10).

To make this more concrete, let's use numbers. We will assume that the stock's price can go up by 11.8% per period or down by 6.46% per period. That is,

$$u = 1.118 \quad \text{and} \quad d = 0.9354$$

Then, as shown in Figure 15.4A, the stock can have three possible prices at the end of two periods:

Price goes up both periods: $uuS = (1.118)(1.118)\$80 = \$100$
Price goes down both periods: $ddS = (0.9354)(0.9354)\$80 = \$70$
Price goes up one period and down the other: $udS = (1.118)(0.9354)\$80 = duS = (0.9354)(1.118)\$80 = \$83.66$

Notice that the first two prices are the same as in the one-period illustration. By breaking the length of time until expiration into two periods rather than one, and adjusting the change in the stock price accordingly, we now have three possible outcomes. If we break down the length of time to expiration into more periods, the number of possible outcomes that the stock price may take on at the expiration date will increase. Consequently, what seemed like an unrealistic assumption about two possible outcomes for each period becomes more realistic with respect to the number of possible outcomes that the stock price may take at the expiration date.

FIGURE 15.4 Two-Period Option Pricing Model Illustration

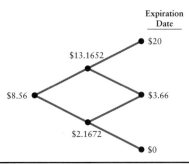

Now we can use the values in Figure 15.4B to calculate C. In our example, we assumed a risk-free interest rate of 10%. When we divide our holding period in two, the risk-free interest rate for one period is now 4.88% because, when compounded, this rate will produce an interest rate of 10% from now to the expiration date (two periods from now). First, consider the calculation of C_u using equation (15.11). From Figure 15.4, we see that

$$C_{uu} = \$20$$

and

$$C_{ud} = \$3.66$$

Therefore,

$$C_u = \left(\frac{1+0.0488-0.9354}{1.118-0.9354}\right)\frac{\$20}{1+0.0488} + \left(\frac{1.118-1-0.0488}{1.118-0.9354}\right)\frac{\$3.66}{1+0.0488}$$
$$= \$13.1652$$

From Figure 15.4,

$$C_{dd} = \$0$$

and

$$C_{du} = \$3.66$$

Therefore,

$$C_d = \left(\frac{1+0.0488-0.9354}{1.118-0.9354}\right)\frac{\$3.66}{1+0.0488} + \left(\frac{1.118-1-0.0488}{1.118-0.9354}\right)\frac{\$0}{1+0.0488}$$
$$= \$2.1672$$

We have inserted the values for C_u and C_d in the bottom panel of Figure 15.4C and can now calculate C by using equation (15.11) as follows:

$$C = \left(\frac{1+0.0488-0.9354}{1.118-0.9354}\right)\frac{\$13.1652}{1+0.0488} + \left(\frac{1.118-1-0.0488}{1.118-0.9354}\right)\frac{\$2.1672}{1+0.0488}$$
$$= \$8.58$$

Dividends can be incorporated into the binomial pricing model by using the dividend amount at each point for the value of the stock. So if the dividend one period from now is expected to be $1, then S_u and S_d in Figure 15.3A would be $S_u + \$1$ and $S_d + \$1$, respectively. In Figure 15.4A, this means the value for the stock one period from now would be $90.44 and $75.832, instead of $89.44 and $74.832.

SENSITIVITY OF THE OPTION PRICE TO A CHANGE IN FACTORS

In employing options in investment strategies, a portfolio manager would like to know how sensitive the price of an option is to a change in any one of the factors that affect its price. Here, we look at the sensitivity of a call option's price to changes in the price of the underlying stock, the time to expiration, and expected stock return volatility.[7]

---

[7] For a detailed explanation of the role of these measures in option strategies, see Whaley (2007).

FIGURE 15.5 Theoretical Call Price and Price of Underlying Stock

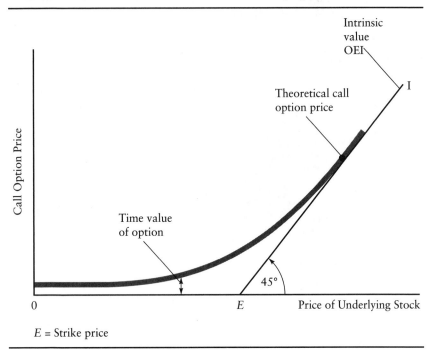

E = Strike price

The Call Option Price and the Price of the Underlying Stock

In developing an option pricing model, we have seen the importance of understanding the relationship between the option price and the price of the underlying stock. Moreover, a portfolio manager employing options to control the price risk of a portfolio wants to know how the option position will change as the price of the underlying stock changes.

Figure 15.5 shows the theoretical price of a call option based on the price of the underlying stock. The horizontal axis is the price of the underlying stock at any point in time. The vertical axis is the call option price. The shape of the curve representing the theoretical price of a call option, given the price of the underlying stock, would be the same regardless of the actual option pricing model used. In particular, the relationship between the price of the underlying stock and the theoretical call option price is convex.

The line from the origin to the strike price on the horizontal axis in Figure 15.5 is the intrinsic value of the call option when the price of the underlying stock is less than the strike price, since the intrinsic value is zero. The 45 degree line extending from the horizontal axis is the intrinsic value of the call option once the price of the underlying stock exceeds the strike price. The reason is that the intrinsic value of the call option will increase by the same dollar amount as the increase in the price of the underlying stock. For example, if the strike price is $100 and the price of the underlying stock increases from $100 to $101, the intrinsic value will increase by $1. If the price of the stock increases from $101 to $110, the intrinsic value of the option will increase from $1 to $10. Thus, the slope of the line representing the intrinsic value after the strike price is reached is 1.

Since the theoretical call option price is shown by the convex line, the difference between the theoretical call option price and the intrinsic value at any given price for the underlying stock is the time value of the option.

Figure 15.6 shows the theoretical call option price, but with a tangent line drawn at the price of p^*. The tangent line in the figure can be used to estimate what the new option price will be (and, therefore, what the change in the option price will be) if the price of the underlying stock changes. Because of the convexity of the relationship between the option price and the price of the underlying stock, the tangent line closely approximates the new option price for a small change in the price of the underlying stock.

FIGURE 15.6 Estimating the Theoretical Option Price with a Tangent Line

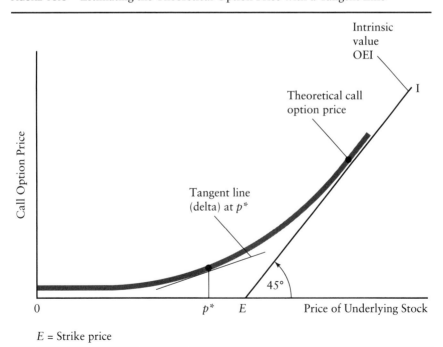

For large changes, however, the tangent line does not provide as good an approximation of the new option price.

The slope of the tangent line shows how the theoretical call option price will change for small changes in the price of the underlying stock. The slope of the tangent line is what we referred to earlier as the hedge ratio. It is more popularly referred to as the *delta* of the option. Specifically,

$$\text{Delta} = \frac{\text{Change in price of call option}}{\text{Change in price of underlying stock}}$$

For example, a delta of 0.4 means that a $1 change in the price of the underlying stock will change the price of the call option by approximately $0.40.

Figure 15.7 shows the curve of the theoretical call option price with three tangent lines drawn. The steeper the slope of the tangent line, the greater the delta. When an option is deep out of the money (that is, the price of the underlying stock is substantially below the strike price), the tangent line is nearly flat (see line 1 in Figure 15.7). This means that delta is close to

FIGURE 15.7 Theoretical Option Price with Three Tangents

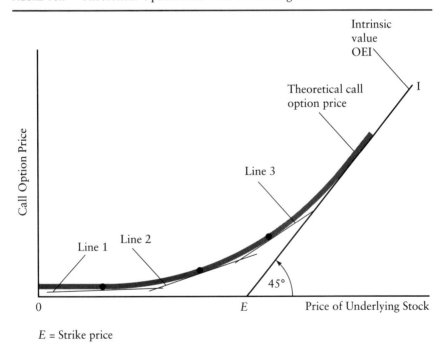

E = Strike price

zero. To understand why, consider a call option with a strike price of $100 and two months to expiration. If the price of the underlying stock is $20, its price would not increase by much, if anything, should the price of the underlying stock increase by $1, from $20 to $21.

For a call option that is deep in the money, the delta will be close to 1. That is, the call option price will increase almost dollar for dollar with an increase in the price of the underlying stock. In terms of the graph in Figure 15.7, the slope of the tangent line approaches the slope of the intrinsic value line after the strike price. As we stated earlier, the slope of that line is 1.

Thus, the delta for a call option varies from zero (for call options deep out of the money) to 1 (for call options deep in the money). The delta for a call option at the money is approximately 0.5.

The curvature of the convex relationship can also be approximated. This is the rate of change of delta as the price of the underlying stock changes. This measure is commonly referred to as *gamma* and is defined as follows:

$$\text{Gamma} = \frac{\text{Change in delta}}{\text{Change in price of underlying stock}}$$

The Call Option Price and Time to Expiration

All other factors remaining constant, the longer the time to expiration, the greater the option price. Since each day the option moves closer to the expiration date, the time to expiration decreases. The *theta* of an option measures the change in the option price as the time to expiration decreases, or, equivalently, it is a measure of *time decay*. Theta is measured as follows:

$$\text{Theta} = \frac{\text{Change in price of option}}{\text{Decrease in time to expiration}}$$

Assuming that the price of the underlying stock does not change (which means that the intrinsic value of the option does not change), theta measures how quickly the time premium of the option changes as the option moves toward expiration.

Buyers of options prefer a low theta so that the option price does not decline quickly as it moves toward the expiration date. An option writer benefits from an option that has a high theta.

The Call Option Price and Expected Stock Return Volatility

All other factors remaining constant, a change in the expected price volatility will change the option price. The *kappa* of an option measures the price change of the option for a 1% change in the expected stock return volatility. That is,

$$\text{Kappa} = \frac{\text{Change in option price}}{1\% \text{ change in expected stock return volatility}}$$

ESTIMATING EXPECTED STOCK RETURN VOLATILITY

The only factor whose value is not known in an option pricing model is expected stock return volatility. Market participants this estimate input into the Black-Scholes option pricing model in one of two ways: (1) by calculating the implied volatility from current option prices or (2) by calculating the standard deviation using historical daily stock returns.

Implied Volatility

An option pricing model relates a given volatility estimate to a unique price for the option. Similarly, if the option price is known, the same option pricing model can be used to determine the corresponding volatility. This is known as *implied volatility*.

In addition to its use as input in an option pricing model to determine the value of another option, implied volatility has other applications in strategies employing options. The most straightforward application is a comparison of implied volatility with the estimate of volatility using historical return data that we describe next. If an investor believes that the estimated volatility using historical data is a better estimate than implied volatility, then the two volatility estimates can be compared to assess whether an option is cheap or expensive. More specifically, if the estimate of volatility using historical data is higher than implied volatility, then the option is cheap; if it is less than implied volatility, then the option is expensive.

In addition to identifying options that may be rich or expensive, implied volatility can be used to compare options on the same underlying stock and time to expiration but with different strike prices. For example, suppose that the implied volatility for a call option with a strike price of 90 is 8% when a call option with a strike of 100 has an implied volatility of 12%. Then, on a relative basis, the call option with a strike of 90 is cheaper than the call option with a strike of 100. Put and call options on the same stock and with the same time to expiration can also be compared using implied volatility.

Calculating Standard Deviation from Historical Data

The second method used to estimate expected stock return volatility is the calculation of the standard deviation of historical daily stock returns. Market practice with respect to the number of days that should be used to calculate the daily standard deviation varies. The number of days can be as few as 10 or as many as 100.

Since market participants are interested in annualized volatility, the daily standard deviation must be annualized as follows:

$$\text{Daily standard deviation} \times \sqrt{\text{Number of days in a year}}$$

Market practice varies with respect to the number of days in the year that should be used in the annualizing formula above. Typically, either 250, 260, or 365 days are used. The first two are used because they represent the number of actual trading days for certain options.

Thus, in calculating an annual standard deviation, a portfolio manager must decide on:

- The number of daily observations to use to calculate the daily standard deviation.
- The number of days in the year to use to annualize the daily standard deviation.

As a result of these two choices, the volatility estimate based on historical daily returns can vary significantly.

SUMMARY

In this chapter, we turned our attention to the pricing of options. There is a relationship between the price of a put option and the price of a call option, called the put-call parity relationship. Several models have been developed to determine the fair value of an option: the Black-Scholes option pricing model, extensions of the Black-Scholes model, and the binomial option pricing model. The arbitrage argument employed in deriving these option pricing models is that the payoff from owning an option can be replicated by a position in the underlying asset and by borrowing funds to create the leverage associated with an option. The cost of the option is then (at most) the cost of creating the portfolio to replicate the option.

The price of an option depends on six factors. The sensitivity of the option price to changes in these factors can be estimated. We discussed several of these measures: The delta and the gamma of an option measure the sensitivity of the option price to a change in the price of the underlying stock; the theta of an option measures the time decay of an option; and the kappa of an option measures the sensitivity of an option's price to a change in expected stock return volatility.

The unknown in an option pricing model is expected stock return volatility. There are two ways to estimate expected stock return volatility: implied volatility and the standard deviation of daily returns from historical data. Implied volatility has several applications in addition to its use in an option pricing model. In estimating the standard deviation based on observed daily returns, a decision must be made about how many daily observations should be used and how the daily standard deviation should be annualized.

REFERENCES

Black, F. 1975. Fact and fantasy in the use of options. *Financial Analysts Journal* (July–August): 36–41, 61–72.

Black, F., and M. Scholes. 1973. Pricing of options and corporate liabilities. *Journal of Political Economy* 81, no. 3: 637–654.

Cox, J. C., S. Ross, and M. Rubinstein. 1979. Option pricing: A simplified approach. *Journal of Financial Economics* 6 (September): 229–263.

Cox, J. C., and S. A. Ross. 1976. The valuation of options for alternative stochastic processes. *Journal of Financial Economics* 3 (March): 145–166.

Cox, J. C., and M. Rubinstein. 1985. *Option markets*. Englewood Cliffs, NJ: Prentice Hall.

Geske, R. 1979. A note on an analytical formula for unprotected American call options on stocks with known dividends. *Journal of Financial Economics* 6 (December): 375–380.

Geske, R. 1981. Comment on Whaley's note. *Journal of Financial Economics* 8 (June): 213–215.

Merton, R. C. 1973. The theory of rational option pricing. *Bell Journal of Economics and Management Science* 4 (Spring): 141–183.

Roll, R. 1977. An analytic formula for unprotected American call options on stocks with known dividends. *Journal of Financial Economics* 4 (November): 251–258.

Whaley, R. E. 1981. On the valuation of American call options on stocks with known dividends. *Journal of Financial Economics* 8 (June): 207–211.

Whaley, R. 2007. *Derivatives: Markets, valuation, risk management*. Hoboken, NJ: John Wiley & Sons.

Part Three

Bond Analysis and Portfolio Management

CHAPTER 16
Bond Fundamentals and Risks

Our focus in Part Two was on managing a common stock portfolio. Now we turn our attention to investing in the other major asset class—bonds. In its simplest form, a bond is a financial obligation of an entity that promises to pay a specified sum of money at specified future dates. The payments are made up of two components: (1) the repayment of the amount of money borrowed and (2) interest. The entity that promises to make the payment is called the issuer of the security or the borrower.

In this chapter, we provide the basic features of bonds and the risks associated with investing in this asset class. In Chapters 17 and 18, we explain the different types of bonds classified according to the issuer. In Chapter 19, we discuss the reasons why interest rates are not the same for all bonds and the factors that affect the interest rate that must be offered on a particular security. Bond valuation and various yield measures are covered in Chapter 20 and in Chapter 22 the valuation of complicated bond structures is explained. One of the major risk factors in managing a bond portfolio is interest rate risk. In Chapter 21, we show how to quantify the exposure of a security and a portfolio to interest rate risk. Bond portfolio strategies are explained in Chapter 23, and the use of derivative instruments for managing bond portfolios is presented in Chapter 24.

FEATURES OF BONDS

The promises of the issuer and the rights of the bondholders are set forth in great detail in the *indenture*. Bondholders would have great difficulty in determining from time to time whether the issuer was keeping all the promises made in the indenture. This problem is resolved for the most part by bringing in a trustee as a third party to the contract. The indenture is made out to the trustee as a representative of the interests of the bondholders; that is, a trustee acts in a fiduciary capacity for bondholders. A trustee is a bond or trust company with a trust department whose officers are experts in performing the functions of a trustee.

Maturity

Unlike common stock, which has a perpetual life, bonds have a date on which they mature. The number of years over which the issuer has promised to meet the conditions of the obligation is referred to as the *term to maturity*. The *maturity* of a bond refers to the date that the debt will cease to exist, at which time the issuer will redeem the bond by paying the amount borrowed. The maturity date of a bond is always identified when describing a bond. For example, a description of a bond might state "due 12/15/2025."

The practice in the bond market is to refer to the "term to maturity" of a bond as simply its "maturity" or "term." Despite sounding like a fixed date in which the bond matures, there are provisions that may be included in the indenture that grants either the issuer or the bondholder the right to alter a bond's term to maturity. These provisions, which will be described later in this chapter, include call provisions, put provisions, conversion provisions, and accelerated sinking fund provisions.

The maturity of a debt instrument is used for classifying two sectors of the market. Debt instruments with a maturity of one year or less are referred to as *money market instruments* and trade in the *money market*. What we typically refer to as the "bond market" includes debt instruments with a maturity greater than one year. The bond market is then categorized further based on the debt instrument's term to maturity: short-term, intermediate-term, and long-term. The classification is somewhat arbitrary and varies amongst market participants. A common classification is that *short-term bonds* have a maturity of from 1 to 5 years, *intermediate-term bonds* have a maturity from 5 to 12 years, and *long-term bonds* have a maturity that exceeds 12 years.

Typically, the maturity of a bond does not exceed 30 years. There are, of course, exceptions. For example, Walt Disney Company issued 100-year bonds in July 1993 and the Tennessee Valley Authority issued 50-year bonds in December 1993.

The term to maturity of a bond is important for two reasons in addition to indicating the time period over which the bondholder can expect to receive interest payments and the number of years before the amount borrowed will be repaid in full. The first reason is that the yield on a bond depends on it. At any given point in time, the relationship between the yield and maturity of a bond (called the *term structure of interest rate*) indicates how bondholders are compensated for investing in bonds with different maturities. This will be explained in Chapter 19. The second reason is that the price of a bond will fluctuate over its life as interest rates in the market change. The degree of price volatility of a bond is dependent on its maturity. More specifically, all other factors constant, the longer the maturity of a bond, the greater the price volatility resulting from a change in interest rates. This will be discussed in more detail in Chapter 21.

Par Value

The *par value* of a bond is the amount that the issuer agrees to repay the bondholder by the maturity date. This amount is also referred to as the *principal, face value, redemption value,* or *maturity value*.

Because bonds can have a different par value, the practice is to quote the price of a bond as a percentage of its par value. A value of 100 means 100% of par value. So, for example, if a bond has a par value of $1,000 and is selling for $850, this bond would be said to be selling at 85. If a bond with a par value of $100,000 is selling for $106,000, the bond is said to be selling for 106.

Coupon Rate

The annual interest rate that the issuer agrees to pay each year is called the *coupon rate*. The annual amount of the interest payment made to bondholders during the term of the bond is called the *coupon* and is determined by multiplying the coupon rate by the par value of the bond. For example, a bond with a 6% coupon rate and a par value of $1,000 will pay annual interest of $60.

When describing a bond issue, the coupon rate is indicated along with the maturity date. For example, the expression "5.5s of 2/15/2024" means a bond with a 5.5% coupon rate maturing on 2/15/2024.

For bonds issued in the United States, the usual practice is for the issuer to pay the coupon in two semiannual installments. Mortgage-backed securities and asset-backed securities, the subject of Chapter 18, typically pay interest monthly. For bonds issued in some markets outside the United States, coupon payments are made only once per year.

In addition to indicating the coupon payments that the investor should expect to receive over the term of the bond, the coupon rate also affects the bond's price sensitivity to changes in market interest rates. All other factors constant, the higher the coupon rate, the less the price will change in response to a change in market interest rates. This will be demonstrated in Chapter 21.

There are securities that have a coupon rate that increases over time according to a specified schedule. These securities are called *step-up notes* because the coupon rate "steps up" over time. For example, a five-year step-up note might have a coupon rate that is 5% for the first two years and 6% for the last three years. Or, the step-up note could call for a 5% coupon rate for the first two years, 5.5% for the third and fourth years, and 6% for the fifth year. When there is only one change (or step up), as in our first example, the issue is referred to as a *single step-up note*. When there is more than one increase, as in our second example, the issue is referred to as a *multiple step-up note*.

Not all bonds make periodic coupon payments. *Zero-coupon bonds*, as the name indicates, do not make periodic coupon payments. Instead, the holder of a zero-coupon bond realizes interest at the maturity date. The aggregate interest earned is the difference between the maturity value and the purchase price. For example, if an investor purchases a zero-coupon bond for 63, the aggregate interest at the maturity date is 37, the difference between the par value (100) and the price paid (63). The reason why certain investors like zero-coupon bonds is that they eliminate one of the risks that we will discuss later, reinvestment risk. The disadvantage of a zero-coupon bond is that the accrued interest earned each year is taxed despite the fact that no actual cash payment is made.

There are issues whose coupon payment is deferred for a specified number of years. That is, there is no coupon payment for the deferred period and then at some specified date coupon payments are made until maturity. These securities are referred to as *deferred interest securities*.

A coupon-bearing security need not have a fixed interest rate over the term of the bond. There are bonds that have an interest rate that is variable. These bonds are referred to as *floating-rate securities*. In fact, another way to classify bond markets is the *fixed-rate bond market* and the *floating-rate bond market*. Floating-rate securities appeal to institutional investors such as depository institutions (banks, savings and loan associations, and credit unions) because they provide a better match against their funding costs which are typically floating-rate debt. Typically, the interest rate is adjusted on specific dates, referred to as the *coupon reset date*. There is a formula for the new coupon rate, referred to as the *coupon reset formula*, that has the following generic formula:

Coupon reset formula = Reference rate + Quoted margin

The quoted margin is the additional amount that the issuer agrees to pay above the reference rate. The most common reference rate is the London Interbank Offered Rate (LIBOR). LIBOR is the interest rate at which major international banks offer each other on Eurodollar certificates of deposit with given maturities. The maturities range from overnight to five years. Suppose that the reference rate is one-month LIBOR and the quoted margin is 80 basis points.[1] Then the coupon reset formula is

$$\text{1-month LIBOR} + 80 \text{ basis points}$$

So, if one-month LIBOR on the coupon reset date is 4.6%, the coupon rate is reset for that period at 5.4% (4.6% plus 80 basis points).

The quoted margin need not be a positive value. It could be subtracted from the reference rate. For example, the reference rate could be the yield on a five-year Treasury security and the coupon rate could reset every six months based on the following coupon reset formula:

$$\text{5-year Treasury yield} - 50 \text{ basis points}$$

While the reference rate for most floating-rate securities is an interest rate or an interest rate index, there are some issues where this is not the case. Instead, the reference rate can be some financial index such as the return on the Standard & Poor's 500 index or a nonfinancial index such as the price of a commodity or the consumer price index.

Typically, the coupon reset formula on floating-rate securities is such that the coupon rate increases when the reference rate increases, and decreases when the reference rate decreases. There are issues whose coupon rate moves in the opposite direction from the change in the reference rate. Such issues are called *inverse floaters* or *reverse floaters*. A general coupon reset formula for an inverse floater is

$$K - L \times (\text{Reference rate})$$

For example, suppose that for a particular inverse floater K is 10% and L is 1. Then the coupon reset formula would be

$$10\% - \text{Reference rate}$$

Suppose that the reference rate is 1-month LIBOR, then the coupon reset formula would be

$$10\% - \text{1-month LIBOR}$$

If in some month one-month LIBOR at the coupon reset date is 5%, the coupon rate for the period is 5%. If in the next month one-month LIBOR declines to 4.5%, the coupon rate increases to 5.5%.

---

[1] A basis point is equal to 0.0001 or 0.01%. Thus, 100 basis points are equal to 1%.

A floating rate security may have a restriction on the maximum coupon rate that will be paid at a reset date. The maximum coupon rate is called a *cap*. Because a cap restricts the coupon rate from increasing, a cap is an unattractive feature for the investor. In the case of an inverse floater, one can see from the general formula that the maximum interest rate would be K. This occurs when the reference rate is zero. In contrast, there could be a *floor* which is the minimum coupon rate specified and this is an attractive feature for the investor.

Not all floating rate securities have the generic coupon reset formula given above. Some have a coupon rate that depends on the range for the reference rate. This type of floating rate security, called a *range note*, has a coupon rate equal to the reference rate as long as the reference rate is within a certain range at the reset date. If the reference rate is outside of the range, the coupon rate is zero for that period. For example, a three-year range note might specify that the reference rate is one-year LIBOR and that the coupon rate resets every year. The coupon rate for the year will be one-year LIBOR as long as one-year LIBOR at the coupon reset date falls within the range as specified below:

	Year 1	Year 2	Year 3
Lower limit of range	4.5%	5.25%	6.00%
Upper limit of range	5.5%	6.75%	7.50%

If one-year LIBOR is outside of the range, the coupon rate is zero. For example, suppose that one-year LIBOR is 5% at the coupon reset date, then the coupon rate for the year is 5%. However, if one-year LIBOR is 6%, the coupon rate for the year is zero since one-year LIBOR is greater than the upper limit for year 1 of 5.5%.

Accrued Interest

In the United States, coupon interest is typically paid semiannual for government bonds, corporate, agency, and municipal bonds. In some countries, interest is paid annually. For mortgage-backed and asset-backed securities, interest is usually paid monthly. The coupon interest payment is made to the bondholder of record. Thus, if an investor sells a bond between coupon payments and the buyer holds it until the next coupon payment, then the entire coupon interest earned for the period will be paid to the buyer of the bond since the buyer will be the holder of record.

The seller of the bond gives up the interest from the time of the last coupon payment to the time until the bond is sold. The amount of interest over this period that will be received by the buyer even though it was earned by the seller is called *accrued interest* In the United States and in many countries, the bond buyer must compensate the bond seller for the accrued interest. The amount that the buyer pays the seller is the agreed-upon price for the bond plus accrued interest. This amount is called the *full price*. The agreed-upon bond price without accrued interest is called the *clean price*.

A bond in which the buyer must pay the seller accrued interest is said to be trading *cum*-coupon. If the buyer forgoes the next coupon payment, the bond is said to be trading *ex*-coupon. In the United States, bonds are always traded *cum*-coupon. There are bond markets outside the United States where bonds are traded *ex*-coupon for a certain period before the coupon payment date.

There are exceptions to the rule that the bond buyer must pay the bond seller accrued interest. The most important exception is when the issuer has not fulfilled its promise to make the periodic payments. In this case, the issuer is said to be in default. In such instances, the bond's price is sold without accrued interest and is said to be traded *flat*.

The appendix to this chapter explains how to calculate accrued interest.

Provisions for Paying Off Bonds

The issuer of a bond agrees to repay the principal by the stated maturity date. The issuer can agree to repay the entire amount borrowed in one lump sum payment at the maturity date. That is, the issuer is not required to make any principal repayments prior to the maturity date. Such bonds are said to have a *bullet maturity*.

Bonds backed by pools of loans (mortgage-backed securities and asset-backed securities) often have a schedule of principal repayments. Such bonds are said to be *amortizing securities*. For many loans, the payments are structured so that when the last loan payment is made, the entire amount owed is fully paid off. Another example of an amortizing feature is a bond that has a *sinking fund provision*. This provision for repayment of a bond may be designed to liquidate all of an issue by the maturity date, or it may be arranged to repay only a part of the total by the maturity date.

A bond issue may have a call provision granting the issuer an option to retire all or part of the issue prior to the stated maturity date. Some issues specify that the issuer must retire a predetermined amount of the issue periodically. These provisions are discussed below.

Call and Refunding Provisions

An issuer generally wants the right to retire a bond issue prior to the stated maturity date because it recognizes that at some time in the future the general level of interest rates may fall sufficiently below the issue's coupon rate so that redeeming the issue and replacing it with another issue with a lower coupon rate would be economically beneficial. This right is a disadvantage to the bondholder since proceeds received must be reinvested at a lower interest rate. As a result, an issuer who wants to include this right as part of a bond offering must compensate the bondholder when the issue is sold by offering a higher coupon rate, or equivalently, accepting a lower price than if the right is not included.

The right of the issuer to retire the issue prior to the stated maturity date is referred to as a *call provision* and is more popularly referred to as a *call option*. A bond with this provision is referred to as a *callable bond*. If an issuer exercises this right, the issuer is said to "call the bond." The price which the issuer must pay to retire the issue is referred to as the *call price*. There may not be a single call price but a *call schedule* which sets forth a call price based on when the issuer may exercise the option to call the bond.

When a bond is issued, the issuer may be restricted from calling the bond for a number of years. In such situations, the bond is said to have a *deferred call*. The date at which the bond may first be called is referred to as the *first call date*. However, not all issues have a deferred call. If a bond issue does not have any protection against early call, then it is said to be a *currently callable issue*. But most new bond issues, even if currently callable, usually have some restrictions against certain types of early redemption. The most common restriction is that prohibiting the refunding of the bonds for a certain number of years. *Refunding* a bond issue means redeeming bonds with funds obtained through the sale of a new bond issue.

Call protection is much more absolute than refunding protection. While there may be certain exceptions to absolute or complete call protection in some cases, it still provides greater assurance against premature and unwanted redemption than does refunding protection. Refunding prohibition merely prevents redemption only from certain sources of funds, namely the proceeds of other debt issues sold at a lower cost of money. The bondholder is only protected if interest rates decline, and the borrower can obtain lower-cost money to pay off the debt.

Bonds can be called in whole (the entire issue) or in part (only a portion). When less than the entire issue is called, the specific bonds to be called are selected randomly or on a pro rata basis. Generally, the call schedule is such that the call price at the first call date is a premium over the par value and scaled down to the par value over time. The date at which the issue is first callable at par value is referred to as the *first par call date*. However, not all issues have a call schedule in which the call price starts out as a premium over par. There are issues where the call price at the first call date and subsequent call dates is par value. In such cases, the first call date is the same as the first par call date.

For zero-coupon bonds, there are three types of call schedules that can be used. The first is a call schedule for which the call price is below par value at the first call date and scales up to par value over time. The second type is one in which the call price at the first call date is above par and scales down to par. The third type is a schedule in which the call price is par value at the first call date and any subsequent call date.

The call prices in a call schedule are referred to as the *regular* or *general redemption prices*. There are also *special redemption prices* for debt redeemed through the sinking fund and through other provisions, and the proceeds from the confiscation of property through the right of eminent domain. The special redemption price is usually par value.

Prepayments

Amortizing securities backed by loans have a schedule of principal repayments. However, individual borrowers typically have the option to pay off all or part of their loan prior to the scheduled principal repayment date. Any principal repayment prior to the scheduled date is called a *prepayment*. The right of borrowers to prepay is called the *prepayment option*.

Basically, the prepayment option is the same as a call option. However, unlike a call option, there is not a call price that depends on when the borrower pays off the issue. Typically, the price at which a loan is prepaid is at par value.

Sinking Fund Provision

A *sinking fund provision* included in a bond indenture requires the issuer to retire a specified portion of an issue each year. Usually, the periodic payments required for sinking fund purposes will be the same for each period. A few indentures might permit variable periodic payments, where payments change according to certain prescribed conditions set forth in the indenture. The alleged purpose of the sinking fund provision is to reduce credit risk. This kind of provision for repayment of debt may be designed to liquidate all of a bond issue by the maturity date, or it may be arranged to pay only a part of the total by the end of the term. If only a part is paid, the remainder is referred to as a *balloon maturity*. Many indentures include a provision that grants the issuer the option to retire more than the amount stipulated for the scheduled sinking fund retirement. This is referred to as an *accelerated sinking fund provision*.

To satisfy the sinking fund requirement, an issuer is typically granted one of following choices: (1) make a cash payment of the face amount of the bonds to be retired to the trustee, who then calls the bonds for redemption using a lottery; or (2) deliver to the trustee bonds purchased in the open market that have a total par value equal to the amount that must be retired. If the bonds are retired using the first method, interest payments stop at the redemption date.

Usually the sinking fund call price is the par value if the bonds were originally sold at par. When issued at a price in excess of par, the call price generally starts at the issuance price and scales down to par as the issue approaches maturity.

There is a difference between the amortizing feature for a bond with a sinking fund provision, and the regularly scheduled principal repayment for a mortgage-backed and an asset-backed security. The owner of a mortgage-backed security and an asset-backed security knows that assuming no default that there will be principal repayments. In contrast, the owner of a bond with a sinking fund provision is not assured that his or her particular holding will be called to satisfy the sinking fund requirement.

Options Granted to Bondholders

A provision in the indenture could grant the bondholder and the issuer an option to take some action against the other party. The most common type of option embedded in a bond is a call option discussed already. This option is granted to the issuer. There are two options that can be granted to the bondholder: the right to put the issue and the right to convert the issue to the issuer's common stock.

A bond with a put provision grants the bondholder the right to sell the bond (that is, force the issuer to redeem the bond) at a specified price on designated dates. A bond with this provision is referred to as a *putable bond*. The specified price is called the *put price*. Typically, a bond is putable at par value if it is issued at or close to par value. For a zero-coupon bond, the put price is below par. The advantage of the put provision to the bondholder is that if after the issue date market rates rise above the issue's coupon rate, the bondholder can force the issuer to redeem the bond at the put price and then reinvest the proceeds at the prevailing higher rate.

A *convertible bond* is an issue giving the bondholder the right to exchange the bond for a specified number of shares of the issuer's common stock. Such a feature allows the bondholder to take advantage of favorable movements in the price of the issuer's common stock. An *exchangeable bond* allows the bondholder to exchange the issue for a specified number of shares of common stock of a corporation different from the issuer of the bond. Convertible bonds are described in Chapter 17.

Currency Denomination

The payments that the issuer makes to the bondholder can be in any currency. For bonds issued in the United States, the issuer typically makes both coupon payments and principal repayments in U.S. dollars. However, there is nothing that forces the issuer to make payments in U.S. dollars. The indenture can specify that the issuer may make payments in some other specified currency. For example, payments may be made in euros or yen.

An issue in which payments to bondholders are in U.S. dollars is called a *dollar-denominated issue*. A *nondollar-denominated issue* is one in which payments are not denominated in U.S. dollars. There are some issues whose coupon payments are in one currency and whose principal payment is in another currency. An issue with this characteristic is called a *dual-currency issue*.

Some issues allow either the issuer or the bondholder the right to select the currency in which a payment will be paid. This option effectively gives the party with the right to choose the currency the opportunity to benefit from a favorable exchange rate movement.

RISKS ASSOCIATED WITH INVESTING IN BONDS

Bonds may expose an investor to one or more of the following risks:

- Interest rate risk
- Call and prepayment risk
- Credit risk
- Liquidity risk
- Exchange rate or currency risk
- Inflation or purchasing power risk

Interest Rate Risk

The price of a typical bond will change in the opposite direction from a change in interest rates. That is, when interest rates rise, a bond's price will fall; when interest rates fall, a bond's price will rise. For example, consider a 6%, 20-year bond. If the yield investors require to buy this bond is 6%, the price of this bond would be $100.[2] However, if the required yield increases to 6.5%, the price of this bond would decline to $94.4479. Thus, for a

---

[2] We will explain how these prices are obtained in Chapter 20.

50 basis point increase in yield, the bond's price declines by 5.55%. If, instead, the yield declines from 6% to 5.5%, the bond's price will rise by 6.02% to $106.0195.

The reason for this inverse relationship between price and changes in interest rates or changes in market yields is as follows. Suppose investor X purchases our hypothetical 6% coupon 20-year bond at par value ($100). The yield for this bond is 6%.[3] Suppose that immediately after the purchase of this bond two things happen. First, market interest rates rise to 6.50% so that if an investor wants to buy a similar 20-year bond, a 6.50% coupon rate would have to be paid by the bond issuer in order to offer the bond at par value. Second, suppose investor X wants to sell the bond. In attempting to sell the bond, investor X would not find an investor who would be willing to pay par value for a bond with a coupon rate of 6%. The reason is that any investor who wanted to purchase this bond could obtain a similar 20-year bond with a coupon rate 50 basis points higher, 6.5%. What can the investor do? The investor cannot force the issuer to change the coupon rate to 6.5%. Nor can the investor force the issuer to shorten the maturity of the bond to a point where a new investor would be willing to accept a 6% coupon rate. The only thing that the investor can do is adjust the price of the bond so that at the new price the buyer would realize a yield of 6.5%. This means that the price would have to be adjusted down to a price below par value. The new price must be $94.4469. While we assumed in our illustration an initial price of par value, the principle holds for any purchase price. Regardless of the price that an investor pays for a bond, an increase in market interest rates will result in a decline in a bond's price.

Suppose instead of a rise in market interest rates to 6.5%, they decline to 5.5%. Investors would be more than happy to purchase the 6% coupon, 20-year bond for par value. However, investor X realizes that the market is only offering investors the opportunity to buy a similar bond at par value with a coupon rate of 5.5%. Consequently, investor X will increase the price of the bond until it offers a yield of 5.5%. That price is $106.0195.

Since the price of a bond fluctuates with market interest rates, the risk that an investor faces is that the price of a bond held in a portfolio will decline if market interest rates rise. This risk is referred to as *interest rate risk* and is a major risk faced by investors in the bond market.

Bond Features that Affect Interest Rate Risk

The degree of sensitivity of a bond's price to changes in market interest rates depends on various characteristics of the issue, such as maturity and coupon rate. Consider first maturity. All other factors constant, the longer the matu-

---

[3] We will explain how the yield of a bond is calculated in Chapter 21.

rity, the greater the bond's price sensitivity to changes in interest rates. For example, we know that for a 6%, 20-year bond selling to yield 6%, a rise in the yield required by investors to 6.5% will cause the bond's price to decline from $100 to $94.4479, a 5.55% price decline. For a 6%, five-year bond selling to yield 6%, the price is $100. A rise in the yield required by investors from 6% to 6.5% would decrease the price to $97.8944. The decline in the bond's price is only 2.11%.

Now let's turn to the coupon rate. A property of a bond is that all other factors constant, the lower the coupon rate, the greater the bond's price sensitivity to changes in interest rates. For example, consider a 9%, 20-year bond selling to yield 6%. The price of this bond would be $112.7953. If the yield required by investors increases by 50 basis points to 6.5%, the price of this bond would fall by 2.01% to $110.5280. This decline is less than the 5.55% decline for the 6%, 20-year bond selling to yield 6%. An implication is that zero-coupon bonds have greater price sensitivity to interest rate changes than same-maturity bonds bearing a coupon rate and trading at the same yield.

Because of default risk (discussed later), different bonds trade at different yields, even if they have the same coupon rate and maturity. How, then, holding other factors constant, does the level of interest rates affect a bond's price sensitivity to changes in interest rates? As it turns out, the higher the level of interest rates that a bond trades, the lower the price sensitivity.

To see this, we can compare a 6%, 20-year bond initially selling at a yield of 6%, and a 6%, 20-year bond initially selling at a yield of 10%. The former is initially at a price of $100, and the latter carries a price of $65.68. Now, if the yield on both bonds increases by 100 basis points, the first bond trades down by 10.68 points (10.68%). After the assumed increase in yield, the second bond will trade at a price of $59.88, for a price decline of only 5.80 points (or 8.83%). Thus, we see that the bond that trades at a lower yield is more volatile in both percentage price change and absolute price change, as long as the other bond characteristics are the same. An implication of this is that, for a given change in interest rates, price sensitivity is lower when the level of interest rates in the market is high, and price sensitivity is higher when the level of interest rates is low.

We can summarize these three characteristics that affect the bond's price sensitivity to changes in market interest rates as follows:

Characteristic 1. For a given maturity and initial yield, the lower the coupon rate the greater the bond's price sensitivity to changes in market interest rates.

Characteristic 2. For a given coupon rate and initial yield, the longer the maturity of a bond the greater the bond's price sensitivity to changes in market interest rates.

Characteristic 3. For a given coupon rate and maturity, the lower the level of interest rates the greater the bond's price sensitivity to changes in market interest rates.

A bond's price sensitivity bond will also depend on any options embedded in the issue. This is explained below when we discuss call risk.

Measuring Interest Rate Risk

Investors are interested in estimating the price sensitivity of a bond to changes in market interest rates. The measure commonly used to approximate the percentage price change is duration. *Duration* gives the approximate percentage price change for a 100 basis point change in interest rates. Chapter 21 explains the concept of duration and its measurement.

The duration for the 6% coupon, five-year bond trading at par to yield 6% is 4.27. Thus, the price of this bond will change by approximately 4.27% if interest rates change by 100 basis points. For a 50 basis point change, this bond's price will change by approximately 2.14% (4.27% divided by 2). As previously explained, this bond's price would actually change by 2.11%. Thus, duration does a good job of approximating the percentage price change. It turns out that the approximation is good the smaller the change in interest rates. The approximation is not as good for a large change in interest rates as explained in Chapter 32.

Call and Prepayment Risk

As explained earlier, a bond may include a provision that allows the issuer to retire or call all or part of the issue before the maturity date. From the investor's perspective, the following are the disadvantages to call provisions:

- The cash flow pattern of a callable bond is not known with certainty.
- Because the issuer will call the bonds when interest rates have dropped, the investor is exposed to *reinvestment risk*. This is the risk that the investor will have to reinvest the proceeds when the bond is called at a lower interest rate.
- The capital appreciation potential of a bond will be reduced because the price of a callable bond may not rise much above the price at which the issuer is entitled to call the bond.

Because of these disadvantages faced by the investor, a callable bond is said to expose the investor *to call risk*. The same disadvantages apply to bonds that can prepay. In this case, the risk is referred to as *prepayment risk*.

Credit Risk

While investors commonly refer to *credit risk* as if it is one dimensional, there are actually three forms of this risk. *Default risk* is the risk that the issuer will fail to satisfy the terms of the obligation with respect to the timely payment of interest and repayment of the amount borrowed. To gauge credit default risk, investors rely on analysis performed by nationally recognized statistical rating organizations (i.e., more popularly known as rating agencies) that perform credit analysis of bond issues and issuers and express their conclusions in the form of a *credit rating*. *Credit spread risk* is the loss or underperformance of an issue or issues due to an increase in the credit spread. *Downgrade risk* is the risk that an issue or issuer will be downgraded, resulting in an increase in the credit spread.

Next we discuss the various forms of credit risk.

Default Risk

We begin our discussion of credit default risk with an explanation of credit ratings and the factors used by rating agencies in assigning a credit rating. We then discuss the rights of creditors in a bankruptcy in the United States and why the actual outcome of a bankruptcy typically differs from the theoretical credit protection afforded under the bankruptcy laws. Finally, we will look at corporate bond *default rates* and *recovery rates* in the United States.

Credit Ratings The prospectus or offer document for an issue provides investors with information about the issuer so that credit analysis can be performed on the issuer before the bonds are placed. Credit assessments take time, however, and also require the specialist skills of credit analysts. Large institutional investors do in fact employ such specialists to carry out credit analysis; however, often it is too costly and time consuming to assess every issuer in every debt market. Therefore, investors often rely on credit ratings.

A credit rating is a formal opinion given by a rating agency of the credit default risk faced by investing in a particular issue of debt securities. For long-term debt obligations, a credit rating is a forward-looking assessment of the probability of default and the relative magnitude of the loss should a default occur. For short-term debt obligations, a credit rating is a forward-looking assessment of the probability of default.

The the three major rating agencies include Moody's Investors Service, Standard & Poor's Corporation, and Fitch Ratings. On receipt of a formal request, the rating agencies will carry out a rating exercise on a specific debt issue. The request for a rating comes from the organization planning the issuance of bonds. Although ratings are provided for the benefit of investors, the issuer must bear the cost. However, it is in the issuer's interest to request a rating as it raises the profile of the bonds, and investors may refuse to buy a bond that is not accompanied by a recognized rating.

Although the rating exercise involves credit analysis of the issuer, the rating is applied to a specific debt issue. This means that, in theory, the credit rating is applied not to an organization itself, but to specific debt securities that the organization has issued or is planning to issue. In practice, it is common for the market to refer to the creditworthiness of organizations themselves in terms of the rating of their debt. A highly rated company, for example, may be referred to as a "triple-A-rated" company, although it is the company's debt issues that are rated as triple A.

The rating systems of the rating agencies use similar symbols. Separate categories are used by each rating agency for short-term debt (with original maturity of 12 months or less) and long-term debt (over one year original maturity). Table 16.1 shows the long-term debt ratings. In all rating systems the term "high grade" means low credit risk or, conversely, high probability of future payments. The highest-grade bonds are designated by Moody's by the letters Aaa, and by the others as AAA. The next highest grade is designated as Aa by Moody's, and by the others as AA; for the third grade, all rating agencies use A. The next three grades are Baa (Moody's) or BBB, Ba (Moody's) or BB, and B, respectively. There are also C grades. Standard and Poor's (S&P) and Fitch use plus or minus signs to provide a narrower credit quality breakdown within each class. Moody's uses 1, 2, or 3 for the same purpose. Bonds rated triple A (AAA or Aaa) are said to be "prime"; double A (AA or Aa) are of "high quality"; single A issues are called "upper medium grade"; and triple B are "medium grade." Lower-rated bonds are said to have "speculative" elements or be "distinctly speculative."

Bond issues that are assigned a rating in the top four categories are referred to as *investment-grade bonds*. Bond issues that carry a rating below the top four categories are referred to as *noninvestment-grade bonds* or more popularly as *high-yield bonds* or *junk bonds*. Thus, the bond market can be divided into two sectors: the *investment-grade sector* and the *noninvestment-grade sector*. *Distressed debt* is a subcategory of noninvestment-grade bonds. These bonds may be in bankruptcy proceedings, may be in default of coupon payments, or may be in some other form of distress.

Factors Considered in Rating Corporate Bond Issues In conducting its examination of corporate bond issues, the rating agencies consider the "four Cs of credit": character, capacity, collateral, and covenants. The meaning of each is as follows:

TABLE 16.1 Summary of Long-Term Bond Rating Systems and Symbols

Fitch	Moody's	S&P	Summary Description
Investment Grade			
AAA	Aaa	AAA	Gilt edged, prime, maximum safety, lowest risk, and when sovereign borrower considered "default-free"
AA+	Aa1	AA+	
AA	Aa2	AA	High grade, high credit quality
AA–	Aa3	AA–	
A+	A1	A+	
A	A2	A	Upper-medium grade
A–	A3	A–	
BBB+	Baa1	BBB+	
BBB	Baa2	BBB	Lower-medium grade
BBB–	Baa3	BBB–	
Speculative Grade			
BB+	Ba1	BB+	
BB	Ba2	BB	Low grade; speculative
BB–	Ba3	BB–	
B+	B1		
B	B	B	Highly speculative
B–	B3		
Predominantly Speculative, Substantial Risk, or in Default			
CCC+		CCC+	
CCC	Caa	CCC	Substantial risk, in poor standing
CC	Ca	CC	May be in default, very speculative
C	C	C	Extremely speculative
		CI	Income bonds—no interest being paid
DDD			
DD			Default
D		D	

- *Character* of management is the foundation of sound credit. This includes the ethical reputation as well as the business qualifications and operating record of the board of directors, management, and executives responsible for the use of the borrowed funds and repayment of those funds.
- *Capacity* is the ability of an issuer to repay its obligations.
- *Collateral* is looked at not only in the traditional sense of assets pledged to secure the debt, but also to the quality and value of those unpledged assets controlled by the issuer. In both senses, the collateral is capable of supplying additional aid, comfort, and support to the debt and the debt holder. Assets form the basis for the generation of cash flow, which services the debt in good times as well as bad.
- *Covenants* set forth restrictions on how management operates the company and conducts its financial affairs. Covenants can restrict management's discretion. A default or violation of any covenant may provide a meaningful early warning alarm enabling investors to take positive and corrective action before the situation deteriorates further. Covenants have value as they play an important part in minimizing risk to creditors. They help prevent the unconscionable transfer of wealth from debt holders to equity holders.

Character analysis involves the analysis of the quality of management. In discussing the factors it considers in assigning a credit rating, Moody's notes the following regarding the quality of management:

> Although difficult to quantify, management quality is one of the most important factors supporting an issuer's credit strength. When the unexpected occurs, it is a management's ability to react appropriately that will sustain the company's performance. (Moody's 1998, 6)

Moody's, for example, assesses management quality by looking at the business strategies and policies formulated by management. Following are factors that are considered: (1) strategic direction, (2) financial philosophy, (3) conservatism, (4) track record, (5) succession planning, and (6) control systems.

In assessing the ability of an issuer to pay, an analysis of the financial statements is undertaken. In addition to management quality, Moody's, for example, looks at (1) industry trends, (2) the regulatory environment, (3) basic operating and competitive position, (4) financial position and sources of liquidity, (5) company structure (including structural subordination and priority of claim), (6) parent company support agreements, and (7) special event risk.

In considering industry trends, the rating agencies look at the vulnerability of the company to economic cycles, the barriers to entry, and the exposure of the company to technological changes. For firms in regulated industries, proposed changes in regulations are analyzed to assess their impact on future cash flows. At the company level, diversification of the product line and the cost structure are examined in assessing the basic operating position of the firm.

The rating agencies look at the capacity of a firm to obtain additional financing and backup credit facilities. There are various forms of backup facilities. The strongest forms of backup credit facilities are those that are contractually binding and do not include provisions that permit the lender to refuse to provide funds.

A corporate debt obligation can be secured or unsecured. In our discussion of creditor rights in a bankruptcy discussed later, we will see that in the case of a liquidation, proceeds from a bankruptcy are distributed to creditors based on the absolute priority rule. However, in the case of a reorganization, the absolute priority rule rarely holds. That is, unsecured creditors may receive distributions for the entire amount of their claim and common stockholders may receive something, while secured creditors may receive only a portion of their claim. The reason is that a reorganization requires approval of all the parties. Consequently, secured creditors are willing to negotiate with both unsecured creditors and stockholders in order to obtain approval of the plan of reorganization.

The question is then, what does a secured position mean in the case of a reorganization if the absolute priority rule is not followed in a reorganization? The claim position of a secured creditor is important in terms of the negotiation process. However, because absolute priority is not followed and the final distribution in a reorganization depends on the bargaining ability of the parties, some credit analysts place less emphasis on collateral compared to the other factors discussed earlier and covenants, which we discuss next.

Covenants deal with limitations and restrictions on the borrower's activities. *Affirmative covenants* call on the debtor to make promises to do certain things. *Negative covenants* are those that require the borrower not to take certain actions. Negative covenants are usually negotiated between the borrower and the lender or their agents. Borrowers want the least restrictive loan agreement available, while lenders should want the most restrictive that is consistent with sound business practices. But lenders should not try to restrain borrowers from accepted business activities and conduct. A borrower might be willing to include additional restrictions (up to a point) if it can get a lower interest rate on the debt obligation. When borrowers seek to weaken restrictions in their favor, they are often willing to pay more interest or give other consideration.

Bankruptcy and Creditor Rights in the United States The holder of a corporate debt instrument has priority over the equity owners in the case of bankruptcy of a corporation. There are creditors who have priority over other creditors. Here, we will provide an overview of the bankruptcy process and then look at what actually happens to creditors in bankruptcies.

There is a federal law governing bankruptcies in the United States and this law is amended periodically. One purpose of the bankruptcy law is to set forth the rules for a corporation to be either liquidated or reorganized. The *liquidation* of a corporation means that all the assets will be distributed to the holders of claims of the corporation and no corporate entity will survive. In a *reorganization*, a new corporate entity will result. Some holders of the claim of the bankrupt corporation will receive cash in exchange for their claims, others may receive new securities in the corporation that results from the reorganization, and others may receive a combination of both cash and new securities in the resulting corporation.

Another purpose of the bankruptcy law is to give a corporation time to decide whether to reorganize or liquidate and then the necessary time to formulate a plan to accomplish either a reorganization or liquidation. This is achieved because when a corporation files for bankruptcy, the law grants the corporation protection from creditors who seek to collect their claims. The petition for bankruptcy can be filed either by the company itself, in which case it is called a *voluntary bankruptcy*, or be filed by its creditors, in which case it is called an *involuntary bankruptcy*. A company that files for protection under the bankruptcy act generally becomes a *debtor-in-possession* (DIP), and continues to operate its business under the supervision of the court.

The bankruptcy law is comprised of 15 chapters, each covering a particular type of bankruptcy. Of particular interest here are two of the chapters, Chapter 7 and Chapter 11. Chapter 7 deals with the liquidation of a company; Chapter 11 deals with the reorganization of a company.

When a company is liquidated, creditors receive distributions based on the "absolute priority rule" to the extent assets are available. The absolute priority rule is the principle that senior creditors are paid in full before junior creditors are paid anything. For secured creditors and unsecured creditors, the absolute priority rule guarantees their seniority to equity holders.

In liquidations, the absolute priority rule generally holds. In contrast, there is a good body of literature that argues that strict absolute priority has not been upheld by the courts or the Securities and Exchange Commission (SEC). Studies of actual reorganizations under Chapter 11 have found that the violation of absolute priority is the rule rather the exception.[4]

---

[4] For a summary of these reasons, see Fabozzi (2009, 176–177).

Consequently, while investors in the debt of a corporation may feel that they have priority over the equity owners and priority over other classes of debtors, the actual outcome of a bankruptcy may be far different from what the terms of the debt agreement state.

Default and Recovery Rates There is a good deal of research published on default rates by rating agencies and academicians. From an investment perspective, default rates by themselves are not of paramount significance: It is perfectly possible for a portfolio of corporate bonds to suffer defaults and to outperform Treasuries at the same time, provided the yield spread of the portfolio is sufficiently high to offset the losses from defaults. Furthermore, because holders of defaulted bonds typically recover a percentage of the face amount of their investment, the *default loss rate* can be substantially lower than the default rate. The default loss rate is defined as follows:

$$\text{Default loss rate} = \text{Default rate} \times (100\% - \text{Recovery rate})$$

For instance, a default rate of 5% and a recovery rate of 30% means a default loss rate of only 3.5% (70% of 5%).

Therefore, focusing exclusively on default rates merely highlights the worst possible outcome that a diversified portfolio of corporate bonds would suffer, assuming all defaulted bonds would be totally worthless.

There have been several studies of default rates, particularly for high-yield corporate bonds, and the reported findings at times appear to be significantly different. The differences in the reported default rates are due to the different approaches used by researchers to measure default rates. As explained by Cheung, Bencivenga, and Fabozzi (1992), the differences in reported default rates are not as great as they might first appear once methodologies employed in these studies are standardized.

Several studies have found that the recovery rate is closely related to the bond's seniority. However, seniority is not the only factor that affects recovery values. In general, recovery values will vary with the types of assets and competitive conditions of the firm, as well as the economic environment at the time of bankruptcy. In addition, recovery rates will also vary across industries. For example, some manufacturing companies, such as petroleum and chemical companies, have assets with a high tangible value, such as plant, equipment, and land. These assets usually have a significant market value, even in the event of bankruptcy. In other industries, however, a company's assets have less tangible value, and bondholders should expect low recovery rates.

To understand why recovery rates might vary across industries, consider two extreme examples: a software company and an electric utility. In the event of bankruptcy, the assets of a software company will probably have little tangible value. The company's products will have a low liquidation value because of the highly competitive and dynamic nature of the industry. The company's major intangible asset, its software developers, may literally disappear as employees move to jobs at other companies. In general, in industries that spend heavily on research and development and in which technological changes are rapid, a company's liquidation value will decline sharply when its products lose their competitive edge. In these industries, bondholders can expect to recover little in the event of default. At the other extreme, electric utility bonds will likely have relatively high recovery values. The assets of an electric company (e.g., generation, transmission, and distribution) usually continue to generate a stream of revenues even after a bankruptcy. In most cases, a bankruptcy of a utility can be solved by changing the company's capital structure, rather than by liquidating its assets. In addition, regulators have a vested interest in maintaining the company as a going concern.

Credit Spread Risk

The *credit spread* is the premium over the government or risk-free rate required by the market for taking on a certain assumed credit exposure. As explained in Chapter 19, the benchmark is often the on-the-run or "active" U.S. Treasury issue for the given maturity or the swap rate curve.

The higher the credit rating, the smaller the credit spread to the benchmark rate all other factors constant. *Credit spread risk* is the risk of financial loss resulting from changes in the level of credit spreads used in the marking-to-market of a debt instrument. Changes in market credit spreads affect the value of the portfolio and can lead to losses for traders or underperformance relative to a benchmark for portfolio managers.

As explained earlier, duration is a measure of the change in the value of a bond when interest rates change. The interest rate that is assumed to change is the benchmark rate. For credit-risky bonds, the yield is equal to the benchmark rate plus the credit spread. A measure of how a credit-risky bond's price will change if the credit spread sought by the market changes is called "spread duration." For example, a spread duration of two for a credit-risky bond means that for a 100 basis point increase in the credit spread (holding the benchmark rate constant), the bond's price will change by approximately 2%.

Downgrade Risk

As explained earlier, market participants gauge the credit default risk of an issue by looking at the credit ratings assigned to issues by the rating agencies. Once a credit rating is assigned to a debt obligation, a rating agency monitors the credit quality of the issuer and can reassign a different credit rating. An improvement in the credit quality of an issue or issuer is rewarded with a better credit rating, referred to as an *upgrade*; a deterioration in the credit rating of an issue or issuer is penalized by the assignment of an inferior credit rating, referred to as a *downgrade*. The actual or anticipated downgrading of an issue or issuer increases the credit spread and results in a decline in the price of the issue or the issuer's bonds. This risk is referred to as *downgrade risk* and is closely related to credit spread risk. A rating agency may announce in advance that it is reviewing a particular credit rating, and may go further and state that the review is a precursor to a possible downgrade or upgrade. This announcement is referred to as "putting the issue under credit watch."

Occasionally, the ability of an issuer to make interest and principal payments changes seriously and unexpectedly because of an unforeseen event. This can include any number of idiosyncratic events that are specific to the corporation or to an industry, including a natural or industrial accident, a regulatory change, a takeover or corporate restructuring, or even corporate fraud. This risk is referred to generically as *event risk* and will result in a downgrading of the issuer by the rating agencies. Because the price of the entity's securities will typically change dramatically or jump in price, this risk is sometimes referred to as *jump risk*.

Rating Migration (Transition) Table The rating agencies periodically publish, in the form of a table, information about how issues that they have rated have changed over time. This table is called a *rating migration table* or *rating transition table*. The table is useful for investors to assess potential downgrades and upgrades. A rating migration table is available for different lengths of time. Table 16.2 shows a hypothetical rating migration table for a one-year period. The first column shows the ratings at the start of the year, and the first row shows the ratings at the end of the year.

Let's interpret one of the numbers. Look at the cell where the rating at the beginning of the year is AA and the rating at the end of the year is AA. This cell represents the percentage of issues rated AA at the beginning of the year that did not change their rating over the year. That is, there were no downgrades or upgrades. As can be seen, 92.75% of the issues rated AA at the start of the year were rated AA at the end of the year. Now look at the cell where the rating at the beginning of the year is AA and at the end of the year is A. This shows the percentage of issues rated AA at the beginning of the year that were downgraded to A by the end of the year. In our hypothetical one-year rating migration table, this percentage is 5.07%. One can view

TABLE 16.2 Hypothetical One-Year Rating Migration Table

Rating at Start of Year	Rating at End of Year								
	AAA	AA	A	BBB	BB	B	CCC	D	Total
AAA	93.20	6.00	0.60	0.12	0.08	0.00	0.00	0.00	100
AA	1.60	92.75	5.07	0.36	0.11	0.07	0.03	0.01	100
A	0.18	2.65	91.91	4.80	0.37	0.02	0.02	0.05	100
BBB	0.04	0.30	5.20	87.70	5.70	0.70	0.16	0.20	100
BB	0.03	0.11	0.61	6.80	81.65	7.10	2.60	1.10	100
B	0.01	0.09	0.55	0.88	7.90	75.67	8.70	6.20	100
CCC	0.00	0.01	0.31	0.84	2.30	8.10	62.54	25.90	100

this figure as a probability. It is the probability that an issue rated AA will be downgraded to A by the end of the year.

A rating migration table also shows the potential for upgrades. Again, using Table 16.2, look at the row that shows issues rated AA at the beginning of the year. Looking at the cell shown in the column AAA rating at the end of the year, there is the figure 1.60%. This figure represents the percentage of issues rated AA at the beginning of the year that were upgraded to AAA by the end of the year.

In general, the following hold for actual rating migration tables. First, the probability of a downgrade is much higher than for an upgrade for investment-grade bonds. Second, the longer the migration period, the lower the probability that an issuer will retain its original rating. That is, a one-year rating migration table will have a lower probability of a downgrade for a particular rating than a five-year rating migration table for that same rating.

Liquidity Risk

Investors who want to sell a bond prior to the maturity date are concerned about whether the price that can be obtained from dealers is close to the true value of the issue. For example, if recent trades in the market for a particular issue have been between 97.25 and 97.75 and market conditions have not changed, investors would expect to sell the bond somewhere in the 97.25 to 97.75 area.

Liquidity risk is the risk that an investor will have to sell a bond below its true value, where the true value is indicated by recent transactions. The primary measure of liquidity is the size of the spread between the bid price (the price at which a dealer is willing to buy a security) and the ask price (the price at which a dealer is willing to sell a security). The wider the bid-ask spread, the greater the liquidity risk.

A liquid market can generally be defined by "small bid-ask spreads which do not materially increase for large transactions" (Gerber 1997, 278). Bid-ask spreads, and therefore liquidity risk, change over time.

For investors who plan to hold a bond until maturity and need not mark a position to market, liquidity risk is not a major concern. An institutional investor that plans to hold an issue to maturity but is periodically marked to market is concerned with liquidity risk. By marking a position to market, it is meant that the security is revalued in the portfolio based on its current market price. For example, mutual funds are required to mark to market at the end of each day the holdings in their portfolio in order to compute the *net asset value* (NAV). While other institutional investors may not mark to market as frequently as mutual funds, they are marked to market when reports are periodically sent to clients or the board of directors or trustees.

Exchange Rate or Currency Risk

For a U.S. investor, nondollar-denominated bond (that is, a bond whose payments are not in U.S. dollars) has unknown U.S. dollar cash flows. The dollar cash flows are dependent on the exchange rate at the time the payments are received. For example, suppose a U.S. investor purchases a bond whose payments are in euros. If the Euro depreciates relative to the U.S. dollar, then fewer dollars will be received. The risk of this occurring is referred to as *exchange rate risk* or *currency risk*. Of course, should the Euro appreciate relative to the U.S. dollar, the investor will benefit by receiving more dollars.

Inflation or Purchasing Power Risk

Inflation risk or *purchasing power risk* arises because of the variation in the value of cash flows from a security due to inflation, as measured in terms of purchasing power. For example, if an investor purchases a bond with a coupon rate of 7%, but the rate of inflation is 8%, the purchasing power of the cash flow has declined. For all but floating rate securities, an investor is exposed to inflation risk because the interest rate the issuer promises to make is fixed for the life of the issue. To the extent that interest rates reflect the expected inflation rate, floating rate securities have a lower level of inflation risk. There are securities indexed to the rate of inflation and these securities are discussed in the next chapter.

SUMMARY

In this chapter, we have described the basic features of bonds and their investment characteristics. Bond prices are quoted as a percentage of par value, with par value equal to 100. The coupon rate is the interest rate that the issuer agrees to pay each year; the coupon is the annual amount of the interest payment and is found by multiplying the par value by the coupon rate. Zero-coupon bonds do not make periodic coupon payments; the bondholder realizes interest at the maturity date equal to the difference between the maturity value and the price paid for the bond. A step-up note is a security whose coupon rate increases over time.

A floating rate security is an issue whose coupon rate resets periodically based on some formula; the typical coupon reset formula is some reference rate plus a spread (referred to as the quoted margin). A floating rate security may have a cap which sets the maximum coupon rate that will be paid at a reset date; a cap is a disadvantage to the bondholder while a floor is an advantage to the bondholder. An inverse floater is an issue whose coupon rate moves in the opposite direction from the change in the reference rate.

Accrued interest is the amount of interest accrued since the last coupon payment and in the United States (as well as in many countries), the bond buyer must pay the bond seller the accrued interest. The full price of a security is the agreed-upon price plus accrued interest; the clean price is the agreed-upon price without accrued interest.

A bond issue may have a call provision granting the issuer an option to retire all or part of the issue prior to the stated maturity date. A call provision is an advantage to the issuer and a disadvantage to the bondholder. When a callable bond is issued, typically the issuer may not call the bond for a number of years; that is, there is a deferred call. Most new bond issues, even if currently callable, usually have some restrictions against refunding. For an amortizing security backed by a pool of loans, the borrowers typically have the right to prepay in whole or in part prior to the scheduled principal repayment date; this provision is called a prepayment option.

A putable bond is one in which the bondholder has the right to sell the issue back to the issuer at a specified price on designated dates. A convertible bond is an issue giving the bondholder the right to exchange the bond for a specified number of shares of the issuer's common stock.

Bonds expose an investor to various risks. The price of a bond changes inversely with a change in market interest rates. Interest rate risk refers to the adverse price movement of a bond as a result of a change in market interest rates; for the owner of a bond it is the risk that interest rates will rise. The coupon rate and maturity of a bond affect its price sensitivity to changes in market interest rates. The duration of a bond measures the approximate percentage price change for a 100 basis point change in interest rates.

Call risk and prepayment risk refer to the risk that a security will be paid off before the scheduled principal repayment date. From an investor's perspective, the disadvantages to call and prepayment provisions are (1) the cash flow pattern is uncertain; (2) reinvestment risk because proceeds received will have to be reinvested at a relatively lower interest rate; and (3) the capital appreciation potential of a bond will be reduced.

While typically market participants think of credit risk in terms of the failure of a borrower to make timely interest and principal payments on a debt obligation, this is only one form of credit risk: credit default risk. Markets participants typically gauge this risk in terms of the credit rating assigned by independent entities called rating agencies. The other types of credit risk are credit spread risk and downgrade risk.

Liquidity risk depends on the ease with which an issue can be sold at or near its true value and is primarily gauged by the bid-ask spread quoted by dealers. From the perspective of a U.S. investor, exchange rate risk is the risk that a currency in which a security is denominated will depreciate relative to

APPENDIX: CALCULATING ACCRUED INTEREST

In this appendix, we explain how to calculate accrued interest. When calculating accrued interest, three pieces of information are needed: (1) the number of days in the accrued interest period, (2) the number of days in the coupon period, and (3) the dollar amount of the coupon payment. The number of days in the accrued interest period represents the number of days over which the investor has earned interest. Given these values, the accrued interest (AI), assuming semiannual payments, is calculated as follows:

$$AI = \frac{\text{Annual coupon}}{2} \times \frac{\text{Days in AI period}}{\text{Days in coupon period}}$$

For example, suppose that (1) there are 50 days in the accrued interest period, (2) there are 183 days in a coupon period, and (3) the annual coupon per $100 of par value is $8. Then the accrued interest is:

$$AI = \frac{\$8}{2} \times \frac{50}{183} = \$1.029$$

It is not simple to determine the number of days in the accrued interest period and the number of days in the coupon period. The calculation begins with the determination of three key dates: (1) trade date, (2) settlement date, and (3) value date. The *trade date* is the date on which the transaction is executed. The *settlement date* is the date a transaction is completed. The settlement date varies by the type of bond. Unlike the settlement date, the *value date* is not constrained to fall on a business day. Interest accrues on a bond from and including the date of the previous coupon up to but excluding the value date.[5] However, this may differ slightly in some non-U.S. markets. For example, in some countries interest accrues up to and including the value date. For a newly issued security, there is no previous coupon payment. Instead, the interest accrues from a date called the *dated date*.

Day Count Conventions

The number of days in the accrued interest period and the number of days in the coupon period may not be simply the actual number of calendar days between two dates. The reason is that there is a market convention for each

---

[5]This is the definition used by the International Securities Market Association (SMA).

type of security that specifies how to determine the number of days between two dates. These conventions are called *day count conventions*.

In calculating the number of days between two dates, the actual number of days is not always the same as the number of days that should be used in the accrued interest formula. The number of days used depends on the day count convention for the particular security. Specifically, there are different day count conventions for Treasury securities than for government agency securities, municipal bonds, and corporate bonds.

For coupon-bearing Treasury securities, the day count convention used is to determine the actual number of days between two dates. This is referred to as the "actual/actual day count convention." For example, consider a coupon-bearing Treasury security whose previous coupon payment was March 1. The next coupon payment would be on September 1. Suppose this Treasury security is purchased with a value date of July 17. The actual number of days between July 17 (the value date) and September 1 (the date of the next coupon payment) is 46 days as shown below:

July 17 to July 31	14 days
August	31 days
September 1	1 day
	46 days

The number of days in the coupon period is the actual number of days between March 1 and September 1, which is 184 days. The number of days between the last coupon payment (March 1) to July 17 is therefore 138 days (184 days − 46 days).

For coupon-bearing agency, municipal, and corporate bonds, a different day count convention is used. It is assumed that every month has 30 days, that any 6-month period has 180 days, and that there are 360 days in a year. This day count convention is referred to as the "30/360 day count convention." For example, consider a security purchased with a value date of July 17, the previous coupon payment on March 1, and the next coupon payment on September 1. If the security is an agency, municipal, or corporate bond rather than a Treasury security, the number of days until the next coupon payment is 44 days as shown below:

July 17 to July 31	13 days
August	30 days
September 1	1 day
	44 days

The number of days from March 1 to July 17 is 136, which is the number of days in the accrued interest period.

REFERENCES

Fabozzi, F. J. 2009. *Bond markets, analysis and strategies*, 7th ed. Upper Saddle River, NJ: Prentice Hall.

Gerber, R. I. 1997. A user's guide to buy-side bond trading. In *managing fixed income portfolios*, edited by F. J. Fabozzi (pp. 277–290). Hoboken, NJ: John Wiley & Sons.

Moody's Investor Service. 1998. Industrial company rating methodology. *Global Credit Research*, July.

CHAPTER 17

Treasury and Agency Securities, Corporate Bonds, and Municipal Bonds

The U.S. bond market is the largest bond market in the world. The major sectors of the bond market are the (1) Treasury securities market, (2) agency securities market, (3) corporate bond market, (4) municipal bonds market, (5) non-U.S. bond market, (6) agency residential mortgage-backed securities market, (7) nonagency residential mortgage securities market, (8) commercial mortgage-backed securities market, and (9) asset-backed securities market. In this chapter, we cover the first five bond sectors. The last four bond sectors are collectively referred to as the *structured product sector* and because these bonds are more complex than the typical bond structure, we cover them in the next chapter.

TREASURY SECURITIES

The securities issued by the U.S. Department of the Treasury (U.S. Treasury hereafter) are called *Treasury securities*, *Treasuries*, or *U.S. government bonds*. Because they are backed by the full faith and credit of the U.S. government, market participants throughout the world view them as having no credit risk. Hence, the interest rates on Treasury securities are the benchmark, default-free interest rates.

Types of Treasury Securities

There are two types of marketable Treasury securities issued: fixed principal securities and inflation-indexed securities. The securities are issued via a regularly scheduled auction process.

Fixed Principal Securities

The U.S. Treasury issues two types of *fixed principal securities*: discount securities and coupon securities. Discount securities are called *Treasury bills*; coupon securities are called *Treasury notes* and *Treasury bonds*.

Treasury bills are issued at a discount to par value, have no coupon rate, and mature at face value. Generally, Treasury bills can be issued with a maturity of up to two years. The U.S. Treasury typically issues only certain maturities. As of January 2009, the practice of the U.S. Treasury is to issue Treasury bills with maturities of four weeks, 13 weeks, 26 weeks, and 52 weeks.

The U.S. Treasury issues securities with initial maturities of two years or more as coupon securities. Coupon securities are issued at approximately par and, in the case of fixed principal securities, mature at par value. They are not callable. *Treasury notes* are coupon securities issued with original maturities of more than two years but no more than 10 years. The U.S. Treasury issues a two-year note, a five-year note, and a 10-year note. Treasuries with original maturities greater than 10 years are called *Treasury bonds*. The U.S. Treasury issues a 30-year bond.

Treasury Inflation-Protected Securities

The U.S. Treasury issues coupon securities that provide inflation protection and are popularly referred to as *Treasury inflation-protected securities* (TIPS). They do so by having the principal increase or decrease based on the rate of inflation such that when the security matures, the investor receives the greater of the principal adjusted for inflation or the original principal. The U.S. Treasury issues a five-year TIPS, a 10-year TIPS, and a 20-year TIPS.

TIPS work as follows. The coupon rate on an issue is set at a fixed rate, the rate being determined via the auction process just like fixed principal Treasury securities. The coupon rate is referred to as the *real rate* because it is the rate that the investor ultimately earns above the inflation rate. The inflation index used for measuring the inflation rate is the nonseasonally-adjusted U.S. City Average All Items Consumer Price Index for All Urban Consumers (CPI-U).

The adjustment for inflation is as follows: The principal that the U.S. Treasury will base both the dollar amount of the coupon payment and the maturity value on is adjusted semiannually. This is called the *inflation-adjusted principal*. For example, suppose that the coupon rate for a TIPS is 3.5% and the annual inflation rate is 3%. Suppose further that an investor purchases on January 1, $100,000 par value (principal) of this issue. The semiannual inflation rate is 1.5% (3% divided by 2). The inflation-adjusted principal at the end of the first six-month period is found by multiplying the original par value by one plus the semiannual inflation rate. In our example, the inflation-adjusted principal at the end of the first six-month period is $101,500. It is this inflation-adjusted principal that is the basis for computing the coupon interest for the first six-month period. The coupon payment is then 1.75% (one-half the real rate of 3.5%) multiplied by the inflation-adjusted principal at the coupon payment date ($101,500). The coupon payment is therefore $1,776.25.

Let's look at the next six months. The inflation-adjusted principal at the beginning of the period is $101,500. Suppose that the semiannual inflation rate for the second six-month period is 1%. Then the inflation-adjusted principal at the end of the second six-month period is the inflation-adjusted principal at the beginning of the six-month period ($101,500) increased by the semiannual inflation rate (1%). The adjustment to the principal is $1,015 (1% times $101,500). So, the inflation-adjusted principal at the end of the second six-month period (December 31 in our example) is $102,515 ($101,500 + $1,015). The coupon interest that will be paid to the investor at the second coupon payment date is found by multiplying the inflation-adjusted principal on the coupon payment date ($102,515) by one-half the real rate (that is, one-half of 3.5%). That is, the coupon payment will be $1,794.01.

As can be seen, part of the adjustment for inflation comes from the coupon payment since it is based on the inflation-adjusted principal. Because of the possibility of disinflation (that is, price declines), the inflation-adjusted principal at maturity may turn out to be less than the original par value. However, the Treasury has structured TIPS so that they are redeemed at the greater of the inflation-adjusted principal and the original par value.

Stripped Treasury Securities

The U.S. Treasury does not issue zero-coupon notes or bonds. However, because of the demand for zero-coupon instruments with no credit risk, the private sector has created such securities using a process called *coupon stripping*.

To illustrate the process, suppose that $2 billion of a 10-year fixed principal Treasury note with a coupon rate of 5% is purchased by a dealer firm to create zero-coupon Treasury securities. The cash flow from this Treasury note is 20 semiannual payments of $50 million each ($2 billion times 0.05 divided by 2) and the repayment of principal of $2 billion 10 years from now. As there are 21 different payments to be made by the U.S. Treasury for this note, a security representing a single payment claim on each payment is issued, which is effectively a zero-coupon Treasury security. The amount of the maturity value or a security backed by a particular payment, whether coupon or principal, depends on the amount of the payment to be made by the U.S. Treasury on the underlying Treasury note. In our example, 20 zero-coupon Treasury securities each have a maturity value of $50 million, and one zero-coupon Treasury security, backed by the principal, has a maturity value of $2 billion. The maturity dates for the zero-coupon Treasury securities coincide with the corresponding payment dates by the U.S. Treasury.

Zero-coupon Treasury securities are created as part of the U.S. Treasury's Separate Trading of Registered Interest and Principal of Securities (STRIPS) program to facilitate the stripping of designated Treasury securities.

FEDERAL AGENCY SECURITIES

Federal agency securities can be classified by the type of issuer—federally related institutions and government-sponsored enterprises. Federal agencies that provide credit for certain sectors of the credit market issue two types of securities: debentures and mortgage-backed securities. We review the former securities here and the latter in the next chapter.

Federally Related Institutions

Federally related institutions are arms of the federal government and generally do not issue securities directly into the marketplace. Federally related institutions include the Export-Import Bank of the United States, the Tennessee Valley Authority, the Commodity Credit Corporation, the Farmers Housing Administration, the General Services Administration, the Government National Mortgage Association, the Maritime Administration, the Private Export Funding Corporation, the Rural Electrification Administration, the Rural Telephone Bank, the Small Business Administration, and the Washington Metropolitan Area Transit Authority.

With the exception of securities of the Tennessee Valley Authority (TVA) and the Private Export Funding Corporation, the securities are backed by the full faith and credit of the U.S. government. The federally related institution that has issued securities in recent years is the TVA.

Government-Sponsored Enterprises

Government-sponsored enterprises (GSEs) are privately owned, publicly chartered entities. They were created by Congress to reduce the cost of capital for certain borrowing sectors of the economy deemed to be important enough to warrant assistance. GSEs issue securities directly in the marketplace.

There are five GSEs that currently issue debentures: Freddie Mac, Fannie Mae, Federal Home Loan Bank System, Federal Farm Credit System, and the Federal Agricultural Mortgage Corporation. Fannie Mae, Freddie Mac, and Federal Home Loan Bank are responsible for providing credit to the housing sectors. The Federal Agricultural Mortgage Corporation provides the same function for agricultural mortgage loans. The Federal Farm Credit Bank System is responsible for the credit market in the agricultural sector of the economy.

With the exception of the securities issued by the Farm Credit Financial Assistance Corporation, GSE securities are not backed by the full faith and credit of the U.S. government, as is the case with Treasury securities. Consequently, investors purchasing GSEs are exposed to credit risk. However, a bailout program for Fannie Mae and Freddie Mac has resulted in some of its debt instruments being backed by the U.S. Treasury.

CORPORATE BONDS

Corporations are classified into five general categories: utilities, transportations, industrials, banks, and finance (nonbanks). Within these five general categories finer breakdowns are often made to create more homogeneous groupings. For example, utilities are subdivided into electric power companies, gas distribution companies, water companies, and communication companies. Transportations are divided further into airlines, railroads, and trucking companies. Industrials are the catchall class and the most heterogeneous of the groupings with respect to investment characteristics because this category includes all kinds of manufacturing, merchandising, and service companies.

Security for Bonds

A corporate bond can be secured or unsecured. In the case of a secured bond, either real property (e.g., real estate) or personal property (e.g. equipment) may be pledged to offer security beyond that of the general credit standing of the issuer. With a *mortgage bond*, the issuer has granted the bondholders a lien against the pledged assets. A *lien* is a legal right to sell mortgaged property to satisfy unpaid obligations to bondholders. Mortgage bonds where the indenture does not limit the total amount of bonds that may be issued is called an *open-ended mortgage*. The mortgage generally is a first lien on the company's real estate, fixed property, and franchises, subject to certain exceptions or permitted encumbrances owned at the time of the execution of the indenture or its supplement. The *after-acquired property clause* also subjects to the mortgage property that is acquired by the company after the filing of the original or supplemental indenture.

In practice, foreclosure and sale of mortgaged property are unusual. If a default occurs, there is usually a reorganization of the issuer in which provision is made for settlement of the debt to bondholders. The mortgage lien is important, though, because it gives the mortgage bondholders a very strong bargaining position relative to other creditors in determining the terms of a reorganization.

Some companies do not own fixed assets or other real property, and so have nothing on which they can give a mortgage lien to secure bondholders. Instead, they own securities of other companies; they are holding companies, and the other companies are subsidiaries. To satisfy the desire of bondholders for security, the issuer grants investors a lien on stocks, notes, bonds, or whatever other kind of financial assets it owns. These assets are termed collateral (or personal property), and bonds secured by such assets are called *collateral trust bonds*.

Debenture bonds are not secured by a specific pledge of property, but that does not mean that bondholders have no claim on the property of issuers. Debenture bondholders have the claim of general creditors on all assets of the issuer not pledged specifically to secure other debt. And they even have a claim on pledged assets to the extent that those assets have value greater than necessary to satisfy secured creditors. *Subordinated debenture bonds* are issues that rank after secured debt, after debenture bonds, and often after some general creditors in the claim on assets and earnings. One of the important protective provisions for debenture bonds is the *negative pledge clause*. This provision prohibits a company from creating or assuming any lien to secure a debt issue without equally securing the subject bond issue(s) (with certain exceptions). Its inclusion in the indenture is designed to prevent other creditors from obtaining a senior position at the expense of existing creditors; however, it is not intended to prevent other creditors from sharing in the position of debenture bondholders.

Table 17.1 provides a summary of claim priority of corporate bondholders. It is important to recognize that while a superior legal status will strengthen a bondholder's chance of recovery in case of default, it will not absolutely prevent bondholders from suffering financial loss when the issuer's ability to generate cash flow adequate to pay its obligations is seriously eroded. Claims against a weak lender are oftentimes satisfied for less than face value.

Some corporate issuers have other companies guarantee their bonds. This is normally done when a subsidiary issues bonds and the investors want the added protection of a third-party guarantee. The use of guarantees makes it easier and more convenient to finance special projects and affiliates, although guarantees are extended to operating company debt. Another credit-enhancing feature is the *letter of credit* (LOC) issued by a bank. An

TABLE 17.1 Claim Priority of Corporate Bondholders

Corporate Bonds	Pledged Property	Priority Claim
Secured		
Mortgage bonds	Fixed assets or real property	First against pledged; then as general claimant against issuer
Collateral trust bonds	Securities	First against pledged property; then as general claimant against issuer
Unsecured		
Debenture bonds	None	As general claimant
Subordinate debentures	None	As claimant after debenture bondholders

LOC requires the bank to make payments to the trustee when requested so that monies will be available for the bond issuer to meet its interest and principal payments when due. Thus, the credit of the bank under the LOC is substituted for that of the bond issuer.

Noninvestment Grade Bonds (Speculative-Grade Bonds)

As explained in the previous chapter, the bond market can be classified into the investment-grade sector and the speculative grade sector. The latter sector—referred to as the *noninvestment grade bond sector*, *high-yield bond sector*, and *junk bond sector*—includes bond issues rated below investment grade by the rating agencies (that is, BBB– and lower by Standard & Poor's and Fitch Ratings and Baa3 and lower by Moody's). They may also be unrated, but not all unrated debt is speculative.

Types of Issuers

Several types of issuers fall into the noninvestment-grade bond sector. These include (1) original issuers, (2) fallen angels, and (3) restructuing and leveraged buyouts.

Original issuers may be young, growing corporations lacking the stronger balance sheet and income statement profile of many established corporations, but often with lots of promise. Also called venture capital situations or growth or emerging market companies, the bond is often sold with a story projecting future financial strength. There are also the established operating firms with financials neither measuring up to the strengths of investment-grade corporations nor possessing the weaknesses of companies on the verge of bankruptcy.

Fallen angels are formerly companies with investment-grade-rated debt that have come upon hard times with deteriorating balance sheet and income statement financial parameters.[1] They may be in default or near bankruptcy. In these cases, investors are interested in the workout value of the debt in a reorganization or liquidation, whether within or without the bankruptcy courts. Some refer to these issues as "special situations." Over the years they have fallen on hard times; some have recovered and others have not. General Motors Corporation and Ford Motor Company are examples of fallen angels. From 1954 to 1981, General Motors Corp. was rated AAA by S&P; Ford Motor Co. was rated AA by S&P from 1971 to 1980. In August 2005, Moody's lowered the rating on both automakers to junk bond status.

Restructurings and leveraged buyouts are companies that have deliberately increased their debt burden with a view toward maximizing shareholder value. The shareholders may be the existing public group to which the company pays a special extraordinary dividend, with the funds coming from borrowings and the sale of assets. Cash is paid out, net worth decreased and leverage increased, and ratings drop on existing debt. Newly issued debt gets junk bond status because of the company's weakened financial condition. In a leveraged buyout (LBO), a new and private shareholder group owns and manages the company. The bond issue's purpose may be to retire other debt from banks and institutional investors incurred to finance the LBO.

Unique Features of Some Issues

Often actions that are taken by management that result in the assignment of a noninvestment-grade bond rating result in a heavy corporate interest payment burden. This places severe cash flow constraints on the firm. To reduce this burden, firms involved with heavy debt burdens have issued bonds with deferred coupon structures that permit the issuer to avoid using cash to make interest payments for a period of three to seven years. There are three types of deferred coupon structures: (1) deferred-interest bonds, (2) step-up bonds, and (3) payment-in-kind bonds. We discussed the first two bond structures in the previous chapter.

Payment-in-kind (PIK) bonds give the issuer an option to pay cash at a coupon payment date or give the bondholder a similar bond (that is, a bond with the same coupon rate and a par value equal to the amount of the coupon payment that would have been paid).

---

[1] Companies that have been upgraded to investment-grade status are referred to as *rising stars*.

Convertible Bonds

A *convertible bond* grants the bondholder the right to convert the bond into a predetermined number of shares of common stock of the issuer. An *exchangeable bond* grants the bondholder the right to exchange the security for the common stock of a firm other than the issuer. Although we refer to convertible bonds throughout out discussion, the principles also apply to exchangeable bonds. Throughout this chapter we use the term convertible bond to refer to both convertible and exchangeable bonds.

The number of shares of common stock that the bondholder will receive from exercising the call option of a convertible bond is called the *conversion ratio*. The conversion privilege may extend for all or only some portion of the convertible bond's life, and the stated conversion ratio may change over time. It is always adjusted proportionately for stock splits and stock dividends.

At the time of issuance of a convertible bond, the issuer effectively grants the bondholder the right to purchase the common stock at a price equal to:

$$\frac{\text{Par value of convertible bond}}{\text{Conversion ratio}}$$

This price is referred to in the prospectus as the *stated conversion price*.

Almost all convertible bonds are callable by the issuer. Typically there is a noncall period (i.e., a time period from the time of issuance that the convertible bond may not be called). There are some issues that have a provisional call feature that allows the issuer to call the issue during the noncall period if the price of the stock reaches a certain price. The call price schedule of a convertible bond is specified at the time of issuance. Typically, the call price declines over time.

A put option grants the bondholder the right to require the issuer to redeem the issue at designated dates for a predetermined price. Some convertible bonds are putable. Put options can be classified as "hard" puts and "soft" puts. A hard put is one in which the convertible bond must be redeemed by the issuer only for cash. In the case of a soft put, the issuer has the option to redeem the convertible bond for cash, common stock, subordinated notes, or a combination of the three.

MUNICIPAL BONDS

Issuers of *municipal bonds* include municipalities, counties, towns and townships, school districts, and special service system districts. Included in the category of municipalities are cities, villages, boroughs, and incorporated towns that received a special state charter. A special purpose service system district, or simply special district, is a political subdivision created to foster economic development or related services to a geographical area. Special districts provide public utility services (water, sewers, and drainage) and fire protection services. Public agencies or instrumentalities include authorities and commissions.

There are both tax-exempt and taxable municipal securities. "Tax-exempt" means that interest on a municipal security is exempt from federal income taxation. The tax exemption of municipal securities applies to interest income, not capital gains. The exemption may or may not extend to taxation at the state and local levels. The state tax treatment depends on (1) whether the issue from which the interest income is received is an "in-state issue" or an "out-of-state issue"; and (2) whether the investor is an individual or a corporation. The treatment of interest income at the state level will be one of the following:

1. Taxation of interest from municipal issues regardless of whether the issuer is in state or out of state.
2. Exemption of interest from all municipal issues regardless of whether the issuer is in state or out of state.
3. Exemption of interest from municipal issues that are in state but some form of taxation where the source of interest is an out-of-state issuer.

Most municipal securities that have been issued are tax exempt. Municipal securities are commonly referred to as tax-exempt securities although taxable municipal securities have been issued and are traded in the market. Municipalities issue *taxable municipal bonds* to finance projects that do not qualify for financing with tax-exempt bonds. An example is a sports stadium. The most common types of taxable municipal bonds are *industrial revenue bonds* and *economic development bonds*. Since there are federally mandated restrictions on the amount of tax-exempt bonds that can be issued, a municipality will issue taxable bonds when the maximum is reached. There are some issuers who have issued taxable bonds in order to take advantage of demand outside of the United States.[2]

Types of Municipal Bonds

Municipal bonds are issued for various purposes. Short-term notes typically are sold in anticipation of the receipt of funds from taxes or receipt

---

[2]There are other types of tax-exempt bonds. These include bonds issued by non-profit organizations. Since the tax-exempt designation is provided pursuant to Section 501(c)(3) of the Internal Revenue Code, the tax-exempt bonds issued by such organizations are referred to as 501(c)(3) obligations. Museums and foundations fall into this category.

of proceeds from the sale of a bond issue, for example. Proceeds from the sale of short-term notes permit the issuing municipality to cover seasonal and temporary imbalances between outlays for expenditures and inflows from taxes. Municipalities issue long-term bonds as the principal means for financing both (1) long-term capital projects such as schools, bridges, roads, and airports, and (2) long-term budget deficits that arise from current operations.

An *official statement* describing the issue and the issuer is prepared for new offerings. Municipal securities have legal opinions that are summarized in the official statement. The importance of the legal opinion is twofold. First, bond counsel determines if the issue is indeed legally able to issue the securities. Second, bond counsel verifies that the issuer has properly prepared for the bond sale by having enacted various required ordinances, resolutions, and trust indentures and without violating any other laws and regulations.

There are basically two types of municipal security structures: tax-backed debt and revenue bonds. We describe each type, as well as variants.

Tax-Backed Debt

Tax-backed debt obligations are secured by some form of tax revenue. The broadest type of tax-backed debt obligation is the general obligation debt. Other types that fall into the category of tax-backed debt are appropriation-backed obligations, debt obligations supported by public credit enhancement programs, and short-term debt instruments.

General Obligation Debt General obligation pledges include unlimited and limited tax general obligation debt. The stronger form is the unlimited tax general obligation debt because it is secured by the issuer's unlimited taxing power (corporate and individual income taxes, sales taxes, and property taxes) and is said to be secured by the full faith and credit of the issuer. A limited tax general obligation debt is a limited tax pledge because for such debt there is a statutory ceiling on the tax rates that may be levied to service the issuer's debt.

There are general obligation bonds that are secured not only by the issuer's general taxing powers to create revenues accumulated in a general fund, but also secured by designated fees, grants, and special charges from outside the general fund. Due to the dual nature of the revenue sources, bonds with this security feature are referred to as "double-barreled in security." As an example, special purpose service systems issue bonds that are secured by a pledge of property taxes, a pledge of special fees/operating revenue from the service provided, or a pledge of both property taxes and special fees and operating revenues.

Appropriation-Backed Obligations Bond issues of some agencies or authorities carry a potential state liability for making up shortfalls in the issuing entity's obligation. While the appropriation of funds must be approved by the issuer's state legislature, and hence they are referred to as *appropriation-backed obligations*, the state's pledge is not binding. Because of this nonbinding pledge of tax revenue, such issues are referred to as *moral obligation bonds*.

Dedicated Tax-Backed Obligations States and local governments have issued increasing amounts of bonds where the debt service is to be paid from so-called dedicated revenues such as sales taxes, tobacco settlement payments, fees, and penalty payments. Many are structured to mimic asset-backed securities discussed in the next chapter.

One type of dedicated tax-backed obligation is a tobacco settlement revenue (TSR) bond. This bond is backed by the tobacco settlement payments owed to the state or local entity resulting from the master settlement agreement between most of the states and the four major U.S. tobacco companies in November 1998.

Revenue Bonds

Revenue bonds are the second basic type of security structure found in the municipal bond market. These bonds are issued for enterprise financings that are secured by the revenues generated by the completed projects themselves, or for general public-purpose financings in which the issuers pledge to the bondholders the tax and revenue resources that were previously part of the general fund. This latter type of revenue bond is usually created to allow issuers to raise debt outside general obligation debt limits and without voter approval.

The trust indenture for a municipal revenue bond details how revenue received by the enterprise will be distributed. This is referred to as the *flow-of-funds structure*. In a typical revenue bond, the revenue is first distributed into a revenue fund. It is from that fund that disbursements for expenses are made.

Revenue bonds can be classified by the type of financing. These include utility revenue bonds, transportation revenue bonds, housing revenue bonds, higher education revenue bonds, health care revenue bonds, seaport revenue bonds, sports complex and convention center revenue bonds, and industrial development revenue bonds.[3]

---

[3]For a more detailed description of these bonds, see Cavallaro (2008), Mincke (2008), Muller (2008), Oliver and Clements (2008), Spiotto (2008), and Van Kuller (2008a, 2008b).

Special Bond Structures

Some municipal securities have special security structures. These include *insured bonds, bank-backed municipal bonds*, and *refunded bonds*.

Insured Bonds Municipal bonds can be credit enhanced by an unconditional guarantee of a commercial insurance company. The insurance cannot be canceled and typically is in place for the term of the bond. The insurance provides for the insurance company writing the policy to make payments to the bondholders of any principal and/or coupon interest that is due on a stated maturity date but that has not been paid by the bond issuer. The insurer's payment is not an advance of the payments due by the issuer but is rather made according to the original repayment schedule obligation of the issuer.[4]

The insurers of municipal bonds are typically monoline insurance companies that are primarily in the business of providing guarantees. While almost half of municipal bonds were insured prior to 2007, beginning in 2008 there was considerably less issuance of such bonds because of the major difficulties faced by monoline insurance companies resulting from the subprime mortgage crisis. With the deteriorating financial difficulties faced by monolines insurers, very little issuance is expected in the future.

Bank-Backed Bonds Municipal issuers have increasingly used various types of facilities provided by commercial banks to credit enhance and thereby improve the marketability of issues.[5] There are three basic types of bank support: letter of credit, irrevocable line of credit, and revolving line of credit. A *letter of credit* (LOC) is the strongest type of support available from a commercial bank. The parties to a LOC agreement are (1) the bank that issues the LOC (that is, the LOC issuer), (2) the municipal issuer who is requesting the LOC in connection with a security (the LOC-backed bonds), and (3) the LOC beneficiary who is typically the trustee. The municipal issuer is obligated to reimburse the LOC issuer for any funds it draws down under the agreement.

There are two types of LOCs: direct-pay LOC and standby LOC. With a *direct-pay LOC*, typically the issuer is entitled to draw upon the LOC in order to make interest and principal payments if a certain event occurs. The LOC beneficiary receives payments from the LOC issuer with the trustee having to request a payment. In contrast, with a *standby LOC*, the LOC beneficiary typically can only draw down on the agreement if the municipal issuer fails to make interest and/or principal payments at the contractual

---

[4]For a further discussion of insured bonds, see Zerega (2008).
[5]For a further discussion of bank-backed bonds, see Cirillo (2008).

due date. The LOC beneficiary must first request payment from the municipal issuer before drawing upon the LOC.

An irrevocable line of credit is not a guarantee of the bond issue, though it does provide a level of security. A revolving line of credit is a liquidity-type credit facility that provides a source of liquidity for payment of maturing debt in the event no other funds of the issuer are currently available. Because a bank can cancel a revolving line of credit without notice if the issuer fails to meet certain covenants, bond security depends entirely on the creditworthiness of the municipal issuer.

Refunded Bonds Municipal bonds are sometimes refunded and such bonds are so-named *refunded bonds*. An issuer may refund a bond issue in order to: (1) reduce funding costs after taking into account the costs of refunding; (2) eliminate burdensome restrictive covenants; and (3) alter the debt maturity structure for budgetary reasons.

Often, a refunding takes place when the original bond issue is escrowed or collateralized by direct obligations guaranteed by the U.S. government. By this it is meant that a portfolio of securities guaranteed by the U.S. government is placed in a trust. The portfolio of securities is assembled such that the cash flows from the securities match the obligations that the issuer must pay. For example, suppose that a municipality has a 5%, $200 million issue with 15 years remaining to maturity. The bond obligation therefore calls for the issuer to make payments of $5 million every six months for the next 15 years and $200 million 15 years from now. If the issuer wants to refund this issue, a portfolio of U.S. government obligations can be purchased that has a cash flow that matches that liability structure: $5 million every six months for the next 15 years and $200 million 15 years from now. Once this portfolio of securities whose cash flows match those of the municipality's obligation is in place, the refunded bonds are no longer general obligation or revenue bonds. Instead, the issue is supported by the cash flows from the portfolio of securities held in an escrow fund. Such bonds, if escrowed with securities guaranteed by the U.S. government, have little, if any, credit risk and are therefore the safest municipal bonds available.

The escrow fund for a refunded municipal bond can be structured so that the refunded bonds are to be called at the first possible call date or a subsequent call date established in the original bond indenture. Such bonds are known as *prerefunded bonds*. While refunded bonds are usually retired at their first or subsequent call date, some are structured to match the debt obligation to the retirement date. Such bonds are known as *escrowed-to-maturity bonds*.[6]

---

[6]For a further discussion of refunded municipal bonds, see Feldstein (2008).

NON-U.S. BONDS

Non-U.S. bonds include government/sovereign bonds, Eurobonds, and European covered bonds.

Sovereign Bonds

While U.S. government securities are not rated by any nationally recognized statistical rating organization, the bonds of other national governments are rated. These ratings are referred to as "sovereign ratings." The two general categories used by rating agencies in deriving their ratings are economic risk and political risk. The former category is an assessment of the ability of a government to satisfy its obligations. Both quantitative and qualitative analyses are used in assessing economic risk. Political risk is an assessment of the willingness of a government to satisfy its obligations. A government may have the ability to pay but may be unwilling to pay. Political risk is assessed based on qualitative analysis of the economic and political factors that influence a government's economic policies.

There are two ratings assigned to each national government. The first is a local currency debt rating and the second is a foreign currency debt rating. The reason for distinguishing between the two types of debt is that, historically, the default frequency differs by the currency denomination of the bond. Specifically, defaults have been greater on foreign currency-denominated debt. The reason for the difference in default rates for local currency debt and foreign currency debt is that if a government is willing to raise taxes and control its domestic financial system, it can generate sufficient local currency to meet its local currency debt obligation. This is not the case with foreign currency–denominated debt. A national government must purchase foreign currency to meet a debt obligation in that foreign currency and therefore has less control with respect to its exchange rate. Thus, a significant depreciation of the local currency relative to a foreign currency in which a debt obligation is denominated will impair a national government's ability to satisfy such obligation.

The implication of this is that the factors rating agencies analyze in assessing the creditworthiness of a national government's local currency debt and foreign currency debt will differ to some extent. In assessing the credit quality of local currency debt, for example, S&P emphasizes domestic government policies that foster or impede timely debt service. The key factors looked at by S&P are:[7]

- Stability of political institutions and degree of popular participation in the political process.

---
[7]See Beers (1997).

- The economic system and structure.
- Living standards and degree of social and economic cohesion.
- Fiscal policy and budgetary flexibility.
- Public debt burden and debt service track record.
- Monetary policy and inflation pressures.
- For foreign currency debt, credit analysis by S&P focuses on the interaction of domestic and foreign government policies.

S&P analyzes a country's balance of payments and the structure of its external balance sheet. The areas of analysis with respect to its external balance sheet are the net public debt, total net external debt, and net external liabilities

The largest government bond market outside of the United States is the Japanese government bond market followed by the markets in Italy, Germany, and France.

As explained earlier, in the U.S. government bond market the interest and one principal payment can be separated and sold as a separate security. Many Euro government bonds can be stripped to create zero-coupon securities.

Sovereign governments also issue inflation-linked bonds. As explained earlier, the U.S. Department of the Treasury issues coupon securities indexed to TIPS. The largest non-U.S. government issuer of inflation-linked bonds is the United Kingdom, followed by France. These bonds, popularly referred to as *linkers* in Europe, are typically linked to a *consumer price index* (CPI).

Eurobonds

A Eurobond has the following four features:

1. They are underwritten by an international syndicate.
2. At issuance they are offered simultaneously to investors in a number of countries.
3. They are issued outside the jurisdiction of any single country.
4. They are not regulated by the single country whose currency is used to pay bondholders.

The Eurobond market is divided into sectors depending on the currency in which the issue is denominated. For example, when Eurobonds are denominated in U.S. dollars, they are referred to as *Eurodollar bonds*. Eurobonds denominated in Japanese yen are referred to as *Euroyen bonds*. Issuers of Eurobonds include national governments and their subdivisions, corporations (financial and nonfinancial), and supranationals.

There are five types of Eurobond structures: straight bonds, subordinated notes, floating rate notes, convertibles, and asset-backed securities.

Euro straights are the traditional fixed rate coupon bonds. They are issued on an unsecured basis and usually issued by high-quality entities. As explained in the previous chapter, with subordinated notes the rights of the bondholder are subordinate to the rights of other creditors.

We discussed the characteristics of floating-rate bonds in the previous chapter. The reference rate for Euro floating-rate notes is either the London Interbank Offered Rate, the bid on LIBOR (referred to as LIBID), or the arithmetic average of LIBOR and LIBID (referred to as LIMEAN). Many issues have either a minimum coupon rate (or floor) that the coupon rate cannot fall below and a maximum coupon rate (or cap) that the coupon rate cannot rise above. Some issues grant the borrower the right to convert from a floating rate to a fixed rate at some time. Moreover, some issues, referred to as *drop-lock bonds*, automatically change the floating coupon rate into a fixed coupon rate under certain circumstances. There are floating-rate notes with a stated maturity date and those with no state maturity date (referred to as *perpetual issues* or *undated issues*).

A convertible Eurobond is one that can be converted into either equity, another bond, or the currency in which the principal or currency can be paid. There are Eurobonds with warrants attached. A warrant is a form of an option that grants the owner of the warrant the right to enter into another financial transaction with the issuer if the owner will benefit as a result of exercising.

Asset-backed securities are explained in the next chapter.

European Covered Bonds

Covered bonds are issued by banks and constitute one of the largest sectors of the European bond market. There are at least 20 European countries with a covered bonds market. The collateral for covered bonds is primarily residential mortgage loans or commercial mortgage loans. The German mortgage-bond market, called the *Pfandbriefe market*, is the largest covered bond market.

The term "covered bonds" is used for this type of bond because there is a pool of loans that is the collateral, which is referred to as the *cover pool*. The loans in the cover pool changes over the bond's life. Here is the way covered bonds work. There are two claims that bondholders have. The first claim is on the cover pool itself. At issuance there is no legal separation of the cover pool from the assets of the issuing bank. However, if after issuance the issuing bank becomes insolvent, at that time the loans that are in the cover pool are segregated from the issuing bank's other assets and held for the benefit of the bondholders. The second claim is against the issuing bank. Covered bonds are typically rated triple A or double A because the loans in the covered pool are of high credit quality and are issued by strong banks.

Covered bonds in many countries are created using the securitization process that will be described in next chapter. Because of this, they are often compared to residential mortgage-backed securities, commercial mortgage-backed securities, and other asset-backed securities. In fact, given the difficulties in the U.S. residential mortgage-backed securities market that began in the summer of 2007, it is expected that there will be greater issuance of covered bonds issued by U.S. entities. The difference between these securities created from a securitization is threefold. While we have not covered securitization yet, we explain the differences anyway. First, at issuance, in a securitization the bank that originated the loans will sell a pool of loans to a special purpose vehicle (SPV). By doing so, the bank has removed the loan pool from its balance sheet. The SPV is the issuer of the securities referred to as mortgage-backed securities. In contrast, with covered bonds, the issuing bank holds the loan pool on its balance sheet and it is only if the issuing bank becomes insolvent that the cover pool is segregated for the benefit of the bondholders. The second difference is that bondholders in mortgage-backed securities do not have recourse to the issuing bank that sold the pool of loans to the SPV. In contrast, bondholders of covered bonds have recourse to the issuing bank. The third difference is that for mortgage-backed securities, the group of loans once assembled does not change whereas it does for covered bonds.

SUMMARY

Treasury coupon securities include fixed-principal and inflation-protected principal securities. Securities issued by the U.S. Treasury are viewed as free of default. While the U.S. Treasury does not issue zero-coupon notes and bonds, these instruments are created by dealers via a coupon stripping process.

Federal agency securities include federally related institutions and government-sponsored enterprises. Federally related institutions are arms of the federal government and generally do not issue securities directly into the marketplace. With the exception of the Tennessee Valley Authority and the Private Export Funding Corporation, federally related institutions are backed by the full faith and credit of the U.S. government. Government-sponsored enterprises are privately owned, publicly chartered entities that do not typically carry the full faith and credit of the U.S. government.

Corporate bonds can represent either secured debt or unsecured debt. Speculative corporate bonds—more commonly referred to as high-yield bonds and junk bonds—have unique structural provisions: deferred interest, step-up, and payment-in-kind. A convertible bond is a bond issue grants the bondholder the right to convert the bond into a predetermined number of shares of common stock of the issuer. Convertible bonds are typically callable and some are putable.

Municipal securities are issued by state and local governments as well as authorities created by them. There are basically two types of municipal security structures: tax-backed debt and revenue bonds. There are also municipal bonds with special structures (insured bonds, bank-backed bonds, and refunded bonds).

Non-U.S. bonds include government/sovereign bonds, Eurobonds, and European covered bonds. These bonds are rated by the three major rating agencies. There are five types of Eurobond structures: straight bonds, subordinated notes, floating-rate notes, convertibles, and asset-backed securities. Covered bonds are issued by banks with the collateral being a pool of residential mortgage loans or commercial mortgage loans (the cover pool).

REFERENCES

Cavallaro, L. 2008. Hospital bond analysis. In *The handbook of municipal bonds,* edited by S. G. Feldstein and F. J. Fabozzi (pp. 845–858). Hoboken, NJ: John Wiley & Sons.

Cirillo, D. K. 2008. How to analyze the municipal bond insurers and the bonds they insure. In *The handbook of municipal bonds,* edited by S. G. Feldstein and F. J. Fabozzi (pp. 1085–1099). Hoboken, NJ: John Wiley & Sons.

Feldstein, S. G. 2008. How to analyze refunded municipal bonds. In *The handbook of municipal bonds,* edited by S. G. Feldstein and F. J. Fabozzi (pp. 1035–1038). Hoboken, NJ: John Wiley & Sons.

Mincke, B. 2008. How to analyze higher education bonds. In *The handbook of municipal bonds,* edited by S. G. Feldstein and F. J. Fabozzi (pp. 1055–1075). Hoboken, NJ: John Wiley & Sons.

Muller, R. H. 2008. Toll road analysis. In *The handbook of municipal bonds,* edited by S. G. Feldstein and F. J. Fabozzi (pp. 981–993). Hoboken, NJ: John Wiley & Sons.

Oliver, W. E., and Clements, D. 2008. How to analyze airport revenue bonds. In *The handbook of municipal bonds,* edited by S. G. Feldstein and F. J. Fabozzi (pp. 813–818). Hoboken, NJ: John Wiley & Sons.

Spiotto, J. E. 2008. Tax-exempt airport finance: Tales from the friendly skies. In S. G. Feldstein and F. J. Fabozzi (eds.), *The Handbook of Municipal Bonds* (pp. 1165–1184). Hoboken, NJ: John Wiley & Sons.

Van Kuller, K. 2008a. Single-family housing bonds. In *The handbook of municipal bonds,* edited by S. G. Feldstein and F. J. Fabozzi (pp. 861–891). Hoboken, NJ: JohnWiley & Sons.

Van Kuller, K. 2008b. Multifamily housing bonds. In *The handbook of municipal bonds*, edited by S. G. Feldstein and F. J. Fabozzi (pp. 893–921). Hoboken, NJ: John Wiley & Sons.

Zerega, T. 2008. The use of letters-of-credit in connection with municipal securities. In *The handbook of municipal bonds*, edited by S. G. Feldstein and F. J. Fabozzi (pp. 1015–1023), Hoboken, NJ: John Wiley & Sons

CHAPTER 18
Structured Products: RMBS, CMBS, and ABS

An *asset-backed security* (ABS) is a debt instrument backed by a pool of loans or receivables. ABSs are also referred to as *structured products*. The process for the creation of asset-backed securities, referred to as securitization begins when the owner of assets sells a pool of assets to a bankruptcy remote vehicle called a *special purpose entity* (SPE). The SPE obtains the proceeds to acquire the asset pool, referred to as the *collateral*, by issuing debt instruments. The cash flow of the asset pool is used to satisfy the obligations of the debt instruments issued by the SPE. The debt instruments issued by the SPE are referred to generically as asset-backed securities, asset-backed notes, asset-backed bonds, or asset-backed obligations.

ABSs issued in a single securitization can have different credit exposure and, based on the credit priority, such securities are described as *senior notes* and *junior notes* (*subordinate notes*). In the prospectus for a securitization transaction, the securities are actually referred to as certificates: *pass-through certificates* or *pay-through certificates*. The distinction between these two types of certificates is the nature of the claim that the investor has on the cash flow generated by the asset pool. If the investor has a direct claim on all of the cash flow and the certificate holder has a proportionate share of the collateral's cash flow, the term "pass-through certificate" (or "beneficial interest certificate") is used. When there are rules that are used to allocate the collateral's cash flow among different classes of investors, the asset-backed securities are referred to as pay-through certificates

There is considerable diversity in the types of assets that have been securitized. These assets can be classified as mortgage assets and nonmortgage assets. Securities backed by residential and commercial mortgage

---

The material in this chapter on residential mortgage-backed securities draws from works coauthored with Anand Bhattacharya and William Berliner.

loans are referred to as *residential mortgage–backed securities* (RMBS) and *commercial mortgage–backed securities* (CMBS), respectively. In turn, RMBS can be further classified as agency RMBS and private-label (or nonagency) RMBS. Agency RMBS are those issued by three government-related entities and is by far the largest sector in the investment-grade bond market (more than 35%). Private-label RMBS are issued by any other entity. Because of the credit risk associated with private-label RMBS, they require credit enhancement to provide some form of credit protection against default on the pool of assets backing a transaction. Credit enhancement mechanisms are typical in ABS transactions. In the case of agency RMBS, the credit enhancement is either a government guarantee or the guarantee of a government-sponsored enterprise. Private-label RMBS are further classified based on the credit quality of the mortgage loans in the pool: prime loans and subprime loans. Subprime loans are loans made to borrowers with impaired credit ratings and RMBS backed by them are referred to as *subprime RMBS*. The market classifies prime loans as part of the nonagency RMBS market and those backed by subprime loans as part of the ABS market.

The mortgage market is considerably larger than the market for non-mortgage ABS. The types of nonmortgage assets that have been securitized are generally classified as traditional assets and nontraditional or emerging assets. Market participants attribute a different meaning as to what is meant by nontraditional assets. Some refer to nontraditional assets as assets other than the major types of assets that have been securitized at the time. In the early years of the ABS market, traditional nonmortgage assets included credit card loans and auto loans. The list of what is viewed as traditional assets has changed as securitization has became a popular vehicle for issuers to raise funds. Others view nontraditional or emerging assets in a more limited way: those assets that are being securitized for the first time or for which there have been very few securitizations. For example, the recording artists David Bowie, James Brown, the Isley Brothers, and Rod Stewart have securitized their future music royalties, the first being by Bowie in 1997.[1]

In this chapter, we explain RMBS and the three largest sectors of the nonmortgage ABS market (credit card receivable-backed securities, auto loan–backed securities, and rate reduction bonds).

---

[1] The $55 million of securities issued were backed by the current and future revenues of Bowie's first 25 music albums (287 songs) recorded prior to 1990. These bonds, popularly referred to as "Bowie bonds," were purchased by Prudential Insurance Company and had a maturity of 10 years. When the bonds matured in 2007, the royalty rights reverted back to David Bowie.

AGENCY RESIDENTIAL MORTGAGE-BACKED SECURITIES

A mortgage is a loan secured by the collateral of some specified real estate property that obliges the borrower to make a predetermined series of payments. The mortgage gives the lender (*mortgagee*) the right, if the borrower (the *mortgagor*) defaults (i.e., fails to make the contractual payments), to foreclose on the loan and seize the property in order to ensure that the debt is paid off. The interest rate on the mortgage loan is called the *note rate*. Our focus in this section is on residential mortgage loans.

The fundamental unit in a mortgage-backed security is the *pool*. At its lowest common denominator, mortgage-backed pools are aggregations of large numbers of mortgage loans with similar (but not identical) characteristics. Loans with a commonality of attributes such as note rate, term to maturity, credit quality, loan balance, and type of mortgage design are combined using a variety of legal mechanisms to create relatively fungible investment vehicles. With the creation of MBS, mortgage loans are transformed from a heterogeneous group of disparate assets into sizeable and homogenous securities that trade in a liquid market.

The transformation of groups of mortgage loans with common attributes into MBS occurs using one of two mechanisms. Loans that meet the underwriting guidelines of three entities—Ginnie Mae, Fannie Mae, and Freddie Mac—are securitized as an *agency pool*. While Ginnie Mae (Government National Mortgage Association) is an agency of the U.S. government, carrying the full faith and credit of U.S. government, Fannie Mae and Freddie Mac are government-sponsored enterprises. Despite this distinction, the MBS issued by these three entities are referred to as *agency MBS* and we review the different types of agency MBS in this section. There are three types of agency MBS: pass-through securities, collateralized mortgage obligations, and stripped mortgage-backed securities.

Loans that either do not qualify for agency pools are securitized in nonagency or "private-label" transactions. These types of securities do not have an agency guaranty, and must therefore be issued under the registration entity or "shelf" of the issuer. We will discuss these types of MBS in the next section.

Cash Flow Characteristics of Residential Mortgage Loan

Although a mortgagor may select from many types of mortgage loans, because our purpose here is to understand the basic cash flow characteristics of a mortgage loan we will use the most common mortgage design: the level payment, fixed rate mortgage. The basic idea behind the design of the level-payment, fixed rate mortgage, or simply level-payment mortgage, is that the borrower pays interest and repays principal in equal installments over an agreed-upon period of time, called the *maturity* or *term of the mortgage*. Thus, at the end of the term, the loan has been fully amortized. For a level-payment mortgage, each monthly mortgage payment is due on the first of each month and consists of:

1. Interest of 1/12 of the fixed annual note rate times the amount of the outstanding mortgage balance at the beginning of the previous month.
2. A repayment of a portion of the outstanding mortgage balance (principal).

The difference between the monthly mortgage payment and the portion of the payment that represents interest equals the amount that is applied to reduce the outstanding mortgage balance. The monthly mortgage payment is designed so that after the last scheduled monthly payment of the loan is made, the amount of the outstanding mortgage balance is zero (i.e., the mortgage is fully repaid). Thus, the portion of the monthly mortgage payment applied to interest declines each month, and the portion applied to reducing the mortgage balance increases.

The reason for this is that because the mortgage balance is reduced with each monthly mortgage payment, the interest on the mortgage balance declines. Since the monthly mortgage payment is fixed, an increasingly larger portion of the monthly payment is applied to reduce the principal in each subsequent month.

For the mortgagee, the cash flow from the mortgage loan is not the same as what the mortgagor pays. This is because of a servicing fee that must be paid. Every mortgage loan must be serviced.

The monthly cash flow from a mortgage loan, regardless of the mortgage design, can, therefore, be divided into three parts: (1) the servicing fee, (2) the interest payment net of the servicing fee, and (3) the scheduled principal repayment (referred to as *amortization*).

Prepayments and Cash Flow Uncertainty

One cannot assume that the mortgagor would not pay off any portion of the mortgage balance prior to the scheduled due date. Payments made in excess of the scheduled principal repayment are called *prepayments*. Prepayments occur for a variety reasons. First, borrowers prepay the entire mortgage balance when they sell their home. Second, borrowers may be economically motivated to pay off the loan as market rates fall below the loan's note rate. This reason for prepaying a mortgage loan is referred to as *refinancing*. Third, in the case of borrowers who cannot meet their mortgage obligations, the property is repossessed and sold. The proceeds from the sale are used to pay off the mortgage loan. Finally, if property is destroyed by fire or if another insured catastrophe occurs, the insurance proceeds are used to pay off the mortgage loan.

The effect of prepayments is that the cash flow from a mortgage is not known with certainty—by this, we mean that the amount and the timing of the cash flow is uncertain. Consequently, ignoring defaults, the mortgagor knows that as long as the loan is outstanding, interest will be received and the principal will be repaid at the scheduled date each month. On the maturity date of the mortgage loan, the investor would recover the amount lent. What the mortgagee does not know—the uncertainty—is for how long the mortgage loan will be outstanding and, therefore, the timing of the principal payments.

Residential Agency Mortgage Pass-Through Securities

In a *mortgage pass-through security*, or simply a *pass-through*, the monthly cash flow from the pool of mortgage loans is distributed on a pro rata basis to the certificate holders. The monthly cash flow that may be distributed to the certificate holders consists of three components:

1. Interest net of the servicing fee.
2. Regularly scheduled principal payments (amortization).
3. Prepayments.

As just noted, the difficulty for a certificate holder in estimating the cash flow is due to prepayments. This risk, as explained in the previous chapter, is called *prepayment risk*.

Prepayments and Prepayment Conventions

In the RMBS market, several conventions have been used as a benchmark for prepayment rates. Today the benchmarks used are the conditional prepayment rate and the Public Securities Association (PSA) prepayment benchmark.

The *conditional prepayment rate* (CPR) as a measure of the speed of prepayments assumes that some fraction of the remaining principal in the mortgage pool is prepaid each month for the remaining term of the collateral. The CPR used for a particular deal is based on the characteristics of the collatral (including its historical prepayment experience) and the current and expected future economic environment.

The CPR is an annual prepayment rate. To estimate monthly prepayments, the CPR must be converted into a monthly prepayment rate, commonly referred to as the *single-monthly mortality rate* (SMM). The following formula is used to determine the SMM for a given CPR:

$$SMM = 1 - [(1 - CPR)^{1/12}]$$

An SMM of w percent means that approximately w percent of the remaining mortgage balance at the beginning of the month, less the scheduled principal payment, will prepay that month. That is,

Prepayment for month t = SMM
× (Beginning mortgage balance for month t (18.1)
− Scheduled principal payment for month t)

One problem with using the CPR is that it assumes a constant prepayment rate from the very outset of the origination of the loans. For example, it is not likely that prepayments might be the largest in dollar amount shortly after loans are originated than later on after loans have seasoned. Yet using a constant CPR makes that assumption. For residential mortgage loans, the PSA prepayment benchmark deals with this problem.[2] The PSA prepayment benchmark is expressed as a monthly series of annual prepayment rates. The basic PSA benchmark model assumes that prepayment rates are low for newly originated loans, then will speed up as the mortgages become seasoned, and then reach a plateau and remain at that level.

The PSA standard benchmark assumes the following prepayment rates for 30-year residential mortgages loans:

- A CPR of 0.2% for the first month, increased by 0.2% per year per month for the next 29 months when it reaches 6% per year.
- A 6% CPR for the remaining years.

All months above are counted with reference to origination of the pool.

This benchmark is referred to as 100% PSA. Mathematically, 100 PSA can be expressed as follows:

If $t \le 30$ months, then CPR = 6%(t/30)
If $t > 30$ months, then CPR = 6%

where t is the number of months since the mortgage originated.

Slower or faster speeds are then referred to as some percentage of PSA. For example, 50% PSA means one-half the CPR of the PSA benchmark

---

[2]The PSA and the CPR approaches are not mutually exclusive alternatives but are mostly used together—the PSA to explain the ramp-up of the expected CPR over the initial months of seasoning. Thereafter, the pool undergoes a constant CPR.

prepayment rate and 165% PSA means 1.65 times the CPR of the PSA benchmark prepayment rate. A prepayment rate of 0% PSA means that no prepayments are assumed.

The PSA benchmark is commonly referred to as a *prepayment model*, suggesting that it can be used to estimate prepayment. However, it is important to note that characterizing this market convention for prepayments as a prepayment model is wrong.

Cash Flow for a Mortgage Pass-Through Security

With this background on prepayments conventions, we can now discuss the structuring of agency deals. To illustrate structuring and how it used to create bonds with different exposure to interest rate and prepayment risk via tranching, we will use a hypothetical pass-through security that will be the collateral for our illustrations. Let us look at the monthly cash flow for a hypothetical pass-through given a PSA assumption. We will assume the following for the underlying mortgages:

- Type: fixed rate, level payment mortgages
- Weighted average coupon (WAC) rate: 6.0%
- Weighted average maturity (WAM): 358 months
- Servicing fee: 0.5%
- Outstanding balance: $660 million

The pass-through security has a coupon rate of 5.5% (WAC of 6% minus the servicing fee of 0.5%).

This first step in structuring requires a projection of the cash flow of the mortgage pool. The cash flow is decomposed into three components:

1. Interest (based on WAC of 6% and pass-through rate of 5.5%).
2. Regularly scheduled principal (i.e., amortization).
3. Prepayments based on some prepayment assumption.

To generate the cash flow for the hypothetical pass-through security we will assume a prepayment speed of 165% PSA. The cash flow is shown in Table 18.1.

Column 2 shows the outstanding mortgage balance at the beginning of the month (i.e., outstanding balance at the beginning of the previous month reduced by the total principal payment in the previous month). Column 3 gives the SMM for 165% PSA.[3] The aggregate monthly mortgage payment

---

[3] Notice that for month 1, the SMM shown in Table 18.1 is for a pass-through security that has been seasoned two months. This is because the WAM is 358 months.

TABLE 18.1 Monthly Cash Flow for a $660 Million Pass-Through Security with a 5.5% Pass-Through Rate, a WAC of 6.0%, and a WAM of 358 Months, Assuming 165% PSA

(1) Month	(2) Outstanding Balance	(3) SMM	(4) Mortgage Payment	(5) Net Interest	(6) Scheduled Prinicipal	(7) Prepayments	(8) Total Principal	(9) Cash Flow
1	660,000,000	0.00083	3,964,947	3,025,000	664,947	546,435	1,211,383	4,236,383
2	658,788,617	0.00111	3,961,661	3,019,448	667,718	728,350	1,396,068	4,415,516
3	657,392,549	0.00139	3,957,277	3,013,049	670,314	909,895	1,580,209	4,593,258
4	655,812,340	0.00167	3,951,794	3,005,807	672,732	1,090,916	1,763,649	4,769,455
5	654,048,691	0.00195	3,945,214	2,997,723	674,970	1,271,261	1,946,231	4,943,954
6	652,102,460	0.00223	3,937,538	2,988,803	677,025	1,450,775	2,127,800	5,116,603
7	649,974,660	0.00251	3,928,768	2,979,051	678,895	1,629,307	2,308,202	5,287,252
8	647,666,458	0.00279	3,918,910	2,968,471	680,578	1,806,703	2,487,281	5,455,752
9	645,179,177	0.00308	3,907,966	2,957,071	682,070	1,982,813	2,664,883	5,621,955
10	642,514,294	0.00336	3,895,943	2,944,857	683,372	2,157,486	2,840,858	5,785,715
11	639,673,436	0.00365	3,882,847	2,931,837	684,480	2,330,573	3,015,053	5,946,890
12	636,658,383	0.00393	3,868,685	2,918,018	685,394	2,501,927	3,187,320	6,105,338
13	633,471,062	0.00422	3,853,466	2,903,409	686,111	2,671,401	3,357,511	6,260,921
14	630,113,551	0.00451	3,837,198	2,888,020	686,630	2,838,851	3,525,482	6,413,502
15	626,588,069	0.00480	3,819,891	2,871,862	686,951	3,004,137	3,691,088	6,562,950
16	622,896,981	0.00509	3,801,557	2,854,944	687,072	3,167,117	3,854,189	6,709,134
17	619,042,792	0.00538	3,782,207	2,837,279	686,993	3,327,655	4,014,648	6,851,928
18	615,028,144	0.00567	3,761,853	2,818,879	686,712	3,485,618	4,172,330	6,991,209
19	610,855,814	0.00597	3,740,509	2,799,756	686,230	3,640,872	4,327,102	7,126,858
20	606,528,712	0.00626	3,718,190	2,779,923	685,546	3,793,290	4,478,836	7,258,760
21	602,049,876	0.00656	3,694,909	2,759,395	684,660	3,942,748	4,627,408	7,386,803
22	597,422,468	0.00685	3,670,684	2,738,186	683,572	4,089,123	4,772,695	7,510,881
23	592,649,773	0.00715	3,645,531	2,716,311	682,282	4,232,298	4,914,580	7,630,892
24	587,735,193	0.00745	3,619,467	2,693,786	680,791	4,372,159	5,052,950	7,746,736
25	582,682,243	0.00775	3,592,511	2,670,627	679,100	4,508,595	5,187,695	7,858,322
26	577,494,549	0.00805	3,564,681	2,646,850	677,208	4,641,501	5,318,709	7,965,560
27	572,175,839	0.00835	3,535,997	2,622,473	675,117	4,770,776	5,445,894	8,068,367
28	566,729,945	0.00865	3,506,479	2,597,512	672,829	4,896,323	5,569,152	8,166,664
29	561,160,793	0.00865	3,476,148	2,571,987	670,344	4,848,172	5,518,516	8,090,503
30	555,642,277	0.00865	3,446,080	2,546,694	667,869	4,800,459	5,468,328	8,015,021

TABLE 18.1 (Continued)

(1) Month	(2) Outstanding Balance	(3) SMM	(4) Mortgage Payment	(5) Net Interest	(6) Scheduled Prinicipal	(7) Prepayments	(8) Total Principal	(9) Cash Flow
100	272,093,325	0.00865	1,875,944	1,247,094	515,478	2,349,114	2,864,592	4,111,686
101	269,228,733	0.00865	1,859,718	1,233,965	513,574	2,324,352	2,837,926	4,071,891
102	266,390,806	0.00865	1,843,631	1,220,958	511,677	2,299,821	2,811,498	4,032,456
103	263,579,308	0.00865	1,827,684	1,208,072	509,788	2,275,518	2,785,306	3,993,378
104	260,794,002	0.00865	1,811,875	1,195,306	507,905	2,251,442	2,759,347	3,954,653
105	258,034,655	0.00865	1,796,203	1,182,659	506,029	2,227,590	2,733,620	3,916,278
200	86,170,616	0.00865	786,913	394,949	356,060	742,285	1,098,345	1,493,293
201	85,072,271	0.00865	780,106	389,915	354,745	732,796	1,087,541	1,477,455
202	83,984,730	0.00865	773,358	384,930	353,435	723,400	1,076,835	1,461,765
203	82,907,896	0.00865	766,669	379,995	352,129	714,097	1,066,226	1,446,221
204	81,841,669	0.00865	760,037	375,108	350,829	704,886	1,055,714	1,430,822
205	80,785,955	0.00865	753,463	370,269	349,533	695,765	1,045,298	1,415,567
300	16,829,401	0.00865	330,091	77,135	245,944	143,445	389,388	466,523
301	16,440,012	0.00865	327,235	75,350	245,035	140,085	385,120	460,470
302	16,054,892	0.00865	324,405	73,585	244,130	136,761	380,891	454,476
303	15,674,001	0.00865	321,599	71,839	243,229	133,474	376,703	448,542
304	15,297,298	0.00865	318,817	70,113	242,330	130,224	372,554	442,667
305	14,924,744	0.00865	316,059	68,405	241,436	127,009	368,444	436,849
350	1,876,871	0.00865	213,790	8,602	204,405	14,467	218,872	227,474
351	1,657,999	0.00865	211,940	7,599	203,650	12,580	216,230	223,829
352	1,441,769	0.00865	210,107	6,608	202,898	10,716	213,614	220,222
353	1,228,154	0.00865	208,290	5,629	202,149	8,875	211,024	216,653
354	1,017,131	0.00865	206,488	4,662	201,402	7,056	208,458	213,120
355	808,672	0.00865	204,702	3,706	200,659	5,259	205,918	209,624
356	602,755	0.00865	202,931	2,763	199,917	3,484	203,402	206,165
357	399,353	0.00865	201,176	1,830	199,179	1,731	200,911	202,741
358	198,442	0.00865	199,436	910	198,444	0	198,444	199,353

is reported in column 4. Notice that the total monthly mortgage payment declines over time, as prepayments reduce the mortgage balance outstanding.[4] Column 5 shows the monthly interest that is determined by multiplying the outstanding mortgage balance at the beginning of the month by the pass-through rate of 5.5% and dividing by 12. The regularly scheduled principal repayment (amortization), shown in column 6 is the difference between the total monthly mortgage payment (column 4) and the gross coupon interest for the month (6.0% multiplied by the outstanding mortgage balance at the beginning of the month, then divided by 12). The prepayment for the month is reported in column 7 and is found by using equation (18.1). The sum of the regularly schedule principal and the prepayment is the total principal payment and is shown in column 8. The projected monthly cash flow is then the sum of the monthly interest plus the total principal payment as shown in the last column of the Table 18.1.

At 165% PSA, the average life for this pass-through security is 8.6 years. The *average life* is a weighted average of the principal cash flows divided by the par value where the weight is the month when the projected principal is expected to be received.

Agency Stripped Mortgage-Backed Securities

A mortgage pass-through distributes the cash flow from the underlying pool of mortgages on a pro rata basis to the securityholders. A *stripped mortgage-backed security* (stripped MBS) is created by altering that distribution of principal and interest from a pro rata distribution to an unequal distribution. In the most common type of stripped MBS, all of the interest is allocated to one class—the *interest only class*—and all of the principal to the other class—the *principal-only class*.

Principal-Only Securities

A principal-only security, also called a *PO* or a *principal-only mortgage strip*, represents the principal component of a pool of underlying mortgages or (in the case of agency-name strips) MBS pools underlying the deal. POs are typically purchased at a substantial discount from par value. The return realized by an investor on a PO is strongly influenced by the prepayment rate of the underlying loans or pools; the faster the prepayment rate (or speed), the greater the return on the investment. If prepayment speeds increase from those assumed at the time of purchase, the investor receives principal

---

[4]In the absence of prepayments, this amount would be constant over the life of the pass-through security. The formula for calculating the total monthly mortgage payment can be found in Chapter 22 of Fabozzi (2006).

(paid at par value) sooner than expected; since this principal was purchased at a discount, the investor's returns are enhanced. Conversely, principal is returned more slowly than expected if prepayment speeds slow, lowering realized returns. This behavior is analogous to that of a zero-coupon bullet-maturity bond. If a five-year zero-coupon bond is called immediately after being purchased at a deep discount, the investor's returns are boosted by the immediate return of principal. Alternatively, if the bond's maturity was somehow extended, the investor's returns would be adversely affected.

Let's look at how the price of the PO would be expected to change as mortgage rates in the market change. When mortgage rates decline below the note rate for the loans in the mortgage pool, prepayments are expected to speed up, accelerating payments to the PO holder. Thus, the cash flow of a PO improves (in the sense that principal repayments are received earlier). The cash flow will also be discounted at a lower interest rate because the mortgage rate in the market has declined. The result is that the PO price will often increase signficantly when mortgage rates decline. When mortgage rates rise above the note rate for the loans in the mortgage pool, prepayments are expected to slow down. The cash flow deteriorates (in the sense that it takes longer to recover principal repayments). Couple this with a higher discount rate, and the price of a PO will normally fall sharply when mortgage rates rise.

Interest-Only Securities

An interest-only class, also called an *IO* or an *interest-only mortgage strip*, has no economic par value. It represents the interest stream generated by the underlying principal, and the investor receives interest only on the amount of principal that remains outstanding. As they are akin to an annuity, their value is increased if prepayment speeds decline, as the interest stream remains outstanding longer. Conversely, their value is reduced by faster prepayments, as the amount of principal generating interest cash flows are more rapidly reduced. In fact, the IO investor may not recover the initial investment in an IO security if prepayments increased significantly, even if the security is held to maturity.

Let's look at the expected price response of an IO to changes in mortgage rates. If mortgage rates decline below the note rate for the loans in the mortgage pool, prepayments are expected to accelerate. This would result in a deterioration of the expected cash flow for an IO. While the cash flow will be discounted at a lower rate, the net effect typically is a decline in the price of an IO. If mortgage rates rise above the note rate for the loans in the mortgage pool, the expected cash flow improves, but the cash flow is discounted at a higher interest rate. The net effect may be either a rise or fall for the IO's price.

Thus, we see an interesting characteristic of an IO: Its price tends to move in the same direction as the change in mortgage rates (1) when mortgage rates fall below the note rate for the loans in the mortgage pool and (2) for some range of mortgage rates above the note rate. (This runs contrary to the normal behavior of bond prices, which usually move opposite the change in interest rates.) Note that while both IOs and POs can have substantial price variability, the combined price changes of the IO and PO must be equal to the price change of the underlying passthrough from which it was created.

Agency Collateralized Mortgage Obligations

A *collateralized mortgage obligation* (CMO) is a security backed by a pool of mortgage pass-through securities. CMOs are structured so that there are several classes of bondholders with varying average lives. The different bond classes are also called *tranches*. The principal payments from the underlying pool of pass-through securities are used to retire the bonds on a priority basis as specified in the prospectus.

Although we will not explain the wide range of bond classes or tranches created in a CMO structure, we will provide a few for the purposes of showing how they are created (structured) and how they alter the investment characteristics relative to the mortgage pass-through securities from which they were created: sequential-pay bonds, planned amortization class bonds, and support bonds. For a more detailed description of the different types of CMO bond classes, see Fabozzi, Bhattacharya, and Berliner (2007).

Sequential-Pay Structures

The simplest type of CMO structure is the *sequential-pay structure*. To illustrate this structure, we will use the $660 million, 5.5% pass-through security (which is comprised of residential mortgage loans that confirm to the underwriting standards of Ginnie Mae, Fannie Mae, and Freddie Mac) to create a simple structure. The following structure is given and we refer to this structure as "Structure 1":

Bond Class	Par Amount	Coupon Rate
A	$320,925,000	5.5%
B	59,400,000	5.5%
C	159,225,000	5.5%
D	120,450,000	5.5%

In structuring an agency deal, there are only rules specified for the distribution of principal and interest. There are no rules for deals with defaults and delinquencies because payments are guaranteed by the issuer. In Structure 1 we will use the following rules:

- *Interest.* The monthly interest is distributed to each bond class on the basis of the amount of principal outstanding at the beginning of the month.
- *Principal.* All monthly principal (i.e., regularly scheduled principal and prepayments) is distributed first to bond class A until it is completely paid off. After bond class A is completely paid off its par amount, all monthly principal payments are made to bond class B until it is completely paid off. After bond class B is completely paid off its par amount, all monthly principal payments are made to bond class C until it is completely paid off its par amount. Finally, after bond C is completely paid off, all monthly principal payments are made to bond class D.

Based on these rules for the distribution of interest and principal, Table 18.2 shows the cash flows for each bond class assuming one prepayment speed, 165% PSA. Note that bond class A is fully paid off in month 78 and in that month principal payments begin for bond class B, which is fully paid off in month 98. Bond class C starts receiving principal payments in month 98.

Before explaining what has been accomplished in Structure 1, a few comments are in order. First, the total par value of the four bond classes in the structure is equal to $660 million which is equal to the par value of the collateral (the pass-through security). Second, we have simplified the illustration by assuming that all bond classes have the same coupon rate. In actual deals, the coupon rate would be determined by prevailing market conditions (i.e., the yield curve) and would not necessarily be equal to each bond class. A condition that must be satisfied is that the total interest to be paid to all the bond classes in a month may not exceed the interest from the collateral otherwise an interest shortfall will occur. Equivalently, the weighted average coupon rate for the bond classes in the structure may not exceed the coupon rate for the collateral (6% in our illustration). Finally, although the payment rules for the distribution of the principal payments are known, the exact amount of monthly principal is not. The monthly principal will depend on the principal cash flows generated by the collateral, which in turn depends on the actual payment rate of the collateral. Thus, in order to project monthly cash flows, a prepayment assumption must be made.

TABLE 18.2 Monthly Cash Flows for Selected Months for Structure 1 Assuming 165% PSA

	A			B		
Month	Beginning Balance	Principal	Interest	Beginning Balance	Principal	Interest
1	320,925,000	1,211,383	1,470,906	59,400,000	0	272,250
2	319,713,617	1,396,068	1,465,354	59,400,000	0	272,250
3	318,317,549	1,580,209	1,458,955	59,400,000	0	272,250
4	316,737,340	1,763,649	1,451,713	59,400,000	0	272,250
5	314,973,691	1,946,231	1,443,629	59,400,000	0	272,250
6	313,027,460	2,127,800	1,434,709	59,400,000	0	272,250
7	310,899,660	2,308,202	1,424,957	59,400,000	0	272,250
8	308,591,458	2,487,281	1,414,378	59,400,000	0	272,250
9	306,104,177	2,664,883	1,402,977	59,400,000	0	272,250
10	303,439,294	2,840,858	1,390,763	59,400,000	0	272,250
11	300,598,436	3,015,053	1,377,743	59,400,000	0	272,250
12	297,583,383	3,187,320	1,363,924	59,400,000	0	272,250
75	14,039,361	3,614,938	64,347	59,400,000	0	272,250
76	10,424,423	3,581,599	47,779	59,400,000	0	272,250
77	6,842,824	3,548,556	31,363	59,400,000	0	272,250
78	3,294,268	3,294,268	15,099	59,400,000	221,539	272,250
79	0	0	0	59,178,461	3,483,348	271,235
80	0	0	0	55,695,114	3,451,178	255,269
81	0	0	0	52,243,936	3,419,293	239,451
82	0	0	0	48,824,643	3,387,692	223,780
83	0	0	0	45,436,951	3,356,372	208,253
84	0	0	0	42,080,579	3,325,330	192,869
85	0	0	0	38,755,249	3,294,564	177,628
95	0	0	0	7,149,734	3,001,559	32,770
96	0	0	0	4,148,175	2,973,673	19,012
97	0	0	0	1,174,502	1,174,502	5,383
98	0	0	0	0	0	0

TABLE 18.2 (Continued)

	C			D		
Month	Beginning Balance	Principal	Interest	Beginning Balance	Principal	Interest
1	96,500,000	0	442,292	73,000,000	0	334,583
2	96,500,000	0	442,292	73,000,000	0	334,583
3	96,500,000	0	442,292	73,000,000	0	334,583
4	96,500,000	0	442,292	73,000,000	0	334,583
5	96,500,000	0	442,292	73,000,000	0	334,583
6	96,500,000	0	442,292	73,000,000	0	334,583
7	96,500,000	0	442,292	73,000,000	0	334,583
8	96,500,000	0	442,292	73,000,000	0	334,583
9	96,500,000	0	442,292	73,000,000	0	334,583
10	96,500,000	0	442,292	73,000,000	0	334,583
11	96,500,000	0	442,292	73,000,000	0	334,583
12	96,500,000	0	442,292	73,000,000	0	334,583
95	96,500,000	0	442,292	73,000,000	0	334,583
96	96,500,000	0	442,292	73,000,000	0	334,583
97	96,500,000	1,073,657	442,292	73,000,000	0	334,583
98	95,426,343	1,768,876	437,371	73,000,000	0	334,583
99	93,657,468	1,752,423	429,263	73,000,000	0	334,583
100	91,905,045	1,736,116	421,231	73,000,000	0	334,583
101	90,168,928	1,719,955	413,274	73,000,000	0	334,583
102	88,448,973	1,703,938	405,391	73,000,000	0	334,583
103	86,745,035	1,688,064	397,581	73,000,000	0	334,583
104	85,056,970	1,672,332	389,844	73,000,000	0	334,583
105	83,384,639	1,656,739	382,180	73,000,000	0	334,583
175				71,179,833	850,356	326,241
176				70,329,478	842,134	322,343
177				69,487,344	833,986	318,484
178				68,653,358	825,912	314,661
179				67,827,446	817,911	310,876
180				67,009,535	809,982	307,127

TABLE 18.2 (Continued)

	C			D		
Month	Beginning Balance	Principal	Interest	Beginning Balance	Principal	Interest
181				66,199,553	802,125	303,415
182				65,397,428	794,339	299,738
183				64,603,089	786,624	296,097
184				63,816,465	778,978	292,492
185				63,037,487	771,402	288,922
350				1,137,498	132,650	5,214
351				1,004,849	131,049	4,606
352				873,800	129,463	4,005
353				744,337	127,893	3,412
354				616,444	126,338	2,825
355				490,105	124,799	2,246
356				365,307	123,274	1,674
357				242,033	121,764	1,109
358				120,269	120,269	551

Now let us look at Structure 1. To see what has been accomplished, a summary of the average life (in years) of the collateral and the four bond classes under a range of prepayment assumptions is shown:

	100%	125%	165%	250%	400%	500%
Collateral	11.2	10.1	8.6	6.4	4.5	3.7
Bond class						
A	4.7	4.1	3.4	2.7	2.0	1.8
B	10.4	8.9	7.3	5.3	3.8	3.2
C	15.1	13.2	10.9	7.9	5.3	4.4
D	24.0	22.4	19.8	15.2	10.3	8.4

Notice the substantial variance of the average life for the collateral. Is this a short-term security that would fit the needs of an institutional investor such as a bank or an intermediate-term security that might be suitable for an insurance company? Basically, the collateral was unappealing to institutional investors concerned with contraction or extension risk given their liability structure. Look at the average life for the four bond classes.

They have average lives that are both shorter and longer than the collateral, thereby attracting institutional investors who have a preference for an average life different from that of the collateral. For example, a depository institution interested in shorter-term paper and concerned with extension risk would find bond class A more appealing than the collateral because within a reasonable range of prepayment speeds, bond class A's average life will be less than five years under slow prepayment speeds while the collateral's average life can extend to a little more than 11 years.[5] At the other end of the maturity preference spectrum, consider a defined benefit pension plan that is seeking longer-term investments and is concerned with contraction risk. That institutional investor would prefer bond class D to the collateral. While bond class D has considerable variance in its average life, the concern of contraction risk is greater for the collateral than for bond class D. To see that, notice in the table above that at the fastest prepayment speed shown in the table (500 PSA) the average life for the collateral can contract to 3.7 years but bond class D to only 8.3 years.

Consequently, we can see that the rules for distribution of principal among the bond classes in this structure, referred to as a sequential pay structure, have redistributed the prepayment risk (i.e., exposure to extension and contraction risk) of the collateral among the bond classes. As a result, an unattractive asset or collateral from the prospective of institutional investors can be used to create securities that better match the needs of those investors, a point that we have stated, but not demonstrated until now.

Planned Amortization Class Bonds and Support Bonds

There are institutional investors who seek securities (bond classes) that have even greater protection against prepayment risk. Investment bankers have created a product for such investors. To understand how this was done by structurers for investment banking firms, look at Table 18.3. The table shows the total principal payment for selected months for our $660 million, 6% collateral assuming a prepayment speed of 100% PSA (column 2) and 250% PSA (column 3). The last column in Table 18.3 shows the minimum total principal payment for each month. That is, if the prepayment speed is constant over the life of the collateral and that constant prepayment speed is between 100% PSA and 250% PSA, then the monthly total principal will be as shown in the last column. If the total of the principal in the last column is summed, it is equal to $470,224,580.

---

[5]Note that the average life is not the expected maturity. Assuming 100% PSA, for example, while bond class A's average life is 4.7 years, it might still take roughly 10 years for bond class A to be completely repaid.

TABLE 18.3 Total Principal Payments at 100% PSA and 250% PSA and Creation of PAC Schedule for Selected Months

Month	100% PSA	250% PSA	PAC Schedule
1	995,525	1,494,837	995,525
2	1,108,446	1,774,008	1,108,446
3	1,221,042	2,052,351	1,221,042
4	1,333,255	2,329,510	1,333,255
5	1,445,026	2,605,129	1,445,026
6	1,556,298	2,878,852	1,556,298
7	1,667,013	3,150,323	1,667,013
8	1,777,113	3,419,190	1,777,113
9	1,886,540	3,685,100	1,886,540
10	1,995,237	3,947,708	1,995,237
11	2,103,149	4,206,667	2,103,149
12	2,210,219	4,461,641	2,210,219
13	2,316,391	4,712,295	2,316,391
14	2,421,610	4,958,303	2,421,610
15	2,525,823	5,199,344	2,525,823
16	2,628,975	5,435,106	2,628,975
17	2,731,013	5,665,285	2,731,013
18	2,831,885	5,889,586	2,831,885
101	2,577,230	2,709,199	2,577,230
102	2,563,858	2,669,922	2,563,858
103	2,550,555	2,631,198	2,550,555
104	2,537,320	2,593,019	2,537,320
105	2,524,154	2,555,377	2,524,154
211	1,451,822	516,114	516,114
212	1,444,240	508,066	508,066
213	1,436,697	500,136	500,136

TABLE 18.3 (Continued)

Month	100% PSA	250% PSA	PAC Schedule
346	712,694	48,340	48,340
347	708,916	47,342	47,342
348	705,158	46,360	46,360
349	701,419	45,394	45,394
350	697,699	44,444	44,444
351	693,998	43,509	43,509
352	690,317	42,591	42,591
353	686,654	41,687	41,687
354	683,010	40,798	40,798
355	679,385	39,924	39,924
356	675,779	39,065	39,065
357	672,191	38,220	38,220
358	668,622	37,388	37,388

The amounts in the last column allows a structurer to create a bond class, referred to as a *planned amortization class bond* (more popularly referred to as a PAC), which has priority over all other bonds classes in the structure with respect to receiving the scheduled principal repayment. For example, for our hypothetical $660 million, 5.5% pass-through security, using a lower prepayment speed of 100% PSA and an upper speed of 250% PSA, the PAC schedule would be shown in the last column. The upper and lower prepayment speeds are referred to as the *structuring speeds* and the range of 100% to 250% PSA is referred to as the *structuring bands*. The non-PAC bond classes in the structure are referred to as the *support bonds* or *companion bonds*, a name given because of their function in the structure as will be explained shortly.

The key in this structure is that the support bonds accept the contraction risk if actual prepayment speeds are fast and accept the extension risk if actual prepayments are slow. Hence, unlike in the sequential pay structure illustrated by Structure 1, where the bond classes are afforded some protection against extension risk or contraction risk but not both, PAC bonds offer prepayment protection against both extension risk and contraction risk.

The prepayment protection in a PAC structure comes from the support bonds. It is the support bonds that receive any excess principal payments beyond the scheduled amount to be paid to the PAC bond classes and must wait to receive principal if there is a principal shortfall—hence, the term *support bonds* to describe this bond class.

To understand the rules for distribution in a PAC structure, consider the following hypothetical structure below that we identify as "Structure 2":

Bond Class	Bond Type	Par Amount	Coupon Rate
P	PAC	$470,224,580	5.5%
S	Support	$189,775,420	5.5%

Notice that the par amount in Structure 2 is the total for a PAC created with a structuring band band of 100% to 250% PSA.

Table 18.3 shows how this is done. Columns 2 and 3 show the monthly principal payments based on prepayment speeds of 100% and 250%, respectively. The last column shows the minimum principal payment for each month. The last column is the schedule of payments to the PAC bond class. It is this schedule, referred to as the PAC schedule, that would be shown in the prospectus.

To understand how the principal payment rules work for a PAC bond class, look at look at month 12. The PAC schedule indicates that for that month the payment to be made to the PAC bond class is $2,210,219. Suppose that actual principal payments for that month are $3,200,000. Then $2,210,219 is paid to the PAC bond class (P) and the balance, $989,781, is distributed to the support bonds.

The following table shows the average life at the time of issuance for the two bond classes:

	PSA Speed					
	50	75	100	165	250	400
P	10.21	8.62	7.71	7.71	7.71	5.52
S	24.85	22.71	20.00	10.67	3.28	1.86
Collateral	14.42	12.68	11.24	8.56	6.44	4.47

Notice that the average life is unchanged for the PAC bond class prepayment speeds from 100% to 250% PSA, the structuring band. Also notice the considerable variation in the average life of the support bond class. Its variability is much greater than that of the collateral for the prepayments speeds shown. This is to be expected because the support bond class is providing prepayment protection for the PAC bond class.

Sequential-Pay PAC Structure In practice, a typical structure may have more than one class of PAC bonds. That is, there may be a series of PAC bonds. For example, consider the following structure that we will refer to as "Structure 3":

Structured Products

Bond Class	Par Amount
P-A	$38,308,710
P-B	153,808,875
P-C	36,116,850
P-D	73,544,130
P-E	107,941,020
P-F	60,505,005
S	189,775,410

The first six bond classes are PAC bonds and their total par value is $470,224,580, the same as the single PAC bond in Structure 2. The rules for the distribution of principal payments is in sequence as follows:

- Pay principal payments received from the collateral to P-A up to its scheduled amount and if there is any excess principal payments, then, if such excess principal payments do not exceed expected principal payments at 250 PSA, distribute them to S or else distribute them to P-A.
- After P-A is fully paid off, pay principal payments received from the collateral to P-B up to its scheduled amount and if there is any excess principal payments, then, if such excess principal payments do not exceed expected principal payments at 250 PSA, distribute them to S, or else, distribute them to P-B.
- After P-B is fully paid off, pay principal payments received from the collateral to P-C up to its scheduled amount and if there is any excess principal payments, then, if such excess principal payments do not exceed expected principal payments at 250 PSA, distribute them to S or else distribute them to P-C.
- And so on.

The average life for each PAC bond assuming various prepayment speeds is provided below:

	PSA Speed					
	50%	75%	100%	165%	250%	400%
P-A	1.3	1.1	1.0	1.0	1.0	1.0
P-B	5.1	4.1	3.5	3.5	3.5	3.1
P-C	8.8	7.1	5.9	5.9	5.9	4.3
P-D	11.1	9.0	7.5	7.5	7.5	5.2
P-E	15.1	12.5	10.9	10.9	10.9	7.3
P-F	19.9	18.5	18.3	18.3	18.3	12.5

Note that the average life is stable for the structuring band for all PAC bonds. This is as to be expected. But note further that the shorter-term PAC bonds such as P-A and P-B have stability over a wider range of prepayment speeds. The reason has to do with the support bonds. In Structure 2, there is $189,775,410 par value of support bonds protecting $470,224,580 par value of a single PAC bond. In Structure 3, since P-A has first priority on the principal payments, this means that from the perspective of P-A, there is $189,775,410 par value of support bonds protecting only $38,308,710 par value of P-A. Hence, there is greater prepayment protection beyond the structuring band. Similarly, for P-B, there is $189,775,410 par value of support bonds protecting only $192,117,585 (sum of par value of P-A and P-B). While the prepayment protection of P-B is provided for a wider range of prepayment speeds compared to the structuring bands, that range is less than for P-A, but greater than for P-C and P-D.

Support Bonds Because of their role in providing protection for PAC bond classes in a structure, support bonds have the greatest prepayment risk in a structure. Investors must be particularly careful in assessing the cash flow characteristics of support bonds to reduce the likelihood of adverse portfolio consequences due to prepayments. Unfortunately, in the early years of the CMO markets, too often buyers of these types of bond classes were not aware of their investment characteristics and were attracted to them because of their high yield based on some specified prepayment assumption rather than analyzing them on an option-adjusted basis.

In the PAC-support structure given by Structure 2, there is only one support bond. In actual deals, the support bonds are often divided into different bond classes. For example, a structurer can create support bonds that payoff in sequence. To provide some support bonds with greater prepayment protection than the other support bonds in a structure, a structurer can even carve up the support bonds to create support bonds with a schedule of principal repayments. That is, support bonds that are PAC support bonds can be created. In a structure with a PAC bond and a support bond with a PAC schedule of principal repayments, the former is called a PAC I bond or Level I PAC bond and the latter a PAC II bond or Level II PAC bond. While PAC II bonds have greater prepayment protection than the support bonds without a schedule of principal repayments, the prepayment protection is less than that provided PAC I bonds.

PRIVATE-LABEL RESIDENTIAL MBS

The private-label CMO market encompasses a variety of product and structuring variations. Technically, any deal that is not securitized under an agency or GSE shelf (i.e., Ginnie Mae, Freddie Mac, or Fannie Mae) can be considered private label as the issuing entity has no connection to the U.S. government (either explicit or implicit). Such deals must have some form of credit enhancement in order to create large amounts of investment-grade bonds. The convention in the markets, however, is to limit the private-label sector to the securitization of prime, first-lien fixed and adjustable rate loans. Other products, such as deals backed by subprime and second-lien loans, are classified as mortgage-related, asset-backed securities, a subset of the ABS category. In some sense, this classification scheme has become fairly arbitrary.

Aside from the presence of credit enhancement, private-label deals share many features and structuring techniques with agency CMOs. There are some important differences, however, due to the nature of the loans collateralizing the deal as well as legal and regulatory issues associated with the different shelves. First, private-label deals can be structured such that derivatives, such as interest rate swaps and caps, can be inserted into the structures as risk mitigators. The GSEs, by contrast, do not allow for their inclusion in deals. Second, the loans collateralizing private-label deals are generally assumed to prepay faster than those in agency pools. The convention in the agency market is to structure deals using a base-case prepayment speed consistent with median prepayment speeds reported by Bloomberg. Private-label deals, by contrast, are structured either to a market convention (i.e., PSA speeds ranging from 250% to 300%) or a predefined ramp (i.e., 6% to 18% CPR ramping over 12 months). The ramp is defined in the prospectus and it is typically called the *prospectus prepayment curve*, or PPC (100% PPC is simply the base ramp defined at the time of pricing). Finally, private-label deals typically have cleanup calls. These are inserted into deals to relieve the trustees from the burden of having to oversee deals with very small remaining balances. The calls are triggered when the current face of the deal and/or collateral group declines below a predetermined level.

In this section, we briefly review the mechanisms involved in creating the internal credit enhancement typically utilized in private-label deals. Note that while the focus in this section is on the structuring of fixed rate mortgage loans as we did in agency deals earlier in this chapter, other mortgage designs can be structured in a similar fashion.

Private-Label Credit Enhancement

The first step in structuring the credit enhancement for a private-label deal is to split the face value of the loans into senior and subordinated interests. The senior bonds have higher priority with respect to both the receipt of interest and principal and the allocation of realized losses, and are generally created with enough subordination to be rated AAA by the credit rating agencies. In most cases, the subordinate interests are subdivided (or tranched) into a series of bonds that decline sequentially in priority. The subordinate classes normally range from AA in rating to an unrated first-loss piece. These securities are often referenced as the six-pack, since there are six broad rating grades generally issued by the rating agencies. In the investment-grade category, bonds range from AA to BBB; noninvestment grade ratings decline from BB to the unrated first-loss piece. The structure (or "splits") of a hypothetical deal is shown in Table 18.4A and B, while a schematic detailing how and losses are allocated within the structure is contained in Figure 18.1.

Internal credit enhancement requires two complimentary mechanisms. The cash flows for deals are allocated through the mechanism of a *waterfall*, which dictates the allocation of principal and interest payments to tranches with different degrees of seniority. At the same time, the allocation of realized losses is also governed by a separate prioritization schedule, with the subordinates (subs) typically being impacted in reverse order of priority.

FIGURE 18.1 Schematic of Hypothetical Structure with Cash Flow and Loss Allocations

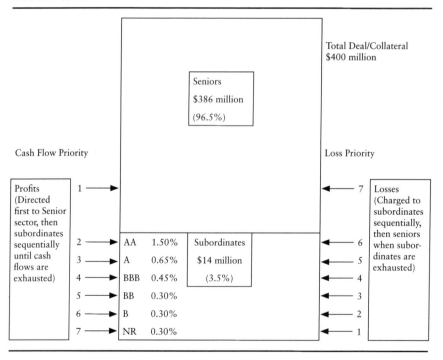

TABLE 18.4 Measuring Subordination by Percentage of Deal Size and Credit Support for a Hypothetical $400 million Deal with 3.5% Initial Subordination

A. Tranche Size as a Percentage of the Total Deal

	Face Value	Percent of Deal
AAA	$386,000,000	96.50%
AA	6,000,000	1.50%
A	2,600,000	0.65%
BBB	1,800,000	0.45%
BB	1,200,000	0.30%
B	1,200,000	0.30%
First Loss (Nonrated)	1,200,000	0.30%
Total Subordination	14,000,000	3.50%

B. Tranche Size Measured by Percentage of Subordination for Each Rating Level (i.e., credit support)

	Face Value	Credit Support (%)[a]
AAA	$386,000,000	3.50%
AA	6,000,000	2.00%
A	2,600,000	1.35%
BBB	1,800,000	0.90%
BB	1,200,000	0.60%
B	1,200,000	0.30%
First Loss (Nonrated)	1,200,000	0.00%

[a]Calculated by summing the deal percentages of all tranches junior in priority. As an example, if cumulative losses on the deal were 0.40%, the First Loss and rated B tranches would be fully exhausted, but the tranches rated BB and above would not be affected.

While the original subordination levels are set at the time of issuance (or, more precisely, at the time the attributes of the deal's collateral are finalized), deals with internal credit enhancement are designed such that the amount of credit enhancement grows over time. Private-label structures generally use a so-called shifting interest mechanism, in which the subordinate classes (or subs) do not receive principal prepayments for a period of time after issuance,

TABLE 18.5 Shifting Interest Example for Subordinates on a Fixed Rate Prime Deal

Months 1–60	Subs completely locked out from prepayments (receive amortization only)
Months 61–72	Subs receive 30% of pro rata share of prepayments
Months 73–84	Subs receive 40% of pro rata share of prepayments
Months 85–96	Subs receive 60% of pro rata share of prepayments
Months 97–108	Subs receive 80% of pro rata share of prepayments
Month 109+	Subs receive 100% of pro rata share of prepayments

Note: Effects of shifting interest structure:
1. Senior bonds paydown faster than subs.
2. Seniors make up proportionately less of the deal.
3. Subordination grows, providing senior bonds more protection.
4. Subordinate bonds have to protect fewer senior bonds (deleveraging).

generally five years for fixed rate deals.[6] After the lockout period expires, the subs begin to receive prepayments on an escalating basis. It is only after 10 years that the subs receive a pro rata allocation of prepayments. Locking out the subs means that as the collateral experiences prepayments, the face value of the subs grows in proportion relative to the senior classes; the senior classes receive all the collateral prepayments during the lockout period and hence decline proportionately over time. A typical shifting interest schedule, along with notes on the effect of the principal reallocation, is shown in Table 18.5.

Deals often have more than one collateral group securitized in the same transaction to minimize costs. Typically, the collateral groups will have different characteristics that make them difficult to commingle. For example, a deal may have separate collateral groups comprised of 30- and 15-year loans. Depending on the collateral in question, the two groups can have separate subordination groups. Alternatively, one set of subs serves as credit support for both groups, in a so-called "Y structure." This creates larger subordinate classes, which generally are more liquid and subsequently trade to tighter spreads.

Private-Label Senior Structuring Variations

Nonaccelerated Senior Bonds

Similar to subordinate tranches, *nonaccelerated senior bonds* or *NAS bonds* do not receive principal payments for the first five years. After year

---
[6]This is the origin of the shifting interest term by which the structuring form is often referenced.

5, the proportional amount of principal received generally scales up on a yearly basis, in the same fashion as the shifting interest, lockout schedule shown in Table 18.5. One difference between NAS and subordinate bonds is that subs receive amortized principal during the first five years, while NAS bonds typically have a complete lockout of both amortized and prepaid principal. After the lockout schedule expires (generally after year 10), the NAS tranches receive their full pro rata share of principal cash flows from the collateral.

NAS tranches typically comprise 10% of original face value of a deal, although some structuring derivations will have original NAS percentages of 20% or higher. Allocation of cash flows is very similar in concept to the shifting interest mechanism utilized in either the senior or sub structure. The principal allocation is accomplished by taking the NAS bonds as a percentage of the outstanding balance of the collateral—the "NAS percentage" in the prospectus—and multiplying it by the proportion of principal it is scheduled to receive, denoted in the prospectus as the "NAS distribution percentage" or "shift percentage." The schedule is generally the same as that used to define the shifting interest mechanism (as illustrated in Table 18.5), although the NAS schedule is referenced in the prospectus separately. As an example, assume that the NAS distribution percentage in month 65 is 30% (meaning it receives 30% of its pro rata share of principal). At that point, the rest of the senior bonds will have partially paid down such that the NAS bond at that point comprises 20% of the deal (growing from the original 10% at origination). Multiplying the 30% distribution percentage by the 20% prevailing NAS percentage suggests that in month 65 the NAS bond receives 6% of the principal generated by the collateral pool.

The presence of NAS bonds (along with the shifting interest subordinates) in a deal changes the profile of the remaining (i.e., senior non-NAS) bonds. These bonds (which are also categorized as *accelerated seniors*) have more volatile average life and duration profiles than those of pure sequentials created through simple time-tranching. This is because the subordinates and NAS bonds (or shifting interest bonds) have schedules; the accelerated seniors only receive principal after the schedule is met, in the same fashion as supports in a PAC/support deal.

MORTGAGE-RELATED, ASSET-BACKED SECURITIES: SUBPRIME MBS

In describing private-label deals, we noted that the emphasis in structures in the mortgage ABS sectors is different from that in structures involving prime first-lien residential loans. Loans that fall into the general category of mortgage ABS are riskier than those in prime deals, either because the loans are granted to borrowers with impaired credit (which greatly increases their expected defaults and losses) or are in an inferior lien position (which creates high-loss severities). As such, these loans are characterized by higher note rates than those in the prime first-lien sector, reflecting risk-based pricing on the part of lenders.

The challenge in structuring mortgage ABS deals is to create cash flow protection and credit enhancement for the senior securities in the most efficient possible way. The optimal form of credit enhancement for deals backed by risky loans with high note rates is the *overcollateralization* (OC) structure. This structure allows the higher note rates associated with these riskier loans to be converted into credit enhancement. In addition to the utilization of excess spread as credit enhancement, deals securitizing these types of risky loans must have higher levels of subordination than in the prime sector. The mechanisms associated with the OC structure are more complex than the traditional shifting interest structures utilized in the prime sector.

For the purposes of our discussion, mortgage ABS deals are collectively referred to as *ABS structures*. As such, these deals should not be confused with ABS deals securitizing assets such as auto loans and credit cards, which have many different features as described later in this chapter. Additionally, the term residential deal is also used interchangeably with prime deal in our discussion, utilizing the admittedly oversimplified terminology used in the market. The following discussion focuses on structures using subprime loans as collateral.

Fundamentals of ABS Structures

ABS deals have various forms of credit enhancement, which is higher than that associated with residential deals. In the residential sector, credit enhancement levels (i.e., the credit support for the senior, AAA tranches) vary depending on the type of loan securitized, but typically do not exceed 10% for the most risky loan categories. In contrast, ABS deals generally have initial enhancement levels in excess of 20%. A challenge with ABS deals is also to efficiently utilize the incrementally higher note rate of the underlying loans in providing credit support, effectively converting interest cash flows into principal. Understanding this requires the introduction of two concepts. One is *excess spread*, which is the difference between interest received from borrowers on the loans and paid to the securities. While all deals technically have excess spread, it is not large enough in residential deals to supplement credit enhancement. However, due to the high note rates associated with risky loans, the amount of excess spread in a typical ABS deal is relatively high. A diagram of a hypothetical deal's cash flows and excess spread is shown in Figure 18.2.

The other concept is overcollateralization, or OC, which refers to the fact that the face value of loans collateralizing the deal is greater than the amount of bonds. OC is created through two mechanisms. One way is to structure a smaller number of bonds at issuance, which is referenced as initial OC. The other mechanism is to utilize some or all of the excess spread to pay down bonds faster than simply through the return of principal. This is called acceleration or turboing. A depiction of the allocation of cash flows with and without turboing is shown in Figure 18.3. These two techniques are utilized (either independently or in conjunction with each other) to augment the subordination of ABS deals.

The credit support mechanisms utilized in ABS deals have a number of implications. Quoting the percentage of credit enhancement in an ABS deal (as is routinely done in residential deals) can be misleading. In part, this is because the excess spread is available to make up losses. Additionally, the credit enhancement includes the amount of OC. Therefore, deals that do not have initial OC but rather achieve the target level through turboing will not have the OC show up in initial enhancement levels. Another difference is that OC by definition is equity in a deal. Therefore, the residual (which represents the deal's equity interest) in an ABS structure has much more importance than that in residential deals. In the latter, the residual usually does not receive any cash flows, since the amount of collateral and bonds

FIGURE 18.2 Gross and Net Interest and Excess Spread for a Hypothetical $100 million Subprime Collateral Pool (8% GWAC, 3.75% net coupon)

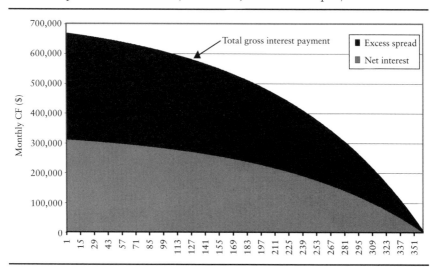

FIGURE 18.3 Normal Cash Flow Allocation and Allocation with Turboing to Create Overcollateralization

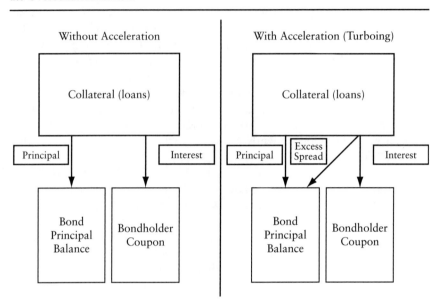

is the same. The residual has value only as an entity for tax purposes and is referred to as noneconomic residual. As such, tax effects generally cause the non-economic residuals to have a negative value at issuance. In an ABS structure, by contrast, the residual has economic value, meaning that it is expected to receive cash flows when other, more senior interests are satisfied. As such, the residual is positioned at the lowest point of the waterfall with respect to cash flow priority.[7] Figure 18.4 shows a graphical depiction of a simple waterfall in an ABS structure.

However, what is commonly referred to as the residual is really a combination of two entities: the excess cash flows (securitized either as the C or XS tranches) and the noneconomic residual (created as an R or NER tranche). While the face value of the R bond is typically small, the C tranche's face value in notional terms can be significant, depending on how much OC is created, either as up-front OC or through the turboing mechanism. In addition, the residual sometimes receives the proceeds from prepayment penalties paid by borrowers. As we will discuss later in this chapter, some

---

[7] A deal's waterfall describes how principal and interest cash flows are allocated within the structure.

FIGURE 18.4 Schematic Representation of Cash Flow Waterfall for Mortgage ABS Deal (with economic residual)

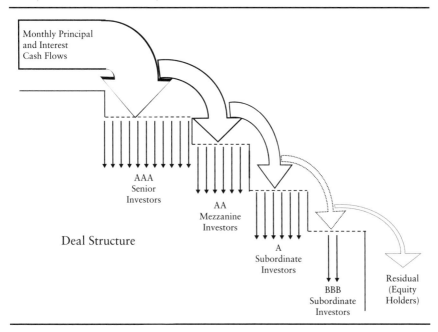

structuring techniques attempt to further enhance execution by effectively tranching the residuals.

Mortgage ABS deals are typically structured such that the senior and subordinate bonds are largely comprised of LIBOR-based floaters. Depending on the composition of the collateral and the level of short interest rates, this type of structure often creates large amounts of excess spread.

COMMERCIAL MORTGAGE-BACKED SECURITIES

Commercial mortgage-backed securities (CMBSs) are backed by a pool of commercial mortgage loans on income-producing property—multifamily properties (i.e., apartment buildings), office buildings, industrial properties (including warehouses), shopping centers, hotels, and health care facilities (i.e., senior housing care facilities). The basic building block of the CMBS transaction is a commercial loan that was originated either to finance a commercial purchase or to refinance a prior mortgage obligation.

Commercial mortgage loans are nonrecourse loans. This means that the lender can only look to the income-producing property backing the loan for interest and principal repayment. If there is a default, the lender looks to the proceeds from the sale of the property for repayment and has no recourse to the borrower for any unpaid balance. Basically, this means that the lender must view each property as a stand-alone business and evaluate each property using measures that have been found to be useful in assessing credit risk.

Regardless of the property type, the two measures that have been found to be key indicators of the potential credit performance are the *debt-to-service coverage* (DSC) ratio and the *loan-to-value* (LTV) ratio. The DSC ratio is the ratio of the property's *net operating income* (NOI) divided by the debt service. The NOI is defined as the rental income reduced by cash operating expenses (adjusted for a replacement reserve). A ratio greater than 1 means that the cash flow from the property is sufficient to cover debt servicing. The higher the ratio, the more likely that the borrower will be able to meet debt servicing from the property's cash flow. In computing the LTV, "value" in the ratio is either market value or appraised value. In valuing commercial property, there can be considerable variation in the estimates of the property's market value. The lower the LTV, the greater the protection afforded the lender.

Another characteristic of the underlying loans that is used in gauging the quality of a CMBS deal is the prepayment protection provisions. We review these provisions later. Finally, there are characteristics of the property that affect quality. Specifically, investors and rating agencies look at the concentration of loans by property type and by geographical location.

As with any securitization transaction, the rating agencies will determine the level of credit enhancement to achieve a desired rating level for each tranche in the structure. For example, if certain DSC and LTV ratios are needed, and these ratios cannot be met at the loan level, then subordination is used to achieve these levels.

Call Protection

The degree of call protection available to a CMBS investor is a function of the following two characteristics: (1) call protection available at the loan level and (2) call protection afforded from the actual CMBS structure. At the commercial loan level, call protection can take the following forms: (1) prepayment lockout, (2) defeasance, (3) prepayment penalty points, and (4) yield maintenance charges.

A *prepayment lockout* is a contractual agreement that prohibits any prepayments during a specified period of time, called the *lockout period*. The lockout period at issuance can be from two to five years. After the lockout period, call protection comes in the form of either prepayment penalty points or yield maintenance charges. Prepayment lockout and defeasance are the strongest forms of prepayment protection.

With *defeasance*, rather than prepaying a loan, the borrower provides sufficient funds for the servicer to invest in a portfolio of Treasury securities that replicates the cash flows that would exist in the absence of prepayments. The substitution of the cash flow of a Treasury portfolio for that of the borrower improves the credit quality of the CMBS deal.

Prepayment penalty points are predetermined penalties that must be paid by the borrower if the borrower wishes to refinance. For example, 5-4-3-2-1 is a common prepayment penalty point structure. That is, if the borrower wishes to prepay during the first year, a 5% penalty for a total of $105 rather than $100 (which is the norm in the residential market) must be paid. Likewise, during the second year, a 4% penalty would apply, and so on.

A *yield maintenance charge*, in its simplest terms, is designed to make the lender indifferent as to the timing of prepayments. The yield maintenance charge, also called the *make-whole charge*, makes it uneconomical to refinance solely to get a lower interest rate. Several methods have been used in practice to compute the yield maintenance charge.

The other type of call protection available in CMBS transactions is structural. That is, because the CMBS bond structures are sequential-pay (by rating), the bonds rated AA cannot pay down until the bonds rated AAA are completely retired, and the bonds rated AA must be paid off before the bonds rated A, and so on. However, principal losses due to defaults are impacted from the bottom of the structure upward.

Balloon Maturity Provisions

Many commercial loans backing CMBS transactions are balloon loans that require substantial principal payment at the end of the term of the loan. If the borrower fails to make the balloon payment, the borrower is in default. The lender may extend the loan, and in so doing may modify the original loan terms. During the workout period for the loan, a higher interest rate will be charged, the "default interest rate."

The risk that a borrower will not be able to make the balloon payment, because either the borrower cannot arrange for refinancing at the balloon payment date or cannot sell the property to generate sufficient funds to pay off the balloon balance, is called *balloon risk*. Since the term of the loan will be extended by the lender during the workout period, balloon risk is also referred to as *extension risk*.

NONMORTGAGE ASSET-BACKED SECURITIES

As explained in the introduction to this chapter, ABS can be classified based on whether the assets are mortgage-related assets or nonmortgage-related assets. The former includes residential mortgage loans and the latter a wide range consumer and business loans and receivables. In this section, we will discuss ABSs for which the collateral is a pool of traditional nonmortgage assets. More specifically, we will describe the three largest sector of the nonmortgage ABS market: credit card receivable–backed securities, auto loan–backed securities, and rate reduction bonds.

Credit Card Receivable–Backed Securities

A major sector of the ABS market is that of securities backed by credit card receivables. Credit cards are issued by banks (e.g., Visa and MasterCard), retailers (e.g., JCPenney and Sears), and travel and entertainment companies (e.g., American Express). Credit card deals are structured as either a discrete trust or master trust. With a master trust the issuer can sell several series from the same trust.

Cash Flow

For a pool of credit card receivables, the cash flow consists of finance charges collected, fees, and principal. Finance charges collected represent the periodic interest the credit card borrower is charged based on the unpaid balance after the grace period. Fees include late payment fees and any annual membership fees.

Interest to security holders is paid periodically (e.g., monthly, quarterly, or semiannually). The interest rate may be fixed or floating. The floating rate is uncapped.

A *credit card receivable–backed security* is a nonamortizing security. For a specified period of time, referred to as the lockout period or revolving period, the principal payments made by credit card borrowers comprising the pool are retained by the trustee and reinvested in additional receivables to maintain the size of the pool. The lockout period can vary from 18 months to 10 years. So, during the lockout period, the cash flow that is paid out to security holders is based on finance charges collected and fees.

After the lockout period, the principal is no longer reinvested but paid to investors. This period is referred to as the principal-amortization period, and the various types of structures are described later.

Performance of the Portfolio of Receivables

Several concepts must be understood in order to assess the performance of the portfolio of receivables and the ability of the issuer to meet its interest obligation and repay principal as scheduled.

The gross yield includes finance charges collected and fees. Charge offs represent the accounts charged off as uncollectible. Net portfolio yield is equal to gross portfolio yield minus charge-offs. The net portfolio yield is important because it is from this yield that the bondholders will be paid. So, for example, if the average yield (WAC) that must be paid to the various tranches in the structure is 5% and the net portfolio yield for the month is only 4.5%, there is the risk that the bondholder obligations will not be satisfied.

Delinquencies are the percentages of receivables that are past due for a specified number of months, usually 30, 60, and 90 days. They are considered an indicator of potential future charge-offs.

The *monthly payment rate* (MPR) expresses the monthly payment (which includes finance charges, fees, and any principal repayment) of a credit card receivable portfolio as a percentage of credit card debt outstanding in the previous month. For example, suppose a $500 million credit card receivable portfolio in January realized $50 million of payments in February. The MPR would then be 10% ($50 million divided by $500 million).

There are two reasons why the MPR is important. First, if the MPR reaches an extremely low level, there is a chance that there will be extension risk with respect to the principal payments on the bonds. Second, if the MPR is very low, then there is a chance that there will not be sufficient cash flows to pay off principal. This is one of the events that could trigger early amortization of the principal (described as follows).

At issuance, portfolio yield, charge-offs, delinquency, and MPR information are provided in the prospectus. Information about portfolio performance is thereafter available from various sources.

Early Amortization Triggers

There are provisions in credit card receivable–backed securities that require early amortization of the principal if certain events occur. Such provisions, which are referred to as either early amortization or rapid amortization, are included to safeguard the credit quality of the issue. The only way that principal cash flows can be altered is by triggering the early amortization provision.

Typically, early amortization allows for the rapid return of principal in the event that the three-month average excess spread earned on the receivables falls to zero or less. When early amortization occurs, the credit card tranches are retired sequentially (that is, first the AAA bond, then the AA bond, and so on). This is accomplished by paying the principal payments made by the credit card borrowers to the investors instead of using them to purchase more receivables. The length of time until the return of principal is largely a function of the monthly payment rate. For example, suppose that a AAA tranche is 82% of the overall deal. If the monthly payment rate is 11%, then the AAA tranche would return principal over a 7.5-month period (82%/11%). An 18% monthly payment rate would return principal over a 4.5-month period (82%/18%).

Monthly information is available on each deal's trigger formula and base rate. The trigger formula is the formula that shows the condition under which the rapid amortization will be triggered. The base rate is the minimum payment rate that a trust must be able to maintain to avoid early amortization.

Auto Loan–Backed Securities

Auto loan–backed securities are issued by:

1. The financial subsidiaries of auto manufacturers (domestic and foreign).
2. Commercial banks.
3. Independent finance companies and small financial institutions specializing in auto loans.

In terms of credit, borrowers are classified as either prime, nonprime, or subprime. Each originator employs its own criteria for classifying borrowers into these three broad groups. Typically, prime borrowers are those that have had a strong credit history that is characterized by timely payment of all their debt obligations. The FICO score of prime borrowers is generally greater than 680. Nonprime borrowers have usually had a few delinquent payments. Nonprime borrowers, also called near-prime borrowers, typically have a FICO score ranging from the low 600s to the mid-600s. When a borrower has a credit history of missed or major problems with delinquent loan payments and the borrower may have previously filed for bankruptcy, the borrower is classified as subprime. The FICO score for subprime borrowers typically is less than the low 600s (Roever 2005).

Cash Flows and Prepayments

The cash flow for auto loan–backed securities consists of regularly scheduled monthly loan payments (interest and scheduled principal repayments) and any prepayments. For securities backed by auto loans, prepayments result from (see Roever 2005):

1. Sales and trade-ins requiring full payoff of the loan.
2. Repossession and subsequent resale of the automobile.
3. Loss or destruction of the vehicle.
4. Payoff of the loan with cash to save on the interest cost.
5. Refinancing of the loan at a lower interest cost.

While refinancings may be a major reason for prepayments of mortgage loans, they are of minor importance for automobile loans. Moreover, the interest rates for the automobile loans underlying some deals are substantially below market rates (subvented rates) since they are offered by manufacturers as part of a sales promotion.

Prepayments for auto loan–backed securities are measured in terms of the *absolute prepayment speed* (ABS). The ABS is the monthly prepayment expressed as a percentage of the original collateral amount. (Note that another measure of prepayments used for other asset classes that have been securitized is the *single monthly mortality rate* (SMM). The SMM is a monthly prepayment rate that expresses prepayments based on the prior month's balance).

Structures

There are two typical structures used in auto ABS structures. In both structures, there are multiple sequential-pay senior classes and a subordinate class. One of the senior classes is a Rule 2a-7 of the Investment Company Act of 1940 eligible money market class. In one typical structure, the senior classes receives all principal until every senior class is paid off. Only after that time is the subordinate class paid any principal. In the other typical structure, once the money market class is paid off, the other senior classes and the subordinate class are paid principal concurrently. However, in this structure, the concurrent payments to the senior classes and subordinate classes require that a performance trigger be reached. If the performance trigger is breached, the principal distribution rules of the second structure will be the same as that for the first structure.

Rate Reduction Bonds

The concept of *rate reduction bonds* (RRBs)—also known as *stranded costs* or *stranded assets*—grew out of the movement to deregulate the electric utility industry and bring about a competitive market environment for electric power. Deregulating the electric utility market was complicated by large amounts of "stranded assets" already on the books of many electric utilities. These stranded assets were commitments that had been undertaken by utilities at an earlier time with the understanding that they would be recoverable in utility rates to be approved by the states' utility commissions. However, in a competitive environment for electricity, these assets would likely become uneconomic, and utilities would no longer be assured that they could charge a high enough rate to recover the costs. To compensate investors of these utilities, a special tariff was proposed. This tariff, which would be collected over a specified period of time, would allow the utility to recover its stranded costs.

This tariff, which is commonly known as the *competitive transition charge* (CTC), is created through legislation. State legislatures allow utilities to levy a fee, which is collected from its customers. Although there is an incremental fee to the consumer, the presumed benefit is that the utility can charge a lower rate as a result of deregulation. This reduction in rates would more than offset the competitive transition charge. In order to facilitate the securitization of these fees, legislation typically designates the revenue stream from these fees as a statutory property right. These rights may be sold to an SPV, which may then issue securities backed by future cash flows from the tariff.

The result is a structured security similar in many ways to other ABS products, but different in one critical aspect: The underlying asset in a RRB deal is created by legislation, which is not the case for other ABS products.

Structure

As noted previously, state regulatory authorities and state legislatures must take the first step in creating RRB issues. State regulatory commissions decide how much, if any, of a specific utility's stranded assets will be recaptured via securitization. They will also decide on an acceptable time frame and collection formula to be used to calculate the CTC. When this legislation is finalized, the utility is free to proceed with the securitization process.

The basic structure of an RRB issue is straightforward. The utility sells its rights to future CTC cash flows to an SPV created for the sole purpose of purchasing these assets and issuing debt to finance this purchase. In most cases, the utility itself will act as the servicer because it collects the CTC payment from its customer base along with the typical electric utility bill. Upon issuance, the utility receives the proceeds of the securitization (less the fees associated with issuing a deal), effectively reimbursing the utility for its stranded costs immediately.

RRBs usually have a "true-up" mechanism. This mechanism allows the utility to recalculate the CTC on a periodic basis over the term of the deal. Because the CTC is initially calculated based on projections of utility usage and the ability of the servicer to collect revenues, actual collection experience may differ from initial projections. In most cases, the utility can re-examine actual collections, and if the variance is large enough (generally a 2% difference), the utility will be allowed to revise the CTC charge. This true-up mechanism provides cash flow stability as well as credit enhancement to the bondholder.

Enhancement Levels

Credit enhancement levels required by the rating agencies for RRB deals are very low relative to other ABS asset classes. Although exact amounts and forms of credit enhancement may vary by deal, most transactions require little credit enhancement because the underlying asset (the CTC) is a statutory asset and is not directly affected by economic factors or other exogenous variables. Furthermore, the true-up mechanism virtually assures cash flow stability to the bondholder.

As an example, the AAA bonds issued by Detroit Edison Securitization Funding 1 in March 2001 were structured with 0.50% initial cash enhancement (funded at closing) and 0.50% overcollateralization (to be funded in equal semiannual increments over the terms of the transactions). This total of 1% credit enhancement is minuscule in comparison to credit cards, for example, which typically require credit enhancement at the AAA level in the 12% to 15% range for large bank issuers.

Unique Risks

RRBs are subject to risks that are very different from those associated with more traditional structured products (e.g., credit cards, home equity loans, and so on). For example, risks involving underwriting standards do not exist in the RRB sector because the underlying asset is an artificial construct. Underwriting standards are a critical factor in evaluating the credit of most other ABS. Also, factors that tend to affect the creditworthiness of many other ABS products—such as levels of consumer credit or the economic environment—generally do not have a direct effect on RRBs. Instead, other unique factors that must be considered when evaluating this sector. The most critical risks revolve around the legislative process and environment plus the long-term ability of the trust to collect future revenues to support the security's cash flows.

SUMMARY

The process of securitization has been used to create various structured products referred to as asset-backed securities. These debt instruments are backed by a pool of loans or receivables. The cash flow of the pool of loans is used to satisfy the obligations of the debt instruments. ABS are classified as mortgage-backed securities and nonmortgage ABS. Residential MBS and commercial MBS fall into the former category.

There are two types of RMBS: agency RMBS and private-label RMBS. Agency RMBS are those issued by three government-related entities (Ginnie Mae, Fannie Mae, and Freddie Mac). There are three types of agency MBS: pass-through securities, CMOs, and stripped MBS. In a mortgage pass-through security, the monthly cash flow from the pool of mortgage loans is distributed on a pro rata basis to the certificate holders. The monthly cash flow that may be distributed to the certificate holders consists of three components: interest net of the servicing fee, regularly scheduled principal payments (amortization), and prepayments. The uncertainty about the cash flow attributable to prepayments is called prepayment risk and this is the major risk in agency RMBS.

A stripped MBS is created by altering the distribution of principal and interest from a pro rata distribution to an unequal distribution. In the most common type of stripped MBS, all of the interest is allocated to one class—the interest only class—and all of the principal to the other class—the principal-only class.

An agency CMO is a security backed by a pool of mortgage pass-through securities. Agency CMOs are structured so that there are several classes of bondholders (tranches) with varying maturities. The principal payments from the underlying pool of pass-through securities are used to retire the bonds on a priority basis as specified in the prospectus. The purpose of a CMO is to redistribute prepayment and interest rate risk among the bond classes within the structure so as to create more appealing securities for investors. There are numerous types of agency CMO bonds, three of which are described in this chapter: sequential-pay bonds, PAC bonds, and support bonds.

Private-label RMBS are issued by any entity other than those issued by Ginnie Mae, Fannie Mae, or Freddie Mac. Because of the credit risk associated with private-label RMBS, they require credit enhancement to provide different degrees of credit protection against defaults on the pool of assets backing a transaction. Private-label RMBS are further classified based on the credit quality of the mortgage loans in the pool: prime loans and subprime loans. Subprime loans are loans made to borrowers with impaired credit ratings and RMBS backed by them are referred to as subprime RMBS.

The market classifies prime loans as part of the nonagency RMBS market and those backed by subprime loans as part of the ABS market.

CMBS are backed by a pool of commercial mortgage loans on income-producing property. Commercial mortgage loans are non-recourse loans. The two measures that have been found to be key indicators of the potential credit performance of commercial mortgage loans are the debt-to-service coverage ratio and the loan-to-value ratio. As with private-label RMBS, credit enhancement is required. With respect to prepayment risk, there is a high level of protection due to the features of commercial mortgage loans (prepayment lockout, defeasance, prepayment penalty points, and yield maintenance charges), as well as at the structure level.

The types of nonmortgage assets that have been securitized are generally classified as traditional assets and nontraditional or emerging assets. The three largest sectors in this market discussed in the chapter are credit card receivable-backed securities, auto loan-backed securities, and rate reduction bonds.

REFERENCES

Fabozzi, F. J. 2006. *Fixed income mathematics: Analytical and statistical techniques.* New York: McGraw-Hill.

Fabozzi, F. J., A. K. Bhattacharya, and W. S. Berliner. 2007. *Mortgage-backed securities: Products, structuring, and analytical techniques.* Hoboken, NJ: John Wiley & Sons.

CHAPTER 19
The Structure of Interest Rates

A casual examination of the financial pages of any newspaper or business magazine will tell you that nobody talks about an "interest rate." There are interest rates reported for borrowing money and investing. These rates are not randomly determined—factors exist that systematically affect how interest rates on different types of loans and debt instruments vary from each other. We refer to this as the *structure of interest rates* and we discuss the factors that affect this structure in this chapter.

THE BASE INTEREST RATE

The securities issued by the U.S. Department of the Treasury, popularly referred to as Treasury securities or simply Treasuries, are backed by the full faith and credit of the U.S. government. At the time of this writing, market participants throughout the world view U.S. Treasuries as being free of default risk, although there is the possibility that unwise economic policy by the U.S. government may alter that perception. While historically Treasury securities have served as the benchmark interest rates throughout the U.S. economy as well as in international capital markets, there are important benchmarks used by market participants that we will discuss later.

We have discussed earlier in this chapter the two theories about the determinants of the level of interest rate, which we will refer to as the base interest rate. A factor that is important in determining the level of rates is the expected rate of inflation. That is, the base interest rate can be expressed as:

Base interest rate = Real interest rate + Expected rate of inflation

The real interest rate is that that would exist in the economy in the absence of inflation.

THE RISK PREMIUM BETWEEN NON-TREASURY AND TREASURY SECURITIES WITH THE SAME MATURITY

In Chapters 17 and 18, we discussed the various sectors of the debt market and explain the myriad of debt instruments. Debt instruments not issued or backed by the full faith and credit of the U.S. government are available in the market at an interest rate or yield that is different from an otherwise comparable maturity Treasury security. We refer the difference between the interest rate offered on a non-Treasury security and a comparable maturity Treasury security as the *spread*. For example, if the yield on a five-year non-Treasury security is 5.4% and the yield on a 10-year Treasury security is 4%, the spread is said to be 1.4%. Rather than referring to the in percentage terms, such as 1.4%, market participants refer to the spread in terms of basis points. A basis point is equal to 0.01%. Consequently, 1% is equal to 100 basis points. In our example, the spread of 1.4% is equal to 140 basis points.

The spread exists because of the additional risk or risks to which an investor is exposed investing in a security that is not issued by the U.S. government. Consequently, the spread is referred to as a *risk premium*. Thus, we can express the interest rate offered on a non-Treasury security with the same maturity as a Treasury security as:

$$\text{Interest rate} = \text{Base interest rate} + \text{Spread}$$

or equivalently,

$$\text{Interest rate} = \text{Base interest rate} + \text{Risk premium}$$

While the spread or risk premium is typically positive, there are factors that can cause the risk premium to be negative as will be explained below. The general factors that affect the risk premium between a non-Treasury security and a Treasury security with the same maturity are:

- The market's perception of the credit risk of the non-Treasury security.
- Any features provided for in the non-Treasury security that make them attractive or unattractive to investors.
- The tax treatment of the interest income from the non-Treasury security.
- The expected liquidity of the non-Treasury issue.

FACTORS AFFECTING THE RISK PREMIUM

The risk premium is affected by the following factors:

- Default risk
- Inclusion of embedded options
- Taxability of interest
- Expected liquidity

We discuss each factor next.

Risk Premium Due to Default Risk

Default risk refers to the risk that the issuer of a debt obligation may be unable to make timely payment of interest or the principal amount when it is due. Although market participants often use default risk and credit risk interchangeably, as explained in Chapter 16 credit risk covers more than just default risk.

Most market participants gauge default risk in terms of credit rating assigned by the three major commercial rating companies: (1) Moody's Investors Service, (2) Standard & Poor's Corporation, and (3) Fitch Ratings. These companies, referred to as *rating agencies*, perform credit analyses of issuer's and issues and express their conclusions by a system of ratings. In all systems the term *high grade* means low credit risk, or conversely, high probability of future payments. The highest-grade bonds are designated by Moody's by the symbol Aaa, and by S&P and Fitch by the symbol AAA. The next highest grade is denoted by the symbol Aa (Moody's) or AA (S&P and Fitch); for the third grade all rating systems use A. The next three grades are Baa or BBB, Ba or BB, and B, respectively. There are also C grades. Moody's uses 1, 2, or 3 to provide a narrower credit quality breakdown within each class, and S&P and Fitch use plus and minus signs for the same purpose. Bond issues that are assigned a rating in the top four categories are referred to as *investment-grade bonds*. Issues that carry a rating below the top four categories are referred to as *noninvestment-grade bonds*, or more popularly as *high-yield bonds* or *junk bonds*.

The spread or risk premium between Treasury securities and non-Treasury securities that are identical in all respects except for credit rating is referred to as a *credit spread*.

For example, on August 5, 2008, finance.yahoo.com reported (based on information supplied by ValuBond) that the five-year Treasury yield was 3.29% and the same day the yield on five-year corporate bonds was as follows:

Credit Rating	Yield
AAA	5.01%
AA	5.50%
A	5.78%

Therefore, the credit spreads were:

Credit Rating	Credit Spread
AAA	5.01% − 3.29% = 1.72% = 172 basis points
AA	5.50% − 3.29% = 2.21% = 221 basis points
A	5.78% − 3.29% = 2.49% = 249 basis points

Note that the lower the credit rating, the higher the credit spread.

Inclusion of Embedded Options

We described the general characteristics of debt instruments in the previous chapter. The terms of the loan agreement may contain provisions that make the debt instrument more or less attractive compared to other debt instruments that do not have such provisions. When there is a provision that is attractive to an investor, the spread decreases relative to a Treasury security of the same maturity. The opposite occurs when there is an unattractive provision: The spread increases relative to comparable-maturity Treasury security.

The three most common features found in bond issues are:

1. Call provision
2. Put provision
3. Conversion provision

A *call provision* grants the issuer the right to retire the bond issue prior to the scheduled maturity date. A bond issue that contains such a provision is said to be a *callable bond*. The inclusion of a call provision benefits the issuer by allowing it to replace that bond issue with a lower interest cost bond issue should interest rates in the market decline. Effectively, a call provision allows the issuer to alter the maturity of the bond issue. A call provision is an unattractive feature for the bondholder because the bondholder will not only be uncertain about maturity, but faces the risk that the issuer will exercise the call provision when interest rates have declined below the interest rate on the bond issue. As a result, the bondholder must reinvest the proceeds received when the bond issue is called into another bond issue paying a lower interest rate. This risk associated with a callable bond is called *reinvestment risk*. For this reason, investors require compensation for accepting reinvestment risk and they receive this compensation in the form of a higher spread or risk premium.

A bond issue with a *put provision* grants the bondholder the right to sell the issue back to the issuer at par value on designated dates. A bond that contains this provision is referred to as a *putable bond*. Unlike a call provision, a put provision is an advantage to the bondholder. The reason is that if interest rates rise after the issuance of the bond, the price of the bond will decline. The put provision allows that bondholder to sell the bond back to the issuer, avoiding a market value loss on the bond and allowing the bondholder to reinvest the proceeds from the sale of the bond at a higher interest rate. Hence, a bond issue that contains a put provision will sell in the market at a lower spread than an otherwise comparable-maturity Treasury security.

A *conversion provision* grants the bondholder the right to exchange the bond issue for a specified number of shares of common stock. A bond with this provision is called a *convertible bond*. The conversion provision allows the bondholder the opportunity to benefit from a favorable movement in the price of the stock into which it can exchange bond. Hence, the conversion provision results in a lower spread relative to a comparable-maturity Treasury issue.

The three provisions we have described are effectively options. Unlike a stand alone option, these provisions are referred to as *embedded options* because they are options embedded in a bond issue.

Taxability of Interest

The U.S. federal tax code specifies that interest income is taxable at the federal income tax level unless otherwise exempted. The federal tax code specifically exempts the interest income from qualified municipal bond issues from taxation at the federal level. Municipal bonds are securities issued by state and local governments and by their creations, such as "authorities" and special districts. The tax-exempt feature of municipal bonds is an attractive feature to an investor because it reduces taxes and hence the spread is often such that the municipal bond issue sells in the market at a lower interest rate than a comparable-maturity bond issue.

For example, on August 5, 2008, finance.yahoo.com reported (based on information supplied by ValuBond) that the five-year Treasury yield was 3.29% and the same day the yield on five-year municipal bonds was as follows:

Credit Rating	Yield
AAA	2.95%
AA	3.04%
A	3.27%

When comparing the yield on a municipal bond issue to that of the yield on a comparable-maturity Treasury issue, the market convention is not to compute the basis point difference (i.e., the spread) between the two bond issues. Instead, the market convention is to compute the ratio of the yield of municipal bond issue to yield of a comparable-maturity Treasury security. The resulting ratio is called the municipal yield ratio. On August 5, 2008, the municipal yield ratio for the three five-year municipal bonds were:

Credit Rating	Municipal Yield Ratio
AAA	2.95%/3.29% = 0.90
AA	3.04%/3.29% = 0.92
A	3.27%/3.29% = 0.99

In selecting between a taxable bond (such as a corporate bond) and a municipal bond with the same maturity and credit rating, an investor can calculate the yield that must be offered on a taxable bond issue to give the same after-tax yield as a municipal bond issue. This yield measure is called the *equivalent taxable yield* and is determined as follows:

$$\text{Equivalent taxable yield} = \frac{\text{Tax-exempt yield}}{(1 - \text{Marginal tax rate})}$$

For example, suppose an investor is considering the purchase of a AA, five-year municipal bond on August 5, 2008 offering a yield of 3.04%. (the tax-exempt yield). Then

$$\text{Equivalent taxable yield} = \frac{0.0304}{(1 - 0.35)} = 4.68\%$$

That is, for an investor in the 35% marginal tax bracket, a taxable bond with a 4.68% yield would provide the equivalent of a 3.04% tax-exempt yield.

Expected Liquidity of a Bond Issue

When an investor wants to sell a particular bond issue, he or she is concerned whether the price that can be obtained from the sale will be close to the "true" value of the issue. For example, if recent trades in the market for a particular bond issue have been between 87.25 and 87.75 and market conditions have not changed, an investor would expect to sell the bond somewhere in the 87.25 to 87.75 range.

The concern that the investor has when contemplating the purchase of a particular bond issue is that he or she will have to sell it below its true value where the true value is indicated by recent transactions. This risk is referred to as *liquidity risk*. The greater the liquidity risk that investors perceive there is with a particular bond issue, the greater the spread or risk premium relative to a comparable-maturity Treasury security. The reason is that Treasury securities are the most liquid securities in the world.

TERM STRUCTURE OF INTEREST RATES

The price of a debt instrument will fluctuate over its life as yields in the market change. As explained and illustrated in Chapter 21, the price volatility of a bond is dependent on its maturity. More specifically, holding all other factors constant, the longer the maturity of a bond the greater the price volatility resulting from a change in market interest rates. The spread between any two maturity sectors of the market is called a *maturity spread*. Although this spread can be calculated for any sector of the market, it is most commonly calculated for the Treasury sector.

For example, this spread on August 6, 2008 Treasury issues for 2-year, 5-year, 10-year, and 30-year issues was follows:

Maturity	Yield
2-year	2.55%
5-year	3.29%
10-year	4.02%
30-year	4.64%

The maturity spreads were then:

5-year/2-year maturity spread: 3.29% − 2.55% = 74 basis points
10-year/2-year maturity spread: 4.02% − 2.55% = 147 basis points
10-year/5-year maturity spread: 4.02% − 3.29% = 73 basis points
30-year/2-year maturity spread: 4.64% − 2.55% = 209 basis points
30-year/5-year maturity spread: 4.64% − 3.29% = 135 basis points
30-year/10-year maturity spread: 4.64% − 4.02% = 62 basis points

FIGURE 19.1 Three Observed Shapes for the Yield Curve

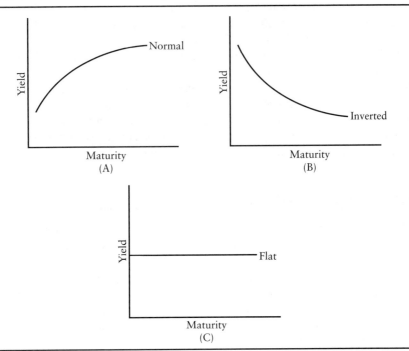

The relationship between the yields on comparable securities but different maturities is called the *term structure of interest rates*. Again, the primary focus is the Treasury market. The graphic that depicts the relationship between the yield on Treasury securities with different maturities is known as the *yield curve* and therefore the maturity spread is also referred to as the *yield curve spread*. Figure 19.1 shows the shape of three hypothetical Treasury yield curves that have been observed from time to time in the United States.

In the next part of this section, we discuss the term structure of interest rates and the various economic theories to explain it.

Forward Rates and Spot Rates

The focus on the Treasury yield curve functions is due mainly because of its role as a benchmark for setting yields in many other sectors of the debt market. However, a Treasury yield curve based on observed yields on the Treasury market is an unsatisfactory measure of the relation between required yield and maturity. The key reason is that securities with the same maturity may actually provide different yields. Hence, it is necessary to develop more accurate and reliable estimates of the Treasury yield curve. Specifically, the key is to estimate the theoretical interest rate that the U.S. Treasury would have to pay assuming that the security it issued is a zero-coupon security. Due its complexity, we will not explain how this is done. However, at this point all that is necessary to know is that there are procedures for estimating the theoretical interest rate or yield that the U.S. Treasury would have to pay for bonds with different maturities. These interest rates are called *Treasury spot rates*.

Valuable information for market participants can be obtained from the Treasury spot rates. These rates are called *forward rates*. First, we will see how these rates are obtained and then we will discuss theories about what determines forward rates. Finally, we will see how issuers can use the forward rates in making financing decisions.

Forward Rates

To see how a forward rate can be computed, consider the following two Treasury spot rates. Suppose that the spot rate for a zero-coupon Treasury security maturing in one year is 4% and a zero-coupon Treasury security maturing in two years is 5%. Let's look at this situation from the perspective of an investor who wants to invest funds for two years. The investor's choices are as follows:

Alternative 1. Investor buys a two-year zero-coupon Treasury security

Alternative 2. Investor buys a one-year zero-coupon Treasury security and when it matures in one year the investor buys another one-year instrument.

With Alternative 1, the investor will earn the two-year spot rate and that rate is known with certainty. In contrast, with Alternative 2, the investor will earn the one-year spot rate, but the one-year spot, one year from now, is unknown. Therefore, for Alternative 2, the rate that will be earned over one year is not known with certainty.

Suppose that this investor expected that one year from now the one-year spot rate will be higher than it is today. The investor might then feel Alternative 2 would be the better investment. However, this is not necessarily true. To understand why it is necessary to know what a forward rate is, let's continue with our illustration.

The investor will be indifferent to the two alternatives if they produce the same total dollars over the two-year investment horizon. Given the two-year spot rate, there is some spot rate on a one-year zero-coupon Treasury security one year from now that will make the investor indifferent between the two alternatives. We will denote that rate by f.

The value of f can be readily determined given the two-year spot rate and the one-year spot rate. If an investor placed $100 in the two-year zero-coupon Treasury security (Alternative 1) earning 5%, the total dollars that will be generated at the end of two years is (i.e., the future value based on compounding):

Total dollars at the end of two years for Alternative 1 = $100(1.05)^2$ = $110.25

The proceeds from investing in the one-year Treasury security at 4% will generate the following total dollars at the end of one year:

Total dollars at the end of two years for Alternative 2 = $100(1.04) = $104

If one year from now this amount is reinvested in a zero-coupon Treasury security maturing in one year, which we denoted f, then the total dollars at the end of two years would be

Total dollars at the end of two years for Alternative 2 = $104(1 + f)$

The investor will be indifferent between the two alternatives if the total dollars are the same. Setting the two equations for the total dollars at end of two years for the two alternatives equal we get

$$\$110.25 = \$104(1 + f)$$

Solving the preceding equation for f, we get

$$f = \frac{\$110.25}{\$104} - 1 = 0.06 = 6\%$$

Here is how we use this rate of 6%. If the one-year spot rate one year from now is less than 6%, then the total dollars at the end of two years would be higher by investing in the two-year zero-coupon Treasury security (Alternative 1). If the one-year spot rate one year from now is greater than 6%, then the total dollars at the end of two years would be higher by investing in a one-year zero-coupon Treasury security and reinvesting the proceeds one year from now at the one-year spot rate at that time (Alternative 2). Of course, if the one-year spot rate one year now is 6%, the two alternatives give the same total dollars at the end of two years.

Now that we have the forward rate f in which we are interested and we know how that rate can be used, let's return to the question we posed at the outset. Suppose that the investor expects that one year from now, the one-year spot rate will be 5.5%. That is, the investor expects that the one-year spot rate one year from now will be higher than its current level. Should the investor select Alternative 2 because the one-year spot rate one year from now is expected to be higher? The answer is no. As we explained in the previous paragraph, if the spot rate is less than 6%, then Alternative 1 is the better alternative. Since this investor expects a rate of 5.5%, then he or she should select Alternative 1 despite the fact that he or she expects the one-year spot rate to be higher than it is today.

This is a somewhat surprising result for some investors. But the reason for this is that the market prices its expectations of future interest rates into the rates offered on investments with different maturities. This is why knowing the forward rates is critical. Some market participants believe that the forward rate is the market's consensus of future interest rates.

Similarly, borrowers need to understand what a forward rate is. For example, suppose a borrower must choose between a two-year loan and a series of two one-year loans. If the forward rate is less than the borrower's expectations of one-year rates one year from now, then the borrower will be better off with a two-year loan. If, instead, the borrower's expectations are that the one-year rate one year from now will be less than the forward rate, the borrower will be better off by choosing a series of two one-year loans.

In practice, a corporate treasurer needs to know both forward rates and what future spreads will be. Recall that a corporation pays the Treasury rate (i.e., the benchmark) plus a spread.

A natural question about forward rates is how well they do at predicting future interest rates. Studies have demonstrated that forward rates do not do a good job in predicting future interest rates. Then, why the big deal about understanding forward rates? The reason, as we demonstrated in our illustration of how to select between two alternative investments, is that the forward rates indicate how an investor's and borrower's expectations must differ from the market consensus in order to make the correct decision.

In our illustration, the one-year forward rate may not be realized. That is irrelevant. The fact is that the one-year forward rate indicated to the investor that if expectations about the one-year rate one month from now are less than 6%, the investor would be better off with Alternative 1.

For this reason, as well as others explained later, some market participants do not refer to forward rates as being market consensus rates. Instead, they refer to forward rates as *hedgeable rates*. For example, by investing in the two-year Treasury security, the investor was able to hedge the one-year rate one year from now. Similarly, a corporation issuing a two-year security is hedging the one-year rate one year from now.[1]

Determinants of the Shape of the Term Structure

At given point in time, if we plot the term structure—the yield to maturity, or the spot rate, at successive maturities against maturity—we would observe one of the three shapes shown in Figure 19.1.

Figure 19.1A shows a yield curve where the yield increases with maturity. This type of yield curve is referred to as an *upward-sloping yield curve* or a *positively sloped yield curve*. Two examples of an upward-sloping yield curve from two days are shown in tabular form below:

Day	3 mos.	6 mos.	1 yr.	2 yrs.	3 yrs.	5 yrs.	7 yrs.	10 yrs.	20 yrs.	30 yrs.
04/15/1992	3.70	3.84	4.14	5.22	5.77	6.66	7.02	7.37	NA	7.87
08/22/2007	3.12	4.08	4.10	4.15	4.19	4.34	4.46	4.63	5.01	4.96
04/18/2008	1.35	1.68	1.85	2.19	2.35	2.95	3.29	3.77	4.52	4.51

A distinction is made for upward sloping yield curves based on the steepness of the yield curve. The steepness of the yield curve is typically measured in terms of the maturity spread between the long-term and short-term yields. While there are many maturity candidates to proxy for long-term and short-term yields, many market participants use the maturity spread between the 6-month and 30-year yield in our example.

The steepness of the two yield curves above is different. The maturity spread between the 30-year and six-month yield was 283 basis points (4.51% − 1.68%) on 4/18/2008 and 403 basis points (7.87% − 3.84%) on 4/14/1992. In practice, a Treasury positively sloped yield curve whose maturity spread as measured by the six-month and 30-year yields is referred to as a *normal yield curve* when the spread is 300 basis points or less. The yield curve on 4/18/2008 is therefore a normal yield curve. When the maturity spread is more than 300 basis points, the yield curve is said to be a *steep yield curve*. The yield curve on 4/15/1992 is a steep yield curve.

Figure 19.1B shows a *downward-sloping* or *inverted yield curve*, where yields in general decline as maturity increases. There have not been many instances in the recent history of the U.S. Treasury market where the yield curve exhibited this characteristic. Examples of downward sloping yield curves include the yield curves in mid-2000 and early 2007. For example:

---

[1] Note, however, that it is only the benchmark interest rate that is being hedged. The spread that the corporation or the issuer will pay can change.

The Structure of Interest Rates   **561**

Day	3 mos.	6 mos.	1 yr.	2 yrs.	3 yrs.	5 yrs.	7 yrs.	10 yrs.	20 yrs.	30 yrs.
02/21/2007	5.18	5.16	5.05	4.82	4.74	4.68	4.68	4.69	4.90	4.79
07/19/2000	6.33	6.15	6.46	6.4	6.31	6.35	6.16	6.29	5.92	6.33

The most notable is on August 14, 1981 Treasury yields at the time were at an historic high. The yield on the two-year was 16.91% and declined for each subsequent maturity until it reached 13.95% for the 30-year maturity.

Figure 19.1C depicts a *flat yield curve*. While the figure suggests that for a flat yield curve the yields are identical for each maturity, that is not what is observed in the maturity. Rather, the yields for all maturities are similar. The yield curves given below in tabular form are examples of a flat yield curve:

Day	3 mos.	6 mos.	1 yr.	2 yrs.	3 yrs.	5 yrs.	7 yrs.	10 yrs.	20 yrs.	30 yrs.
01/03/1990	7.89	7.94	7.85	7.94	7.96	7.92	8.04	7.99	N/A	8.04
05/23/2007	4.91	5.01	4.96	4.85	4.79	4.79	4.8	4.86	5.09	5.01

Notice the very small six-month/30-year maturity spread of less than 10 basis points.

A variant of the flat yield is one in which the yield on short-term and long-term Treasuries are similar but the yield on intermediate-term Treasuries are much lower than the six-month and 30-year yields. Such a yield curve is referred to as a *humped yield curve*. Examples of humped yield curves are the following:

Day	3 mos.	6 mos.	1 yr.	2 yrs.	3 yrs.	5 yrs.	7 yrs.	10 yrs.	20 yrs.	30 yrs.
11/24/2000	6.34	6.12	5.86	5.74	5.63	5.7	5.63	5.86	5.67	6.34
01/01/2007	5.87	5.58	5.11	4.87	4.82	4.76	4.97	4.92	5.46	5.35

Economic Theories of the Term Structure of Interest Rates

There are two major economic theories that have evolved to account for the observed shapes of the yield curve: the *expectations theory* and the *market segmentation theory*.

Expectations Theories

There are several forms of the expectations theory:

1. Pure expectations theory
2. Biased expectations theory

Both theories share an hypothesis about the behavior of short-term forward rates and also assume that the forward rates in current long-term bonds are closely related to the market's expectations about future short-term rates. The two theories differ, however, on whether or not other factors also affect forward rates, and how. The pure expectations theory postulates that no systematic factors other than expected future short-term rates affect forward rates; the biases expectations theory asserts that there are other factors.

Pure Expectations Theory According to the pure expectations theory, the forward rates exclusively represent the expected future rates. Thus, the entire term structure at a given time reflects the market's current expectations of the family of future short-term rates. Under this view, a rising term structure, as in Figure 19.1A, must indicate that the market expects short-term rates to rise throughout the relevant future. Similarly, a flat term structure reflects an expectation that future short-term rates will be mostly constant, while a falling term structure must reflect an expectation that future short rates will decline steadily.

A major shortcoming of the pure expectations theory is that is ignores the risks inherent in investing in debt instruments. If forward rates were perfect predictors of future interest rates, then the future prices of bonds would be known with certainty. The return over any investment period would be certain and independent of the maturity of the debt instrument initially acquired and of the time at which the investor needed to liquidate the debt instrument. However, with uncertainty about future interest rates and hence about future prices of bonds, these debt instruments become risky investments in the sense that the return over some investment horizon is unknown.

Similarly, from a borrower's perspective, the cost of borrowing for any required period of financing would be certain and independent of the maturity of the debt instrument if the rate at which the borrower must refinance debt in the future is known. But with uncertainty about future interest rates, the cost of borrowing is uncertain if the borrower must refinance at some time over the periods in which the funds are initially needed.

Biased Expectations Theory Biased expectations theories take into account the shortcomings of the pure expectations theory. The two theories are:

- The liquidity theory
- Preferred habitat theory

According to the *liquidity theory*, the forward rates will not be an unbiased estimate of the market's expectations of future interest rates because they embody a premium to compensate for risk; this risk premium is referred to as a *liquidity premium*. Thus, an upward-sloping yield curve may reflect expectations that future interest rates either (1) will rise or (2) will be flat or even fall, but with a liquidity premium increasing fast enough with maturity so as to produce an upward-sloping yield curve.

The *preferred habitat theory* also adopts the view that the term structure reflects the expectation of the future path of interest rates as well as a risk premium. However, the preferred habitat theory rejects the assertion that the risk premium must rise uniformly with maturity. Proponents of the habitat theory say that the latter conclusion could be accepted if all investors intend to liquidate their investment at the first possible date, while all borrowers are eager to borrow long. However, this is an assumption that can be rejected for a number of reasons. The argument is that different financial institutions have different investment horizons and have a preference for the maturities in which they invest. The preference is based on the maturity of their liabilities. To induce a financial institution out of that maturity sector, a premium must be paid. Thus, the forward rates include a liquidity premium and compensation for investors to move out of their preferred maturity sector. Consequently, forward rates do not reflect the market's consensus of future interest rates.

Market Segmentation Theory

The *market segmentation theory* also recognizes that investors have preferred habitats dictated by saving and investment flows. This theory also proposes that the major reason for the shape of the yield curve lies in asset and liability management constraints (either regulatory or self-imposed) and creditors (borrowers) restricting their lending (financing) to specific maturity sectors. However, the market segmentation theory differs from the preferred habitat theory because the market segmentation theory assumes that neither investors nor borrowers are willing to shift from one maturity sector to another to take advantage of opportunities arising from differences between expectations and forward rates. Thus, for the segmentation theory, the shape of the yield curve is determined by supply of and demand for securities within each maturity sector.

Swap Rate Yield Curve

Another benchmark that is used by global investors is the swap rate. (Chapter 24 describes interest rate swaps, a derivative instrument.) In a generic interest rate swap, the parties exchange interest rate payments on specified dates: One party pays a fixed rate and the other party a floating rate over the life of the swap. In a typical swap, the floating rate is based on a reference rate and the reference rate is typically the London Interbank Offered Rate (LIBOR). The fixed interest rate that is paid by the fixed rate counterparty is called the *swap rate*. The relationship between the swap rate and maturity of a swap is called the *swap rate yield curve*, or more commonly referred to as the *swap curve*. Because it the reference rate is typically LIBOR, the swap curve is also called the *LIBOR curve*.

The swap curve is used as a benchmark in many countries outside the United States. Unlike a country's government bond yield curve, however, the swap curve is not a default-free yield curve. Instead, it reflects the credit risk of the counterparty to an interest rate swap. Since the counterparty to an interest rate swap is typically a bank-related entity, the swap curve reflects the average credit risk of representative banks that provide interest rate swaps. More specifically, a swap curve is viewed as the *interbank yield curve*. It is also referred to as the *AA yield curve* because the banks that borrow money from each other at LIBOR have credit ratings of Aa/AA or above.

We see the effect of this credit risk when we compare the yield curve based on U.S. Treasuries with the swap rate curve. For example, consider the rates for August 22, 2008:

	1 yr.	2 yrs.	3 yrs.	4 yrs.	5 yrs.	7 yrs.	10 yrs.	30 yrs.
Yield curve, U.S. Treasuries	2.15	2.35	2.62	NA	3.07	3.39	3.82	4.44
Swap curve		3.05	3.38	3.73	3.95	4.10	4.36	4.58	4.92

The spread between these two curves ranges from 48 basis points for 30-year yield to 111 basis points for 3-year yield.

There are reasons why investors prefer to use a country's swap curve if it available than a country's yield curve obtained from its government bonds. We will not describe these reasons here.[2]

SUMMARY

Interest rates are determined by the base rate (rate on a Treasury security) plus a spread or risk premium. The factors that affect the risk premium for a non-Treasury security with the same maturity as a Treasury security are (1) the perceived creditworthiness of the issuer; (2) inclusion of provisions such

---

[2]These reasons are provided in Ron (2002).

as a call provision, put provision, or conversion provision; (3) taxability of interest; and (4) expected liquidity of an issue.

The term structure of interest rates shows the relationship between the yield on a bond and its maturity; the yield curve is the graph of the relationship between the yield on bonds of the same credit quality but different maturities. Valuable information for issuers and investors is provided in forward rates. Two major theories are offered to explain the observed shapes of the yield curve: the expectations theory and the market segmentation theory. There are two forms of the expectations theory: pure expectations theory and biased expectations theory. The two forms of the biased expectations theory are the liquidity theory and the preferred habit theory.

REFERENCES

Ron, U. 2002. A practical guide to swap curve construction. Chap. 6 in *Interest rate, term structure, and valuation modeling*, edited by F. J. Fabozzi. New York: John Wiley & Sons.

CHAPTER 20
Bond Pricing and Yield Measures

In previous chapters, we discussed the fundamental characteristics of bonds and the wide range of bonds available in the market. In this chapter and the one to follow, we explain the fundamental analytical tools necessary to understand how to analyze bonds and assess their potential performance.

This chapter illustrates how to determine the price of a bond as well as the relationship between price and yield. Then we discuss various yield measures and their meaning for evaluating the potential performance over some investment horizon. In particular, we explain the various conventions for measuring the yield of a bond, and then demonstrate why conventional yield measures fail to identify the potential return from investing in a bond over some investment horizon. A better measure for assessing the potential return from investing in a bond is the total return. We see how to calculate the potential total return from investing in a bond over some investment horizon. In Chapter 21, we explain the price volatility characteristics of a bond and describe measures to quantify price volatility.

PRICING OF OPTION-FREE BONDS

The price of any financial instrument is equal to the present value of the expected cash flows from the financial instrument. Therefore, determining the price requires:

1. An estimate of the expected cash flows.
2. An estimate of the appropriate required yield.

The expected cash flows for some financial instruments are simple to compute; for others, the task is more difficult. The *required yield* reflects the yield for financial instruments with comparable risk.

The first step in determining the price of a bond is to estimate its cash flow. The cash flow for a bond that the issuer cannot retire prior to its stated maturity date (that is, an option-free bond) consists of:

1. Periodic coupon interest payments to the maturity date.
2. The par value at maturity.

Our illustrations of bond pricing use three assumptions to simplify the analysis:

1. The coupon payments are made every six months. (For most U.S. bond issues, coupon interest is in fact paid semiannually.)
2. The next coupon payment for the bond is received exactly six months from now.
3. The coupon interest is fixed for the term of the bond.

While our focus in this chapter is on option-free bonds, in Chapter 22 we explain how to value bonds with embedded options.

Consequently, the cash flows for an option-free bond consist of an annuity of a fixed coupon interest payment paid semiannually and the par, or maturity, value. For example, a 20-year bond with a 10% coupon rate and a par, or maturity, value of $1,000 has the following cash flows from coupon interest:

$$\text{Annual coupon interest} = \$1{,}000 \times 0.10 = \$100$$

$$\text{Semiannual coupon interest} = \$100/2 = \$50$$

Therefore, there are 40 semiannual cash flows of $50, and there is a $1,000 cash flow 40 six-month periods from now.

Notice the treatment of the par value. It is not treated as if it is received 20 years from now. Instead, it is treated on a basis consistent with the coupon payments, which are semiannual.

The required yield is determined by investigating the yields offered on comparable bonds in the market. In this case, comparable investments would be option-free bonds of the same credit quality and the same maturity. The required yield typically is expressed as an annual interest rate. When the cash flows occur semiannually, the market convention is to use one-half the annual interest rate as the periodic interest rate with which to discount the cash flows.

Given the cash flows of a bond and the required yield, we have all the information needed to price a bond. Because the price of a bond is the pres-

Bond Pricing and Yield Measures

ent value of the cash flows, it is determined by adding these two present values:

1. The present value of the semiannual coupon payments.
2. The present value of the par, or maturity, value at the maturity date.

In general, the price of a bond can be computed using the following formula:

$$P = \frac{C}{(1+r)^1} + \frac{C}{(1+r)^2} + \frac{C}{(1+r)^3} + \cdots + \frac{C}{(1+r)^n} + \frac{M}{(1+r)^n}$$

or

$$P = \sum_{t=1}^{n} \frac{C}{(1+r)^t} + \frac{M}{(1+r)^n} \tag{20.1}$$

where

- P = price (in \$)
- n = number of periods (number of years × 2)
- C = semiannual coupon payment (in \$)
- r = periodic interest rate (required annual yield ÷ 2)
- M = maturity value
- t = time period when the payment is to be received

Because the semiannual coupon payments are equivalent to an ordinary annuity, the present value of the coupon payments can be determined from the following formula:

$$\text{Present value of coupon payments} = C \left[\frac{1 - \frac{1}{(1+r)^n}}{r} \right] \tag{20.2}$$

To illustrate how to compute the price of a bond, consider a 20-year 10% coupon bond with a par value of \$1,000. Let's suppose that the required yield on this bond is 11%. The cash flows for this bond are as follows:

1. 40 semiannual coupon payments of \$50.
2. \$1,000 to be received 40 six-month periods from now.

The semiannual or periodic interest rate (or periodic required yield) is 5.5% (11% divided by 2).

The present value of the 40 semiannual coupon payments of $50, discounted at 5.5%, is $802.31, calculated as

$$C = \$50 \quad n = 40 \quad r = 0.055$$

$$\text{Present value of coupon payments} = \$50 \left[\frac{1 - \frac{1}{(1.055)^{40}}}{0.055} \right]$$

$$= \$50 \left(\frac{1 - 0.117463}{0.055} \right) = \$802.31$$

The present value of the par, or maturity, value of $1,000 received 40 six-month periods from now, discounted at 5.5%, is $117.46, as follows:

$$\frac{\$1,000}{(1.055)^{40}} = \frac{\$1,000}{8.51332} = \$117.46$$

The price of the bond is then equal to the sum of the two present values:

```
Present value of coupon payments       = $802.31
+ Present value of par (maturity value) =  117.46
Price                                   = $919.77
```

Suppose that instead of an 11% required yield, the required yield is 6.8%. The price of the bond would then be $1,347.04, demonstrated as follows: The present value of the coupon payments, using a periodic interest rate of 3.4% (6.8%/2), is

$$\text{Present value of component payments} = \$50 \left[\frac{1 - \frac{1}{(1.034)^{40}}}{0.034} \right] = \$1,084.51$$

The present value of the par, or maturity, value of $1,000 received 40 six-month periods from now, discounted at 3.4%, is

$$\frac{\$1,000}{(1.034)^{40}} = \$262.53$$

The price of the bond is then

```
Present value of coupon payments       = $1,084.51
+ Present value of par (maturity value) =    262.53
Price                                   = $1,347.04
```

If the required yield is equal to the coupon rate of 10%, it can be demonstrated that the price of the bond would be its par value, $1,000.

Zero-coupon bonds do not make any periodic coupon payments. Instead, the investor realizes interest as the difference between the maturity value and the purchase price. The price of a zero-coupon bond is calculated by substituting zero for C in equation (20.1):

$$P = \frac{M}{(1+r)^n} \qquad (20.3)$$

Equation (20.3) states that the price of a zero-coupon bond is simply the present value of the maturity value. In the present value computation, however, the number of periods used for discounting is not the number of years to maturity of the bond, but rather, double the number of years. The discount rate is one-half the required annual yield.

Price/Yield Relationship

A fundamental property of a bond is that its price changes in the opposite direction from the change in the required yield. The reason is that the price of the bond is the present value of the cash flows. As the required yield increases, the present value of the cash flows decreases; hence, the price decreases. The opposite is true when the required yield decreases: The present value of the cash flows increases, and, therefore, the price of the bond increases. This can be seen by examining the price for the 20-year, 10% bond when the required yield is 11%, 10%, and 6.8%. Table 20.1 shows the price of the 20-year, 10% coupon bond for various required yields.

If we graph the price/required yield relationship for any option-free bond, we will find that it has the bowed shape shown in Figure 20.1. This shape is referred to as *convex*. The convexity of the price/yield relationship has important implications for the investment properties of a bond, as we explain later in this chapter.

Relationship between Coupon Rate, Required Yield, and Price

As yields in the marketplace change, the only variable that can change to compensate an investor in an existing bond is the price of that bond. When the coupon rate is equal to the required yield, the price of the bond will be equal to its par value as we state earlier.

When yields in the marketplace rise above the coupon rate at a given point in time, the price of the bond adjusts so that the investor can realize some additional interest. This is accomplished by the price falling below its

TABLE 20.1 Price/Yield Relationship for a 20-Year, 10% Coupon Bond

Yield	Price	Yield	Price
0.045	$1,720.32	0.110	$919.77
0.050	1,627.57	0.115	883.50
0.055	1,541.76	0.120	849.54
0.060	1,462.30	0.125	817.70
0.065	1,388.65	0.130	787.82
0.070	1,320.33	0.135	759.75
0.075	1,256.89	0.140	733.37
0.080	1,197.93	0.145	708.53
0.085	1,143.08	0.150	685.14
0.090	1,092.01	0.155	663.08
0.095	1,044.41	0.160	642.26
0.100	1,000.00	0.165	622.59
0.105	958.53		

FIGURE 20.1 Shape of the Price/Yield Relationship

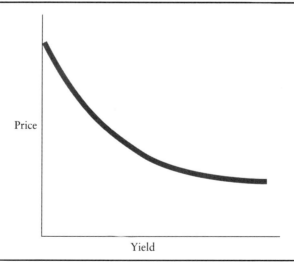

par value. The capital appreciation realized by holding the bond to maturity represents a form of interest to the investor to compensate for a coupon rate that is lower than the required yield. When a bond sells below its par value, it is said to be selling at a *discount*. In our earlier calculation of bond price, we saw that when the required yield is greater than the coupon rate, the price of the bond is always lower than the par value ($1,000).

When the required yield in the market is below the coupon rate, the bond must sell above its par value. This is because investors who would have the opportunity to purchase the bond at par would be getting a coupon rate in excess of what the market requires. As a result, investors would bid up the price of the bond because its yield is so attractive. The price would eventually be bid up to a level where the bond offers the required yield in the market. A bond whose price is above its par value is said to be selling at a *premium*.

The relationship between coupon rate, required yield, and price can be summarized as follows:

Coupon rate < Required yield: Price < Par (discount bond)

Coupon rate = Required yield: Price = Par

Coupon rate > Required yield: Price > Par (premium bond)

Relationship between Bond Price and Time If Interest Rates Are Unchanged

If the required yield does not change between the time the bond is purchased and the maturity date, what will happen to the price of the bond? For a bond selling at par value, the coupon rate is equal to the required yield. As the bond moves closer to maturity, the bond will continue to sell at par value. The price of a bond will not remain constant for a bond selling at a premium or a discount, however. A discount bond's price increases as it approaches maturity, assuming the required yield does not change. For a premium bond, the opposite occurs. For both bonds, the price will equal par value at the maturity date.

Reasons for the Change in the Price of a Bond

The price of a bond will change for one or more of the following three reasons:

1. There is a change in the required yield owing to changes in the credit quality of the issuer. That is, the required yield changes because the

market now compares the bond yield with yields from a different set of bonds with the same credit risk.
2. There is a change in the price of the bond selling at a premium or a discount without any change in the required yield, simply because the bond is moving toward maturity.
3. There is a change in the required yield owing to a change in the yield on comparable bonds. That is, market interest rates change.

Complications

The framework for pricing a bond discussed in this chapter assumes that:

1. The next coupon payment is exactly six months away.
2. The cash flows are known.
3. One rate is used to discount all cash flows.

Let's look at the implications for the pricing of a bond if each assumption is not true.

Next Coupon Payment Due in Less Than Six Months

When an investor purchases a bond whose next coupon payment is due in less than six months, the accepted method for computing the price of the bond is as follows:

$$P = \sum_{t=1}^{n} \frac{C}{(1+r)^v (1+r)^{t-1}} + \frac{M}{(1+r)^v (1+r)^{n-1}} \quad (20.4)$$

where

$$v = \frac{\text{Days between settlement and next coupon}}{\text{Days in six-month period}}$$

Note that when v is 1 (that is, when the next coupon payment is six months away), equation (20.4) reduces to equation (20.1).

The Cash Flows May Not Be Known

For option-free bonds, assuming that the issuer does not default, the cash flows are known. For some bonds, however, the cash flows are not known with certainty. This is because an issuer may have an option to call a bond before the stated maturity date. With callable bonds, the cash flows will, in fact, depend on the future level of interest rates relative to the coupon rate.

Bond Pricing and Yield Measures

For example, the issuer will typically call a bond when interest rates drop far enough below the coupon rate so that it is economic to retire the bond issue prior to maturity and issue new bonds at a lower coupon rate.[1] Consequently, the cash flows of bonds that may be called prior to maturity are dependent on future interest rates in the marketplace.

Different Discount Rates Apply to Each Cash Flow

Our pricing analysis has assumed that it is appropriate to discount each cash flow using the same discount rate. A bond can be viewed as a package of zero-coupon bonds, in which case a unique discount rate should be used to determine the present value of each cash flow. As will be explained in Chapter 22, this means discounting each cash flow at the spot rate for the period when the cash flow is expected to be received.

Price Quotes

We have assumed in our illustrations that the maturity, or par, value of a bond is $1,000. A bond may have a maturity, or par, value greater or less than $1,000. Consequently, when quoting bond prices, traders quote the price as a percentage of par value. A bond selling at par is quoted as 100, meaning 100% of its par value. A bond selling at a discount will be selling for less than 100; a bond selling at a premium will be selling for more than 100.

The procedure for converting a price quote to a dollar price is as follows:

(Price per $100 of par value/100) × par value

For example, if a bond is quoted at 96½ and has a par value of $100,000, then the dollar price is

(96.5/100) × $100,000 = $96,500

If a bond is quoted at 103^{19}/$_{32}$ and has a par value of $1 million, then the dollar price is

(103.59375/100) × $1,000,000 = $1,035,937.50

As explained in Chapter 16, when an investor purchases a bond between coupon payments, the investor must compensate the seller for the accrued

---

[1] Mortgage-backed securities are another example; the borrower has the right to prepay all or part of the obligation prior to maturity.

interest. How accrued interest is calculated is explained in the appendix to Chapter 16.

CONVENTIONAL YIELD MEASURES

Related to the price of a bond is its yield. The price of a bond is calculated from the cash flows and the required yield. The yield of a bond is calculated from the cash flows and the market price plus accrued interest. In this section, we discuss various yield measures and their meaning for evaluating the relative attractiveness of a bond.

There are three bond yield measures commonly quoted by dealers and used by portfolio managers: (1) current yield, (2) yield to maturity, and (3) yield to call. In our illustrations below we assume that the next coupon payment is six months from now and therefore there is no accrued interest.

Current Yield

Current yield relates the annual coupon interest to the market price. The formula for the current yield is

$$\text{Current yield} = \frac{\text{Annual dollar coupon interest}}{\text{Price}}$$

For example, the current yield for a 15-year, 7% coupon bond with a par value of $1,000 selling for $769.40 is 9.10%, as shown:

$$\text{Current yield} = \frac{\$70}{\$769.40} = 0.091\% = 9.1\%$$

The current yield calculation takes into account only the coupon interest and no other source of return that will affect an investor's yield. No consideration is given to the capital gain that the investor will realize when a bond is purchased at a discount and held to maturity; nor is there any recognition of the capital loss that the investor will realize if a bond purchased at a premium is held to maturity. The time value of money is also ignored.

Yield to Maturity

The *yield to maturity* is the interest rate that will make the present value of a bond's remaining cash flows (if held to maturity) equal to the price (plus accrued interest, if any). Mathematically, the yield to maturity, y, for a bond that pays interest semiannually and that has no accrued interest is found by solving the following equation:

$$P = \frac{C}{(1+y)^1} + \frac{C}{(1+y)^2} + \frac{C}{(1+y)^3} + \cdots + \frac{C}{(1+y)^n} + \frac{M}{(1+y)^n}$$

This expression can be rewritten in shorthand notation as

$$P = \sum_{t=1}^{n} \frac{C}{(1+y)^t} + \frac{M}{(1+y)^n} \qquad (20.5)$$

Since the cash flows are every six months, the yield to maturity y found by solving equation (20.5) is a semiannual yield to maturity. This yield can be annualized by either (1) doubling the semiannual yield or (2) compounding the yield. The market convention is to annualize the semiannual yield by simply doubling its value. The yield to maturity computed on the basis of this market convention is called the *bond-equivalent yield*. It is also referred to as a yield on a *bond-equivalent basis*.

The computation of the yield to maturity requires an iterative procedure. To illustrate the computation, consider the bond that we used to compute the current yield. The cash flow for this bond is (1) 30 coupon payments of $35 every six months and (2) $1,000 to be paid 30 six-month periods from now. To get y in equation (20.5), different interest rates must be tried until the present value of the cash flows is equal to the price of $769.42. The present value of the cash flows of the bond for several periodic interest rates is shown in Table 20.2.

When a 5% semiannual interest rate is used, the present value of the cash flows is $769.42. Therefore, y is 5%, and is the semiannual yield to maturity. As noted before, the convention in the market is to double the

TABLE 20.2 Iterative Procedure for Calculating the Yield to Maturity

Annual Interest Rate (2y)	Semiannual Rate (y)	Present Value of 30 Payments of $35	Present Value of $1,000 30 Periods from Now	Present Value of Cash Flows
9.00	4.50	570.11	267.00	837.11
9.50	4.75	553.71	248.53	802.24
10.00	5.00	538.04	231.38	769.42[a]
10.50	5.25	532.04	215.45	738.49
11.00	5.50	508.68	200.64	709.32

[a] Market price.

TABLE 20.3 Relationship between Coupon Rate, Current Yield, Yield to Maturity, and Bond Price

Bond Selling At	Relationship
Par	Coupon rate = Current yield = Yield to maturity
Discount	Coupon rate < Current yield < Yield to maturity
Premium	Coupon rate > Current yield > Yield to maturity

semiannual yield to obtain an annualized yield. Thus, the yield on a bond-equivalent basis for our hypothetical bond is 10%.

It is much easier to compute the yield to maturity for a zero-coupon bond. To find the yield to maturity, we substitute zero for the coupon in equation (20.5) and solve for y:

$$y = \left(\frac{M}{P}\right)^{1/n} - 1 \qquad (20.6)$$

For example, for a 10-year zero-coupon bond with a maturity value of $1,000, selling for $439.18:

$$y = \left(\frac{\$1,000}{\$439.18}\right)^{1/20} - 1 = 0.042 = 4.2\%$$

Note that the number of periods is equal to 20 semiannual periods, which is double the number of years. The number of years is not used because we want a yield value that may be compared with alternative coupon bonds. To get the bond-equivalent annual yield, we must double y, which gives us 8.4%.

The yield-to-maturity calculation takes into account not only the current coupon income but also any capital gain or loss the investor will realize by holding the bond to maturity. In addition, the yield to maturity considers the timing of the cash flows.

The relationship among the coupon rate, current yield, yield to maturity, and bond price is shown in Table 20.3.

Yield to Call

As explained in Chapter 16, the issuer may be entitled to call a bond prior to the stated maturity date. When the bond may be called and at what price is specified in the indenture. The price at which the bond may be called is referred to as the *call price*. For some issues, the call price is the same regardless of when the issue is called. For other callable issues, the call price depends on when the issue is called. That is, there is a *call schedule* that specifies a call price for each call date.

Bond Pricing and Yield Measures

For callable issues, the practice has been to calculate a *yield to call* as well as a yield to maturity. The yield to call assumes that the issuer will call the bond at some assumed call date, and the call price is then the call price specified in the call schedule. Typically, investors calculate a *yield to first call* and a *yield to par call*. The yield to first call assumes that the issue will be called on the first call date. The yield to first par call assumes that the issue will be called the first time on the call schedule when the issuer is entitled to call the bond at par value.

The procedure for calculating the yield to any assumed call date is the same as for any yield calculation: Determine the interest rate that will make the present value of the expected cash flows equal to the price plus accrued interest. In the case of yield to first call, the expected cash flows are the coupon payments to the first call date and the call price. For the yield to first par call, the expected cash flows are the coupon payments to the first date at which the issuer may call the bond at par.

Mathematically, the yield to call can be expressed as follows:

$$P = \frac{C}{(1+y_c)^1} + \frac{C}{(1+y_c)^2} + \frac{C}{(1+y_c)^3} + \cdots + \frac{C}{(1+y_c)^{n^*}} + \frac{M^*}{(1+y_c)^{n^*}}$$

$$P = \sum_{t=1}^{n^*} \frac{C}{(1+y_c)^t} + \frac{M^*}{(1+y_c)^{n^*}} \quad (20.7)$$

where

M^* = call price (in \$) at the assumed call date
n^* = number of periods until the assumed call date
y_c = yield to call

For a bond that pays coupon interest semiannually, doubling y_c gives the yield to call on a bond-equivalent basis.

To illustrate the computation, consider an 18-year, 11% coupon bond with a maturity value of \$1,000 selling for \$1,168.97. Suppose that the first call date is 13 years from now and that the call price is \$1,055. The cash flows for this bond if it is called in 13 years are (1) 26 coupon payments of \$55 every six months and (2) \$1,055 due in 26 six-month periods from now.

The value for y_c—the yield to first call in this example—in equation (20.7) is the one that will make the present value of the cash flows to the first call date equal to the bond's price of \$1,168.97. In this case, that periodic interest rate is 4.5%. Therefore, the yield to first call on a bond-equivalent basis is 9%.

Investors typically compute both the yield to call and the yield to maturity for a callable bond selling at a premium. They then select the lower of the two as the yield measure. The lowest yield based on every possible call date and the yield to maturity is referred to as the *yield to worst*.

Potential Sources of a Bond's Dollar Return

An investor who purchases a bond can expect to receive a dollar return from one or more of these sources:

1. The periodic coupon interest payments made by the issuer.
2. Income from reinvestment of the periodic interest payments (the interest-on-interest component).
3. Any capital gain (or capital loss—negative dollar return) when the bond matures, is called, or is sold.

Any measure of a bond's potential yield should take into consideration each of these three potential sources of return. The current yield considers only the coupon interest payments. No consideration is given to any capital gain (or loss) or to interest-on-interest. The yield to maturity takes into account coupon interest and any capital gain (or loss). It also considers the interest-on-interest component; implicit in the yield-to-maturity computation, however, is the assumption that the coupon payments can be reinvested at the computed yield to maturity. The yield to maturity, therefore, is a *promised yield;* that is, it will be realized only if (1) the bond is held to maturity and (2) the coupon interest payments are reinvested at the yield to maturity. If either (1) or (2) fails to occur, the actual yield realized by an investor can be greater than or less than the yield to maturity when the bond is purchased.

The yield to call also takes into account all three potential sources of return. In this case, the assumption is that the coupon payments can be reinvested at the computed yield to call. Therefore, the yield-to-call measure suffers from the same drawback inherent in the implicit assumption of the reinvestment rate for the coupon interest payments. Also, it assumes that the bond will be held until the assumed call date, at which time the bond will be called.

Determining the Interest-on-Interest Dollar Return

The interest-on-interest component can represent a substantial portion of a bond's potential return. Letting r denote the semiannual reinvestment rate, we can find the interest-on-interest plus the total coupon payments from the following formula:[2]

---

[2] This is the formula for the future value of an annuity.

$$\text{Coupon interest} + \text{Interest-on-interest} = C\left[\frac{(1+r)^n - 1}{r}\right] \quad (20.8)$$

The total dollar amount of coupon interest is found by multiplying the semiannual coupon interest by the number of periods:

$$\text{Total coupon interest} = nC$$

The interest-on-interest component is then the difference between the coupon interest plus interest-on-interest and the total dollar coupon interest, as expressed in equation (20.9):

$$\text{Interest-on-interest} = C\left[\frac{(1+r)^n - 1}{r}\right] - nC \quad (20.9)$$

The yield-to-maturity measure assumes that the reinvestment rate is the yield to maturity. For example, let's consider the 15-year, 7% bond that we have used to illustrate how to compute the current yield and yield to maturity. The yield to maturity for this bond is 10%. Assuming an annual reinvestment rate of 10%, or a semiannual reinvestment rate of 5%, the interest-on-interest plus total coupon payments using equation (20.8) is

$$\text{Coupon interest} + \text{Interest-on-interest} = \$35\left[\frac{(1.05)^{30} - 1}{0.05}\right] = \$2,325.36$$

Using equation (20.9), we calculate the interest-on-interest component as

$$\text{Coupon interest} = 30\,(\$35) = \$1,050.00$$

$$\text{Interest-on-interest} = \$2,325.36 - \$1,050 = \$1,275.36$$

Yield to Maturity and Reinvestment Risk

Let's look at the potential total dollar return from holding this bond to maturity. As mentioned earlier, the total dollar return comes from three sources. In our example:

1. Total coupon interest of $1,050 (coupon interest of $35 every six months for 15 years).
2. Interest-on-interest of $1,275.36 earned from reinvesting the semiannual coupon interest payments at 5% every six months.
3. A capital gain of $230.60 ($1,000 par value minus $769.40 purchase price).

The potential total dollar return if the coupons can be reinvested at the yield to maturity of 10% is then $2,555.96.

Notice that if an investor places the money that would have been used to purchase this bond, $769.40, in a savings account earning 5% semiannually for 15 years, the future value of the savings account would be

$$\$769.40(1.05)^{30} = \$3,325.30$$

For the initial investment of $769.40, the total dollar return is $2,555.96.

So an investor who invests $769.40 for 15 years at 10% per year (5% semiannually) expects to receive at the end of 15 years the initial investment of $769.40 plus $2,555.96. This is precisely what we found by breaking down the dollar return on the bond, assuming a reinvestment rate equal to the yield to maturity of 10%. Thus, it can be seen that for the bond to yield 10%, the investor must generate $1,275.36 by reinvesting the coupon payments. This means that to generate a yield to maturity of 10%, approximately half ($1,275.36/$2,555.96) of this bond's total dollar return must come from the reinvestment of the coupon payments.

The investor will realize the yield to maturity at the time of purchase only if the bond is held to maturity and the coupon payments can be reinvested at the yield to maturity. The risk that the investor faces is that future reinvestment rates will be less than the yield to maturity at the time the bond is purchased. This risk is called *reinvestment risk*.

Two characteristics of a bond determine the importance of the interest-on-interest component and, therefore, the degree of reinvestment risk: maturity and coupon. For a given yield to maturity and a given coupon rate, the longer the maturity, the more dependent the bond's total dollar return is on the interest-on-interest component in order to realize the yield to maturity at the time of purchase. In other words, the longer the maturity, the greater the reinvestment risk. The implication is that the yield-to-maturity measure for long-term coupon bonds tells little about the potential yield that an investor may realize if the bond is held to maturity. For long-term bonds, the interest-on-interest component may be as high as 80% of the bond's potential total dollar return.

Turning to the coupon rate, for a given maturity and a given yield to maturity, the higher the coupon rate, the more dependent the bond's total dollar return will be on the reinvestment of the coupon payments in order to produce the yield to maturity anticipated at the time of purchase. This means that when maturity and yield to maturity are held constant, premium bonds are more dependent on the interest-on-interest component than are bonds selling at par. Discount bonds are less dependent on the interest-on-interest component than are bonds selling at par. For zero-coupon bonds,

Bond Pricing and Yield Measures

none of the bond's total dollar return is dependent on the interest-on-interest component. So a zero-coupon bond has no reinvestment risk if held to maturity. Thus, the yield earned on a zero-coupon bond held to maturity is equal to the promised yield to maturity.

PORTFOLIO YIELD MEASURES

Two conventions have been adopted by practitioners to calculate a portfolio yield: (1) weighted-average portfolio yield and (2) internal rate of return.

Weighted Average Portfolio Yield

Probably the most common—and most flawed—method for calculating a portfolio yield is the *weighted average portfolio yield*. It is found by calculating the weighted average of the yield of all the bonds in the portfolio. The yield is weighted by the proportion of the portfolio that a security makes up. In general, if we let

w_i = the market value of bond i relative to the total market value of the portfolio
y_i = the yield on bond i
K = the number of bonds in the portfolio

then the weighted-average portfolio yield is

$$w_1 y_1 + w_2 y_2 + w_3 y_3 + \ldots + w_K y_K$$

For example, consider the three-bond portfolio in Table 20.4. In this illustration, the total market value of the portfolio is $57,259,000, K is equal to 3, and

TABLE 20.4 Three-Bond Portfolio

Bond	Coupon Rate (%)	Maturity (years)	Par Value ($)	Market Value ($)	Yield to Maturity (%)
B1	7.0	5	10,000,000	9,209,000	9.0
B2	10.5	7	20,000,000	20,000,000	10.5
B3	6.0	3	30,000,000	28,050,000	8.5
Total			60,000,000	57,259,000	

$w_1 = \$9{,}209{,}000/\$57{,}259{,}000 = 0.161 \qquad y_1 = 0.090$

$w_2 = \$20{,}000{,}000/\$57{,}259{,}000 = 0.349 \qquad y_2 = 0.105$

$w_3 = \$28{,}050{,}000/\$57{,}259{,}000 = 0.490 \qquad y_3 = 0.085$

The weighted average portfolio yield is then

$$0.161\,(0.090) + 0.349\,(0.105) + 0.490\,(0.085) = 0.0928 = 9.28\%$$

While it is the most commonly used measure of portfolio yield, the average yield measure provides little insight into the potential return of a portfolio. To see this, consider a portfolio consisting of only two bonds: a six-month bond offering a yield to maturity of 11%, and a 30-year bond offering a yield to maturity of 8%. Suppose that 99% of the portfolio is invested in the six-month bond, and 1% in the 30-year bond. The weighted average yield for this portfolio would be 10.97%. But what does this yield mean? How can it be used within any asset/liability framework? The portfolio is basically a six-month portfolio even though it has a 30-year bond. Would a manager of a depository institution feel confident offering a two-year CD with a yield of 9%? This would suggest a spread of 197 basis points above the yield on the portfolio based on the weighted average portfolio yield. This would be an imprudent policy because the yield on this portfolio over the next two years will depend on interest rates six months from now.

Portfolio Internal Rate of Return

Another measure used to calculate a portfolio yield is the *portfolio internal rate of return*. It is computed by first determining the cash flows for all the bonds in the portfolio, and then finding the interest rate that will make the present value of the cash flows equal to the market value of the portfolio.

To illustrate how to calculate a portfolio's internal rate of return, we will use the three-bond portfolio in Table 20.4. To simplify the illustration, it is assumed that the coupon payment date is the same for each bond. The cash flow for each bond and the portfolio's cash flows are shown in Table 20.5. The portfolio's internal rate of return is the interest rate that will make the present value of the portfolio's cash flows (the last column in Table 20.5) equal to the portfolio's market value of \$57,259,000. The interest rate is 4.77%. Doubling this rate to 9.54% gives the portfolio's internal rate of return on a bond-equivalent basis.

The portfolio internal rate of return, while superior to the weighted average portfolio yield, suffers from the same problems as yield measures

TABLE 20.5 Cash Flow of Three-Bond Portfolio

Period Cash Flow Received	Bond B1	Bond B2	Bond B3	Portfolio
1	$350,000	$1,050,000	$900,000	$2,300,000
2	350,000	1,050,000	900,000	2,300,000
3	350,000	1,050,000	900,000	2,300,000
4	350,000	1,050,000	900,000	2,300,000
5	350,000	1,050,000	900,000	2,300,000
6	350,000	1,050,000	30,900,000	32,300,000
7	350,000	1,050,000	—	1,400,000
8	350,000	1,050,000	—	1,400,000
9	350,000	1,050,000	—	1,400,000
10	10,350,000	1,050,000	—	11,400,000
11	—	1,050,000	—	1,050,000
12	—	1,050,000	—	1,050,000
13	—	1,050,000	—	1,050,000
14	—	21,050,000	—	21,050,000

in general that we discussed earlier: It assumes that the cash flows can be reinvested at the calculated yield. In the case of a portfolio internal rate of return, it assumes that the cash flows can be reinvested at the calculated internal rate of return. Moreover, it assumes that the portfolio is held till the maturity of the longest-maturity bond in the portfolio. For example, if, in our illustration, one of the bonds had a maturity of 30 years, it is assumed that the portfolio is held for 30 years and that all interim cash flows (coupon interest and maturing principal) are reinvested at a rate equal to 9.54%.

TOTAL RETURN

At the time of purchase, an investor is promised a yield, as measured by the yield to maturity, if both of the following conditions are satisfied: (1) The bond is held to maturity, and (2) all coupon interest payments are reinvested at the yield to maturity.

We focused on the second assumption, and we showed that the interest-on-interest component for a bond may constitute a substantial portion of the bond's total dollar return. Therefore, reinvesting the coupon interest payments at a rate of interest less than the yield to maturity will produce a lower yield than the yield to maturity.

TABLE 20.6 Four Alternative Bond Investments

Bond	Coupon	Maturity	Yield to Maturity
A	5%	3 years	9.0%
B	6	20	8.6
C	11	15	9.2
D	8	5	8.0

Rather than assume that the coupon interest payments are reinvested at the yield to maturity, an investor can make an explicit assumption about the reinvestment rate based on expectations. The *total return* is a measure of yield that incorporates an explicit assumption about the reinvestment rate.

Let's take a careful look at the first assumption—that a bond will be held to maturity. Suppose, for example, that an investor who has a five-year investment horizon is considering the four bonds shown in Table 20.6. Assuming that all four bonds are of the same credit quality, which one is the most attractive for this investor? An investor who selects bond C because it offers the highest yield to maturity is failing to recognize that the investment horizon calls for selling the bond after five years at a price that depends on the yield required in the market for 10-year, 11% coupon bonds at the time. Hence, there could be a capital gain or capital loss that will make the return higher or lower than the yield to maturity promised now. Moreover, the higher coupon on bond C relative to the other three bonds means that more of this bond's return will be dependent on the reinvestment of coupon interest payments.

Bond A offers the second highest yield to maturity, but matures before the investment horizon is reached. On the surface, it seems to be particularly attractive because it eliminates the problem of realizing a possible capital loss when the bond must be sold prior to the maturity date. Moreover, the reinvestment risk seems to be less than for the other three bonds because the coupon rate is the smallest. However, the investor would not be eliminating the reinvestment risk because, after three years, the proceeds received at maturity must be reinvested for two more years. The yield that the investor will realize depends on interest rates after three years on two-year bonds when the proceeds must be rolled over.

The yield to maturity does not seem to be helping us to identify the best bond. How, then, do we find out which is the best bond? The answer depends on the investor's expectations. Specifically, it depends on the interest rate at which the coupon interest payments can be reinvested until the end of the investor's planned investment horizon. Also, for bonds with a maturity longer than the investment horizon, it depends on the investor's expectations about required yields in the market at the end of the planned investment horizon. Consequently, any of these bonds can be the best alternative, depending on some reinvestment rate and some future required yield at the end of the planned investment horizon. The total return measure takes these expectations into account and will determine the best investment for the investor depending on portfolio manager's expectations.

Computing the Total Return for a Bond

The idea underlying total return is simple. The objective is first to compute the total future dollars that will result from investing in a bond assuming a particular reinvestment rate. The total return is then computed as the interest rate that will make the initial investment in the bond grow to the computed total future dollars.

The procedure for computing the total return for a bond held over some investment horizon can be summarized as follows.

Step 1. Compute the total coupon payments plus the interest-on-interest based on the assumed reinvestment rate using equation (20.8). The reinvestment rate in this case is one-half the annual interest rate that the investor assumes can be earned on the reinvestment of coupon interest payments.

Step 2. Determine the projected sale price at the end of the planned investment horizon. The projected sale price will depend on the projected required yield at the end of the planned investment horizon. The projected sale price will be equal to the present value of the remaining cash flows of the bond, discounted at the projected required yield.

Step 3. Sum the values computed in steps 1 and 2. The sum is the total future dollars that will be received from the investment given the assumed reinvestment rate and the projected required yield at the end of the investment horizon.

Step 4. Obtain the semiannual total return using the formula:

$$\left(\frac{\text{Total future dollars}}{\text{Purchase price of bond}}\right)^{1/h} - 1 \qquad (20.10)$$

where h is the number of six-month periods in the investment horizon.

Step 5. The semiannual total return found in step 4 must be annualized. There are two alternatives. The first is simply to double the semiannual total return found in step 4. The resulting interest rate is the total return on a bond-equivalent yield basis. The second is to calculate the annual return by compounding the semiannual total return. This is done as follows:

$$(1 + \text{semiannual total return})^2 - 1 \qquad (20.11)$$

A total return calculated using equation (20.11) is called a total return on an *effective rate basis*.

Determination of how to annualize the semiannual total return depends on the situation at hand. The first approach is just a market convention. If an investor is comparing the total return with the return either on other bonds or on a bond index in which yields are calculated on a bond-equivalent basis, then this approach is appropriate. However, if the portfolio objective is to satisfy liabilities that the institution is obligated to pay, and if those liabilities are based on semiannual compounding, then the second approach is appropriate.

To illustrate computation of the total return, suppose that an investor with a three-year investment horizon is considering purchasing a 20-year, 8% coupon bond for $828.40. The yield to maturity for this bond is 10%. The investor expects to be able to reinvest the coupon interest payments at an annual interest rate of 6%, and, at the end of the planned investment horizon, the then-17-year bond will be selling to offer a yield to maturity of 7%. The total return for this bond is found as follows.

Step 1. Compute the total coupon payments plus the interest-on-interest, assuming an annual reinvestment rate of 6%, or 3% every six months. The coupon payments are $40 every six months for three years, or six periods (the planned investment horizon). Applying equation (20.8), we get the total coupon interest plus interest-on-interest, which is $258.74.

Step 2. Determining the projected sale price at the end of three years, assuming that the required yield to maturity for 17-year bonds is 7%, is accomplished by calculating the present value of 34 coupon payments of $40 plus the present value of the maturity value of $1,000, discounted at 3.5%. The projected sale price is $1,098.51.

Step 3. Adding the amounts in steps 1 and 2 gives total future dollars of $1,357.25.

Step 4. To obtain the semiannual total return, compute the following:

$$\left(\frac{\$1,357.25}{\$828.40}\right)^{1/6} - 1 = 0.0858, \text{ or } 8.58\%$$

Step 5. Doubling 8.58% gives a total return on a bond-equivalent basis of 17.16%. Using equation (20.11), we get the total return on an effective rate basis:

$$(1.0858)^2 - 1 = 17.90\%$$

Applications of Total Return (Horizon Analysis)

The total return measure allows a portfolio manager to project the performance of a bond on the basis of the planned investment horizon and expectations concerning reinvestment rates and future market yields. This permits the portfolio manager to evaluate which of several potential bonds considered for acquisition will perform the best over the planned investment horizon. As we have emphasized, this cannot be done using the yield to maturity.

Using total return to assess performance over some investment horizon is called *horizon analysis*. When a total return is calculated over an investment horizon, it is referred to as a *horizon return*. In this book, we use the terms horizon return and total return interchangeably.

An often cited objection to the total return measure is that it requires the portfolio manager to formulate assumptions about reinvestment rates and future yields, as well as to think in terms of an investment horizon. Unfortunately, some portfolio managers find comfort in measures such as the yield to maturity and yield to call simply because they do not require incorporating any particular expectations. The horizon analysis framework, however, enables the portfolio manager to analyze the performance of a bond under different interest rate scenarios for reinvestment rates and future market yields. This procedure is referred to as *scenario analysis*. Only by investigating multiple scenarios can the portfolio manager see how sensitive the bond's performance will be to each scenario.

To illustrate scenario analysis, consider a portfolio manager who is deciding on whether to purchase a 20-year, 9% option-free bond selling at $109.896 per $100 of par value. The yield to maturity for this bond is 8%. Assume also that the portfolio manager's investment horizon is three years, and that the portfolio manager believes the reinvestment rate can vary from 3% to 6.5%, and the projected yield at the end of the investment horizon can vary from 5% to 12%. Table 20.7A shows different projected yields at the end of the three-year investment horizon, and the second panel gives the corresponding price for the bond at the end of the investment horizon. (This is step 2 in the total return calculation discussed earlier.) For example, consider the 10% projected yield at the end of the investment horizon. The price of a 17-year option-free bond with a coupon rate of 9% would be

TABLE 20.7 Scenario Analysis

Bond A: 9% coupon, 20-year option-free bond
Price: $109.896
Yield to maturity: 8%
Investment horizon: Three years

A. Projected Yield at End of Investment Horizon

5.00%	6.00%	7.00%	8.00%	9.00%	10.00%	11.00%	12.00%

B. Projected Sale Price at End of Investment Horizon

145.448	131.698	119.701	109.206	100.000	91.9035	84.763	78.4478

C. Total Future Dollars

Reinv. Rate	5.00%	6.00%	7.00%	8.00%	9.00%	10.00%	11.00%	12.00%
3.0%	173.481	159.731	147.734	137.239	128.033	119.937	112.796	106.481
3.5%	173.657	159.907	147.910	137.415	128.209	120.113	112.972	106.657
4.0%	173.834	160.084	148.087	137.592	128.387	120.290	113.150	106.834
4.5%	174.013	160.263	148.266	137.771	128.565	120.469	113.328	107.013
5.0%	174.192	160.443	148.445	137.950	128.745	120.648	113.508	107.193
5.5%	174.373	160.623	148.626	138.131	128.926	120.829	113.689	107.374
6.0%	174.555	160.806	148.809	138.313	129.108	121.011	113.871	107.556
6.5%	174.739	160.989	148.992	138.497	129.291	121.195	114.054	107.739

D. Total Return (Effective Rate)

Reinv. Rate	5.00%	6.00%	7.00%	8.00%	9.00%	10.00%	11.00%	12.00%
3.0%	16.44	13.28	10.37	7.69	5.22	2.96	0.87	21.05
3.5%	16.48	13.32	10.41	7.73	5.27	3.01	0.92	20.99
4.0%	16.52	13.36	10.45	7.78	5.32	3.06	0.98	20.94
4.5%	16.56	13.40	10.50	7.83	5.37	3.11	1.03	20.88
5.0%	16.60	13.44	10.54	7.87	5.42	3.16	1.08	20.83
5.5%	16.64	13.49	10.59	7.92	5.47	3.21	1.14	20.77
6.0%	16.68	13.53	10.63	7.97	5.52	3.26	1.19	20.72
6.5%	16.72	13.57	10.68	8.02	5.57	3.32	1.25	20.66

1. Price of a 9%, 17-year option-free bond selling to yield the assumed projected yield at the end of the investment horizon.
2. Projected sale price at the end of the investment horizon plus coupon interest plus interest-on-interest at the assumed reinvestment rate.
3. Semiannual total return calculated as follows:

$$\left(\frac{\text{Total future dollars}}{\$109.896}\right)^{1/6} - 1$$

$$\text{Total return(effective rate)} = (1 + \text{Semiannual total return})^2 - 1$$

$91.9035. Table 20.7C shows the total future dollars at the end of three years under various scenarios for the reinvestment rate and the projected yield at the end of the investment horizon. (This is step 3 in the total return calculation discussed above.) For example, with a reinvestment rate of 4% and a projected yield at the end of the investment horizon of 10%, the total future dollars would be $120.290. Table 20.7D shows the total return on an effective rate basis for each scenario.

Table 20.7 is useful for a portfolio manager in assessing the potential outcome of a bond (or a portfolio) over the investment horizon. For example, a portfolio manager knows that the maximum and minimum total return for the scenarios shown in the table will be 16.72% and –1.05%, respectively, and also knows the scenarios under which each will be realized.

Another way to use scenario analysis is in assessing the likelihood that an investment objective will not be realized. For example, suppose that a life insurance company has issued a three-year guaranteed investment contract in which it has guaranteed an effective annual interest rate of 7.02%. (This insurance contract is explained in Chapter 25.) Suppose that the premiums are invested in the bond analyzed in Table 20.7, and that the portfolio manager's investment objective is a minimum return of 7.02% plus a spread of 100 basis points. The spread represents the profit that the life insurance company seeks to earn. Thus the minimum return is 8.02%. From Table 20.7, the portfolio manager can see that if the yield at the end of the investment horizon is 8% or greater, and that if the reinvestment rate over the three-year investment horizon is less than 6.5%, a total return on an effective rate basis will be less than the investment objective of a minimum return of 8.02%.

Total Return and Bond Price Volatility

Earlier, we explained the three sources of return from investing in a bond. The importance of each source of return from holding a bond over some investment horizon depends on the characteristics of the bond (coupon and maturity) and the length of the investment horizon. For long investment horizons, a coupon bond's reinvestment income will be a major component of the total return. For short investment horizons, reinvestment income is not an important source of return. However, for short investment horizons, the potential price change is of major importance. This can be seen from the first two panels of Table 20.7. The price at the beginning of the investment horizon is $109.896. The projected price at the end of the investment horizon can vary from $145.448 to $78.4478 if the projected yield at the investment horizon is between 5% and 12%.

Because of the importance of the price volatility of a bond on its total return over some investment horizon, it is critical to understand the characteristics of a bond that affect its price volatility and to know how to quantify potential price volatility. This is the subject of the next chapter.

SUMMARY

The price of a bond is the present value of the bond's cash flows, the discount rate being equal to the yield offered on comparable bonds. For an option-free bond, the cash flows are the coupon payments and the maturity value. For a zero-coupon bond, there are no coupon payments and therefore the price is equal to the present value of the maturity value. The higher (lower) the required yield, the lower (higher) the price of a bond. Therefore, a bond's price changes in the opposite direction from the change in the required yield. When the coupon rate is equal to the required yield, the bond will sell at its par value. When the coupon rate is less (greater) than the required yield, the bond will sell for less (more) than its par value and is said to be selling at a discount (premium).

The conventional yield measures commonly used by bond market participants are the current yield, yield to maturity, and yield to call. We reviewed the three potential sources of dollar return from investing in a bond—coupon interest, interest-on-interest, and capital gain (or loss)—and showed that none of the three conventional yield measures deals satisfactorily with all these sources. The current yield measure fails to consider both interest-on-interest and capital gain (or loss). The yield to maturity considers all three sources, but it is deficient in assuming that all coupon interest can be reinvested at the yield to maturity. Reinvestment risk is the risk that the coupon payments will be reinvested at a rate less than the yield to maturity. The yield to call has the same shortcoming; it assumes that the coupon interest can be reinvested at the yield to call.

There are two measures of a portfolio yield: weighted-average yield to maturity and portfolio internal rate of return. Both these measures are deficient in that they offer little insight into the potential return from holding a portfolio over some investment horizon.

The total return measure is more meaningful than either yield to maturity or yield to call for assessing the relative attractiveness of a bond given the portfolio manager's expectations and planned investment horizon. Scenario analysis can be used to assess the performance of a bond under various sets of assumptions and the conditions under which an investment objective may not be satisfied.

CHAPTER 21

Bond Price Volatility and the Measurement of Interest Rate Risk

As we explained in the previous chapter, a fundamental property of a bond is that its price will change in the opposite direction from the change in the required yield for the bond. This property follows from the fact that the price of a bond is equal to the present value of its expected cash flows. Although all bonds change in price when the required yield changes, they do not change by the same percentage. For example, when the required yield increases by 100 basis points for two bonds, the price of one might fall by 15%, while that of the other might fall by only 1%. To effectively implement bond portfolio strategies, it is necessary to understand why bonds react differently to yield changes. In addition, it is necessary to quantify how a bond's price might react to yield changes. Ideally, a portfolio manager would like a measure that indicates the relationship between changes in required yields and changes in a bond's price. That is, a manager would want to know how a bond's price is expected to change if yields change by, say, 100 basis points.

In this chapter, we discuss the characteristics of a bond's price that affect its price volatility. We present two measures that are used to quantify a bond's price volatility. One of these measures, duration, is a measure of the approximate percentage change in a bond's price if yield changes by 100 basis points. Duration, however, provides only an approximation of how the price will change. Duration can be supplemented with another measure that we will discuss, convexity. Together, duration and convexity do an effective job of estimating how a bond's price will change when yields change. In later chapters, we will use these two measures in bond portfolio management strategies.

PRICE VOLATILITY PROPERTIES OF OPTION-FREE BONDS

The inverse relationship between bond price and yield for an option-free bond is illustrated in Table 21.1 for six hypothetical bonds. The bond prices are shown assuming a par value of $100. When the price/yield relationship for any option-free bond is graphed, it exhibits the convex shape shown in Figure 20.1 of Chapter 20. The price/yield relationship is for a given point in time. We know from the properties of a bond described in the previous chapter that over time, the price of a bond changes as its maturity changes.

Table 21.2 shows for the six hypothetical bonds in Table 21.1, the percentage change in each bond's price for various changes in the required yield, assuming that the initial yield for all six bonds is 9%. For example, consider the 9%, 25-year bond. If the bond is selling to yield 9%, its price would be 100 (see Table 21.1). If the required yield declines to 8%, the price of that bond would be 110.741 (see Table 21.1). Thus a decline in yield from 9% to 8% would increase the price by 10.74% [(110.741 − 100)/100]. This is the value shown in Table 21.2.

An examination of Table 21.2 reveals several properties concerning the price volatility of an option-free bond.

> *Property 1.* For very small changes in the required yield, the percentage price change for a given bond is roughly the same, whether the required yield increases or decreases.

TABLE 21.1 Price/Yield Relationship for Six Hypothetical Option-Free Bonds

Required Yield	Price at Required Yield Coupon/Maturity in Years					
	9%/5	9%/25	6%/5	6%/25	0%/5	0%/25
6.00%	112.7953	138.5946	100.0000	100.0000	74.4094	22.8107
7.00	108.3166	123.4556	95.8417	88.2722	70.8919	17.9053
8.00	104.0554	110.7410	91.8891	78.5178	67.5564	14.0713
8.50	102.0027	105.1482	89.9864	74.2587	65.9537	12.4795
8.90	100.3966	100.9961	88.4983	71.1105	64.7017	11.3391
8.99	100.0395	100.0988	88.1676	70.4318	64.4236	11.0975
9.00	100.0000	100.0000	88.1309	70.3570	64.3928	11.0170
9.01	99.9604	99.9013	88.0943	70.2824	64.3620	11.0445
9.10	99.6053	99.0199	87.7654	69.6164	64.0855	10.8093
9.50	98.0459	95.2339	86.3214	66.7773	62.8723	9.8242
10.00	96.1391	90.8720	84.5565	63.4881	61.3913	8.7204
11.00	92.4624	83.0685	81.1559	57.6712	58.5431	6.8767
12.00	88.9599	76.3572	77.9197	52.7144	55.8395	5.4288

TABLE 21.2 Instantaneous Percentage Price Change for Six Hypothetical Bonds

Six Hypothetical Bonds, Priced Initially to Yield 9%

9% coupon,	5 years to maturity,	Price =	100.0000
9% coupon,	25 years to maturity,	Price =	100.0000
6% coupon,	5 years to maturity,	Price =	88.1309
6% coupon,	25 years to maturity,	Price =	70.3570
0% coupon,	5 years to maturity,	Price =	64.3928
0% coupon,	25 years to maturity,	Price =	11.0710

Required Yield Changes to	Change in Basis Points	Percentage Price Change, Coupon/Maturity in Years					
		9%/5	9%/25	6%/5	6%/25	0%/5	0%/25
6.00%	−300	12.80	38.59	13.47	42.13	15.56	106.04
7.00	−200	8.32	23.46	8.75	25.46	10.09	61.73
8.00	−100	4.06	10.74	4.26	11.60	4.91	27.10
8.50	−50	2.00	5.15	2.11	5.55	2.42	12.72
8.90	−10	0.40	1.00	0.42	1.07	0.48	2.42
8.99	−1	0.04	0.10	0.04	0.11	0.05	0.24
9.01	1	−0.04	−0.10	−0.04	−0.11	−0.05	−0.24
9.10	10	−0.39	−0.98	−0.41	−1.05	−0.48	−2.36
9.50	50	−1.95	−4.75	−2.05	−5.09	−2.36	−11.26
10.00	100	−3.86	−9.13	−4.06	−9.76	−4.66	−21.23
11.00	200	−7.54	−16.93	−7.91	−18.03	−9.08	−37.89
12.00	300	−11.04	−23.64	−11.59	−25.08	−13.28	−50.96

Property 2. For large changes in the required yield, the percentage price change is not the same for an increase in the required yield as it is for a decrease in the required yield.

Property 3. For a large change in basis points, the percentage price increase is greater than the percentage price decrease. The implication of this property is that if an investor owns a bond, the price appreciation that will be realized if the required yield decreases is greater than the capital loss that will be realized if the required yield rises by the same number of basis points.

An explanation for these three properties of bond price volatility lies in the convex shape of the price/yield relationship. We will investigate this in more detail later in the chapter.

FACTORS THAT AFFECT A BOND'S PRICE VOLATILITY

Two features of an option-free bond determine its price volatility: coupon and term to maturity. In addition, the yield level at which a bond trades affects its price volatility. This is demonstrated next.

The Effect of the Coupon Rate

Consider the three 25-year bonds in Table 21.2. For a given change in yield, the zero-coupon bond has the largest price volatility, and the largest coupon bond (the 9% coupon bond) has the smallest price volatility. This is also true for the three five-year bonds. In general, for a given term to maturity and initial yield, the lower the coupon rate, the greater the price volatility of a bond.

The Effect of Maturity

Consider the two 9% coupon bonds in Table 21.2. For a given change in yield, the 25-year bond has the largest price volatility, and the shortest-maturity bond (the five-year bond) has the smallest price volatility. This is also true for the two 6% coupon bonds and the two zero-coupon bonds in Table 21.2. In general, for a given coupon rate and initial yield, the longer the maturity, the greater the price volatility of a bond.

Effects of Yield to Maturity on Price Volatility

The price volatility of a bond is also affected by the level of interest rates in the economy. Specifically, the higher the level of yields, the lower the price volatility. To illustrate this, let's compare the 9%, 25-year bond trading at two yield levels: 7% and 13%. If the yield increases from 7% to 8%, the bond's price declines by 10.3%; but if the yield increases from 13% to 14%, the bond's price declines by 6.75%.

MEASURING INTEREST RATE RISK USING THE PRICE VALUE OF A BASIS POINT

To control the interest rate risk of a bond portfolio or a trading position, it is essential to have a measure that quantifies a bond's exposure to changes in interest rates. A portfolio manager can measure the exposure to interest rate changes of a portfolio or trading position by revaluing the bonds held based on various interest rate scenarios. However, the typical way in which interest rate risk is measured is by approximating the impact of a change in interest rates on a bond or a bond portfolio. The two popular measures used are (1) the price value of a basis point and (2) duration and convexity. However, both measures suffer from the problem that they measure only an exposure to a parallel shift in interest rates. That is, it is assumed that the interest rate for all the bonds held will change by the same number of basis of points. There are measures that are used to assess the exposure to changes in the yield curve that we discuss later in this chapter. In this section, we focus on the the price value of a basis point.

The *price value of a basis point* (PVBP), also referred to as the *dollar value of an 01* (DV01), measures the change in the price of the bond if the required yield changes by 1 basis point. Note that this measure of price volatility indicates dollar price volatility as opposed to percentage price volatility (price change as a percentage of the initial price). Typically, the price value of a basis point is expressed as the absolute value of the change in price. Owing to property 1 of the price/yield relationship, price volatility is the same for an increase or a decrease of 1 basis point in required yield.

We can illustrate how to calculate the price value of a basis point by using the six bonds in Table 21.1. For each bond, the initial price, the price after increasing the yield by 1 basis point (from 9% to 9.01%), and the price value of a basis point (the difference between the two prices) are shown in Table 21.3.

Because this measure of price volatility is in terms of dollar price change, dividing the price value of a basis point by the initial price gives the percentage price change for a 1 basis point change in yield. We will see how to use this measure in Chapter 24, when we demonstrate how to hedge a position in a bond.

TABLE 21.3 Price Value of a Basis Point

Bond	Initial Price (9% Yield)	Price at 9.01%	Price Value of a Basis Point[a]
5 years, 9% coupon	100.0000	99.9604	0.0396
25 years, 9% coupon	100.0000	99.9013	0.0987
5 years, 6% coupon	88.1309	88.0945	0.0364
25 years, 6% coupon	70.3570	70.2824	0.0746
5 years, zero coupon	64.3928	64.3620	0.0308
25 years, zero coupon	11.0710	11.0445	0.0265

[a]Absolute value per $100 of par value.

MEASURING INTEREST RATE RISK USING DURATION AND CONVEXITY

The most commonly used approach to measure interest rate risk exposure of a portfolio or a trading position is by approximating the impact of a change in interest rates on a bond or a bond portfolio using duration. Duration is a first approximation. To improve upon this approximation, a second measure is estimated and is referred to as convexity. In this section, we explain how duration is estimated for bonds and portfolios. There are different types of duration measures for individual bonds and portfolios. We also explain the limitations of duration. We then discuss how the duration measure can be improved by using a measure called convexity.

Duration

The most obvious way to measure the price sensitivity as a percentage of the security's current price to changes in interest rates is to change rates (i.e., "shock" rates) by a small number of basis points and calculate how a security's value will change as a percentage of the current price. The name popularly used to refer to the approximate percentage price change is duration. The following formula can be used to estimate the duration of a security:

$$\text{Duration} = \frac{V_- - V_+}{2V_0(\Delta y)} \quad (21.1)$$

where

Δy = the change (or shock) in interest rates (in decimal form)
V_0 = the current price of the bond
V_- = the estimated price of the bond if interest rates are decreased by the change in interest rates
V_+ = the estimated price of the bond if interest rates are increased by the change in interest rates

Throughout this chapter, when we use "change in interest rate" and "change in yield" interchangeably.

It is important to understand that the two values in the numerator of equation (21.1) are the estimated values if interest rates change obtained from a valuation model. Consequently, the duration measure is only as good as the valuation model employed to obtain the estimated values in equation (21.1). The more difficult it is to estimate the value a bond, the less confidence a portfolio manager may have in the estimated duration. We will see that the duration of a portfolio is nothing more than a market-weighted average of the duration of the bonds comprising the portfolio. Hence, a portfolio's duration is sensitive to the estimated duration of the individual bonds.

To illustrate the duration calculation, consider the following option-free bond: a 6% coupon five-year bond trading at par value to yield 6%. The current price is $100. Suppose the yield is changed by 50 basis points. Thus, $\Delta y = 0.005$ and $V_0 = \$100$. This is simple bond to value if interest rates or yield is changed. If the yield is decreased to 5.5%, the price of this bond would be $102.1600. If the yield is increased to 6.5%, the value of this bond would be $97.8944. That is, $V_- = \$102.1600$ and $V_+ = \$97.8944$. Substituting into equation (21.1), we obtain

$$\text{Duration} = \frac{\$102.1600 - \$97.8944}{2(\$100)(0.005)} = 4.27$$

There are various ways in that practitioners have interpreted what the duration of a bond is. We believe the most useful way to think about a bond's duration is as the approximate percentage change in the bond's price for a 100 basis point change in interest rates. Thus a bond with a duration of say 5 will change by approximately 5% for a 100 basis point change in interest rates (i.e., if the yield required for this bond changes by approximately 100 basis points). For a 50 basis point change in interest rates, the bond's price will change by approximately 2.5%; for a 25 basis point change in interest rates, 1.25%, and so on.

Dollar Duration

In estimating the sensitivity of the price of bond to changes in interest rates, we looked at the percentage price change. However, for two bonds with the same duration but trading at different prices, the dollar price change will not be the same. To see this, suppose that we have two bonds, B_1 and B_2, that both have a duration of 5. Suppose further that the current price of B_1 and B_2 are $100 and $90, respectively. A 100 basis point change for both bonds will change the price by approximately 5%. This means a price change of $5 (5% times $100) for B_1 and a price change of $4.5 (5% times $90) for B_2.

The dollar price change of a bond can be measured by multiplying duration by the full dollar price and the number of basis points (in decimal form) and is called the *dollar duration*. That is,

Dollar duration = Duration × Dollar price × Change in rates in decimal

The dollar duration for a 100 basis point change in rates is

$$\text{Dollar duration} = \text{Duration} \times \text{Dollar price} \times 0.01 \qquad (21.2)$$

So, for bonds B_1 and B_2, the dollar duration for a 100 basis point change in rates is

For bond B_1: Dollar duration = 5 × $100 × 0.01 = $5.0
For bond B_2: Dollar duration = 5 × $90 × 0.01 = $4.5

Knowing the dollar duration allows a portfolio manager to neutralize the risk of bond position. For example, consider a position in bond B_2. If a trader wants to eliminate the interest rate risk exposure of this bond (i.e., hedge the exposure), the trader will look for a position in another financial instrument(s) (for example, an interest rate derivative described in Chapter 24) whose value will change in the opposite direction to bond B_2's price by an amount equal to $4.5. So if the trader has a long position in B_2, the position will decline in value by $4.5 for a 100 basis point increase in interest rates. To hedge this risk exposure, the trader can take a position in another financial instrument whose value increases by $4.5 if interest rates increase by 100 basis points.

The dollar duration can also be computed without having to know a bond's duration. This is done by simply looking at the average price change for a bond when interest rates are increased and decreased by the same number of basis points. This can be done easily for interest rate derivatives. For example, the dollar duration for an interest rate futures contract and an interest rate swap can be computed by changing interest rates and determining how the price of the derivative changes on average. This is important because when trying to control the interest rate risk of a position, a portfolio manager or risk manager will employ interest rate derivatives.

Modified Duration, Macaulay Duration, and Effective Duration

A popular form of duration that is used by practitioners is modified duration. *Modified duration* is the approximate percentage change in a bond's price for a 100 basis point change in interest rates, assuming that the bond's cash flows do not change when interest rates change. What this means is that in calculating the values used in the numerator of the duration formula, the cash flows used to calculate the current price are assumed. Therefore, the change in the bond's value when interest rates change by a small number of basis points is due solely to discounting at the new yield level.

Modified duration is related to another measure commonly cited in the bond market: *Macaulay duration*. The formula for this measure, first used by Frederick Macaulay (1938), is rarely used in practice so it will not be produced here. For a bond that pays coupon interest semiannually, modified duration is related to Macaulay duration as follows:

$$\text{Modified duration} = \text{Macaulay duration}/(1 + \text{yield}/2)$$

where yield is the bond's yield to maturity in decimal form. Practically speaking, there is very little difference in the computed values for modified duration and Macaulay duration.

The assumption that the cash flows will not change when interest rates change makes sense for option-free bonds because the payments by the issuer are not altered when interest rates change. This is not the case for callable bond, putable bonds, bonds with accelerated sinking fund options, mortgage-backed securities, and certain types of asset-backed securities (i.e., mortgage related securities). For these securities, a change in interest rates may alter the expected cash flows.

The price-yield relationship for callable bonds and prepayable securites is shown in Figure 21.1. As market rates (yields) decline, investors become concerned that they will decline further so that the issuer or homeowner will benefit from calling the bond. The precise yield level where investors begin to view the issue likely to be called may not be known, but we do know that there is some level. In Figure 21.1, at yield levels below y^*, the price-yield relationship for the callable bond departs from the price-yield relationship for the option-free bond. If, for example, the market yield is such that an option-free bond would be selling for $109, but since it is callable would be called at

FIGURE 21.1 Price-Yield Relationship for an Option-Free Bond and a Callable Bond

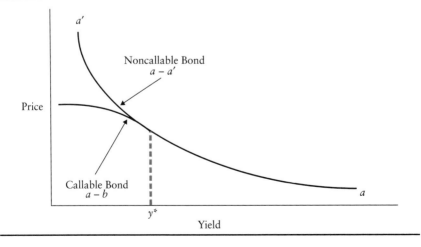

$104, investors would not pay $109. If they did, and the bond is called, investors would receive $104 (the call price) for a bond they purchased for $109. Notice that for a range of yields below y^*, there is price compression (i.e., there is limited price appreciation as yields decline). The portion of the callable bond price-yield relationship below y^* is said to be *negatively convex*.

Negative convexity means that the price appreciation will be less than the price depreciation for a large change in yield of a given number of basis points. In contrast, a bond that is option-free exhibits positive convexity. This means that the price appreciation will be greater than the price depreciation for a large change in yield.

For bonds with embedded options, there are valuation models that take into account how changes in interest rates will affect cash flows that we will describe in the next section. When the values used in the numerator of equation (21.1) are obtained from a valuation model that takes into account both the discounting at different interest rates and how the cash flows can change, the resulting duration is referred to as *effective duration* or *option-adjusted duration*.

Spread Duration for Fixed Rate Bonds

Duration is a measure of the change in the value of a bond when rates change. The interest rate that is assumed to shift is the Treasury rate. However, for non-Treasury securities, the yield is equal to the Treasury yield plus a spread to the Treasury yield curve. The price of a bond exposed to credit risk can change even though Treasury yields are unchanged because the spread required by the market changes. A measure of how a non-Treasury issue's price will change if the spread sought by the market changes is called *spread duration*. For example, a spread duration of 2.2 for a security means that if the Treasury rate is unchanged but spreads change by 100 basis points, the security's price will change by approximately 2.2%.

Portfolio Duration

Portfolio duration can be obtained by calculating the weighted average of the duration of the bonds in the portfolio. The weight is the proportion of the portfolio that a security comprises. Mathematically, portfolio duration can be calculated as follows:

$$\text{Portfolio duration} = w_1 D_1 + w_2 D_2 + \ldots + w_N D_N \qquad (21.3)$$

where

w_i = market value of bond i/market value of the portfolio
D_i = duration of bond i
N = number of bonds in the portfolio

To illustrate this calculation, consider the $240,220,000 10-bond portfolio shown in Table 21.4. The table shows the market value of each bond, the percentage that each bond is of the portfolio, and the duration of each bond. The fifth column gives the product of the weight and the duration. The last row in that column shows the portfolio duration as given by equation (21.3): 5.21.

A portfolio duration of 5.21 means that for a 100 basis point change in the yield for all 10 bonds, the market value of the portfolio will change by approximately 5.21%. But keep in mind that the yield on all 10 bonds must change by 100 basis points for the duration measure to be most useful. The assumption that all interest rates must change by the same number of basis points is a critical assumption, and its importance cannot be overemphasized. Market practitioners refer to this as the *parallel yield curve shift assumption*.

Portfolio duration can also be computed by using dollar duration as given by equation (21.2). This is done by computing the dollar duration for each bond in the portfolio. The sixth column of Table 21.4 gives the dollar

TABLE 21.4 Calculation of Portfolio Duration and Contribution to Portfolio Duration

Bond	Market Value ($)	Percent of Portfolio	Duration	Duration × Percent of Portfolio = Contribution to Portfolio Duration	Dollar Duration ($)
1	10,000,000	4.1629	4.70	0.20	470,000
2	18,500,000	7.7013	3.60	0.28	666,000
3	14,550,000	6.0569	6.25	0.38	909,375
4	26,080,000	10.8567	5.42	0.59	1,413,536
5	24,780,000	10.3155	2.15	0.22	532,770
6	35,100,000	14.6116	3.25	0.47	1,140,750
7	15,360,000	6.3941	6.88	0.44	1,056,768
8	26,420,000	10.9983	6.50	0.71	1,717,300
9	40,000,000	16.6514	4.75	0.79	1,900,000
10	29,430,000	12.2513	9.23	1.13	2,716,389
Port.	240,220,000	100.0000		5.21	12,522,888

duration for each bond in the portfolio. The portfolio duration as shown in the last row of the sixth column of the table is $12,522,888. This means that for a 100 basis point change in interest rates, the change in the portfolio's value will be approximately $12,522,888. Since the market value of the portfolio is $240,220,000, this means that the percentage change in the value of the portfolio for a 100 basis point change in interest rates is 5.21% ($12,522,888/$240,220,000). Since duration is the approximate percentage change in value for a 100 basis point change in interest rates, we can see that the portfolio duration is 5.21%, the same duration obtained from using equation (21.3).

To appreciate why it is helpful to know the portfolio dollar duration, suppose that the portfolio manager wants to change the current duration of 5.21 for the 10-bond portfolio to a duration of 4. What this means is that the portfolio manager wants a dollar duration for of 4% of $240,220,000 or $9,608,800. But the current portfolio duration is $12,522,888. To get the portfolio to 4, the portfolio manager must get rid of $2,914,088 ($12,522,888 − $9,608,800). To do this, the portfolio manager, if authorized to use interest rate derivatives), will take a position in one or more derivatives whose dollar duration is −$2,914,088.

Contribution to Portfolio Duration

Portfolio managers commonly assess their exposure to an issue in terms of the percentage of that issue in the portfolio. A better measure of exposure of an individual issue to changes in interest rates is in terms of its *contribution to portfolio duration*. This is found by multiplying the percentage that the individual issue is of the portfolio by the duration of the individual issue. That is,

$$\text{Contribution to portfolio duration} = \frac{\text{Market value of issue}}{\text{Market value of portfolio}} \times \text{Duration of issue} \quad (21.4)$$

Notice the contribution to portfolio duration is simply the individual components in portfolio duration formula given by equation (21.3). In Table 21.4, the contribution to portfolio duration for each bond is shown in the fifth column.

While we shown how to compute the contribution to portfolio duration for each bond in a portfolio, the same formula can be used to determine the contribution to portfolio duration for each bond sector represented in a portfolio.

The contribution to the spread duration of a portfolio can also be computed using spread duration of an issue in equation (21.4).

Approximating Percentage

The approximate percentage price change of a bond using duration is found as follows:

$$\text{Approximate percentage price change} = -\text{Duration} \times (\Delta y) \times 100 \quad (21.5)$$

where Δy is the change (or shock) in interest rates (in decimal form).

The reason for the negative sign on the right-hand side of equation (21.5) is due to the inverse relationship between price change and yield change.

For example, consider the 6%, 25-year bond trading at 70.3570 to yield 9% whose duration can be shown to be 10.6. The approximate percentage price change for a 10 basis point increase in yield (i.e., $\Delta y = +0.001$) is

$$\text{Approximate percentage price change} = -10.6 \times (+0.001) \times 100 = -1.06\%$$

How good is this approximation? The actual percentage price change is −1.05% (as shown in Table 21.2 when yield increases to 9.10%). Duration, in this case, did an excellent job in estimating the percentage price change. We would come to the same conclusion if we used duration to estimate the percentage price change if the yield declined by 10 basis points (i.e., $\Delta y = -0.001$). In this case, the approximate percentage price change would be +1.06% (i.e., the direction of the price change is reversed but the magnitude of the change is the same). Table 21.2 shows that the actual percentage price change is +1.07%.

Let's look at how well duration does in estimating the percentage price change if the yield increases by 200 basis points instead of 10 basis points. In this case, Δy is equal to +0.02. Substituting into equation (21.5), we have

$$\text{Approximate percentage price change} = -10.6 \times (+0.02) \times 100 = -21.2\%$$

How good is this estimate? From Table 21.2 we see that the actual percentage price change when the yield increases by 200 basis points to 11% is −18.03%. Thus, the estimate is not as good as when we used duration to approximate the percentage price change for a change in yield of only 10 basis points. How about if we use duration to approximate the percentage price change when the yield decreases by 200 basis points? The approximate percentage price change in this scenario is +21.2%, but the actual percentage price change as shown in Table 21.2 is +25.46%.

Notice also in the two scenarios where we changed the yield by 200 basis points that the approximate percentage price change overestimated how much the bond's price would actually decline if the yield increased by 200 basis points and underestimates how much the bond's price would actually increase if the yield decreased by 200 basis points. This will always be the case.

Convexity

The duration measure indicates that regardless of whether interest rates increase or decrease, the approximate percentage price change is the same. However, this does not agree with Property 3 of a bond's price volatility. Specifically, while for small changes in yield the percentage price change will be the same for an increase or decrease in yield, for large changes in yield this is not true. This suggests that duration is only a good approximation of the percentage price change for a small change in yield.

The reason for this is that duration is in fact a first approximation for a small change in yield. The approximation can be improved by using a second approximation. This approximation is referred to as "convexity." The use of this term in the industry is unfortunate since the term convexity is also used to describe the shape or curvature of the price/yield relationship. The convexity measure of a security can be used to approximate the change in price that is not explained by duration.

Convexity Measure

The convexity measure of a bond can be approximated using the following formula:

$$\text{Convexity measure} = \frac{V_+ + V_- - 2V_0}{2V_0 (\Delta y)^2} \qquad (21.6)$$

where the notation is the same as used earlier for duration as given by equation (21.1).

For our hypothetical 6%, 25-year bond selling to yield 9%, we know from Table 21.1 that for a 10 basis point change in yield ($\Delta y = 0.001$):

$$V_0 = 70.3570, \ V_- = 71.1105, \text{ and } V_+ = 69.6164$$

Substituting these values into the convexity measure given by equation (21.6):

$$\text{Convexity measure} = \frac{69.6164 + 71.1105 - 2(70.3570)}{2(70.3570)(0.001)^2} = 91.67$$

We'll see how to use this convexity measure shortly. Before doing so, there are three points that should be noted. First, there is no simple interpretation of the convexity measure as there is for duration. Second, it is more common for market participants to refer to the value computed in equation (21.6) as the "convexity of a bond" rather than the "convexity measure of a bond." Finally, the convexity measure reported by dealers and vendors will differ for an option-free bond. The reason is that the value obtained from equation (21.6) will be scaled for the reason explained later.

The procedure for calculating the convexity measure for a portfolio is the same as for calculating a portfolio's duration. That is, the convexity measure for each bond in the portfolio is computed. Then the weighted average of the convexity measure for the bonds in the portfolio is computed to get the portfolio's convexity measure.

Convexity Adjustment to Percentage Price Change

Given the convexity measure, the approximate percentage price change adjustment due to the bond's convexity (i.e., the percentage price change not explained by duration) is

$$\text{Convexity adjustment to percentage price change} = \text{Convexity measure} \times (\Delta y)^2 \times 100 \quad (21.7)$$

For example, for the 6%, 25-year bond selling to yield 9%, the convexity adjustment to the percentage price change based on duration if the yield increases from 9% to 11% is

$$91.67 \times (0.02)^2 \times 100 = 3.67$$

If the yield decreases from 9% to 7%, the convexity adjustment to the approximate percentage price change based on duration would also be 3.67%.

The approximate percentage price change based on duration and the convexity adjustment is found by adding the two estimates. So, for example, if yields change from 9% to 11%, the estimated percentage price change would be:

Estimated change approximated by duration	= −21.20%
Convexity adjustment	= +3.66%
Total estimated percentage price change	= −17.54%

The actual percentage price change from Table 21.2 is −18.03%. Hence, the approximation has improved.

For a decrease of 200 basis points, from 9% to 7%, the approximate percentage price change would be as follows:

Estimated change approximated by duration = +21.20%
Convexity adjustment = +3.66%
Total estimated percentage price change = +24.86%

The actual percentage price change from Table 21.2 is +25.46%. Once again, we see that duration combined with the convexity adjustment does a good job of estimating the sensitivity of a bond's price change to large changes in yield.

Positive vs. Negative Convexity

Notice that when the convexity measure is positive, we have the situation described earlier that the gain is greater than the loss for a given large change in rates. When a bond (or a bond portfolio) exhibits this behavior, it is said to have *positive convexity*. We can see this in the example above. However, if the convexity measure is negative, we have the situation where the loss will be greater than the gain. For example, suppose that a callable bond has an effective duration of 4 and a convexity measure of −30. This means that the approximate percentage price change for a 200 basis point change is 8%. The convexity adjustment for a 200 basis point change in rates is then

$$-30 \times (0.02)^2 \times 100 = -1.2$$

Therefore, the convexity adjustment is −1.2%, and the approximate percentage price change after adjusting for convexity is:

Estimated change approximated by duration = −8.0%
Convexity adjustment = −1.2%
Total estimated percentage price change = −9.2%

For a decrease of 200 basis points, the approximate percentage price change would be as follows:

Estimated change approximated by duration = +8.0%
Convexity adjustment = −1.2%
Total estimated percentage price change = +6.8%

Notice that the loss is greater than the gain—a property called *negative convexity*.

What does the sign of the convexity mean for a bond portfolio? It means that for a portfolio that has positive convexity, for a large change in interest rates, the absolute value of the change in the portfolio's value will be greater when interest rates decline than when they increase. The opposite is true for a portfolio that has negative convexity.

Scaling the Convexity Measure

The convexity measure as given by equation (21.6) means nothing in isolation. It is the substitution of the computed convexity measure into equation (21.7) that provides the estimated adjustment for convexity. Therefore, it is possible to scale the convexity measure in any way and obtain the same convexity adjustment.

For example, in some books the convexity measure is defined as follows:

$$\text{Convexity measure} = \frac{V_+ + V_- - 2V_0}{V_0 (\Delta y)^2} \qquad (21.8)$$

Equation (21.8) differs from equation (21.6) since it does not include 2 in the denominator. Thus the convexity measure computed using equation (21.8) will be double the convexity measure using equation (21.6). So, for our earlier illustration, since the convexity measure using equation (21.6) is 91.67, the convexity measure using equation (21.8) would be 183.34.

Which is correct, 91.67 or 183.24? Both are correct. The reason is that the corresponding equation for computing the convexity adjustment would not be given by equation (21.7) if the convexity measure is obtained from equation (21.8). Instead, the corresponding convexity adjustment formula would be equation (21.7) divided by 2.

Some dealers and vendors scale in a different way. Consequently, the convexity measure for our hypothetical bond could be reported as 9.17 or 18.3. It is the modification of equation (21.7) that assures that regardless of how the convexity measure is scaled, it will produce the same approximate percentage change due to convexity.

Standard Convexity and Effective Convexity

The prices used in equation (21.6) to calculate the convexity measure can be obtained by either assuming that when the yield changes the expected cash flows do not change or they do change. In the former case, the resulting convexity is referred to as *standard convexity*. (Actually, in the industry, convexity is not qualified by the adjective "standard.") *Effective convexity*, in contrast, assumes that the cash flows do change when yields change. This is the same distinction made for duration.

As with duration, for bonds with embedded options, there can be quite a difference between the calculated standard convexity and effective convexity. In fact, for all option-free bonds, either convexity measure will have a positive value. For bonds with embedded options, the calculated effective convexity can be negative when the calculated modified convexity is positive.

MEASURING EXPOSURE TO YIELD CURVE CHANGES KEY RATE DURATION

As explained earlier, duration assumes that when interest rates change, all yields on the yield curve change by the same amount. This is a problem when using duration for a portfolio that will typically have bonds with different maturities. Consequently, it is necessary to be able to measure the exposure of a bond or bond portfolio to shifts in the yield curve. There have been several approaches to measuring yield curve risk. One way is to simply look at the cash flows of the portfolio. We will see this in Chapter 23. The most commonly used measure is *key rate duration* introduced by Ho (1992).

The basic principle of key rate duration is to change the yield for a particular maturity of the yield curve and determine the sensitivity of either an individual bond or a portfolio to that change holding all other yields constant. The sensitivity of the change in the bond's value or portfolio's value to a particular change in yield is called *rate duration*. There is a rate duration for every point on the yield curve. Consequently, there is not one rate duration. Rather, there is a set of durations representing each maturity on the yield curve. The total change in value of a bond or a portfolio if all rates change by the same number of basis points is simply the duration of a bond or portfolio.

Ho's approach focuses on 11 key maturities of the Treasury yield curve. These rate durations are called *key rate durations*. The specific maturities on the spot rate curve for which a key rate duration is measured are 3 months, 1 year, 2 years, 3 years, 5 years, 7 years, 10 years, 15 years, 20 years, 25 years, and 30 years. Changes in rates between any two key rates are calculated using a linear approximation.

A key rate duration for a particular portfolio maturity should be interpreted as follows: Holding the yield for all other maturities constant, the key rate duration is the approximate percentage change in the value of a portfolio (or bond) for a 100 basis point change in the yield for the maturity whose rate has been changed. Thus, a key rate duration is quantified by changing the yield of the maturity of interest and determining how the value or price changes. In fact, equation (21.1) is used. The prices denoted by V_- and V_+ in the equation are the prices in the case of a bond and the portfolio values in the case of a bond portfolio found by holding all other interest rates constant and changing the yield for the maturity whose key rate duration is sought.

SUMMARY

The price/yield relationship for all option-free bonds is convex. There are three properties of the price volatility of an option-free bond: (1) For small changes in yield, the percentage price change is symmetric; (2) for large changes in yield, the percentage price change is asymmetric; and (3) for large changes in yield, the price appreciation is greater than the price depreciation for a given change in yield.

The price volatility of an option-free bond is affected by two characteristics of a bond—maturity and coupon—and the yield level at which a bond trades. For a given maturity and yield, the lower the coupon rate, the greater the price volatility. For a given coupon rate and yield, the lower the coupon rate, the greater the price volatility. For a given coupon rate and maturity, the price volatility is greater the lower the yield.

There are two measures of bond price volatility: price value of a basis point and duration/convexity. We focused on the various duration measures—Macaulay duration, modified duration, and dollar duration—showing the relationship between bond price volatility and each of these measures. Duration is the approximate percentage change in price for a 100 basis point change in yield. The dollar duration is the approximate dollar price change.

Duration is the first approximation as to how the price of a bond or value of a portfolio will change when rates change. A second approximation can be used to improve the estimate of the price change obtained from duration. The second approximation is sometimes called "convexity." More specifically, a convexity measure can be computed and then the convexity adjustment to the percentage price change can be made. By adjustment it is meant that the approximate percentage price change as estimated by duration is adjusted. The convexity adjustment formula depends on how the convexity measure is defined. Thus dealers and vendors may report different convexity measures for an option-free bond but come up with the same convexity adjustment for a given change in yield. As with duration, a modified convexity and effective convexity measure can be computed.

The duration of a portfolio is the weighted average duration of the bonds constituting the portfolio. When a portfolio manager attempts to gauge the sensitivity of a bond portfolio to changes in interest rates by computing a portfolio's duration, it is assumed that the interest rate for all maturities changes by the same number of basis points. The most commonly used approach for estimating the sensitivity of a bond portfolio to unequal changes in interest rates is key rate duration. A rate duration is the approximate change in the value of a portfolio (or bond) to a change in the interest rate of a particular maturity assuming that the interest rate for all other maturities is held constant. Practitioners compute a key rate duration, which is simply the rate duration for key maturities.

REFERENCES

Ho, T. S. Y. 1992. Key rate durations: Measures of interest rate risks. *Journal of Fixed Income* 2 (September): 29–44.

Macaulay, F. 1939. *Some theoretical problems suggested by the movement of interest rates, bond yields, and stock prices in the U.S. since 1856.* New York: National Bureau of Economic Research.

CHAPTER 22
Valuing Bonds with Embedded Options

As explained in Chapter 20, the complication in valuing bonds with embedded options and option-type derivatives is that cash flows depend on interest rates in the future. Academicians and practitioners have attempted to capture this interest rate uncertainty through various models, often designed as one- or two-factor processes. These models attempt to capture the stochastic behavior of interest rates.

The lattice framework provides a means for implementing interest rate models, providing for the valuation of interest rate instruments with embedded options and interest rate option-like derivatives. Effectively, the lattice specifies the distribution of short-term interest rates over time. The lattice holds all the information required to perform the valuation of certain option-like interest rate products. First, the lattice is used to generate the cash flows across the life of the security. Next, the interest rates on the lattice are used to compute the present value of those cash flows.

There are several interest rate models that have been used in practice to construct an interest rate lattice. In each case, interest rates can realize one of several possible levels when we move from one period to the next. A lattice model that allows only two rates in the next period is called a *binomial model*. A lattice model that allows three possible rates in the next period is called a *trinomial model*. There are even more complex models that allow more than three possible rates in the next period.

Regardless of the underlying assumptions, each model shares a common restriction. In order to be "arbitrage-free," the interest rate tree generated must produce a value for an on-the-run, option-free bond that is consistent with the current par yield curve. In effect, the value generated by the model must be equal to the observed market price for the optionless instrument. Under these conditions the model is said to be "arbitrage free." A lattice

---

This chapter is coauthored with Andrew Kalotay and Michael Dorigan.

that produces an arbitrage-free valuation is said to be "fair." The lattice is used for valuation only when it has been calibrated to be fair as detailed later in this chapter.

We also demonstrate how a lattice is used to value an option-free bond and then apply the model to value bonds with embedded options.

THE INTEREST RATE LATTICE

In our illustration, we represent the lattice as a binomial tree, the simplest lattice form. Figure 22.1 provides an example of a binomial interest rate tree, which consists of a number of "nodes" and "legs." Each leg represents a one-year interval over time. A simplifying assumption of one-year intervals is made to illustrate the key principles. The methodology is the same for smaller time periods. In fact, in practice the selection of the length of the time period is critical, but we need not be concerned with this nuance here.

FIGURE 22.1 Four-Year Binomial Interest Rate Tree

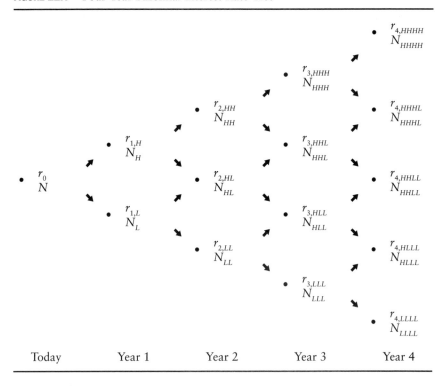

Valuing Bonds with Embedded Options **615**

The distribution of future interest rates is represented on the tree by the nodes at each point in time. Each node is labeled as N and has a subscript, a combination of Ls and Hs. The subscript indicates whether the node is lower or higher on the tree, respectively, relative to the other nodes. Thus node N_{HH} is reached when the one-year rate realized in the first year is the higher of the two rates for that period, then the highest of the rates in the second year.

The root of the tree is N, the only point in time at which we know the interest rate with certainty. The one-year rate today (that is, at N) is the current one-year spot rate, which we denote by r_0.

We must make an assumption concerning the probability of reaching one rate at a point in time. For ease of illustration, we have assumed that rates at any point in time have the same probability of occurring. In other words, the probability is 50% on each leg.

The interest rate model we will use to construct the binomial tree assumes that the one-year rate evolves over time based on a lognormal random walk with a known (stationary) volatility. Technically, the tree represents a one-factor model. Under the distributional assumption, the relationship between any two adjacent rates at a point in time is calculated via the following equation:

$$r_{1,H} = r_{1,L} e^{2\sigma\sqrt{t}}$$

where σ is the assumed volatility of the one-year rate, t is the length of the time period in years, and e is the base of the natural logarithm. Since we assume a one-year interval, that is, $t = 1$, we can disregard the calculation of the square root of t in the exponent.

For example, suppose that $r_{1,L}$ is 4.4448% and σ is 10% per year, then

$$r_{1,H} = 4.4448\%(e^{2\times 0.10}) = 4.4448\%(1.2214) = 5.4289\%$$

In the second year, there are three possible values for the one-year rate. The relationship between $r_{2,LL}$ and the other two one-year rates is as follows:

$$r_{2,HH} = r_{2,LL}(e^{4\sigma}) \text{ and } r_{2,HL} = r_{2,LL}(e^{2\sigma})$$

So, for example, if $r_{2,LL}$ is 4.6958%, and assuming once again that σ is 10%, then

$$r_{2,HH} = 4.6958\%(e^{4\times 0.10}) = 7.0053\%$$

and

$$r_{2,HL} = 4.6958\%(e^{2\times0.10}) = 5.7354\%$$

This relationship between rates holds for each point in time, Figure 22.2 shows the interest rate tree using this new notation.

Determining the Value at a Node

In general, to get a security's value at a node we follow the fundamental rule for valuation: The value is the present value of the expected cash flows. The appropriate discount rate to use for cash flows one year forward is the one-year rate at the node where we are computing the value. Now there are two present values in this case: The present value of the cash flows in the state where the one-year rate is the higher rate, and one where it is the lower rate state. We have assumed that the probability of both outcomes is 50%.

FIGURE 22.2 Four-Year Binomial Interest Rate Tree with One-Year Rates[a]

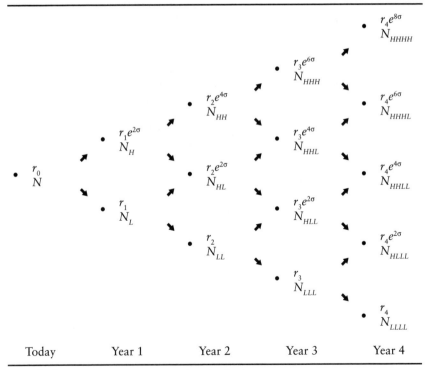

[a] r_t is the lowest one-year rate at each point in time.

Valuing Bonds with Embedded Options

FIGURE 22.3 Calculating a Value at a Node

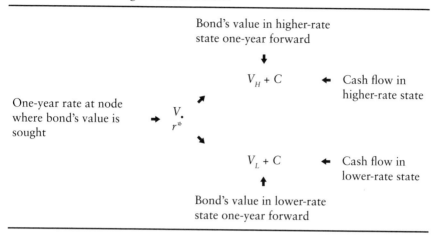

Figure 22.3 provides an illustration for a node assuming that the one-year rate is r^* at the node where the valuation is sought and letting:

V_H = the bond's value for the higher one-year rate state
V_L = the bond's value for the lower one-year rate state
C = coupon payment

From where do the future values come? Effectively, the value at any node depends on the future cash flows. The future cash flows include (1) the coupon payment one year from now and (2) the bond's value one year from now, both of which may be uncertain. Starting the process from the last year in the tree and working backwards to get the final valuation resolves the uncertainty. At maturity, the instrument's value is known with certainty—par. The final coupon payment can be determined from the coupon rate, or from prevailing rates to which it is indexed. Working back through the tree, we realize that the value at each node is quickly calculated. This process of working backward is often referred to as *recursive valuation*.

Using our notation, the cash flow at a node is either

$V_H + C$ for the higher one-year rate

or

$V_L + C$ for the lower one-year rate

The present value of these two cash flows using the one-year rate at the node, r^*, is

$$\frac{V_H + C}{(1+r^*)} = \text{Present value for the higher one-year rate}$$

and

$$\frac{V_L + C}{(1+r^*)} = \text{Present value for the lower one-year rate}$$

Then, the value of the bond at the node is found as follows:

$$\text{Value at a node} = \frac{1}{2}\left[\frac{V_H + C}{(1+r^*)} + \frac{V_L + C}{(1+r^*)}\right]$$

CALIBRATING THE LATTICE

We noted above the importance of the no-arbitrage condition that governs the construction of the lattice. To assure this condition holds, the lattice must be calibrated to the current par yield curve, a process we demonstrate here. Ultimately, the lattice must price optionless par bonds at par.

Assume the on-the-run par yield curve for a hypothetical issuer as it appears in Table 22.1 The current one-year rate is known, 3.50%. Hence, the next step is to find the appropriate one-year rates one year forward. As before, we assume that volatility, σ, is 10% and construct a two-year tree using the two-year bond with a coupon rate of 4.2%, the par rate for a two-year security.

Figure 22.4 shows a more detailed binomial tree with the cash flow shown at each node. The root rate for the tree, r_0, is simply the current one-year rate, 3.5%. At the beginning of Year 2 there are two possible one-year rates, the higher rate and the lower rate. We already know the relationship between the two. A rate of 4.75% rate at N_L has been arbitrarily chosen as a starting point. An iterative process determines the proper rate (that is, trial and error). The steps are described and illustrated below. Again, the goal is a rate that, when applied in the tree, provides a value of par for the two-year, 4.2% bond.

TABLE 22.1 Issuer Par Yield Curve

Maturity	Par Rate	Market Price
1 year	3.50%	100
2 years	4.20%	100
3 years	4.70%	100
4 years	5.20%	100

FIGURE 22.4 The One-Year Rates for Year 1 Using the Two-Year 4.2% On-the-Run Issue: First Trial

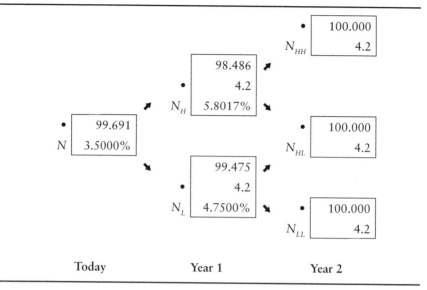

Step 1. Select a value for r_1. Recall that r_1 is the lower one-year rate. In this first trial, we arbitrarily selected a value of 4.75%.

Step 2. Determine the corresponding value for the higher one-year rate. As explained earlier, this rate is related to the lower one-year rate as follows: $r_1 e^{2\sigma}$. Since r_1 is 4.75%, the higher one-year rate is 5.8017% (= 4.75% $e^{2 \times 0.10}$). This value is reported in Figure 22.4 at node N_H.

Step 3. Compute the bond value's one year from now as follows:

a. Determine the bond's value two years from now. In our example, this is simple. Since we are using a two-year bond, the bond's value is its maturity value ($100) plus its final coupon payment ($4.2). Thus, it is $104.2.

b. Calculate V_H. Cash flows are known. The appropriate discount rate is the higher one-year rate, 5.8017% in our example. The present value is $98.486 (= $104.2/1.058017).

c. Calculate V_L. Again, cash flows are known—the same as those in Step 3b. The discount rate assumed for the lower one-year rate is 4.75%. The present value is $99.475 (= $104.2/1.0475).

Step 4. Calculate V:

a. Add the coupon to both V_H and V_L to obtain the values at N_H and N_L, respectively. In our example we have $102.686 for the higher rate and $103.675 for the lower rate.

b. Calculate V. The one-year rate is 3.50%. (Note: At this point in the valuation, r^* is the root rate, 3.50%). Therefore, $99.691 = ½($99.214 + $100.169)

Step 5: Compare the value in Step 4 to the bond's market value. If the two values are the same, then the r_1 used in this trial is the one we seek. If, instead, the value found in Step 4 is not equal to the market value of the bond then r_1 in this trial is not the one-year rate that is consistent with the current yield curve. In this case, one year from now the five steps are repeated with a different value for r_1.

When r_1 is 4.75%, a value of $99.691 results in Step 4, which is less than the observed market price of $100. Therefore, 4.75% is too large and the five steps must be repeated trying a lower rate for r_1.

Let's jump right to the correct rate for r_1 in this example and rework steps 1 through 5. This occurs when r_1 is 4.4448%. The corresponding binomial tree is shown in Figure 22.5. The value at the root is equal to the market value of the two-year issue (par).

FIGURE 22.5 The One-Year Rates for Year 1 Using the Two-Year 4.2% On-the-Run Issue

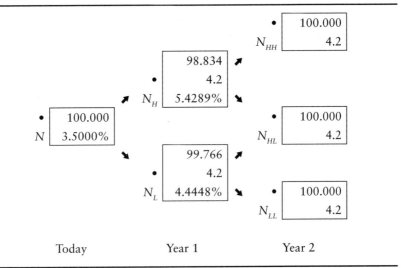

FIGURE 22.6 Information for Deriving the One-Year Rates for Year 2 Using the Three-Year 4.7% On-the-Run Issue

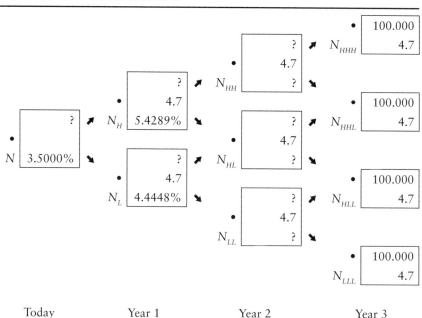

We can "grow" this tree for one more year by determining r_2. Now we will use the three-year on-the-run issue, the 4.7% coupon bond, to get r_2. The same five steps are used in an iterative process to find the one-year rates in the tree two years from now. Our objective is now to find the value of r_2 that will produce a bond value of $100. Note that the two rates one year from now of 4.4448% (the lower rate) and 5.4289% (the higher rate) do not change. These are the fair rates for the tree one-year forward.

The problem is illustrated in Figure 22.6. The cash flows from the three-year, 4.7% bond are in place. All we need to perform a valuation are the rates at the start of Year 3. In effect, we need to find r_2 such that the bond prices at par. Again, an arbitrary starting point is selected, and an iterative process produces the correct rate.

The completed version of Figure 22.6 is found in Figure 22.7. The value of r_2, or equivalently $r_{2,LL}$, which will produce the desired result is 4.6958%. The corresponding rates $r_{2,HL}$ and $r_{2,HH}$ would be 5.7354% and 7.0053%, respectively. To verify that these are the correct one-year rates two years from now, work backwards from the four nodes at the right of the tree in Figure 22.7. For example, the value in the box at N_{HH} is found by taking the value of $104.7 at the two nodes to its right and discounting at 7.0053%.

FIGURE 22.7 The One-Year Rates for Year 2 Using the 3-Year 4.7% On-the-Run Issue

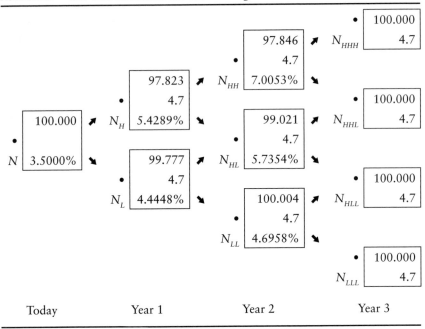

The value is $97.846. Similarly, the value in the box at N_{HL} is found by discounting $104.70 by 5.7354% and at N_{LL} by discounting at 4.6958%.

USING THE LATTICE FOR VALUATION

To illustrate how to use the lattice for valuation purposes, consider a 6.5% option-free bond with four years remaining to maturity. Since this bond is option-free, it is not necessary to use the lattice model to value it. All that is necessary to obtain an arbitrage-free value for this bond is to discount the cash flows using the spot rates obtained from bootstrapping the yield curve shown in Table 22.1. (All calculations are highly sensitive to the number of decimal places shown.) The spot rates are shown in Table 22.2.

As explained in Chapter 20, the required yield for each cash flow need not be the same. For pricing a bond, the cash flows should be discounted at the spot rates. Let's see how that is done to value the 6.5%, four-year option free bond with a par value of $100 using the spot rates in Table 22.2. The computation is as follows:

$$\frac{\$6.5}{(1.03500)} + \frac{\$6.5}{(1.042247)^2} + \frac{\$6.5}{(1.047345)^3} + \frac{\$106.5}{(1.052707)^4} = \$104.643$$

Valuing Bonds with Embedded Options

The numerator is the cash flow for each year and the denominator uses the spot rates in Table 22.2 as the discount rate to compute the present value of the cash flow. The price of this option-free bond is $104.643 and this should agree with any price we obtain by valuing this bond using the lattice.

Figure 22.8 contains the fair tree for a four-year valuation. Figure 22.9 shows the various values in the discounting process using the lattice in Figure 22.8. The root of the tree shows the bond value of $104.643, the same value found by discounting at the spot rate. This demonstrates that the lat-

TABLE 22.2 Spot Rates

Maturity	Spot Rate
1-year	3.5000%
2-year	4.2147%
3-year	4.7345%
4-year	5.2707%

All calculations are highly sensitive to the number of decimal places shown.

FIGURE 22.8 Binomial Interest Rate Tree for Valuing Up to a Four-Year Bond for Issuer (10% volatility assumed)

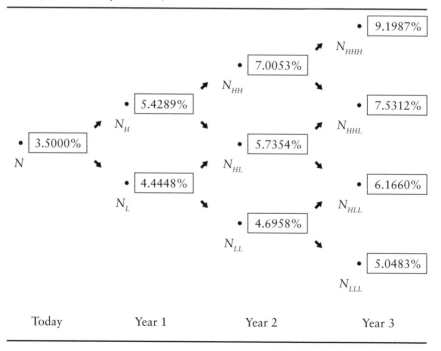

FIGURE 22.9 Valuing an Option-Free Bond with Four Years to Maturity and a Coupon Rate of 6.5% (10% volatility assumed)

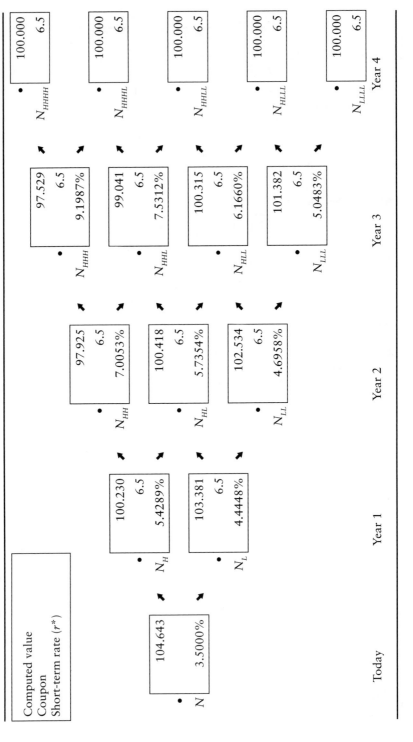

tice model is consistent with the valuation of an option-free bond when using spot rates.

Later in this chapter the lesson here is applied to more complex instruments, those with option features that require the lattice-based process for proper valuation. Regardless of the security or derivative to be valued, the generation of the lattice follows the same no-arbitrage principles outlined here. Subsequently, cash flows are determined at each node, the recursive valuation process undertaken to arrive at fair values. Hence, a single lattice and a valuation process prove to be robust means for obtaining fair values for a wide variety of fixed income instruments.

USING THE LATTICE MODEL TO VALUE BONDS WITH EMBEDDED OPTIONS

Now we will demonstrate how the lattice framework provides a robust means for valuing bonds with embedded options. In addition, we extend the application of the interest rate tree to the calculation of the option-adjusted spread, as well as the effective duration and convexity of a bond.[1]

The valuation of bonds with embedded options proceeds in the same fashion as in the case of an *option-free bond*. However, the added complexity of an embedded option requires an adjustment to the cash flows on the tree depending on the structure of the option. A decision on whether to call or put must be made at nodes on the tree where the option is eligible for exercise. Examples for both callable and putable bonds follow. The analysis can be extended to cases where there are several embedded options such as callable bond with an accelerated sinking fund provision.

Valuing a Callable Bond

In the case of a call option, the call will be made when the *present value* (PV) of the future cash flows is greater than the call price at the node where the decision to exercise is being made. Effectively, the following calculation is made:

$$V_t = \text{Min}[\text{Call price}, \text{PV}(\text{Future cash flows})]$$

where V_t represents the PV of future cash flows at the node. This operation is performed at each node where the bond is eligible for call.

---

[1] The model describe below was first introduced by Kalotay, Williams, and Fabozzi (1993).

For example, consider a 6.5% bond with four years remaining to maturity that is callable in one year at $100. We will value this bond, as well as the other instruments in this chapter, using a binomial tree. The on-the-run yield curve for the issuer used to construct the tree is given in Table 22.1. The methodology for constructing the binomial interest rate tree from the yield curve was explained earlier. Application of the methodology results in the binomial interest-rate free in Figure 22.8 assuming that interest rate volatility is 10% and that cash flows occur at the end of the year.

Figure 22.10 shows two values are now present at each node of the binomial tree. The discounting process is used to calculate the first of the two values at each node. The second value is the value based on whether the issue will be called. To simplify the analysis, it is assumed that the issuer calls the issue if the PV of future cash flows exceeds the call price. This second value is incorporated into the subsequent calculations.

In Figure 22.11 certain nodes from Figure 22.10 are highlighted. Figure 22.11A shows nodes where the issue is not called (based on the simple call rule used in the illustration) in year 2 and year 3. The values reported in this case are the same as in the valuation of an option-free bond. Panel (b) of the figure shows some nodes where the issue is called in year 2 and year 3. Notice how the methodology changes the cash flows. In year 3, for example, at node N_{HLL} the recursive valuation process produces a PV of 100.315. However, given the call rule, this issue would be called. Therefore, 100 is shown as the second value at the node and it is this value that is then used as the valuation process continues. Taking the process to its end, the value for this callable bond is 102.899.

The value of the call option is computed as the difference between the value of an option-free bond and the value of a callable bond. In our illustration, the value of the option-free bond has been shown to be 104.643. The value of the callable bond is 102.899. Hence, value of the call option is 1.744 (= 104.634 − 102.899).

Valuing a Putable Bond

A putable bond is one in which the bondholder has the right to force the issuer to pay off the bond prior to the maturity date. The analysis of the putable bond follows closely that of the callable bond. In the case of the putable, we must establish the rule by which the decision to put is made. The reasoning is similar to that for the callable bond. If the PV of the future cash flows is less than the put price (that is, par), then the bond will be put. In equation form,

$$V_t = \text{Max}[\text{Put price}, \text{PV(Future cash flows)}]$$

FIGURE 22.10 Valuing a Callable Bond with Four Years to Maturity, a Coupon Rate of 6.5%, and Callable after the First Year at 100 (10% volatility assumed)

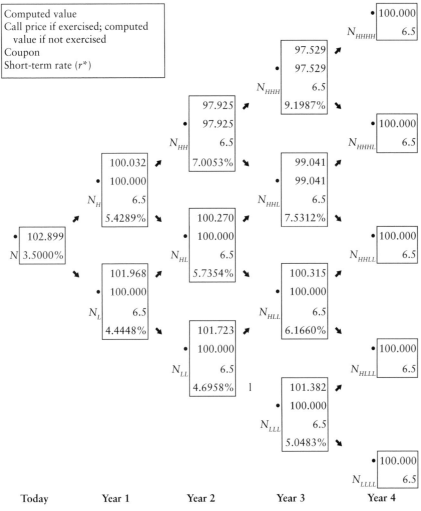

Figure 22.12 is analogous to Figure 22.11. It shows the binomial tree with the values based on whether or not the investor exercises the put option at each node. The bond is putable any time after the first year at par. The value of the bond is 105.327. Note that the value is greater than the value of the corresponding option-free bond.

With the two values in hand, we can calculate the value of the put option. Since the value of the putable bond is 105.327 and the value of the

FIGURE 22.11 Highlighting Nodes in Years 2 and 3 for a Callable Bond
A. Nodes Where Call Option Is Not Exercised

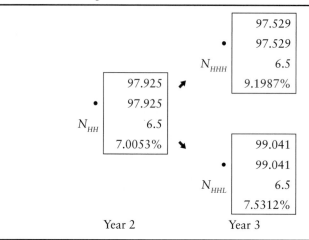

B. Selected Nodes Where the Call Option Is Exercised

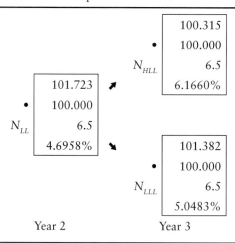

corresponding option-free bond is 104.643, the value of the embedded put option purchased by the investor is effectively 0.684.

Suppose that a bond is both putable and callable. The procedure for valuing such a structure is to adjust the value at each node to reflect whether the issue would be put or called. Specifically, at each node there are two decisions about the exercising of an option that must be made. If it is called, the value at the node is replaced by the call price. The valuation procedure then continues using the call price at that node. If the call option is not exer-

FIGURE 22.12 Valuing a Putable Bond with Four Years to Maturity, a Coupon Rate of 6.5%, and Putable after the First Year at 100 (10% volatility assumed)

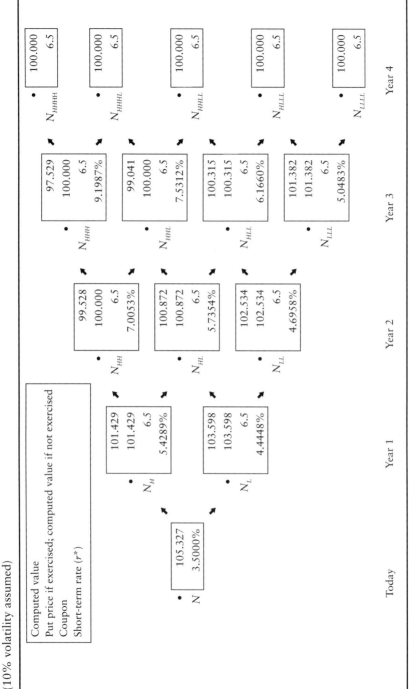

cised at a node, it must be determined whether or not the put option will be exercised. If it is exercised, then the put price is substituted at that node and is used in subsequent calculations.

EXTENSIONS

We next demonstrate how to compute the option-adjusted spread, effective duration, and the convexity for a bond with an embedded option.

Option-Adjusted Spread

We have concerned ourselves with valuation to this point. However, financial market transactions determine the actual price for a fixed income instrument, not a series of calculations on an interest rate lattice. If markets are able to provide a meaningful price (usually a function of the liquidity of the market in which the instrument trades), this price can be translated into an alternative measure of value, the option-adjusted spread (OAS).

The OAS for a security is the fixed spread (usually measured in basis points) over the benchmark rates that equates the output from the valuation process with the actual market price of the security. For an optionless security, the calculation of OAS is a relatively simple, iterative process. The process is much more analytically challenging with the added complexity of optionality. And, just as the value of the option is volatility dependent, the OAS for a fixed income security with embedded options or an option-like interest rate product is volatility dependent.

Recall our illustration in Figure 22.10 where the value of a callable bond was calculated as 102.899. Suppose that we had information from the market that the price is actually 102.218. We need the OAS that equates the value from the lattice with the market price. Since the market price is lower than the valuation, the OAS is a positive spread to the rates in the exhibit, rates we assume to be benchmark rates.

The solution in this case is 35 basis points, which is incorporated into Figure 22.13 that shows the value of the callable bond after adding 35 basis points to each rate. The simple, binomial tree provides evidence of the complex calculation required to determine the OAS for a callable bond. In Figure 22.10, the bond is called at N_{HLL}. However, once the tree is shifted 35 bps in Figure 22.13, the PV of future cash flows at N_{HLL} falls below the call price to 99.985, so the bond is not called at this node. Hence, as the lattice structure grows in size and complexity, the need for computer analytics becomes obvious.

Valuing Bonds with Embedded Options

FIGURE 22.13 Demonstration that the Option-Adjusted Spread is 35 Basis Points for a 6.5% Callable Bond Selling at 102.218 (assuming 10% volatility)[a]

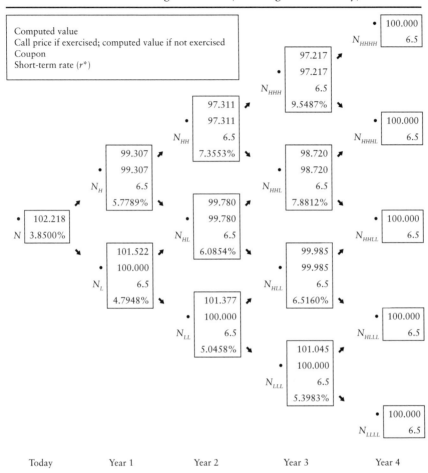

[a] Each one-year rate is 35 basis points greater than in Figure 22.10.

Effective Duration and Effective Convexity

Duration and convexity provide a measure of the interest rate risk inherent in a fixed income security. We rely on the lattice model to calculate the effective duration and effective convexity of a bond with an embedded option and other option-like securities. The equations for these two risk measures as given in Chapter 21 are reproduced here:

$$\text{Effective duration} = \frac{V_- - V_+}{2V_0(\Delta r)}$$

$$\text{Effective convexity} = \frac{V_+ - V_- - 2V_0}{2V_0(\Delta r)^2}$$

where V_- and V_+ are the values derived following a parallel shift in the yield curve down and up, respectively, by a fixed spread. The model adjusts for the changes in the value of the embedded call option that result from the shift in the curve in the calculation of V_- and V_+.

Note that the calculations must account for the OAS of the security. Below we provide the steps for the proper calculation of V_+. The calculation for V_- is analogous.

Step 1. Given the market price of the issue, calculate its OAS.
Step 2. Shift the on-the-run yield curve up by a small number of basis points (Δr).
Step 3. Construct a binomial interest rate tree based on the new yield curve from Step 2.
Step 4. Shift the binomial interest rate tree by the OAS to obtain an "adjusted tree." That is, the calculation of the effective duration and convexity assumes a constant OAS.
Step 5. Use the adjusted tree in Step 4 to determine the value of the bond, V_+.

We can perform this calculation for our four-year callable bond with a coupon rate of 6.5%, callable at par selling at 102.218. We computed the OAS for this issue as 35 basis points. Figure 22.14 holds the adjusted tree following a shift in the yield curve up by 25 basis points, and then adding 35 basis points (the OAS) across the tree. The adjusted tree is then used to value the bond. The resulting value, V_+ is 101.621.

To determine the value of V_-, the same five steps are followed except that in Step 2, the on-the-run yield curve is shifted down by a small number of basis points (Δr). It can be demonstrated that for our callable bond, the value for V_- is 102.765.

The results are summarized next:

$r = 0.0025$
$V_+ = 101.621$
$V_- = 102.765$
$V_0 = 102.218$

Valuing Bonds with Embedded Options

FIGURE 22.14 Determination of V_+ for Calculating Effective Duration and Convexity[a]

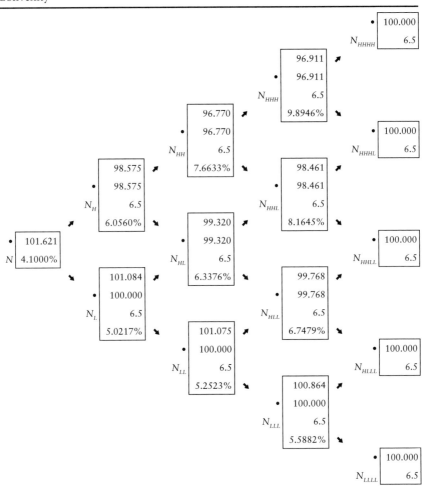

[a] +25 basis point shift in on-the-run yield curve.

Therefore,

$$\text{Effective duration} = \frac{102.765 - 101.621}{2(102.218)(0.0025)} = 2.24$$

$$\text{Effective convexity} = \frac{101.621 + 102.765 - 2(102.218)}{2(102.218)(0.0025)^2}$$

$$= -39.1321$$

Notice that this callable bond exhibits negative convexity.

SUMMARY

Several models have been developed to value bonds with embedded options. The most common model is a one-factor model. The lattice provides a framework for implementing interest rate models. The lattice uses an arbitrage-free interest rate lattice or tree to generate the cash flows over the life of the financial instrument and, subsequently, to determine the present value of the cash flow. The present value of the cash flow is then the fair value of the financial instrument. The lattice must be constructed so as to be consistent with (that is, calibrated to) the observed market value of an on-the-run option-free issue.

The valuation of an option-free bond is straightforward. However, once there is a provision in the bond structure that grants the issuer and the investor an option, valuation becomes more difficult. The standard technology employed to value bonds with options that depend on future interest rates, such as calls and puts, is the lattice framework. The initial step in the lattice approach is to generate an arbitrage-free lattice or interest rate tree from an appropriate on-the-run yield curve. Based on rules specified by the modeler for when an option will be exercised, a lattice of future cash flows is obtained and then valued using the interest rates in the lattice.

Other useful analytical measures can be obtained using the lattice model. These measures include option-adjusted spread—a measure of relative value—and effective duration and effective convexity—measures of price sensitivity to changes in interest rates.

REFERENCES

Kalotay, A. J., G. O. Williams, and F. J. Fabozzi. 1993. A model for the valuation of bonds and embedded options. *Financial Analysts Journal* 49, no. 3: 35–46.

CHAPTER 23
Bond Portfolio Strategies

With an understanding of the investment features of bonds and how to quantify the exposure of a bond portfolio to interest rate risk, we now turn to bond portfolio strategies. As in the case of equity portfolio strategies, bond portfolio strategies can be classified as active strategies and passive strategies. Both types of strategies are discussed in this chapter.

We begin this chapter with a discussion of the various bond market indexes. The spectrum of bond portfolio strategies can be understood in terms of the degree of mismatch that is permitted between the index and the managed portfolio.

BOND MARKET INDEXES

The wide range of bond market indexes available can be classified as broad-based bond market indexes and specialized bond market indexes. We discuss each type below.

Broad-Based Bond Market Indexes

The three broad-based bond market indexes most commonly used by institutional investors are the Barclays Capital U.S. Aggregate Index (previously the Lehman Brothers U.S. Aggregate Index), the Salomon Smith Barney Broad Investment-Grade Bond Index (SSB BIG), and the Merrill Lynch Domestic Market Index. There are more than 5,500 issues in each index. Reilly and Wright (2005) report that the correlation of annual returns between the three broad-based indexes to be around 98%.

The three broad-based indexes are computed daily and are market value weighted. This means that for each issue, the ratio of the market value of an issue relative to the market value of all issues in the index is used as the weight of the issue in all calculations. The securities in the SSB BIG index are all trader priced. For the two other indexes, the securities are either trader priced or model priced. Each index has a different way in which it handles intra-month cash flows that must be reinvested. For the SSB BIG index, these cash flows are assumed to be reinvested at the one-month Treasury bill rate while for the Merrill Lynch index, they are assumed to be reinvested in the specific issue. There is no reinvestment of intra-month cash flows for the Barclays Capital index.

Each index is broken into sectors. The Barclays Capital index, for example, is divided into the following six sectors: (1) Treasury, (2) agency, (3) mortgage, (4) commercial mortgage-backed securities, (5) asset-backed securities, and (6) credit. Table 23.1 shows the percentage composition of the index as of October 17, 2008.

The agency sector includes agency debentures, not mortgage-backed issued by federal agencies. The credit sector includes domestic corporate issues and U.S. dollar denominated bonds of European issuers. The four sectors within the credit sector are (1) financial, (2) utility, (3) industrial, and (4) noncorporates. All three indexes exclude issues that are noninvestment grade (i.e., below BBB) and issues that have a maturity of one year or less. To be included in the Barclays Capital index, the size of the issue must be more than $150 million; for the Merrill Lynch and SSB indexes, the issue size need only be $50 million. Only taxable issues are included in the broad-based bond market indexes.

The mortgage sector consists of only agency pass-through securities: Ginnie Mae, Fannie Mae, and Freddie Mac pass-through securities. Thus, agency collateralized mortgage obligations and agency stripped mortgage-backed securities are not included. The reason why these mortgage derivatives products are not included is that it would be double counting since they are created from agency pass-through securities. In constructing the index for the mortgage sector for the Barclays Capital index, for example, it groups more than 800,000 individual mortgage pools with a fixed rate coupon into generic aggregates. These generic aggregates are defined in terms of agency (i.e., Gin-

TABLE 23.1 Sectors of the Barclays Capital U.S. Aggregate Index as of October 17, 2008

Sector	Percent of Market Value
Treasury	21.95
Agency	9.89
Mortgage	38.95
Commercial mortgage-backed securities	5.02
Asset-backed securities	0.78
Credit	23.41
Total	100.00

nie Mae, Fannie Mae, and Freddie Mac), program type (i.e., 30-year and 15-year mortgages), price relative to par, coupon rate for the pass-through, and the year the pass-through was originated. For an issue to be included it must have a minimum amount outstanding of $100 million and a minimum weighted average maturity of one year. Agency pass-throughs backed by pools of adjustable-rate mortgages are not included in the mortgage index. Table 23.2 shows the breakdown of this sector by program and price.

TABLE 23.2 Percentage Composition of the Mortgage Sector of the Barclays Capital U.S. Aggregate Index as of October 17, 2008

Program	Price	Percent of Market Value
GNMA		
30-year		
	<98	0.05
	98 to <102	1.87
	102 to <106	1.64
	106+	0.10
15-year		
	<98	0.01
	98 to <102	0.06
	102 to <106	0.02
	106+	0.00
GNMA Total		3.75
Fannie Mae and Freddie Mac		
30-year		
	<98	0.77
	98 to <102	16.19
	102 to <106	9.62
	106+	0.30
15-year		
	<98	0.45
	98 to <102	3.71
	102 to <106	0.95
	106+	0.00
Fannie Mae and Freddie Mac Total		31.99
Total pass-throughs		41.04

Specialized Bond Market Indexes

The specialized bond market indexes focus on one sector of the bond market or a subsector of the bond market. Indexes on sectors of the market are published by the three firms that produce the broad-based bond market indexes, as well as other brokerage firms and nonbrokerage firms.

Moreover, there is a family of U.S. bond municipal indexes. The Barclays Capital municipal bond indexes are the ones most commonly used by institutional investors. There is a broad-based index the Barclays Capital Municipal Bond Index that includes long-term, tax-exempt bonds that are investment grade. The index is divided into the following four main sectors: (1) state and local general obligation bonds, (2) revenue bonds, (3) insured bonds, and (4) prerefunded bonds. The revenue sector in turn is divided into the following subindexes or sectors: electric, housing, industrial development and PCR, transportation, eduction, water and sewer, resource recovery, leasing, and special tax. There are subindexes by the maturity of the bonds comprising the index and by credit rating: AAA, AA, A, and BAA. There are specialized index such as the "managed money" and "insurance industry" tax-exempt indexes to serve the benchmark needs of investor groups whose permissible investments in the tax-exempt municipal bond market are not likely to be met by the Barclays Capital Municipal Bond Index.

International Bond Indexes

There are specialized international bond indexes that fall into three categories. The first is an index that includes both U.S. and non-U.S. bonds. Such indexes are referred to as "global bond indexes" or "world bond indexes." The Barclays Capital Global Aggregate Bond Index is an example. Table 23.3 shows the sectors of that index as of October 17, 2008. The "Collateralised" sector is the German covered bond market. Table 23.4 shows the breakdown of the index by the currency of the issuer.

The second type includes only non-U.S. bonds and are commonly referred to as "international bond indexes" or "ex-U.S. bond indexes." The third type includes specialized bond indexes for particular non-U.S. bond sectors. Two examples of this third type of index are Barclays Capital's Pan-European Aggregate Index and the Asian-Pacific Aggregate Index. Table 23.5 shows the composition of the latter index as of October 17, 2008.

Indexes can be reported on a currency hedged basis and/or an unhedged currency hedged basis.

TABLE 23.3 Sectors of the Barclays Capital Global Aggregate Index as of October 17, 2008

Sector	Percent of Market Value
Treasury	47.48
Agency	9.93
Credit	21.72
U.S. mortgage	13.72
ABS/CMBS	1.83
Collateralized (Pfandbrief)	5.32
Total	100.00

TABLE 23.4 Barclays Capital Global Aggregate Index by Currency of Issuer as of October 17, 2008

	Percent of Market Value	Number of Issues
U.S. Dollar	38.0	5,714
Euro	32.1	2,854
Japanese Yen	16.6	1,548
British Pound	5.4	939
Canadian Dollar	2.6	513
Australian Dollar	0.6	147
New Zealand Dollar	0.1	20
Swedish Krona	0.6	50
Danish Krone	0.4	39
Norwegian Krone	0.1	10
Singapore Dollar	0.2	20
Korean Won	1.1	158
South African Rand	0.2	42
Hong Kong Dollar	0.0	1
Chile Peso	0.0	6
Mexican Peso	0.3	18
Slovakia Koruna	0.0	6
Hungarian Forint	0.2	19
Czech Koruna	0.2	15
Polish Zloty	0.4	14
Taiwan Dollar	0.4	69
Malaysia Ringgit	0.2	23
Swiss Franc	2.0	11
Total	99.8	12,225

TABLE 23.5 Barclays Capital Asian-Pacific Aggregate Index by Currency of Issuer as of October 17, 2008

	Percent of Market Value	Number of Issues
Japanese Yen	84.5	1,482
Australian Dollar	2.9	125
New Zealand Dollar	0.5	15
Singapore Dollar	0.9	19
Korean Won	7.7	131
Hong Kong Dollar	0.0	2
Taiwan Dollar	2.4	70
Malaysia Ringgit	1.0	26
Total	100.0	1,870

THE SPECTRUM OF STRATEGIES

A good way to understand the spectrum of bond portfolio strategies and the key elements of each strategy is in terms of the benchmark established by the client. This is depicted in Figure 23.1. The figure, developed by Volpert of the Vanguard Group, shows the risk and return of a bond strategy versus a benchmark. Volpert classifies the strategies as follows:

1. Pure bond index matching
2. Enhanced indexing/matching primary risk factors approach
3. Enhanced indexing/minor risk factor mismatches
4. Active management/larger risk factor mismatches
5. Active management/full-blown active

We discuss each of these strategies below.

The difference between indexing and active management is the extent to which the portfolio can deviate from the primary risk factors that impact the performance of an index. The primary risk factors associated with an index are:

1. The duration of the index
2. The present value distribution of the cash flows
3. Percent in sector and quality
4. Duration contribution of sector
5. Duration contribution of credit quality

6. Sector/coupon/maturity cell weights
7. Issuer exposure control

The first primary risk factor deals with the sensitivity of the value of the index to a parallel shift in interest rates. The second factor is important for controlling the yield curve risk associated with an index. Table 23.6 shows how these primary risk factors apply to the three major sectors of the broad-based bond market indexes.

FIGURE 23.1 Bond Management Risk Spectrum

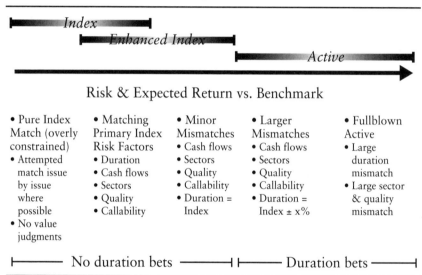

Source: Exhibit 1 in Volpert (1997, 192).

TABLE 23.6 Primary Bond Index Matching Factors

	Government	Corporate	MBS
Modified adjusted duration	X	X	
Present value of cash flows	X	X	
Percent in sector and quality	X		
Duration contribution of sector	X		
Duration contribution of credit quality	X		
Sector/coupon/maturity cell weights		X	X
Issuer exposure control		X	

Source: Exhibit 7 in Volpert (1997, 199).

Pure Bond Indexing Strategy

In terms of risk and return, a pure bond index matching strategy involves the least risk of underperforming the index. Several factors explain the popularity of bond indexing. First, the empirical evidence suggests that historically the overall performance of active bond managers has been poor. The second factor is the lower advisory management fees charged for an indexed portfolio compared to active management advisory fees. Advisory fees charged by active managers typically range from 15 to 50 basis points. The range for indexed portfolios, in contrast, is 1 to 20 basis points (with the upper range representing the fees for enhanced indexing discussed later). Some pension plan sponsors have decided to do away with advisory fees and to manage some or all of their funds in-house following an indexing strategy. Lower nonadvisory fees, such as custodial fees, is the third explanation for the popularity of bond indexing.

Critics of indexing point out that while an indexing strategy matches the performance of some index, the performance of that index does not necessarily represent optimal performance. Moreover, matching an index does not mean that the manager will satisfy a client's return requirement objective. For example, if the objective of a life insurance company or a pension fund is to have sufficient funds to satisfy a predetermined liability, indexing only reduces the likelihood that performance will not be materially worse than the index. The return on the index is not necessarily related to the liability.

The pure bond indexing strategy involves creating a portfolio so as to replicate the issues comprising the index. This means that the indexed portfolio is a mirror image of the index. However, a manager pursuing this strategy will encounter several logistical problems in constructing an indexed portfolio. First of all, the prices for each issue used by the organization that publishes the index may not be execution prices available to the manager. In fact, they may be materially different from the prices offered by some dealers. In addition, the prices used by organizations reporting the value of indexes are based on bid prices. Dealer ask prices, however, are the ones that the manager would have to transact at when constructing or rebalancing the indexed portfolio. Thus there will be a bias between the performance of the index and the indexed portfolio that is equal to the bid-ask spread.

Furthermore, there are logistical problems unique to certain sectors in the bond market. Consider first the corporate bond market. There are typically about 5,000 issues in the corporate bond sector of a broad-based bond market index. Because of the illiquidity for many of the issues, not only may the prices used by the organization that publishes the index be unreliable, but also many of the issues may not even be available. Next, consider the mortgage sector. There are over 800,000 agency pass-through issues. As explained earlier, the organizations that publish indexes aggregate all these issues into a few hundred generic issues. The manager is then faced with the difficult task of finding pass-through securities with the same risk-return profile of these hypothetical generic issues.

Finally, recall that the total return depends on the reinvestment rate available on interim cash flows received prior to month end. If the organization publishing the index regularly overestimates the reinvestment rate, then the indexed portfolio could underperform the index.

Enhanced Indexing/Matching Primary Risk Factors Approach

An enhanced indexing strategy can be pursued so as to construct a portfolio to match the primary risk factors without acquiring each issue in the index. This is a common strategy used by smaller funds because of the difficulties of acquiring all of the issues comprising the index. Generally speaking, the fewer the number of issues used to replicate the index, the smaller the tracking error due to transaction costs but the greater the tracking error risk because of the difficulties of matching the primary risk factors perfectly. In contrast, the more issues purchased to replicate the index, the greater the tracking error due to transaction costs, but the smaller the tracking error risk due to the mismatch of the primary factors between the indexed portfolio and the index.

While, in the spectrum of strategies defined by Volpert, this strategy is called an "enhanced strategy," some investors refer to this as simply an indexing strategy. For example, the following is from the summary of key features of Vanguard Total Bond Market, ETF, an an exchange-traded class of shares issued by Vanguard Total Bond Market Index Fund filed with the SEC:[1]

INVESTMENT OBJECTIVE
The Fund seeks to track the performance of a broad, market-weighted bond index.

PRIMARY INVESTMENT STRATEGIES
The Fund employs a *"passive management"*—or indexing—investment approach designed to track the performance of the Lehman Brothers Aggregate Bond Index. This Index measures a wide spectrum of public, investment-grade, taxable, fixed income securities in the United States—including government, corporate, and international dollar-denominated bonds, as well as mortgage-backed and asset-backed securities—all with maturities of more than 1 year.

---
[1] Vanguard Bond Index Funds, · 485APOS , on 1/17/07, p. 4.

INVESTMENT STRATEGY

The Fund employs a "passive" management approach, investing in a portfolio of assets whose performance is expected to match approximately the performance of the Lehman Aggregate Index before the deduction of Fund expenses. Under normal circumstances, the Fund invests at least 80% of the value of its net assets in a statistically selected sampling of bonds and other fixed-income securities that are included in or correlated with the Lehman Aggregate Index, as well as derivatives linked to that index.

There are two methodologies used to construct a portfolio to replicate an index: the stratified sampling and the optimization approach. Both approaches assume that the performance of an individual bond depends on a number of systematic factors that affect the performance of all bonds and on a factor unique to the individual issue. This last risk is diversifiable risk. The objective of the two approaches is to construct an indexed portfolio that eliminates this diversifiable risk.

Stratified Sampling Approach

With the stratified sampling approach (or cellular approach) to indexing, the index is divided into cells representing the primary risk factors. The objective is then to select from all of the issues in the index one or more issues in each cell that can be used to represent that entire cell. The total dollar amount purchased of the issues from each cell will be based on the percentage of the index's total market value that the cell represents. For example, if X% of the market value of all the issues in the index is made up of corporate bonds, then X% of the market value of the indexed portfolio should be composed of corporate bond issues. In the quote from the Vanguard SEC filing, it is mentioned that Vanguard uses this approach.

The number of cells that the indexer uses will depend on the dollar amount of the portfolio to be indexed. In indexing a portfolio of less than $50 million, for example, using a large number of cells would require purchasing odd lots of issues. This increases the cost of buying the issues to represent a cell, and thus would increase the tracking error risk. Reducing the number of cells to overcome this problem increases tracking error risk because the major risk factors of the indexed portfolio may differ materially from those of the index.

Optimization Approach

In the optimization approach, the manager seeks to design an indexed portfolio that will match the cell breakdown just as described and also satisfy other constraints, but also optimize some objective. An objective might be to maximize convexity or to maximize expected total returns or to minimize tracking error. Constraints, other than matching the cell breakdown, might include not purchasing more than a specified amount of one issuer or group of issuers within the same strategy.

The computational technique used to derive the optimal solution to the indexing problem in this approach is mathematical programming. When the objective function that the manager seeks to optimize is a linear function, linear programming (a specific form of mathematical programming) is used. If the objective function is quadratic, then the particular mathematical programming technique used is quadratic programming. When the object is to minimize tracking error in constructing the indexed portfolio, because tracking eror is a quadratic function (the difference between the benchmark return and the indexed portfolio's return, squared), quadratic programming is used to find the optimal indexed portfolio.

Although on the surface the stratified sampling approach is easier to use than the optimization approach, it is extremely difficult to implement the stratified sampling approach when large, diversified portfolios are taken as the benchmark. In this case, many cells are required, and the problem becomes complex. Also, because the handpicking of issues to match each cell is subjective, large tracking errors may result. Mathematical programming reduces the complexity of the problem when well-defined constraints are employed, allowing the manager to analyze large quantities of data optimally.

The investment objective of StateStreetGlobal Advisors' (SSgA) World Government Bond Index strategy "is to match the total return of the Citigroup World Government Bond Index," although the this firm notes that this strategy can also be employed if the JPMorgan Global Governments Index or another third-party global governments index is selected by a client. The firm's approach to matching the index is as follows:

> Since the individual bonds that compose the Index are highly correlated, we do not employ full replication but, instead, use a combination of optimization and stratified sampling techniques to construct portfolios to replicate this Index. Our methods are geared to constructing diversified portfolios that match the duration, sector, country and currency weights and quality of the investment benchmark. Once these constraints are in place, there still remains a choice of eligible securities for purchase. At this point, we utilize our relative value and trading capabilities to choose those securities that we consider optimal from the available universe. This is, those bonds that encapsulate the desired risk characteristics, but also offer the best relative value and liquidity among the universe of eligible securities.

We employ a suite of advanced third party and proprietary risk software in the management of these portfolios to ensure the summary risk characteristics of the portfolio are in line with the Index and that the ex-ante portfolio tracking error is within our guideline level.

As explained, the approach by SSgA uses both methodologies where, in the optimization approach, the objective is to minimize tracking error.

Enhanced Indexing/Minor Risk Factor Mismatches

Another enhanced strategy is one where the portfolio is constructed so as to have minor deviations from the risk factors that affect the performance of the index. For example, there might be a slight overweighting of issues or sectors where the manager believes there is relative value. However, it is important to point out that the duration of the constructed portfolio is matched to the duration of the index. This is depicted in Table 23.6 which shows that there are no duration bets for the pure index match strategy and the two enhanced index strategies.

Active Management/Larger Risk Factor Mismatches

Active bond strategies are those that attempt to outperform the market by intentionally constructing a portfolio that will have a greater index mismatch than in the case of enhanced indexing. The decision to pursue an active strategy or to engage a client to request a portfolio manager to pursue an active strategy must be based on the belief that there is some type of gain from such costly efforts; for there to be a gain, pricing inefficiencies must exist. The particular strategy chosen depends on why the portfolio manager believes this is the case.

Volpert classifies two types of active strategies. In the more conservative of the two active strategies, the portfolio manager makes larger mismatches relative to the index in terms of risk factors. This includes minor mismatches of duration. Typically, there will be a limitation as to the degree of duration mismatch. For example, the portfolio manager may be constrained to be within ±1 of the duration of the index. So, if the duration of the index is 4, the portfolio manager may have a duration between 3 and 5. To take advantage of an anticipated reshaping of the yield curve, there can be significant differences in the cash flow distribution between the index and the portfolio constructed by the manager. As another example, if the portfolio manager believes that, within the corporate sector, issues rated A will outperform issues rated AA, the portfolio manager may overweight the A issues and underweight AA issues.

Active Management/Full-Blown Active

In the full-blown active management case, the portfolio manager is permitted to make a significant duration bet without any constraint. The portfolio manager can have a duration of zero (i.e., be all in cash) or can leverage the portfolio to a high multiple of the duration of the index. The portfolio manager can decide not to invest in only one or more of the major sectors of the broad-based bond market indexes. The portfolio manager can make a significant allocation to sectors not included in the index. For example, there can be a substantial allocation to nonagency mortgage-backed securities.

We discuss various strategies used in active portfolio management in the next section.

VALUE-ADDED STRATEGIES

Active portfolio strategies and enhanced indexing/minor risk factor mismatch strategies seek to generate additional return after adjusting for risk. This additional return is popularly referred to as *alpha*. We shall refer to these strategies as *value-added strategies*. These strategies can be classified as strategic strategies and tactical strategies.

Strategic strategies, sometimes referred to as *top-down value-added strategies*, involve the following:

1. Interest rate expectations strategies
2. Yield curve strategies
3. Inter- and intrasector allocation strategies

Tactical strategies, sometimes referred to as *relative value strategies*, are short-term trading strategies. They include:

1. Strategies based on rich/cheap analysis
2. Yield curve trading strategies
3. Return enhancing strategies employing futures and options

Below we discuss these strategies. In addition, there are strategies involving futures and options for adding incremental return.

To help understand strategic strategies, we use the portfolio recommended by Barclays Capital to its clients in an October 20, 2008, publication. This recommended portfolio, shown in Table 23.7, is for a portfolio manager whose benchmark was the Barclays Capital U.S. Aggregate Index and is based on the percent of market value. Table 23.8 provides the same information but on a duration-weighted basis.

TABLE 23.7 Recommend Portfolio Asset Allocation Based on Market Value as of October 17, 2008

Option-Adjusted Duration	Spread Duration
102%	104%

U.S. Aggregate Core Portfolio

Approx. Maturity/Duration	T-bills/ 0–1 yr		2 yr/1–2 yr		3 yr/2–3 yr		4 yr/3–4 yr		5–6 yr/4–5 yr		6–10 yr/ 5–7 yr		10–20 yr/ 7–10 yr		20–30 yr/ 10+ yr		Total		% Over- (+)/ Under- Weight (−)
	Index	Rec.	Index	Rec.	Index	Rec.	Index	Rec.	Index	Rec.	Index	Rec.	Index	Rec.	Index	Rec.	Index	Rec.	
Treasury	0.45	0.00	5.49	4.95	2.23	0.00	2.34	0.00	2.23	6.71	3.39	0.00	2.98	1.78	2.78	1.22	21.89	14.66	−33
Agency	1.03	0.00	2.54	0.00	1.94	6.08	0.91	0.58	0.96	3.03	1.11	0.25	0.73	0.22	0.46	0.00	9.68	10.16	5
Mtg. Pass-throughs	0.85	0.00	4.37	0.05	10.15	13.58	15.10	13.68	7.16	8.26	1.56	7.51	0.00	0.00	0.00	0.00	39.19	43.08	10
CMBS	0.02	0.00	0.45	0.00	0.52	0.00	0.68	0.00	0.55	0.00	2.85	4.12	0.23	1.71	0.00	0.00	5.30	5.83	10
ABS	0.03	0.04	0.24	0.35	0.18	0.24	0.09	0.06	0.07	0.09	0.09	0.00	0.07	0.03	0.01	0.00	0.78	0.81	4
Credit	0.09	0.00	1.93	6.35	2.96	2.59	2.98	4.16	2.69	3.79	4.24	2.89	3.51	1.56	4.74	4.11	23.14	25.45	10
Total	2.47	0.04	15.02	11.70	17.98	22.49	22.10	18.48	13.66	21.88	13.24	14.77	7.52	5.30	7.99	5.33	100.00	100.00	
% Over- (+)/ Underweight (−)		−98		−22		25		−16		60		12		−30		−33			

Source: Barclays Capital, Fixed Income Research, *Global Relative Value*, October 20, 2008, p.4.

TABLE 23.8 Recommend Portfolio Asset Allocation on a Duration-Weighted Basis as of October 17, 2008

Option-Adjusted Duration	Spread Duration
102%	104%

U.S. Aggregate Core Portfolio

Approx. Maturity/Duration	Percent of Market Value by Duration Range												% Over-(+)/ Under- Weight (−)	Contribution to Spread Duration						% Over-(+)/ Under- Weight (−)
	0–2		2–4		4–7		7–9		9+		Total			Option-Adj. Duration			Spread Duration			
	Index	Rec.	Index	Rec.	Index	Rec.	Index	Rec.	Index	Rec.	Index	Rec.		Index	Rec.	Diff.	Index	Rec.	Diff.	
Treasury	5.96	5.05	4.40	0.00	5.67	8.34	2.67	2.38	3.25	1.52	21.95	17.29	−21	1.11	0.95	−0.16	0.00	0.00	0.00	—
Agency	3.55	0.00	3.08	5.37	2.17	4.64	0.60	0.84	0.50	0.00	9.89	10.85	10	0.35	0.43	0.09	0.35	0.40	0.05	16
Mtg. Pass-throughs	2.95	0.05	16.72	14.16	19.29	29.70	0.00	0.00	0.00	0.00	38.95	43.91	13	1.62	1.99	0.37	1.58	2.04	0.46	29
CMBS	0.47	0.00	1.18	0.00	3.35	5.02	0.02	0.00	0.00	0.00	5.02	5.02	0	0.24	0.32	0.09	0.23	0.31	0.08	36
ABS	0.24	0.38	0.31	0.27	0.16	0.09	0.06	0.03	0.01	0.00	0.78	0.78	0	0.03	0.02	−0.01	0.02	0.02	−0.01	−27
Credit	2.00	5.78	6.23	6.85	7.16	5.29	2.90	1.15	5.11	3.11	23.41	22.17	−5	1.47	1.19	−0.28	1.48	1.03	−0.45	−30
Total	15.16	11.26	31.92	26.64	37.80	53.07	6.25	4.41	8.87	4.63	100.00	100.00		4.81	4.91	0.10	3.66	3.80	0.15	4
% Over-(+)/ Underweight (−)		−26		−17		40		−29		−48										

Source: Barclays Capital, Fixed Income Research, *Global Relative Value*, October 20, 2008, p.3.

Interest Rate Expectations Strategies

A portfolio manager who believes that he or she can accurately forecast the future level of interest rates will alter the portfolio's duration based the forecast. Because duration is a measure of interest rate sensitivity, this involves increasing a portfolio's duration if interest rates are expected to fall and reducing duration if interest rates are expected to rise. For those portfolio managers whose benchmark is a bond market index, this means increasing the portfolio duration relative to the benchmark index if interest rates are expected to fall and reducing it if interest rates are expected to rise. The degree to which the duration of the managed portfolio is permitted to diverge from that of the benchmark index may be limited by the client. Interest rate expectations strategies are commonly referred to as *duration strategies*.

A portfolio's duration may be altered in the cash market by swapping (or exchanging) bonds in the portfolio for other bonds that will achieve the target portfolio duration. Alternatively, a more efficient means for altering the duration of a bond portfolio is to use interest rate futures contracts. As we explain in Chapter 24, buying futures increases a portfolio's duration, while selling futures decreases it.

The key to this active strategy is, of course, an ability to forecast the direction of future interest rates. The academic literature does not support the view that interest rates can be forecasted so that risk-adjusted excess returns can be consistently realized. It is doubtful whether betting on future interest rates will provide a consistently superior return.

Tables 23.7 and 23.8 show the "option-adjusted duration" for the U.S. Aggregate Index and the recommended portfolio. The "option-adjusted duration" is the term used by Barclays Capital rather than effective duration. As can be seen, the recommended duration for a U.S. aggregate portfolio was 4.91 versus 4.81 for the index. That is, the recommended portfolio duration was 1.02% of the index so basically the recommended portfolio is pretty much market neutral.

Yield Curve Strategies

The yield curve for U.S. Treasury securities shows the relationship between maturity and yield. The shape of the yield curve changes over time. A shift in the yield curve refers to the relative change in the yield for each Treasury maturity. A parallel shift in the yield curve refers to a shift in which the change in the yield for all maturities is the same. A nonparallel shift in the yield curve means that the yield for every maturity does not change by the same number of basis points.

Top down yield curve strategies involve positioning a portfolio to capitalize on expected changes in the shape of the Treasury yield curve. There are three yield curve strategies: (1) bullet strategies, (2) barbell strategies, and (3) ladder strategies. In a *bullet strategy*, the portfolio is constructed so that the maturity of the bonds in the portfolio are highly concentrated at one point on the yield curve. In a *barbell strategy*, the maturity of the bonds included in the portfolio is concentrated at two extreme maturities. Actually, in practice when managers refer to a barbell strategy it is relative to a bullet strategy. For example, a bullet strategy might be to create a portfolio with maturities concentrated around 10 years while a corresponding barbell strategy might be a portfolio with 5-year and 20-year maturities. In a *ladder strategy* the portfolio is constructed to have approximately equal amounts of each maturity. So, for example, a portfolio might have equal amounts of bonds with one year to maturity, two years to maturity, and so on.

Each of these strategies will result in different performance when the yield curve shifts. The actual performance will depend on both the type of shift and the magnitude of the shift. Thus, no general statements can be made about the optimal yield curve strategy.

When this strategy is applied by a portfolio manager whose benchmark is a broad-based bond market index, there is a mismatching of maturities relative to the index in one or more of the bond sectors. This can be seen in Table 23.8 which shows the recommended portfolio on a duration-weighted basis relative to the index. Notice that the recommended portfolio underweighted on the sectors with less than four years to maturity and greater than seven years to maturity. That is, the short and long end of the yield curve were underweighted relative to the index. The four- to seven-year maturity sector is overweighted. The recommended portfolio is constructed to be more like a bullet portfolio than the index.

Inter- and Intrasector Allocation Strategies

A manager can allocate funds among the major bond sectors that is different from that the allocation in the index. This is referred to as an *intersector allocation strategy*. For example, Table 23.8 shows the portfolio allocation on a duration-weighted basis by sector for the recommended portfolio versus the index. As can be seen, there is an underweighting of the Treasury sector and the credit sector and an overweighting of the agency and mortgage sectors. The recommended portfolio is neutral relative to the index with respect to the CMBS and ABS sectors.

Several duration measures that we discussed in Chapter 21 and reported in Table 23.8 provide us with information about the level of exposure to spread risk. First is the difference in the spread duration between the index

(3.66) and the recommended portfolio (3.80). The second is the difference in the contribution to spread duration for each sector in the index and the corresponding sector in the recommended portfolio.

In an intrasector allocation strategy, the portfolio manager's allocation of funds within a sector differs from that of the index. Tables 23.9 and 23.10 show for the credit sector (the corporate sector) and the mortgage and CMBS sector, respectively, the allocation. Table 23.9 shows the intrasector allocation recommendation on October 17, 2008 for the corporate sector in terms of contribution to spread duration for each credit quality and by sector (financial, utility, industrials, and noncorporates).

Table 23.10 shows the recommended allocation for the mortgage sector in terms of market value and spread duration by program and price. The differences in allocation by price reflect differences in prepayment risk exposure. For example, consider the 30-year programs. There is an underweighting of premium products (i.e., pass-throughs trading above par value). This suggests that the allocation in the mortgage sector is such that there is concern that prepayments will accelerate causing premium products (i.e., high coupon mortgages) to underperform low coupon and par coupon mortgages. In contrast, for the 15-year mortgage products, there is an overweighting of premium products. Also shown in Table 23.10 is the recommended overweighting of CMBS.

Next we discuss factors that managers consider in making inter- and intrasector allocations.

Considerations in Inter- and Intrasector Allocations

In making inter- and intrasector allocations, a portfolio manager is anticipating how spreads will change. Spreads reflect differences in credit risk, call risk (or prepayment risk), and liquidity risk. When the spread for a particular sector or subsector is expected to decline or "narrow," a portfolio manager may decide to overweight that particular sector or subsector. It will be underweighted if the portfolio manager expects the spread to increase or "widen."

Credit spreads change because of expected changes in economic prospects. Credit spreads between Treasury and non-Treasury issues widen in a declining or contracting economy and narrow during economic expansion. The economic rationale is that in a declining or contracting economy, corporations experience a decline in revenue and cash flow, making it difficult for corporate issuers to service their contractual debt obligations. To induce investors to hold non-Treasury securities, the yield spread relative to Treasury securities must widen. The converse is that during economic expansion and brisk economic activity, revenue and cash flow pick up, increasing

TABLE 23.9 Corporate Sector Recommendation in Terms of Spread Duration Contribution as of October 17, 2008

	Aaa–Aa				A				Baa				Total			% Over (+)/
	Index	Rec.	Diff.	Index	Rec.	Diff.	Index	Rec.	Diff.	Index	Rec.	Diff.	Index	Rec.	Diff.	Underweight (−)
Spread Duration																
0–3	0.11	0.06	−0.05	0.03	0.07	0.04	0.02	0.03	0.00	0.17	0.16	−0.01				−6
3–5	0.09	0.07	−0.02	0.07	0.20	0.13	0.07	0.06	−0.01	0.23	0.32	0.10				43
5–7	0.07	0.00	−0.07	0.10	0.15	0.05	0.10	0.03	−0.07	0.27	0.18	−0.09				−33
7–10	0.10	0.18	0.08	0.08	0.06	−0.02	0.08	0.00	−0.08	0.26	0.24	−0.02				−6
10+	0.11	0.02	−0.10	0.24	0.22	−0.01	0.20	0.09	−0.11	0.55	0.33	−0.22				−40
Total	0.48	0.32	−0.16	0.52	0.70	0.18	0.47	0.20	−0.27	1.47	1.23	−0.24				−16
% Over- (+)/ Underweight (−)			−33			35			−57			−16				
Sector																
Financial	0.22	0.05	−0.17	0.19	0.16	−0.03	0.05	0.00	−0.05	0.46	0.21	−0.25				−55
Utility	0.00	0.00	0.00	0.05	0.12	0.07	0.09	0.00	−0.09	0.14	0.12	−0.02				−14
Industrials	0.06	0.09	0.03	0.25	0.41	0.15	0.29	0.12	−0.17	0.61	0.62	0.01				2
Non-Corp.	0.12	0.18	0.06	0.03	0.01	−0.01	0.03	0.08	0.05	0.18	0.28	0.10				52
Total	0.41	0.32	−0.08	0.52	0.71	0.18	0.47	0.20	−0.27	1.40	1.23	−0.17				−12
% Over- (+)/ Underweight (−)			−21			35			−57			−12				

Notes: Market Value and duration contribution statistics reflect values as of the prior business day. Overweight and underweight percentages highlighted in shaded area represent current date recommendations.

Source: Barclays Capital, Fixed Income Research, *Global Relative Value*, October 20, 2008, p. 4.

TABLE 23.10 Mortgage and CMBS Sector Recommendation in Terms of Spread Duration Contribution as of October 17, 2008

		Index		Recommend.		Difference		% Over- (+)/ Underweight (−)	
Program and Price		% Mkt. Val.	% Sprd. Dur.	% Mkt. Val.	% Sprd. Dur.	% Mkt. Val.	% Sprd. Dur.	% Mkt. Val.	% Sprd. Dur.
GNMA									
30-year									
	<98	0.05	0.00	0.98	0.06	0.93	0.06	1,860	2,349
	98 to <102	1.87	0.09	3.96	0.21	2.09	0.12	112	142
	102 to <106	1.64	0.07	0.00	0.00	−1.64	−0.07	−100	−100
	106+	0.10	0.00	0.00	0.00	−0.10	0.00	−100	−100
15-year									
	<98	0.01	0.000	0.00	0.00	−0.01	0.00	−100	−100
	98 to <102	0.06	0.002	0.00	0.00	−0.06	0.00	−100	−100
	102 to <106	0.02	0.001	0.05	0.00	0.03	0.00	150	157
	106+	0.00	0.000	0.00	0.00	0.00	0.00	—	—
GNMA Summary		3.75	0.16	4.99	0.28	1.24	0.11	33	69

TABLE 23.10 (Continued)

Program and Price	Index		Recommend.		Difference		% Over- (+)/ Underweight (−)	
	% Mkt. Val.	% Sprd. Dur.	% Mkt. Val.	% Sprd. Dur.	% Mkt. Val.	% Sprd. Dur.	% Mkt. Val.	% Sprd. Dur.
Fannie Mae and Freddie Mac								
Conventional 30-year								
<98	0.77	0.04	4.46	0.24	3.69	0.20	479	516
98 to <102	16.19	0.71	15.35	0.65	−0.84	−0.06	−5	−8
102 to <106	9.62	0.33	10.37	0.37	0.75	0.04	8	12
106+	0.30	0.01	0.00	0.00	−0.30	−0.01	−100	−100
Conventional 15-year								
<98	0.45	0.01	2.90	0.13	2.45	0.11	544	757
98 to <102	3.71	0.12	2.97	0.11	−0.74	−0.01	−20	−6
102 to <106	0.95	0.03	0.81	0.02	−0.14	0.00	−15	−6
106+	0.00	0.00	0.00	0.00	0.00	0.00	—	—
Conventional Summary	31.99	1.25	36.86	1.52	4.87	0.27	15	21
Total Pass-throughs	35.74	1.41	41.87	1.79	6.13	0.37	17	26
CMBS	5.30	0.25	5.83	0.38	0.53	0.13	10	50
Total	41.04	1.67	47.70	2.16	6.66	0.50	16	30

Source: Barclays Capital, Fixed Income Research, *Global Relative Value*, October 20, 2008, p. 4.

the likelihood that corporate issuers will have the capacity to service their contractual debt obligations. Yield spreads between Treasury and federal agency securities will vary depending on investor expectations about the prospects that an implicit government guarantee will be honored.

A portfolio manager, therefore, can use economic forecasts of the economy in developing forecasts of credit spreads. Also, some managers base forecasts on historical credit spreads. The underlying principle is that there is a "normal" credit spread relationship that exists. If the current credit spread in the market differs materially from that "normal" credit spread, then the portfolio manager should position the portfolio so as to benefit from a return to the "normal" credit spread. The assumption is that the "normal" credit spread is some type of average or mean value and that mean reversion will occur. If, in fact, there has been a structural shift in the marketplace, this may not occur as the normal spread may change.

A portfolio manager will also look at technical factors to assess relative value. For example, a manager may analyze the prospective supply and demand for new issues on spreads in individual sectors or issuers to determine whether they should be overweighted or underweighted. This commonly used tactical strategy is referred to as *primary market analysis*.

Now let's look at spreads due to call or prepayment risk. Expectations about how these spreads will change will affect the intersector allocation decision between Treasury securities (with noncallable securities) and spread products that have call risk. Corporate and agency bonds have callable and noncallable issue, all mortgages are prepayable, and asset-backed securities have products that are callable but borrowers may be unlikely to exercise the call. Consequently, with sectors having different degrees of call risk, expectations about how spreads will change also affect intraallocation decisions. They affect (1) the allocation between callable and noncallable bonds within the corporate bond sector and (2) within the agency, corporate, mortgage, and ABS sectors the allocation among premium (i.e., high coupon), par, and discount (i.e., low coupon) bonds.

Spreads due to call risk will change as a result of expected changes in (1) the direction of the change in interest rates and (2) interest rate volatility. An expected drop in the level of interest rates will widen the yield spread between callable bonds and noncallable bonds as the prospects that the issuer will exercise the call option increase. The reverse is true: The spread narrows if interest rates are expected to rise. An increase in interest rate volatility increases the value of the embedded call option and thereby increases the spread between (1) callable bonds and noncallable bonds and (2) premium and discount bonds. Trades where the portfolio manager anticipates better performance due to the embedded option of individual issues or sectors are referred to as *structure trades*.

Individual Security Selection Strategies

Once the allocation to a sector or subsector has been made, the portfolio manager must decide on the specific issues to select. This is because a manager will typically not invest in all issues within a sector or subsector. Instead, depending on the dollar size of the portfolio, the manager will select a representative number of issues.

It is at this stage that a portfolio manager makes an intrasector allocation decision to the specific issues. The portfolio manager may believe that there are securities that are mispriced within a subsector and therefore will outperform over the investment horizon other issues within the same sector. There are several active strategies that portfolio managers pursue to identify mispriced securities. The most common strategy identifies an issue as undervalued because either (1) its yield is higher than that of comparably rated issues; or (2) its yield is expected to decline (and price therefore rise) because credit analysis indicates that its rating will be upgraded.

Once a portfolio is constructed, a portfolio manager may undertake a swap that involves exchanging one bond for another bond that is similar in terms of coupon, maturity, and credit quality, but offers a higher yield. This is called a *substitution swap* and depends on a capital market imperfection. Such situations sometimes exist in the bond market owing to temporary market imbalances and the fragmented nature of the non-Treasury bond market. The risk the portfolio manager faces in making a substitution swap is that the bond purchased may not be truly identical to the bond for which it is exchanged. Moreover, typically bonds will have similar but not identical maturities and coupon. This could lead to differences in the convexity of the two bonds.

What is critical in assessing any potential swaps is to compare positions that have the same dollar duration. To understand why, consider two bonds, X and Y. Suppose that the price of bond X is 80 and has a duration of 5 while bond Y has a price of 90 and has a duration of 4. Since duration is the approximate percentage change per 100 basis point change in yield, a 100 basis points change in yield for bond X would change its price by about 5%. Based on a price of 80, its price will change by about $4 per $80 of market value. Thus, its dollar duration for a 100 basis point change in yield is $4 per $80 of market value. Similarly, for bond Y, its dollar duration for a 100 basis point change in yield per $90 of market value can be determined. In this case it is $3.6. So, if bonds X and Y are being considered as alternative investments or in some swap transaction other than one based on anticipating interest rate movements, the amount of each bond involved should be such that they will both have the same dollar duration.

To illustrate this, suppose that a portfolio manager owns $10 million par value of bond X which has a market value of $8 million. The dollar duration of bond X per 100 basis point change in yield for the $8 million market value is $400,000. Suppose further that this manager is considering exchanging bond X that it owns in its portfolio for bond Y. If the portfolio manager wants to have the same interest rate exposure (i.e., dollar duration) for bond Y that she currently has for bond X, she will buy a market value amount of bond Y with the same dollar duration. If the portfolio manager purchased $10 million of par value of bond Y and therefore $9 million of market value of bond Y, the dollar price change per 100 basis point change in yield would be only $360,000. If, instead, the portfolio manager purchased $10 million of market value of bond Y, the dollar duration per 100 basis point change in yield would be $400,000. Since bond Y is trading at 90, $11.11 million of par value of bond Y must be purchased to keep the dollar duration of the position from bond Y the same as for bond X.[2]

Failure to adjust a swap so as to hold the dollar duration the same means that the return will be affected by not only the expected change in the spread but also a change in the yield level. Thus, a portfolio manager would be making a conscious spread bet and possibly an unintentional bet on changes in the level of interest rates.

USING FACTOR MODELS TO MANAGE A PORTFOLIO

In Chapter 11, we demonstrated how a factor model can be used in common stock portfolio management. In this section, we explain how a factor model can be used in bond portfolio management. Taken together the information in the tables discussed below allow a bond portfolio manager to assess the portfolio's risk relative to a benchmark and reconstruct or rebal-

---

[2]Mathematically, this problem can be expressed as follows. Let

$\$D_X$ = dollar duration per 100 basis point change in yield for bond X for the market value of bond X held

D_Y = duration for bond Y

MV_Y = market value of bond Y needed to obtain the same dollar duration as bond X

Then, the following equation sets the dollar duration for bond X equal to the dollar duration for bond Y:

$\$D_X = (D_Y/100)MV_Y$

Solving for MVY,

$MV_Y = \$D_X/(D_Y/100)$

Dividing by the price per $1 of par value of bond Y gives the par value of bond Y that has an approximately equivalent dollar duration as bond X.

ance a portfolio if the risk exposures are unacceptable. The information for the illustration in this section was provided by Vadim Konstantinovsky of Barclays Capital using that firm's factor model.

Risk Characteristics of the Portfolio Relative to the Benchmark

In our illustration, we use an actual bond portfolio consisting of 40 bond issues. The bonds issues are shown in Table 23.11. The last column of the table shows the percentage (weight) of each issue in terms of market value as of September 17, 2008. Table 23.12 provides the breakdown of the portfolio by sector. The benchmark that will be used in this illustration is the Barclays Capital U.S. Aggregate Index. The last column of the table shows the difference by sector between the portfolio and the benchmark. A negative sign indicates an underweighting of the sector in the portfolio relative to the benchmark; a positive sign indicates an overweighting of the sector in the portfolio relative to the benchmark. As can be seen, this portfolio is underweighted in all sectors except for the financial sector and the mortgage sector (i.e., agency pass-through securities).

The allocation of the portfolio by credit quality is reported in Table 23.13, which also shows the credit quality of the benchmark. "MBS" credit means the exposure to agency MBS. The portfolio has only exposure to MBS issued by Fannie Mae and Freddie Mac while the benchmark includes exposure to all three issuers in the mortgage sector: Ginnie Mae, Fannie Mae, and Freddie Mac. Because of the substantial exposure to the mortgage sector, it is important to understand the allocation within this sector compared to the benchmark. The MBS sectors are shown in terms of coupon rate and type.

The duration for the 40-bond portfolio and the benchmark is 5.56 and 4.84, respectively. Table 23.14 shows the duration by sector for the portfolio and the benchmark. Using the information about the weight of each sector and its duration, the contribution to portfolio duration and contribution duration can be computed. For example, consider the mortgage sector. This sector is 64.78% of the portfolio and 37.17% of the benchmark. The durations are 5.65 and 5.23 for the portfolio and benchmark, respectively. Therefore, the contributions to durations are

$$\text{Contribution to portfolio duration} = 0.6478 \times 5.65 = 3.66$$

and

$$\text{Contribution to benchmark duration} = 0.3717 \times 5.23 = 1.94$$

TABLE 23.11 40-Bond Portfolio as of September 17, 2008

Cusip	Issuer Name	Coupon	Maturity	Moody's	S&P	Sector	Market Value (%)
FGB06006	FHLM Gold Guar Single F.	6	3/1/2036	AAA	AAA	FHb	9.29
FNA05005	FNMA Conventional Long T.	5	2/1/2035	AAA	AAA	FNa	8.84
FNA05407	FNMA Conventional Long T.	5.5	5/1/2037	AAA	AAA	FNa	8.46
FNA05405	FNMA Conventional Long T.	5.5	3/1/2035	AAA	AAA	FNa	8.33
FGB05005	FHLM Gold Guar Single F.	5	2/1/2035	AAA	AAA	FHb	7.67
002824AT	ABBOTT LABORATORIES-GLOBA	5.875	5/15/2016	A1	AA	IND	6.18
FNA06006	FNMA Conventional Long T.	6	4/1/2036	AAA	AAA	FNa	6.15
912828CT	US TREASURY NOTES	4.25	8/15/2014	AAA	AAA	UST	6.11
FNA05403	FNMA Conventional Long T.	5.5	8/1/2032	AAA	AAA	FNa	6.03
060505DP	BANK OF AMERICA CORP	5.75	12/1/2017	AA2	AA	FIN	5.73
172967CQ	CITIGROUP INC-GLOBAL	5	9/15/2014	A1	A+	FIN	5.16
FNA06007	FNMA Conventional Long T.	6	6/1/2037	AAA	AAA	FNa	5.12
FNA05003	FNMA Conventional Long T.	5	9/1/2032	AAA	AAA	FNa	4.90
912828BH	US TREASURY NOTES	4.25	8/15/2013	AAA	AAA	UST	1.60
912828BR	US TREASURY NOTES	4.25	11/15/2013	AAA	AAA	UST	1.56
912828CA	US TREASURY NOTES	4	2/15/2014	AAA	AAA	UST	1.42
912828CJ	US TREASURY NOTES	4.75	5/15/2014	AAA	AAA	UST	1.39
912828DC	US TREASURY NOTES	4.25	11/15/2014	AAA	AAA	UST	1.27
912828DM	US TREASURY NOTES	4	2/15/2015	AAA	AAA	UST	1.24
912828DV	US TREASURY NOTES	4.125	5/15/2015	AAA	AAA	UST	1.22
31359MJH	FEDERAL NATL MTG ASSN-GLO	6	5/15/2011	AAA	AAA	USA	0.20
31359MFG	FEDERAL NATL MTG ASSN-GLO	7.25	1/15/2010	AAA	AAA	USA	0.19

TABLE 23.11 (Continued)

Cusip	Issuer Name	Coupon	Maturity	Moody's	S&P	Sector	Market Value (%)
31359MEY	FEDERAL NATL MTG ASSN	6.625	9/15/2009	AAA	AAA	USA	0.18
3134A35H	FEDERAL HOME LN MTG CORP-	6.875	9/15/2010	AAA	NR	USA	0.15
31359MEV	FEDERAL NATL MTG ASSN-GLO	6.375	6/15/2009	AAA	AAA	USA	0.15
3137EAAT	FEDERAL HOME LN MTG CORP-	5	6/11/2009	AAA	AAA	USA	0.13
369604AY	GENERAL ELECTRIC CO-GLOBA	5	2/1/2013	AAA	AAA	IND	0.13
369604BC	GENERAL ELECTRIC CO-GLOBA	5.25	12/6/2017	AAA	AAA	IND	0.10
36962GYY	GENERAL ELECTRIC CAPITAL-	6	6/15/2012	AAA	AAA	FIN	0.09
17275RAC	CISCO SYSTEMS INC-GLOBAL	5.5	2/22/2016	A1	A+	IND	0.08
459200GJ	INTL BUSINESS MACHINES-GL	5.7	9/14/2017	A1	A+	IND	0.08
00209TAA	AT&T BROADBAND CORP - GLO	8.375	3/15/2013	BAA2	BBB+	IND	0.07
172967EM	CITIGROUP INC-GLOBAL	6.125	11/21/2017	AA3	AA-	FIN	0.07
22541LAB	CREDIT SUISSE FB USA INC	6.125	11/15/2011	AA1	AA-	FIN	0.07
437076AP	HOME DEPOT INC-GLOBAL	5.4	3/1/2016	BAA1	BBB+	IND	0.07
617446GM	MORGAN STANLEY DEAN WITTE	6.75	4/15/2011	A1	A+	FIN	0.07
61748AAE	MORGAN STANLEY DEAN WITTE	4.75	4/1/2014	A2	A	FIN	0.07
25152CMN	DEUTSCHE BANK AG	6	9/1/2017	AA1	AA-	FIN	0.06
78387GAP	SBC COMMUNICATIONS INC-GL	5.1	9/15/2014	A2	A	IND	0.06
233835AW	DAIMLERCHRYSLER NORTH AME	6.5	11/15/2013	A3	A-	IND	0.05
29078EAB	EMBARQ CORP	7.082	6/1/2016	BAA3	BBB-	IND	0.05
68402LAC	ORACLE CORP	5.25	1/15/2016	A2	A	IND	0.05
852061AD	SPRINT NEXTEL CORP	6	12/1/2016	BAA3	BB	IND	0.05
88732JAH	TIME WARNER CABLE INC-GLO	5.85	5/1/2017	BAA2	BBB+	IND	0.05
65332VBG	NEXTEL COMMUNICATIONS	7.375	8/1/2015	BAA3	BB	IND	0.04

TABLE 23.12 Sector Composition of Portfolio and Benchmark

Sector	% of Portfolio	% of Benchmark	Overweight (+)/Underweight (−)
Treasury	15.81	22.66	−6.85
Agencies	1.00	10.12	−9.12
Financial institutions	11.27	7.83	3.44
Industrials	7.08	7.52	−0.44
Utilities	0.00	1.98	−1.98
Non-U.S. credit	0.06	6.95	−6.89
Mortgage	64.78	37.17	27.61
Asset backed	0.00	0.79	−0.79
CMBS	0.00	4.98	−4.98
Totals	100.00	100.00	

TABLE 23.13 Credit Quality of the Portfolio and Benchmark

Credit Quality	% of Portfolio	% of Benchmark	Overweight (+)/Underweight (−)
MBS	64.79	37.17	27.62
AAA	17.13	41.06	−23.93
AA	5.94	4.87	1.07
A	11.81	9.21	2.60
BAA	0.24	7.69	−7.45
BA	0.09	0.00	0.09
Totals	100.00	100.00	

TABLE 23.14 Duration and Contribution to Duration by Sector

	Portfolio			Benchmark			Difference	
Sector	% of Port.	Dur.	Cntrb. to Dur.	% of Port.	Dur.	Cntrb. to Dur.	% of Port.	Cntrb. to Dur.
Treasury	15.81	5.13	0.81	22.66	5.21	1.19	−6.85	−0.38
Agencies	1.00	1.40	0.01	10.12	3.98	0.35	−9.12	−0.34
Financial Inst.	11.27	5.89	0.66	7.83	5.25	0.42	3.44	0.24
Industrials	7.08	6.00	0.42	7.52	6.48	0.49	−0.44	−0.07
Utilities	0.00	0.00	0.00	1.98	7.32	0.15	−1.98	−0.15
Non-U.S. credit	0.06	6.88	0.00	6.95	5.90	0.41	−6.89	−0.41
Mortgage	64.78	5.65	3.66	37.17	5.23	1.58	27.61	2.08
Asset backed	0.00	0.00	0.00	0.79	3.15	0.02	−0.79	−0.02
CMBS	0.00	0.00	0.00	4.98	4.60	0.23	−4.98	−0.23
Totals	100.00		5.56	100.00		4.84		0.72

Duration provides a measure of the exposure of a portfolio or a benchmark index to changes in the level of interest rates but fails to measure the exposure of a portfolio or a benchmark index to changes in the shape of the yield curve. In Chapter 19, we discussed the various types of yield curve changes (i.e., shifts). A simple way to get a feel for the yield curve risk exposure of a portfolio relative to a benchmark is by looking at the distribution of the present values of the cash flows for the portfolio and the benchmark index. Table 23.15A shows the distribution of the difference in the present values of the cash flows for the 40-bond portfolio and for the Barclays Capital U.S. Aggregate Index. The difference seems to suggest that the portfolio is constructed like a bullet portfolio concentrated in the 5- to 10-year range.

TABLE 23.15 Estimating Yield Curve Risk Exposure Relative to Benchmark

A. Difference in Present Value of Cash Flow Structure (Portfolio − Benchmark)

Years	Difference (%)
0.00	0.181
0.25	0.569
0.50	0.363
0.75	0.849
1.00	−1.095
1.50	−3.958
2.00	−2.923
2.50	−2.343
3.00	−1.655
3.50	−1.518
4.00	−2.500
5.00	0.668
6.00	10.340
7.00	1.938
10.00	1.233
15.00	0.736
20.00	−0.013
25.00	−0.344
30.00	−0.505
40.00	−0.009

TABLE 23.15 (Continued)
B. Difference in Key Rate Durations (Portfolio − Benchmark)

Years	Difference
0.50	−0.003
2.00	−0.214
5.00	0.485
10.00	0.257
20.00	−0.185
30.00	−0.359

TABLE 23.16 Difference in Contribution to Spread Duration by Sector

Sector	Difference
Treasury	−0.34
Agencies	−0.35
Financial institutions	0.36
Industrials	−0.04
Utilities	−0.14
Non-U.S. credit	−0.38
Mortgage	0.98
Asset backed	−0.03
CMBS	−0.29

A superior approach the assessing yield curve risk exposure is to determine the key rate durations of the portfolio and the benchmark. Key rate duration is the sensitivity of a portfolio's value to the change in a particular key spot rate. The specific maturities on the spot rate curve for which key rate durations are measured vary from vendor to vendor. The six key rate durations reported in Table 23.15B shows the difference in key rate durations between the portfolio and the benchmark. It is clear that there is underweighting of the short and long end of the portfolio and overweighting of the five-year and 10-year sectors.

The spread duration for a portfolio or a bond index is computed as a market weighted average of the spread duration for each sector. The difference in the spread duration by sector for the 40-bond portfolio and for the benchmark are shown in Table 23.16. Notice that the spread duration is higher for the financial institutions and mortgage sectors and lower for every other sector.

Some corporate bonds and agency debentures have embedded options—call and put options. These options impact the performance of a portfolio and a benchmark. The adverse effect on performance resulting from these embedded options is referred to as *optionality risk*. The optionality risk exposure of a bond occurs because a change in interest rates changes the value of the embedded option, which, in turn changes the value of the bond. The same is true at the portfolio and benchmark levels. Optionality risk can be quantified using measures commonly used in the option pricing. In option pricing theory, the delta of an option is an estimate of the sensitivity of the value of the option to changes in the price of the underlying instrument. For bonds, delta can be computed for each issue that has an embedded option and then these deltas can be aggregated to obtain an estimate of the delta for a portfolio or a benchmark. Table 23.17 reports the delta of the 40-bond portfolio and the benchmark index, as well as the difference between the two. The percentage of the portfolio represents all holdings other than the mortgage sector. (Thus, the value of 35.22% for the portfolio is 100% minus the mortgage holdings of 64.78%.) Notice that the holdings are partitioned in terms of the embedded option and how the securities trade. Bullet bonds do not have embedded options and, therefore, the delta for these bonds is zero. A security with an embedded call option is classified as trading either to its call date or to its maturity date, depending on its market price. In this context, "trading to" indicates that the price of the security is such that the market is pricing the security either as if it will be called or as if it will not be called. The same is true for securities with a put option—they are classified as either trading to the put date or trading to maturity.

The largest deviation of the hypothetical portfolio and the benchmark is in the mortgage sectors. The three major risk of investing in this sector are sector risk, prepayment risk, and convexity risk. The subsectors of the mortgage sector are generally based on the coupon rate. The motivation for using this

TABLE 23.17 Optionality Exposure for Benchmark

Option Delta	Benchmark (excluding MBS)			Difference	
	% of Port.	Delta	Cntrb. to Delta	% of Port.	Cntrb. to Delta
Bullet	41.48	0.0000	0.0000	−13.18	0.0000
Callable traded to maturity	14.62	0.0639	0.0093	−7.70	−0.0093
Callable traded to call	0.93	0.8354	0.0078	−0.93	−0.0078
Putable traded to maturity	0.02	0.2380	0.0000	−0.02	0.0000
Putable traded to put	0.02	0.4283	0.0001	−0.02	−0.0001
Totals	57.07		0.0172	−21.85	−0.0172

classification is that the coupon rate relative to the prevailing mortgage rate has an impact on prepayments and therefore on the spread at which a pass-through security trades relative to Treasuries. In turn, prepayments are also impact how long the underlying mortgage pools have been outstanding. This characteristic is referred to as the seasoning of the underlying mortgage pool. This characteristic can be classified as unseasoned, moderately seasoned, and seasoned. For the hypothetical portfolio, the difference in the contribution to duration between the 40-bond portfolio and the benchmark index is 1.31.

With respect to prepayment risk—the risk of an adverse price change due to changes in expected prepayments—the benchmark used for prepayments is the PSA prepayment benchmark discussed in Chapter 18. One measure of prepayment risk is *prepayment sensitivity* which is the basis point change in the price of an MBS for a 1% increase in prepayments. For example, suppose that, for some mortgage product at 300 PSA, the price is 110.08. A 1% increase in the PSA prepayment rate means that the PSA increases from 300 PSA to 303 PSA. Suppose that, at 303 PSA, the price is recomputed using a valuation model and found to be 110.00. Therefore, the price decline is –0.08, in terms of basis points, –8, so that the prepayment sensitivity is –8. Some mortgage products increase in value when prepayments increase and some products decrease in value when prepayments increase. Examples of the former are pass-through securities trading at a discount (i.e., pass-through securities whose coupon rate is less than the prevailing mortgage rate) and principal-only mortgage strips. These securities have positive prepayment sensitivity. Examples of mortgage products that decrease in value when prepayments increase are pass-through securities trading at a premium (i.e., pass-through securities whose coupon rate is greater than the prevailing mortgage rate) and interest-only mortgage strips. These securities have negative prepayment sensitivity. A portfolio manager can compute the risk exposure in terms of the difference in the contribution to prepayment sensitivity for the 40-bond portfolio and the benchmark. For the 40-bond portfolio, it is 0.34.

Finally, let's look at the third risk by investing in the mortgage sector: convexity risk. The sector of the mortgage market that tends to exhibit negative convexity is pass-through securities. Consequently, a portfolio manager should assess the convexity of a portfolio compared to the benchmark index. A portfolio manager's allocation to the mortgage sector might be the same as that of the benchmark index with the same effective duration, and yet performance can be quite different if the portfolio has different exposure to convexity. This concept is referred to as *convexity risk*. Exposure to convexity risk in the mortgage sector is measured by the difference between the convexity of a portfolio and the convexity of the benchmark index and for the 40-bond portfolio it is –0.54. This means that the portfolio has greater negative convexity than the index.

Tracking Error

As explained in Chapter 11, a factor model attempts to identify the specific risks that contribute to the forward-looking tracking error. All of the risks are quantified in terms of forward-looking tracking error as opposed to backward-look tracking error. The tracking error for our hypothetical portfolio based on the Barclays' model is 62 basis points. We can decompose the tracking error in order to understand where the risks are. The analysis begins with a decomposition of the risks into two general categories—*systematic risk* and *nonsystematic risk* (also referred to as *residual risk*). For our hypothetical portfolio, the following was determined:

Forward-looking tracking error due to systematic risk
= 58 basis points

Forward-looking tracking error due to non-systematic risk
= 20 basis points

This may seem inconsistent with a 62 basis point tracking error for the portfolio given that the sum of these two risks exceeds 62 basis points. The reason for this is that tracking errors represent variances. Consequently, it is not the sum of these two risks that must sum to the portfolio's tracking error. Rather, it is the squares of these two tracking errors when added equal the square of the portfolio's tracking error. Or equivalently, the square root of the sum of the square of the two tracking errors will equal the portfolio's tracking error; that is, $[(58)^2 + (20)^2]^{0.5} = 61.35$ or 62 basis points (rounded).

The adding of variances requires that an assumption be made. The assumption is that there is a zero correlation between the factors (i.e., the factors are statistically independent). If this is not the case, the correlation between the factors must be taken into account in estimating the tracking error.

Systematic risk can be decomposed into two risks: term structure factor risk and non-term structure factor risk. A portfolio's exposure to changes in the general level of interest rates is measured in terms of exposure to (1) a parallel shift in the yield curve and (2) a nonparallel shift in the yield curve. Taken together, this risk exposure is referred to as *term structure risk*. We know that the duration of the 40-bond portfolio is greater than the benchmark duration (5.56 versus 4.84). The difference between the yield curve risk for the portfolio and for the benchmark was shown Table 23.15, based on the distribution of the present value of the cash flows and key rate durations. The factor model indicates that the forward-looking tracking error due to term structure risk is 52 basis points.

The other systematic risk that is not due to exposure to changes in the term structure is called *nonterm structure risk*. These risk factors include sector risk, quality risk, optionality risk, coupon risk, and MBS risk (sector, prepayment, and convexity risks). For the 40-bond portfolio, the factor model indicates that the tracking error due to the non-term structure risk is 60 basis points. We now know that forward-looking tracking error due to systematic risk is 58 basis points, consisting of:

Forward-looking tracking error due to term structure risk
= 52 basis points

Forward-looking tracking error due to non-term structure risk
= 60 basis points

As noted, the predicted tracking error due to systematic risk is not equal to the sum of these two components of tracking error. If the term structure factor and the non-term structure factors are statistically independent, then the total forward-looking tracking error from all the systematic factors is 79 basis points. However, when the correlations are taken into account, the forward-looking tracking error due to systematic risk is 58 basis points.

In Table 23.18, the forward-looking tracking error subcomponents are reported for the systematic risk in two different ways. In the column labeled "Isolated Tracking Error," the tracking error was estimated considering only

TABLE 23.18 Decomposition of Systematic Tracking Error (in basis points)

	Isolated Tracking Error	Cumulative Tracking Error	Change in Cumulative
Tracking error term structure	52	52	52
Nonterm structure	60		
Tracking error sector	18	59	8
Tracking error quality	9	64	5
Tracking error optionality	2	64	0
Tracking error coupon	3	65	0
Tracking error MBS sector	59	52	−13
Tracking error MBS volatility	33	53	1
Tracking error MBS prepayments	8	58	5
Total systematic tracking error			58

the effect of each risk factor in isolation. For example, the 9 basis points for the tracking error for quality considers only the mismatch between the portfolio exposure and benchmark exposure due to quality and taking into consideration the correlations only of quality exposure for the different quality ratings. The last two columns in the table with the headings "Cumulative Tracking Error" and "Change in Cumulative" report the second way in which the tracking error is decomposed. The cumulative tracking error is computed by incrementally introducing one group of risk factors at a time to the tracking error calculation. For example, in the first row the 52 basis points represents the tracking error due to term structure exposure. The third row shows the tracking error due to sector exposure. The cumulative tracking error of 59 basis points represents the combined tracking error due to both term structure exposure (52 basis points) and sector exposure taken together but ignoring all other systematic risk factors. Since the increase in tracking error by adding sector exposure to the term structure exposure is 7 basis points, the change in the cumulative tracking error is 7 basis points. A value of 8 is reported in the last column of the table only because there was rounding involved in the interim numbers. Because of the way in which the calculations were performed, the cumulative tracking error shown for all the systematic risk factors in the next-to-the last column of 58 basis points, and the same value reported in the last column for the "Total Systematic Tracking Error," take into consideration the correlations among the systematic risk factors. However, it should be remembered that while the total systematic tracking error will be the same regardless of the order in which the systematic risk factors are introduced, the interim values in the last two columns of the table will differ depending on the order in which the systematic risk factors are introduced.

Nonsystematic risk is divided into those risks that are issuer specific and components that are issue specific. This risk is due to the fact that the portfolio has greater exposure to specific issues and issuers than the benchmark index. To understand these non-systematic risks, look at the last column of Table 23.11 which reports the percentage of the 40-bond portfolio's market value invested in each issue. Since there are only 40 issues in the portfolio, each issue makes up a non-trivial fraction of the portfolio. Specifically, look at the exposure to three corporate issuers, Abbott Laboratories, Bank of America, and Citicorp. They individually represent more than 5% of the portfolio. If any of three issuers is downgraded, this would cause large losses in the 40-bond portfolio, but it would not have a significant effect on the benchmark which includes more than 5,000 issues. Consequently, a large exposure to a specific corporate issuer represents a material mismatch between the exposure of the portfolio and the exposure of a benchmark index that must be taken into account in assessing a portfolio's risk relative to a benchmark index. The nonsystematic tracking error for the 40-bond portfolio is 21 basis points, consisting of issuer-specific tracking error of 20 basis points and issue-specific tracking error of 20 basis points.

Constructing and Rebalancing a Portfolio

So far we have seen how a factor model can be utilized by a portfolio manager to quantify the risk exposure of a portfolio to the factors that will impact the performance of a portfolio relative to a benchmark. We started with a 40-bond portfolio and then described the portfolio risks. However, in practice, the factor model is employed to construct the portfolio and then typically used to rebalance or restructure the portfolio.

The initial construction of the portfolio using a factor model involves using an optimizer. Portfolio optimizer software obtains the optimal value for an objective function subject to constraints. Although a discussion of the software is beyond the scope of this chapter, what is important to understand is that once a portfolio manager specifies an objective, the optimizer will compute the optimal portfolio. The two illustrations below using the 40-bond portfolio will illustrate how a portfolio can be rebalanced using a factor model and a portfolio optimizer.

In our first illustration, suppose that the portfolio manager wants to reduce the forward-looking tracking error significantly. For our 40-bond portfolio, the tracking error is 62 basis points. Assume that the portfolio manager wants to rebalance the portfolio in such a manner that its tracking error is 33 basis points. The goal is to rebalance the portfolio in a cost efficient manner. A portfolio optimizer can be used to identify trades that reduce tracking error in a cost efficient way. The portfolio optimizer begins with a universe of market prices for acceptable securities (i.e., those permitted by the investment guidelines). The portfolio optimizer is designed to select a trade that identifies a 1-for-1 bond swap with the greatest reduction in tracking error per unit of each bond acquired in the trade. In the case of our 40-bond portfolio, the portfolio optimizer identified the first trade in Table 23.19. This one trade reduced the tracking error from 62 basis points to 47 basis. The five swaps in the table reduce in the most cost efficient manner the tracking error to 33 basis points.

In our second illustration, we will see how a portfolio optimizer can also be used to structure a portfolio so as to incorporate a market view. Let's suppose that a portfolio manager follows a top down approach to the selection of sectors. Consequently, the portfolio manager seeks exposure to sector risk, while at the same time, seeking to minimize exposure to other risk factors such as term structure risk and non-sector non-term structure systematic risk. A portfolio optimizer can be used to rebalance the current

TABLE 23.19 Portfolio Optimizer Identified Swaps to Reduce Tracking Error from 62 to 33 Basis Points

Initial tracking error: 62 basis points
Targeted tracking error: 33 basis points

Swap #1:
Sell: $90,426,000 of FNMA Conventional Long T. 5.000 2035/02/01
Buy: $86,931,000 of Federal Home Ln Mtg Corp 5.375 2014/01/09
Cost of Trade: $443,392
New Tracking Error: 47 bps

Swap #2: New Tracking Error:
Sell: $31,199,000 of FNMA Conventional Long T. 6.000 2037/06/01
Buy: $32,186,000 of Unilever Capital Corp-Glo 5.900 2032/11/15
Cost of Trade: $158,462
New Tracking Error: 41 bps

Swap #3:
Sell: $44,621,000 of FNMA Conventional Long T. 5.500 2037/05/01
Buy: $32,186,000 of Unilever Capital Corp-Glo 5.900 2032/11/15
Cost of Trade: $219,553
New Tracking Error: 37 bps

Swap #4:
Sell: $19,337,000 of FNMA Conventional Long T. 6.000 2036/04/01
Buy: $17,278,000 of US Treasury Bonds 5.500 2028/08/15
Cost of Trade: $91,537
New Tracking Error: 34 bps

Swap #5:
Sell: $13,676,000 of Bank Of America Corp 5.750 2017/12/01
Buy: $12,233,000 of Federal Natl Mtg Assn-Glo 7.250 2010/01/15
Cost of Trade: $64,772
New Tracking Error: 33 bps

Cumulative cost of five swaps: $977,717

portfolio in a manner that maintains the current tracking error for sector risk but reduces the tracking error for the other systematic risks. The portfolio optimizer is set up so that there is a substantial penalty for reducing exposure to sector risk. For example, consider the 40-bond portfolio with a forward-looking tracking error of 62 basis points and the forward-looking tracking error due to sector risk of 18 basis points. The portfolio optimizer was run to keep the tracking error due to sector risk as close as possible to

18 basis points while reducing the tracking error due to the other risk factors. The seven bond swaps in Table 23.20 were identified by the portfolio optimizer. After these seven bond swaps, the predicted tracking error for the portfolio declines from 62 basis points to 56 basis points with the sector tracking error remaining the same and tracking error for the other systematic risks changing.

LIABILITY-DRIVEN STRATEGIES

Thus far, the bond portfolio strategies discussed in this chapter have focused on managing funds relative to a benchmark that is a market index. In a liability-driven strategy, the goal is to manage funds to satisfy contractual liabilities. Insurance companies have historically used liability-driven strategies for certain products that they sold. The two strategies are immunization and cash flow matching. Sponsors of defined benefit pension plans have used these strategies. However, due to the fact that pension liabilities are not fixed in the future, plan sponsors have found that these two strategies do not accomplish their objectives. We conclude this chapter with a discussion of the various types of liability-driven strategies.

Immunization Strategy for a Single-Period Liability

Immunization is a hybrid strategy having elements of both active and passive strategies. Classical immunization can be defined as the process by which a bond portfolio is created having an assured return for a specific time horizon irrespective of interest rate changes. In a concise form, the following are the important characteristics: (1) a specified time horizon; (2) an assured rate of return during the holding period to a fixed horizon date; and (3) insulation from the effects of potential adverse interest rate changes on the portfolio value at the horizon date.

The fundamental mechanism underlying immunization is a portfolio structure that balances the change in the value of the portfolio at the end of the investment horizon with the return from the reinvestment of portfolio cash flows (coupon payments and maturing securities). That is, immunization requires offsetting interest rate risk and reinvestment risk. To accomplish this balancing act requires controlling duration. By setting the duration of the portfolio equal to the desired portfolio time horizon, the offsetting of positive and negative incremental return sources can under certain circumstances be assured. This is a necessary condition for effectively immunized portfolios. Figure 23.2 summarizes the general principles of classical immunization.

TABLE 23.20 Portfolio Optimizer Identified Swaps to Reduce Tracking Error but Maintain Tracking Error of Sector Risk

Initial tracking error: 62 basis points
Required tracking error for sector risk: 18 basis points

Swap #1:
Sell: $6,649,000 of Bank Of America Corp   5.750 2017/12/01
Buy: $6,174,000 of Federal Home Ln Mtg Corp   5.250 2012/03/15
Cost of Trade: $32,057
New Tracking Error: 60 bps

Swap #2:
Sell: $4,659,000 of FNMA Conventional Long T.   5.000 2035/02/01
Buy: $6,174,000 of Federal Home Ln Mtg Corp   5.250 2012/03/15
Cost of Trade: $24,647
New Tracking Error: 59 bps

Swap #3:
Sell: $773,000 of Intl Business Machines-Gl   5.700 2017/09/14
Buy: $786,000 of Federal Home Ln Mtg Corp   5.250 2012/03/15
Cost of Trade: $3,898
New Tracking Error: 59 bps

Swap #4:
Sell: $773,000 of Cisco Systems Inc-Global   5.500 2016/02/22
Buy: $764,000 of Federal Home Ln Mtg Corp   5.250 2012/03/15
Cost of Trade: $3,842
New Tracking Error: 59 bps

Swap #5:
Sell: $515,000 of Oracle Corp   5.250 2016/01/15
Buy: $500,000 of Federal Home Ln Mtg Corp   5.250 2012/03/15
Cost of Trade: $2,537
New Tracking Error: 59 bps

Swap #6:
Sell: $11,560,000 of Abbott Laboratories-Globa   5.875 2016/05/15
Buy: $11,937,000 of Federal Home Ln Mtg Corp   5.450 2013/11/21
Cost of Trade: $58,743
New Tracking Error: 57 bps

Swap #7:
Sell: $7,176,000 of FNMA Conventional Long T.   5.000 2035/02/01
Buy: $8,026,000 of Travelers Cos Inc   6.250 2017/03/15
Cost of Trade: $38,005
New Tracking Error: 56 bps

Cumulative cost of swaps: $163,730

FIGURE 23.2 General Principles of Classical Immunization

Goal: Lock in a minimum target rate of return and target investment value regardless of how interest rates change over the investment horizon.

Risk when interest rates change: (1) reinvestment risk and (2) interest rate or price risk

Principle:

   Scenario 1: Interest rates increase

    Implications:
    1. Reinvestment income increases.
    2. Value of bonds in the portfolio with a maturity greater than the investment horizon declines in value.

   Goal: Gain in reinvestment income = Loss in portfolio value

   Scenario 2: Interest rates decline

    Implications:
    1. Reinvestment income decreases.
    2. Value of bonds in the portfolio with a maturity greater than the investment horizon increases in value.

   Goal: Loss in reinvestment income = Gain in portfolio value

Assumption: Parallel shift in the yield curve (i.e., all yields rise and fall uniformly)

How often should the portfolio be rebalanced to adjust its duration? On the one hand, the more frequent rebalancing increases transaction costs, thereby reducing the likelihood of achieving the target return. On the other hand, less frequent rebalancing will result in the portfolio's duration wandering from the target duration, which will also reduce the likelihood of achieving the target return. Thus a portfolio manager faces a trade-off: Some transaction costs must be accepted to prevent the portfolio duration from wandering too far from its target, but some maladjustment in the portfolio duration must be lived with, or transaction costs will become prohibitively high.

In the actual process leading to the construction of an immunized portfolio, the selection of the universe is extremely important. The lower the credit quality of the securities considered, the higher the potential risk and return. Immunization theory assumes there will be no defaults and that securities will be responsive only to overall changes in interest rates. The lower the credit quality permitted in the portfolio, the greater the likelihood that these assumptions will not be met. Furthermore, securities with embedded options such as call features and mortgage-backed prepayments complicate and may even prevent the accurate measure of cash flows and, therefore, duration, which frustrates the basic requirements of immunization. Finally, liquidity is a consideration for immunized portfolios because, as just noted, they must be rebalanced over time.

Perhaps the most critical assumption of the classical immunization strategy concerns the assumption regarding the type of interest rate change. A property of a classically immunized portfolio is that the target value of the investment is the lower limit of the value of the portfolio at the horizon date if there is a parallel shift in the yield curve. This would appear to be an unrealistic assumption. According to the theory, if there is a change in interest rates that does not correspond to this shape-preserving shift, matching the duration to the investment horizon no longer assures immunization.

A natural extension of classical immunization theory is a technique for modifying the assumption of parallel shifts in the yield curve. One approach is a strategy that can handle any arbitrary interest rate change so that it is not necessary to specify an alternative duration measure. The approach developed by Fong and Vasicek (1984) establishes a measure of *immunization risk* against any arbitrary interest rate change. The immunization risk measure can then be minimized subject to the constraint that the duration of the portfolio be equal to the investment horizon, resulting in a portfolio with minimum exposure to any interest rate movements.

One way of minimizing immunization risk is shown in Figure 23.3. The spikes in the two panels of the exhibit represent actual portfolio cash flows. The taller spikes depict the actual cash flows generated by matured securities while the smaller spikes represent coupon payments. Both portfolio A and portfolio B are composed of two bonds with a duration equal to the investment horizon. Portfolio A is, in effect, a barbell portfolio—a portfolio comprising short and long maturities and interim coupon payments. For portfolio B, the two bonds mature very close to the investment horizon and the coupon payments are nominal over the investment horizon. As explained earlier in this chapter, a portfolio with this characteristic is called a bullet portfolio.

It is not difficult to see why the barbell portfolio should be riskier than the bullet portfolio. Assume that both portfolios have durations equal to the horizon length, so that both portfolios are immune to parallel rate changes. This immunity is attained as a consequence of balancing the effect of changes in reinvestment rates on payments received during the investment horizon against the effect of changes in market value of the portion of the portfolio still outstanding at the end of the investment horizon. When

FIGURE 23.3 Immunization Risk Measure

Portfolio A. High-Risk Immunized Portfolio

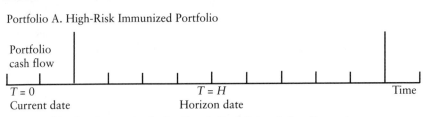

Note: Portfolio duration matches horizon length. Portfolio's cash flow dispersed.

Portfolio B. Low-Risk Immunized Portfolio

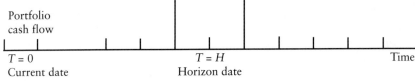

Note: Portfolio duration matches horizon length. Portfolio's cash flow concentrated around horizon dates.

interest rates change in an arbitrary nonparallel way, however, the effect on the two portfolios is very different. Suppose, for instance, that short rates decline while long rates go up. Both portfolios would realize a decline of the portfolio value at the end of the investment horizon below the target investment value, since they experience a capital loss in addition to lower reinvestment rates. The decline, however, would be substantially higher for the barbell portfolio for two reasons. First, the lower reinvestment rates are experienced on the barbell portfolio for longer time intervals than on the bullet portfolio, so that the opportunity loss is much greater. Second, the portion of the barbell portfolio still outstanding at the end of the investment horizon is much longer than that of the bullet portfolio, which means that the same rate increase would result in a much greater capital loss. Thus the bullet portfolio has less exposure to whatever the change in the interest rate structure may be than the barbell portfolio.

It should be clear from the foregoing discussion that immunization risk is the risk of reinvestment. The portfolio that has the least reinvestment risk will have the least immunization risk. When there is a high dispersion of cash flows around the horizon date, as in the barbell portfolio, the portfolio is exposed to higher reinvestment risk. However, when the cash flows are concentrated around the horizon date, as in the bullet portfolio, the portfolio is subject to minimum reinvestment risk.

Contingent Immunization Strategy

There are variants of the classical immunization strategy. A *contingent immunization strategy* involves the identification of both the available immunization target rate and a lower safety net level return with which the client would be minimally satisfied. The portfolio manager can continue to pursue an active strategy until an adverse investment experience drives the then-available potential return—combined active return (from actual past experience) and immunized return (from expected future experience)—down to the safety net level; at such time the portfolio manager would be obligated to completely immunize the portfolio and lock in the safety net level return. As long as this safety net is not violated, the portfolio manager can continue to actively manage the portfolio. Once the immunization mode is activated because the safety net is violated, the portfolio manager can no longer return to the active mode unless, of course, the contingent immunization plan is abandoned.

The key considerations in implementing a contingent immunization strategy are (1) establishing accurate immunized initial and ongoing available target returns; (2) identifying a suitable and immunizable safety net; and (3) implementing an effective monitoring procedure to ensure that the safety net is not violated.

Cash Flow Matching Strategy

The immunization strategy described previously is used to immunize a portfolio created to satisfy a single liability in the future against adverse interest rate movements. However, it is more common in situations to have multiple future liabilities. One example is the liability structure of pension funds. Another example is a life insurance annuity contract. When there are multiple future liabilities, it is possible to extend the principles of immunization to such situations. However, it is more common in practice to use a *cash flow matching strategy*. This strategy is used to construct a portfolio designed to fund a schedule of liabilities from portfolio return and asset value, with the portfolio's value diminishing to zero after payment of the last liability.

A cash flow matching strategy can be described intuitively as follows. A bond is selected with a maturity that matches the last liability. An amount of principal equal to the amount of the last liability is then invested in this bond. The remaining elements of the liability stream are then reduced by the coupon payments on this bond, and another bond is chosen for the next-to-last liability, adjusted for any coupon payments of the first bond selected. Going backward in time, this sequence is continued until all liabilities have been matched by payments on the securities selected for the portfolio. Figure 23.4 provides a simple illustration of this process for a five-year liability

FIGURE 23.4 Illustration of Cash Flow Matching Process

Assume: Five-year liability stream and cash flow from bonds are annual.

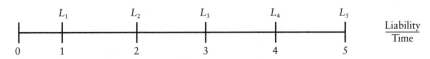

Step 1:
Cash flow from Bond A selected to satisfy L_5
  Coupons = A_C; Principal = A_p and $A_C + A_p = L_5$
Unfunded liabilities remaining:

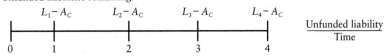

Step 2:
Cash flow from Bond B selected to satisfy L_4
  Unfunded liability = $L_4 - A_C$
  Coupons = B_C; Principal = B_p and $B_C + B_p = L_4 - A_C$
Unfunded liabilities remaining:

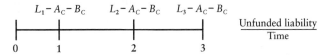

Step 3:
Cash flow from Bond C selected to satisfy L_3
  Unfunded liability = $L_3 - A_C - B_C$
  Coupons = C_C; Principal = C_p and $C_C + C_p = L_3 - A_C - B_C$
Unfunded liabilities remaining:

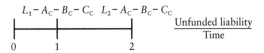

Step 4:
Cash flow from Bond D selected to satisfy L_2
  Unfunded liability = $L_2 - A_C - B_C - C_C$
  Coupons = D_C; Principal = D_p and $D_C + D_p = L_2 - A_C - B_C - C_C$
Unfunded liabilities remaining:

$L_1 - A_C - B_C - C_C - D_C$

|—————|
0   1

Unfunded liability / Time

Step 4:
Select Bond E with a cash flow of $L_1 - A_C - B_C - C_C - D_C$

stream. Optimization techniques can be employed to construct a least-cost cash flow matching portfolio from an acceptable universe of bonds.

Liability-Driven Strategies for Defined Benefit Pension Plans

Although some sponsors of defined benefit pension plans have used the cash flow matching strategy, since the dramatic decline in interest rates, this strategy is used less frequently. Moreover, the problem with employing a traditional cash flow matching strategy is that the liabilities are uncertain due to factors such as changes in the contractual benefits provided by the plan sponsor, the decision by plan beneficiaries to retire early, and the impact of inflation on benefits.

A measure of the performance of a pension fund is the *funding ratio* which is equal to

$$\text{Funding ratio} = \frac{\text{Market value of the plan assets}}{\text{Value of the plan liabilities}}$$

The value of the liabilities is the discounted cash flow of the liabilities (i.e., present value of the liabilities) using a suitable discount rate.

Despite the importance of the funding ratio, historically plan sponsors have focused on the plan's assets using market benchmarks as a measure of performance without consideration of the relationship between the plan's liability profile. Basically, the asset allocation decision used the mean-variance optimization model of Markowitz (1952) without considering liabilities. Historically, a commonly used allocation was a 60/40 stock/bond mix.

There are two views as to the appropriate investment strategy that plan sponsors should utilize in the allocation of plan funds to the major asset classes: bond-only view and bond-equity view. Proponents of the bond-only view favors the cash flow matching strategy discussed earlier. Proponents of the bond-equity view argue that the liability characteristics of pension funds require an exposure to equities. Both views, however, agree that the benchmark should be the liabilities, not general market benchmarks for major asset classes that are too often used.

Basically, those who espouse the bond-equity view believe that the plan sponsor use the classical the mean-variance optimization framework but that the liability benchmark must be incorporated into the analysis. In mean-variance optimization, a portfolio manager determines the efficient frontier. The efficient frontier is the set of efficient portfolios where an efficient portfolio is the portfolio with the highest expected return for a given level of risk. To determine which efficient portfolio to select, the Sharpe ratio is used. As explained in Chapter 7, the Sharpe ratio is the excess return of the portfolio divided by the standard deviation of the excess return. The excess return is the difference between the expected return of the portfolio minus the risk-free rate, the risk-free rate being a Treasury rate. Proponents of the bond-equity view argue that rather than measuring the excess return in terms of a benchmark such as the risk-free rate, the benchmark should be an index that reflects the liability structure of the pension plan.

Ross, Bernstein, Ferguson, and Dalio (2008) propose the following liability-driven strategy for a pension plan which involves two steps. In the first step, the plan sponsor in consultation with its advisor creates a cash flow matched strategy in order to hedge the adverse consequences associated with the exposure to the liabilities attributable to a change in interest rates. In the second step, the plan sponsor in consultation with its advisor works with asset managers to create portfolios that generate a return that exceeds the return on the immunizing portfolio. Such portfolios are referred to as "excess return portfolios." The total return for the pension plan is then

Total plan return = Return on liability-immunizing portfolio
+ Return on excess return portfolios − Return on liabilities

The return on liabilities is the change in the present value of the liabilities. If the immunizing portfolio is properly created, its return should be closed to the return on the liabilities. (Recall it is not a simple task to completely immunize.) Hence, the volatility of the liabilities is neutralized to a great extent. What remains is then the return on the excess return portfolio.

SUMMARY

In this chapter, bond portfolio strategies are discussed. We started with a description of the bond market indexes available. These indexes can be classified as broad-based bond market indexes or specialized market indexes. The three broad-based bond market indexes most commonly used by institutional investors are the Barclays Capital U.S. Aggregate Index, the Salomon Smith Barney Broad Investment-Grade Bond Index, and the Merrill Lynch Domestic Market Index.

The spectrum of bond portfolio strategies and the key elements of each strategy can be understood in terms of the risk and return of a strategy versus a benchmark established by the client. Strategies can be classified as follows: (1) pure bond index matching; (2) enhanced indexing/matching primary risk factors approach; (3) enhanced indexing/minor risk factor mismatches; (4) active management/larger risk factor mismatches; and (5) active management/full-blown active.

The difference between indexing and active management is the extent to which the portfolio can deviate from the primary risk factors associated with the index. The primary risk factors associated with an index are: (1) the duration of the index; (2) the present value distribution of the cash flows; (3) percent in sector and quality; (4) duration contribution of sector; (5) duration contribution of credit quality; (6) sector, coupon, or maturity cell weights; and (7) issuer exposure control.

A pure bond index matching strategy involves the least risk of underperforming the index and involves creating a portfolio so as to replicate the issues comprising the index. A portfolio manager pursuing a pure index matching strategy will encounter several logistical problems in constructing an indexed portfolio that will cause tracking error.

An enhanced indexing strategy can be pursued so as to construct a portfolio to match the primary risk factors without acquiring each issue in the index. There are three methodologies used to construct a portfolio to replicate an index: the stratified sampling or cellular approach, the optimization approach, and the variance minimization approach.

Enhanced indexing/minor risk factor mismatches is an enhanced strategy where the portfolio is constructed so as to have minor deviations from the risk factors that affect the performance of the index but the duration of the constructed portfolio is matched to the duration of the index.

Active bond strategies are those that attempt to outperform the market by intentionally constructing a portfolio that will have a greater index mismatch than in the case of enhanced indexing. One active bond strategy the portfolio manager makes larger mismatches relative to the index in terms of risk factors, including minor mismatches of duration. In the full blown active management case, the portfolio manager is permitted to make a significant duration bet without any constraint and can make a significant allocation to sectors not included in the index.

Value-added strategies are those that seek to enhance return relative to an index and can be strategic or tactical. Strategic strategies include interest rate expectations strategies, yield curve strategies, and inter- and intrasector allocation strategies. Tactical strategies are short-term trading strategies that include strategies based on rich/cheap analysis, yield curve trading strategies, and return enhancing strategies employing futures and options.

Interest rate expectations strategies involve adjusting the duration of the portfolio relative to the index based on expected movements in interest rates. Top down yield curve strategies involve positioning a portfolio to capitalize on expected changes in the shape of the Treasury yield curve following either a bullet strategy, barbell strategy, or ladder strategy.

An intersector allocation strategy involves a manager's allocation of funds among the major bond sectors. In making inter- and intrasector allocations, a manager is anticipating how spreads due to differences in credit risk, call risk (or prepayment risk), and liquidity risk will change. In undertaking a swap to enhance returns via intrasector allocation, it is critical in evaluating potential swaps that the trade be constructed so as maintain the same dollar duration as the initial position so as to avoid an unintentional interest rate bet.

A factor model that encompasses more than term structure risk exposure can be used to construct and analyze a portfolio relative to a benchmark. A factor model can be used to determine the forward-looking tracking error of systematic risk factors relative to a benchmark and the exposure to nonsystematic risk factors.

The liability structure of a defined benefit pension plans is uncertain. There are two liability-driven strategies advocated for defined benefit pension plans. One approach argues that only bonds should be acquired and a dedicated portfolio strategy should be used. The other approach is a liability-driven strategy that uses bonds and equities but uses the liabilities as a benchmark in determining the best asset allocation.

REFERENCES

Fong, H. G., and O. A. Vasicek. 1984. A risk minimizing strategy for portfolio immunization. *Journal of Finance* 30: 1541–1546.

Markowitz, H. M. 1952. Portfolio selection. *Journal of Finance* 7, no. 1: 77–91.

Ross, P., D. Bernstein, N. Ferguson, and R. Dalio. 2008. Creating an optimal portfolio to fund pension liabilities. In *Handbook of finance*, vol. 2, edited by F. J. Fabozzi (pp. 463–484). Hoboken, NJ: John Wiley & Sons.

Volpert, K. E. Managing indexed and enhanced indexed bond portfolios. In *Managing fixed income portfolios,* edited by F. J. Fabozzi (pp. 191–211). Hoboken, NJ: John Wiley & Sons.

CHAPTER 24

Using Derivatives in Bond Portfolio Management

For many types of strategies employed in investment management, derivative instruments provide a more efficient vehicle for obtaining exposure to an asset class. Our focus in Chapters 13 and 14 is on the use of equity derivatives in equity portfolio management. In this chapter, we explain how interest rate derivatives—futures, options, swaps—and credit derivatives can be used in bond portfolio management. We do not review the basics of futures and options because they are covered in Chapters 13 and 14, respectively.

USING TREASURY BOND AND NOTE FUTURES CONTRACTS IN BOND PORTFOLIO MANAGEMENT

There are several interest rate futures contracts that are available to portfolio managers. The contracts typically used to control the risk of bond portfolio is the Treasury bond and note futures contracts. We describe these contracts here, their pricing in terms of deviations from the basic futures pricing model, and how they are used.

Basic Features of Treasury Bond and Note Futures Contracts

The Treasury bond and note futures contracts are traded on the Chicago Board of Trade (CBOT). The underlying instrument for the bond futures contract is $100,000 par value of a hypothetical 20-year, 6% coupon bond. This hypothetical bond's coupon rate is called the *notional coupon*. There are three Treasury note futures contracts: 10-year, five-year, and two-year. All three contracts are modeled after the Treasury bond futures contract and are traded on the CBOT. The underlying instrument for the 10-year Treasury note contract is $100,000 par value of a hypothetical

10-year, 6% Treasury note. Treasury futures contracts trade with March, June, September, and December settlement months. The futures price is quoted in terms of par being 100. Since the bond and notes futures contract are similar, for the remainder of our discussion we focus on the bond futures contract.

We have been referring to the underlying instrument as a hypothetical Treasury bond. While some interest rate futures contracts can only be settled in cash, the seller (the short) of a Treasury bond futures contract who chooses to make delivery rather than liquidate his/her position by buying back the contract prior to the settlement date must deliver some Treasury bond. This begs the question "which Treasury bond?" The CBOT allows the seller to deliver one of several Treasury bonds that the CBOT specifies are acceptable for delivery. A trader who is short a particular bond is always concerned with the risk of being unable to obtain sufficient securities to cover their position.

The bond issues that meet the delivery requirements for a particular contract are referred to as *deliverable issues*. The CBOT makes its determination of the Treasury issues that are acceptable for delivery from all outstanding Treasury issues that have at least 15 years to maturity from the first day of the delivery month. For settlement purposes, the CBOT specifies that a given issue's term to maturity is calculated in complete three month increments (that is, complete quarters). For example, if the actual maturity of an issue is 15 years and 5 months, it would be rounded down to a maturity of 15 years and 1 quarter (three months). Moreover, all bonds delivered by the seller must be of the same issue.

Keep in mind that, while the underlying Treasury bond for this contract is a hypothetical issue and therefore cannot itself be delivered into the futures contract, the bond futures contract is not a cash settlement contract. The only way to close out a Treasury bond futures contract is to either initiate an offsetting futures position or to deliver one of the deliverable issues.

The delivery is as follows. On the settlement date, the seller of the futures contract (the short) is required to deliver to the buyer (the long) $100,000 par value of a 6%, 20-year Treasury bond. As noted, no such bond exists, so the seller must choose one of the deliverable issues to deliver to the long. Suppose the seller selects a 5% coupon, 20-year Treasury bond to settle the futures contract. Since the coupon of this bond is less than the notional coupon of 6%, this would be unacceptable to the buyer who contracted to receive a 6% coupon, 20-year bond with a par value of $100,000. Alternatively, suppose the seller is compelled to deliver a 7% coupon, 20-year bond. Since the coupon of this bond is greater than the notional coupon of 6%, the seller would find this unacceptable. How does the exchange adjust for the fact that deliverable issues have coupons and maturities that differ from the notional coupon of 6%?

To make delivery equitable to both parties, the CBOT publishes conversion factors for adjusting the price of each deliverable issue for a given contract. Given the conversion factor for a deliverable issue and the futures price, the adjusted price is found by multiplying the conversion factor by the futures price. The adjusted price is called the *converted price*. That is,

$$\text{Converted price} = \text{Contract size} \times \text{Futures settlement price} \times \text{Conversion factor}$$

For example, suppose the settlement price of a Treasury bond futures contract is 110 and the deliverable issue selected by the short has a conversion factor of 1.25. Given the contract size is $100,000, the converted price for the deliverable issue is

$$\$100{,}000 \times 1.10 \times 1.25 = \$137{,}500$$

The price that the buyer must pay the seller when a the deliverable issue is delivered is called the *invoice price*. The invoice price is the converted price plus the deliverable issue's accrued interest. That is, the invoice price is:

$$\text{Invoice price} = \text{Contract size} \times \text{Futures settlement price} \times \text{Conversion factor} + \text{Accrued interest}$$

In selecting the issue to be delivered, the short will select from all the deliverable issues the one that will give the largest rate of return from a *cash-and-carry strategy*. We explained this strategy in Chapter 13 where we derived the theoretical futures price. In the case of Treasury bond futures, a cash-and-carry strategy is one in which a cash bond that is acceptable for delivery is purchased with borrowed funds and simultaneously the Treasury bond futures contract is sold. The bond purchased can be delivered to satisfy the short futures position. Thus, by buying the Treasury issue that is acceptable for delivery and selling the futures, an investor has effectively sold the bond at the delivery price (that is, the converted price).

A rate of return can be calculated for this strategy. This rate of return is referred to as the *implied repo rate*. Once the implied repo rate is calculated for each deliverable issue, the issue selected for delivery will be the one that has the highest implied repo rate (that is, the issue that gives the maximum return in a cash-and-carry strategy). The issue with the highest return is

TABLE 24.1 Summary of Delivery Options for the Treasury Bond and Note Futures Contract

Delivery Option	Description
Quality or swap option	Choice of which deliverable issue to deliver
Timing option	Choice of when in delivery month to deliver
Wild card option	Choice to deliver after the closing price of the futures contract is determined

referred to as the *cheapest-to-deliver issue* (CTD issue). This issue plays a key role in the pricing of a Treasury futures contract.[1]

In addition to the choice of which acceptable Treasury issue to deliver—sometimes referred to as the *quality option* or *swap option*—the short has at least two more options granted under CBOT delivery guidelines. The short is permitted to decide when in the delivery month, delivery actually will take place. This is called the *timing option*. The other option is the right of the short to give notice of intent to deliver up to 8:00 P.M. Chicago time after the closing of the exchange (3:15 P.M. Chicago time) on the date when the futures settlement price has been fixed. This option is referred to as the *wildcard option*. The quality option, the timing option, and the wildcard option—in sum referred to as the *delivery options*—mean that the long position can never be sure which Treasury bond issue will be delivered or when it will be delivered. These three delivery options are summarized in Table 24.1.

Pricing of Treasury Bond and Note Futures Contracts

In Chapter 13, we explained the basic pricing model for a generic futures contract. We also explained how the model must be modified for stock index futures. Let's look at how the specifics of the Treasury futures contract necessitate the refinement of the theoretical futures pricing model. The assumptions that require a refinement of the model are the assumptions that (1) there are no interim cash flows and (2) the deliverable asset and the settlement date are known.

With respect to interim cash flows, for a Treasury futures contract the underlying is a Treasury note or a Treasury bond. Unlike a stock index futures contract, the timing of the interest payments that will be made by the

---

[1]While a particular Treasury bond may be the CTD issue today, changes in interest rates, for example, may cause some other issue to be the CTD issue at a future date. A sensitivity analysis can be performed to determine how a change in yield affects the CTD issue. In particular, sensitivity analysis identifies which deliverable issue is cheapest to deliver following various shocks to the yield curve.

U.S. Department of the Treasury for every issue that is acceptable as deliverable for a contract is known with certainty and can be incorporated into the pricing model. However, the reinvestment interest that can be earned from the coupon payment from the payment dates to the settlement date of the contract is unknown and depends on prevailing interest rates at each payment date.

Now let's look at the implications regarding a known deliverable and known settlement date. Neither assumption is consistent with the delivery rules for some futures contracts. For U.S. Treasury note and bond futures contracts, for example, the contract specifies deliverable issues that can be delivered to satisfy the contract. Although the party that is long the contract (that is, the buyer of the contract) does not know the specific Treasury issue that will be delivered, the long can determine the CTD issue from amongst the deliverable issues. It is this issue that is used in obtaining the theoretical futures price. The net effect of the short's option to select the issue to deliver to satisfy the contract is that it reduces the theoretical future price by an amount equal to the value of the delivery option granted to the short.

Moreover, unlike other futures contract, the Treasury bond and note contracts do not have a delivery date. Instead, there is a delivery month. The short has the right to select when in the delivery month to make delivery. The effect of this option granted to the short is once again to reduce the theoretical futures price. More specifically,

> Theoretical futures price adjusted for delivery options
> = Cash market price + (Cash market price) × (Financing cost − Cash yield)
> − Value of the delivery options granted to the short

Bond Portfolio Management Applications

There are various ways an asset manager can use interest rate futures contracts in addition to speculating on the movement of interest rates. Prior to the introduction of Treasury bond and note futures contracts, Treasury securities were used. Before describing the use of Treasury futures, let's first address why these contracts are used rather than using Treasury securities.

There are four reasons why it is preferable to use Treasury futures rather than Treasury securities. First, Treasury futures are more liquid than Treasury securities and therefore executing in the Treasury futures market results in lower transactions costs. Second, often when taking a position in Treasury securities it may be expensive if the instrument used to control interest rate risk is a Treasury security that is on "special," or if an off-the-run Treasury needs to be utilized. Under such circumstances, the cost of establishing a position in a Treasury security may be expensive because of low reverse-repo rates or wide bid-ask spreads. Third, margin requirements for establishing futures positions are less than margin requirements for buying Treasury securities on margin. Finally, if the position that is required involves a short position in the market, it is far easier to short Treasury futures than Treasury securities.

Controlling the Interest Rate Risk of a Portfolio

Asset managers can use interest rate futures to alter the interest rate sensitivity, or duration, of a portfolio. Those with strong expectations about the direction of the future course of interest rates will adjust the duration of their portfolios so as to capitalize on their expectations. Specifically, a money manager who expects rates to increase will shorten duration; a money manager who expects interest rates to decrease will lengthen duration. While asset managers can use cash market instruments to alter the durations of their portfolios, using futures contracts provides a quicker and less expensive means for doing so (on either a temporary or permanent basis).

A formula to approximate the number of futures contracts necessary to adjust the portfolio duration to some target duration is

$$\frac{\left(\begin{array}{c}\text{Target portfolio}\\ \text{duration}\end{array} - \begin{array}{c}\text{Current portfolio}\\ \text{duration}\end{array}\right) \times \text{Market value of the portfolio}}{\text{Dollar duration of the futures contract}}$$

The dollar duration of the futures contract is the dollar price sensitivity of the futures contract to a change in interest rates.

Notice that if the asset manager wishes to increase the portfolio's current duration, the numerator of the formula is positive. This means that futures contracts will be purchased. That is, buying futures increases the duration of the portfolio. The opposite is true if the objective is to shorten the portfolio's current duration: The numerator of the formula is negative and this means that futures must be sold. Hence, selling futures contracts reduces the portfolio's duration.

Hedging

Hedging is a special case of risk control where the target duration sought is zero. If cash and futures prices move together, any loss realized by the hedger from one position (whether cash or futures) will be offset by a profit on the other position. When the net profit or loss from the positions is exactly as anticipated, the hedge is referred to as a *perfect hedge*.

In practice, hedging is not that simple as demonstrated in Chapter 13 for stock index futures. In bond portfolio management, typically the bond to be hedged is not identical to the bond underlying the futures contract and therefore there is cross hedging. This may result in substantial basis risk.

Conceptually, cross hedging is somewhat more complicated than hedging deliverable securities because it involves two relationships. In the case of Treasury bond futures contracts, the first relationship is between the CTD issue and the futures contract. The second is the relationship between the security to be hedged and the CTD issue.

The key to minimizing risk in a cross hedge is to choose the right hedge ratio. The hedge ratio depends on volatility weighting, or weighting by relative changes in value. The purpose of a hedge is to use gains or losses from a futures position to offset any difference between the target sale price and the actual sale price of the security.

Accordingly, the hedge ratio is chosen with the intention of matching the volatility (that is, the dollar change) of the Treasury bond futures contract to the volatility of the bond to be hedged. Consequently, the hedge ratio for a bond is given by

$$\text{Hedge ratio} = \frac{\text{Volatility of bond to be hedged}}{\text{Volatility of Treasury bond futures contract}} \qquad (24.1)$$

For hedging purposes, we are concerned with volatility in absolute dollar terms. To calculate the dollar volatility of a bond, one must know the precise time that volatility is to be calculated (because volatility generally declines as a bond moves toward its maturity date), as well as the price or yield at which to calculate volatility (because higher yields generally reduce dollar volatility for a given yield change). The relevant point in the life of the bond for calculating volatility is the point at which the hedge will be lifted. Volatility at any other point is essentially irrelevant because the goal is to lock in a price or rate only on that particular day. Similarly, the relevant yield at which to calculate volatility initially is the target yield. Consequently, the "volatility of bond to be hedged" referred to in equation (24.1) for the hedge ratio is the price value of a basis point for the bond on the date the hedge is expected to be delivered.

Illustration We will use an illustration to show how to calculate the hedge ratio and then verify that it will do an effective job in hedging a bond position.[2] We will assume that on December 24, 2007, a bond portfolio manager wants to hedge a position in a Procter & Gamble (P&G) 5.55% of 3/5/2037 bond that he anticipates selling on March 31, 2008. The par value of the P&G bonds is $10 million. The portfolio manager decides that he will use the March 2008 Treasury bond futures to hedge the bond position

---

[2]Peter Ru of Morgan Stanley provided this illustration.

which he can settle on March 31, 2008. Because the portfolio manager is trying to protect against a decline in the value of the P&G bonds between December 24, 2007 and the anticipated sale date, he will short (sell) a number of March 2008 Treasury bond futures contracts. Because the bond to be hedged is a corporate bond and the hedging instrument is a Treasury bond futures contract, this is an example of a cross hedge.

On December 24, 2007, the P&G bond was selling at 97.127 and offering a yield of 5.754%. Since the par value of the P&G bond held in the portfolio is $10 million, this means that the market value of the bond is $9,712,700 (97.127 × $10,000,000). The price of the March 2008 Treasury bond futures contract on December 24, 2007 was 114.375. The portfolio manager determines that the Treasury 6.25s of 8/15/2023 issue was the CTD issue for the March 2008 Treasury bond futures contract. The price of this Treasury issue is 117.719 (a yield of 4.643%) and the conversion factor for this Treasury issue is 1.0246. The yield spread between the P&G bond and the CTD issue was 111.1 basis points (5.754% − 4.643%). To simplify the analysis, the portfolio manager assumes that this 111.1 yield spread will remain the same over the period the bond is hedged.

What target price is the portfolio manager seeking to lock in for the P&G bonds? One might think it is the current market price of the P&G bonds, 97.127. However, that is not correct. The target price is determined by the March 2008 Treasury bond futures contract that is being shorted. Some calculations are required to determine the target price. We begin by determining the target price for the CTD issue. Given the conversion factor for the CTD issue (1.0246) and the futures price for the March 2007 contract (114.375), the target price for the CTD issue is found by multiplying these two values. that is, the target price for the CTD issue is 117.1886. But there is a target yield for the CTD issue that corresponds to the price of 117.1886. For the Treasury 6.25s of 8/15/2023 issue, the yield if the price is 117.1886 on March 31, 2008 (the settlement date) is 4.670%. Thus, the target yield for the CTD issue is 4.670%.

Given the target for yield for the CTD issue of 4.670%, the portfolio manager can calculate the target yield for the P&G bond. Here the portfolio manager makes use of the assumption that yield spread between the P&G bond and the CTD issue remains at 111.1 basis points. For the target yield for the CTD issue of 4.670%, the portfolio manager adds the 111.1 basis point spread, giving a target yield for the P&G bond of 5.781%. The final step to estimate the target price for the P&G bond as of March 31, 2008 is to determine the price for the P&G bond on the settlement date given a target yield of 5.781%. This is a straightforward calculation given the coupon and maturity date of the P&G bond. The target price is 96.788. For a $10

Using Derivatives in Bond Portfolio Management

million par value holding of the P&G bond, the target market value that the portfolio manager seeks is about $9,678,000.

To calculate the hedge ratio, the portfolio manager needs to know the volatility of the March 2008 Treasury bond futures contract. Fortunately, knowing the volatility of the bond to be hedged relative to the CTD issue and the volatility of the cheapest-to-deliver bond relative to the futures contract, we can modify the hedge ratio given by equation (24.1) as follows:

$$\text{Hedge ratio} = \frac{\text{Volatility of bond to be hedged}}{\text{Volatility of CTD issue}} \times \frac{\text{Volatility of CTD bond}}{\text{Volatility of Treasury bond futures contract}} \quad (24.2)$$

The second ratio above can be shown to equal the conversion factor for the CTD issue. Assuming a fixed yield spread between the bond to be hedged and the CTD issue, equation (24.2) can be rewritten as

$$\text{Hedge ratio} = \frac{\text{PVBP of bond to be hedged}}{\text{PVBP of CTD issue} \times \text{Conversion factor for CTD issue}} \quad (24.3)$$

where PVBP is equal to the price value of a basis point. As explained in Chapter 21, the PVBP is computed by changing the yield of a bond by one basis point and determining the change in the bond's price. It is a measure of price volatility to interest rate changes and related to duration.

The portfolio manager can calculate the PVBP of the P&G bond and the CTD issue from the target yield and the target price for the bonds at the settlement date. For the CTD issue it is 0.1207 and for the P&G bond it is 0.1363. Substituting these two values plus the conversion factor for the CTD issue (1.0246) into equation (24.3), we get

$$\text{Hedge ratio} = \frac{0.1363}{0.1207} \times 1.0246 = 1.157$$

Given the hedge ratio, the number of contracts that must be short is determined as follows:

$$\text{Number of contracts} = \text{Hedge ratio} \times \frac{\text{Par value to be hedged}}{\text{Par value of the futures contract}}$$

Because the amount to be hedged is $10 million and each Treasury bond futures contract is for $100,000 par value, this means that the number of futures contracts that must be sold is

$$\text{Number of contracts} = \text{Hedge ratio} \times \frac{\$10,000,000}{\$100,000}$$
$$= 1.157 \times 100 = 116 \text{ contracts (rounded)}$$

Table 24.2 shows that if the simplifying assumptions that were made in this illustration to calculate the hedge ratio are satisfied, a futures hedge wherein 116 futures contracts are shorted very nearly locks in the target market value of $9,678,000 for $10 million par value of the P&G bond. There are refinements that can be made to the hedging procedure to improve this hedge.[3] However, these are unimportant for a basic understanding of hedging with Treasury bond futures contracts.

USE OF INTEREST RATE OPTIONS IN BOND PORTFOLIO MANAGEMENT

Interest rate options can be written on a fixed income security or an interest rate futures contract. The former options are called *options on physicals* and the latter are called *futures options*. The most liquid exchange-traded options on a fixed income security is an option on Treasury bonds traded on the Chicago Board of Trade (CBOT). For reasons to be explained later, options on interest rate futures have been far more popular than options on physicals. However, portfolio managers have made increasingly greater use of over-the-counter (OTC) options. Typically they are purchased by institutional investors who want to hedge the risk associated with a specific security or index. Besides options on fixed income securities, there are OTC options on the shape of the yield curve or the yield spread between two securities. A discussion of these OTC options is beyond the scope of this chapter.

Exchange-Traded Futures Options

A futures option gives the buyer the right to buy from or sell to the writer a designated futures contract at the strike price. If the futures option is a call option, the buyer has the right to purchase one designated futures contract at the strike price. That is, the buyer has the right to acquire a long futures position in the designated futures contract. If the buyer exercises the call option, the writer acquires a corresponding short position in the futures contract.

A put option on a futures contract grants the buyer the right to sell one designated futures contract to the writer at the strike price. That is,

---
[3] See Fabozzi (2009).

TABLE 24.2 Hedge of the $10 million Par Value of Procter & Gamble 5.55% 3/5/20037 with March 2008 Treasury Bond Futures Contract with Settlement on March 31, 2008

Actual Sale Price of P&G Bond	Yield at Sale	Yield of Treasury[a]	Price of Treasury	Futures Price[b]	Gain (loss) on 116 contracts	Effective Sale Price[c]
8,000,000	7.204%	6.093%	101.544	99.106	1,771,194	9,771,194
8,200,000	7.010%	5.899%	103.508	101.023	1,548,862	9,748,862
8,400,000	6.824%	5.713%	105.438	102.907	1,330,323	9,730,323
8,600,000	6.645%	5.534%	107.341	104.764	1,114,875	9,714,875
8,800,000	6.472%	5.361%	109.224	106.601	901,748	9,701,748
9,000,000	6.306%	5.195%	111.071	108.404	692,606	9,692,606
9,200,000	6.144%	5.033%	112.914	110.203	484,008	9,684,008
9,400,000	5.989%	4.878%	114.714	111.960	280,164	9,680,164
9,600,000	5.838%	4.727%	116.504	113.707	77,476	9,677,476
9,800,000	5.691%	4.580%	118.282	115.442	(123,809)	9,676,191
10,000,000	5.550%	4.439%	120.021	117.139	(320,633)	9,679,367
10,200,000	5.412%	4.301%	121.755	118.831	(516,925)	9,683,075
10,400,000	5.278%	4.167%	123.469	120.505	(711,032)	9,688,968
10,600,000	5.149%	4.038%	125.149	122.144	(901,256)	9,698,744
10,800,000	5.022%	3.911%	126.832	123.787	(1,091,785)	9,708,215
11,000,000	4.899%	3.788%	128.490	125.405	(1,279,473)	9,720,527
11,200,000	4.780%	3.669%	130.120	126.996	(1,464,047)	9,735,953
11,400,000	4.663%	3.552%	131.749	128.586	(1,648,452)	9,751,548
11,600,000	4.550%	3.439%	133.347	130.145	(1,829,358)	9,770,642

[a] By assumption, the yield on the CTD issue (6.25% of 8/15/2003) is 111.1 basis points lower than the yield on the P&G bond.
[b] By convergence, the futures price equals the price of the CTD issue divided by 1.0246 (the conversion factor).
[c] Transaction costs and the financing of margin flows are ignored.

the option buyer has the right to acquire a short position in the designated futures contract. If the put option is exercised, the writer acquires a corresponding long position in the designated futures contract. Table 24.3 summarizes these positions. There are futures options on all the Treasury bond and note futures contracts.

TABLE 24.3 Call and Put Futures Options

Type	Buyer Has the Right to:	If Exercised, the Seller Has:	If Exercised, the Seller Pays the Buyer:
Call	Purchase one futures contract at the strike price	A short futures position	Current futures price − Strike price
Put	Sell one futures contract at the strike price	A long futures position	Strike price − Current futures price

The CBOT's Treasury bond futures contracts have delivery months of March, June, September, and December. As with stock index futures contracts, there are *flexible Treasury futures options*. These futures options allow counterparties to customize options within certain limits. Specifically, the strike price, expiration date, and type of exercise (American or European) can be customized subject to CBOT constraints.

Mechanics of Trading Futures Options

Because the parties to the futures option will realize a position in a futures contract when the option is exercised, the question is, what will the futures price be? That is, at what price will the long be required to pay for the instrument underlying the futures contract, and at what price will the short be required to sell the instrument underlying the futures contract?

Upon exercise, the futures price for the futures contract will be set equal to the strike price. The position of the two parties is then immediately marked to market in terms of the then-current futures price. Thus, the futures position of the two parties will be at the prevailing futures price. At the same time, the option buyer will receive from the option seller the economic benefit from exercising. In the case of a call futures option, the option writer must pay to the buyer of the option the difference between the current futures price and the strike price. In the case of a put futures option, the option writer must pay the option buyer the difference between the strike price and the current futures price. This is summarized in Figure 24.3.

For example, suppose an investor buys a call option on some futures contract in which the strike price is 85. Assume also that the futures price is 95 and that the buyer exercises the call option. Upon exercise, the call buyer is given a long position in the futures contract at 85, and the call writer is assigned the corresponding short position in the futures contract at 85. The futures positions of the buyer and the writer are immediately marked to market by the exchange. Because the prevailing futures price is 95 and the strike price is 85, the long futures position (the position of the call buyer) realizes a gain of 10, while the short futures position (the position of the call writer) realizes a loss of 10. The call writer pays the exchange 10, and the call buyer receives 10 from the exchange. The call buyer, who now has a long futures position at 95, can either liquidate the futures position at 95 or maintain a long futures position. If the former course of action is taken, the call buyer sells a futures contract at the prevailing futures price of 95. There is no gain or loss from liquidating the position. Overall, the call buyer realizes a gain of 10. The call buyer who elects to hold the long futures position will face the same risk and reward of holding such a position, but still realizes a gain of 10 from the exercise of the call option.

Suppose, instead, that the futures option is a put rather than a call, and the current futures price is 60 rather than 95. If the buyer of this put option exercises it, the buyer would have a short position in the futures contract at 85; the option writer would have a long position in the futures contract at 85. The exchange then marks the position to market at the then-current futures price of 60, resulting in a gain to the put buyer of 25, and a loss to the put writer of the same amount. The put buyer, who now has a short futures position at 60, can either liquidate the short futures position by buying a futures contract at the prevailing futures price of 60 or maintain the short futures position. In either case, the put buyer realizes a gain of 25 from exercising the put option.

Reasons for the Popularity of Futures Options

There are three reasons why futures options on Treasuries are preferred to options on physicals as the options vehicle of choice for institutional investors.[4] First, unlike options on Treasury securities, options on Treasury futures do not require payments for accrued interest to be made. Consequently, when a futures option is exercised, the call buyer and the put writer need not compensate the other party for accrued interest. Second, futures options are believed to be "cleaner" instruments because of the reduced likelihood of delivery squeezes. Market participants who must deliver a Treasury security are concerned that at the time of delivery, the Treasury to be delivered will be in short supply, resulting in a higher price to acquire the security. Because the deliverable supply of futures contracts is more than adequate for futures options currently traded, there is no concern about a delivery squeeze. Finally, in order to price any option, it is imperative to know at all times the price of the underlying instrument. In the bond market, current prices are not as easily available as price information on the futures contract. The reason is that Treasury securities

---

[4] The reasons are given by Goodman (1985, 13–14).

Pricing Models on Options on Physicals and Futures Options

In Chapter 15, we discussed the Black-Scholes option pricing model. In this section, we will provide an overview of pricing models for options on physicals and futures options. In general, these options are much more complex than options on stocks or stock indexes because of the need to take into consideration the term structure of interest rates.

Black-Scholes Model for Valuing Options on Treasury Securities

As explained in Chapter 15, by imposing certain assumptions and using arbitrage arguments, the Black-Scholes model computes the fair (or theoretical) price of a European call option on a nondividend-paying stock. Let's see if we can use the same model to price an option on a Treasury bond. Because the basic Black-Scholes model is for a noncash-paying security, let's apply it to a Treasury strip (i.e., zero-coupon Treasury) with three years to maturity. Assume the following values:

Strike price = $88.00
Time remaining to expiration = 2 years
Current price[5] = $83.96
Expected price volatility = standard deviation = 10%
Risk-free rate = 6%

In terms of the values in the Black-Scholes formula presented in Chapter 15:

$S = \$83.96$
$K = 88.00$
$t = 2$
$s = 0.10$
$r = 0.06$

Substituting these values into the Black-Scholes formula would produce a price of $8.12. There is no reason to suspect that this estimated value is unreasonable. However, let's change the problem slightly. Instead of a strike price of $88, let's make the strike price for the call option on this Treasury strip $100.25. Substituting the new strike price into the Black-Scholes for-

---
[5]The current price is $83.96, which is the present value of the maturity value of $100 discounted at 6% (i.e., $100/(1.06)³).

mulas would give a value of $2.79. Thus, the Black-Scholes model tells us that this call option has a fair value of $2.79. Is there any reason to believe this is unreasonable? Well, consider that this is a call option on a Treasury strip that will never have a value greater than its maturity value of $100 (it makes no coupon payments). Consequently, a call option with a strike price of $100.25 must have a value of zero. Yet the Black-Scholes model tells us that the value is $2.79! In fact, with a higher volatility assumption, the model would give an even greater value for the call option.

The reason for obtaining an unrealistic value for this option is the underlying assumptions of the model. There are three assumptions underlying the Black-Scholes model that limit its use in pricing options on Treasury securities. First, the probability distribution for the prices assumed by the Black-Scholes model permits some probability—no matter how small—that the price can take on any positive value. But in the case of a Treasury strip, the price cannot take on a value above $100. In the case of a Treasury coupon bond, we know that the price cannot exceed the sum of the coupon payments plus the maturity value. Thus, unlike stock prices, Treasury prices have a maximum value. So any probability distribution for prices assumed by an option pricing model that permits Treasury prices to be higher than the maximum value could generate nonsensical option prices. The Black-Scholes model does allow Treasury prices to exceed the maximum bond value.

The second assumption of the Black-Scholes model is that the short-term interest rate is constant over the life of the option. Yet the price of a Treasury security will change as interest rates change. A change in the short-term interest rate changes the rates along the yield curve. Therefore, to assume that the short-term rate will be constant is inappropriate for Treasury options.

The third assumption is that the variance of prices is constant over the life of the option. However, as a bond moves closer to maturity, its price volatility declines. Therefore, the assumption that price variance is constant over the life of a Treasury option is inappropriate.

Black Model for Treasury Futures Options

The most commonly used model for futures options is the one developed by Black (1976). The Black model was initially developed for valuing European options on forward contracts. There are two problems with this model. First, the Black model does not overcome the problems just identified for the Black-Scholes model. Failing to recognize the yield curve means that there will not be a consistency between pricing Treasury futures and options on Treasury futures. Second, the Black model was developed for pricing European options on futures contracts. Treasury futures options, however, are

American options. The second problem can be overcome. The Black model was extended by Barone-Adesi and Whaley (1987) to American options on futures contracts. This is the model used by the CBOT to settle the flexible Treasury futures options. However, this model was also developed for equities and is subject to the first problem noted above. Despite its limitations, the Black model is the most popular option pricing model for options on Treasury futures

Applications to Bond Portfolio Management

In our explanation of how to use options in equity portfolio management, we explained how they can be used in risk management and return enhancement. We will not repeat an explanation of the applications here. Instead, we will illustrate how futures options can be used for hedging and return enhancement. More specifically, we will illustrate a protective put strategy (a risk management application) and a covered call writing strategy (a return enhancement application). As will be seen, the applications are complicated by the fact that the option is not an option on a physical but a futures option.

Protective Put Buying Strategy with Futures Options

Buying puts on Treasury futures options is one of the easiest ways to purchase protection against rising rates. As explained in Chapter 14, this strategy is called a protective put buying strategy. To illustrate this strategy, we use the P&G bond that we used earlier in this chapter to demonstrate how to use Treasury bond futures for hedging. We also compare hedging using Treasury bond futures with hedging using Treasury futures options.

In our illustration, we assumed that the portfolio manager owns $10 million par value of the P&G 5.55%, 3/5/2037 bond and used Treasury bond futures to lock in a sale price for those bonds on a futures delivery date. The P&G bond was selling at a yield of 5.74%. The specific contract used for hedging was the Treasury bond futures contract with settlement in March 2008. The CTD issue for the Treasury bond futures contract was the Treasury 6.25%, 8/15/2023 bond selling to yield 4.643%.

Now we want to show how the portfolio manager could have used Treasury bond futures options instead of Treasury bond futures to protect against rising rates. In this illustration, we will assume that the portfolio manager uses a put option on the March 2008 Treasury bond futures contract. The put options for this contract expire on February 22, 2008. For simplicity, we assumed that this yield spread between the CTD issue and the P&G bonds remain at 111.1 basis points.

Using Derivatives in Bond Portfolio Management

To hedge using puts on Treasury bond futures, the portfolio manager must determine the minimum price for the P&G bond. In the illustration, it is assumed that the minimum price is 96.219 per bond or $9,621,900 for $10 million of par value. Thus, 96.219 becomes the target price for the P&G bond. However, the problem is that the portfolio manager is not purchasing a put option on the P&G bond but a put option on a Treasury bond futures contract. Therefore, the hedging process requires that the portfolio manager must determine the strike price for a put option on a Treasury bond futures contract that is equivalent to a strike price of 96.219 for the P&G bond.

The process involves several steps. These steps are shown in Figure 24.1. Because the minimum price is 96.219 (Box 1 in Figure 24.1) for the P&G bond, this means that the portfolio manager is seeking to establish a maximum yield of 5.821%. We know this because given the price, coupon, and maturity of the bond, the yield can easily be computed. This gets us to Box 2 in Figure 24.1. Now we have to make use of the assumption that the yield spread between the P&G bond and the CTD issue is 111.1 basis points. By subtracting this yield spread from the maximum yield of 5.821%, we get the maximum yield for the CTD issue of 4.710%. This gets us to Box 3 in Figure 24.1.

Now we move on to Box 4 in the figure. Given the yield of 4.710% for the CTD issue, the minimum price can be determined. Because the CTD issue is the Treasury 6.25% 8/15/2023, a 4.710% yield means a target price for

FIGURE 24.1 Calculating Equivalent Prices and Yields for Hedging with Futures Options

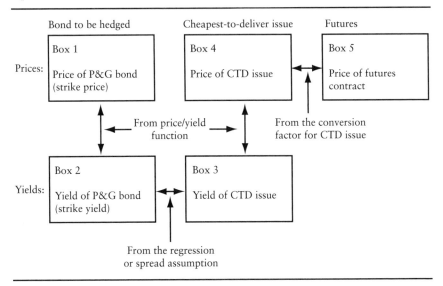

that issue is 116.8044. The corresponding futures price is found by dividing the price of the CTD issue by the conversion factor. This gets us to Box 5 in the figure. The conversion factor for the CTD issue is 1.0246. Therefore, the futures price is about 114.373 (116.8044 divided by 1.0246). Now the portfolio manager must look to the options market to determine what strike prices are available because there are a limited number of strike prices available on the exchange. In this illustration, we will assume that the strike price available to the portfolio manager is a strike price of 114 for a put option on a Treasury bond futures contract. This means that a put option on a Treasury bond futures contract with a strike price of 114 is roughly equivalent to a put option on the P&G bond with a strike price of 96.219.

The steps identified in Figure 24.1 and described above are always necessary to identify the appropriate strike price on a put futures option. The process involves simply (1) the relationship between price and yield; (2) the assumed relationship between the yield spread between the bonds to be hedged and the CTD issue; and (3) the conversion factor for the CTD issue. As with hedging with futures illustrated earlier in this chapter, the success of the hedging strategy will depend on (1) whether the CTD issue changes and (2) the yield spread between the bonds to be hedged and the CTD issue.

The hedge ratio is determined using equation (24.3) because we will assume a constant yield spread between the bond to be hedged and CTD issue. To compute the hedge ratio, the portfolio manager must calculate the price values of a basis point at the option expiration date (assumed to be February 22, 2008) and at the yields corresponding to the futures' strike price of 114 (4.710% yield for the CTD issue and 5.821% for the P&G bond). The price value of a basis point per $100 par value for the P&G bond and the CTD issue were 0.1353 and 0.1208, respectively. This results in a hedge ratio of 1.148 for the protective put hedge, or 1.15 with rounding. Because the par value of the futures option is $100,000 and the par value to be protected is $10,000, 115 put options on the Treasury bond futures contract should be purchased. At the time of the hedge, December 24, 2007, the price quote for this put option was 1.972. This means the dollar cost of each option is $197.2. Since 115 contracts would have to be purchased, the total cost of the put options (ignoring commissions) would be $22,678.

To create a table for the protective put hedge, we can use some of the numbers from Table 24.2. The first column in Table 24.4 repeats the numbers in the first column of Table 24.2; the second column in Table 24.4 reproduces the futures price from the fifth column of Table 24.2. The rest of the columns in Table 24.4 are computed. The value of the put options shown in the third column of the table is easy to calculate because the value of each option at expiration is the strike price of the futures option (114) minus the futures price (or zero if that difference is negative). The difference

Using Derivatives in Bond Portfolio Management

TABLE 24.4 Hedge of the $10 million Par Value of Procter & Gamble 5.55% 3/5/20037 Using a Protective Put Option Strategy

Actual Sale Price of P&G Bonds	Futures Price[a]	Value of 115 Put Options[b]	Cost of 115 Put Options	Effective Sale Price[c]
8,000,000	99.139	1,709,040	22,678	9,686,362
8,200,000	101.054	1,488,827	22,678	9,666,149
8,400,000	102.946	1,271,207	22,678	9,648,529
8,600,000	104.812	1,056,651	22,678	9,633,973
8,800,000	106.647	845,619	22,678	9,622,941
9,000,000	108.469	636,036	22,678	9,613,358
9,200,000	110.265	429,516	22,678	9,606,838
9,400,000	112.042	225,118	22,678	9,602,440
9,600,000	113.787	24,502	22,678	9,601,824
9,800,000	115.519	0	22,678	9,777,322
10,000,000	117.237	0	22,678	9,977,322
10,200,000	118.938	0	22,678	10,177,322
10,400,000	120.608	0	22,678	10,377,322
10,600,000	122.269	0	22,678	10,577,322
10,800,000	123.908	0	22,678	10,777,322
11,000,000	125.522	0	22,678	10,977,322
11,200,000	127.135	0	22,678	11,177,322
11,400,000	128.721	0	22,678	11,377,322
11,600,000	130.303	0	22,678	11,577,322

[a] These numbers are approximate because futures trade in even 32nds.
[b] From $115 \times \$1,000 \times \text{Max}[(114 - \text{futures price}), 0]$.
[c] Does not include transaction costs or the financing of the options position.

is then multiplied by $1,000. Let's see why by looking at the first row that corresponds to a future price of 99.139. Since the strike price for the put option is 114, the value of the put option is 14.861 (114.000 − 99.139) per $100 of par value. Because the par value for the Treasury bond futures contract is $100,000, the 14.861 must be multiplied by $1,000. Thus, the value of the contract is 14.861 times $1,000 or $14,861. For the 115 contracts purchased for this strategy, the total value is $1,709,015. The value of the 115 put options shown in the third column of $1,709,040 differs by $25 due to rounding in earlier calculation.

The next-to-the-last column of Table 24.4 shows the cost of the 115 put options. The effective sale price for the P&G bond can then be computed. It is equal to the sum of the actual market price for the P&G bond and the value of the 115 put options at expiration, reduced by the cost of the 115 put options. The effective sale price is shown in the last column of the table. This effective sale price is never less than $9,601,824. Recall that we established a minimum price of $9,621,900. This minimum effective sale price is something that can be calculated prior to the implementation of the hedge. Note that as prices decline, the effective sale price actually exceeds the projected effective minimum sale price by a small amount. This is due to rounding and the fact that the hedge ratio is left unaltered, although the relative price values of a basis point that go into the hedge ratio calculation change as yields change. As prices increase, however, the effective sale price of the P&G bond increases as well; unlike the futures hedge shown in Table 24.2, the protective put buying strategy protects the portfolio manager if rates rise but allows the portfolio manager to profit if rates fall.

Table 24.5 compares the hedging strategy involving shorting Treasury bond futures with that of the protective put buying strategy.

Covered Call Writing Strategy

To see how covered call writing with futures options works, we assume that the portfolio manager owns the P&G bond used in our previous illustration. With futures selling around 114.375, a futures call option with a strike price of a 120 might be appropriate. The price for the March call options with a strike of 120 expiring on 2/22/2008 was 0.512. As before, it is assumed that the P&G bond will remain at a 111.11 basis point spread off the CTD issue. The number of options contracts sold will be the same as in the protective put strategy, 115.

Table 24.4 shows the results of the covered call writing strategy given these assumptions. To calculate the effective sale price of the bonds in the covered call writing strategy, the premium received from the sale of the call options is added to the actual sale price of the bonds, and the liability associated with the short call position is subtracted from the actual sale price. The liability associated with each call is the futures price minus the strike price of 120 (or zero if this difference is negative), all multiplied by $1,000. The middle column in the table is just this value multiplied by 115, the number of options sold.

Just as the minimum effective sale price can be calculated beforehand for the protective put strategy, the maximum effective sale price can be calculated beforehand for the covered call writing strategy. The maximum effective sale price will be the price of the P&G bond corresponding to the

TABLE 24.5 Comparison of Hedging with Treasury Bond Futures and Protective Put Buying Strategy

Actual Sale Price of P&G Bonds	Effective Sale Price with Futures Hedge	Effective Sale Price with Protective Puts
8,000,000	9,767,401	9,686,362
8,200,000	9,745,273	9,666,149
8,400,000	9,725,761	9,648,529
8,600,000	9,709,339	9,633,973
8,800,000	9,696,472	9,622,941
9,000,000	9,685,066	9,613,358
9,200,000	9,676,751	9,606,838
9,400,000	9,670,575	9,602,440
9,600,000	9,668,215	9,601,824
9,800,000	9,667,281	9,777,322
10,000,000	9,668,034	9,977,322
10,200,000	9,670,700	10,177,322
10,400,000	9,676,990	10,377,322
10,600,000	9,684,253	10,577,322
10,800,000	9,694,165	10,777,322
11,000,000	9,706,975	10,977,322
11,200,000	9,719,797	11,177,322
11,400,000	9,735,913	11,377,322
11,600,000	9,752,347	11,577,322

strike price of the call option sold, plus the premium received. In this case the strike price on the futures call option was 120. A futures price of 120 corresponds to a price of 122.9520 (from 120 times the conversion factor of 1.0246), and a corresponding yield of 4.126% for the CTD issue. The equivalent yield for the P&G bond is 111.11 basis points higher, or 5.3271%, for a corresponding price of 103.273. Adding on the premium received, 0.512, the final maximum effective sale price will be about 103.785 or $10,378,500. While not shown here, it can demonstrated that if the P&G bond does trade at 111.1 basis points over the CTD issue as assumed, the maximum effective sale price for the P&G bond is, in fact, slightly more than that amount. The discrepancies shown in the table are due to rounding and the fact that the position is not adjusted even though the relative price values of a basis point change as yields change.

USING INTEREST RATE SWAPS IN BOND PORTFOLIO MANAGEMENT[6]

In Chapter 13, we explained equity swaps. The use of such swaps are far less common than that for interest rate swaps. In this section, we explain how bond portfolio managers can control interest rate risk using interest rate swaps. Although different types of interest rate swaps exist, including vanilla swaps, basis swaps, indexed-amortizing swaps, and callable swaps, to name a few, here our focus is on generic interest rate swaps as hedge instruments.

We begin with a brief description of the characteristics of interest rate swaps and how a swap can be viewed as a financed bond position. This alternate view is particularly useful for understanding how interest rate swaps can be used to control interest rate risk. We then focus on the valuation and interest rate sensitivity of swaps and go on to develop hedge ratios and hedge strategies using swaps. As we shall illustrate, hedging with swaps is very similar to hedging with Treasury securities and interest rate futures contracts. An example of constructing a hedge for corporate bonds is provided. We conclude by comparing the effectiveness of interest rate swaps as hedge instruments with alternate hedge instruments such as Treasury securities and interest rate futures.

Characterizing Interest Rate Swaps

In its most basic form, an interest rate swap is an agreement between two parties to exchange cash flows periodically. In a plain vanilla swap, one party pays a fixed rate of interest based on a notional amount in return for the receipt of a floating rate of interest based on the same notional amount from the counterparty. These cash flows are exchanged periodically for the life (also known as the tenor) of the swap. Typically, no principal is exchanged at the beginning or end of a swap.

The fixed rate on a swap is ordinarily set at a rate such that the net present value of the swap's cash flow is zero at the start of the swap contract. This type of swap is also known as a *par swap* and the fixed rate is also called the swap rate. The difference between the swap rate and the yield on an equivalent-maturity Treasury is called the *swap spread*.

The floating rate on a swap is typically benchmarked off the London Interbank Offered Rate (LIBOR) or constant maturity Treasury (CMT) rate. In a plain vanilla swap, the floating rate is 3-month LIBOR, which resets and pays quarterly in arrears on an actual/360 daycount basis. The fixed

---

[6] This section is coauthored with Shrikant Ramamurthy, Managing Director, RBS Greenwich Capital.

rate is paid semiannually on a 30/360 daycount basis, which is similar to the convention in the corporate bond market.[7]

Interest rate swaps also can be callable prior to maturity by one of the parties in the swap. These types of swaps are called *callable swaps* and the fixed rate is adjusted to reflect the value of the call option and the nature (long or short) of the option position.

Swaps as Financed Bond Positions

Conceptually, from the propsective of the fixed rate receiver (floating rate payer), a position in an interest rate swap can be viewed as a long fixed rate bond position that is totally financed at short-term interest rates, such as term repurchase (repo) rates or LIBOR. In a fully financed long bond position, fixed rate interest payments are received and floating rate financing costs are paid periodically, with the final principal payment from the bond used to repay the initial financing of the bond purchase. On a net basis, a fully financed bond position has zero cost, like a swap, and the periodic cash flows replicate the cash flows on a swap. In fact, a swap from the perspective of the fixed rate receiver is a fully leveraged bond position where the financing rate is equivalent to the floating rate on a swap. Hence, this alternate view of an interest rate swap from the perspective of the fixed rate receiver is appealing because it implies that a swap can be used as an alternative hedging vehicle to Treasury securities and futures contracts to manage interest rate risk.

The position of a floating rate payer (fixed rate receiver) is equivalent to shorting a fixed rate bond and investing the proceeds in a floating rate bond. Once again, this is applying because it suggests that swaps can be used as an alternative instrument to manage interest rate risk.

Pricing of Interest Rate Swaps

The pricing of a swap requires the same financial tools that are used in the pricing of debt instruments. Essentially, the value of a generic swap is the present value of a series of uncertain net cash flows that are dependent on interest rates. In a generic interest rate swap, the cash flows on the fixed component are known at the inception of the swap. However, the future cash flows on the floating component are unknown.

The future floating rates for purposes of valuing a swap are derived from forward rates that are embedded in the current yield curve. For float-

---

[7]Paid in arrears means that the floating rate for a particular quarter is set at the beginning of the quarter and the associated cash flow is exchanged at the end of the quarter.

ing rates based off of LIBOR benchmarks, forward rates also can be determined from the various Eurodollar futures contracts.

A Eurodollar CD is a dollar-denominated CD issued outside of the United States, typically by a European bank. The interest rate paid on Eurodollar CDs is LIBOR. Three-month LIBOR is the underlying for the Eurodollar futures contract. That is, the parties are agreeing to buy and sell "three-month LIBOR."

Eurodollar futures contracts trade with four maturities each year for approximately 10 years and each contract is settled into the three-month spot LIBOR at the maturity of the contract. Although forward rates may or may not be good predictors of future rates, forward rates can be realized in future time periods via simple hedging strategies. As a result, the uncertainty associated with floating rate cash flows in a swap can be addressed and hedged.

By utilizing forward rates, a swap net cash flow can be derived throughout the life of a swap. The sum of these cash flows discounted at the corresponding forward rate for each time period is the current value of the swap. Mathematically, the value of a swap position is

$$\text{Swap value} = \sum_{i=1}^{n} PV_i[\text{Fixed cash flow}(i) - \text{Floating cash flow}(i)] \quad (24.4)$$

The discount rates used to value the future cash flows from a swap are typically forward LIBOR rates irrespective of the counterparties involved. The counterparty risk in a swap is usually accounted for through collateral arrangements that guarantee future net cash flows, and these collateral amounts vary depending on each counterparty's credit risk. As a result, swap rates are generic and do not vary between differently rated counterparties.

Equation (24.4) also can be used to determine swap rates. The swap rate is the fixed rate on a par swap. Fair swap rates for specific maturities can be computed by finding the fixed rate in equation (24.4) that provides a swap value of zero. Table 24.6 illustrates the cash flows for a hypothetical two-year swap and utilizes equation (24.4) to determine the value of the swap. At a fixed rate of 6.225%, the swap has zero value and is a fair swap.

The value of a swap can be computed alternatively by viewing the swap as an equivalent bond position as discussed earlier. In this approach, the value of a swap is simply the difference between the value of a fixed rate bond with a coupon equal to the fixed rate on the swap and a floating rate bond that pays a coupon equal to the floating rate on the swap. Again the bonds and each of their cash flows are priced against LIBOR discount rates in keeping with the convention in the swap market. In this approach, the value of the swap is given mathematically by:

Using Derivatives in Bond Portfolio Management

TABLE 24.6 Pricing of a Two-Year Interest Rate Swap

Maturity	2 years
Fixed rate	6.225%, semiannually, 30/360
Floating rate	3-month LIBOR, quarterly, 30/360
Notional amount	$100

Time (years)	Implied 3 Mo. LIBOR (%)	Cash Flows ($) Fixed	Cash Flows ($) Floating	Net Cash Flows ($)	Present Value of $1 ($)	Present Value of Net Cash Flows ($)
0.00	5.750				1.0000	0.0000
0.25	5.875	0.0000	1.4375	−1.4375	0.9858	−1.4171
0.50	6.000	3.1125	1.4688	1.6438	0.9716	1.5970
0.75	6.125	0.0000	1.5000	−1.5000	0.9572	−1.4358
1.00	6.250	3.1125	1.5313	1.5813	0.9428	1.4907
1.25	6.375	0.0000	1.5625	−1.5625	0.9283	−1.4504
1.50	6.500	3.1125	1.5938	1.5188	0.9137	1.3877
1.75	6.625	0.0000	1.6250	−1.6250	0.8991	−1.4610
2.00	6.750	3.1125	1.6563	1.4563	0.8844	1.2880
				Value of swap [equation (24.4)] =		0.00

Note: Typically, the floating rate on a swap is paid on an Actual/360 day-count basis. In this table, the floating rate is assumed to be paid on a 30/360 daycount basis for convenience.

$$\text{Swap value} = \text{Fixed rate bond} - \text{Floating rate bond} \quad (24.52)$$

In a generic interest rate swap, the value of the floating rate bond on each reset date is equal to par. This is because, going forward from each reset date, the interest cash flows on the floating rate bond are equal to LIBOR rates and the discount rates used to present value future interest and principal cash flows are also LIBOR rates. Essentially, going forward from each reset date, the floating rate bond provides a coupon equal to what is expected by the marketplace. As a result, by definition, on these dates the value of the floating rate bond should be equal to par. Incorporating this into equation (24.5), we can restate the value of a generic swap on a reset date to be equal to:

$$\text{Swap value on reset date} = \text{Value of fixed rate bond} - 100 \quad (24.6)$$

Any of these equations (24.4), (24.5), and (24.6) can be used to value a swap. Typically, on a reset date, it is easier to value a swap using equation (24.6) given that forward floating rate coupons need not be determined. Between reset dates, equation (24.5) can be a simple way to value a swap given that the value of the floating rate component can be estimated as a fixed rate bond that matures at par on the next reset date. In this approach also, forward floating rate coupons do not have to be determined.

Interest Rate Sensitivity of a Swap

Although the value of a swap is a function of both long- and short-bond positions, it is still very sensitive to interest rates. Figure 24.2 shows the price profile of a currently par priced swap to changes in interest rates. The swap in is the same as the swap in Table 24.6. For comparison purposes, the values of the fixed rate and floating rate bonds that make up the equivalent portfolio are shown as well.

The swap currently has no value and both the fixed and floating rate bonds are priced at par. As rates decline, the value of the swap increases as the fixed rate cash-flow receipts become more valuable in the lower-rate

FIGURE 24.2 Price Sensitivity of a Two-Year Interest Rate Swap

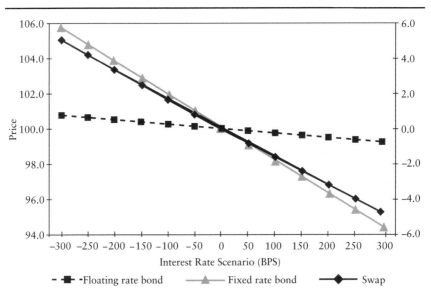

Note: The pricing on the floating rate bond assumes that the coupon for the first period has already been set.

environment. The value of the swap does not increase as much as that of the fixed rate bond because the increase in the value of the swap in declining-rate scenarios is constrained by the increase in the value of the floating rate bond. However, given that the increase in the floating rate bond is minimal, the change in the value of the swap is similar to the change in the value of the fixed rate bond. In environments where rates rise, the value to the swap falls like that of the fixed rate bond; however, the decline in value is slightly reduced by the short floating rate position.

Like a fixed rate bond, an interest rate swap displays positive convexity, which, as explained in Chapter 21, means that the increase in the value of a swap for a decline in rates is larger than the loss associated with a similar increase in rates. The similar price profile between a fixed rate bond and a swap is important to note because it is this similarity that makes swaps an efficient and alternate hedge instrument for bonds.

PVBP of a Swap

The *price value of a basis point* (PVBP) of a swap measures the dollar sensitivity of a swap for changes in interest rates. The PVBP of a swap is the change in the value of a swap for a 1 basis point change in rates. As it was for using Treasury futures and options for hedging, the PVBP is the key measure in developing a hedge ratio when using interest rate swaps.

The PVBP of a swap can be computed using equation (24.5) as follows:

PVBP(Swap) = PVBP(Fixed rate bond) − PVBP(Floating rate bond) (24.7)

The PVBP using equation (24.7) is usually computed on a notional amount of $1 million. Implicitly, the PVBP computation assumes that rate movements are parallel, with the entire yield curve shifting in equal fashion. Typically, PVBP is computed using increments of 10 to 25 basis points. Since PVBP is computed using scenarios where rates rise and fall, the PVBP computation is an average sensitivity measure and will not measure exactly the sensitivity in either scenario.

Table 24.7 shows the PVBP computation for the two-year swap example used in Table 24.6 and Figure 24.2. The PVBP of the swap is $160.71—slightly less than the PVBP of a two-year fixed rate bond at $185.36. The PVBP of a swap is slightly less than that of fixed rate bond to account for the short position in the floating rate bond, which has a PVBP of $24.65. Equation (24.7) provides the PVBP for the swap.

In general, the PVBP of a swap is approximately equal to the PVBP of a fixed rate bond with maturity spanning from the next reset date to the maturity date of the swap. The PVBP of a five-year swap is similar to the PVBP of

TABLE 24.7 PVBP Computation for a Swap

Maturity	2 years
Fixed rate	6.225%, semiannually, 30/360
Floating rate	3-month LIBOR, quarterly, 30/360
Notional amount	$1 million

	Total Value ($)		
	Rate Down 10 BPs	No Change	Rates Up 10 BPs
Swap	1,609.25	0.00	−1,604.95
Fixed rate bond	1,001,855.77	1,000,000	998,148.65
Floating rate bond	1,000,246.52	1,000,000	999,753.60

Note: PVBP computation using equation (24.7):

$$\text{PVBP}_{\text{Swap}} = \text{PVBP (fixed rate bond)} - \text{PVBP (floating rate bond)}$$

$$= \frac{1{,}001{,}855.77 - 998{,}148.65}{20} - \frac{1{,}000{,}246.52 - 999{,}753.60}{20}$$

$$= 185.36 - 24.65$$

$$= \$160.71$$

a 4.75-year fixed rate bond; the PVBP of a 2.25-year swap is similar to the PVBP of a two-year fixed rate bond.

Although the PVBP of a swap is similar to that of a slightly shorter fixed rate bond, the PVBP of a swap will change differently over time from the PVBP on a fixed rate bond. This is important to note in the hedging context. The PVBP of a swap just prior to a reset date will be identical to the PVBP of a fixed rate bond because, at this time, the PVBP of the floating rate bond is zero. However, just after the reset date, the floating rate bond will have a PVBP that is similar to the PVBP of a fixed rate bond to the next reset date. As a result, just after the reset date, the PVBP on a swap will immediately decline by the PVBP of the floating rate bond. Between reset periods, the PVBP of the swap will not change much as both the PVBP of the fixed rate bond and the floating rate bond will decline in similar fashion. This is very different from the PVBP of a fixed rate bond that declines steadily over time.

Figure 24.3 displays, over time, the PVBP for the swap and fixed rate bond used in Tables 24.6 and 24.7, and Figure 24.2. As the tables and figure illustrate, the PVBP of the fixed rate bond declines as a function of time, while the PVBP of the swap declines in a jump fashion around the reset date of the floating rate on the swap. The PVBP is relatively stable between reset

FIGURE 24.3 PVBP of a Two-Year Swap and Fixed Rate Bond over Time

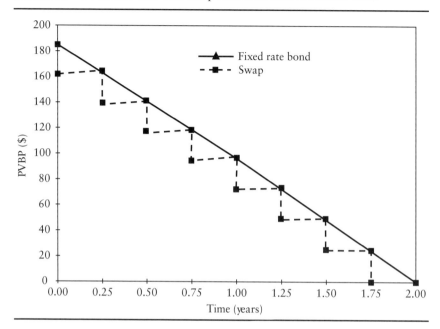

dates and actually increases incrementally as the next reset date approaches. The PVBP of a swap actually increases slightly between reset dates because the PVBP of a floating rate note declines slightly faster than the PVBP of a fixed rate bond during these time periods.[8]

Hedging with Interest Rate Swaps

Hedging bonds with interest rates swaps is similar to hedging bonds with Treasury notes or futures contracts as we illustrated earlier in this chapter. To hedge a long position in a bond, an asset manager needs to establish a pay-fixed swap position since changes in the value of a swap are inversely related to changes in the value of the bond being hedged. Recall that in a pay-fixed swap position, which is analogous to a short-bond position, the asset manager pays a fixed rate to receive a floating rate. In designing a hedge using interest rate swaps, the maturity of the interest rate swap should

---

[8]The modified duration and PVBP of a bond is a concave monotonic function of maturity, that is the duration and PVBP increase at a decreasing rate as a function of maturity. As a result, the PVBP of a floating rate bond, which essentially behaves like a short dated fixed rate bond, decreases faster over time than the PVBP of a long dated fixed rate bond.

match the maturity of the instrument that is used as the pricing reference for the security being hedged. This is analogous to hedging in the Treasury market.

For example, if a two-year corporate bond is priced relative to the two-year Treasury, the corporate bond's price changes as yield spreads change and as the yield on the two-year Treasury changes. The appropriate swap hedge for this corporate bond is a two-year swap since it is also priced relative to the two-year Treasury. A two-year swap's value changes as swap spreads change and as the two-year Treasury's yield changes. As a result of using a two-year swap to hedge the corporate bond, the interest rate risk of the two-year corporate bond that is attributable to movements in two-year Treasury yields can be mitigated. To the extent that the two-year corporate bond's yield spread is correlated to two-year swap spreads, spread risk also may be mitigated.

Hedge Ratio

The hedge ratio for hedging a bond using interest rate swaps is a function of the PVBPs of the swap and the security to be hedged, and is expressed as:

$$\text{Hedge ratio} = \frac{\text{PVBP of security to be hedged}}{\text{PVBP of swap}} \quad (24.8)$$

Recall that the PVBP of an interest rate swap is similar to that of a fixed rate bond with a maturity from the swap's next reset date to the swap's maturity date. Thus, the hedge ratio using interest rate swaps generally will be slightly higher than the hedge ratio using Treasuries.

Corporate Bond Swap Hedge Illustration

Table 24.8 describes a hedge for a long position in TCI Corporation 9.25s of April 15, 2002, as of June 16, 1997. Since the TCI notes are priced off five-year Treasury rates, the appropriate hedge instrument using swaps is a five-year interest rate swap, which is similarly affected by movements in five-year yields. The hedge ratio using swaps is 1.061, implying that approximately $1.061 million notional amount of five-year swaps need to be sold in order to hedge $1 million TCI corporate notes. If five-year Treasuries are used as a substitute, the hedge ratio will be slightly smaller because the five-year Treasury has a higher PVBP.

If the TCI position is not hedged, the portfolio can gain or lose approximately $21,000 if rates move 50 basis points. In contrast, the hedged portfolio provides substantial protection against interest rate movements. If rates

TABLE 24.8 Hedging a Corporate Bond Using Interest Rate Swaps

Objective: Hedge $1 million par amount TCI Corp 9.25s of April 15, 2002, using five-year interest rate swaps.

Issue	Coupon/ Swap Rate (%)	Maturity	Price[a]	Yield (%)	Spread (bps)	PVBP per $1 million Par Amount ($)
TCI Corp	9.25	04/15/02	107.915	7.27	+100	420.27
5-Year Swap	6.53	06/19/02	0.000	—	+26	396.20

$$\text{Hedge Ratio} = \frac{420.27}{396.20} = 1.061$$

Change in Portfolio Value[a]

	Unhedged Portfolio	Hedged Portfolio
Rates increase by 50 basis points	1,058,390 − 1,079,150 = −20,760	(1,058,390 − 1,079,150) − 1,061(−19,550) = 17.45
Rates decrease by 50 basis points	1,100,420 − 1,079,150 = 21,270	(1,100,420 − 1,079,150) − 1.061(20,080) = −34.88

[a] Prices as of June 16, 1997.

move 50 basis points, the hedged portfolio moves minimally in value. This analysis assumes that yield spreads are unchanged and does not account for any bid-offer spread in the markets. If spread changes on the corporate bond position are accompanied by similar spread changes on the five-year swap, the swap hedge will also eliminate spread risk. If corporate spreads are negatively correlated with swap spreads, then a swap-based hedge will increase the exposure to spread risk. Generally though, swap spreads move in the same direction as corporate spreads and provide protection against general movements in corporate spreads. Of course, given the generic nature of swap spreads, they will never provide protection against the idiosyncratic risk of any particular corporate credit.

One point to note when using swaps as a hedge instrument is that the PVBP of a swap declines on a reset date (see Figure 24.3). This implies that on swap reset dates, the existing swap position may need to be adjusted by shorting additional swaps with the same remaining term-to-maturity to match the PVBP of the security being hedged.

Swaps vs. Other Hedge Instruments

Usually, bonds are hedged in the cash market using Treasury securities or in the futures markets with Treasury futures. The Treasury market can provide effective and similar protection as interest rate swaps when hedging against interest rate risk. The advantage of the Treasury market is that it is a highly liquid market with very small bid-offer costs, especially in on-the-run maturities. It is also easy to enter into and liquidate Treasury positions quickly and efficiently. In contrast, interest rate swaps, although liquid, have higher bid-offer costs (typically one basis point in yield) and are more time consuming to enter and exit. Since swaps are customized contracts between two parties and are not exchange traded, they cannot be sold and actually have to be terminated, which is time consuming and can be less efficient. Alternatively, a swap position can be effectively terminated by entering into an opposite position in another interest rate swap; however, this strategy is not efficient. For short-term hedging purposes, Treasuries may be more desirable hedge instruments.

Many times in the hedging context, however, hedging in the Treasury market may be expensive for one of the reasons cited earlier in this chapter: if a Treasury security that is on "special" or if an off-the-run Treasury needs to be utilized in the hedge. Interest rate swaps can be cheaper alternatives in these cases. Swaps can be structured for any off-the-run maturity and supply is never an issue given the liquidity in the Eurodollar market, especially five years and in.

Swaps have other advantages over Treasury securities. Swaps are off-balance-sheet instruments, unlike Treasury securities, and therefore should not affect the capital structure. In addition, to the extent that swap spreads are correlated with the spread of the security being hedged, an interest rate swap will provide some protection against spread risk, unlike both Treasury securities and Treasury futures contracts. Another advantage of an interest rate swap is that, because it is a structured agreement, call options and amortization can be embedded into a swap. This is particularly useful when hedging amortizing and/or callable securities.

The behavior of the PVBP of a swap can be both an advantage and disadvantage versus other hedge instruments. Recall that the PVBP of a swap is fairly constant between the reset dates of the swap. This is unlike a Treasury security whose PVBP declines continuously over time. Thus, when hedging a constant-duration portfolio (e.g., an indexed bond portfolio), an interest rate swap is an attractive hedging instrument as the hedge ratio does not change as a function of time between reset dates.

In comparing futures contracts with swaps, futures do not have any liquidity constraints. However, the use of futures in the hedging context exposes the hedged portfolio to basis risk. Basis risk refers to the scenario in which movements in futures prices do not exactly correspond to movements in cash Treasury prices. A futures contract's price movements generally are related to price movements in the Treasury security that is the cheapest to deliver into the futures contract, which typically is not an on-the-run Treasury. Thus, when hedging a security that is priced relative to an on-the-run Treasury with a futures contract, there is the risk that movements in futures prices will not fully hedge price movements in the bond. An interest rate swap does not have the basis risk that is inherent in a futures contract since on-the-run swaps are priced relative to on-the-run Treasuries. From a basis risk standpoint, interest rate swaps are better hedging instruments than futures contracts.

USING STOCK INDEX FUTURES AND TREASURY BOND FUTURES TO IMPLEMENT AN ASSET ALLOCATION DECISION

As explained in Chapter 1, one of the major tasks in investment management is the allocation of funds among major asset classes. As the asset allocation of a client changes, it is necessary to shift funds among the asset classes. Funds can be shifted in one of two ways. The most obvious is by buying or selling the amount specified in the asset mix in the cash market. The costs associated with shifting funds in this manner are the transaction costs with respect to commissions, bid-ask spreads, and market impact. Moreover, there will be a disruption of the activities of the asset managers who are managing funds for each asset class. For example, a pension sponsor typically engages certain assets managers for managing equity funds, and different ones for managing bond funds. An asset allocation decision requiring the reallocation of funds will necessitate the withdrawal of funds from some asset managers and the placement of funds with others. If the shift is temporary, there will be a subsequent revision of the asset allocation, further disrupting the activities of the asset managers.

An alternative approach is to use the futures market to change an exposure to an asset class. As we explained in this chapter and in Chapter 13, buying futures contracts increases exposure to the asset class underlying the futures contract, while selling futures contracts reduces it. For the major asset classes, equities and bonds, a client can use stock index futures and Treasury bond futures to alter the asset mix. The advantages of using financial futures contracts over transacting in the cash market for each asset class are (1) transaction costs are lower; (2) execution is faster in the futures market; (3) market impact costs are avoided or reduced because the the asset manager has more time to buy and sell securities in the cash market; and (4) activities of the asset managers employed by the client are not disrupted. A strategy of using futures for asset allocation to avoid disrupting the activities of asset managers is sometimes referred to as an *overlay strategy*.

USING CREDIT DEFAULT SWAPS TO MANAGE CREDIT RISK

Thus far, our focus has been on using derivatives to control interest rate risk. Another major risk exposure of a bond portfolio is credit risk. There are derivatives instruments that are available to provide credit protection or to obtain credit exposure. The general name for these types of derivatives is *credit derivatives*. The type of credit derivative that is the most commonly used is a *credit default swap* (CDS). Here our focus will be only this type of credit derivative. More specifically, there are two types of CDS: single-name CDS and credit default swap index. We will describe the features of these two credit default swaps and how they can be used to manage credit risk. It is important to emphasize that a CDS is an OTC instrument. Therefore, while this derivative can be used to control credit risk, there is counterparty risk in a CDS trade that must be taken into account.

Single-Name Credit Default Swaps

A credit default swap is employed to shift credit exposure to a credit protection seller. A CDS that involves only one entity for which credit protection is being transferred is called a *single-name credit default swap*. The entity that is the underlying for the contract is either referred to as the reference entity or reference obligation. The *reference entity* is the issuer of the bond and hence is also referred to as the *reference issuer*. For example, the reference issuer could be Procter & Gamble. Rather than a reference entity, the underlying for a single-name CDS could be a specific bond issue. In such cases, the underlying is referred to as the *reference obligation*. For example, Procter & Gamble has many bond issues outstanding. Any one of those issues could be the reference obligation for a single-name CDS. Typically, the underlying for a single-name CDS involving a corporate entity is a reference entity.

The mechanics of a single-name CDS are as follows. There are two parties to the contract: the buyer of the CDS and the seller of the CDS. The buyer of the CDS is the party that is seeking credit protection for the reference entity. The seller of the CDS is the party that is providing protection to the CDS buyer for the reference entity. The credit protection being sought is against the occurrence of a *credit event*. That is, if a credit event occurs with respect to the reference entity, the protection seller (i.e., seller of the CDS) must compensate the protection buyer (i.e., buyer of the CDS). To understand the mechanics of the contract we need to understand: (1) what a credit event is and (2) what the potential cash flows are for the two parties to the contract.

One might think that a credit event is the default or bankruptcy of the reference entity. However, that is not true. Default or bankruptcy are only two types of credit events. What constitutes a credit event is defined in the legal documentation for a CDS trade. That documentation, which is the standard contract for a CDS trade developed by the International Swap and Derivatives Association (ISDA), defines eight credit events that attempt to capture every type of situation that could cause the credit quality of the reference entity to deteriorate, or cause the value of the bonds of the reference entity to decline in value. These eight events include (1) bankruptcy, (2) failure to pay, (3) repudiation/moratorium, (4) downgrade, (5) restructuring, (6) credit event upon merger, (7) cross acceleration, and (8) cross default.

Here is a brief description of the first five credit events that are probably the most important in a CDS. *Bankruptcy* is defined as a variety of acts that are associated with bankruptcy or insolvency laws. *Failure to pay* means that the reference entity fails to make one or more required payments on any debt obligation when due. To understand a *repudiation/moratorium*, some background information is needed. When a reference entity breaches a covenant, it has defaulted on its obligation. When a default occurs, the obligation becomes due and payable prior to the scheduled due date had the reference entity not defaulted and this is referred to as an *obligation acceleration*. When a reference entity disaffirms or challenges the validity of its obligation, this is covered by repudiation/moratorium. A *downgrade* means the lowering of the credit rating of the reference entity's obligations. The most controversial credit event is restructuring of an obligation. A *restructuring* occurs when the terms of the obligation are altered so as to make the new terms less attractive to the debt holder than the original terms. The terms that can be changed would typically include, but are not limited to, one or more of the following: (1) a reduction in the interest rate; (2) a reduction in the principal; (3) a rescheduling of the principal repayment schedule (e.g., lengthening the maturity of the obligation) or postponement of an interest payment; or (4) a change in the level of seniority of the obligation in the reference entity's debt structure.

The above definitions are set forth in more detail in the *1999 ISDA Credit Derivatives Definitions* as modified in 2001 by the *Restructuring Supplement to the 1999 ISDA Credit Derivatives Definitions* and then in 2003 by the *2003 ISDA Credit Derivative Definitions*. In the documentation for a specific CDS trade, there is checkbox whereby the counterparties to the trade specify the credit events that are applicable.

Now let's look at the cash flows for a single-name CDS trade. The protection buyer pays a premium periodically (typically every quarter) to the credit protection seller in return for the right to receive a payment conditional upon the occurrence of a credit event by the reference entity. The premium is called the *swap payment*. If no credit event occurs over the life of the contract, then the credit protection buyer makes the payments up to the contract's maturity date. At that time, the contract terminates. If a credit event occurs, the credit protection buyer is responsible for the accrued premium up to the date of the credit event and the credit protection seller must perform depending on the settlement procedure set forth in the legal documentation. The contract terminates after the credit event occurs.

The settlement procedure involves either (1) a payment by the credit protection seller to the credit protection buyer for the deterioration in the value of an obligation of the reference entity or (2) the purchase at par value of a bond delivered by the credit protection buyer to the credit protection seller. The first form of settlement is referred to as *cash settlement*; the second form is called *physical settlement*.

With cash settlement, the methods used to determine the amount of the payment that the credit protection seller must make varies. A single-name CDS can specify at the trade date the exact amount of the payment that will be made by the protection seller should a credit event occur. Conversely, the trade can be structured so that the amount of the swap payment is determined after the credit event. Under these circumstances, the amount payable by the protection seller is determined based upon the observed prices of similar debt obligations of the reference entity in the market.

When there is physical settlement, the credit protection buyer has the right to select from a preset of *deliverable obligations*, the particular issue to deliver. Just as with Treasury futures contract, there will be a cheapest-to-deliver issue.

In a typical credit default swap, the protection buyer pays for the protection premium over several settlement dates rather than upfront, typically quarterly. In the case of quarterly payments, the payment is computed as follows:

$$\begin{aligned}&\text{Quarterly swap premium payment}\\&= \text{Notional amount swap rate (in decimal form)}\\&\quad \times \text{Actual no. of days in quarter}/360\end{aligned}$$

How Asset Managers Can Use Single-Name CDS

The most obvious way for an asset manager to use a single-name CDS is to acquire credit protection for the holding of a credit name in its portfolio. The question is why doesn't the asset manager just sell the bonds? There are two reasons. First, the market for corporate bonds is not very liquid. The asset manager may find it beneficial to acquire protection rather than sell the bond when there is poor liquidity. Second, there may be a tax reason for doing so. For example, the asset manager may have to hold a corporate bond for say two months in order to benefit from a favorable capital gains treatment. A single-name CDS can be used to provide protection against credit risk during that two month period.

If an asset manager wants to purchase the obligation of a corporate entity (i.e., gain long exposure), then the most obvious way to do so is to purchase the bond in the cash market. However, as just noted, because of the illiquidity of the corporate bond market, there may be better execution by transacting in the CDS market. More specifically, the selling of credit protection on a corporate entity provides long credit exposure to that entity. To understand why, consider what happens when an asset manager sells credit protection on a reference entity. The asset manager receives the swap premium and if there is no credit event, the swap premium is received over the life of the CDS contract. However, this is equivalent to buying the bond of the corporate entity. Instead of receiving coupon interest payments, the asset manager receives the swap premium payments. If there is a credit event, then the asset manager under the terms of the CDS must make a payment to the credit protection buyer. However, this is equivalent to a loss that would be realized if the bond was purchased. Hence, selling credit protection via a single-name CDS is economically equivalent to a long position in the reference entity.

Suppose that an asset manager wants to short a corporate bond because it is believed that the corporation is going to experience a credit event that will cause a decline in the value of the bond. In the absence of a CDS, the asset manager would have to short the bonds in the cash market. However, it is extremely difficult to short corporate bonds. With a liquid single-name CDS, it is easy to effectively short the bond of a corporate entity. Remember that shorting a bond involves making payments to another party and then if the investor is correct and the bond's price declines, sells the bond at a higher price (i.e., realizes a gain). That is precisely what occurs when a single-name CDS is purchased: the investor makes payments (the swap premium payments) and realizes a gain if a credit event occurs. Hence, buying credit protection via a single-name CDS is equivalent to shorting.

Finally, for an asset manager seeking a leveraged position in a corporate bond, this can be achieved by selling credit protection. As just noted, selling credit protection is equivalent to a long position in the reference entity. Moreover, as with other derivatives, CDS allows this to be done on a leveraged basis.

Credit Default Swap Index

Unlike a single-name CDS, the underlying for a *credit default swap index* (CDX) is a standardized basket of reference entities. There are standardized CDX compiled and managed by Dow Jones. For the corporate bond indexes, there are separate indexes for investment-grade corporate entities, the most actively traded being the North America Investment Grade Index (denoted by DJ.CDX.NA.IG). As the index name suggests, the reference entities in this index are those with an investment-grade rating. The index includes 125 corporate names in North America with each corporate name having an equally weight in the index (0.8%). The index is updated semiannually by Dow Jones.

The mechanics of a CDX are different from that of a single-name CDS. For both types of CDS, there is a swap premium that is paid periodically. If a credit event occurs, the swap premium payment ceases in the case of a single-name CDS and the contract is terminated. In contrast, for a CDX, the swap payment continues to be made by the credit protection buyer. However, the amount of the quarterly swap premium payment is reduced. This is because the notional amount is reduced as result of a credit event for a reference entity.

For example, suppose that a portfolio manager is the protection buyer for a DJ.CDX.NA.IG and the notional amount is $100 million. The formula given earlier for the quarterly swap premium payment is used to compute the payment for a CDX. At the outset of the CDX trade (before a credit event), the premium would be based on a notional amount of $100 million. If a credit event occurs for one of the reference entity, the notional amount for computing future swap premium payments is reduced by $80,000 (0.8% times $100 million) to $99,920,000.

How Asset Managers Can Use CDX

What we said earlier about how an asset manager can use a single-name CDX applies equally to CDX. However, rather than managing exposure to a single entity, a CDX allows the management of exposure to a diversified portfolio of investment-grade corporate names. Thus, an asset manager seeking credit protection for the investment-grade corporate sector of a portfolio can obtain that protection by buying a CDX. This is the same as reducing credit exposure to that sector. A corporate manager seeking to increase exposure to the investment-grade corporate sector can do so by selling a CDX.

SUMMARY

In this chapter, we described how derivatives can be employed in bond portfolio management. Treasury bond and note futures contract are typically used to control the interest rate risk of a portfolio. The price of a Treasury bond and note futures contract differs from the basic model for determining the theoretical futures price of a Treasury bond futures contract because of delivery options associated with these contracts.

Interest rate options include options on bonds (physical options) and options on interest rate futures contracts (futures options). In bond portfolio manager, futures options are the preferred exchange-traded vehicle for implementing investment strategies.

An interest rate swap, when broken into its individual components, can be shown to be economically equivalent to a fully financed fixed rate bond position. Given this view, swaps can be utilized like other bonds and have hedging applications. Interest rate swaps are similar to Treasuries as hedge instruments, although the price value of a basis point of a swap can differ over time from the PVBP of a similar-maturity Treasury. Although just like Treasury and futures contracts, interest rate swaps can be used effectively to manage the interest rate risk in bonds, to the extent that bond spreads are correlated with swap spreads, they can also provide protection from spread risk.

In addition to their use in managing a portfolio of equities and bonds, stock index futures and Treasury bond futures can be employed in an overlay strategy by a client to implement an asset allocation decision.

The Black-Scholes option pricing model has limitations in valuing options on bonds due to the assumptions underlying the model. For valuing options on futures, the most popular model is the Black model.

Hedging bonds with interest rates swaps is similar to hedging bonds with Treasury notes or futures contracts. To hedge a long position in a bond, it is necessary for an asset manager to establish an interest rate swap position in which it receives fixed and pays floating. This is because a pay-fixed swap position is analogous to a short bond position. Compared to employing Treasury futures contracts, hedging with interest rate swaps does not expose the hedged portfolio to basis risk.

Credit derivatives are available to allow an asset manager to obtain credit protection or to take on credit exposure. The most commonly used credit derivative is a credit default swap of which there are two types: single-name CDS and credit default swap index. The buyer of a CDS is the party that is seeking credit protection while the seller of the CDS is the party that is providing protection. The credit protection being sought is against the occurrence of a credit event that is covered by the CDS trade.

Asset managers can use a single-name CDS to acquire credit protection for the holding of a single corporate credit in the portfolio or, in the case of CDX, protection against a specified portfolio of corporate credits. The advantage of doing so with a CDS is that the market for corporate bonds is not very liquid compared to the CDS market for some corporate names. By buying credit protection if the underlying reference entity or entities is not owned, an asset manager can take a short position, something difficult to accomplish in the cash market. By selling a CDS, an asset manager can gain exposure to a corporate entity or a portfolio of corporate entities. More specifically, the selling of credit protection provides long credit exposure.

REFERENCES

Barone-Adesi, G., and R. E. Whaley. 1987. Efficient analytic approximation of American option values. *Journal of Finance* 42, no. 2: 301–320.

Black, F. 1976. The pricing of commodity contracts. *Journal of Financial Economics* 3 (March): 161–179.

Buetow, G. W., Jr., and F. J. Fabozzi. 2001. *Valuation of interest rate swaps and swaptions.* Hoboken, NJ: John Wiley & Sons.

Fabozzi, F. J., S. V. Mann, and M. Choudhry. 2005. Interest-rate swaps and swaptions. In *The handbook of fixed income securities*, 7th ed., edited by F. J. Fabozzi (pp. 1301–1334). New York: McGraw-Hill.

Goodman, L. S. 1985. Introduction to debt options. In *Winning the interest rate game: A guide to debt options,* edited by F. J. Fabozzi (pp. 3–24). Chicago, IL: Probus Publishing.

Part Four

Investment Companies, Exchange-Traded Funds, and Alternative Investments

CHAPTER 25

Investment Companies, Exchange-Traded Funds, and Investment-Oriented Life Insurance

In Part Three of this book, we discuss investments that are alternatives to directly investing in either stocks or bonds. In this chapter we focus on three investment vehicles: investment companies, exchange-traded funds, and investment-oriented insurance. In Chapter 26, the book's final chapter, we turn our attention to three types of alternative assets—hedge funds, private equity, and commodities.

INVESTMENT COMPANIES

Investment companies include open-end mutual funds, closed-end funds, and unit trusts. Shares in investment companies are sold to the public and the proceeds invested in a diversified portfolio of securities. The value of a share of an investment company is called its net asset value. The two types of costs borne by investors in mutual funds are the shareholder sales charge or loads and the annual fund operating expense. Two major advantages of the indirect ownership of securities by investing in mutual funds are (1) risk reduction through diversification; and (2) reduced cost of contracting and processing information because an investor purchases the services of a presumably skilled financial advisor at less cost than if the investor directly and individually negotiated with such an advisor. There is a wide-range of investment companies that invest in different asset classes and with different investment objectives.

This chapter is coauthored with Frank J. Jones.

Types of Investment Companies

There are three types of investment companies: open-end funds, closed-end funds, and unit trusts.

Open-End Funds (Mutual Funds)

Open-end funds, commonly referred to simply as *mutual funds*, are portfolios of securities, mainly stocks, bonds, and money market instruments. There are several important aspects of mutual funds. First, investors in mutual funds own a pro rata share of the overall portfolio. Second, the investment manager of the mutual fund manages the portfolio, that is, buys some securities and sells others (this characteristic is unlike unit investment trusts, discussed later).

Third, the value or price of each share of the portfolio, called the *net asset value* (NAV), equals the market value of the portfolio minus the liabilities of the mutual fund divided by the number of shares owned by the mutual fund investors. That is,

$$NAV = \frac{\text{Market value of portfolio} - \text{Liabilities}}{\text{Number of shares outstanding}}$$

For example, suppose that a mutual fund with 20 million shares outstanding has a portfolio with a market value of $315 million and liabilities of $15 million. The NAV is

$$NAV = \frac{\$315,000,000 - \$15,000,000}{20,000,000} = \$15$$

Fourth, the NAV or price of the fund is determined only once each day, at the close of the day. For example, the NAV for a stock mutual fund is determined from the closing stock prices for the day. Business publications provide the NAV each day in their mutual fund tables. The published NAV's are the closing NAV's.

Fifth, and very importantly, all new investments into the fund or withdrawals from the fund during a day are priced at the closing NAV (investments after the end of the day or on a non-business day are priced at the next day's closing NAV).

The total number of shares in the fund increases if there are more investments than withdrawals during the day, and vice versa. This is the reason such a fund is called an "open-end" fund. For example, assume that at the beginning of a day a mutual fund portfolio has a value of $1 million, there are no liabilities, and there are 10,000 shares outstanding. Thus, the NAV of the fund is $100. Assume that during the day $5,000 is deposited into the fund, $1,000 is withdrawn, and the prices of all the securities in the portfolio remain constant. This means that 50 shares were issued for the $5,000 deposited (since each share is $100) and 10 shares redeemed for $1,000 (again, since each share is $100). The net number of new shares issued is then 40. Therefore, at the end of the day there will be 10,040 shares and the total value of the fund will be $1,004,000. The NAV will remain at $100.

If, instead, the prices of the securities in the portfolio change, both the total size of the portfolio and, therefore, the NAV will change. In the previous example, assume that during the day the value of the portfolio doubles to $2 million. Since deposits and withdrawals are priced at the end-of-day NAV, which is now $200 after the doubling of the portfolio's value, the $5,000 deposit will be credited with 25 shares ($5,000/$200) and the $1,000 withdrawn will reduce the number of shares by 5 shares ($1,000/$200). Thus, at the end of the day there will be 10,020 shares in the fund with an NAV of $200, and the value of the fund will be $2,004,000. (Note that 10,020 shares × $200 NAV equals $2,004,000, the portfolio value).

Overall, the NAV of a mutual fund will increase or decrease due to an increase or decrease in the prices of the securities in the portfolio, respectively. The number of shares in the fund will increase or decrease due to the net deposits into or withdrawals from the fund, respectively. And the total value of the fund will increase or decrease for both reasons.

Closed-End Funds

The shares of a *closed-end fund* are very similar to the shares of common stock of a corporation. The new shares of a closed-end fund are initially issued by an underwriter for the fund. And after the new issue, the number of shares remains constant. This is the reason such a fund is called a "closed-end" fund. After the initial issue, there are no sales or purchases of fund shares by the fund company as there are for open-end funds. The shares are traded on a secondary market, either on an exchange or in the over-the-counter market.

Investors can buy shares either at the time of the initial issue (as discussed below), or thereafter in the secondary market. Shares are sold only on the secondary market. The price of the shares of a closed-end fund are determined by the supply and demand in the market in which these funds are traded. Thus, investors who transact closed-end fund shares must pay a brokerage commission at the time of purchase and at the time of sale.

The NAV of closed-end funds is calculated in the same way as for open-end funds. However, the price of a share in a closed-end fund is determined by supply and demand, so the price can fall below or rise above the net asset value per share. Shares selling below NAV are said to be "trading at a discount," while shares trading above NAV are "trading at a premium." Newspapers list quotations of the prices of these shares under the heading "Closed-End Funds." Some sources also list the NAV and the discount or premium of the shares.

Consequently, there are two important differences between open-end funds and closed-end funds. First, the number of shares of an open-end fund varies because the fund sponsor will sell new shares to investors and buy existing shares from shareholders. Second, by doing so, the share price is always the NAV of the fund. In contrast, closed-end funds have a constant number of shares outstanding because the fund sponsor does not redeem shares and sell new shares to investors (except at the time of a new underwriting). Thus, the price of the fund shares will be determined by supply and demand in the market and may be above or below NAV, as discussed above.

Although the divergence of the price from NAV is often puzzling, in some cases the reasons for the premium or discount are easily understood. For example, a share's price may be below the NAV because the fund has a large built-in tax liability and investors are discounting the share's price for that future tax liability. (We'll discuss this tax liability issue later in this chapter.) A fund's leverage and resulting risk may be another reason for the share's price trading below NAV. A fund's shares may trade at a premium to the NAV because the fund offers relatively cheap access to, and professional management of, stocks in another country about which information is not readily available to or transactions are difficult or expensive for small investors.

Under the Investment Company Act of 1940, closed-end funds are capitalized only once. They make an initial IPO (initial public offering) and then their shares are traded on the secondary market, just like any corporate stock, as discussed earlier. The number of shares is fixed at the IPO; closed-end funds cannot issue more shares. In fact, many closed-end funds become leveraged to raise more funds without issuing more shares.

An important feature of closed-end funds is that the initial investors bear the substantial cost of underwriting the issuance of the funds' shares. The proceeds that the managers of the fund have to invest equals the total paid by initial buyers of the shares minus all costs of issuance. These costs, which average around 7.5% of the total amount paid for the issue, normally include selling fees or commissions paid to the retail brokerage firms that distribute them to the public. The high commissions are strong incentives for retail brokers to recommend these shares to their retail customers, and also for investors to avoid buying these shares on their initial offering.

As explained later in this chapter, exchange-traded funds pose a threat to both mutual funds and closed-end funds. ETFs are essentially hybrid closed-end vehicles, which trade on exchanges but which typically trade very close to NAV.

Since closed-end funds are traded like stocks, the cost to any investor of buying or selling a closed-end fund is the same as that of a stock. The obvious charge is the stock broker's commission. The bid-offer spread of the market on which the stock is traded is also a cost.

Unit Trusts

A *unit trust* is similar to a closed-end fund in that the number of unit certificates is fixed. Unit trusts typically invest in bonds. They differ in several ways from both mutual funds and closed-end funds that specialize in bonds. First, there is no active trading of the bonds in the portfolio of the unit trust. Once the unit trust is assembled by the sponsor (usually a brokerage firm or bond underwriter) and turned over to a trustee, the trustee holds all the bonds until they are redeemed by the issuer. Typically, the only time the trustee can sell an issue in the portfolio is if there is a dramatic decline in the issuer's credit quality. As a result, the cost of operating the trust will be considerably less than costs incurred by either a mutual fund or a closed-end fund. Second, unit trusts have a fixed termination date, while mutual funds and closed-end funds do not. (There are, however, exceptions. Target term closed-end funds have a fixed termination date.) Third, unlike the mutual fund and closed-end fund investor, the unit trust investor knows that the portfolio consists of a specific portfolio of bonds and has no concern that the trustee will alter the portfolio. While unit trusts are common in Europe, they are not common in the United States.

All unit trusts charge a sales commission. The initial sales charge for a unit trust ranges from 3.5% to 5.5%. In addition to these costs, there is the cost incurred by the sponsor to purchase the bonds for the trust that an investor indirectly pays. That is, when the brokerage firm or bond underwriting firm assembles the unit trust, the price of each bond to the trust also includes the dealer's spread. There is also often a commission if the units are sold.

In the remainder this chapter of our primary focus chapter is on open-end (mutual) funds.

Fund Sales Charges and Annual Operating Expenses

There are two types of costs borne by investors in mutual funds. The first is the *shareholder fee*, usually called the *sales charge* or *load*. For securities transactions, this charge is called a *commission*. This cost is a "one-time" charge debited to the investor for a specific transaction, such as a purchase, redemption or exchange. The type of charge is related to the way the fund is sold or distributed. The second cost is the annual fund operating expense, usually called the *expense ratio*, which covers the funds' expenses, the largest of which is for investment management. This charge is imposed annually. This cost occurs on all funds and for all types of distribution. We discuss each cost next.

Sales Charges or Loads

Sales charges on mutual funds are related to their method of distribution. The current menu of sales charges and distribution mechanisms has evolved significantly and is now much more diverse than it was a decade ago. To understand the current diversity and the evolution of distribution mechanisms, consider initially the circumstances of a decade ago. At that time, there were two basic methods of distribution, two types of sales charges, and the type of the distribution was directly related to the type of sales charge.

The two types of distribution were sales force and direct. *Sales-force distribution* occurred via an intermediary, that is via an agent, a stockbroker, insurance agent, or other entity who provided investment advice and incentive to the client, actively "made the sale," and provided subsequent service. This distribution approach is active, that is the fund is typically sold, not bought.

The other approach is *direct* (from the fund company to the investor), whereby there is no intermediary or salesperson to actively approach the client, provide investment advice and service, or make the sale. Rather, the client approaches the mutual fund company, most likely by a "1-800" telephone contact, in response to media advertisements or general information, and opens the account. Little or no investment counsel or service is provided either initially or subsequently. With respect to the mutual fund sale, this is a *passive* approach, although these mutual funds may be quite active in their advertising and other marketing activities. Funds provided by the direct approach are bought, not sold.

There is a *quid pro quo*, however, for the service provided in the sales-force distribution method. The *quid pro quo* is a sales charge borne by the customer and paid to the agent. The sales charge for the agent-distributed fund is called a *load*. The traditional type of load is called a *front-end load*, since the load is deducted initially or "up-front." That is, the load is deducted from the amount invested by the client and paid to the agent/distributor. The remainder is the net amount invested in the fund in the client's name. For example, if the load on the mutual fund is 5% and the investor invests $100, the $5 load is paid to the agent and the remaining $95 is the net amount invested in the mutual fund at NAV. Importantly, only $95, not $100, is invested in the fund. The fund is, thus, said to be "purchased above NAV" (i.e., the investor pays $100 for $95 of the fund). The $5 load compensates the sales agent for the investment advice and service provided to the client by the agent. The load to the client, of course, represents income to the agent.

Let's contrast this with directly placed mutual funds. There is no sales agent and, therefore, there is no need for a sales charge. Funds with no sales charges are called *no-load mutual funds*. In this case, if the client provides $100 to the mutual fund, $100 is invested in the fund in the client's name. This approach to buying the fund is called buying the fund "at NAV," that is, the whole amount provided by the investor is invested in the fund.

Previously, many observers speculated that load funds would become obsolete and no-load funds would dominate because of the sales charge. Increasingly financially sophisticated individuals, the reasoning went, would make their own investment decisions and not need to compensate agents for their advice and service. But the actual trend has been quite different.

Why has the trend not been away from the more costly agent-distributed funds as many expected? There are two reasons. First, many investors have remained dependent on the investment counsel and service, and perhaps more importantly, the initiative of the sales agent. Second, sales-force distributed funds have shown considerable ingenuity and flexibility in imposing sales charges, which both compensate the distributors and are acceptable to the clients. Among the recent adaptations of the front-end sales load are *back-end loads* and *level loads*. While the front-end load is imposed at the time of the purchase of the fund, the back-end load is imposed at the time fund shares are sold or redeemed. Level loads are imposed uniformly each year. These two alternative methods both provide ways to compensate the agent. However, unlike with the front-end load, both of these distribution mechanisms permit the client to buy a fund at NAV—that is, not have any of their initial investment debited as a sales charge before it is invested in their account.

The most common type of back-end load currently is the *contingent deferred sales charge* (CDSC). This approach imposes a gradually declining load on withdrawal. For example, a common "3,3,2,2,1,1,0" CDSC approach imposes a 3% load on the amount withdrawn within one year, 3% within the second year, 2% within the third year, and so on. There is no sales charge for withdrawals after the sixth year. Thus, the sales charge is postponed or deferred, and it is contingent upon how long the investment is held.

The third type of load is neither a front-end load at the time of investment nor a (gradually declining) back-end load at the time of withdrawal, but a constant load each year (e.g., a 1% load every year). This approach is called a *level load*. Most mutual fund families are strictly either no-load (direct) or load (sales-force).

Many load type mutual fund families often offer their funds with all three types of loads—that is, front-end loads (usually called *A shares*); back-end loads (often called *B shares*); and level loads (often called *C shares*). These families permit the distributor and its client to select the type of load they prefer.[1] These different types of load shares are called share *classes*. A recent type of share class is *F shares*. F shares have no front, level or back loads. In this way they are like C shares. But F shares have considerably lower annual expenses than C shares, as will be seen below. F shares are designed for financial planners who charge annual fees (called fee-based financial planners) rather than sales charges such as commissions or loads. F shares of a fund family may only be sold by investment dealers and their representatives which have an arrangement with the fund family.

According to the National Association of Securities Dealers (NASD), the maximum allowable sales charge is 8.5%, although most funds impose lower charges.

The sales charge for a fund applies to most, even very small, investments (although there is typically a minimum initial investment). For large investments, however, the sales charge may be reduced. For example, a fund with a 4.5% front-end load may reduce this load to 3.0% for investments over $1 million. At some level of investment the front-end load will be 0%. There may be in addition further reductions in the sales charge at greater investments. The amount of investment needed to obtain a reduction in the sales charge is called a *breakpoint*—the breakpoint is $1 million in this example. There are also mechanisms whereby the total amount of the investment necessary to qualify for the breakpoint does not need to be invested up front, but only over time (according to a "letter of intent" signed by the investor).[2] Fund returns are calculated without subtracting sales charges since different individual investors have different sales charges (e.g., may have different breakpoints).

The sales charge is, in effect, paid by the client to the distributor. How does the fund family, typically called the sponsor or manufacturer of the fund, cover its costs and make a profit? This is the topic of the second type of "cost" to the investor, the fund annual operating expense.

Annual Operating Expenses (Expense Ratio)

The *operating expense*, also called the *expense ratio*, is debited annually from the investor's fund balance by the fund sponsor. The three main categories of annual operating expenses are the management fee, distribution fee, and other expenses.

The *management fee*, also called the *investment advisory fee*, is the fee charged by the investment advisor for managing a fund's portfolio. If the investment advisor is part of a company separate from the fund sponsor, some or all of this investment advisory fee is passed on to the investment advisor by

---

[1] See O'Neal (1999).
[2] See Inro, Jaing, Ho, and Lee (1999).

the fund sponsor. In this case, the fund manager is called a *subadvisor*. The management fee varies by the type of fund, specifically by the risk of the asset class of the fund. For example, the management fee as well as the risk may increase from money market funds to bond funds, to U.S. growth stock funds, to emerging market stock funds, as illustrated by examples to come.

In 1980, the SEC approved the imposition of a fixed annual fee, called the *12b-1 fee*, which is, in general, intended to cover *distribution costs*, also including continuing agent compensation and manufacturer marketing and advertising expenses. Such l2b-1 fees are now imposed by many mutual funds. By law, 12b-1 fees cannot exceed 1% of the fund's assets per year. The 12b-1 fee may also include a service fee of up to 0.25% of assets per year to compensate sales professionals for providing services or maintaining shareholder accounts. The major rationale for the component of the l2b-1 fee which accrues to the selling agent is to provide an incentive to selling agents to continue to service their accounts after having received a transaction-based fee such as a front-end load. As a result, a 12b-1 fee of this type is consistent with sales-force sold, load funds, not with directly sold, no-load funds. The rationale for the component of the 12b-1 fee which accrues to the manufacturer of the fund is to provide incentive and compensate for continuing advertising and marketing costs.

Other expenses include primarily the costs of (1) custody (holding the cash and securities of the fund); (2) the transfer agent (transferring cash and securities among buyers and sellers of securities and the fund distributions, etc.); (3) independent public accountant fees; and (4) directors' fees.

The sum of the annual management fee, the annual distribution fee, and other annual expenses is called the expense ratio or annual operating expense. All the cost information on a fund, including selling charges and annual expenses, are included in the fund prospectus. In addition to the annual operating expenses, the fund prospectus provides the fees which are imposed only at the time of a fund transaction.

As we explained earlier, many agent-distributed funds are provided in different forms, typically the following: (1) A shares: front-end load; (2) B shares: back-end load (contingent deferred sales charge); (3) C shares: level load; and (4) F shares: fee-based program. These different forms of the same fund are called share classes. Table 25.1 provides an example of hypothetical sales charges and annual expenses of funds of different classes for an agent-distributed stock mutual fund. The sales charge accrues to the sales agent. The management fee accrues to the mutual fund manager. The 12b-1 fee accrues to the sales agent and the fund sponsor. Other expenses, including custody and transfer fees and the fees of managing the fund company, accrue to the fund sponsor to cover expenses. All of these expenses are deducted from fund returns on an annual basis.

TABLE 25.1 Hypothetical Sales Charges and Annual Expenses of Funds of Different Classes for an Agent-Distributed Stock Mutual Fund

	Sales Charge			Annual Operating Expenses			
	Front	Back	Level	Management Fee	Distribution (12b-1 fee)	Other Expenses	Expense Ratio
A	4.5%	0	0%	0.90%	0.25%	0.15%	1.30%
B	0	a	0%	0.90%	1.00%	0.15%	2.05%
C	0	0	1%	0.90%	1.00%	0.15%	2.05%
F	0	0	0	0.90%	0.25%	0.15%	1.30%

a 3%, 3%, 2%, 2%, 1%, 0%

Multiple-Share Classes

Share classes were first offered in 1989 following the SEC's approval of multiple-share class. Initially, share classes were used primarily by sales-force funds to offer alternatives to the front-end load as a means of compensating brokers. Later, some of these funds used additional share classes as a means of offering the same fund or portfolio through alternative distribution channels in which some fund expenses varied by channel. Offering new share classes was more efficient and less costly than setting up two separate funds.[3]

Advantages of Investing in Mutual Funds

There are several advantages of the indirect ownership of securities by investing in mutual funds. The first is risk reduction through diversification. By investing in a fund, an investor can obtain broad-based ownership of a sufficient number of securities to reduce portfolio risk. While an individual investor may be able to acquire a broad-based portfolio of securities, the degree of diversification will be limited by the amount available to invest. By investing in an investment company, however, the investor can effectively achieve the benefits of diversification at a lower cost even if the amount of money available to invest is not large.

The second advantage is the reduced cost of contracting and processing information because an investor purchases the services of a presumably skilled financial advisor at less cost than if the investor directly and individually negotiated with such an advisor. The advisory fee is lower because of the larger size of assets managed, as well as the reduced costs of searching for an investment manager and obtaining information about the securities. Also,

---

[3] See Reid (2000).

the costs of transacting in the securities are reduced because a fund is better able to negotiate transactions costs; and custodial fees and recordkeeping costs are less for a fund than for an individual investor. For these reasons, there are said to be economies of scale in investment management.

Third, and related to the first two advantages, is the advantage of the professional management of the mutual fund. Fourth is the advantage of liquidity. Mutual funds can be bought or liquidated any day at the closing NAV. Fifth is the advantage of the variety of funds available, in general, and even in one particular funds family, as discussed later.

Finally, money market funds and some other types of funds provide payment services by allowing investors to write checks drawn on the fund, although this facility may be limited in various ways.

Types of Funds by Investment Objective

Mutual funds have been provided to satisfy the various investment objectives of investors. In general, there are stock funds, bond funds, money market funds, and others. Within each of these categories, there are several subcategories of funds. There are also U.S.-only funds, international funds (no U.S. securities), and global funds (both U.S. and international securities). There are also passive and active funds. Passive (or indexed) funds are designed to replicate an index, such as: the S&P 500 Stock Index; the Lehman Aggregate Bond Index; or the Morgan Stanley Capital International EAFE Index (Europe, Australasia, and the Far East). Active funds, on the other hand, attempt to outperform an index by actively trading the fund portfolio. There are also many other categories of funds, as discussed below. Each fund's objective is stated in its prospectus, as required by the SEC and the "1940 Act," as discussed below.

Stock funds differ by:

- The average market capitalization ("market cap") (large, mid, and small) of the stocks in the portfolio.
- Style (growth, value, and blend).
- Sector—"sector funds" specialize in one particular sector or industry, such as technology, healthcare or utilities.

With respect to style, stocks with high price-to-book value and price/earnings ratios are considered growth stocks, and stocks with low price-to-book value and price/earnings ratios are considered value stocks, although other variables may also be considered. There are also blend stocks with respect to style.

Bond funds differ by the creditworthiness of the issuers of the bonds in the portfolio (for example, U.S. government and investment-grade and high-yield corporates) and by the maturity (or duration) of the bonds (long, intermediate, and short.) There is also a category of bond funds called municipal bond funds whose interest income is exempt from federal income taxes. Municipal funds may be single state (that is, all the bonds in the portfolio were issued by issuers in the same state) or multistate or national.

There are also other categories of funds such as asset allocation, hybrid, target date, and balanced funds (all of which hold both stocks and bonds), and convertible bond funds.

Another subcategory of the stock/bond hybrid category that is a recent addition to the types of mutual funds is the *target-date fund*. This type of fund, popularly referred to as a *life-cycle fund*, establishes its asset allocation on a specific date, the assumed retirement date for the investor, and then rebalances to a more conservative allocation as that date approaches.[4] The first generation of target-date funds had fairly simple asset allocations. For example, in 2010 a 30-year old investor who planned to retire at 65 would invest in a 2045 target date fund. A specific target date fund might specify a 70%/30% U.S. stocks/bonds allocations. Such an allocation prompts two types of questions. First is whether 70%/30% is the optimal asset mix. This issue could never be resolved in a "one size fits all" product such as a target date fund. To better address this issue, the risk tolerance on an individual investor basis should be considered. The second question relates to the overall asset allocation. What proportion of international stocks should be in the allocation? Of this, what is the share of emerging markets? Should there be real estate, commodities, or other inflation-protected assets in the portfolio? Again, these issues cannot be resolved on a one-size-fits-all basis. Although target-date funds are superior to an extreme portfolio allocation such as 100% to one asset class, they are inferior to an individually designed portfolio for an investor. Target-date funds at least provide some diversification and become more conservative as retirement approaches. Currently, there are significant differences with respect to both stock and bond mix and degree of diversification for target-date funds with the same retirement date.

Although not as popular as the target-date fund, a related type of fund is the *target-risk fund*. This type of mutual fund determines its asset allocation around pre-specified levels of risk (such as aggressive, moderate, or conservative) and subsequently rebalances the fund's portfolio to maintain this risk level.

---

[4]Target-date funds are actually "funds of funds," whereby the overall target-date fund is a combination of stock funds, bond funds and, in some cases, other funds. These individual funds can be either active or passive funds.

There is also a category of money market funds (maturities of one year or less) which provide protection against interest rate fluctuations. These funds may have some degree of credit risk (except for the U.S. government money market category). Many of these funds offer check-writing privileges. In addition to taxable money market funds, there are also tax-exempt municipal money market funds.

Among the other fund offerings are index funds and funds of funds. Index funds, as discussed above, attempt to passively replicate an index. Funds of funds invest in other mutual funds not in individual securities.

Several organizations provide data on mutual funds. The most popular ones are *Morningstar* and *Lipper*. These firms provide data on fund expenses, portfolio managers, fund sizes, and fund holdings. But perhaps most importantly, they provide performance (that is, rate of return) data and rankings among funds based on performance and other factors. To compare fund performance on an "apples to apples" basis, these firms divide mutual funds into several categories which are intended to be fairly homogeneous by investment objective. The categories provided by Morningstar and Lipper are similar but not identical. Morningstar's performance ranking system whereby each fund is rated on the basis of return and risk from one-star (the worst) to five-stars (the best) relative to the other funds in its category is well known.

Mutual fund data are also provided by the Investment Company Institute, the national association for mutual funds.

Taxation of Mutual Funds

Mutual funds must distribute at least 90% of their net investment income earned (bond coupons and stock dividends) exclusive of realized capital gains or losses to shareholders (along with meeting other criteria) to be considered a *regulated investment company* (RIC) and, thus, not be required to pay taxes at the fund level prior to distributions to shareholders. Consequently, funds always make these distributions. Taxes, if this criterion is met, are then paid on distributions, only at the investor level, not the fund level. Even though many mutual fund investors choose to reinvest these distributions, the distributions are taxable to the investor, either as ordinary income or capital gains (long term or short term), whichever is relevant.

Capital gains distributions must occur annually, and typically occur late during the calendar year. The capital gains distributions may be either long-term or short-term capital gains, depending on whether the fund held the security for a year or more. Mutual fund investors have no control over the size of these distributions and, as a result, the timing and amount of the taxes paid on their fund holdings is largely out of their control. In particular, withdrawals by some investors may necessitate sales in the fund, which in turn cause realized capital gains and a tax liability to accrue to investors who maintain their holding.

New investors in the fund may assume a tax liability even though they have no gains. That is, all shareholders as of the date of record receive a full year's worth of dividends and capital gains distributions, even if they have owned shares for only one day. This lack of control over capital gains taxes is regarded as a major limitation of mutual funds. In fact, this adverse tax consequence is one of the reasons suggested for a closed-end company's price selling below par value. Also, this adverse tax consequence is one of the reasons for the popularity of exchange traded funds to be discussed later.

Of course, the investor must also pay ordinary income taxes on distributions of income. Finally, when the fund investors sell the fund, they will have long-term or short-term capital gains, taxes, depending on whether they held the fund for a year or less.

Structure of a Fund

A mutual fund organization is structured as follows:

- A *board of directors* (also called the *fund trustees*), which represents the *shareholders* who are the owners of the mutual fund.
- The mutual fund, which is an entity based on the Investment Company Act of 1940.
- An *investment advisor*, which manages the fund's portfolios and is a *registered investment advisor* (RIA) according to the Investment Advisor's Act of 1940.
- A *distributor* or broker-dealer, which is registered under the Securities Act of 1934.
- Other service providers, both external to the fund (the independent public accountant, custodian, and transfer agent) and internal to the fund (marketing, legal, reporting, etc.).

The role of the board of directors is to represent the fund shareholders. The board is composed of both "interested" (or "inside") directors who are affiliated with the investment company (current or previous management) and "independent" (or "outside") directors who have no affiliation with the investment company. Currently, regulations require that more than half of the board be composed of independent directors and that the chairperson can be either an interested or independent director.

The mutual fund enters into a contract with an investment advisor to manage the fund's portfolios. The investment advisor can be an affiliate of a brokerage firm, an insurance company, a bank, an investment management firm, or an unrelated company.

The distributor, which may or may not be affiliated with the mutual fund or investment advisor, is a broker-dealer.

The role of the custodian is to hold the fund assets, segregating them from other accounts to protect the shareholders' interests. The transfer agent processes orders to buy and redeem fund shares, transfers the securities and cash, collects dividends and coupons, and makes distributions. The independent public accountant audits the fund's financial statements.

EXCHANGE-TRADED FUNDS

There are two criticisms that have been leveled again mutual funds. First, because mutual fund (open-end fund) shares are priced only at the closing (i.e., end of trading day), an investor who wants to transact in mutual funds can only do so at the close of the day at the closing price. That is, because there are no intraday prices, transactions (i.e., purchases and sales) prior to the close of the day are not allowed. Second, from an investor's perspective, mutual funds are an inefficient tax structure: redemptions by current shareholders of the fund can trigger taxable capital gains (or losses) for shareholders who remain in the fund.

Unlike mutual funds, because closed-end funds are listed on an exchange, they trade throughout the trading day. That does not mean that the first criticism of mutual funds does not apply to closed-end funds. This is because there is typically a difference, in some cases a large difference, between the NAV of the closed-end's underlying portfolio and the closed-end fund's market price. When the NAV exceeds the fund's market price, it is said to be trading at a discount; when the NAV is less than the fund's market price it is said to be selling at a premium.

Consequently, mutual funds and closed-end funds have an NAV but the latter are exchange traded and therefore a market value is available throughout the trading day. This permits investors to use trading strategies such as shorting and levering with closed-fund funds. In contrast, mutual fund shares are always exchanged at a price equal to NAV because at the end of each trading day the sponsor will always issue new fund shares or redeem outstanding fund shares at the NAV.

It would be ideal to have an investment vehicle that embodied a combination of the desirable aspects of mutual funds (open-end funds) and also closed-end funds. That is, it would be ideal to have an investment vehicle that can be transacted throughout the trading day like a stock (as is a closed-end fund) at a price equal to the continuously known NAV (that is, the price is not at a premium or discount to its NAV). An investment vehicle with these two attributes exists: an *exchange-traded fund* (ETF). Like mutual funds, ETFs require a sponsor.[5] In addition to providing seed money to initiate the ETF and advertising and marketing the ETF, a sponsor (or provider) must do the following:

- Develop or select the index that the ETF's portfolio will seek to match the performance.
- Retain a key player, authorized participants (whose function is explained next).
- Manage the portfolio.

Most ETFs employ an index which was previously developed by another company.[6] Therefore, most ETFs are essentially index funds, but differ from conventional index funds in that (1) they are traded throughout the day on an exchange (just like a stock); (2) the types of orders described in Chapter 6 (market, limit, and stop-loss orders) can be executed (just as with individual stocks); and (3) they can be sold short or bought on margin (i.e., with borrowed money). Moreover, it is even possible to trade options on many ETFs. As explained below, the number of shares outstanding can change, a characteristic ETFs share with open-end funds.

Another characteristic of open-end funds sought is that they trade throughout the day at a price that is very close to their NAV. What mechanism will force an ETF's market price to trade very close to the portfolio's NAV? This is accomplished as follows. An agent is commissioned to arbitrage between the ETF's stock price and the NAV to keep their values equal. The agent, referred to as an *authorized participant*, would do this by buying the cheap ETF and selling the expensive underlying portfolio (at NAV) when the ETF's price is below the NAV, and vice versa. This arbitrage performed by the authorized participant would tend to maintain the ETF's price very close (or equal) to that of the NAV. In practice, there is more than one authorized participant. Authorized participants are mainly large institutional traders who have contractual agreements with ETF providers

For the arbitrage mechanism to work, the composition and the NAV of the ETF's portfolio must be known and continuously traded throughout the trading day. When the portfolio is a known index (such as the S&P 500

---

[5]The four largest ETF sponsors by size are Barclays Global Investors, State Street, PowerShares, and Vanguard.

[6]The index providers are paid a commission by the sponsor for the use of their index.

Index), this requirement is met. For example, for the S&P 500, the 500 stocks in the index are very liquid and their prices and the value of the index are quoted continuously throughout the trading day. The arbitrage process is not feasible for the typical actively managed mutual fund because the composition of the fund's portfolios is not known throughout the trading day. The reason is that mutual funds are only required to make the fund's holdings public only four times a year and then only 45 days after the date of the portfolio report.

Consequently, ETFs are feasible for indexes on broad liquid security indexes but not on typical actively managed mutual funds. The original ETFs were based on well known stock and bond indexes, both U.S and international. The first ETF, which began trading on the American Stock Exchange on January 1, 1993, was based on the S&P 500 Index and popularly referred to as the "Spider." This was followed by ETFs based on narrower sector indexes covering financial, health care, industrial, natural resources, precious metals, technology, utilities, real estate and others. These were, in turn, followed by ETFs based on new and often narrow indexes, specifically designed for ETFs. There is now an effort to develop ETFs on actively managed funds.

The Creation and Redemption Process for ETFs

The purchase of shares of a mutual fund and an ETF by individual investors is quite different. A purchase of a mutual fund's share by an individual investor is done by buying it directly from the fund company. The price paid is equal to the fund's NAV as of the end of the trading day. For an ETF, a share is not purchased by an individual investor from the ETF provider. Instead, an ETF share is purchased from a current investor in the ETF via an exchange at a price determined by supply and demand for the ETF, not the ETF's underlying NAV as is the case for a mutual fund. The NAV of the underlying portfolio, however, remains calculable and available, and is dependent on the forces in the underlying securities markets.

While individual investors do not deal directly with the provider of the ETF, authorized participants do. When an authorized participant wants to sell ETF shares, it delivers its ETF shares to the provider and in return receives the underlying portfolio of securities. That is, no cash changes hands between the authorized participant selling ETF shares and the provider. In the case of a purchase of ETF shares by an authorized participant, the authorized participant assembles a portfolio of the securities (in the same proportion that they are held in the ETF's portfolio) and delivers the portfolio to the ETF provider, who then delivers the new ETF shares to the authorized participant.

Thus, only authorized participants may create or redeem ETF shares with the ETF sponsor and then only in large, specified quantities called *creation/redemption units*. These unit sizes range from approximately 50,000 to 100,000 ETF shares and because of the large sums involved, authorized participants must be large institutional investors. The authorized participant may create new ETF shares by providing the fund with a specified basket of securities (that is, a creation unit) and the fund responds by transferring the corresponding number of the ETF shares to the authorized participant. Similarly, an authorized participant can redeem ETF shares by providing the fund with a specific number of ETF shares (a *redemption unit*), and the fund will transfer to the authorized participant the specific basket of securities. From the perspective of the U.S. tax code, there is no tax consequence. This is because any such transfers qualify as "in-kind transfers" of assets and have no cost or tax impact. Herein lies one of the major advantages of ETFs relative to mutual funds that helps keep an ETF's market price close to its NAV. If there is a disparity in the ETF's market price and its NAV, this creates an opportunity for authorized participants to generate an arbitrage profit. This activity by authorized participants to exploit that opportunity drives the market price and NAV closer together.

Let's look at the dynamics of the relationship between the authorized participants, on the one hand, and either the markets for the individual stock which determine the NAV of the underlying portfolio or the ETF sponsor on the other. Assume that the NAV and market price for a particular ETF are the same. Suppose that there is subsequently a large demand for the ETF shares. This would cause the ETF's market price to rise above the ETF's NAV. Under this scenario, authorized participants will earn a small arbitrage profit by buying the basket of securities (which are cheap relative to the ETF price), and then engaging in an in-kind transfer of the basket of securities for the ETF units. As a result, there are fewer ETF shares outstanding, making the NAV increase and more ETF units available on the market, both of which make the differential between the ETF's price and the ETF's NAV disappear. Figure 25.1 shows where the ETF's price exceeds the ETF's NAV, while part B of the figure illustrates the situation where the ETF's price is less than the ETF's NAV, resulting in the redemption of ETF shares.

As should be clear, the role of authorized participants is critical in accomplishing the objective that the investor in ETF expects: Keeping the ETF's price very close to the ETF's NAV. This will result in the ETF's return matching that of the ETF's targeted index. If the authorized participant fails to closely track the ETF's NAV, an investor will realize a return that may be either greater or less than the targeted index.

Investment Companies, ETFs, and Investment-Oriented Life Insurance

FIGURE 25.1 The ETF Creation/Redemption Process
A. Creation of New ETF Units

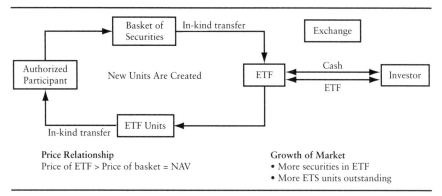

B. Redemption of Outstanding ETF Shares

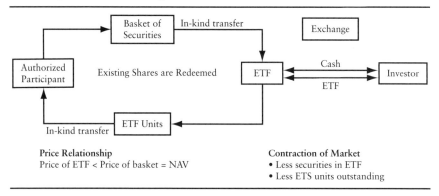

For this process to work effectively, the underlying securities need to be known and be liquid. If an authorized participant cannot trade the underlying securities in the exact proportions as they are in the NAV of the portfolio, the share price of an ETF and its NAV could diverge. If the composition of the underlying portfolio is not known exactly throughout the trading day, the arbitrage will be difficult. As noted earlier, ETFs that are currently available target a passive index and there have been only a few actively managed ETFs. Given the role we just described of the authorized participant, it should be clear why it is difficult to offer an actively managed ETF: the difficulty of tracking an actively managed portfolio.

Institutional investors are constantly monitoring the ETF market to take advantage of discounts and premiums when they develop. A high degree of transparency is required to make this process possible so that the authorized participants are always aware of what each ETF owns and what its shares are worth. Consequently, ETFs are required to publish their NAVs every 15 seconds throughout the trading day.

ETFs vs. Mutual Funds

The pros and cons of mutual funds and ETF's are summarized in Table 25.2. Table 25.3 considers the tax differences in more detail. Overall, the ETFs have the advantages of intraday pricing and tax management, and many, but not all, have lower expenses than their corresponding index mutual funds. However, since open-ended funds are "transacted" through the fund sponsor and ETFs are traded on an exchange, the commissions on each ETF trade may make them unattractive for a strategy that involves several small purchases, as for instance, would result from strategies such as dollar cost averaging or monthly payroll deductions. However, ETFs may provide a viable alternative to mutual funds for many other purposes.

INVESTMENT-ORIENTED LIFE INSURANCE

Insurance and investments are distinct concepts. This distinction leads to the development of various insurance and investment products. In practice, however, there is an overlap between some types of insurance products and investment products. This overlap occurs due partially to specific tax advantages provided to investment-oriented life insurance products. In this section, we do not consider any of the pure life insurance products. Rather, we consider only various types of investment-oriented life insurance products. These products are listed in Table 25.4.

Cash Value Life Insurance

With *cash value life insurance*, each year's premium is segregated into two components by the insurance company. The first is the amount needed to pay for the pure insurance, which, as indicated, increases each year. The second goes into the insured's investment account, which is the cash value of the life insurance contract. An investment return is earned on this cash value, which further increases the cash value. The buildup of this *cash value* and the ability to borrow against it both have tax advantages, as discussed below. Two important observations can be made here.

First, a common marketing or sales advantage attributed to cash value life insurance is that the higher premium paid will "force" the individuals to save, whereas if they did not pay the higher insurance premium, they would

TABLE 25.2 Mutual Funds vs. Exchange-Traded Funds

	Mutual Funds	ETFs
Variety	Wide choice	Choices currently limited to stock and bond indexes, but there are such indexes
Taxation	Subject to taxation on dividend and realized capital gains. May have gains/losses when other investors redeem funds. May have gains/losses when securities in the portfolio are changed	Subject to taxation on dividend and realized capital gain; no gains/losses when other investors redeem funds; and may have gains/losses when securities in the portfolio are changed
Valuation	NAV, based on actual price	Creations and redemptions at NAV. Secondary market price may be valued somewhat above or below NAV, but deviation typically small due to arbitrage
Pricing	End-of-day	Continuous
Expenses	Low for index funds	Low and, in some cases, even lower, than for index mutual funds
Transaction cost	None for no-load funds; sales charge for load funds	Commission or brokerage charge
Management fee	Depends on fund; even index funds have a range of management fees	Depends on fund; tends to be very low on many index funds

TABLE 25.3 Taxes: Mutual Funds versus Exchange Traded Funds

	Mutual Funds	ETFs
Holding/Maintaining	—	—
Taxes on dividend, income and realized capital gains	Fully taxable	Fully taxable
Turnover of portfolio	Withdrawal by other investor may necessitate portfolio sales and realized capital gains for holder	Withdrawal by others does not cause portfolio sales and, thus, no realized capital for holder
Disposition	—	—
Withdrawal of investment	Capital gains tax on difference between sales and purchase price	Capital gains tax on difference between sales and purchase price
Overall	Due to some portfolio turnover, will realize capital gains	Due to very low portfolio turnover, will not realize significant capital gains

TABLE 25.4 Investment-Oriented Insurance Product

1. *Cash Value Life Insurance*

    Whole life
    Variable life
    Universal life
    Variable universal life

2. *Annuities*

    Variable
    Fixed
    GICs

use their income for consumption rather than savings. According to this rationale, the higher insurance premium is, thus, *forced savings*.

Whether or not this first observation has merit, the second observation unequivocally does. The federal government encourages the use of cash value life insurance by providing significant tax advantages. Thus the second advantage of cash value life insurance is *tax-advantaged* savings.

There are several tax advantages to cash value life insurance. The first and major tax advantage is called *inside buildup*. This means that the returns on the investment component of the premium, both income and capital gains, are not subject to taxation (income or capital gains) while held in the insurance contract. Inside buildup is a significant advantage to "saving" via a cash value life insurance policy rather than, for example, saving via a mutual fund.

The second tax advantage of a cash value life insurance policy relates to borrowing against the policy. In general, an amount equal to the cash value of the policy can be borrowed. However, there are some tax implications. The taxation of life insurance is covered in more detail in a following section. In addition to the above, the *death benefit*, that is the amount paid to the beneficiary of the life insurance contract at the death of the insured, is exempt from income taxes, although it may be subject to estate taxes. This benefit applies both to cash value and pure life insurance.

Term insurance has become much more of a commodity product and, in fact, there are websites that provide premium quotes for term life insurance for various providers. Cash value life insurance, due to its complexity and multiple features, is not, however, a commodity.

Obviously, the cost of annual term life insurance is much lower than that of whole life insurance, particularly for the young and middle-aged. For example, while there is a wide range of premiums for both term and whole life insurance, for a 35-year-old male, the annual cost of $500,000 of annual term insurance may be $400 and the cost of whole life insurance may be $5,000.

Stock and Mutual Insurance Companies

There are two major forms of life insurance companies, stock and mutual. A stock insurance company is similar in structure to any corporation (also called a public company). Shares (of ownership) are owned by independent shareholders and may be traded publicly. The shareholders care only about the performance of their shares, that is the stock appreciation and the dividends over time. Their holding period and, thus, their view may be short term or long term. The insurance policies are simply the products or businesses of the company in which they own shares.

In contrast, mutual insurance companies have no stock and no external owners. Their policyholders are their owners. The owners, that is the policyholders, care primarily or even solely about the performance of their insurance policies, notably the company's ability to eventually pay on the policy and to, in the interim, provide investment returns on the cash value of the policy, if any. Since these payments may occur considerably into the future, the policyholders' view will be long term. Thus, while stock insurance companies have two constituencies, their stockholders and their policyholders, mutual insurance companies only have one, since their policyholders and their owners are the same. Traditionally, the largest insurance companies have been mutual, but recently there have been many demutualizations, that is, conversions by mutual companies to stock companies. Currently several of the largest life insurance companies are stock companies.

The debate on which is the better form of insurance company, stock or mutual, is too involved to be considered in any depth here. However, consider selected comments on this issue. First, consider this issue from the perspective of the policyholder. Mutual holding companies have only one constituency, their policyholder or owner. The liabilities of many types of insurance companies are long term, particularly the writers of whole life insurance. Thus, mutual insurance companies can appropriately have a long time horizon for their strategies and policies. They do not have to make short-term decisions to benefit their shareholders, whose interests are usually short term, via an increase in the stock price or dividend, in a way that might reduce their long-term profitability or the financial strength of the insurance company. In addition, if the insurance company earns a profit, it can pass the profit onto its policyholders via reduced premiums. (Policies that benefit from an increased profitability of the insurance company are called *participating policies*, as discussed later.) These increased profits do not have to accrue to stockholders because there are none.

Finally, mutual insurance companies can adopt a longer time frame in their investments, which will most likely make possible a higher return. Mutual insurance companies, for example, typically hold more common stock in their portfolios than stock companies. However, whereas the long time frame of mutual insurance companies may be construed an advantage over stock companies, it may also be construed as a disadvantage. Rating agencies and others assert that, due to their longer horizon and their long time frame, mutual insurance companies may be less efficient and have higher expenses than stock companies. Empirically, rating agencies and others assert that mutual insurance companies have typically significantly reduced their expenses shortly before and after converting to stock companies.

Overall, it is argued, mutual insurance companies have such long planning horizons that they may not operate efficiently, particularly with respect to expenses. Stock companies, on the other hand, have very short planning horizons and may operate to the long-term disadvantage of their policyholders to satisfy their stockholders in the short run. Recently, however, mutual insurance companies have become more cost conscientious.

General Account vs. Separate Account Products

The general account of an insurance company refers to the overall resources of the life insurance company, mainly its investment portfolio. Products "written by the company itself" are said to have a "general account guarantee," that is, they are a liability of the insurance company. When the rating agencies (Moody's, Standard & Poor's, Fitch) provide a credit rating, these ratings are on products written by or guaranteed by the general account, specifically on the "claims-paying ability" of the company. Typical products written by and guaranteed by the general account are whole life, universal life, and fixed annuities (including GICs). Insurance companies must support the guaranteed performance of their general account products to the extent of their solvency. These are called *general account products*.

Other types of insurance products receive no guarantee from the insurance company's general account, and their performance is based, not on the performance of the insurance company's general account, but solely on the performance of an investment account separate from the general account of the insurance company, often an account selected by the policyholder. These products are called *separate account products*. Variable life insurance and variable annuities are separate account products. The policyholder selects specific investment portfolios to support these separate account products. The performance of the insurance product depends almost solely on the performance of the portfolio selected, adjusted for the fees or expenses of the insuring company (which do depend on the insurance company). The performance of the separate account products, thus, is not affected by the performance of the overall insurance company's general account portfolio.

Most general account insurance products, including whole life insurance, participate in the performance of the company's general account performance. For example, whereas a life insurance company provides the guarantee of a minimum dividend on its whole life policies, the policies' actual dividend may be greater if the investment portfolio performs well. This is called the "interest component" of the dividend. (The other two components of the dividend are the expense and mortality components.) Thus, the performance of the insurance policy participates in the overall company's performance. Such a policy is called a *participating policy*, in this case a participating whole life insurance policy.

In addition, the performance of some general account products may not be affected by the performance of the general account portfolio. For example, disability income insurance policies may be written on a general account, and while their payoff depends on the solvency of the general account, the policy performance (for example, its premium) may not participate in the investment performance of the insurance companies' general account investment portfolio.

Both stock and mutual insurance companies write both general and separate account products. However, most participating general account products tend to be written in mutual companies.

Overview of Cash Value Whole Life Insurance

The details of *cash value whole life insurance* (CVWLI) are very complex. This section provides a simple overview of CVWLI, partially by contrasting it with term life insurance.

As discussed above, in annual term life insurance, the owner of the policy, typically also the insured, pays an annual premium which reflects the actuarial risk of death during the year. The premium, thus, increases each year. If the insured dies during the year, the death benefit is paid to the insurer's beneficiary. If the insured does not die during the year, the term policy has no value at the end of the year.

The construction and performance of CVWLI and term life insurance are quite different. Primarily, the owner of the CVWLI policy pays a constant premium. This premium on the CVWLI policy is initially much higher than the initial premium on a term policy (the pure insurance cost) because the constant premium must cover not only lower insurance risk early in the policy but also higher insurance risk later in the policy when the insured has a higher age and the annual cost of the pure insurance exceeds the level premium. However, assuming the same interest and mortality assumptions on both products, the CVWLI premium should be lower than the average of the term premium over time. This is because in the early years, the excess of the level CVWLI premium over the term premium can earn interest, which lowers the overall premium needed to fund the policy; and some CVWLI policy holders paying the level premium die in the early years, leaving funds (from the excess of the level premium over the early life insurance cost) available to the remaining policy holders, which can be used to decrease the CVWLI premium.

In the early years of the policy, the excess of the premium over the pure insurance cost is invested by the insurance company in its general account portfolio. In the later years, there is a shortfall in the premiums relative to the pure insurance cost and the previous cash value buildup is used to fund this shortfall. This portfolio generates a return which accrues to the policy owner's cash value. Typically, the insurance company guarantees a minimum increase in cash value, called the *guaranteed cash value buildup*. The insurance company, however, may provide an amount in excess of the guaranteed cash value buildup based on earnings for participating policies. What happens to this excess? Assume that the insurance company has a mutual structure, that is, it is owned by the policyholders. In this case, with no stockholders, the earnings accrue to the policyholders as dividends.

The arithmetic of the development of the cash value in a life insurance contract follows:

> \+ Premium
> − Cost of insurance (mortality) (denoted by M)
> − Expenses (denoted by E)
> \+ Guaranteed (minimum) cash value buildup
> \+ (Participating) dividend
> ─────────────────────────
> = Increase (buildup) in cash value

Note that the overall dividend is calculated from the investment income, the cost of paying the death benefit (the mortality expense denoted by M), and the expense of running the company (denoted by E). The latter two together are called the *M&E charges*.

If the insurance company is owned by stockholders, some or all of the earnings might go to the stockholders as dividends.

The returns to the insurance company and, therefore, the dividends to the policyholder can increase if: (1) investment returns increase; (2) company expenses decrease; or (3) mortality costs decrease (that is, the life expectancy of the insured increases).

The dividends can be "used" by the policyholder in either of two ways. The first is to decrease the annual premium. In this case, the death benefit remains constant. The second is to increase the death benefit and the cash value of the policy. Such increases are called *paid-up additions* (PUAs). In this case, the annual premium remains constant. Most policies are written in the second way.

The intended way for the life insurance policy to terminate is for the insured to die and the life insurance company to pay the death benefit to the beneficiary. There are other ways, however. First, the policy can be *lapsed* (alternatively called *forfeited* or *surrendered*). In this case, the owner of the policy withdraws the cash value of the policy and the policy is terminated.

There are also two *nonforfeiture options*—that is methods whereby an insurance policy for the insured remains. The owner can use the cash value of the policy to buy *extended term insurance* (the amount and term of the resulting term insurance policy depends on the cash value). In addition, the cash value of the policy can be used to buy a reduced amount of fully paid (that is, no subsequent premiums are due) whole life insurance—this is called *reduced paid up*.

In addition to the forfeiture option and the two non-forfeiture options of terminating the CVWLI policy, the policy could be left intact and borrowed against. This is called a *policy loan*. An amount equal to the cash value of the policy can be borrowed. There are two effects of the loan on the policy. First, the dividend is paid only on the amount equal to the cash value of the policy minus the loan. Second, the death benefit of the policy paid is the policy death benefit minus the loan.

The taxation of the death benefit payout, a policy lapse, and borrowing against the loan are considered next. For taxation of life insurance, it is important to recall that the insurance premium is paid by the policy owner with after-tax dollars (this is often called the *cost* of the policy). But the cash value is allowed to build up inside the policy with taxes deferred (or usually tax-free), often called the *return* on the policy.

Taxability of Life Insurance

A major attraction of life insurance as an investment product is its taxability. Consider the four major tax advantages of life insurance.

The first tax advantage is that when the death benefit is paid to the beneficiary of the insurance policy, the benefit is free of income tax. If the life insurance policy is properly structured in an estate plan, the benefit is also free of estate taxes.

The second tax advantage is called "inside buildup"—that is, all earnings (interest, dividend, and realized capital gains) are exempt from income and capital gains taxes. Thus, these earnings are tax deferred (and when included in the death benefit become income tax free, and in some cases also estate tax free).

The third relates to the lapse of a policy. When the policy is lapsed, the owner receives the cash value of the policy. The amount taxed is the cash value minus the cost of the policy (the total premiums paid plus the dividends, if paid in cash). That is, the tax basis of the policy is the cost (accumulated premiums) of the policy. The cost, thus, increases the basis and is recovered tax-free. (Remember, however, that these costs were paid with after-tax dollars.) And, the remainder was allowed to accumulate without taxation but is taxed at the time of the lapse.

The fourth tax issue relates to borrowing against the policy—that is, a policy loan. The primary tax issue is the distinction between the cost (accumulated premium) and the excess of the policy cash value over the cost (call it the excess). When a policy loan is made, the cost is deemed to be borrowed first (that is, FIFO—first in-first out—accounting is employed). The amount up to the cash value of the policy can be borrowed and not be subject to the ordinary income tax. (An exception to this practice is for a Modified Endowment Contract (MEC). If the loan is outstanding at the time of the policy lapse, the loan is treated on a FIFO basis whereby the cost basis is assumed to be borrowed first and is not taxable, and when the cost basis is exhausted by the loan, the remainder of the loan—up to the cash value of the policy—is taxable.)

Although CVWLI has both insurance and investment characteristics, Congress provided insurance policies tax advantages because of their insurance, not their investment, characteristics. And Congress does not wish to apply these insurance-directed tax benefits to primarily investment products. In this regard, in the past some activities related to borrowing against insurance policies were considered abuses by Congress and tax law changes were made to moderate these activities. These abuses originated with a product called *single-premium life insurance*. This policy is one in which only a single premium is paid for a whole life insurance policy. The premium creates an immediate cash value. This cash value and the resulting investment income earned are sufficient to pay the policy's benefits. The excess investment income accumulates tax-free.

Products

The major investment-oriented insurance products can be divided into two categories—cash value life insurance and annuities. Each has several types, which are listed in Table 25.5. These products are described in the following sections.

Cash Value Life Insurance

Cash value life insurance was introduced above. There are two dimensions of cash value life insurance policies. The first is whether the cash value is *guaranteed* (called whole life) or *variable* (called variable life). The second is whether the required premium payment is *fixed* or *flexible*, that is whether it has a universal (flexible) feature or not. They can be combined in all ways.

TABLE 25.5 Types of Universal Life Insurance

Premium	Guaranteed	Variable
Fixed	Whole life	Variable life
Flexible	Universal life	Variable universal life

Thus, there are four combinations, which we discuss next. The broad classification of cash value life insurance, called whole life insurance, in addition to providing pure life insurance (as does term insurance), builds up a cash value or investment value inside the policy.

Traditional cash value life insurance, usually called whole life insurance, has a *guaranteed* buildup of cash value based on the investment returns on the general account portfolio of the insurance company. That is, the cash value in the policy is guaranteed to increase by a specified minimum amount each year. This is called the *cash value buildup*. (The guaranteed cash value buildup of many U.S. CVWLI policies tend to be in the range of 3%–4%.) The cash value may grow by more than this minimum amount if a dividend is paid on the policy. Dividends, however, are not guaranteed. There are two types of dividends, participating and nonparticipating. Participating dividends depend on (that is, participate in) the investment returns of the general account of the insurance company portfolio (the insurance company M&E charges also affect the dividend).

The participating dividend *may be* used to increase the cash value of the policy by more than its guaranteed amount. Actually, there are two potential uses of the dividend. The first is to reduce the annual premium paid on the policy. In this case, while the premium decreases, the cash value of the policy increases by only its guaranteed amount (and the face value the death benefit remains constant).

The second use is to buy more life insurance with the premium, called *paid-up additions* (PUA). In this case, the cash value of the entire policy increases by more than the guaranteed amount on the original policy (and the face value of the current policy is greater than the face value of the original policy).

In either case, the performance of the policy over time may be substantially affected by the participating dividends.

Contrary to the guaranteed or fixed cash value policies based on the general account portfolio of the insurance company, *variable life insurance* polices allow the policyowners to allocate their premium payments to and among several separate investment accounts maintained by the insurance company, and also to be able to shift the policy cash value among these separate accounts. As a result, the amount of the policy cash value depends on the investment results of the separate accounts the policyowners have selected. Thus, there is no guaranteed cash value or death benefit. Both depend on the performance of the selected investment portfolio.

The types of separate account investment options offered in their variable life insurance policies vary by insurance companies. Typically, the insurance company offers a selection of common stock and bond fund investment opportunities, often managed by the company itself and also by other investment managers. If the investment options perform well, the cash value buildup in the policy will be significant. However, if the policyholder selects investment options that perform poorly, the variable life insurance policy will perform poorly. There could be little or no cash value buildup, or, in the worst case, the policy could be terminated because there is not enough value in the contract to pay the mortality charge. This type of cash value life insurance is called *variable life insurance*.

The key element of *universal life* is the flexibility of the premium for the policyowner. The flexible premium concept separates the pure insurance protection (term insurance) from the investment (cash value) element of the policy. The policy cash value is set up as a cash value fund (or accumulation fund) to which the investment income is credited and from which the cost of term insurance for the insured (the mortality charge) is debited. The policy expenses are also debited.

This separation of the cash value from the pure insurance is called the "unbundling" of the traditional life insurance policy. Premium payments for universal life are at the discretion of the policyholder, that is, are flexible with the exceptions that there must be a minimum initial premium to begin the coverage, and there must also be at least enough cash value in the policy each month to cover the mortality charge and other expenses. If not, the policy will lapse. Both guaranteed cash value and variable life can be written on a flexible premium or fixed premium basis.

The universal feature—flexible premiums—can be applied to either guaranteed value whole life (called simply universal life) or to variable life (called variable universal life). These types are summarized in Table 25.5. Variable universal life insurance combines the features of variable life and universal life policies—that is, the choice of separate account investment products and flexible premiums.

Over the last decade, term and variable life insurance have been growing at the expense of whole life insurance. The most common form of variable life is variable universal.

Most whole life insurance policies are designed to pay death benefits when one specified insured dies. An added dimension of whole life policies is that two people (usually a married couple) are jointly insured, and the policy pays the death benefit not when the first person dies, but when the second person (the "surviving spouse") dies. This is called *survivorship insurance* or *second-to-die insurance*. This survivorship feature can be added to standard cash value whole life, universal life, variable life, and variable universal life policies. Thus, each of the four policies discussed could also be written on a survivorship basis.

In general, the annual premium for a survivorship insurance policy is lower than for a policy on a single person because, by construction, the second of two people to die has a longer life span than the first. Survivorship insurance is typically sold for estate planning purposes.

Table 25.6 provides a summary of the various types of cash value life insurance, with (annual renewable) term insurance included for contrast.

Annuities

By definition, an annuity is simply a series of periodic payments. Annuity contracts have been offered by insurance companies and, more recently, by other types of financial institutions such as mutual fund companies.

There are two phases to annuities according to cash flows, the accumulation period and the liquidation period. During the accumulation period, the investor is providing funds, or investing. Annuities are considered primarily accumulation products rather than insurance products. During the liquidation period, the investor is withdrawing funds, or liquidating the annuity. One type of liquidation is annuitization, or withdrawal via a series of fixed payments, as discussed below. This method of liquidation is the basis for the name of annuities.

There are several ways to classify annuities. One is the method of paying premiums. Annuities are purchased with *single premiums*, *fixed periodic premiums*, or *flexible periodic premiums* during the accumulation phase. All three are used in current practice.

A second classification is the time the income payments commence during the liquidation phase. An *immediate annuity* is one in which the first benefit payment is due one payment interval (month, year or other) from the purchasing date. Under a *deferred annuity*, there is a longer period before the benefit period begins. While an immediate annuity is purchased with a single premium, a deferred annuity may be purchased with a single, fixed periodic, or flexible periodic payments, although the flexible periodic payment is most common.

An important basis for annuities is whether they are fixed or variable annuities. Fixed annuities, as discussed in more detail below, are expressed in a fixed number of dollars, while variable annuities are expressed in a fixed number annuity units, each unit of which may have a different and changing market value. Fixed versus variable annuities is the key distinction between annuities currently provided.

Now we will look at the various types of annuities. The most common categories are *variable annuities* and *fixed annuities*.

While cash value life insurance has the appearance of life insurance with an investment feature, annuities, in contrast, have the appearance of an investment product with an insurance feature. The major advantage of an annuity is its inside buildup, that is, its investment earnings are tax deferred. However, unlike life insurance where the death benefit is not sub-

TABLE 25.6 Life Insurance Comparison (by type and element)

Type	Description	Death Benefit	Premium	Cash Value (CV)	Advantages to Owner	Disadvantages to Owner
Annual renewable term	"Pure" life insurance with no cash value; initially, the highest death benefit for the lowest premium; premium increases exponentially	Fixed, constant	Increases exponentially	None	Low premium for coverage	Increasing premium; most term insurance is lapsed
Whole life	Known maximum cost and minimum death benefit; dividends may: reduce premiums; pay-up policy; buy paid-up additions; accumulate at interest; or be paid in cash	Fixed, constant	Fixed, constant	Fixed	Predictable; forced savings and conservative investment	High premiums given death benefit
Variable life	Whole life contract; choice of investment assets; death benefits depend on investment results	Guaranteed minimum; can increase based on investment performance	Fixed, constant	Based on investment performance; not guaranteed	Combines life insurance and investments on excess premiums	All investment risk is to the owner
Universal life	Flexible premium, current assumption adjustable death benefit policy; policy elements unbundled	Adjustable; Two options: 1. like ordinary life; 2. like ordinary life plus term rider equal to cash value	Flexible at option of policyowner	Varies depending on face amount and premium; minimum guaranteed interest; excess increases cash value	Flexibility	Some investment risk to owner
Variable universal life	Features of universal and variable life	Adjustable	Flexible at option of policyowner	Varies depending on face amount, premium, and investment performance; not guaranteed	Flexibility and choice of investments	All investment risk is to owner

ject to income taxes, withdrawals from annuities are taxable. There are also restrictions on withdrawals. Specifically, there are IRS requirements for the taxability of early withdrawals (before age 59.5) and required minimum withdrawals (after age 70.5). These requirements and the other tax issues of annuities are very complex and considered only briefly here.

The most common types of annuities, variable and fixed annuities, are discussed below.

Variable Annuities   *Variable annuities* are, in many ways, similar to mutual funds. Given the above discussion, variable annuities are often considered to be "mutual funds in an insurance wrapper." The return on a variable annuity depends on the return of the underlying portfolio. The returns on annuities are, thus, in a word, "variable." In fact, many investment managers offer similar or identical funds separately in both a mutual fund and an annuity format. Thus, variable annuity offerings are approximately as broad as mutual fund offerings. For example, consider a large capitalization, blended stock fund. The investment manager may offer this fund in both a mutual fund and annuity format. But, of course, the two portfolios are segregated. The portfolios of these two products may be identical and, thus, the portfolio returns will be identical.

Before considering the differences, however, there is one similarity. Investments in both mutual funds and annuities are made with after-tax dollars; that is, taxes are paid on the income before it is invested in either a mutual fund or an annuity.

But there are important differences to investors in these two products. First, all income (dividend and interest) and realized capital gains generated in the mutual fund are taxable, even if they are not withdrawn. On the other hand, income and realized capital gains generated in the annuity are not taxable until withdrawn. Thus, annuities benefit from the same *inside buildup* as cash value life insurance.

There is another tax advantage to annuities. If a variable annuity company has a group of annuities in its family (called a "contract"), an investor can switch from one annuity fund to another in the contract (for example from a stock fund to a bond fund) and the switch is not a taxable event. However, if the investor shifts from a stock fund in one annuity company to a bond fund in another annuity company, it is considered a withdrawal and a reinvestment, and the withdrawal is a taxable event (there are exceptions to this, however, as will be discussed). The taxation of annuity withdrawals will also be considered.

While the inside buildup is an advantage of annuities, there are offsetting disadvantages. For comparison, there are no restrictions on withdrawals from (selling shares of) a mutual fund. Of course, withdrawals from a mutual fund are a taxable event and will generate realized capital gains or losses, which will generate long-term or short-term gains or losses and, thus, tax consequences. There are, however, significant restrictions on withdrawals from annuities. First, withdrawals before age 59.5 are assessed a 10% penalty (there are, however, some "hardship" exceptions to this). Second, withdrawals must begin by age 70.5 according to the IRS *required minimum distribution rules* (RMD). These mandatory withdrawals are designed to eventually produce tax revenues on annuities to the IRS. Mutual funds have no disadvantages to withdrawing before 59.5 nor requirements to withdraw after 70.5.

There is an exception to the taxation resulting from a shift of funds from one variable annuity company to another. Under specific circumstances, funds can be so moved without causing a taxable event. Such a shift is called a *1035 exchange* after the IRS rule that permits this transfer.

Another disadvantage of annuities is that all gains on withdrawals, when they occur, are taxed as ordinary income, not capital gains, whether their source was income or capital gains. For many investors, their income tax rate is significantly higher than the long-term capital gains tax rate and this form of taxation is therefore a disadvantage.

The final disadvantage of annuities is that the heirs of a deceased owner receive them with a cost basis equal to the purchase price (which means that the gains are taxed at the heir's ordinary income tax rate) rather than being stepped up to a current market value as with most investments.

Why has the IRS given annuities the same tax advantage of inside buildup that insurance policies have? The answer to this question is that annuities are structured to have some of the characteristics of life insurance, commonly called "features." There are many such features. The most common feature is that the minimum value of an annuity fund that will be paid at the investor's death is the initial amount invested. Thus, if an investor invests $100 in a stock annuity, the stock market declines such that the value of the fund is $90, and the investor dies, the investor's beneficiary will receive $100, not $90. This is a life insurance characteristic of an annuity.

The above feature represents a *death benefit* (DB), commonly called a return of premium. However, new, and often more complicated, death benefits have been introduced, including a periodic lock-in of gains (called a *stepped-up DB*); a predetermined annual percentage increase (called a *rising floor DB*); or a percentage of earnings to offset estate taxes and other death expenses (called an *earnings enhancement DB*). In addition to these death benefit features, some *living benefit* features have also been developed, including premium enhancements and minimum accumulation guarantees.

Obviously these features have value to the investor and, as a result, a cost to the provider. The value of a feature depends on its design and can be high or approximately worthless. And the annuity company will charge the investor for the value of these features.

The cost of the features relates to another disadvantage of annuities, specifically their expenses. The insurance company will impose a charge for the potential death benefit payment (called *mortality*) and other expenses, overall called M&E charges, as discussed previously for insurance policies. These M&E charges will be in addition to the normal investment management, custody, and other expenses experienced by mutual funds. Thus, annuity expenses will exceed mutual fund expenses by the annuity's M&E charges. The annuity investor does, however, receive the value of the insurance feature for the M&E charge.

Thus, the overall trade-offs between mutual funds and annuities can be summarized as follows. Annuities have the advantages of inside buildup and the particular life insurance features of the specific annuity. But annuities also have the disadvantages of higher taxes on withdrawal (ordinary income versus capital gains), restrictions on withdrawals, and higher expenses. For short holding periods, mutual funds will have a higher after-tax return. For very long holding periods, the value of the inside buildup will dominate and the annuity will have a higher after-tax return.

What is the breakeven holding period, that is, the holding period beyond which annuities have higher after-tax returns? The answer to this question depends on several factors, such as the tax rates (income and capital gains), the excess of the expenses on the annuity, and others.

Fixed Annuities There are several types of fixed annuities but, in general, the invested premiums grow at a rate—the credited rate—specified by the insurance company in each. This growth is accrued and added to the cash value of the annuity each year (or more frequently, such as monthly) and is not taxable as long as it remains in the annuity. Upon liquidation, it is taxed as ordinary income (to the extent that is represents previously untaxed income).

The two most common types of fixed annuities are the *flexible premium deferred annuity* (FPDA) and the *single premium deferred annuity* (SPDA). The FPDA permits contributions which are flexible in amount and timing. The interest rate paid on these contracts—the credited rate—varies and depends on the insurance company's current interest earnings and its desired competitive position in the market. There are, however, two types of limits on the rate. First, the rate is guaranteed to be no lower than a specified contract guaranteed rate, often in the range 3% to 4%. Second, these contracts often have *bail-out provisions*, which stipulate that if the credited rate decreases below a specified rate, the owner may withdraw all the funds (lapse the contract) without a surrender charge. Bail-out credited rates are often set at 1% to 3% below the current credited rate and are designed to limit the use of a "teaser rate" (or "bait and switch" practices), whereby an insurance company offers a high credited rate to attract new investors and then reduces the credited rate significantly, with the investor limited from withdrawing the funds by the surrender charges.

An initial credited rate, a minimum guaranteed rate, and a bailout rate are set initially on the contract. The initial credited rate, thus, may be changed by the insurance company over time. The *reset* (or renewal) *period* must also be specified—this is, the frequency with which the credited rate can be changed.

Another important characteristic of annuities is the basis for the valuation of withdrawals prior to maturity. The traditional method has been book value, that is, withdrawals are paid based on the purchase price of the bonds (bonds rather than stocks are used to fund annuities). Thus, if yields have increased, the insurance company will be paying the withdrawing investor more than the bonds are currently worth. And at this time, there is an incentive for the investor to withdraw and invest in a new higher yielding fixed annuity. Thus, book value fixed annuities provide risk to the insurance company. Surrender charges, discussed next, mitigate this risk. Another way to mitigate this risk is via *market value–adjusted* (MVA) annuities, whereby early withdrawals are paid on the basis of the current market value of the bond portfolio rather than the book value. This practice eliminates the early withdrawal risk to the insurance company. (Obviously, all variable annuities are paid on the basis of market value rather than bonds value.)

Another characteristic of both variable and fixed annuities relates to one aspect of their sales charges. These charges are very similar for annuities and mutual funds. Mutual funds and annuities were originally provided with front-end loans, that is, sales charges imposed on the initial investment. For example, with a 5% front-end load of a $100 initial investment, $5 would be retained by the firm for itself and the agent, and $95 invested in the fund for the investor.

More recently, back-end loads have been used as an alternative to front-end loads. With a back-end load, the fixed percentage charge is imposed at the time of withdrawal. Currently, the most common form of back-end load is the contingent deferred sales charge, also called a *surrender charge*. This approach imposes a load which is gradually declining over time. For example, a common CDSC is a "7%/6%/5%/4%/3%/2%/1%/0%" charge according to which a 7% load is imposed on withdrawals during the first year, 6% during the second year, 5% during the third year, and so forth. There is no charge for withdrawals after the seventh year.

Finally, there are level loads, which impose a constant load (1% for example) every year. Currently on annuities, a front-end load is often used along with a CDSC surrender charge.

Annuities have become very complex instruments. This section provides only an overview.

Guaranteed Investment Contracts

The first major investment-oriented product developed by life insurance companies, and a form of fixed annuity, was the *guaranteed investment contract* (GIC). GICs were used extensively for retirement plans. With a GIC, a life insurance company agrees, in return for a single premium, to pay the principal amount and a predetermined annual crediting rate over the life of the investment, all of which are paid at the maturity date of the GIC. For example, a $10 million five-year GIC with a predetermined crediting rate of 10% means that at the end of five years, the insurance company pays the guaranteed crediting rate and the principal. The return of the principal depends on the ability of the life insurance company to satisfy the obligation, just as in any corporate debt obligation. The risk that the insurer faces is that the rate earned on the portfolio of supporting assets is less than the guaranteed rate.

The maturity of a GIC can vary from 1 year to 20 years. The interest rate guaranteed depends on market conditions and the rating of the life insurance company. The interest rate will be higher than the yield on U.S. Treasury securities of the same maturity. These policies are typically purchased by pension plan sponsors as a pension investment.

A GIC is a liability of the life insurance company issuing the contract. The word guarantee does not mean that there is a guarantor other than the life insurance company. Effectively, a GIC is a zero-coupon bond issued by a life insurance company and, as such, exposes the investor to the same credit risk. This credit risk has been highlighted by the default of several major issuers of GICs. The two most publicized defaults were Mutual Benefit, a New Jersey-based insurer, and Executive Life, a California-based insurer, which were both seized by regulators in 1991.

The basis for these defaults is that fixed annuities are insurance company general account products and variable annuities are separate account products. For fixed annuities, the premiums become part of the insurance company, are invested in the insurance company's general account (which are regulated by state laws), and the payments are the obligations of the insurance company. Variable annuities are separate account products, that is, the premiums are deposited in investment vehicles separate from the insurance company, and are usually selected by the investor. Thus fixed annuities are general account products and the insurance company bears the investment risk, while variable annuities are separate account products and the investor bears the investment risk.

SPDAs and GICs   SPDAs and GICs with the same maturity and crediting rate have much in common. For example, for each the value of a $1 initial investment with a five-year maturity and a fixed crediting rate for the five years at $r\%$ would have a value at maturity of $(1 + r)^5$.

However, there are also significant differences. SPDAs have elements of an insurance product and so its inside buildup is not taxed as earned (it is taxed as income at maturity). SPDAs are not qualified products, that is, they must be paid for in after tax-dollars. GICs are not insurance products. GICs, however, are typically put into pension plans (defined benefit or defined contribution), which are qualified. In this case, thus, the GIC investments are paid for in after-tax dollars and receive the tax deferral of inside buildup. SPDAs are also put into qualified plans. Specifically, banks often sell IRAs funded with SPDAs.

Another difference between SPDAs and GICs is that since SPDAs are annuities, they usually have surrender charges, typically the 7%/6%/5%/4%/3%/2%/1%/0%, mentioned previously. Thus, if a five-year SPDA is withdrawn after three years, there is a 4% surrender charge. GICs do not have surrender charges and can be withdrawn with no penalty (under benefit responsive provisions).

Another feature of SPDAs is the reset period, the period after which the credited rate can be changed by the writer of the product. For example, a five-year SPDA may have a reset period after three years, at which time the credited rate can also be increased or decreased. For SPDAs, there can also be an interaction between the reset period and the surrender charge. For example, a five-year SPDA with a three-year reset period could be liquidated after three years due to a lowered crediting rate, but only with a 4% surrender charge. GICs have no reset period, that is, the credited rate is constant throughout the contract's life. Early withdrawals of GICs are at book value; they are interest rate insensitive.

SPDAs typically have a reset period of one year but with an initial M-year minimum guarantee ($M = 1, 2, 3, 5, 7, 9$). SPDAs typically have a maturity based on the age of the annuitant (such as age 90 or 95), not a fixed number of years. Thus, while SPDAs typically have a maturity greater than the guarantee period, for GICs the maturity period equals the guarantee period. Common maturities for GICs and SPDAs are one, three, five, and seven years.

SUMMARY

A share in an investment company represents a pro rata interest in the net asset value of the portfolio. The net asset value is equal to the market value of the securities in the portfolio reduced by the liabilities divided by the total number of shares outstanding. The three types of investment companies are open-end (more popularly referred to as mutual funds), closed-end funds, and unit trusts. Mutual fund shares can only be transacted at the end of the trading day and at the NAV calculated at that time. Closed-end funds are traded on an exchange and therefore can be transacted at any time during the trading day at a price determined by supply and demand, just like any other stock. The NAV of a closed-end fund can be less than, equal to, or greater than the fund's NAV.

A wide range of funds with many different investment objectives is available. A fund must clearly set forth its investment objective in its prospectus, and the objective identifies the type or types of assets the fund will invest in. Mutual funds and closed-end funds provide two crucial economic functions associated with financial intermediaries: risk reduction via diversification and lower costs of contracting and information processing.

There are drawbacks to mutual funds and closed-end funds from the perspective of investors. Exchange-traded funds overcome these problems. The advantages of ETFs over mutual funds is that they can be traded throughout the trading day on an exchange and thus having continuous pricing. This allows an investor to sell ETFs short, buy on margin, and placed the types of orders that investors are accustomed to in trading stocks. Moreover, compared to a mutual fund, there are tax advantages that include not being subject to capital gains tax when the investor does not liquidate a position and they typically have lower management fees. ETFs are based on portfolios which track an index, that is they are passive vehicles although active ETFs are being developed. Authorized participants play a critical role in ETFs because it is their arbitrage activities that keep the ETF's price from deviating from the ETF's NAV.

Basically, there is a distinction between investment and life insurance products. The former provide returns on an initial investment; the latter provide risk protection against a wide variety of risks and have no cash value. However, there are two types of products that have attributes of both investments and insurance: cash value life insurance and annuities. Cash value life insurance is a combination of pure life insurance with a buildup of cash value as a result of the higher premium paid relative to a pure life insurance policy. The types of cash value life insurance include whole life and variable life, and universal versions of both of these. The second type is annuities—variable and fixed. A variable annuity is effectively a mutual fund in an insurance wrapper, with insurance elements that may include both death benefits and living benefits. The difference between a fixed annuity and a variable annuity is that the return on a fixed annuity is specified at the time of the investment and is certain, while that of a variable annuity depends on the performance of the investment portfolio selected by the investor. The investment element of these hybrid insurance/investment products benefits from their tax advantages with the chief tax advantage being the inside buildup, although cash value life insurance products also have other significant tax benefits.

REFERENCES

Inro, D. C., C. X. Jaing, M. Y. Ho, and W. Y. Lee. 1999. Mutual fund performance: Does fund size matter? *Financial Analysts Journal* 55 (May–June): 74–87.

O'Neal, E. S. 1999. Mutual fund share classes and broker incentives. *Financial Analysts Journal* 55 (September–October): 76–87.

Reid, B. 2000. The 1990s: A decade of expansion and changes in the U.S. mutual fund industry. *Perspectives: Investment Company Institute* 6, no. 3: 1–20.

CHAPTER 26
Alternative Assets

In Chapter 1, we described asset classes and mentioned the types of investment vehicles that fall into the category of what is referred to as *alternative assets*. Part of the difficulty of working with alternative asset classes is defining them. Are they a separate asset class or a subset of an existing asset class? Do they allow investors to push out the efficient frontier? That is, do they give the investor the opportunity to increase the expected portfolio return for a given level of risk compared to what is available in the absence of alternative assets? Are they listed on an exchange or do they trade in the over-the-counter market?

In most cases, alternative assets are a subset of an existing asset class. This may run contrary to the popular view that alternative assets are separate asset classes. However, we take the view that what many consider separate "classes" are really just different investment strategies within an existing asset class. Access to alternative assets is less straightforward than it is to purchase stocks and bonds; therefore, alternative assets are often overlooked because they require more work to invest in than traditional asset classes.

In this chapter, we will explain three types of the best known alternative assets: hedge funds, private equity, and commodities.

HEDGE FUNDS

The U.S. securities law does not provide a definition of the pools of investment funds run by asset managers that are referred to as "hedge funds."[1] These

---

[1] The term *hedge fund* was first used by *Fortune* in 1966 to describe the private investment fund of Alfred Winslow Jones. In managing the portfolio, Jones sought to "hedge" the market risk of the fund by creating a portfolio that was long and short the stock market by an equal amount.

The sections on hedge funds and private equity are coauthored with Mark J. P. Anson. The section on commodities is coauthored with Roland Füss and Dieter G. Kaiser.

entities as of this writing are not regulated. George Soros, chairman of Soros Fund Management, a firm that advises a privately owned group of hedge funds (the Quantum Group of Funds), defines a hedge fund as follows:

> Hedge funds engage in a variety of investment activities. They cater to sophisticated investors and are not subject to the regulations that apply to mutual funds geared toward the general public. Fund managers are compensated on the basis of performance rather than as a fixed percentage of assets. "Performance funds" would be a more accurate description. (Soros 2000, 32)

The first page of a report by the President's Working Group on Financial Markets, *Hedge Funds, Leverage, and the Lessons of Long-Term Capital Management* published in April 1999, provides the following definition:

> The term "hedge fund" is commonly used to describe a variety of different types of investment vehicles that share some common characteristics. Although it is not statutorily defined, the term encompasses any pooled investment vehicle that is privately organized, administered by professional money managers, and not widely available to the public.

The above definitions, however, do not begin to describe the activities of hedge funds. The following is a description of hedge funds offered by the United Kingdom's Financial Services Authority, the regulatory body of all providers of financial services in that country:[2]

> The term can also be defined by considering the characteristics most commonly associated wih hedge funds. Usually, hedge funds:
>
> - Are organised as private investment partnerships or offshore investment corporations.
> - Use a wide variety of trading strategies involving position-taking in a range of markets.
> - Employ an assortment of trading techniques and instruments, often including short-selling, derivatives and leverage.
> - Pay performance fees to their managers.
> - Have an investor base comprising wealthy individuals and institutions and a relatively high minimum investment limit (set at US$100,000 or higher for most funds).

---

[2]Financial Services Authority, *Hedge Funds and the FSA*, Discussion Paper 16, 2002, p. 8.

The definitions reproduced above help us understand several attributes of hedge funds. First and foremost, the word "hedge" in hedge funds is misleading because it is not a characteristic of hedge funds today. Second, hedge funds use a wide range of trading strategies and techniques in an attempt to not just generate abnormal returns but rather attempt to generate stellar returns regardless of how the market moves. The strategies used by a hedge fund can include one or more of the following:

- Leverage, which is the use of borrowed funds.
- Short selling, which is the sale of a financial instrument not owned in anticipation of a decline in that financial instrument's price.
- Derivatives to create leverage and/or to control risk.
- Simultaneous buying and selling of related financial instruments to realize a profit from the temporary misalignment of their prices.

Third, in evaluating hedge funds, investors are interested in the absolute return generated by the asset manager, not the relative return. *Absolute return* is simply the return realized rather than *relative return* which is the difference between the realized return and the return on some benchmark or index which is quite different from the criterion used when evaluating the performance of an asset manager.[3]

Fourth, the management fee structure for hedge funds is a combination of a fixed fee based on the market value of assets managed plus a share of the positive return. The latter is a performance-based compensation referred to as an *incentive fee*.

We define *hedge fund* as a privately organized investment vehicle that manages a concentrated portfolio of public and private securities and derivative instruments on those securities, that can invest both long and short and can apply leverage.

In this section, we will discuss the various types of hedge funds according to the investment strategies that they pursue and considerations in investing in hedge funds. We begin by first comparing hedge funds with mutual funds.

---

[3] The term *absolute return* comes from the skill-based nature of the industry. Hedge fund managers generally claim that their investment returns are derived from their skill at security selection rather than that of broad asset classes. This is due to the fact that most hedge fund managers build concentrated portfolios of relatively few investment positions and do not attempt to track a stock or bond index. The work of Fung and Hsieh (1997) shows that hedge funds generate a return distribution that is very different from mutual funds.

Hedge Funds Versus Mutual Funds

There are six key elements of hedge funds that distinguish them from their more traditional counterpart, the mutual fund.

First, hedge funds are private investment vehicles that pool the resources of sophisticated investors. One of the ways that hedge funds avoid the regulatory scrutiny of the Securities and Exchange Commission (SEC) or the Commodities Futures Trading Commission (CFTC) is that they are available only for high-net-worth investors. Under SEC rules, hedge funds cannot have more than 100 accredited investors in the fund.[4]

There is a penalty, however, for the privacy of hedge funds. They cannot raise funds from investors via a public offering. Additionally, hedge funds may not advertise broadly or engage in a general solicitation for new funds.

Second, hedge funds tend to have portfolios that are much more concentrated than their mutual fund brethren. Most hedge funds do not have broad securities benchmarks. One reason is that most hedge fund managers claim that their style of investing is "skill based" and cannot be measured by a market return. Consequently, hedge fund managers are not forced to maintain security holdings relative to a benchmark; they do not need to worry about "benchmark" risk. This allows them to concentrate their portfolio only on those securities that they believe will add value to the portfolio.

Another reason for the concentrated portfolio is that hedge fund managers tend to have narrow investment strategies. These strategies tend to focus on only one sector of the economy or one segment of the market. They can tailor their portfolio to extract the most value from their smaller investment sector or segment. Furthermore, the concentrated portfolios of hedge fund managers generally are not dependent on the direction of the financial markets, in contrast to long-only managers.

Third, hedge funds tend to use derivative strategies much more predominately than mutual funds. The use of derivative strategies may require more sophisticated risk management techniques to control these risks.

Fourth, hedge funds may go both long and short securities. The ability to short public securities and derivative instruments is one of the key distinctions between hedge funds and traditional money managers. Hedge fund managers incorporate their ability to short securities explicitly into their investment strategies. For example, equity long/short hedge funds tend to buy and sell securities within the same industry to maximize their return

---

[4] An accredited investor is defined as an individual that has a minimum net worth in excess or $1,000,000, or income in each of the past two years of $200,000 ($300,000 for a married couple) with an expectation of earning at least that amount in the current year.

but also to control their risk. This is very different from traditional money managers that are tied to a long-only securities benchmark.

Fifth, many hedge fund strategies invest in nonpublic securities, that is, securities that have been issued to investors without the support of a prospectus and a public offering.

Finally, hedge funds use leverage, sometimes, large amounts. Mutual funds, for example, are limited in the amount of leverage they can employ; they may borrow up to 33% of their net asset base. Hedge funds do not have this restriction. Consequently, it is not unusual to see some hedge fund strategies that employ leverage up to 10 times their net asset base.

Categories of Hedge Funds

Everyone has their own classification scheme for hedge funds.[5] This merely reflects the fact that hedge funds are a bit difficult to "box in." Here we break down hedge funds into broad categories as depicted in Figure 26.1.

We classify hedge funds into four broad buckets: market directional, corporate restructuring, convergence trading, and opportunistic. *Market directional hedge funds* are those that retain some amount of systematic risk exposure. For example, *equity long/short* (or, as it is sometime called, *equity hedge*) are hedge funds that typically contain some amount of net long market exposure. Thus they retain some amount of systematic risk exposure that will be affected by the direction of the stock market.

Corporate restructuring hedge funds take advantage of significant corporate transactions like a merger, acquisition, or bankruptcy. These funds earn their living by concentrating their portfolios in a handful of companies where it is more important to understand the likelihood that the corporate transaction will be completed than it is to determine whether the corporation is under or over valued.

Convergence trading hedge funds are the hedge funds that practice the art of arbitrage. In fact the specialized subcategories within this bucket typically contain the word *arbitrage* in their description such as statistical arbitrage, fixed income arbitrage, or convertible arbitrage. In general these hedge funds make bets that two similar securities but with dissimilar prices will converge to the same value over the investment holding period.

Last, we have the *opportunistic* category. We include in this category global macrohedge funds, global tactical asset allocation hedge funds, and multi-strategy hedge funds. These funds are designed to take advantage of whatever opportunities present themselves—hence the word "opportunistic."

---

[5]See, for example, Lhabitant (2004).

FIGURE 26.1 Categories of Hedge Funds

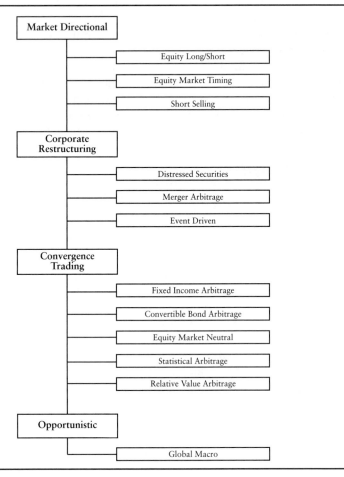

Hedge Fund Strategies

Hedge funds invest in the same equity and fixed income securities as traditional long-only managers. Therefore, it is not the alternative "assets" in which hedge funds invest that differentiates them from long-only managers, but rather, it is the alternative investment strategies that they pursue. Below we provide more detail on the types of strategies pursued by hedge fund managers.

Market Direction Hedge Funds

The strategies in this bucket of hedge funds either retain some systematic market exposure associated with the stock market such as equity long/short or are specifically driven by the movements of the stock market such are market timing or short selling.

Equity Long/Short Equity long/short managers build their portfolios by combining a core group of long stock positions with short sales of stock or stock index options and futures. Their net market exposure of long positions minus short positions tends to have a positive bias. That is, equity long/short managers tend to be long market exposure. The length of their exposure depends on current market conditions. For instance, during the great stock market surge of 1996 to 1999, these managers tended to be mostly long their equity exposure. However, as the stock market turned into a bear market in 2000 to 2002, these managers decreased their market exposure as they sold more stock short or sold stock index options and futures.

The ability to go both long and short in the market is a powerful tool for earning excess returns. The ability to fully implement a strategy not only about stocks and sectors that are expected to increase in value but also stocks and sectors that are expected to decrease in value allows the hedge fund manager to maximize the value of her market insights.

Equity long/short hedge funds essentially come in two flavors: fundamental and quantitative. *Fundamental long/short hedge funds* conduct traditional economic analysis on a company's business prospects compared to its competitors and the current economic environment. These shops will visit with management, talk with Wall Street analysts, contact customers and competitors and essentially conduct bottom-up analysis. The difference between these hedge funds and long-only managers is that they will short the stocks that they consider will be poor performers and buy those stocks that are expected to outperform the market. In addition, they may leverage their long and short positions.

Fundamental long/short equity hedge funds tend to invest in one economic sector or market segment. For instance, they may specialize in buying and selling internet companies (sector focus) or buying and selling small market capitalization companies (segment focus).

In contrast, *quantitative equity long/short hedge fund managers* tend not to be sector or segment specialists. In fact, quite the reverse: quantitative hedge fund managers like to cast as broad a net as possible in their analysis. These managers are often referred to as statistical arbitrage managers because they base their trade selection on the use of quantitative statistics instead of fundamental stock selection.

Market Timers Market timers, as their name suggest, attempt to time the most propitious moments to be in the market, and invest in cash otherwise.

More specifically, they attempt to time the market so that they are fully invested during bull markets and strictly in cash during bear markets.

Unlike equity long/short strategies, market times use a top-down approach as opposed to a bottom-up approach. Market-timing hedge fund managers are not stock pickers. They analyze fiscal and monetary policy as well as key macroeconomic indicators to determine whether the economy is gathering or running out of steam.

Macroeconomic variables they may analyze are labor productivity, business investment, purchasing managers' surveys, commodity prices, consumer confidence, housing starts, retail sales, industrial production, balance of payments, current account deficits and surpluses, and durable good orders. They use this macroeconomic data to forecast the expected *gross domestic product* (GDP) for the next quarter.

Once market timers have their forecast for the next quarter(s), they position their investment portfolio in the market according to their forecast. Construction of their portfolio is quite simple. They do not need to purchase individual stocks. Instead, they buy or sell stock index futures and options to increase or decrease their exposure to the market as necessary. At all times, contributed capital from investors is kept in short-term, risk-free interest-bearing accounts. Treasury bills are often purchased which not only yield a current risk-free interest rate, but also can be used as margin for taking positions in stock index futures.

When a market timer's forecast is bullish, he may purchase stock index futures with an economic exposure equivalent to the contributed capital. He may apply leverage by purchasing futures contracts that provide an economic exposure to the stock market greater than that of the underlying capital. However, market timers generally do not borrow investment capital.

When the hedge fund manager is bearish, he will trim his market exposure by selling futures contracts. If he is completely bearish, he will sell all of his stock index futures and call options and just sit on his cash portfolio. Some market timers may be more aggressive and short stock index futures and buy stock index put options to take advantage of an anticipated bear market.

In general though, market timers tend to have long exposure to the market at all times, making them market directional. However, they attempt to trim this exposure when markets appear bearish.

Short Selling *Short-selling hedge funds* have the opposite exposure of traditional long-only managers. In that sense, their return distribution should be the mirror image of long-only managers: they make money when the stock market is declining and lose money when the stock market is gaining.

These hedge fund managers may be distinguished from equity long/short managers in that they generally maintain a net short exposure to the stock market. However, short selling hedge funds tend to use some form of market timing. That is, they trim their short positions when the stock market is increasing and go fully short when the stock market is declining. When the stock market is gaining, short sellers maintain that portion of their investment capital not committed to short selling in short-term interest bearing accounts.

Corporate Restructuring Hedge Funds

As the name suggests, the focal point of corporate restructuring hedge funds is some form of corporate restructuring such as a merger, acquisition, or bankruptcy. Companies that are undergoing a significant transformation generally provide an opportunity for trading around that event. These strategies are driven by the deal, not by the market.

Distressed Securities *Distressed debt hedge funds* invest in the securities of a corporation that it is in bankruptcy, or is likely to fall into bankruptcy. Companies can become distressed for any number of reasons such as too much leverage on their balance sheet, poor operating performance, accounting irregularities, and even competitive pressure. Some of these strategies can overlap with private equity strategies that we will discuss later in this chapter. The key difference here is that hedge funds are less concerned with the fundamental value of a distressed corporation and, instead, concentrate on trading opportunities surrounding the company's outstanding stock-and-bond securities.

There are many variations on how to play a distressed situation but most fall into three categories. In its simplest form, the easiest way to profit from a distressed corporation is to sell its stock short. This requires the hedge fund manager to borrow stock from its prime broker and sell in the marketplace stock that it does not own with the expectation that the hedge fund manager will be able to purchase the stock back at a later date and at a cheaper price as the company continues to spiral downward in its distressed situation. This is nothing more than "sell high and buy low" strategy.

However, the short selling of a distressed company exposes the hedge fund manager to significant risk if the company's fortunes should suddenly turnaround. Therefore, most hedge fund managers in this space typically use a hedging strategy within a company's capital structure.

A second form of distressed securities investing is called *capital structure arbitrage*. Consider Company A that has four levels of outstanding capital: senior secured debt, junior subordinated debt, preferred stock, and common stock. A standard distressed security investment strategy would be to:

1. Buy the senior secured debt and short the junior subordinated debt.
2. Buy the preferred stock and short the common stock.

In a bankruptcy situation, the senior secured debt stands in line in front of the junior subordinated debt for any bankruptcy determined payouts. The same is true for the preferred stock compared to Company A's common stock. Both the senior secured debt and the preferred stock enjoy a higher standing in the bankruptcy process than either junior debt or common equity. Therefore, when the distressed situation occurs or progresses, senior secured debt should appreciate in value relative to the junior subordinated debt. In addition, there should be an increase in the spread of prices between preferred stock and common stock. When this happens, the hedge fund manager closes out her positions and locks in the profit that occurs from the increase in the spread.

Finally, distressed securities hedge funds can become involved in the bankruptcy process to find significantly undervalued securities. This is where an overlap with private equity firms can occur. To the extent that a distressed securities hedge fund is willing to learn the arcane workings of the bankruptcy process and to sit on creditor committees, significant value can be accrued if a distressed company can restructure and regain its footing.

Merger Arbitrage Merger arbitrage is perhaps the best-known corporate restructuring investment strategy among investors and hedge fund managers. Merger arbitrage, sometimes referred to as *risk arbitrage*, generally entails the buying the stock of the firm that is to be acquired and selling the stock of the firm that is the acquirer. Merger arbitrage managers seek to capture the price spread between the current market prices of the merger partners and the value of those companies upon the successful completion of the merger.

The stock of the target company usually trades at a discount to the announced merger price. The discount reflects the risk inherent in the deal; other market participants are unwilling to take on the full exposure of the transaction-based risk. Merger arbitrage is then subject to event risk. There is the risk that the two companies will fail to come to terms and call off the deal. There is the risk that another company will enter into the bidding contest, ruining the initial dynamics of the arbitrage. There is also regulatory risk. Various U.S. and foreign regulatory agencies may not allow the merger to take place for antitrust reasons. Merger arbitrageurs specialize in assessing event risk and building a diversified portfolio to spread out this risk. Merger arbitrageurs conduct significant research on the companies involved in the merger.

The term *arbitrage* is used loosely. As discussed above, there is plenty of event risk associated with a merger announcement. The profits earned from merger arbitrage are not riskless. Consider the saga of the purchase of MCI Corporation by Verizon Communications. Throughout 2005, Verizon was in a bidding war against Qwest Communications for the purchase of MCI. On February 3, 2005, Qwest announced a $6.3 billion merger offer for MCI. This bid was quickly countered by Verizon on February 10 that matched the $6.3 billion bid established by Qwest. The bidding war raged back and forth for several months before Verizon finally won the day in October 2005 with an ultimate purchase price of $8.44 billion.

Some merger arbitrage managers only invest in announced deals. However, other hedge fund managers will put on positions on the basis of rumor or speculation. The deal risk is much greater with this type of strategy, but so too, is the merger spread (the premium that can be captured).

To control for risk, most merger arbitrage hedge fund managers have some risk of loss limit at which they will exit positions. Some hedge fund managers concentrate only in one or two industries, applying their specialized knowledge regarding an economic sector to their advantage. Other merger arbitrage managers maintain a diversified portfolio across several industries to spread out the event risk.

Merger arbitrage is deal driven rather than market driven. Merger arbitrage derives its return from the relative value of the stock prices between two companies as opposed to the status of the current market conditions. Consequently, merger arbitrage returns should not be highly correlated with the general stock market.

Special Situation *Special situation hedge funds* are very similar in their approach to investing as in distressed securities and merger arbitrage. The only difference is that their mandate is broader than the other two corporate-restructuring strategies. Event-driven transactions include mergers and acquisitions, spin-offs, tracking stocks, accounting write-offs, reorganizations, bankruptcies, share buy-backs, special dividends, and any other significant market event. Event-driven managers are nondiscriminatory in their transaction selection.

By their very nature, these special events are nonrecurring. Therefore, the financial markets typically do not digest the information associated with these transactions on a timely manner. The financial markets are simply less efficient when it comes to large, isolated transactions. This provides an opportunity for event-driven managers to act quickly and capture a premium in the market. Additionally, most of these events may be subject to certain conditions such as shareholder or regulatory approval. Therefore, there is significant deal risk associated with this strategy for which a savvy hedge fund manager can earn a return premium. The profitability of this type of strategy is dependent upon the successful completion of the corporate transaction within the expected timeframe.

Convergence Trading Hedge Funds

As explained above, hedge fund managers tend to use the word "arbitrage" somewhat loosely. Arbitrage is defined simply as riskless profits requiring no initial outlay. It is the purchase of a security for cash at one price and the immediate resale for cash of the same security at a higher price. Alternatively, it may be defined as the simultaneous purchase of security A for cash at one price and the selling of an identical security B for cash at a higher price. In both cases, the arbitrageur has no risk. There is no market risk because the holding of the securities is instantaneous. There is no basis risk because the securities are identical, and there is no credit risk because the transaction is conducted in cash.

Instead of riskless profits, in the hedge fund world, arbitrage is generally used to mean low-risk investments. Instead of the purchase and sale of identical instruments, there is the purchase and sale of similar instruments. The securities also may not be sold for cash, so there may be credit risk during the collection period. Finally, the purchase and sale may not be instantaneous. The arbitrageur may need to hold onto its positions for a period of time, thereby having exposure to market risk.

Fixed Income Arbitrage Fixed income arbitrage involves purchasing one fixed income security and simultaneously selling a similar fixed income security with the expectation that over the investment holding period, the two security prices will converge to a similar value. Hedge fund managers search continuously for these pricing inefficiencies across all fixed income markets. This is nothing more than buying low and selling high and waiting for the undervalued security to increase in value or the overvalued security to decline in value, or wait for both to occur.

The sale of the second security is done to hedge the underlying market risk contained in the first security. Typically, the two securities are related either mathematically or economically such that they move similarly with respect to market developments. Generally, the difference in pricing between the two securities is small, and this is what the fixed income arbitrageur hopes to gain. By buying and selling two fixed income securities that are tied together, the hedge fund manager hopes to capture a pricing discrepancy that will cause the prices of the two securities to converge over time.

However, because the price discrepancies can be small, the way hedge fund managers add more value is to leverage their portfolio through direct borrowings from their prime broker, or by creating leverage through swaps and other derivative securities. Bottom line, they find pricing anomalies then "crank up the volume" through leverage.

Fixed income arbitrage does not need to use exotic securities. For example, it can be nothing more than buying and selling U.S. Treasury bonds. In the bond market, the most liquid securities are the *on-the-run* Treasury bonds. These are the most currently issued bonds issued by the U.S. Treasury Department. However, there are other U.S. Treasury bonds outstanding that have very similar characteristics to the on-the-run Treasury bonds. The difference is that *off-the-run* bonds were issued at an earlier date, and are now less liquid as the on-the-run bonds. As a result, price discrepancies occur. The difference in price may be no more than one-half or one quarter of a point ($25) but can increase in times of uncertainty when investor money shifts to the most liquid U.S. Treasury bond. During the Russian bond default crisis, for example, on-the-run U.S. Treasuries were valued as much as $100 more than similar, off-the-run U.S. Treasury bonds of the same maturity. Nonetheless, when held to maturity, the prices of these two bonds will converge to the same value. Any difference will be eliminated by the time they mature, and any price discrepancy may be captured by the hedge fund manager.

Fixed income arbitrage is not limited to the U.S. Treasury market. It can be used with corporate bonds, municipal bonds, sovereign debt, or mortgage-backed securities.

What should be noted about fixed income arbitrage strategies is that they do not depend on the direction of the general financial markets. Arbitrageurs seek out pricing inefficiencies between two securities instead of making bets on market direction. However, these strategies do depend heavily on the ability to lever the portfolio and therefore on obtaining financing.

Convertible Bond Arbitrage Convertible bonds combine elements of both stock and bonds in one package. As explained in Chapter 17, convertible bond is a bond that contains an embedded option to convert the bond into the underlying company's stock.

Convertible arbitrage funds build long positions of convertible bonds and then hedge the equity component of the bond by selling the underlying stock or options on that stock. The equity risk of this strategy can be hedged by selling the appropriate ratio of stock underlying the convertible option. As explained in Chapters 13 and 14, this hedge ratio is known as the "delta" and is designed to measure the sensitivity of the convertible bond value to movements in the underlying stock.

Convertible bonds that trade at a low premium to their conversion value tend to be more correlated with the movement of the underlying stock. These convertibles then trade more like stock than they do a bond. Consequently, a high hedge ratio, or delta, is required to hedge the equity risk contained in the convertible bond. Convertible bonds that trade at a premium to their conversion value are highly valued for their bond-like protection. Therefore, a lower delta hedge ratio is necessary.

However, convertible bonds that trade at a high conversion act more like fixed income securities and therefore have more interest rate exposure than those with more equity exposure. This risk must be managed by selling interest rate futures, interest rate swaps or other bonds. Furthermore, it should be noted that the hedging ratios for equity and interest rate risk are not static, they change as the value of the underlying equity changes and as interest rates change. Therefore, the hedge fund manager must continually adjust his hedge ratios to ensure that the arbitrage remains intact.

If this all sounds complicated, it is, but that is how hedge fund managers make money. They use sophisticated option pricing models and interest rate models to keep track of the all of moving parts associated with convertible bonds. Hedge fund managers make arbitrage profits by identifying pricing discrepancies between the convertible bond and its component parts, and then continually monitoring these component parts for any change in their relationship.

The amount of leverage used in convertible arbitrage will vary with the size of the long positions and the objectives of the portfolio. Leverage is also inherent in the shorting strategy because the underlying short equity position must be borrowed. Convertible arbitrage leverage has a minimum of two times the amount of invested capital. This may seem significant, but it is lower than other forms of arbitrage.

Convertible bonds earn returns for taking on exposure to a number of risks such as (1) liquidity (convertible bonds are typically issued as private securities); (2) credit risk (convertible bonds are usually issued by less than investment grade companies); (3) event risk (the company may be downgraded or declare bankruptcy); (4) interest rate risk (as a bond it is exposed to interest rate risk); (5) negative convexity (most convertible bonds are callable); and (6) model risk (it is complex to model all of the moving parts associated with a convertible bond). These events are only magnified when leverage is applied.

Market Neutral *Market-neutral hedge funds* go long and short the market. The difference, is that they maintain integrated portfolios, which are designed to neutralize market risk. This means being neutral to the general stock market as well as having neutral risk exposures across industries. Security selection is all that matters.

Market-neutral hedge fund managers generally apply the rule of one alpha.[6] This means that they build an integrated portfolio designed to produce only one source of alpha. This is distinct from equity long/short managers that build two separate portfolios: one long and one short, with two sources of alpha. The idea of integrated portfolio construction is to neutralize market and industry risk and concentrate purely on stock selection. In other words, there is no beta risk in the portfolio either with respect to the broad stock market or with respect to any industry. Only stock selection, or alpha, should remain.

Market-neutral hedge fund managers generally hold equal positions of long and short stock positions. Therefore, the manager is dollar neutral; there is no net exposure to the market either on the long side or on the short side. Additionally, market-neutral managers generally apply no leverage because there is no market exposure to leverage. However, some leverage is always inherent when stocks are borrowed and shorted. Nonetheless, the nature of this strategy is that it does not have credit risk.

Generally, market-neutral managers follow a three-step procedure in their strategy. The first step is to build an initial screen of "investable" stocks. These are stocks traded on the hedge fund manager's local exchange, with sufficient liquidity so as to be able to enter and exit positions quickly, and with sufficient float so that the stock may be borrowed from the hedge fund manager's prime broker for short positions. Additionally, the hedge fund manager may limit his universe to a capitalization segment of the equity universe such as the midcap range.

Second, the hedge fund manager typically builds factor models as explained in Chapter 11. Their purpose is to find those financial variables that influence stock prices. These are bottom-up models that concentrate solely on corporate financial information as opposed to macroeconomic data. This is the source of the manager's skill—his stock selection ability.

The last step is portfolio construction. The hedge fund manager will use a computer program to construct his portfolio in such a way that it is neutral to the market as well as across industries. The hedge fund manager may use a commercial "optimizer"—computer software designed to measure exposure to the market and produce a trade list for execution based on a manager's desired exposure to the market—or he may use his own computer algorithms to measure and neutralize risk.

Most market-neutral managers use optimizers to neutralize market and industry exposure. However, more sophisticated optimizers attempt to keep the portfolio neutral to several risk factors. These include size, book to value, price/earnings ratios, and market price to book value ratios. The idea

---

[6]See Jacobs and Levy (1995).

is to have no intended or unintended risk exposures that might compromise the portfolio's neutrality.

We would expect market-neutral managers to produce returns independent of the general market (they are neutral to the market).

Statistical Arbitrage   A close cousin to equity market-neutral hedge fund managers is *statistical arbitrage*. The key difference is the amount of quantitative input. While equity market-neutral is based more on fundamental research, statistical arbitrage is driven purely by quantitative factor models.

These managers use mathematical analysis to review past company performance in light of several quantitative factors. For instance, these managers may build regression models to determine the impact of market price to book value (price/book ratio) on companies across the universe of stocks as well as different market segments or economic sectors. Or they may analyze changes in dividend yields on stock price performance.

These are linear and quadratic regression equations designed to identify those economic factors that consistently have an impact on share prices. This process is very similar to that discussed with respect to equity long/short hedge fund managers. Indeed, the two strategies are very similar in their stock selection methods. The difference is that equity long/short managers tend to have a net long exposure to the market while market-neutral managers have no exposure.

Typically, these managers build factor models to identify those economic factors that have a consistent impact on share prices. If the model proves successful on historical data, the hedge fund manager will then conduct an "out of sample" test of the model. This involves testing the model on a subset of historical data that was not included in the model building phase.

If a hedge fund manager identifies a successful quantitative strategy, it will apply its model mechanically. Buy and sell orders will be generated by the model and submitted to the order desk. In practice, the hedge fund manager will put limits on its model such as the maximum short exposure allowed or the maximum amount of capital that may be committed to any one stock position. In addition, quantitative hedge fund managers usually build in some qualitative oversight to ensure that the model is operating consistently.

Statistical arbitrage programs tend to be labeled "black boxes." This is a term for sophisticated computer algorithms that lack transparency. The lack of transparency associated with these investment strategies comes in two forms. First, hedge fund managers, by nature, are secretive. They are reluctant to reveal their proprietary trading programs. Second, even if a hedge fund manager were to reveal his proprietary computer algorithms, these algorithms are often so sophisticated and complicated that they are difficult to comprehend.

Note that this strategy does not share in the large up and down cycles of the stock market. It earns a steady return, not as great as the stock market, but in excess of U.S. Treasuries. Remember the goal of this strategy is to neutralize market risk and to profit on small price discrepancies between stocks in the same industry or sector. Consistent profits are the key; large bets are avoided.

Relative Value Arbitrage Relative value arbitrage might be better named the smorgasbord of arbitrage. This is because relative value hedge fund managers are catholic in their investment strategies; they invest across the universe of arbitrage strategies. The best known of these managers was Long-Term Capital Management. Once the story of this hedge fund unfolded, it was clear that its trading strategies involved merger arbitrage, fixed income arbitrage, volatility arbitrage, stub trading, and convertible arbitrage.

In general, the strategy of relative value managers is to invest in spread trades: the simultaneous purchase of one security and the sale of another when the economic relationship between the two securities (the "spread") has become mispriced. The mispricing may be based on historical averages or mathematical equations. In either case, the relative arbitrage manager purchases the security that is "cheap" and sells the security that is "rich." It is called relative value arbitrage because the cheapness or richness of a security is determined *relative* to a second security. Consequently, relative value managers do not take directional bets on the financial markets. Instead, they take focused bets on the pricing relationship between two securities.

Relative value managers attempt to remove the influence of the financial markets from their investment strategies. This is made easy by the fact that they simultaneously buy and sell similar securities. Therefore, the market risk embedded in each security should cancel out. Any residual risk can be neutralized through the use of options or futures. What is left is pure security selection: the purchase of those securities that are relatively cheap and the sale of those securities that are relatively rich. Relative value managers earn a profit when the spread between the two securities returns to normal. They then unwind their positions and collect their profit.

We have already discussed fixed income arbitrage, convertible arbitrage, and statistical arbitrage. Two other popular forms of relative value arbitrage are stub trading and volatility arbitrage. They are described in Anson (2008).

Volatility arbitrage involves options and warrant trading. Option prices contain an *implied* number for volatility. That is, it is possible to observe the market price of an option and back out the value of volatility implied in the current price using various option pricing models. The arbitrageur can then compare options on the same underlying stock to determine if the volatility implied by their prices are the same.

The implied volatility derived from option pricing models should represent the expected volatility of the underlying stock that will be realized over the life of the option. Therefore, two options on the same underlying stock should have the same implied volatility. If they do not, an arbitrage opportunity may be available. Additionally, if the implied volatility is significantly different from the historical volatility of the underlying stock, then relative value arbitrageurs expect the implied volatility will revert back to its historical average.

Volatility arbitrage generally is applied in one of two models. The first is a mean-reversion model. This model compares the implied volatility from current option prices to the historical volatility of the underlying security with the expectation that the volatility reflected in the current option price will revert to its historical average and the option price will adjust accordingly.

A second volatility arbitrage model applies a statistical technique called Generalized Autoregressive Conditional Heteroscedasticity (GARCH). GARCH models use prior data points of conditional volatility to forecast future volatility. The GARCH forecast is then compared to the volatility implied in current option prices.

Both models are designed to allow hedge fund managers to determine which options are priced "cheap" versus "rich." Once again, relative value managers sell those options that are rich based on the implied volatility *relative* to the historical volatility and buy those options with cheap volatility relative to historical volatility.

Opportunistic Hedge Fund Strategies

Along the lines of the smorgasbord comment for relative value hedge funds, *opportunistic hedge fund strategies* have the broadest mandate across the financial, commodity, and futures markets. These all encompassing mandates can lead to specific bets on currencies or stocks as well as a well-diversified portfolio. We describe one type of such hedge fund here.

Global Macro As their name implies, global macrohedge funds take a macroeconomic approach on a global basis in their investment strategy. These are top-down managers who invest opportunistically across financial markets, currencies, national borders, and commodities. They take large positions depending upon the hedge fund manager's forecast of changes in interest rates, currency movements, monetary policies, and macroeconomic indicators.

Global macro hedge fund managers have the broadest investment universe. They are not limited by market segment or industry sector, nor by geographic region, financial market, or currency. Global macro hedge fund managers also may invest in commodities. In fact, a fund of global macrohedge funds offers the greatest diversification of investment strategies.

Global macrohedge funds tend to have large amounts of investor capital. This is necessary to execute their macroeconomic strategies. In addition, they may apply leverage to increase the size of their macro bets. As a result, global macrohedge funds tend to receive the greatest attention and publicity in the financial markets.

Funds of Hedge Funds

Funds of hedge funds are hedge fund managers that invest their capital in other hedge funds. These managers practice tactical asset allocation; reallocating capital across hedge fund strategies when they believe that certain hedge fund strategies will do better than others.

One drawback of fund of funds is the double layer of fees. Investors in hedge fund of funds typically pay a management plus profit sharing fees to the hedge fund of funds managers in addition to the management and incentive fees that must be absorbed from the underlying hedge fund managers. This double layer of fees makes it difficult for fund of fund managers to outperform some of the more aggressive individual hedge fund strategies. However, the trade-off is better risk control from a diversified portfolio.

Selecting a Hedge Fund Manager

Beyond performance numbers, there are three fundamental questions that every hedge fund manager should answer during the initial screening process. The answers to these three questions are critical to understanding the nature of the hedge fund manager's investment program. The three questions are:

1. What is the investment objective of the hedge fund?
2. What is the investment process of the hedge fund manager?
3. What makes the hedge fund manager so smart?

A hedge fund manager should have a clear and concise statement of its investment objective. Second, the hedge fund manager should identify its investment process. For instance, is it quantitatively or qualitatively based? Last, the hedge fund manager must demonstrate that he or she is smarter than other money managers.

The questions presented are threshold issues. These questions are screening tools designed to reduce an initial universe of hedge fund managers down to a select pool of potential investments. They are not, however, a substitute for a thorough due diligence review.

PRIVATE EQUITY

Private equity provides the long-term equity base of a company that is not listed on any exchange and therefore cannot raise capital via the public stock market. Private equity provides the working capital that is used to help private companies grow and succeed. It is a long-term investment process that requires patient due diligence and hands on monitoring.

Here we focus on the best known of the private equity categories: venture capital. Venture capital is the supply of equity financing to start-up companies that do not have a sufficient track record to attract investment capital from traditional sources (e.g., the public markets or lending institutions). Entrepreneurs that develop business plans require investment capital to implement those plans. However, these start-up ventures often lack tangible assets that can be used as collateral for a loan. In addition, start-up companies are unlikely to produce positive earnings for several years. Negative cash flows are another reason why banks and other lending institutions as well as the public stock market are unwilling to provide capital to support the business plan.

It is in this uncertain space where nascent companies are born that venture capitalists operate. Venture capitalists finance these high-risk, illiquid, and unproven ideas by purchasing senior equity stakes while the firms are still privately held. Venture capitalists are willing to underwrite new ventures with untested products and bear the risk of no liquidity only if they can expect a reasonable return for their efforts. Often venture capitalists set expected target rates of return of 33% or more to support the risks they bear. Venture capitalists have two roles within the industry. Raising money from investors is just the first part. The second is to invest that capital with start-up companies. Venture capitalists are not passive investors. Once they invest in a company, they take an active role either in an advisory capacity or as a director on the board of the company. They monitor the progress of the company, implement incentive plans for the entrepreneurs and management, and establish financial goals for the company. Besides providing management insight, venture capitalists usually have the right to hire and fire key managers, including the original entrepreneur. They also provide access to consultants, accountants, lawyers, investment bankers, and most importantly, other business that might purchase the start-up company's product.

Venture Capital Fees

Venture capitalists earn fees two ways: management fees and a percentage of the profits earned by the venture fund. Management fees can range anywhere from 1% to 3.5%, with most venture capital funds in the 2% to

2.5% range. Management fees are used to compensate the venture capitalist while looking for attractive investment opportunities for the venture fund.

A key point is that the management fee is assessed on the amount of committed capital, not invested capital. Consider the following example: a venture capitalist raises $100 million in committed capital for her venture fund. The management fee is 2.5%. To date, only $50 million dollars of the raised capital has been invested. The annual management fee that the venture capitalist collects is $2.5 million—2.5% × $100 million—even though not all of the capital has been invested. Investors pay the management fee on the amount of capital they have agreed to commit to the venture fund whether or not that capital has actually been invested.

Consider the implications of this fee arrangement. The venture capitalist collects a management fee from the moment that an investor signs a subscription agreement to invest capital in the venture fund—even though no capital has actually been contributed by the limited partners yet. Furthermore, the venture capitalist then has a call option to demand—according to the subscription agreement—that the investors contribute capital when the venture capitalist finds an appropriate investment for the fund. This is a great deal for the venture capitalist—he is paid a large fee to have a call option on the limited partners' capital. Not a bad business model. We will see later that this has some keen implications for leveraged buyout funds.

The second part of the remuneration for a venture capitalist is the profit sharing or incentive fees. This is really where the venture capitalist makes money. Incentive fees provide the venture capitalist with a share of the profits generated by the venture fund. The typical incentive fee is 20% but the better known venture capital funds can charge up to 35%. That is, the best venture capitalists can claim 1/3 of the profits generated by the venture fund.

The incentive fees for venture capital funds are a free option. If the venture capitalist generates profits for the venture fund, he can collect a share of these profits. If the venture fund loses money, the venture capitalist does not collect an incentive fee. This option has significant value to the venture capitalist. Furthermore, valued within an option context, venture capital profit sharing fees provide some interesting incentives to the venture capitalist.

For example, one way to increase the value of a call option is to increase the volatility of the underlying asset. This means that the venture capitalist is encouraged to make riskier investments with the pool of capital in the venture fund to maximize the value of his incentive fee. This increased risk may run counter to the desires of the limited partners to maintain a less risky profile. It is also fascinating to realize that this incentive fee is costless to the venture capitalist—he does not pay any price for the receipt of this option. Indeed, the venture capitalist gets paid a management fee in addition to this free call option on the profits of the venture fund. As we noted previously, this is not a bad business model for the venture capitalist.

Fortunately, there is a check and balance on incentive fees in the venture capital world. Most, if not all, venture capital limited partnership agreements include some restrictive covenants on when incentive fees may be paid to the venture capitalist. There are three primary covenants that are used.

First, most venture capital partnership agreements include a clawback provision. A *clawback covenant* allows the limited partners to clawback previously paid incentive fees to the venture capitalist if, at the end/liquidation of the venture fund, the limited partners are still out of pocket some costs or lost capital investment. This prevents the venture capitalist from making money if the limited partners do not earn a profit.

Second, there is often an escrow agreement where a portion of the venture capitalist incentive fees are held in a segregated escrow account until the fund is liquidated. Again this ensures that the venture capitalist does not walk away with any profit unless the limited partners also earn a profit. If a profit is earned by every limited partner, the escrow proceeds are released to the venture capitalist.

Finally, there is often a prohibition on the distribution of profit sharing fees to the venture capitalist until all committed capital is paid back to the limited partners. In other words, the limited partners must first be paid back their invested capital before profits may be shared in the venture fund. Sometimes this covenant provides that all management fees must also be recouped by the limited partners before the venture capitalist can collect his incentive fees.

The Business Plan

The venture capitalist has two constituencies: investors on the one hand, and start-up portfolio companies on the other. In the prior section, we discussed the relationship between the venture capitalist and his investors.

The most important document upon which a venture capitalist will base his decision to invest in a start-up company is the business plan. The business plan must be comprehensive, coherent, and internally consistent. It must clearly state the business strategy, identify the niche that the new company will fill, and describe the resources needed to fill that niche.

The business plan also reflects the start-up management team's ability to develop and present an intelligent and strategic plan of action. The business plan not only describes the business opportunity but also gives the venture capitalist an insight into the viability of the management team.

Last, the business plan must be realistic. One part of every business plan is the assumptions about revenue growth, cash-burn rate, additional rounds of capital injection, and expected date of profitability and/or IPO (initial public offering) status. The financial goals stated in the business plan must be achievable. Additionally, financial milestones identified in the business plan can become important conditions for the vesting of management equity, the release of deferred investment commitments, and the control of the board of directors.

In this section, we review the key elements of a business plan for a start-up venture. This is the heart and sole of the venture capital industry—it is where new ideas are born and capital is committed.

The executive summary is the opening statement of any business plan. In this short synopsis, it must be clear what is the unique selling point of the start-up venture. Is it a new product, distribution channel, manufacturing process, chip design, or consumer service? Whatever it is, it must be spelled out clearly for a nontechnical person to understand.[7]

The executive summary should quickly summarize the eight main parts of the business plan:

1. The market
2. The product/service
3. Intellectual property rights
4. The management team
5. Operations and prior operating history
6. Financial projections
7. Amount of financing
8. Exit opportunities

Each of these is described in more detail in Anson (2008).

Venture Capital Investment Vehicles

As the interest for venture capital investments has increased, venture capitalists have responded with new vehicles for venture financing. These include limited partnerships, limited liability companies, corporate venture funds, and venture capital fund of funds.

Limited Partnerships

The predominant form of venture capital investing in the United States is the limited partnership. Venture capitalists operate either as "3(c)(1)" or "3(c)(7)" funds to avoid registration as an investment company under the Investment Company Act of 1940. As a limited partnership, all income and capital gains flow through the partnership to the limited partner investors.

---

[7]See the British Venture Capital Association (2004).

The partnership itself is not taxed. The appeal of the limited partnership vehicle has increased since 1996 with the "Check the Box" provision of the U.S. tax code.

Previously, limited partnerships had to meet several tests to determine if their predominant operating characteristics resembled more a partnership than a corporation. Such characteristics included, for instance, a limited term of existence. Failure to qualify as a limited partnership would mean double taxation for the investment fund—first, at the fund level and second, at the investor level.

This changed with the U.S. Internal Revenue Services decision to let entities simply decide their own tax status by checking a box on their annual tax form as to whether they wished to be taxed as a corporation or as a partnership. "Checking the box" greatly encouraged investment funds to establish themselves as a limited partnership.

Limited partnerships are generally formed with an expected life of 10 years with an option to extend the limited partnership for another one to five years. The limited partnership is managed by a general partner who has day to day responsibility for managing the venture capital fund's investments as well as general liability for any lawsuits that may be brought against the fund. Limited partners, as their name implies, have only a limited (investor) role in the partnership. They do not partake in the management of the fund and they do not bear any liability beyond their committed capital.

All partners in the fund will commit to a specific investment amount at the formation of the limited partnership. However, the limited partners do not contribute money to the fund until it is called down or "taken down" by the general partner. Usually, the general partner will give one to two months notice of when it intends to make additional capital calls on the limited partners. Capital calls are made when the general partner has found a start-up company in which to invest. The general partner can make capital calls up to the amount of the limited partners' initial commitments.

An important element of limited partnership venture funds is that the general partner/venture capitalist has also committed investment capital to the fund. This assures the limited partners of an alignment of interests with the venture capitalist. Typically, limited partnership agreements specify a percentage or dollar amount of capital that the general partner must commit to the partnership.

Limited Liability Companies

Another financing vehicle in the venture capital industry is the *limited liability company* (LLC). Similar to a limited partnership, all items of net income or loss as well as capital gains are passed through to the shareholders in the LLC. Also, like a limited partnership, an LLC must adhere to the safe harbors of the Investment Company Act of 1940. In addition, LLCs usually have a life of 10 years with possible options to extend for another one to five years.

The managing director of an LLC acts like the general partner of a limited partnership. He has management responsibility for the LLC including the decision to invest in start-up companies the committed capital of the LLC's shareholders. The managing director of the LLC might itself be another LLC or a corporation. The same is true for limited partnerships; the general partner need not be an individual, it can be a legal entity like a corporation.

In sum, LLCs and limited partnerships accomplish the same goal—the pooling of investor capital into a central fund from which to make venture capital investments. The choice is dependent upon the type of investor sought. If the venture capitalist wishes to raise funds from a large number of passive and relatively uninformed investors, the limited partnership vehicle is the preferred venue. However, if the venture capitalist intends to raise capital from a small group of knowledgeable investors, the LLC is preferred.

The reason is twofold. First, LLCs usually have more specific shareholder rights and privileges. These privileges are best utilized with a small group of well-informed investors. Second, an LLC structure provides shareholders with control over the sale of additional shares in the LLC to new shareholders. This provides the shareholders with more power with respect to the twin issues of increasing the LLC's pool of committed capital and from whom that capital will be committed.

Venture Capital Fund of Funds

A venture capital fund of funds is a venture pool of capital that, instead of investing directly in start-up companies, invests in other venture capital funds. The venture capital fund of funds is a relatively new phenomenon in the venture capital industry. The general partner of a fund of funds does not select start-up companies in which to invest. Instead, the general partner selects the best venture capitalists with the expectation that they will find appropriate start-up companies to fund.

A venture capital fund of funds offers several advantages to investors. First, the investor receives broad exposure to a diverse range of venture capitalists, and in turn, a wide range of start-up investing. Second, the investor receives the expertise of the fund of funds manager in selecting the best venture capitalists with whom to invest money. Last, a fund of funds may have better access to popular, well-funded venture capitalists whose funds may be closed to individual investors. In return for these benefits, investors pay a management fee (and, in some cases, an incentive fee) to the fund of funds manager. The management fee can range from 0.5% to 2% of the net assets managed.

Fund of fund investing also offers benefits to the venture capitalists. First, the venture capitalist receives one large investment (from the venture fund of funds) instead of several small investments. This makes fund raising and investor administration more efficient. Second, the venture capitalist interfaces with an experienced fund of funds manager instead of several (potentially inexperienced) investors.

The Life Cycle of a Venture Capital Fund

A venture capital fund is a long-term investment. Typically, investors' capital is locked up for a minimum of 10 years—the standard term of a venture capital limited partnership. During this long investment period, a venture capital fund will normally go through five stages of development.

The first stage is the fund raising stage where the venture capital firm raises capital from outside investors. Capital is committed—not collected. This is an important distinction noted above. Investors sign a legal agreement (typically a subscription) that legally binds them to make cash investments in the venture capital fund up to a certain amount. This is the committed, but not yet drawn, capital. The venture capital firm/general partner will also post a sizeable amount of committed capital. Fundraising normally takes six months to a year.

The second stage consists of sourcing investments, reading business plans, preparing intense due diligence on start-up companies and determining the unique selling point of each start-up company. This period begins the moment the fund is closed to investors and normally takes up the first five years of the venture fund's existence. During stage two, no profits are generated by the venture capital fund. In fact, quite the reverse, the venture capital fund generates losses because the venture capitalist continues to draw annual management fees (which can be up to 3.5% a year on the total committed capital). These fees generate a loss until the venture capitalist begins to extract value from the investments of the venture fund.

Stage three is the investment of capital. During this stage, the venture capitalist determines how much capital to commit to each start-up company, at what level of financing, and in what form of investment (convertible preferred shares, convertible debentures, etc.). At this stage the venture capitalist will also present capital calls to the investors in the venture fund to draw on the capital of the limited partners. Note that no cash flow is generated yet, the venture fund is still in a deficit.

Stage four begins after the funds have been invested and lasts almost to the end of the term of the venture capital fund. During this time the venture

Alternative Assets **793**

capitalist works with the portfolio companies in which the venture capital fund has invested. The venture capitalist may help to improve the management team, establish distribution channels for the new product, refine the prototype product to generate the greatest sales, and generally position the start-up company for an eventual public offering or sale to a strategic buyer. During this time period, the venture capitalist will begin to generate profits for the venture fund and its limited partner investors. These profits will initially offset the previously collected management fees until a positive net asset value is established for the venture fund.

The last stage of the venture capital fund is its windup and liquidation. At this point, all committed capital has been invested and now the venture capitalist is in the harvesting stage. Each portfolio company is either sold to a strategic buyer, brought to the public markets in an initial public offering, or liquidated through a Chapter 7 bankruptcy liquidation process. Profits are distributed to the limited partners and the general partner/venture capitalist now collects incentive and profit sharing fees.

These stages of a venture capital firm lead to what is known as the *J-curve effect*. Figure 26.2 demonstrates the J-curve. We can see that during the early life of the venture capital fund, it generates negative revenues (losses) but eventually, profits are harvested from successful companies and these cash flows overcome the initial losses to generate a net profit for the fund. Clearly, given the initial losses that pile up during the first four to five years of a venture capital fund, this type of investing is only for patient, long-term investors.

FIGURE 26.2 The Life Cycle of a Venture Capital Fund

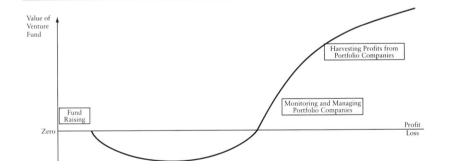

Specialization within the Venture Capital Industry

Like any industry that grows and matures, expansion and maturity lead to specialization. The trend towards specialization in the venture capital industry exists on several levels: by industry, geography, stage of financing, and "special situations."

Stage of Financing

While some venture capital firms classify themselves by geography or industry, by far the most distinguishing characteristic of venture capital firms is the stage of financing. Some venture capitalists provide first stage, or "seed capital" while others wait to invest in companies that are further along in their development. Still other venture capital firms come in at the final round of financing before the IPO. A different level of due diligence is required at each level of financing because the start-up venture has achieved another milestone on its way to success. In all, there are five discrete stages of venture capital financing: angel investing, seed capital, early stage capital, late stage/expansion capital, and mezzanine financing. We discuss each of these separately below.

Angel Investing

Angel investors often come from friends and family. At this stage of the new venture, typically there is a lone entrepreneur who has just an idea. There is no formal business plan, no management team, no product, no market analysis—just an idea.

In addition to family and friends, angel investors can also be wealthy individuals who "dabble" in start-up companies. This level of financing is typically done without a private placement memorandum or subscription agreement. It may be as informal as a "cocktail napkin" agreement. Yet without the angel investor, many ideas would wither on the vine before reaching more traditional venture capitalists.

At this stage of financing, the task of the entrepreneur is to begin the development of a prototype product or service. In addition, the entrepreneur begins the draft of the business plan, assesses the market potential, and may even begin to assemble some key management team members. No marketing or product testing is done at this stage.

The amount of financing at this stage is very small—$50,000 to $500,000. Any more than that would strain family, friends, and other angels. The funds are used primarily to flush out the concept to the point where an intelligent business plan can be constructed.

Seed Capital

Seed capital is the first stage where venture capital firms invest their capital. At this stage, a business plan is completed and presented to a venture capital firm. Some parts of the management team have been assembled at this point, a market analysis has been completed, and other points of the business plan are addressed by the entrepreneur and the small team assembled. Financing is provided to complete the product development and, possibly, to begin initial marketing of the prototype to potential customers. This phase of financing usually raises $1 to $5 million.

At this stage of financing, a prototype may have been developed and the testing of a product with customers may have begun. This is often referred to as "beta testing," and is the process where a prototype product is sent to potential customers free of charge to get their input into the viability, design, and user friendliness of the product.

Very little revenue has been generated at this stage, and the company is definitely not profitable. Venture capitalists invest in this stage based on their due diligence of the management team, their own market analysis of the demand for the product, the viability of getting the product to the market while there is still time and not another competitor, the additional management team members that will need to be added, and the likely timing for additional rounds of capital from the same venture capital firm for from other venture capital funds.

Early Stage Venture Capital

At this point, the start-up company should have a viable product that has been beta tested. Alpha testing may have already begun. This is the testing of the second generation prototype with potential end users. Typically, a price is charged for the product or a fee for the service. Revenues are being generated and the product or service has now demonstrated commercial viability. Early stage venture capital financing is usually $2 million and more.

Early stage financing is typically used to build out the commercial scale manufacturing services. The product is no longer being produced out of the entrepreneur's garage or out of some vacant space above a grocery store. The company is now a going concern with an initial, if not complete, management team. At this stage, there will be at least one venture capitalist sitting on the board of directors of the company.

The goal of the start-up venture is to achieve market penetration with its product. Some of this will have already been accomplished with the beta and alpha testing of the product. However, additional marketing must now be completed. In addition, distribution channels should be identified by now and the product should be established in these channels. Reaching a break-even point is the financial goal.

Late Stage/Expansion Venture Capital

At this point, the start-up company may have generated its first profitable quarter, or be just at the breakeven point. Commercial viability is now established. Cash flow management is critical at this stage, as the company is not yet at the level where its cash flows can self sustain its own growth.

Last stage/expansion capital fills this void. This level of venture capital financing is used to help the start-up company get through its cash crunch. The additional capital is used to tap into the distribution channels, establish call centers, expand the manufacturing facilities, and to attract the additional management and operational talent necessary to the make the start-up company a longer-term success. Because this capital comes in to allow the company to expand, financing needs are typically greater than for seed and early stage. Amounts may be in the $5 million to $15 million range.

At this stage, the start-up venture enjoys the growing pains of all successful companies. It may need additional working capital because it has focused on product development and product sales, but now finds itself with a huge backload of accounts receivable from customers upon which it must now collect. Inevitably, start-up companies are very good at getting the product out of the door but very poor at collecting receivables and turning sales into cold hard cash.

Again, this is where expansion capital can help. Late stage venture financing helps the successful start-up get through its initial cash crunch. Eventually, the receivables will be collected and sufficient internal cash will be generated to make the start-up company a self-sustaining force. Until then, one more round of financing may be needed.

Mezzanine Stage

Mezzanine venture capital is the last stage before a start-up company goes public or is sold to a strategic buyer. At this point, a second generation product may already be in production if not distribution. The management team is together and solid, and the company is working on managing its cash flow better. Manufacturing facilities are established, and the company may already be thinking about penetrating international markets. Amounts vary depending on how long the bridge financing is meant to last but generally is in the range of $5 to $15 million.

The financing at this stage is considered "bridge" or mezzanine financing to keep the company from running out of cash until the IPO or strategic sale. The start-up company may still have a large inventory of uncollected accounts receivable that need to be financed in the short term. Profits are being recorded, but accounts receivable are growing at the same rate of sales.

Mezzanine financing may be in the form of convertible debt. In addition the company may have sufficient revenue and earning power that traditional bank debt may be added at this stage. This means that the start-up company may have to clean up its balance sheet as well as its statement of cash flows. Commercial viability is more than just generating sales, it also requires turning accounts receivable into actual dollars.

The J-Curve for a Start-Up Company

Figure 26.3 presents the J-curve for a start-up company. Similar to the J-curve for a venture capital fund, the initial years of a start-up company generate a loss. Money is spent turning an idea into a prototype product and from there beta testing the product with potential customers. Little or no revenue is generated during this time. It is not until the product goes into alpha testing that revenues may be generated and the start-up becomes a viable concern.

Once a critical mass is generated—where sales are turned into profits and accounts receivable is turned into cash—then it becomes a matter of timing until the start-up company achieves a public offering. Additional rounds of financing may be needed to get the company to its IPO "nirvana." At this point commercial viability is established, but managing the cash crunch becomes critical.

FIGURE 26.3 The Life Cycle of a Start-Up Company

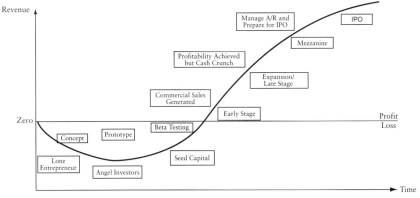

COMMODITY INVESTMENTS

According to the academic literature, investments in commodity markets are considered an effective way for investors to diversify traditional portfolios. The diversification benefits of commodities come from their low (and sometimes even negative) correlation with equity and bond markets, as well as from their high positive correlation with inflation. Therefore, during times of price increases, commodities as real assets can function as effective inflation hedges. Moreover, the low correlation with stocks and bonds in general remains even in downward-trending markets (i.e., during phases when it is needed most). However, because commodities can be characterized as a heterogeneous asset class, commodity sector risk and return profiles can vary quite significantly, and may even move in opposite directions. In addition, the complexity of commodity investments can be revealed when considering the different ways investors can obtain exposure to this asset class. Commodity stocks, commodity funds, commodity futures, and futures indexes all provide specific advantages and specific disadvantages. In this section, we discuss the fundamentals of commodity investments.

Commodity Sectors

Investments in global commodity markets differ greatly from other investments in several important ways. First, commodities are real assets—primarily consumption and not investment goods. They have an intrinsic value, and provide utility by use in industrial manufacturing or in consumption. Furthermore, supply is limited because in any given period, commodities have only a limited availability. For example, renewable commodities like grains can be produced virtually without limitation. However, their yearly harvest is strictly limited. In addition, the supply of certain commodities shows a strong seasonal component. While metals can be mined almost all year, agricultural commodities like soybeans depend on the harvesting cycle.

Another important aspect of commodities as an asset class is its heterogeneity. The quality of commodities is not standardized; every commodity has its own specific properties. A common way to classify them is to distinguish between soft and hard commodities. *Hard commodities* are products from the energy, precious metals, and industrial metals sectors. *Soft commodities* are usually weather-dependent, perishable commodities from the agricultural sector serving consumptional purposes, such as grains, soybeans, or livestock such as cattle or hogs. Figure 26.4 shows the classification of commodity sectors.

FIGURE 26.4 Classification of Commodity Sectors

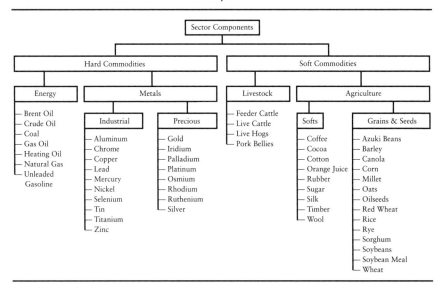

Storability and availability (or renewability) are also important features of commodities. Since storability plays a decisive role in pricing, we distinguish between storable and nonstorable commodities. A commodity is said to have a high degree of storability if it is nonperishable and the costs of storage remain low with respect to its total value. Industrial metals such as aluminium or copper are prime examples: They fulfill both criteria to a high degree. In contrast, livestock is storable to only a limited degree, as it must be continuously fed and housed at current costs, and is only profitable in a specific phase of its lifecycle.

Commodities such as silver, gold, crude oil, and aluminium are nonrenewable. The supply of nonrenewable commodities depends on the ability of producers to mine raw material in both sufficient quantity and quality.

The availability of commodity manufacturing capacities also influences supply. For some metals (excluding precious metals) and crude oil, the discovery and exploration of new reserves of raw materials is still an important issue. For a given supply, the price of nonrenewable resources depends strongly on current investor demand, while the price of renewable resources depends more on estimated future production costs.

The monetary benefit from holding a commodity physically instead of being long the respective futures is called the *convenience yield*. The convenience yield reflects market participants' expectations regarding a possible future scarcity of a short-term nonrenewable commodity.

Commodities as an Asset Class of Their Own

There is a broad consensus among academics and practitioners that commodities compared to other alternative assets can be considered—in a portfolio context—as an asset class of their own. By definition, an asset class consists of similar assets that show a homogeneous risk-return profile (a high internal correlation), and a heterogeneous risk-return profile toward other asset classes (a low external correlation). The key properties are common value drivers, and not necessarily common price patterns. This is based on the idea that a separate asset class contains a unique risk premium that cannot be replicated by combining other asset classes.[8] Furthermore, it is generally required that the long-term returns and liquidity from an asset class are significant to justify an allocation.

To describe existing asset classes, Greer (1997) explains the decomposition into so-called super classes: *capital assets*, *store of value assets*, and *consumable or transferable assets*. Continuous performance is a characteristic of capital assets. Equity capital like stocks provides a continuous stream of dividend payments, while fixed income guarantees regular interest payments in the absence of the default of the obligor. Common to all capital assets is that their valuation follows the net present value method by discounting expected future cash flows. Store of value assets cannot be consumed, nor do they generate income; classic examples are foreign exchange, art, and antiquities.

Commodities belong to the third super class—consumable or transferable (C/T) assets. In contrast to stocks and bonds, physical commodities like energy, grains, or livestock, do not generate continuous cash flows, but rather have an economic value. Grains, for example, can be consumed or used as input goods; crude oil is manufactured into a variety of products. This difference is what makes commodities a unique asset class.

Hence, it is obvious that commodity prices cannot be determined by discounting future cash flows. Thus, interest rates have only a minor influence on the value of commodities. Moreover, commodity prices are the result of the interaction between supply and demand on specific markets.[9]

The line between the super classes is blurred in the case of gold. On the one hand, gold as a commodity is used in such things as electrical circuitry because of its excellent conductivity. On the other hand, gold as a store of value asset is a precious metal and is used for investment, similarly to currencies.

Another specific criterion that differentiates commodities from capital assets is that commodities are denominated worldwide in U.S. dollars. Furthermore, the value of a specific commodity is determined through global

---

[8]See Scherer and He (2008).
[9]See Scott (1994).

Alternative Assets

rather than regional supply and demand. In comparison, equity markets reflect the respective economic development within a country or a region.

Prospects for Commodity Market Participation

In general, there are several ways to participate in commodity markets via a number of different kinds of financial instruments. The most important are (1) direct investment in the physical good; (2) indirect investment in stocks of natural resource companies; (3) commodity mutual funds; (4) an investment in commodity futures; and (5) an investment in structured products on commodity futures indexes.

Buying the Physical Good

First, it seems obvious to invest directly in commodities by purchasing the physical goods at the spot market. However, the immediate or within two days delivery is frequently not practical for investors. According to Geman (2005), precious metals like gold, silver, or platinum are an exception, as they do not have high current costs and do not require storage capacity. However, a portfolio consisting solely of precious metals would not be a sufficiently diversified portfolio for investors to hold.

Commodity Stocks

An investment in commodity stocks (*natural resource companies*), which generate a majority of their profits by buying and selling physical commodities, may conceivably be considered an alternative investment strategy. In general, the term *commodity stock* cannot be clearly differentiated. It consists of listed companies that are related to commodities (i.e., those that explore, mine, refine, manufacture, trade, or supply commodities to other companies). Such an indirect investment in commodities (e.g., the purchase of petrochemical stocks) is only an insufficient substitute for a direct investment. By investing in such stocks, investors do not receive direct exposure to commodities because listed natural resource companies all have their own characteristics and inherent risks, and take action in oder not to be exposed too strongly to their commodity product by hedging appropriately.

Georgiev (2005) shows that these sector-specific stocks are only slightly correlated with commodity prices, and hence prices of commodity stocks do not completely reflect the performance of the underlying market. This is because stocks reflect other price-relevant factors such as the strategic position of the company, management quality, capital structure (the debt/equity ratio), the expectations and ratings of company and profit growth, risk sensitivity, as well as information transparency and information credibility.

Stock markets also show quick and more sensible reactions to expected developments that can impact company value. Hence, other causes of independent price discovery exist that differ from a pure commodity investment. Moreover, there may be temporary market disequilibriums, especially for stocks with low free float where few buy and sell transactions can already cause major price reactions. Finally, natural resource companies are subject to operational risk caused by human or technical failure, internal regulations, or external events. This means that when investing in a company listed on the stock exchange, both the associated market risk as well as any idiosyncratic risk must be considered carefully. Also note that the majority of large oil and energy companies hedge the risk associated with buying and selling oil products in order to smooth yearly profits.

However, the risk of commodity stocks is not completely reflected in the price volatility. First, particularly in the energy and metal sectors, there is the paradox that companies threaten their own business fundamentals by extracting exhaustible resources. On the one hand, long-term decreasing total reserves mean rising prices and a positive prospective for investors and commodity producers. On the other hand, commodity producers will suffer when resources are depleted.

Second, there is always the risk of a total loss if prices decrease below total production costs and the extraction of a commodity is stopped. By constructing an index consisting of commodity stocks, Gorton and Rouwenhorst (2006) show empirically that observed return correlations with commodity futures are even lower than those with the S&P 500. Furthermore, the commodity stock index exhibits lower historical returns than a direct commodity investment. For example, the returns of European oil companies covary strongly with EuroStoxx, but less with oil price returns. Exceptions are gold and silver stocks, whose beta to the domestic stock index is smaller than the beta to the gold and silver price.

Commodity Funds

In contrast to an investment in commodity stocks, one can actively invest in commodity funds, realizing an adequate diversification benefit with moderate transaction costs. Commodity funds differ in terms of management style, allocation strategy, geographic and temporal investment horizon in the denominated currency, and investment behavior. It is also important for investors to distinguish between active and passive funds (i.e., index tracking funds). Commodity stock indexes (e.g., the MSCI World Materials, the FTSE World Mining, the HSBC Global Mining, the Morgan Stanley Commodity Related Index, the FTSE World Oil, and Gas or the FTSE Goldmines) and commodity futures indexes can be used to benchmark actively managed commodity funds. Commodity trading advisors (CTAs) also present an alternative to actively managed investment products. Today, there are also about 400 hedge funds with energy- and commodity-related trading strategies.

Investors can choose from an increasing number of investible commodity futures indexes as a passive form of investing in commodities (see Table 26.1). Commodities have an exceptional position among alternative investments because they provide investible indexes for a broad universe of commodity sectors.

TABLE 26.1 Commodity Futures Indexes

	Reuters/Jefferies Commodity Research Bureau (RJ/CRB)	Standard & Poor's Goldman Sachs Commodity Index (SPGSCI)	Dow Jones/AIG Commodity Index (DJ-AIGCI)
Introduced in:	2005	1991	1998
Historical data available since:	1982	1970	1991
Number of commodities	19	24	19
Weighting scheme	Within a graduated system of four groups, based on liquidity and economic relevance	Rolling five-year average of world production	Liquidity data, in conjunction with dollar-weighted production from the past five years
Rebalancing frequency	Monthly	Yearly	Yearly
Allocation restrictions	None	None	33% Maximum per sector; 2% market minimum per commodity
Relevant futures price on which the index calculation is based	Next futures contract/delivery month	Next month with sufficient liquidity	Next futures contract/delivery month
Roll period	4 days	5 days	5 days
Calculation method	Arithmetic	Arithmetic	Arithmetic

For the majority of investors, an index-oriented investment represents the most reasonable way to obtain exposure to commodities or an individual commodity sector. Such an investment can be done cost-effectively using the following two types of financial products:

- Exchange-traded funds (ETFs) on commodity indexes, and
- Commodity index certificates closely tied to commodity indexes.

Index funds have the advantage of being relatively easy to trade and reasonably priced. Another advantage of funds over certificates is the nonexisting credit risk of the issuer. Because ETFs represent special assets, investor deposits are safe even if the investment company goes bankrupt.

Certificates constitute legal obligations that can be quickly and fairly cheaply issued by banks. In the case of commodity index certificates, the issuing institution invests in futures markets and rolls the futures contracts for a fee. The term of a certificate is normally restricted to a fixed date (e.g., rainbow certificates, whose underlyings are different subindexes or asset classes, or discount and bonus certificates). But there are also open-end certificates.

However, because the indexes, like the commodities themselves, are denominated in U.S. dollars, investors are exposed to currency risk. Quanto certificates, discount certificates with a currency hedge, can be used to mitigate this risk.

The main disadvantage of index certificates is that they often use excess return indexes as the underlying instrument. These indexes do not consider all the return components, in contrast to total return indexes, which may lead to lower returns during periods of high interest rates. Investing in a low performance excess return index compared to a total return index can nevertheless be an advantage because the latter bears little or no initial costs and no yearly management fees. Hence, for investors with short-term investment horizons, certificates on excess return indexes with lower returns can be a smart choice during periods of low interest rates.

Another disadvantage of index-based commodity investments is that due to their construction, they can only consider short-term futures contracts. Commodity funds not linked to commodity indexes, however, can freely determine their optimal term by investing directly in commodity futures contracts. And similarly to purchasing rainbow certificates on different asset classes, there is also the possibility of purchasing commodity funds that do not invest exclusively in commodity indexes, but also include commodity stocks to a certain extent.

Commodity Futures

In addition to options and other derivatives, commodity products are based primarily on futures contracts. Contract sizes in the commodity market are standardized. The smallest tradable unit represents a contract, and the smallest possible price change of a futures is called a *tick*. The value of the minimum price change is the U.S. dollar and cent-denominated tick, multiplied by the contract size (also known as the point value) of the commodity. As explained in Chapter 13, it is common practice to deposit a margin for every futures contract. The amount is determined by the exchange, but it is usually between 2% and 10% of the contract. (Futures commission merchants may charge higher margins than the exchanges.)

Generally, for commodity futures, there are two forms of settlement: delivery of the commodity at maturity, which happens in about 2% of the cases, and closing the futures position (i.e., buying or selling the same amount of contracts before maturity). The following are the contract specifications published regularly by the futures exchanges:

- *The type and quality of the futures underlying.* The type of commodity, abbreviation, and futures exchange.
- *The contract size.* The amount and units of the underlying asset per futures contract.
- *Price determination.* The formal notation of futures prices at the futures exchange.
- *Trading hours.*
- *The tick.* The minimum permissible price fluctuation.
- *The currency.* In which the futures contract is quoted.
- *The daily price limit.*
- *The last trading date.*
- *Delivery regulations.* Such as delivery month, type of settlement and the like.

Investors in commodity futures can profit from price movements of the underlying commodity without having to fulfill the logistical or storage requirements connected with a direct purchase. However, this is only possible if the position is closed before maturity. The advantages of futures investments lie especially in the tremendous flexibility and leveraged nature of the futures position due to the low capital requirements. Thus, a shift of an existing futures position is possible at any time, even in the short term. By holding long or short positions, investors can profit from rising and falling markets. Furthermore, the futures markets are characterized by a high degree of liquidity and low transaction costs.

Despite the numerous advantages of an active investment in commodity futures, it is not always advisable for a private investor to take futures positions in such volatile commodities. Even if diversification by a large number of different futures contracts were guaranteed, the investor would still face the problem of maintaining an exposure to commodity prices without the liability of physical delivery of the underlying contract. This requires continuously closing existing futures positions and re-establishing new positions by opening more futures contracts. This is referred to as *rolling of futures contracts*, and it may be quite costly depending on the forward curve of the futures market. An active, indirect investment in commodities can be achieved by purchasing futures contracts and closing them prior to maturity. In order to keep an exposure to commodities, investors must buy another futures contract with a later maturity date (this is called *rolling*, and must be repeated before each maturity date).

In addition, falling futures prices may constantly trigger margin calls (although margins can be withdrawn if the futures prices increase). Overall, however, compared to traditional assets, managing futures positions requires a great deal of time and effort. It is also possible to invest in commodity swaps and forwards. These instruments, however, are of minor liquidity since they are tailor-made for individual investors. Furthermore, these derivatives are not exchange traded, and commodity investment strategies of individual investors cannot be publicly observed.

SUMMARY

In this chapter, we provide an overview of three alternative investment vehicles: hedge funds, private equity, and commodities.

With respect to hedge funds, the distinguishing feature of hedge fund managers is the strategies they employ compared to traditional portfolio managers. There are many different hedge fund strategies. Which types are best for an investor will depend on the strategic approach that the investor wishes to take. Some investors may be more focused on equity-based strategies. For them, equity long/short funds or market timing might be appropriate. For an investor with a fixed income bias, convertible arbitrage, fixed income arbitrage, or relative-value arbitrage may be appropriate. Suffice it to say that there is sufficient variety in the hedge fund marketplace to suit most investors. Within the four broad categories of hedge fund strategies described in this chapter can be many different substrategies that try to exploit a security pricing inefficiency, an informational advantage, or a misalignment of values across global asset classes.

The private equity sector purchases the private stock or equity-linked securities of nonpublic companies that are expected to go public or provides the capital for public companies (or their divisions) that may wish to go private. The key component in either case is the private nature of the securities purchased. Private equity, by definition, is not publicly traded. Therefore, investments in private equity are illiquid. Investors in this marketplace must be prepared to invest for the long haul—investment horizons may be as long as 5 to 10 years. The term "private equity" is a generic term that encompasses several distinct strategies in the market for private investing.

An allocation to commodities offers not only a hedge against inflation, but also effective diversification because of their low correlation with traditional asset classes. These advantages hold for passive investment in commodity futures indexes, which are considered indicators of commodity market price movements. In general, there are several ways to participate in commodity markets via one or more of the following financial instruments, the most important being (1) direct investment in the physical good; (2) indirect investment in stocks of natural resource companies; (3) commodity mutual funds; (4) an investment in commodity futures; and (5) an investment in structured products on commodity futures indexes.

REFERENCES

Anson, M. J. P. 2008. *The handbook of alternative assets*, 3rd ed. Hoboken, NJ: John Wiley & Sons.

British Venture Capital Association. 2004. A guide to private equity. White paper, October.

Fung, W., and D. A. Hsieh. 1997. Empirical characteristics of dynamic trading strategies: The case of hedge funds. *Review of Financial Studies* 10 (Summer): 275–302.

Georgiev, G. 2005. Benefits of commodity investment. Working Paper.

Geman, H. 2005. *Commodities and commodity derivatives: Modeling and pricing for agriculturals, metals and energy*. Chichester, UK: John Wiley & Sons.

Gorton, G., and K. G. Rouwenhorst. 2006. Facts and fantasies about commodity futures. *Financial Analysts Journal* 62, no. 2: 47–68.

Greer, R. J. 1997. What is an asset class, anyway? *Journal of Portfolio Management* 23, no. 2: 86–91.

Jacobs, B., and K. Levy. 1995. The law of one alpha. *Journal of Portfolio Management* 21 (Summer): 78–79.

Lhabitant, F.-S. 2004. *Hedge funds: Quantitative insights*. Chichester, UK: John Wiley & Sons.

Scherer, B. and He, L. 2008. The diversification benefits of commodity futures indexes: A mean-variance spanning test. In *The handbook of commodity investing*, edited by F. J. Fabozzi, R. Füss, and D. G. Kaiser (pp. 241–265). Hoboken, NJ: John Wiley & Sons.

Scott, J. H. 1994. Managing asset classes. *Financial Analysts Journal* 50 (January–February): 62–69.

APPENDIX

Measuring and Forecasting Yield Volatility

In this appendix, we look at how to measure and forecast yield volatility. As explained in Chapter 22, yield volatility is an important input into the valuation modeling of bonds with embedded options and in Chapter 24 its role in the valuation of options on bonds is explained. Volatility is measured in terms of the standard deviation or variance. We begin this appendix with an explanation of how yield volatility as measured by the daily percentage change in yields is calculated from historical yields. We will see that there are several issues confronting a trader or investor in measuring historical yield volatility. Next we turn to modeling and forecasting yield volatility, looking at the state-of-the-art statistical techniques that can be employed.

CALCULATING THE STANDARD DEVIATION FROM HISTORICAL DATA

The variance of a random variable using historical data is calculated using the following formula:

$$\text{Variance} = \sum_{t=1}^{T} \frac{(X_t - \bar{X})^2}{T-1} \quad \text{(A.1)}$$

and then

$$\text{Standard deviation} = \sqrt{\text{Variance}}$$

where

X_t = observation t on variable X

This appendix is coauthored by Wai Lee.

$\overline{X}$ = the sample mean for variable X
T = the number of observations in the sample

Our focus in this chapter is on yield volatility. More specifically, we are interested in the percentage change in daily yields. So, X_t will denote the percentage change in yield from day t and the prior day, $t-1$. If we let y_t denote the yield on day t and y_{t-1} denote the yield on day $t-1$, then X_t which is the natural logarithm of percentage change in yield between two days, can be expressed as

$$X_t = 100[\ln(y_t/y_{t-1})]$$

For example, assume that the yield on some day was 6.56% and on the next day it was 6.59%. Therefore, the natural logarithm of X is

$$X = 100[\ln(6.593/6.555)] = 0.5780$$

To illustrate how to calculate a daily standard deviation from historical data, consider the hypothetical yield data in Table A.1 for 26 trading days. From the 26 observations, 25 days of daily percentage yield changes are calculated in the third column. The fourth column shows the square of the deviations of the observations from the mean. The bottom of the table shows the calculation of the daily mean for the 25 observations, the variance, and the standard deviation. The daily standard deviation is 0.6360%.

The daily standard deviation will vary depending on the 25 days selected. The appropriate number depends on the situation at hand. For example, traders concerned with overnight positions might use the 10 most recent days (i.e., two weeks). A bond portfolio manager who is concerned with longer term volatility might use 25 days (about one month).

If serial correlation is not significant, the daily standard deviation can be annualized by multiplying it by the square root of the number of days in a year. That is,

$$\text{Daily standard deviation} \times \sqrt{\text{Number of days in a year}}$$

Market practice varies with respect to the number of days in the year that should be used in the annualizing formula above. Typically, either 250 days, 260 days, or 365 days are used.

Thus, in calculating an annual standard deviation, the manager must decide on:

TABLE A.1 Calculation of Daily Standard Deviation Based on 25 Daily Observations

t	y_t	$X_t = 100[\ln(y_t/y_{t-1})]$	$(X_t - \bar{X})^2$
0	6.694		
1	6.699	0.06720	0.02599
2	6.710	0.16407	0.06660
3	6.675	−0.52297	0.18401
4	6.555	−1.81311	2.95875
5	6.583	0.42625	0.27066
6	6.569	−0.21290	0.01413
7	6.583	0.21290	0.09419
8	6.555	−0.42625	0.11038
9	6.593	0.57804	0.45164
10	6.620	0.40869	0.25270
11	6.568	−0.78860	0.48246
12	6.575	0.10652	0.04021
13	6.646	1.07406	1.36438
14	6.607	−0.58855	0.24457
15	6.612	0.07565	0.02878
16	6.575	−0.56116	0.21823
17	6.552	−0.35042	0.06575
18	6.515	−0.56631	0.22307
19	6.533	0.27590	0.13684
20	6.543	0.15295	0.06099
21	6.559	0.24424	0.11441
22	6.500	−0.90360	0.65543
23	6.546	0.70520	0.63873
24	6.589	0.65474	0.56063
25	6.539	−0.76173	0.44586
	Total	−2.35020	9.7094094

Sample mean = $\bar{X} = \dfrac{-2.35020}{25} = -0.09401\%$

Variance = $\dfrac{9.7094094}{25-1} = 0.4045587$

Std = $\sqrt{0.4045587} = 0.6360\%$

1. The number of daily observations to use.
2. The number of days in the year to use to annualize the daily standard deviation.

Let's address the question of what mean should be used in the calculation of the forecasted standard deviation. Suppose at the end of Day 12 an investor is interested in a forecast for volatility using the 10 most recent days of trading and updating that forecast at the end of each trading day. What mean value should be used? An investor can calculate a 10-day moving average of the daily percentage yield change.

Table A.2 shows the 10-day moving average calculated for Days 12 to 24 in Table A.1. Notice the considerable variation which is typically observed in the market.

Rather than using a moving average, it is more appropriate to use an expectation of the average. Longerstacey and Zangari (1995) argue that it would be more appropriate to use a mean value of zero. In that case, the variance as given by equation (A.1) simplifies to

$$\text{Variance} = \sum_{t=1}^{T} \frac{X_t^2}{T-1} \tag{A.2}$$

TABLE A.2 10-Day Moving Daily Average

10 Trading Days Ending	Daily Average (%)
Day 12	−0.203
Day 13	−0.044
Day 14	0.079
Day 15	0.044
Day 16	0.009
Day 17	−0.047
Day 18	−0.061
Day 19	−0.091
Day 20	−0.117
Day 21	−0.014
Day 22	−0.115
Day 23	−0.152
Day 24	−0.027
Day 25	−0.111

TABLE A.3 Moving Daily Standard Deviation Based on 10 Days of Observations

10 Trading Days Ending	Daily Standard Deviation (%)
Day 12	0.757
Day 13	0.819
Day 14	0.586
Day 15	0.569
Day 16	0.595
Day 17	0.602
Day 18	0.615
Day 19	0.591
Day 20	0.577
Day 21	0.520
Day 22	0.600
Day 23	0.536
Day 24	0.544
Day 25	0.600

The daily standard deviation given by equations (A.1) and (A.2) assigns an equal weight to all observations. So, if an investor is calculating volatility based on the most recent 10 days of trading, each day is given a weight of 10%.

For example, suppose that an investor is interested in the daily volatility of the yields in Table A.1 and decides to use the 10 most recent trading days. Table A.3 reports the 10-day volatility for various days using the yields in Table A.1 and the formula for the variance given by equation (A.2).

There is reason to suspect that market participants give greater weight to recent movements in yield when determining volatility. To give greater importance to more recent information, observations further in the past should be given less weight. This can be done by revising the variance as given by equation (A.2) as follows:

$$\text{Variance} = \sum_{t=1}^{T} \frac{W_t X_t^2}{T-1} \quad (A.3)$$

where W_t is the weight assigned to observation t such that the sum of the weights is equal to one (i.e., $\Sigma W_t = 1$) and the further the observation from today, the lower the weight.

The weights should be assigned so that the forecasted volatility reacts faster to a recent major market movement and declines gradually as we move away from any major market movement. The approach by RiskMetrics™ is to use an *exponential moving average*. The formula for the weight W_t in an exponential moving average is

$$W_t = (1 - \beta)\beta^t$$

where β is a value between 0 and 1. The observations are arrayed so that the closest observation is $t = 1$, the second closest is $t = 2$, and so on.

For example, if β is 0.90, then the weight for the closest observation ($t = 1$) is

$$W_1 = (1 - 0.90)(0.90)^1 = 0.09$$

For $t = 5$ and β equal to 0.90, the weight is

$$W_5 = (1 - 0.90)(0.90)^5 = 0.05905$$

The parameter β is measuring how quickly the information contained in past observations is "decaying" and hence is referred to as the "decay factor." The smaller the β, the faster the decay. What decay factor to use depends on how fast the mean value for the random variable X changes over time. A random variable whose mean value changes slowly over time will have a decay factor close to one. A discussion of how the decay factor should be selected is beyond the scope of this appendix.

MODELING AND FORECASTING YIELD VOLATILITY

Generally speaking, there are two ways to model yield volatility. The first way is by estimating historical yield volatility by some time series model. The resulting volatility is called *historical volatility*. The second way is to estimate yield volatility based on the observed prices of interest rate derivatives. Yield volatility calculated using this approach is called *implied volatility*. In this section, we discuss these two approaches, with more emphasis on historical volatility. As will be explained later, computing implied volatility from interest rate derivatives is not as simple and straightforward as from derivatives of other asset classes such as equity. Apart from assuming that a particular option pricing model is correct, we also need to model the time evolution of the complete term structure and volatilities of yields of different maturities. This relies on state-of-the-art modeling techniques as well as superior computing power.

Historical Volatility

We begin the discussion with a general stochastic process of which yield, or interest rate, is assumed to follow:

$$dy = \mu(y,t)dt + \sigma(y,t)dW \tag{A.4}$$

where y is the yield, μ is the expected instantaneous change (or drift) of yield, σ is the instantaneous standard deviation (volatility), and W is a standard Brownian motion such that the change in $W(dW)$ is normally distributed with mean zero and variance of dt. Both μ and σ are functions of the current yield y and time t.

Since we focus on volatility in this appendix, we leave the drift term in its current general form. It can be shown that many of the volatility models are special cases of this general form. For example, assuming that the functional form of volatility is

$$\sigma(y,t) = \sigma_0 y \tag{A.5}$$

such that the yield volatility is equal to the product of a constant, σ_0, and the current yield level, we can rewrite equation (A.4) as[1]

$$d\ln y = \mu'(y,t)dt + \sigma_0 dW \tag{A.6}$$

The discrete time version of this process will be

$$\ln y_{t+1} = \ln y_t + \mu' + \sigma_0(W_{t+1} - W_t) \tag{A.7}$$

Thus, when we calculate yield volatility by looking at the natural logarithm of percentage change in yield between two days as in the earlier section, we are assuming that yield follows a log-normal distribution, or, the natural logarithm of yield follows a normal distribution. The parameter σ_0 in this case can be interpreted as the *proportional yield volatility*, as the yield volatility is obtained by multiplying σ_0 with the current yield. In this case, yield volatility is proportional to the level of the yield. We call the above model the *Constant Proportional Yield Volatility Model* (CP).

---

[1] Equation (A.6) is obtained by application of Ito's Lemma. We omit the details here.

This simple assumption offers many advantages. Since the natural logarithm of a negative number is meaningless, a log-normal distribution assumption for yield guarantees that yield is always non-negative. Evidence also suggests that at high interest rate levels, volatility of yield increases with the level of yield. A simple intuition is for scale reasons. Thus, while the volatility of changes in yield is unstable over time since the level of yield changes, the volatility of changes in natural logarithm of yield is relatively stable, as it already incorporates the changes in yield level. As a result, the natural logarithm of yield can be a more useful process to examine.[2]

A potential drawback of the CP model is that it assumes that the proportional yield volatility itself is constant, which does not depend on time nor on the yield level. In fact, there exists a rich class of yield volatility models that includes the CP model as a special case. We call this group the *Power Function Model*.[3]

Power Function Model

For simplicity of exposition, we write the yield volatility as σ_t, which is understood to be a function of time and level of yield. For example, consider the following representation of yield volatility:

$$\sigma_t = \sigma_0 y_{t-1}^{\gamma} \tag{A.8}$$

In this way, yield volatility is proportional to a power function of yield. The following are examples of the volatility models assumed in some well-known interest rate models, which can be represented as special cases of equation (A.8):

1. $\gamma = 0$: Vasicek (1977) and Ho and Lee (1986)
2. $\gamma = 0.5$: Cox, Ingersoll, and Ross (1985)
3. $\gamma = 1$: Black (1976) and Brennan and Schwartz (1979)

The Vasicek model and Ho-Lee model maintain an assumption of a normally distributed interest rate process. Simply speaking, yield volatility is assumed to be constant, independent of time, and independent of yield level. Theoretically, when the interest rate is low enough while yield volatility remains constant, this model allows the interest rate to go below zero.

The Cox-Ingersoll-Ross (CIR) model assumes that yield volatility is a constant multiple of the square root of yield. Its volatility specification

---

[2] See Coleman, Fisher, and Ibbotson (1993) for a similar conclusion.
[3] In the finance literature, this is also known as the *Constant Elasticity of Variance Model*.

is thus also known as the *Square Root Model*. Since the square root of a negative number is meaningless, the CIR model does not allow yield to become negative. Strictly speaking, the functional form of equation (A.8) only applies to the instantaneous interest rate, but not to any yield of longer maturities within the CIR framework. To be specific, when applied to, say, the 10-year yield, yield volatility is obtained from the stochastic process of the 10-year yield, which can be derived from the closed-form solution for the bond price. To simplify the discussion, we go with the current simple form instead.

The volatility assumption in the Black model and Brennan-Schwartz model is equivalent to the previous CP model. In other words, yield is assumed to be log-normally distributed with constant proportional yield volatility.

Many of these functional forms for yield volatility are adopted primarily because they lead to closed-form solutions for the pricing of bonds, bond options, and other interest rate derivatives, as well as for simplicity and convenience. There is no simple answer for which form is the best. However, it is generally thought that $\gamma = 0$, or a normal distribution with constant yield volatility, is an inappropriate description of an interest rate process, even though the occasions of observing negative interest rate in the model is found to be rare. As a result, many practitioners adopt the CP model, as it is straightforward enough, while it eliminates the drawback of the normal distribution.

One critique of the Power Function Model is the fact that while it allows volatility to depend on the yield level, it does not incorporate the observation that a volatile period tends to be followed by another volatile period, a phenomenon known as *volatility clustering*. Nor does it allow past yield shocks to affect current and future volatility. To tackle these problems, we introduce a very different class of volatility modeling and forecasting tool.

Generalized Autoregressive Conditional Heteroscedasticity Model

Generalized Autoregressive Conditional Heteroscedasticity (GARCH) Model is probably the most extensively applied family of volatility models in empirical finance. As explained in Chapter 4, it is well known that statistical distributions of many financial prices and returns series exhibit fatter tails than a normal distribution. These characteristics can be captured with a GARCH model. In fact, some well-known interest rate models, such as the Longstaff-Schwartz model, adopt GARCH to model yield volatility, which is allowed to be stochastic.[4] Here "conditional" means that the value of the

---

[4] Longstaff and Schwartz (1992). Longstaff and Schwartz (1993) explains the practical implementation of the model and how yield volatility is modeled by GARCH.

variance depends on or is conditional on the information available, typically by means of the realized values of other random variables. "Heteroscedasticity" means that the variance is not the same for all values of the random variable at different time periods.

If we maintain the assumption that the average daily yield change is zero, as before, the standard GARCH(1,1) model can be written as

$$y_t - y_{t-1} = \varepsilon_t$$

$$E[\varepsilon_t^2] = \sigma_t^2 = a_0 + a_1 \varepsilon_{t-1}^2 + a_2 \sigma_{t-1}^2 \qquad (A.9)$$

where ε_t is just the daily yield change, interpreted as a yield shock, $E[.]$ denotes the statistical expectation operator, and a_0, a_1, and a_2 are parameters to be estimated. In this way, yield volatility this period depends on the yield shock as well as yield volatility in the last period. The GARCH model also estimates the long-run equilibrium variance, ω, as

$$E[\varepsilon_t^2] = \bar{\omega} = \frac{a_0}{1 - a_1 - a_2} \qquad (A.10)$$

The GARCH model is popular not only for its simplicity in specification and its parsimonious nature in capturing time series properties of volatilities, but also because it is a generalization of some other measures of volatility. For example, it has been shown that equal-weighted rolling sample measure of variance and exponential smoothing scheme of volatility measure are both special cases of GARCH, but with different restrictions on the parameters. Other technical details of GARCH are beyond the scope of this appendix.[5]

Experience has shown that a GARCH(1,1) specification generally fits the volatility of most financial time series well, and is quite robust.

Implied Volatility

The second way to estimate yield volatility is based on the observed prices of interest rate derivatives, such as options on bond futures, or interest rate caps and floors. Yield volatility calculated using this approach is called *implied volatility*.

The implied volatility is based on some option pricing model. One of the inputs to any option pricing model in which the underlying is a Treasury security or Treasury futures contract is expected yield volatility. If the observed price of an option is assumed to be the fair price and the option

---
[5] See, for example, Engle (1993) for further details.

pricing model is assumed to be the model that would generate that fair price, then the implied yield volatility is the yield volatility that when used as an input into the option pricing model would produce the observed option price. Because of their liquidity, options on Treasury futures, Eurodollar futures, and caps and floors on LIBOR are typically used to extract implied volatilities.

Computing implied volatilities of yield from interest rate derivatives is not as straight forward as from derivatives of, say, stock prices. Later in this section, we will explain that these implied volatilities are not only model-dependent, but on some occasions they are also difficult to interpret, and can be misleading as well. For the time being, we follow the common practice in the industry of using the Black option pricing model for futures discussed in Chapter 24.[6]

Although the Black model has many limitations and inconsistent assumptions, it has been widely adopted. Traders often quote the exchange-traded options on Treasury or Eurodollar futures in terms of implied volatilities based on the Black model. These implied volatilities are also published by some investment houses, and are available through data vendors. For illustration purposes, we use the data of CBOT traded call options on 30-year Treasury bond futures as of April 30, 1997. The contract details, as well as the extracted implied volatilities based on the Black model, are listed in Table A.5.

Since the options are written on futures prices, the implied volatilities computed directly from the Black model are thus the implied price volatilities of the underlying futures contract. To convert the implied price volatilities to implied yield volatilities, we need the duration of the corresponding cheapest-to-deliver Treasury bond.[7] The conversion is based on the simple standard relationship between percentage change in bond price and change in yield:

$$\frac{\Delta P}{P} \approx -\text{Duration} \times \Delta y$$

which implies that the same relationship also holds for price volatility and yield volatility.

Looking at the implied yield volatilities of the options with the same delivery month, one can immediately notice the well-documented "volatility smile." For example, for the options with a delivery month in June 1997, the implied yield volatility starts at a value of 0.98% for the deep in-the-money option with a strike price of 105, steadily drops to a minimum of 0.84% for

---

[6]Black (1976).
[7]See Chapter 24 for a discussion of Treasury futures contracts and the cheapest-to-deliver issue.

TABLE A.5 Call Options on 30-Year Treasury Bond Futures on April 30, 1997

Delivery Month	Futures Price	Strike Price	Option Price	Implied Price Volatility	Duration	Implied Yield Volatility
1997:6	109.281	105	4.297	9.334	9.57	0.975
1997:6	109.281	106	3.328	9.072	9.57	0.948
1997:6	109.281	107	2.406	8.811	9.57	0.921
1997:6	109.281	108	1.594	8.742	9.57	0.913
1997:6	109.281	109	0.938	8.665	9.57	0.905
1997:6	109.281	110	0.469	8.462	9.57	0.884
1997:6	109.281	111	0.188	8.205	9.57	0.857
1997:6	109.281	112	0.062	8.129	9.57	0.849
1997:6	109.281	113	0.016	7.993	9.57	0.835
1997:6	109.281	114	0.016	9.726	9.57	1.016
1997:6	109.281	116	0.016	13.047	9.57	1.363
1997:6	109.281	118	0.016	16.239	9.57	1.697
1997:6	109.281	120	0.016	19.235	9.57	2.010
1997:6	109.281	122	0.016	22.168	9.57	2.316
1997:6	109.281	124	0.016	25.033	9.57	2.616
1997:6	109.281	126	0.016	27.734	9.57	2.898
1997:6	109.281	128	0.016	30.392	9.57	3.176
1997:6	109.281	130	0.016	33.01	9.57	3.449
1997:9	108.844	100	8.922	8.617	9.54	0.903
1997:9	108.844	102	7.062	8.750	9.54	0.917
1997:9	108.844	104	5.375	8.999	9.54	0.943
1997:9	108.844	106	3.875	9.039	9.54	0.947
1997:9	108.844	108	2.625	9.008	9.54	0.944
1997:9	108.844	110	1.656	8.953	9.54	0.938
1997:9	108.844	112	0.969	8.913	9.54	0.934
1997:9	108.844	114	0.516	8.844	9.54	0.927
1997:9	108.844	116	0.250	8.763	9.54	0.919
1997:9	108.844	118	0.109	8.679	9.54	0.910
1997:9	108.844	120	0.047	8.733	9.54	0.915
1997:9	108.844	122	0.016	8.581	9.54	0.899

TABLE A.5 (Continued)

Delivery Month	Futures Price	Strike Price	Option Price	Implied Price Volatility	Duration	Implied Yield Volatility
1997:9	108.844	124	0.016	9.625	9.54	1.009
1997:9	108.844	126	0.016	10.646	9.54	1.116
1997:9	108.844	128	0.016	11.65	9.54	1.221
1997:12	108.469	98	10.562	7.861	9.51	0.827
1997:12	108.469	106	4.250	9.036	9.51	0.950
1997:12	108.469	108	3.125	9.070	9.51	0.954
1997:12	108.469	110	2.188	9.006	9.51	0.947
1997:12	108.469	112	1.469	8.953	9.51	0.941
1997:12	108.469	114	0.938	8.881	9.51	0.934
1997:12	108.469	116	0.594	8.949	9.51	0.941
1997:12	108.469	118	0.359	8.973	9.51	0.944
1997:12	108.469	120	0.234	9.232	9.51	0.971
1997:12	108.469	122	0.141	9.340	9.51	0.982
1997:12	108.469	128	0.031	9.793	9.51	1.030

the out-of-money option with a strike price of 113, and rises back to a maximum of 3.45% for the deep out-of-money option with a strike price of 130. Since all the options with the same delivery month are written on the same underlying bond futures, the only difference is their strike prices. The question is, which implied volatility is correct? While the answer to this question largely depends on how we accommodate the volatility smile,[8] standard practice suggests that we use the implied volatility of the at-the-money, or the nearest-the money option. In this case, the implied yield volatility of 0.91% of the option with a strike price of 109 should be used

What is the meaning of an "implied yield volatility of 0.91%"? To interpret this number, one needs to be aware that this number is extracted from the observed option price based on the Black model. As a result, the meaning of this number not only depends on the assumption that the market correctly prices the option, but also the fact that the market prices the option in accordance with the Black model. Neither of these assumptions need to hold. In fact, most probably, both assumptions are unrealistic. Given these assumptions, one may interpret that the option market expects a *constant*

---

[8]Current research typically uses either a jump diffusion process, a stochastic volatility model, or a combination of both to explain volatility smile. The details are beyond the scope of this appendix.

annualized yield volatility of 0.91% for 30-year Treasury from April 30, 1997, to the maturity date of the option.

Caps and floors can also be priced by the Black model when they are interpreted as portfolios of options written on forward interest rates. Accordingly, implied volatilities can be extracted from cap prices and floor prices, but subjected to the same limitations of the Black model.

Limitations of the Black Model

There are two major assumptions of the Black model that makes it unrealistic. First, interest rates are assumed to be constant. Yet, the assumption is used to derive the pricing formula for the option which derives its payoff precisely from the fact that future interest rates (forward rates) are stochastic. It has been shown that the Black model implies a time evolution path for the term structure that leads to arbitrage opportunities. In other words, the model itself implicitly violates the no-arbitrage spirit in derivatives pricing.

Second, volatilities of futures prices, or forward interest rates, are assumed to be constant over the life of the contract. This assumption is in sharp contrast to empirical evidence as well as intuition. It is well understood that a forward contract with one month to maturity is more sensitive to changes in the current term structure than a forward contract with one year to maturity. Thus the volatility of the forward rate is inversely related to the time to maturity.

Finally, on the average, implied volatilities from the Black model are found to be higher than the realized volatilities during the same period of time.[9] A plausible explanation is that the difference in the two volatilities represents the fee for the financial service provided by the option writers, while the exact dynamics of the relationship between implied and realized volatilities remains unclear.

Practical Uses of Implied Volatilities from the Black Model

Typically, implied volatilities from exchange-traded options with sufficient liquidity are used to price over-the-counter interest rate derivatives such as caps, floors, and swaptions. Apart from the limitations as discussed above, another difficulty in practice is the fact that only options with some fixed maturities are traded. For example, in Table A.5, the *constant* implied volatilities only apply to the time periods from April 30, 1997 to the delivery dates in June, September, and December 1997, respectively. For instance, on May 1, 1997, we need a volatility input to price a three-month cap

---

[9] See Goodman and Ho (1997) for a comparison of implied versus realized volatility.

on LIBOR. In this case, traders will either use the implied volatility from options with maturities closest to three months, or make an adjustment/judgment based on the implied volatilities of options with maturities just shorter than three months, and options with maturities just longer than three months.

The finance industry is not unaware of the limitations of the Black model and its implied volatilities. Due to its simplicity and its early introduction to the market, it has become the standard in computing implied volatilities. However, there has been a tremendous amount of rigorous research going on in interest rate and interest rate derivatives models. While a comprehensive review of this research is not provided here, it is useful to highlight the broad classes of models which can help us understand where implied volatilities related research is going.

Broadly speaking, there are two classes of models. The first class is known as the *Equilibrium Model*. Some noticeable examples include the Vasciek model, CIR model, Brennan-Schwartz model, and Longstaff-Schwartz model, as mentioned earlier in this chapter. This class of models attempts to specify the equilibrium conditions by assuming that some state variables drive the evolution of the term structure. By imposing other structure and restrictions, closed-form solutions for equilibrium prices of bonds and other interest rate derivatives are then derived. Many of these models impose a functional form to interest rate volatility, such as the power function as discussed and estimated earlier, or assume that volatility follows certain dynamics. In addition, the models also specify a particular dynamics on how interest rate drifts up or down over time. To implement these models, one needs to estimate the parameters of the interest rate process, including the parameters of the volatility function, based on some advanced econometric technique applied to historical data.

There are two major shortcomings of this class of models. First, these models are not preference-free, which means that we need to specify the utility function in dictating how investors make choices. Second, since only historical data are used in calibrating the models, these models do not rule out arbitrage opportunities in the current term structure. Due to the nature of the models, volatility is an important input to these models rather than an output that we can extract from observed prices. In addition, it has been shown that the term structure of spot yield volatilities can differ across one-factor versions of these models despite the fact that all produce the same term structure of cap prices.[10]

The second class of models is known as the *No-Arbitrage Model*. The *Ho-Lee Model* is the first model of this class. Other examples include the

---

[10]See Canabarro (1995).

Black-Derman-Toy model,[11] Black-Karasinski model,[12] Kalotay-Williams-Fabozzi model,[13] and the Heath-Jarrow-Morton model (HJM).[14] In contrast to the equilibrium models which attempt to model equilibrium, these no-arbitrage models are less ambitious. They take the current term structure as given, and assume that no arbitrage opportunities are allowed during the evolution of the entire term structure. All interest rate sensitive securities are assumed to be correctly priced at the time of calibrating the model. In this way, the models, together with the current term structure and the no-arbitrage assumption, impose some restrictions on how interest rates of different maturities will evolve over time. Some restrictions on the volatility structure may be imposed in order to allow interest rates to mean-revert, or to restrict interest rates to be positive under all circumstances. However, since these models take the current bond prices as given, more frequent recalibration of the models is required once bond prices change.

The HJM model, in particular, has received considerable attention in the industry as well as in the finance literature. Many other no-arbitrage models are shown to be special cases of HJM. In spirit, the HJM model is similar to the well-celebrated Black-Scholes model in the sense that the model does not require assumptions about investor preferences.[15] Much like the Black-Scholes model that requires volatility instead of expected stock return as an input to price a stock option, the HJM model only requires a description of the volatility structure of forward interest rates, instead of the expected interest rate movements in pricing interest rate derivatives. It is this feature of the model that, given current prices of interest rate derivatives, make extraction of implied volatilities possible.

Amin and Morton (1994) and Amin and Ng (1997) use this approach to extract a term structure of implied volatilities. Several points are noteworthy. Since the no-arbitrage assumption is incorporated into the model, the extracted implied volatilities are more meaningful than those from the Black model. Moreover, interest rates are all stochastic instead of being assumed constant. On the other hand, these implied volatilities are those of forward interest rates, instead of spot interest rates. Furthermore, interest rate derivatives with different maturities and sufficient liquidity are required to calibrate the model. Finally, the HJM model is often criticized as too

---

[11] Black, Derman, and Toy (1990).
[12] Black and Karasinski (1991).
[13] Kalotay, Williams, and Fabozzi (1993).
[14] Heath, Jarrow, and Morton (1992).
[15] This by no means implies that the Black-Scholes model is a no-arbitrage model. Although no-arbitrage condition is enforced, the Black-Scholes model does require equilibrium settings and market clearing conditions. Further details are beyond the scope of this appendix.

complicated for practitioners, and is too slow for real-time practical applications.[16]

SUMMARY

Yield volatility estimates play a critical role in the valuation of bonds with embedded options and interest rate options, as well as interest rate risk management. In this chapter, we have discussed how historical yield volatility is calculated and the issues that are associated with its estimate. These issues include the number of observations and the time period to be used, the number of days that should be used to annualize the daily standard deviation, the expected value that should be used, and the weighting of observations. We then looked at modeling and forecasting yield volatility. The two approaches we discussed are historical volatility and implied volatility. For the historical volatility approach, we discussed various models, their underlying assumptions, and their limitations. These models include the Power Function Models and GARCH Models. While many market participants talk about implied volatility, we explained that unlike the derivation of this measure in equity markets, deriving this volatility estimate from interest rate derivatives is not as simple and straightforward. The implied volatility estimate depends not only on the particular option pricing model employed, but also on a model of the time evolution of the complete term structure and volatilities of yields of different maturities.

REFERENCES

Amin, K. I., and A. J. Morton. 1994. Implied volatility functions in arbitrage-free term structure models. *Journal of Financial Economics* 35, no. 2: 141–180.

Amin, K. I., and V. K. Ng. 1997. Inferring future volatility from the information in implied volatility in eurodollar options: A new approach. *Review of Financial Studies* 10: 333–367.

Black, F. 1976. The pricing of commodity contracts. *Journal of Financial Economics* 3, no. 1: 167–179.

Black, F., E. Derman, and W. Toy. 1990. A one-factor model of interest rates and its applications to Treasury bond options. *Financial Analysts Journal* 46 (January–February): 33–39.

Black, F., and P. Karasinski. 1991. Bond and option pricing when short rates are lognormal. *Financial Analysts Journal* 47 (July–August): 52–59.

Brennan, M., and E. Schwartz. 1979. A continuous time approach to the pricing of bonds. *Journal of Banking and Finance* 3: 133–155.

---

[16] See Heath, Jarrow, Morton, and Spindel (1992) for a response to this critique.

Canabarro, E. 1995. Where do one-factor interest rate models fail? *Journal of Fixed Income* 5 (September): 31–52.

Coleman, T. S., K. Fisher, and R. G. Ibbotson. 1993. A note on interest rate volatility. *Journal of Fixed Income* 2 (March): 97–101.

Cox, J. C., J. E. Ingersoll, and S. A. Ross. 1985. A theory of the term structure of interest rates. *Econometrica* 53: 385–407.

Engle, R. F. 1993. Statistical models for financial volatility. *Financial Analysts Journal* 49 (January–February): 72–78.

Goodman, L. S., and J. Ho. 1997. Are investors rewarded for shorting volatility? *Journal of Fixed Income* 7 (June): 38–42.

Heath, D., R. Jarrow, A. Morton, and M. Spindel. 1992. Easier done than said. *Risk* 5 (October): 77–80.

Heath, D., R. Jarrow, and A. Morton. 1992. Bond pricing and the term-structure of interest rates: A new methodology. *Econometrica* 60: 77–105.

Ho, T. S. Y., and S-B. Lee. 1986. Term structure movements and pricing interest rate contingent claims. *Journal of Finance* 41, no. 5: 1011–1029.

Kalotay, A. J., G. O. Williams, and F. J. Fabozzi. 1993. A model for the valuation of bonds and embedded options. *Financial Analysts Journal* 49 (May–June): 35–46.

Longerstacey, J. P., and P. Zangari. 1995. *Five questions about RiskMetrics*^{TM}. JPMorgan Research Publication.

Longstaff, F. A., and E. S. Schwartz. 1992. Interest rate volatility and the term structure: A two-factor general equilibrium model. *Journal of Finance* 47, no. 5: 1259–1282.

Longstaff, F. A., and E. S. Schwartz. 1993. Implementation of the Longstaff-Schwartz interest rate model. *Journal of Fixed Income* (September): 7–14.

Vasicek, O. 1977. An equilibrium characterization of the term structure. *Journal of Financial Economics* 5, no. 2: 177–188.

Index

AA yield curve, 564
Abnormal return, 147
Absolute prepayment speed (ABS), 543
Absolute priority rule, 476–477
Absolute return, 769
Accelerated seniors, 533
Accelerated sinking fund provision, 465–466
Access Rule, 138
Accounting Principles Board (APB), *APB Opinion No. 19*, 224
Accounts receivable
 collection, 215
 cycling, number, 214
 management, 213–214
Accounts receivable turnover ratio, 213–214, 215
Accrued interest (AI), 462–463
 absence, 577
 calculation, 484–486
Acid-test ratio, 208
Active equity strategies, 175
Active management
 full-blown active example, 647
 larger risk factor mismatches, 646
 return, 186
Active mutual funds, 56
Active portfolio strategy, 9
Active return
 calculation, 300, 301t
 data, 301t
Active risk decomposition, 314–315
 flowchart, 315f
Active strategies, classification (Volpert), 646
Active systematic-active residual risk decomposition, 315
 flowchart, 316f
Active U.S. Treasury issue, benchmark, 478
Activity, evaluation, 194
Activity ratios, 213–215
Actual/actual day count convention, 485
Additive growth model, 257–258
Additive stochastic DDM, 258
Adjustable rate loans, securitization, 529
Adjusted cash flow, example, 226t
Adverse stock price movements, hedging, 381–389
Affirmative covenants, 475
After-acquired property clause, 491

Agency CMOs, 518–528
 structuring techniques, 529
Agency debentures, 636
 embedded options, inclusion, 665
Agency incentive arrangement, 337
Agency MBS, 509
Agency pass-throughs, adjustable-rate mortgages backing, 637
Agency pool, 509
Agency RMBS, 508, 509–528
 market, 487
Agency securities, 487
 market, 487
Agency stripped MBS, 516–518
Agent-distributed funds, 731
Agent-distributed stock mutual fund, 734t
Algorithmic trading (algo), 338–339
 dark pools, comparison, 339
All-or-nothing options, 425
Alpha
 average active return, 304
 data/calculation, 301t
 tracking error, combination, 304
Alternative assets, 767
Alternative display facility (ADF), 139–140
Alternative electronic markets, 134–137
Alternative return measures, 176–179
Alternative trading systems (ATS), 135–139
Amazon.com, adjusted cash flow, 226t
American listed options, 421–422
American option, 398
 contracts, obligations/rights, 398t
American Stock Exchange (Amex), 130, 152
 ETF trading, 741
Amortization, 510
Amortizing securities, 463
Angel investing, 794
Annualized returns, historical performance (usage), 42t
Annualized standard deviations, historical performance (usage), 44t
Annual management fee, sum, 733
Annual operating expenses, 729–734
 expense ratio, 732–734
Annual premium, 755–756
Annual term life insurance, cost, 747

827

Annuities, 756–762
  disadvantages, 759
  inside buildup advantage, 758–759
  IRS tax advantage, 759
  phases, 756
  tax advatnages, 758
Applied equity valuation, 245
Appropriation-backed obligations, 497, 498
Arbitrage, 771
  mechanism, 740–741
  opportunity, production, 103–104
  principle, 103–105
  profit, capture, 376
  term, usage, 777
Arbitrage pricing theory (APT), 89
  model, 102–107
    derivation, 114–117
    formulation, 105–106
Arithmetic average (mean) rate of return, 179–180
Arithmetic random walk, 284
Artificial intelligence (AI), 288
A shares, 731–732
  front-end load, 733
Asian option, 421–422
Asian-Pacific Aggregate Index, 638
Asking prices, 122
Ask prices, sorting, 348
Asset allocation
  decision, 4
    implementation, stock index futures/Treasury
      bond futures (usage), 715
  division, 4
  portfolio theory, application, 46–53
Asset-allocation models, transaction costs (incorporation), 355–356
Asset-backed securities (ABS), 503, 507
  asset classes, 545
  credit support mechanisms, usage, 535
  market, 487
  sectors, 651–652
  structures, 534
    fundamentals, 534–537
Asset-based factors, 354–355
Asset classes, 5–7, 46
  classification, 6–7
  definition, 5
Asset correlations, importance, 28
Asset manager
  CDX usage, 720
  short hedge, usage, 382
  single-name CDS usage, 718–719
Asset pricing model, characteristics, 90–91
Asset pricing theory, 89
  principles, 107–108
Asset returns
  correlation, 26
  distribution, 66
  probability distribution, specification, 21

Assets
  alternatives, 767
  book value, 268
  cash price, 378
  inclusion, 27
  inputs, 46
  management, 1, 214–215
  market price, 413
  variability, definition (Sharpe), 99
  variance, 99
As-you-like-it option, 424
Atlantic option, 398
At-the-money market price, 411
Authorized participant, 740
Autocorrelation, 285–286
Auto loan-backed securities, 508, 542–543
  cash flows/prepayments, 542–543
  structures, 543
Autoregressive (AR) model, 291
Autoregressive conditional heteroskedasticity
    (ARCH), 71
  hidden-variable model, relationship, 292
Average credit sales per day, 206
Average day's cost of goods sold, 204–205
Average day's purchases on credit, amount (determination), 206–207
Average life, 516
  variance, 522–523
Average measures, 349–350
Average price per performance-measure dollar,
    computation, 269
Average yield measure, 584

Bachelier, Louis, 278
Back-end loads, 731
Backward-looking tracking error, forward-looking
    tracking error (contrast), 303–304
Bail-out provision, 760–761
Bait and switch practices, 761
Balance sheet, example, 195t
Balloon maturity, 465
  provisions, 539
Balloon risk, 539
Bank-backed bonds, 499–500
Bank-related entity, 564
Bankruptcy, 476–477
  event, 717
  prediction, cash flow analysis (importance), 240
Barbell portfolio, risk, 675–676
Barbell strategy, 651
Barclays Capital Asian-Pacific Aggregate Index,
    640t
Barclays Capital Global Aggregate Bond Index,
    638
Barclays Capital Global Aggregate Index
  issuer currency, 639t
Barclays Capital Global Aggregate Index, sectors,
    639t

Index

Barclays Capital Municipal Bond Index, long-term tax-exempt bonds (inclusion), 638
Barclays Capital portfolio, 647
Barclays Capital U.S. Aggregate Index, 635
  intra-month cash flows, reinvestment (absence), 636
  mortgage sector, percentage composition, 637t
  sectors, 636
    ranking, 636t
Barra E3 model risk definitions, 311t
Barra fundamental factor model (E3 model), 310
Barrier options, 423
Base interest rate, 549
Basic earning power
  calculation, 199–200
  ratio, 196
Basis risk, 383
Basket options, 424–425
Basket trades, 336
Bayesian approach, 280
Behavioral finance, 80–82
  theory, 160
Benchmark, 3–4
  broad-based bond market index, 651
  construction, 172–173
  credit quality, 662t
  exposure, portfolio exposure (material mismatch), 669–670
  index
    agency responsibility, 7
    exposure (measure), duration (usage), 663
  optionality exposure, 665t
  portfolios, 184
    market cap/style, relationship, 306
    risk characteristics, relationship, 659–667
  risk, 770
  sector composition, 662t
  sector deviation, 306
  selection, 170–171
Beneficial interest certificate, 507
Berkshire Hathaway, 275
Bermuda option, 398
Best bid and offer (BBO), 141
Beta, 91, 307–308
  ratio estimate, 101
  tracking error, relationship, 308f
  values, 92
Beta testing, 795
Biased expectations theory, 561, 562–563
Bid-ask spreads, 342–343, 481, 688
Bid-offer costs, 714
Bid-offer spread, 143, 713–715
Bid prices, sorting, 348
Bid quote, 121
BIDS, 136
Binary options, 425
Binomial interest rate tree, 623f
Binomial model, 613

Binomial option pricing model, 438–447
Binomial stochastic DDM, 257
Binomial stochastic model, 257–259
Binomial tree, evidence, 630
Black boxes, 782
Black-Derman-Toy model, 824
Black-Karasinski model, 824
Black model
  implied volatilities, uses, 822–825
  limitations, 822
    awareness, absence, 823
Black-Scholes call option price, comparison, 435t
Black-Scholes option pricing model, 432–436, 696
  adjustment, 438
  assumptions, 436–438, 696–697
  drawbacks, 431–432
  option price, derivation, 433
  taxes/transaction costs, 438
Block trades, 144, 335–336
Board of directors, 738
Bond-equity view, 679
Bond-equivalent basis, 577
  internal rate of return, 584
Bond-equivalent yield, 577
Bondholders, options (grant), 466–467
Bond issues
  features, 552
  liquidity, expectation, 555–556
  refunding, 464
Bond market indexes, 635–640
  specialization, 638
Bond-only view, 679
Bond portfolio management
  applications, 687–692, 698–703
  derivatives, usage, 683
  interest rate options, usage, 692–703
  interest rate swaps, usage, 704–715
  Treasury bond/note futures contracts, usage, 683–692
Bond prices
  change, reasons, 573–574
  complications, 574–575
  computation, 569
  fluctuation, 468
  present values, equivalence, 570
  quotes, 575–576
  sensitivity, 469–470
    estimation, 599–600
  time, relationship, 573
Bond price volatility, 593
  degree, 459
  factors, 596
  impact, 596
  total return, relationship, 591–592
  yield to maturity, impact, 596
Bonds
  arbitrage-free value, obtaining, 622
  capital appreciation, 470

Bonds (*Cont.*)
  cash flows, 568–569
    present value, 576–577
  convexity, 607
  discount sale, 573
  dollar return, sources, 580–583
  embedded options, inclusion, 602
  features, 457–467
  fundamentals/risks, 457
  indexing, popularity, 642
  instantaneous percentage price change, example, 595t
  investment
    alternatives, 586t
    risks, 467–482
  issuers, creditworthiness, 736
  management risk spectrum, 641f
  maturity, 458–459
  payoff, provisions, 463–466
  percentage price change, approximation, 605–606
  pools, backing, 463
  portfolio strategies, 635
    classification (Volpert), 640
    spectrum, 640–647
  position risk, neutralization, 600
  price/yield relationship, 571
  pricing, 567
    assumptions, 568
  sale, premium, 573
  security, 491–493
  seller, 462–463
  structures, 499–500
  total dollar return, 585
  total return
    computation, 587–589
    discovery, 588–589
  valuation, embedded options
    inclusion, lattice model (usage), 625–630
    usage, 613
  valuation, extensions, 630–634
  value, computation, 619
  volatility, 689
Book value, example, 217
Borrowing
  dependence, 236
  rates, lending rates (contrast), 379–380
Bottom-up approaches, top-down approaches (contrast), 152–153
Boundary conditions, tightening, 431
Bowie bonds, 508
Break-even recovery price, 420
Bridge financing, 796–797
Broad-based bond market index, 635–637
  benchmark, impact, 651
Broad-based securities portfolio, acquisition, 734
Broad-based stock market index, 390
Brokerage firm, 337
  trade execution, 337–338

Broker-dealer, disadvantages, 340
Broker loan rate, 334
B shares, 731–732
  back-end load, 733
Buffett, Warren, 275
Bullet maturity, 463
Bullet strategy, 651
Burlington Large Order Cross (BLOX), 136
Business plan, 788–789
  parts, 789
Business risk, 215–216
Buy hedge, 382
Buying on margin, 334
Buy limit order, 332–333
Buy orders, sell orders (imbalance), 129
Buy stop order, 333
Buy-write strategy, 420

Calendar effects, 164
Callable bond, 464, 552
  cash flow pattern, 470
  example, 628, 630
  nodes, highlighting, 628f
  noncallable bond, spread, 656
  price-yield relationship, 601–602
    illustration, 601f
  sale, premium, 579–580
  valuation, 625–626
    example, 627f
Callable issue, 464
Call auction, 122
Call futures options, 694t
Call money rate, 334
Call option, 397, 464
  illustration, 820t–821t
  profit/loss profile, comparison, 405
  purchase, 402, 405
  sale, 402
  valuation, 438
  value
    computation, 626
    increase, 787–788
  writing, 405–406
Call option price
  computation, 433–436
  derivation, 443–444
  expected stock return volatility, relationship, 451–452
  solution, 445
  time to expiration, relationship, 451
Call price, 579
Call protection, 464, 538–539
Call provisions, 463–465, 552–553
Call risk, 470
Call schedule, 464, 579
  types, 465
Cap, 462
  pricing, 822

Index

Capacity, 472, 474
Capital appreciation, 470
Capital asset pricing model (CAPM), 89, 91–102
　assumptions, 92–94
　derivation, 92–102
　empirical analogue, 290
　formula, 91
　modifications, 93
　r generation, 250
　systematic risk statement, 106
　tests, 102
　zero-beta version (Black), 109–112
Capital assets, 800
Capital calls, making, 790
Capital commitment, 792
Capital expenditures coverage ratio, 238
Capital gain, 581–582
　call/sale, 580
Capital gains
　distribution, 737–738
　ordinary income, contrast, 760
　tax, 341–342
　treatment, 718–719
Capital injection, 789
Capital investment, 792
Capitalization method, 174
Capital loss, 580
Capital market line (CML), 94–99
　illustration, 95f
　no risk-free asset/zero-beta portfolios, 111f
　optimal portfolio, relationship, 96f
　risk premium, 98–99
Capital markets, investors, 110
Capital municipal bond indexes, 638
Capital spending, financing sources, 236
Capital structure arbitrage, 775–776
Carry (cost of carry), 378
Cash-and-carry strategy, 685
Cash-and-carry trade, 376
Cash-burn rate, 788
Cash concept, 225
Cash conversion cycle (CCC), 207
Cash enhancement, 545
Cash flow
　allocation, 536f
　analysis, 193, 223–235
　　importance, 240
　change, absence (assumption), 601
　company classification, 228
　company comparisons, 231
　direct method, 225
　discount rates, application, 575
　estimates, 224
　FCDF, contrast, 266
　indirect method, 225
　information, usage, 238–240
　interest coverage ratio, 219, 236, 238
　interest expense, relationship, 225
　knowledge, absence, 574–575
　management, 796
　matching process, illustration, 678f
　matching strategy, 677–679
　measurement, difficulty, 223–234
　measures, usage, 238–239
　present value, 568–569
　　calculation, 577
　reporting, 223
　schematic, 530f
　sources, patterns, 227t
　statement, 224–229, 797
　　example, 197t
　　reformatting, 227, 228t
　structure, present value (difference), 663t–664t
　uncertainty, 510–511
　usage, 540
　waterfall, schematic representation, 537f
　yield, requirement, 622–623
Cash flow generating performance measure, 266–267
Cash flow to capital expenditures ratio, 238
Cash flow to debt ratio, 238
　cash flow estimates, usage, 239f
Cash market price, usage, 389
Cash market transaction, 378
Cash-or-nothing options, 425
Cash-secured put strategies, 419–420
Cash settlement contracts, 369
　stock index futures contracts, comparison, 373–374
Cash taxes, deduction, 234–235
Cash value buildup, 754
Cash value life insurance, 744, 747
　introduction, 753–756
　life insurance appearance, 756
Cash value whole life insurance (CVWLI)
　characteristics, 753
　construction/performance, 750
　overview, 750–752
　policies, 754
Cash yield, 377–378
Central value/location, measure, 61
Chaos theory, 156
Chapter 7 bankruptcy, 476
Chapter 11 bankruptcy, 476
Character, 472, 474
　analysis, 474
Characteristic line, 101
Charge-offs, 541
Cheapest-to-delivery (CTD) issue, 686
　determination, 687
　presence, 718
　target yield, 690–691
Chicago Board of Trade (CBOT)
　constraints, 694
　conversion factors, publication, 685
　delivery guidelines, 686

Chicago Board of Trade (*Cont.*)
   traded call options, 819
   Treasury bond/note futures contracts trading, 683–684
   Treasury bonds trading, 692
Choice, economic theory, 16
Chooser options, 424
Citigroup World Government Bond Index, 645
Classical immunization
   principles, 674f
   strategy, assumption, 675
   theory, extension, 675
Classical safety-first, 76
Clawback covenant, 788
Clean price, 463
Clearance, 142
Clearinghouse, role, 369
Client-imposed constraints, 8
Closed-end funds, 727–729
   listing, 739
   NAV, 727–728
   open-end funds, contrast, 728
Clustering, 288
Cognitive biases, 81
Coherent risk measure
   axiomatic properties, 72–74
   property, 74
Collars
   design, 418
   profit equation, 419
   strategy, 419f
Collar strategies, 418–419
Collateral, 472, 474, 507
   average life, variance, 522–523
   impact, 519
Collateralized mortgage obligations (CMOs), 509
Collateral trust bonds, 492
Commercial mortgage-backed securities (CMBS), 507, 508, 537–539
   call protection, 539
   market, 487
   sector recommendations, spread duration, 654t–655t
   sectors, 651–652
Commission, 729
   arrangements, 336–337
Commission broker, 127
Commissions, 144
Commodities
   asset class, 798
      status, 800–801
   holding, monetary benefit, 799
   investments, 798–806
   market penetration, prospects, 801–806
   sectors, 798–799
      classification, 799f
   storability/availability, 799
   super class, 800

Commodities Futures Trading Commission (CFTC), 770
Commodity funds, 802–804
   management style, differences, 802–803
Commodity futures, 805–806
   indexes, 803t
Commodity indexes
   certificates, 804
   ETFs, 804
Commodity stocks, 801–802
   risk, 802
Commodity trading advisors (CTAs), 803
Common risk factors, 313
Common shareholder, dividend situation, 248
Common-size analysis, 220–221
Common-size balance sheet
   example, 221t
   indication, 221
Common-size income statement, 222
   example, 222t
Common stock portfolio, management
   fundamental factor models, usage, 299
   transaction costs/trade execution, 331
Common stocks
   purchase price calculation, 495
   shorting, 776
Companion bonds, 525
Company, liquidation, 476
Company-specific risk, 99
Competitive market makers, 422–423
Competitive transition charge (CTC), 544-545
Component payments, present value, 570
Component percentage ratios, 216–217
Compound growth rate, calculation, 253
Compound options, 423
Conditional expectation, 282–283
Conditional expected value, 283
Conditional mean, 283
Conditional order, 333
Conditional prepayment rate (CPR), 511–512
   ramping, 529
Conditional probability, 282–283
   distribution, determination, 283
Conditional value at risk (CVaR), 77
Confidence level, 185
Consolidated Quotation System (CQS), 141
Consolidated Tape Association (CTA), 141
   securities, 139
Consolidated Tape System (CTS), 141
Constant annualized yield volatility, 821–822
Constant discount rate, assumption, 249–250
Constant growth dividend discount model, 251–254
   problems, 254
Constant implied volatilities, 822
Constant maturity Treasury (CMT) rate, 704
Constant Proportional Yield Volatility Model (CP), 815–816

Index

Constant rate DDM, misvaluation, 254
Constrained efficient frontier maximum allocation, composition, 52f
Constraints, addition, 36
Consumable assets, 800
Consumable/transferable (C/T) assets, 800
Consumer price index (CPI), 461
　linkage, 502
Contingent deferred sales charge (CDSC), 731, 733
Contingent immunization strategy, 677
Continuous market, 122
Continuous trading, advantage, 122
Contrarian strategy, 158
Convenience yield, 799
Conventional yield measures, 576–583
Convergence trading hedge funds, 771, 778–784
Conversion
　provision, 552, 553
　ratio, 495
Converted price, 685
Convertible arbitrage, 783
　funds, 779
Convertible bonds, 466–467, 495
　arbitrage, 779–780
　returns, earning, 780
　trading, 780
Convertible debt, 797
Convertibles, 503
Convexity, 606–610
　adjustment, 607–608
　measure, 606–607
　　scaling, 609
　risk, 665
　usage, 598–610
Corporate bondholders, claim priority, 492
　ranking, 493t
Corporate bonds, 487, 491–495
　embedded options, inclusion, 665
　hedging, interest rate swaps (usage), 713t
　issues, rating factors, 472–475
　market, 487, 642–643
Corporate bond swap hedge, illustration, 712–713
Corporate credit, 713
Corporate debt obligation, 475
Corporate restructuring hedge funds, 771, 775–778
Corporate sector recommendations, spread duration, 653t
Corporation, liquidation, 476
Correlation, covariance (relationship), 25–26
Cost management, 415
Cost of carry, 378
Cost of goods sold (average day), 204–205
Cost trade-offs, 357f
Counterparty risk, 365
　exposure, 372
Countries, payments balance (S&P analysis), 502
Coupon-bearing Treasury securities, 485
Coupon bond, price/yield relationship, 572t

Coupon payment
　determination, coupon rate (usage), 617–618
　due date, 574
Coupon payment, calculation, 489
Coupon rate, 459–462
　bond price
　　relationship, 578t
　　volatility, impact, 596
　change, 469
　current yield, relationship, 578t
　price, relationship, 571–573
　real rate, 488
　required yield, relationship, 571–573
　yield to maturity, relationship, 578t
Coupon reset date, 460
Coupon reset formula, 460
Coupon stripping, 489
Covariance, 24–25
　correlation, relationship, 25–26
　structure, index model approximations, 36–39
Covenants, 472, 474
Coverage ratios, 217–219
Covered bonds, 503–504
Covered calls, 419–420
　strategy, 420
　writing strategy, 702–703
Cover pool, 503–504
Cox-Ingersoll-Ross (CIR) model, 816–817
Creation/redemption units, 742
Credit
　analysis, 472
　event, 716
　four Cs, 472, 474
　rating, 471–472
　support
　　mechanisms, usage, 535
　　subordination, measurement, 531t
Credit card receivable-based securities, 508, 540–542
　cash flow, 540
　early amortization triggers, 541–542
　portfolio, performance, 541
Credit default swap (CDS), 716
　contract life, 719
Credit default swap index (CDX), 719–720
　asset manager usage, 720
　mechanics, 720
Credit derivatives, 716
Creditor rights, 476–477
Credit risk, 365, 780
　management, credit default swaps (usage), 716–720
　reference, 471
Credit-risky bond, 478
Credit spread, 478
　change, 652, 656
　risk, 471, 478
Cross acceleration, event, 717

834 INDEX

Cross default, event, 717
Cross hedge risk, minimization, 689
Cross hedging, 383–384
  complication, 689
Crossing networks, 135–137
Cross order, 342
C shares, 731–732
  level load, 733
C tranches, 536
Cumulative probability distribution, 60–61
Currency denomination, 467
Currency risk, 482
Current assets, level, 209
Currently callable issue, 464
Current portfolio duration, 688
Current ratio, 208
Current yield, 576
Custodial costs, 391–392
Custodian, role, 739
Custody, 733

Daily standard deviation, 453
Dark pools, 137
  algos, comparison, 339
Dated date, 484
DAX 20 return time series, 72f
Day count conventions, 484–486
Days payables outstanding (DPO), 207
Days sales in inventory (DSI), 205
Days sales outstanding (DSO), 206
Dealer option, 399
Dealers, 122
Deal size, subordination (measurement), 531t
Death benefit (DB), 747, 759
Debenture bonds, 492
Debt/equity ratio, 801–802
Debt-for-stock exchange, 230
Debt instruments, 458
Debt obligation issuer, interest payment failure, 551
Debtor-in-possession (DIP), 476
Debt repayment, provision, 465
Debt securities, issues, 471
Debt-to-assets ratio, 216, 219
Debt-to-equity ratio, 216, 219
Debt-to-service coverage (DSC) ratio, 538
Decision trees, 288
Dedicated tax-backed obligations, 497, 498
Deep-in-the-money call option, 451
Default interest rate, 539
Default loss rate, 477
Default probability, forward-looking assessment, 471
Default rate, 477–478
Default risk, 469, 471–478
  impact, 551–552
Defeasance, 538, 539
Deferred annuity, 756
Deferred call, 464
Deferred-interest bonds, 494

Deferred interest securities, 460
Defined benefit pension plans, liability-driven strategies, 679–680
Delinquency, 541
Deliverable asset, knowledge, 686–687
Deliverable date, implications, 687
Deliverable issues, 684
  price adjustment, conversion factors (CBOT publication), 685
Deliverable obligations, 718
Delivery date, 367
Delivery options, 686
Delta, 449–451
Depository Trust and Clearing Corporation (DTTC), 142
Depreciation rules, artificiality, 265
Derivative contracts, risk-reward characteristics, 399–400
Derivatives
  process, 366–367
  usage, 683
Descriptors, usage, 310
Designated Order Turnaround (DOT), 125–126
Detroit Edison Securitization Funding a, bonds, 545
Developed market foreign stocks/bonds, 6
Deviations, probability-weighted function, 77
Diffusion process, 437
Digital options, 425
Directional effect, 160–161
Direct Market Access (DMA), 140
Direct method, usage, 225
Directors' fees, 733
Direct-pay LOC, 499–500
Discount, 573
Discounted cash flow (DCF)
  methods, RV methods (contrast), 272–275
  models, 245–256
  sensitivity analysis, necessity, 274–275
  valuation, 275
  usefulness, 272–273
Discount rates
  application, 575
  change, 252
  expected return, relationship, 262
  usage, 250
Dispersion measures, 75
Distressed debt hedge funds, 775
Distressed securities, 775–776
Distributed lag models, 291
Distributor, 738
  affiliation, 739
Diversifiable risk, 99
  factors, 91
Dividend discount model (DDM), 246, 248–263
  calculation, 248–249
  complications, 263–264
  earnings per share approach, 263–264
  expected returns, relationship, 261–263

Index

Dividend payout ratio, 247
Dividends, 437–438
 consideration, 410
 growth rate, 254
 measures, 246–247
 models, comparison, 260t
 operating cash flow classification, 225
 payout, 246
 stock prices, relationship, 247–248
 tax, 341–342
 usage, 751
 yield, 246–247
Dividends per share, 246
Dollar-denominated CD, issuance, 706
Dollar-denominated issue, 467
Dollar-denominated LIBOR, exchange, 393
Dollar duration, 599–600
Dollar return, sources, 580–583
Dollar-weighted rate of return, 182–183
Double-barreled in security, 497
Dow, Charles, 156
Dow Jones Industrial Average (DJIA), 149, 157
 S&P500 Index, relationship, 388–389
Dow Jones Wilshire 5000, usage, 38
Downgrade, 479
 event, 717
 risk, 471, 478–481
Downside protection, 420
Downside risk, 23, 77
 portfolio manager concern, 416
Downward-sloping yield curve, 560–561
Dow Theory
 strategies, 156–158
 testing, difficulty, 157–158
Dramatic underperformance, probability (increase), 306–307
Drop-lock bonds, 503
DuPont system, 199–202
 application, 203f
Duration, 470, 598–606
 calculation, illustration, 599
 control, 672
 duration/contribution, 662t
 sector analysis, 662t
 usage, 598–610
Dynamic asset allocation, 4–5
Dynamic factor models, 292

E3 model, 310
Early amortization triggers, 541–542
Early stage venture capital, 795–796
Earnings before interest, taxes, depreciation, amortization (EBITDA), 224
Earnings before interest and taxes (EBIT), 196, 218, 268
 consideration, 219
 reduction, 219
Earnings before taxes, earnings before interest and taxes (ratio), 201
Earnings per share (EPS)
 approach, 263–264
 dependence, 270
Earnings quality, 236
Earnings surprise strategies, 161
Earnings usage (scaling basis), 271
Earnings yield, 264
 factor exposures, 327t–329t
Economic development bonds, 496
Economic forecasts, usage, 656
Effective convexity, 609–610, 631–634
 calculation, V determination, 633f
Effective duration, 600–602, 631–634
 calculation, V determination, 633f
Effective rate basis, 588
Efficiency, levels, 148
Efficient frontier, 46–49
 composition, 50f
 constraining, benefits/costs, 53
 expansion, 49–53
  asset classes, usage, 50f
 obtaining, 93
 U.S. bonds/U.S. large-cap equity, usage, 47f
Efficient market, 147–148
Efficient portfolio, 30, 31–33
 construction, 10, 30–31
 example, 32f
 set, 17–18
 solving, 45
Efficient set, 32
 optimal portfolio, selection, 34–36
Electronic communication networks (ECNs), 134, 339
Electronic markets, alternatives, 134–137
Embedded options
 inclusion, 552–553
 usage, 613
Emerging market
 meaning, 7
 transaction costs, 352
Emerging market foreign stocks/bonds, 6
Ending inventory, representation, 205
Enhanced index fund, contrast, 302
Enhanced indexing, 646
 minor risk factor mismatches, 646
 risk factors approach, 643–646
Enhanced strategy, 643
Equilibrium Model, 823
Equilibrium value, determination, 116
Equity derivative, 365
Equity hedge, 771
Equity indexing, motivation, 169–170
Equity long/short, 773
 hedge funds, 770–771
 managers, portfolio construction, 773
Equity market, sectors, 152–153
Equity multiplier, 201–202

Equity options
  pricing models, 429
  usage, 397
Equity portfolio management, stock index futures/equity swaps (usage), 365
Equity REIT, 324
Equity styles, 153
  evolution, 166–167
  investing, 166–169
Equity swaps, 393–394
  structures, 393
  usage, 365
Equity trade, usage, 346–347
Equivalent prices/yields, calculation, 699f
Error terms, 284–285
  testing, 285
Eurobonds, 502–503
  structures, types, 503
Eurodollar bonds, 502
Eurodollar CD, 706
Eurodollar certificates of deposit, 460–461
Eurodollar futures contracts, 706
European call, 423
  options, valuation, 431–432
European covered bonds, 503–504
European listed options, 421–422
European option, 398
  usage, 436
Euro straights, 503
Euroyen bonds, 502
Evaluation period, 176
Event risk, 479, 780
Ex ante return, 20
Ex ante tracking error, 303
Excess returns, predictability (impact), 294–295
Excess risk-adjusted returns, generation, 277
Excess spread, 534–535
Exchangeable bond, 466–467, 495
Exchange market structures, 121–124
Exchange rate risk, 482
Exchanges, 125–133
Exchange-traded derivatives, 365
Exchange-traded funds (ETFs), 725, 739–744
  creation/redemption process, 741–744
    flowchart, 743f
  mutual funds, contrast, 744
  outstanding shares, redemption, 743f
  provider, interaction, 741
  purchase, 53
  shares
    creation/redemption, authorization, 742
    outstanding, 742
Exchange-traded futures options, 692–696
Exchange-traded options, 399
Exchange trading, priority rule, 332
Ex-coupon, 463
Execution risk, portfolio risk (combination), 358
Executive summary, 789

Exercise price, 397
Exercise style, 398
Exotic equity options, usage, 425–426
Exotics, 422–425
Exotic securities, usage (absence), 779
Expansion venture capital, 796
Expectations, linear predictions, 285
Expectations theories, 561–563
  forms, 561
Expected future cash flows, concept, 267
Expected portfolio returns, 15, 79
Expected return, 359–360
  DDMs, relationship, 261–263
  decline, 52–53
  dispersion, 22
  term, usage, 20
Expected shortfall, 77
Expected stock return volatility, 436–437, 447
  call option price, relationship, 451–452
  estimation, 452–453
Expected tail loss, 77
Expected terminal price, 250
Expected value, 62–63
Expected volatility, 414
Expense ratio, 729–730, 732–734
Expiration date, 397
  inclusion, 399
Explicit costs, 331
Explicit transaction costs, 341–343
  bid-ask spreads, 342–343
  commission/fees, 341
  taxes, 341–342
Ex post tracking error, 303
Extended term insurance, 751–752
Extra-market risk, 114
Ex-U.S. bond indexes, 638

Face value, 459
Factor exposures, 324t–326t
Factor risk exposures, assessment, 317–318
Factor risk models (factor models), 299
Factors, linear regressions, 289
Fair and orderly market, 129
Fair Isaac Corporation (FICO) scores, 542
Fair market benchmark, 349
Fallen angels, 493, 494
Fama, Eugene, 279
Feasible portfolios, 31–33
  example, 32f
February-May-August-November (FMAN) expiring options, 400
Federal agency securities, 490–491
  classification, 490
Federal Home Loan Mortgage Corporation (FHLMC), 509
Federally related institutions, 490
Federal National Mortgage Association (FNMA), 509
Fill-or-kill order, 334

Index

Financial analysis, 193
  cash flows, usefulness, 235–240
Financial economic theory, 16
Financial Industry Regulation Authority (FINRA), 142
Financial leverage
  evaluation, 194
  ratio, 215–220
Financial products, types, 804
Financial ratio
  analysis, 193, 194–223
  usage, 222–223
  usage, 216–217
Financial risk, 215–216
Financial Services Authority (United Kingdom), 768
Financing, stage, 794
Finite life general dividend discount model, 249–251
  constant discount rate, assumption, 249–250
  illustration, 261
  inputs, requirement, 250
  relative value, assessment, 251
Firm valuation, 271–272
First central moment, 62–63
First-generation OTC options, 421–422
First in-first out (FIFO), 753
First-lien fixed loans, securitization, 529
First par call date, 464–465
Fitch Ratings, rating agency, 471–472, 551
Fixed annual fee, SEC imposition, 733
Fixed annuities, 756, 760–762
  characteristic, 761–762
Fixed asset turnover, 214–215
Fixed asset turnover ratio, 215
Fixed charge coverage ratio, 218, 219
Fixed charges, consideration, 218–219
Fixed costs, variable costs (contrast), 331
Fixed income arbitrage, 778–779, 783
Fixed-income securities, 6
Fixed periodic premiums, 756
Fixed premium payment, 753
Fixed principal securities, 487–488
  types, issuance, 488
Fixed rate bond, PVBP, 710–711
  illustration, 711f
Fixed-rate bond market, 460
Fixed rate bonds, spread duration, 602
Fixed rate mortgage, 509
Fixed rate prime deal, 532t
Flat yield curve, 561
FLexible EXchange (FLEX) Options, 400, 401–402
  listed option, 421–422
Flexible periodic premiums, 756
Flexible premium deferred annuity (FPDA), 760–761
Flexible premiums, 755
  payment, 753
Flexible Treasury futures options, 694
Floating rate bond, PVBP, 710

Floating-rate bond market, 460
Floating-rate notes, 503
Floating-rate securities, 460
Floor, 462
  pricing, 822
Floor brokers, function, 127
Flow-of-funds structure, 498
Forced savings, 747
Forecasting, modeling market (impact), 352–355
Foreign currency, debt obligation, 501
40-bond portfolio, 660t–661t
  duration, 659
  tracking error, example, 670
Forward contracts
  features, 372–373
  futures contract, contrast, 372
  pricing, 374–378
  valuation, 374–375
Forward interest rates, volatilities, 822
Forward-looking forecast, 279
Forward looking inputs, 46t
Forward-looking tracking error
  backward-looking tracking error, contrast, 303–304
  non-systematic risk, impact, 667
  subcomponents, 668–669
  systematic risk, impact, 667
Forward rates, 556–560
  examination, 559
  future short-term rates, impact, 562
  question, 559
  realization, failure, 559–560
  usage, 706
Fourth central moment, 63
Four-year binomial interest rate tree, 614f
  one-year rates, inclusion, 616f
Four-year valuation, fair tree, 623, 625
Frame dependence, 81
Free cash flow DCF model, 264–266
Free cash flow (FCF), 230–231, 264
  calculation, 231–233
  cash flow, contrast, 266–267
  company income, relationship, 233
  theory, development, 230
Frequentist interpretation, 280
Frictions, 94
Front-end load, reduction, 732
Front-running, 337
  minimization, 338
F shares, 732
  fee-based program, 733
Full price, 463
Fully leveraged bond positions, 705
Fully rational approach, 82
Fundamental analysis
  strategies, 161–166
Fundamental analysis, technical analysis (contrast), 153–154

Fundamental factor models, 107
  description/estimation, 309–312
  descriptors, usage, 310
  usage, 299
  usefulness, 312
Fundamental long/short hedge funds, 773
Funding ratio, 679
Funds of hedge funds, 785
Future cash flows
  present value, 625–626
  value, discount rates (usage), 706
Future floating rates, 705–706
Future interest rates, distribution (representation), 615
Futures
  leveraging, 372
  prices, 367
    volatilities, 822
  pricing, 374–378
  valuation, 374–375
Futures contracts
  arbitrageur profit, 377
  dollar duration, 688
  expense, 392
  features, 367–373
  forward contracts, contrast, 372
  futures prices, 694
  options, contrast, 399–400
  party choices, 368–369
  put option, 692–693
  swaps, contrast, 714–715
Futures options, 692
  popularity, reasons, 695–696
  pricing models, 696–698
  trading, mechanics, 694–695
Futures/T-Bill portfolio, 391t
Future values, origination, 617

Gamma, 451
Gaussian distribution, 63
General account products, 749–750
Generalized autoregressive conditional heteroskedasticity (GARCH), 292, 784, 817–818
Generally accepted accounting principle (GAAP), 265
General obligation debt, 497
General redemption prices, 465
Genetic algorithms, 288
Geometric growth model, 257–258
Geometric mean, calculation, 253
Geometric random walk, 286
Global macrohedge funds, 784–785
Good-till-canceled order, 334
Government National Mortgage Association (GNMA), 509
Government-sponsored enterprises (GSEs), 490–491
  shelf, 529

Graham, Benjamin, 154, 162, 165
Gross domestic product (GDP), expectation, 774
Gross profit margin
  operating performance, relationship, 211–212
  production, 210–211
Gross yield, inclusion, 541
Growth, value (contrast), 354
Growth company, 166–167
Growth stocks, 6
  manager, performance, 166–167
Guaranteed cash value, 753
  buildup, 751
Guaranteed investment contract (GIC), 3, 749, 762–763
  life insurance company liability, 762

Half spread, 342
Hamilton model, 293
Hard commodities, 798
Hard dollars, payment, 340
Hard puts, 495
Heath-Jarrow-Morton (HJM) model, 824
Hedge, term (usage), 769
Hedgeable rates, 559–560
Hedged portfolio, 438
  payoff, 443
Hedged position, return, 382–383
Hedged stock portfolio, effectiveness (determination), 383
Hedge funds, 767–785
  categories, 771
    flowchart, 772f
  characteristic, 769
  definition, 769
  investment objective, 785
  manager, 778
    market exposure, 774
    selection, 785
  mutual funds, contrast, 770–771
  opportunistic category, 771
  privacy, 770
  strategies, 771, 772–785
Hedge Funds, Leverage, and the Lessons of Long-Term Capital Management (President's Working Group on Financial Markets), 768
Hedge ratio, 384–389, 712–713
  calculation, example, 689–692
  derivation, 439–442
  determination, 700
  selection, 689
Hedging, 688–692
  futures contracts, employment, 381
  futures options, usage, 699f
  protective put buying strategy, comparison, 703t
  Treasury bond futures buying strategy, comparison, 703t
Heuristic-driven biases, 81
Heuristics, concept, 80–81

Index

Hidden-variable predictive return model (hidden-variable models), 288, 292–293
High-credit-quality entities, 373
High-expected return stocks, 162–163
High grade, term (usage), 551
High-yield bonds, 472, 551
Historical data, usage, 278–279
Historical performance, usage (problems), 43
Historical returns, usage, 45–46
Historical volatility, 814–818
Holding period, 747
  rate of return, 672
  return, 19
Ho-Lee Model, 823–824
Homogeneous expectations assumption, 30
Horizon analysis, applications, 589–591
Horizontal common-size analysis, 220
Hulbert, Mark, 155–156
Humped yield curve, 561
Hybrid markets, 123–124

Immediate annuity, 756
Immunization principles, 674f
Immunization risk
  measures, 676f
  minimization, 675
  reinvestment risk, relationship, 676
Immunized portfolio, construction, 674–675
Imperfect substitution, 343–344
Implementation shortfall approach, 351
Implicit transaction costs, 341, 343–346
  investment delay, 343
  market impact costs, 343–345
  market timing costs, 345
  opportunity costs, 346
  price movement risk, 345
Implied repo rate, 685–686
Implied volatility, 452, 818–825
  Black model uses, 822–825
  computation, 819
Implied yield volatilities, 819
  meaning, 821–822
Incentive fee, 769
  check/balance, 788
Income statement, example, 196t
Income taxes, operating cash flow classification, 225
Indenture, bond price specification, 578
Independent and identically distributed (IID) variables, 283
Independent public accountant fee, 733
Index-based commodity investments, 804
Index certificates, disadvantage, 804
Index dollar value, 401
Indexed portfolio
  construction, 389–392
  design, optimization approach, 644–646
Indexes
  options, 400–401

risk factors, 640–641
value, sensitivity, 641
Index fund manager strategies, 390
Index funds, advantages, 804
Indexing
  criticism, 642
  problem, optimal solution (computational technique), 645
Indifference curves, 16–17, 96
  example, 17f
Indirect method, usage, 225
Industrial revenue bonds, 496
Inflation, expected rate, 549
Inflation-adjusted principal, 488–489
Inflation-indexed securities, 487
Inflation risk, 482
Information
  contracting/processing, cost reduction, 725
  advantage, 734–735
  decay, 814
Information ratio, 304
  data/calculation, 301t
Initial margin, 369
  absence, 375
  requirement, 334
Initial public offering (IPO)
  financing, 794
  status, 789
In-kind transfers, 742
Innovation process, 284–285
Input estimation, historical data (usage), 42–46
Inside buildup, 747, 752
  advantage, 758–759
Instantaneous standard deviation, 815
In-state issue, 496
Instinet Crossing Network, 136
Institutional investors
  attraction, 523
  investment objectives, classification, 2–3
  trading arrangements, 335–340
Institutional investors, inclusion, 2
Institutional Network, 134
Institutional trades, types, 335
Insurance company returns, 751
Insured bonds, 499
Integrated portfolio management, 359–360
Intelligent Investor (Graham), 162
Intensity effect, 160–161
Interbank yield curve, 564
Interest
  component, 749
  coverage ratio, 217–218, 219
  rules, 519
  taxability, 553–554
Interest-bearing debt, 216
Interest income, operating cash flow classification, 225
Interest-on-interest, 581

Interest-on-interest component, 580
　level, 582
Interest-on-interest dollar return, determination, 580–581
Interest-only (IO) class, 516
Interest-only (IO) mortgage strip, 517
　price response, expectation, 517–518
Interest-only (IO) securities, 517–518
Interest rate derivatives, usage, 600
Interest rate risk, 467–470, 780
　bonds, impact, 468–470
　control, 688
　measurement, 470, 593
　　duration/convexity, usage, 598–610
　　price value of a basis ponit, usage, 596–597
　offsetting, 672
Interest rates
　basis point change, 604, 608
　calculation, 550
　change, 601
　direction, change, 656
　distribution, representation, 615
　expectations strategies, 650
　exposure, 513
　futures contracts, cash settlement, 684
　lattice, 614–618
　price/changes, inverse relationship, 468
　structure, 549
　term structure, 458–459, 555–564
　　economic theories, 561–563
　　shape, determinants, 560–561
　Treasury spot rates, relationship, 557
　tree, arbitrage-free characteristic, 613
　volatility, spread, 656
Interest rate swaps
　callability, 704
　characterization, 704–705
　hedging, 711–712
　pricing, 705–711
　usage, 704–715
Interim cash flows, 379
　absence, 686–687
Intermarket Trading System (ITS), 138
Intermediate-term bonds, 458
Internal credit enhancement, 530
　usage, 531
Internalization, 139
Internal rate of return, 182
International bond indexes, 638–640
　inclusion, 638
International markets, penetration, 796–797
International Swap and Derivatives Association (ISDA), CDS trade documentation, 717
International trading costs, measurement/analysis, 351
Intersector allocation strategies, 651–658
　considerations, 652–656
Intra-day pricing, advantages, 744

Intrasector allocation strategies, 651–658
　considerations, 652–656
Intrinsic value, 411
Invariance, 72
Inventory
　effects, 343–344
　flow, 215
　illiquidity, 209
　management, 213
Inventory turnover ratio, 213, 215
Inverse floaters, 461
Inverted yield curve, 560–561
Investible commodity futures indexes, number (increase), 803
Investment
　advisor, 738
　advisory fee, 732–733
　companies, 725–739
　　types, 726–729
　constraints, 7–9
　delay, 343
　dimensions, 107
　horizon, 49
　　bond sale, 586
　　bond total return computation, 587–588
　objective, likelihood, 591
　policy, establishment, 4–9
　risk measures, features, 68–74
　strategy, change, 336
　style, requirements, 353
　tax considerations, 8–9
　vehicle, 739–740
Investment companies, 725
Investment Company Act of 1940, 738, 789
　Rule 2a-7, 543
Investment-grade bonds, 472, 529, 551
Investment-grade sector, 472
Investment management
　equity options, usage, 397
　overview, 1
　process, activities, 1
Investment objectives
　classification, 2–3
　setting, 2–4
Investment-oriented insurance product, 746t
　categories, 753–763
Investment-oriented life insurance, 725, 744–763
Investment Technologies Group (ITG), 136
Investors
　equity, 369
　mental account, maintenance, 81
　preference, 35
　retirement date, 736
　risk-return profile, alteratoin, 407
　venture capitalist constituency, 788
Invoice price, 685
Involuntary bankruptcy, 476
Irrevocable LOC, 500

Index

ISDA Credit Derivatives Definitions (1999/2003), 717
Issuer
  credit analysis, 472
  par yield curve, 618t
Iterative process, 618–619

January-April-July-October (JAJO) expiring options, 400
J-curve effect, 793
JPMorgan Global Governments Index, 645
Jump risk, 479
Junior notes, 507
Junior subordinated debt, shorting, 776
Junk bonds, 472, 551

Kahneman, Daniel, 80, 82
Kalotay-Williams-Fabozzi model, 824
Kappa, 451–452
Keynes, John Maynard, 80
Key rate duration, 610–611
Knock-in options, 423
Knock-out options, 423
Konstantinovsky, Vadim, 659
Krispy Kreme Doughnuts, Inc.
  cash flows, 237f
  financial results, 236
  income, 237f
Kurtosis, 62
  illustration, 66f

Ladder strategy, 651
Lagged values, 291
Lagged variables, 291
Large-cap stocks, active trading, 354
Late stage/expansion venture capital, 796
Lattice, 613–614
  calibration, 618–622
  usage, 622–625
Law of one price, 103
Leavens, D.H., 27
Legs, 614
Lehman Aggregate Bond Index, 735
Lehman Brothers U.S. Aggregate Index, 635
Lending rates, borrowing rates (contrast), 379–380
Letter of credit (LOC), 492–493
  support, 499
  types, 499–500
Letter of intent, 732
Level loads, 731
Level-payment mortgage, 509
Leverage, 310
  amount, 780
  increase, 405
Leveraged buyouts (LBOs), 493, 494
Leveraged portfolio, 95
Liability, 3
Liability-driven objectives, 2
Liability-driven strategies, 9, 672, 679–680
  proposal, 680
Lien, 491
Life-cycle fund, 736
Life insurance companies, investment-oriented products, 3
Life insurance comparisoni, 757t
Life insurance contract, cash value (development), 751
Life insurance policy, forefeit/surrender, 751
Life insurance taxability, 752–753
Like-kind firms, selection, 269–270
Limited liability companies (LLCs), 790–791
Limited partners, capital, 792
Limited partnerships, 789–790
  tests, 790
  venture funds, importance, 790
Limit orders, 121, 128, 740
  placement, 332–333
Linear autoregressive predictive return model (linear autoregressive model), 288, 291–292
Linear optimization problems, 356
Linear payoff, 400
Linear regressions, 289
  equations, 782
Lipper performance ranking system, 737
Liquidation, 476
Liquidity, 780
  concession, 343
  evaluation, 194
  measures, 208–209
  premium, 563
  ratios, 209–210
  risk, 481, 555
    measure, 358
  short-term obligation ability, 202–210
  theory, 562, 563
  transaction costs, relationship, 347–349
LiquidNet, 136
Listed derivatives, 365
Listed equity options
  usage, 415–421
Listed equity options, features, 400–402
Listed options, 399
  risk/return characteristics, 402–410
Loan-to-value (LTV) ratio, 538
Lockout period, 532, 538–539
Log-normal distribution, 815–816
London Interbank Offered Rate bid (LIBID), 503
London Interbank Offered Rate (LIBOR), 460–462
  benchmarking, 704–705
  curve, 564
  discount rates, 706
  LIBOR-based floaters, 537
  reference rate, 564
  three-month cap, 822–823
London Interbank Offered Rate/London Interbank Offered Rate bid, arithmetic mean (LIMEAN), 503

Long call option, expiration (profit/loss profile), 403t–404t
Long call positions, expiration (profit/loss profile), 406f
Long futures, 367
Long hedge, 381–382
　usage, 382
Long-only managers, 158–159
　contrast, 770
Long-only portfolios, 36
Long position, 367
　financing cost, 430
　profit/loss profile, 430t
Long put option
　expiration, profit/loss profile, 407t–408t
　position, profit/loss profile, 430t
Long put position, expiration (profit/loss profile), 406t, 408t, 409t
Long-short portfolios, 36
Long stock option, expiration (profit/loss profile), 403t–404t
Long-term bond rating systems/symbols, summary, 473t
Long-term bonds, 458, 497
Long-term budget deficits, 497
Long-term capital gains tax rate, 759
Long-term capital projects, 497
Long-term Equity Anticipation Securities (LEAPS), 400, 401–402
Long-term value strategies, 353
Lookback options, 422, 424
Loss allocations, schematic, 530f
Lower partial moment, 76
Low-expected return stocks, 162–163
Low latency, 339
Low-price-earnings-ratio effect, 164
　strategy, 165
Lucky saving, 342

Macaulay, Frederick, 601
Macaulay duration, 600–602
Machine learning, 288
Magnitude effect, 160–161
Maintenance margin, 370
　requirement, 370–371
Management fee, 732–733
　assessment, 787
March-June-September-December (MJSD) expiring options, 400
Marginal contributions, 308–309
Margin requirements, 369–371
Margin transactions, 334–335
Market anomaly strategies, 164–166
Market capitalization, 6, 354
Market-clearing price, generation, 245
Market directional hedge funds, 771
Market direction hedge funds, 772–775

Market efficiency, 147–148
　question, 170
　semistrong form, 148
　strong form, 148
　weak form, 148
Market-if-touched order, 333–334
Market impact
　empirical findings, 349–352
　measurements, 349–352
　　approaches, 351
　opportunity cost, contrast, 357f
　reduction, 137
　trading, 356
Market impact cost, 331, 343–345
　result, 350
　sell order, 344f
　trade timing, 353–354
　variation, 347
Market index, 7
　purchase, 53
Market makers, 122
Market-neutral hedge funds, 780–782
Market-neutral long-short strategy, 162–164
Market orders, 121, 126–127, 740
　danger, 332–333
　order type, 332
Market overreaction, 160
　strategies, 156
Market portfolio, 91
Market risk, 91, 106
Markets
　agents, population, 287
　forecasters, idealized behavior, 294
　forecasting, value, 293–295
　impact costs, 343–345
　participants, 551
　timers, 773–774
　trader information, 338
　volatility, 306–307
Market segmentation theory, 561, 563
Market timing costs, 345
Market turn, occurrence, 157
Market value-adjusted (MVA) annuities, 761
Market value to book value (MV/BV) ratio, 267
Markov switching-vector autoregressive (MS-VAR) models, 293
Markowitz diversification
　principle, 29–30
　strategy, 28
Markowitz efficient frontier, 109–110
Mark-to-market procedure, 371
Martingales
　definition, 284
　difference sequence, 283
　idea, 286
　model, application, 287
　random walks, relationship, 284

Index

Matching primary risk factors approach, 643–646
Maturity, 458–459, 510
  bond price volatility, impact, 596
  date, statement, 574–575
  par value, 568
  spread, 555
  value, 459
    purchase price, contrast, 571
Mean absolute deviation (MAD), 61, 75
Mean (measure), usage, 61
Mean-standard deviation, 75
Mean-variance analysis, 59
  application, 41
Mean-variance efficient portfolio, 32
Mean-variance framework, extension, 355
Mean-variance optimization, 78
  framework, 679–680
Mean-variance portfolio analysis (mean-variance analysis), 16, 23
Merger
  arbitrage, 776–777
  credit event, 717
Mezzanine venture capital, 796–797
Microsoft Corporation, DuPont system (application), 203f
Minimum-variance zero-beta portfolio, 112
Minor risk factor mismatches, 646
Modeling market, impact, 352–355
Modeling techniques, asset management firm adoption, 278
Model risk, 780
Modern portfolio theory, principles, 107–108
Modified duration, 600–602
Modified Endowment Contract (MEC), 753
Moments, 62–63
Momentum portfolios, 159
Momentum strategies, 156, 158–161
Money, time value (consideration), 410
Money machine, absence, 105
Money management, 1
Money managers, performance attribution analysis, 186t
Money market funds, 737
Money market instruments, 458
Monotonicity, 72
  property, requirement, 73
Monthly cash flow, 514t–515t, 520t–522t
Monthly payment rate (MPR), 541
Moody's Investors Service, rating agency, 471–472, 551
Moral obligation bonds, 498
Moratorium, event, 717
Morgan Stanley Capital International (MSCI) EAFE
  constraint, 52
  Index, 735
  index, 42
  international equity, inclusion, 49–51
Morningstar performance ranking system, 737

Mortality and expense (M&E) charges, 751, 760
Mortgage ABS
  deal, cash flow waterfall (schematic representation), 537f
  sectors, 533–534
Mortgage-backed securities, interest payment, 450
Mortgage bond, 491
Mortgaged property, foreclosure/sale, 492
Mortgagee/mortgagor, 509
Mortgage loans, groups (transformation), 509
Mortgage market, increase, 508
Mortgage pass-through security, cash flow, 513, 516
Mortgage pool, cash flow (projection), 513
Mortgage rate, coupon rate (relationship), 666
Mortgage-related ABS, 533–537
Mortgage sector
  investment risk, 666–667
  recommendations, spread duration, 654t–655t
Mortgage term, 510
Most distant futures contract, 368
Moving daily average, 812t
  deviation, 813t
Multifactor CAPM (Merton), 112–114
Multifactor risk models, 106–107, 303
Multi-index market models, 38–39
Multiphase dividend discount models, 255–257
  three-stage growth model, 256–257
  two-stage growth model, 255–256
Multiple assets
  feasible/efficient portfolios, example, 33f
  portfolio risk measurement, 26
Multiples
  bases, selection, 270
  determination, 270–271
Multiple-share classes, 734
Multiple step-up note, 460
Municipal bonds, 487, 495–500
  issuers, 495–496
  market, 487
  securities, 553
  types, 496–500
Music royalties, securitization, 508
Mutual funds, 726–727
  annual operating expenses, 729–734
  contracts, 739
  direct placement, 731
  ETFs, contrast, 745t, 746t
  hedge funds, contrast, 770–771
  investment, advantages, 734–735
  investors, 737–738
  market price, NAV excess, 739
  professional management, advantage, 735
  purchase, 53
  sales, growth, 336
  sales charges, 729–734
  structure, 738–739
  taxation, 737–738
  tax liability, assumption, 738

Mutual funds (*Cont.*)
  trustees, 738
  types, investment objective category, 735–737
Mutual insurance companies, 747–749
  stock external owners, absence, 748

Narrow-based stock index futures contract, 373
National Association of Securities Dealers (NASD), ADF operation, 139
National Association of Securities Dealers Quotations (NASDAQ), 124
  BBOs, 141
  stock market, 130–132
National Association of Securities Dealers Quotations National Market (NNM), 133
National Association of Securities Dealers Quotations Small Cap Market, 133
National best bid and offer (NBBO), 123, 137
National exchanges, 125–130, 133
National governments, ratings (assignation), 501
National Market System (NMS), SEC (contrast), 138–139
National Securities Clearance Corporation (NSCC), 142
Natural buyers/sellers, 121
Natural resource companies, 801
Nearby futures contract, 368
Negative carry, 378
Negative convexity, 780
  meaning, 602
  positive convexity, contrast, 608–609
Negative covenants, 475
Negative dollar return, 580
Negative earnings surprise, 161
Negative pledge clause, 492
Neglected-firm effect, 164, 165
NER tranche, 536–537
Net asset value (NAV), 481, 726–727
  price divergence, 728
Net earnings, 268
Net financing cost, 378
Net free cash flow (NFCF), 233–235
Net income, calculation, 200–201
Net operating income (NOI), 538
Net profit margin, calculation, 212
Net working capital cushion, 210
Net working capital-to-sales ratio, 208–209
Neural networks, 288
New York Stock Exchange (NYSE), 125–129
  block trades, 335–336
  NYSE-assigned specialists, roles, 128–129
  OpenBook, 349
  Rule 127, 336
  specialists, 128–129
Next futures contract, 368
Nikkei 225, finance, 394
No-arbitrage condition, importance, 618
No-Arbitrage Model, 823

Nodes, 614
  value
    calculation, 617f
    determination, 616–618
Noise, assumptions, 285
Noise traders, 68
Nonaccelerated senior (NAS) bonds, 532–533
  presence, 533
Nonaccelerated senior (NAS) distribution percentage, 533
Nonaccelerated senior (NAS) percentage, 533
Nonaccelerated senior (NAS) tranches, deal face value, 533
Nonamortizing security, 540
Noncallable bond, callable bond (spread), 656
Noncash-paying security, 696–697
Nondisplayed liquidity, 137
Nondollar-denominated issue, 467
Nonexchange indexes, 151t
Nonfactor error term, measurement, 312
Nonforfeiture options, 751–752
Nonintermediated markets, naturals involvement, 122
Noninvestment-grade bonds, 472, 493–495, 551
  issuers, types, 493–494
  issues, features, 494–495
Noninvestment-grade sector, 472
Nonliability-driven objectives, 2
Nonlinear programming algorithm, 355
Nonmortgage asset-backed securities, 540–545
Nonrecourse loans, 537–538
Nonrenewable commodities, 799
Nonsystematic risk, 99–100, 667
  division, 669–670
Nonterm structure risk, 668
Non-Treasury securities
  Treasury securities, risk premium, 550
  yield, 602
Non-U.S. bonds, 501–504
  inclusion, 638
  market, 487
Normal credit spread, 656
Normal probability distribution (normal distribution), 63–64
  contrast, 66f
  empirical evidence, 65–67
  example, 63f
  theoretical distributions, 67–68
Normal yield curve, 560
North America Investment Grade Index, 720
Note rate, 509
No-trade price, 349
Number of days of inventory, 205
Number of days of purchases, 207

Odd-lot purchases, problems, 172
Offer quote, 121
Off-exchange markets, 134–137

Index

Official statement, 497
Off-the-run bonds, 779
Off-the-run maturity, 714
Off-the-run U.S. Treasury bonds, 779
One-period illustration, 445
One-period investment horizon, assumption, 93
One-period option pricing model, 442f
    illustration, 442f
One-year rating migration table, 480t
On-the-run benchmark, 478
On-the-run issue, one-year rates, 619f, 620f, 622f
    derivation, information, 621f
On-the-run pay yield curve, 618
On-the-run Treasury bonds, 779
On-the-run U.S. Treasury bonds, 779
OpenBook, 128, 349
Open-ended mortgage, 491
Open-end funds, 726–727
    closed-end funds, contrast, 728
    ETFs, comparison, 740
Open interest, 369
Open order, 334
Operating cash flow
    classifications, 225
    usage, 240
Operating cycle, 204–207
    calculation, 206
    information, example, 209
    investment conversion, 207
    length, measurement, 204
    measurement, 205
    phases, 204
Operating earnings, 196
Operating expense, 732–733
Operating financial condition, aspects, 194
Operating performance
    condition, aspects, 194
    evaluation, 211
Operating profit
    decline, example, 200
    margin, 211
        operating performance, relationship, 211–212
Opportunistic hedge fund strategies, 784–785
Opportunity cost, 331, 346
    market impact, contrast, 357f
    trading, 356
Optimal execution, models, 358
Optimal portfolio, 17–18
    CML, relationship, 96f
    implementation, 53–56
        active strategies, usage, 56
    passive implementation, 53–55
        example, 54t
    selection, 34–36
        example, 34f
        indifference curves, usage, 35f
Optimal trading, 356–359

Optimization
    approach, 644–646
    method, 327
Optimization technology, 78
Option-adjusted basis, 528
Option-adjusted duration, 602
    example, 650
Option-adjusted spread (OAS), 630
    demonstration, 631f
Optionality exposure, 665t
Option buyer, 397
    option position value realization, 412–413
Option-free bonds
    cash flows, 568
    price volatility properties, 593–595
    price-yield relationship, 601f
    price/yield relationship, example, 594t
    pricing, 567–576
    valuation, 624f
Option life
    anticipated cash payments, 414–415
    return, expected volatility, 414
    short-term risk-free interest rate, 414
Option position, comparisons, 410
Option price, 410–415
    components, 411–413
    factors, 413–415
        illustration, 413t
    sensitivity, 447–452
Option pricing models, 431–447
    inputs, 452
Options
    cost management applications, 426
    delta, 450
    features, 397–400
    futures contracts, contrast, 399–400
    intrinsic value, 412t
    involvement, 783–784
    positions, profit/loss (summary), 409
    pricing, 444
    returns management applications, 426
    risk management applications, 426
    theta, 451
    time premium, 412–413
    time to expiration, 414
    time value, 412
    value, calculation, 434, 436
Option seller, 397
Option writer, 397
Order-driven markets, 121–122
    quote-driven markets, contrast, 123–124
Orderly market, maintenance, 128
Order Protection Rule, 138
Orders
    list, 347–348
    types, 332–334
Ordinary income, capital gains (contrast), 760

INDEX

Original issuers, 493
Original stock price, 417
Out-of-state issue, 496
Out-of-the-money market price, 411
Out-of-the-money option, 416
  strike price, 821
Overcollateralization (OC), 535
  structure, 534
  turboing, 536f
Overperformance option, 423–424
Over-the-counter Bulletin Board (OTCBB), 133
Over-the-counter (OTC) derivative, 372
Over-the-counter (OTC) equity options, 421–425
  first generation, 422
Over-the-counter (OTC) interest rate derivatives, 822–823
Over-the-counter (OTC) issues, 152
Over-the-counter (OTC) markets, 123–133, 365, 399
Over-the-counter (OTC) option, 399, 692
  cost, increase, 399
  structures, 422
Overweighting, 172–173
Overwrites, 419–420
  strategy, 420

Paid-up additions (PUA), 754
Pan-European Aggregate Index, 638
Paper portfolio, 351
Par, present value, 569–570
Parallel yield curve shift assumption, 603
Par swap, 704
Participating dividend, 754
Participating policies, 748, 749
Par value, 459
Par value at maturity, 568
Passive management
  approach, 644
  employment, 643
Passive portfolio strategy, 9
Passive strategies, 169–175
Pass-through certificates, 507
Pass-through security
  average life, 516
  discovery, 643
  monthly cash flow, 514t–515t
Payment failure, event, 717
Payment-in-kind (PIK), 494
  bonds, 494
Pay-now-choose-later option, 424
Pay-through certificates, 507
Pennies, adoption, 339
Pension funds
  liability structure, 677
  performance measure, 679
Pension plans
  liability-driven strategy, proposal, 680
  types, 3

Percentage price change
  convexity adjustment, 607–608
  estimation, 605–606
Perfect hedge, 381, 688–689
Performance attribution
  analysis, 176, 185, 186t
  models, 185–187
Performance evaluation, 11, 147, 176, 183–187
Performance funds, 768
Performance measurement, 11, 176–183
Periodic coupon interest payments, 568
  issuance, 580
Periodic coupon payments, absence, 571
Periodic interest payments, interest-on-interest component, 580
Periodic interest rate, 569–570
Permanent price impact cost, 344
Perpetual issues, 503
Pfandbriefe market, 503
Physical good, purchase, 801
Physicals, pricing models, 696–698
Physical settlement, 718
Pink Sheets, 133
Pipeline, 136
Planned amortization class II (PAC II) bond, 528
Planned amortization class (PAC)
  PAC-support structure, 528
  schedule, creation, 524t–525t
  structure
    distribution rules, 526
    prepayment protection, 525
Planned amortization class (PAC) bonds, 523–528
Policy asset allocation decision, 4
Policy loan, 752
Political institutions, stability, 501
Portfolio
  asset allocation, recommendation, 648t, 649t
  beta, 307–308
  construction, 10, 670–672
    applications, 316–329
  convexity, portfolio manager assessment, 666
  creation, 103–104
    pure bond indexing strategy, involvement, 642
  credit quality, 662t
    allocation, 659
  current duration, increase, 688
  deviation, 665–667
  diversification, 26–30
  example, 318t
  expected return
    example, 31t
    measurement, 19–21
  exposure, benchmark exposure (material mismatch), 669–670
  factor exposures, 327t–329t
  feasible set, 31
  holdings, 318t

Index

interest rate risk, control, 688
internal rate of return, 584–585
market cap/style, benchmark (contrast), 306
market value, 604
monitoring, 10
nonsystematic risk (reduction), diversification (impact), 99–100
optimizer, usage, 670–672
  examples, 671t, 673t
  rebalancing, 54, 670–672
return, 177
  calculations, 178
risk-return portfolio, 319t
risk-return trade-off, 48t
sector composition, 662t
securities, prices, 727
spread duration, 665
standard deviations, example, 31t
stocks, number (inclusion), 305
strategy, 640–647
  selection, 9–10
structure, 672
theory, behavioral finance (contrast), 80–82
tilting, 326–327
time horizon, 672
total risk, decomposition, 313
tracking error, 300, 667
  determination, 300, 302
  index, relationship, 302
  S&P500, relationship, 302
value, 713t
  comparison, 391t
yield, 541
  measures, 583–585
Portfolio duration, 602–604
  alteration, 650
  calculation, 603t
    dollar duration, usage, 603–604
  contribution, 603t, 604–605
  value, 603
Portfolio exposure
  analysis, 320t–323t
  assessment, 316–319
  measure, duration (usage), 663–667
Portfolio M, 98
Portfolio management, 1
  contrast, 360f
  factor models, usage, 658–672
  integration, 359–360
  listed equity options, usage, 415–421
  strategies, 419–420
Portfolio managers
  bond ownership, 657–658
  economic forecasts, usage, 656
  performance, 43
Portfolio risk, 359–360
  acceptable levels, 15
  asset returns, correlation (effect), 29–30
  change, 115
  characteristics, benchmark (relationship), 659–667
  correlation, relationship, 28–29
  execution risk, combination, 358
  measurement, 21–26, 300
Portfolio selection
  alternative risk measures, 74–77
  concepts, 16–1816
  higher moments, 77–78
  Markowitz theory, 82
  process, schematic presentation, 41f
  theory, 15
    contribution, 28
    extensions, 77–79
    issues, 59
Position, liquidation, 368–369
Posit (ITG), 136
Positive carry, 378
Positive convexity, negative convexity (contrast), 608–609
Positive earnings surprise, 161
Positive free cash flow, 231
Positive homogeneity, 72
  property, 73
Positively sloped yield curve, 560
Posttrade measures, 349
Power Function Model, 816–817
  criticism, 817
Predictability, importance, 294–295
Predicted tracking error, 303
Predictive regressive models, 289, 291
Predictive return models, 287–293
  classification, 288
Preditability
  concept, 279–286
  usage, 281
  statistical concepts, 282–286
Preferred habitat theory, 562, 563
Preferred shareholder, dividend situation, 248
Premium, 573
  excess, 750–751
Prepayable securities, price-yield relationship, 601–602
Prepayments, 465
  allocation, 532
  assumptions, 522–523
  cash flow uncertainty, relationship, 510–511
  conventions, 511–513
  impact, 511
  lockout, 538–539
  option, 465
  penalty points, 538, 539
  protection provisions, 538
  risk, 470, 665
    examination, 666
  sensitivity, 666
  speed, assumption, 523

Prerefunded bonds, 500
Present value (PV), level, 625–626
President's Working Group on Financial Markets, 768
Pretrade measures, 349
Price/earnings (P/E) ratio, 267
  strategies, 162
Price impact cost, 343
Price momentum, 354
  strategy, 158
Price movement risk, 331, 345
Price per dollar of book value, usage, 271
Price per restaurant, usage, 271
Price quotes, 575–576
Price reporting, 141
Price reversal strategy, 158
Price-to-book (P/B) value, 167
Price-to-earnings (P/E) ratios, 735
Price-to-earnings (P/E) value, 167
Price value of a basis point (PVBP)
  calculation, 691
  computation, 710t
  illustration, 597t
  usage, 596–597
Price volatility, 354
  measure, 597
Price/X ratio, 267–268
Price/yield relationship, 571
  illustration, 572t
  shape, 572f
Pricing models, examination, 286–287
Primary bond index matching factors, 641t
Primary market analysis, 656
Prime loans, securitization, 529
Principal
  reference, 459
  rules, 519
Principal cash flows (generation), collateral (impact), 519
Principal-only (PO) class, 516
Principal-only (PO) mortgage strip, 516–517
  price, change, 517
Principal-only (PO) securities, 516–517
Principal payments
  payment/receipt, 527
  rules, 526
Principals, 122
Private equity, 786–797
Private-label credit enhancement, 529–532
Private-label RMBS, 508, 528–533
Private-label senior structuring variations, 532–533
Private-label transactions, 509
Probability
  function, 60
  relative frequency concept, 280
Probability distribution, 60
  description, 61–63

  function, information, 62–63
  illustration, 21t, 25t
Probability theory, 16
  conceptual tools, 280
  review, 60–64
Procter & Gamble (P&G)
  adjusted cash flow, 226t
  bonds
    effective sale price, 702
    price, determination, 690–691
    sale, 690
    strike prices, 700
  cash flow, 225
    estimate, 223–224
  depreciation/amortization, 232
  free cash flow, calculation, 234t
  growth, maintenance, 232
  par value, 693t
    hedge, 701t
  position, hedging, 689–690
Production cost, changes, 211
Profitability, 416–417
  evaluation, 194
  expected date, 789
  predictability, impact, 294–295
  ratios, 210–213
Profit margin ratios, 210
Profit sharing fees, distribution (prohibition), 788
Program trades, 335, 336–338
Progressive adaptation, 288
Projected performance, conversion, 269
Project performance, valuation, 269
Promised yield, 580
Propagation effect, 71–72
Prospective prepayment curve (PPC), 529
Prospect theory, 80
Protective put buying strategy, usage, 703t
Protective put hedge, table (creation), 700–701
Protective put strategies, 416–418
  illustration, 418f
  profitability, 417
Psychological approach, 82
Public orders, 332
Public Securities Association (PSA), 511
  benchmark, assumptions, 512–513
  monthly cash flows, 520t–522t
  prepayment rate, 666
  total principal payments, 524t–525t
Purchasing power risk, 482
Pure bond indexing strategy, 642–643
Pure expectations theory, 561, 562
Pure index fund, 170
Pure order-driven market, 121
Putable bond, 466
  usage, example, 628, 630
  valuation, 626–630
    example, 629f
Put-call parity relationship, 429–431

Index

Put futures options, 694t
    option writer payment, 694
Put option, 397
    classification, 495
    price, computation, 436
    purchase, 402, 406–407
        involvement, 416
    sale, 402
    writing, 409
Put price, 466
Put provision, 552, 553

Quadratic optimization method, 174
Quadratic optimization problems, 356
Quadratic programming, usage, 30–31
Quadratic regression equation, 782
Quality option, 686
Quantitative analysis, 193
Quantitative equity long/short hedge fund managers, 773
Quantitative statistics, usage, 773
Quantum Group of Funds, 768
Quick ratio, 208, 209
Quid pro quo, 730
Quote-driven dealer market, 123f
Quote-driven markets, 121–123
    order-driven markets, contrast, 123–124

Rainbow options, 423–424
Random variable, 60
    variance, 809
Random walks, martingales (relationship), 284
RAS Asset Management, 345
Rate of return, calculation, 685–686
Rate reduction bonds (RRBs), 508, 543–545
    enhancement levels, 545
    issue, structure, 544
    risks, 545
    structure, 544–545
    true-up mechanism, 545
Rating agencies, 551
    rating systems, 472
Rating migration/transition table, 479, 481
Ratio analysis, 236, 238
Rational investors, 68
Ratios, classification, 194–220
Real interest rate, 549
Real rate, 488
Real-world investors, forecasting techniques (usage), 294
Rebalancing, frequency, 55f
Receivables portfolio, performance, 541
Recovery rate, 477–478
    variation, 477–478
Recursive valuation, 617
Redemption unit, 742
Redemption value, 459
Reduced paid up, 752

Reference entity, 716
Reference issuer, 716
Reference obligation, 716
Reference rate, 461, 564
Refinancing, 510–511
Refunded bonds, 500
Refunding, 464
    provisions, 463–465
Regional exchanges, 130, 133
Registered investment advisor (RIA), 738
Registered traders, 127
Regression analysis, usage, 37–38
Regressive predictive return model (regressive model), 288, 289–291
Regular redemption prices, 465
Regulation, 141–142
Regulatory constraints, 8
Reinvestment risk, 460, 470, 553
    immunization risk, relationship, 676
    increase, 582
    offsetting, 672
    yield to maturity, relationship, 581–583
Relative return, 769
Relative valuation (RV)
    methods, 266–272
        DCF methods, contrast, 272–275
    models, 245
    principles, 268–269
    sensitivity analysis, necessity, 274–275
    steps, 269–272
    usefulness, 273–274
Relative value
    arbitrage, 783–784
    assessment, 251
    strategies, 647
Renewal period, 761
Reorganization, 476
Replicating portfolio
    benchmark construction, relationship, 172–173
    capitalization method, 174
    construction
        considerations, 171–173
        methods, 173–174
    maintenance, 172
    management, implications, 173
    quadratic optimization method, 174
    stratified method, 174
    tracking error risk, 171–172
    transaction costs, 171–172
Repudiation, event, 717
Required minimum distribution (RMD) rules, 759
Required yield, 567–568
    coupon rate, relationship, 571–573
    price, relationship, 571–573
Reset options, 422
Reset period, 761
Residential agency mortgage pass-through securities, 511–516

Residential mortgage-backed securities (RMBS), 507, 508
Residential mortgage loan, cash flow characteristics, 509–511
Residual risk, 99
  contrast, 314
Restructurings, 493, 494
  event, 717
Return
  annualizing, 183
  arithmetic average (mean) rate, 179–180
  calculation, 177–178
  dollar-weighted rate, 182–183
  enhancement, 415
    strategies, 420–421
  fluctuation, 282
  internal rate, 182
  measures, alternatives, 176–179
  rate, calculation, 685–686
  risk, trade-off, 47
  static multifactor models, 290
  time-weighted return, 180–182, 183
Return distribution, tails, 65–66
Return generating function, 310
Return on assets
  calculation, 197–198
  examination, 199–200
Return-on-assets ratio, 196–197
Return on equity (ROE)
  calculation, 198
  decomposition, 202
  firms, 167
  ratio, 201–202
Return on investment
  evaluation, 194
  ratios, 196, 198–199
Revenue bonds, 498
Revenue generation, 795
Revenue growth, assumptions, 788
Reverse cash-and-carry trade, 377
  theoretical futures price calculation, 379
Reverse floaters, 461
Reverse-repo rates, 688
Reward-risk ratio, 304
Rising floor death benefit, 759
Risk
  arbitrage, 776
  asymmetry, 69
  control, 106, 777
    applications, 316–329
  decomposition, 312–316
    overview, 317f
    summary, 316
  extra-market sources, 113
  factors, 90
    descriptors, contrast, 310
    mismatches, 646
    usage, 310

  indexes, 310
  management strategies, 415–419
  reduction, diversification (impact), 725
  relativity, 69
  sources, intertemporal dependence/correlation, 69–72
  uncertainty, 70
Risk-adjusted returns, generation, 277
Risk assets, risk-free assets (contrast), 18
Risk-averse investors, 17–18
Risk-controlled active management, 175
Risk/expected tail loss, conditional value, 76
Risk-free asset
  assumption, 110
  availability, 94
  beta, 110
  existence, 93, 110
  introduction, 95–96
  variance, 97
Risk-free interest rate, 437
  assumption, 446
Risk-free rate
  absence, 94
  borrowing/lending, 112
  estimation, 252
Riskless arbitrage, 376
Riskless assets, 18
Riskless hedge, 441
Risk measurement (risk measures), 64–68
  axiomatic properties, 72–74
  categorization, 68
  features, 69
  variance/standard deviation, 22
Risk multidimensionality, 69
Risk premium, 90–91
  components, 91–92
  default risk, impact, 551–552
  factors, 551–555
Risk-return decomposition, example, 319t
Risk-return profile, alteration, 407
Risky assets, portfolio, 30–36
  expected return, 20–21
Risky efficient portfolios, composition, 51t
Robust estimator, 79
Robust portfolio optimization, 78–79
Round lot, 334
R tranche, 536–537
Rule 10A-1, adoption, 143
Rule 10b-21, SEC adoption, 144
Rule of one alpha, application, 781

Safety-first risk measures, 75–77
Sales charge/load, 729–732
Sales charges/annual expenses, 734t
Sales-force distribution, occurrence, 730
Sales price, changes, 211, 212
Sales volume, changes, 211, 212

Index

Salomon Smith Barney Broad Investment-Grade Bond Index (SSB BIG), 635
Same-day measures, 349–350
Samuelson, Paul, 279
Scenario analysis, 589, 590t, 591
Second central moment, 63
Second-generation OTC options, 422–425
Second-lien loans, 529
Second-to-die insurance, 755
Sector risk, 665
Sector-specific stocks, 801–802
Secured corporate debt obligation, 475
Securities
 auto loan backing, 543
 basket, delivery, 38–381
 broad-based portfolio, acquisition, 734
 OAS, 630
  calculations, impact, 632–634
 PVBP, 712
 sale, 778
 selection strategies, 657–658
 supply/demand schedule, 348f
Securities Act amendments (1975), 138
Securities Act of 1933 (Securities Act), 141–142
Securities Act of 1934 (Exchange Act), 141–142
Securities Exchange Act of 1934, 334
Securities Exchange Commission (SEC)
 formal/information soft dollar limitations, 340
 NMS, contrast, 138–139
 12b-1 fee, 733
Securitization transaction, 538
Security Analysis (Graham), 154
Security market line (SML), 100–102
Seed capital, 795
Self-regulating organizations (SROs), 142
Sell hedge, 381–382
Sell limit order, 333
Sell orders, buy orders (imbalance), 129
Sell stop order, 333
Semiannual cash flows, 568
Semiannual coupon payments
 annuity, equivalence, 569
 present value, 569–570
Semiannual interest rate, 569–570
 usage, 577
Semiannual payments, assumption, 484
Semiannual total return, annualization process (determination), 588
Semivariance, 23
Senior notes, 507
Sensitivity analysis, necessity, 274–275
Separate account investment options, types, 754–755
Separate account products, 749–750
Separate Trading of Registered Interest and Principal of Securities (STRIPS), 490
Sequential-pay PAC structures, 526–528
Sequential-pay structures, 518–523
Serial correlation, 810

Settlement, 142
 futures price, convergence, 390
 price, determination, 369–370
 procedure, 718
Settlement date, 367, 383
 futures contracts seller requirement, 684–685
 implications, 687
 knowledge, 686–687
 transaction completion, 484
Shareholder fee, 729
Shares, exchange-traded class, 643
Sharpe, William, 82, 185
Sharpe ratio, 184–185
Shift percentage, 533
Shock rates, 598
Short-bond position, 711–712
Short call option position, profit/loss profile, 430t
Short call positions, expiration (profit/loss profile), 406f
Short futures, 367
Short hedge, 381–382
 usage, 382
Short position, 367
Short put position, expiration (profit/loss profile), 409t
Short selling, 380, 774–775
Short-selling hedge funds, 774–775
Short-selling rules, 143–144
Short stock position, expiration (profit/loss profile), 407t–408t
Short-term bonds, 458
Short-term notes, 496–497
Short-term obligations
 meeting, cushion, 208–209
 satisfaction, 203
Short-term risk-free interest rate, 414
Short-term signal, 353
Simple filter rules strategies, 156, 158
Single-index market model, 37–38
Single-index performance evaluation measures, 184–185
Single-monthly mortality (SMM) rate, 512, 543
Single-name credit default swaps, 716–719
 asset manager usage, 718–719
 mechanics, 716
 trade, cash flows, 717–718
Single-period liability, immunization strategy, 672–677
Single-period portfolio return, measurement, 19–20
Single premium deferred annuity (SPDA), 760, 763
Single-premium life insurance, 753
Single premiums, usage, 756
Single step-up note, 460
Sinking fund call price, par value, 466
Sinking fund provision, 463, 465–466
Sinking fund requirement, 466
Six-pack securities, 530
Skewed distribution, 62f

Skewness, 61–62
Skill based investing, 770
Small-cap stocks, comparison, 354
Small-firm effect, 164
  strategy, 165
Soft commodities, 798
Soft dollars
  arrangement, 339–340
  payment, 340
  SEC limitations, 340
Soft puts, 495
Soros, George, 768
Soros Fund Management, 768
Sourcing investments, 792
Sovereign bonds, 501–502
Special bond structures, 499–500
Specialists, 122
  responsibility, 129
Specialized bond market indexes, 638
Special purpose vehicle (SPV), 504
Special redemption prices, 465
Special situation hedge funds, 777–778
Specific risk, 313
Speculative-grade bonds, 493–495
  issuers, types, 493–494
  issues, features, 494–495
Spider, 741
Spot rates, 556–560
  example, 557–558
Spread, 550
  call risk, impact, 656
  duration, 478, 602
  option, 423–424
Spread duration, contribution (difference), 664t
Square root model, 817
Stable Paretian distribution, 65
Standard and Poor's 100 (OEX), 401
Standard and Poor's 500
  benchmark, 317–318
  expected return, 302
  Index, DJIA (relationship), 388–389
  index, MSCI EAFE index (correlation), 44t
  index fund, costs, 174–175
  portfolio, comparison, 382–383
  returns, distribution, 67f
  return time series, 70f, 71f
  risk exposures, analysis, 320t–323t
  Stock Index, 735
  tracking error, 302
  usage, 171
Standard and Poor's Corporation, rating agency, 471–472, 551
Standard convexity, 609–610
Standard deviation, 22–26, 61
  calculation
    historical data, usage, 453, 809–814
    observations, basis, 811t

  risk measure, 48
  variation, 810
Standby LOC, 499–500
Start-up company, J-curve, 797
Start-up portfolio companies, venture capitalist constituency, 788
Start-up venture, goal, 795–796
Stated conversion price, 495
Statement of cash flows, 224–229, 797
  reformatting, 227, 228t
Statement of Financial Accounting Standards (SFAS), No. 95, 225
StateStreetGlobal Advisors (SSgA) World Government Bond Index strategy, 645
Static multifactor models, 290
Static regressive models, 289–291
Stationary time-series process, 283
Statistical arbitrage, 782–783
Statistical concepts, importance, 285–286
Statistical factor model, 106–107
Statistical models, description, 352
Statistical moments, 62–63
Statistical theory, 16
Steep yield curve, 560
Stepped-up death benefit, 759
Step-up bonds, 494
Stochastic dividend discount model (stochastic DDM), 257–263
  advantages, 260–261
  applications, 260
  binomial stochastic model, 257–259
  dividend discount models, 261–263
  expected returns, 261–263
  trinomial stochastic model, 259–260
  usage, 261
Stochastic process, usage, 437
Stock funds, difference, 735
Stock index, performance, 380–381
Stock index future contracts
  cash settlement contracts, comparison, 373–374
  dollar value, 373
  pricing correctness, 379
Stock index futures
  applications, 381–392
  features, 373–381
  stock index basis, 383
  usage, 389, 715
Stock index futures, usage, 365
Stock insurance companies, 747–749
Stock markets
  block trades, 144
  clearance/settlement, 142
  commissions, 144
  functioning, 140–144
  index, risk control, 319, 324
  indicators, 149–152
    classification, 149

Index **853**

practices, evolution, 138–140
price reporting, 141
reactions, 802
regulation, 141–142
short-selling rules, 143–144
structure, 124f
tick size, 142–143
Stock options, 400
price, 401
Stock portfolio
factor exposures, 324t–326t
hedging, 383–384
risk, control, 381
Stock prices
example, 439
fixed drift, 286
generation, stochastic process (usage), 437
increase, 430
martingales, relationship, 287
movements, hedging, 381–389
original price, 417
Stock replacement strategy, 392
Stock returns
forecasting, 277
merits, debate, 280
predictions, example, 281–282
volatility, expectation, 434, 436–437
Stocks
basket, trading, 336
direct purchase, 391t
fair value, expected return (relationship), 262f
public orders, 128
purchases, simultaneity, 164
strategies, 147
Stop-limit order, 333
Stop-loss orders, 740
Stop order, 128, 333
dangers, 333
Straight bonds, 503
Stranded assets, 544
Strategic strategies, 647
Stratified method, 174
Stratified sampling approach, 644
Strict random walk, 284
Strict white noise, 284
Strike price, 397, 421
fixation, 414
Stripped MBS, 509
Stripped Treasury securities, 489–490
Structured portfolio strategies, 9
Structured products, 507
sector, 487
Structure trades, 656
Structuring bonds, 525
Structuring speeds, 525
Stub trading, 783
Style indexes, 152
Subadditivity, 72

property, 73
Subordinated debenture bonds, 492
Subordinated notes, 503
Subordinate notes, 507
Subordinates, shifting interest, 532t
Subperiod return, 178–179
averaging methods, 179t
Subprime collateral pool, characteristics, 535f
Subprime loans, 529
Subprime MBS, 533–537
Substitution swap, 657
Super classes, 800
SuperDOT system, 127–128
Support bonds, 523–528
usage, 528
Support vector machines, 288
Supranationals, 502
Surviving spouse, 755
Survivorship insurance, 755
policy, annual premium, 755–756
Swap curve, benchmark usage, 564
Swap rate, 564
curve, 478
yield curve, 563–564
Swaps
assessment, 657–658
floating rate, benchmarking, 704–705
futures contracts, comparison, 714–715
hedge instruments, contrast, 713–715
identification, portfolio optimizer (usage), 671t, 673t
option, 686
payment, 717–718
PVBP
behavior, 714
computation, 710t
value, 706
Systematic portfolio risk, 100f
Systematic-residual risk decomposition, 314
flowchart, 314f
Systematic risk, 91, 99, 667
decomposition, 667
factor, excess return, 105–106
term structure changes, exposure, 668
Systematic tracking error, decomposition, 668t

Tactical strategies, 647
Target-date fund, 736
Target portfolio duration, 688
Taxable municipal bonds, 496
Taxable municipal securities, 496
Tax-advantaged savings, 747
Tax-backed debt obligations, 497–498
Tax-exempt municipal securities, 496
Teaser rate, 761
Technical analysis, 154
empirical studies, 156
fundamental analysis, contrast, 153–154

Technical analysis (*Cont.*)
  strategies, 154–161
  value, debate, 155
10-day moving daily average, 812t
Tennessee Valley Authority, 50-year bonds, 458
Term insurance, commodity product, 747
Term repurchase (repo) rates, 705
Term structure
  shape, determinants, 560–561
Term to maturity, 458
Text mining, 288
Theoretical call option price, 449
  curve, 450
Theoretical call price, 448f
Theoretical futures price, 377
  borrowing rate basis, 379
  calculation, 389
  examination, 378–381
  securities basket, delivery, 380–381
  short selling, 380
  transaction costs, 380
Theoretical option price
  estimation, tangent line (usage), 449f
  tangents, usage, 450f
Theory fishing, 82
Theory of Speculation, The (Bachelier), 278
Theta, 451
Third central moment, 63
20-year Treasury bond futures, call options, 820t–821t
30/360 day count convention, 485–486
Three-bond portfolio
  cash flow, 585t
  example, 583t
Three-month LIBOR, purchase/sale, 706
Three-stage DDM, 256
Three-stage growth model, 256–257
Tick size, 142–143
Tilted portfolio, creation, 175
Tilt exposure, 327
Time decay, measure, 451
Time horizon, specification, 672
Time premium, 412–413
Times interest-covered ratio, 217–218
Time to expiration, call option price (relationship), 451
Time value of money, consideration, 410
Time-weighted rate of return, 180–182
Timing option, 686
Tobacco settlement revenue (TSR), 498
Top-down approaches, bottom-up approaches (contrast), 152–153
Top-down value-added strategies, 647
Top-down yield curve strategies, 651
Total asset turnover ratio, 214–215
  equity multiplier, multiplication, 202
Total coupon interest, 581
Total debt-to-assets ratio, 216

Total excess return, 313
Total excess risk, 313
Total firm valuation, 264–266
Total loss, risk, 802
Total principal payments, 524t–525t
Total return, 585–592
  applications, 589–591
  bond price volatility, relationship, 591–592
Total risk decomposition, 313–314
  flowchart, 313f
Tracking error, 300–309, 667–670
  benchmark stocks, contrast, 305f
  beta, relationship, 308f
  determinants, 304–308
  determination, 300, 302
  dramatic shortfall, relationship, 307f
  increase, 307
  marginal contribution, 308–309
  nonbenchmark stocks, contrast, 306f
  risk, 171–172
Trade-based factors, 353–354
Trade date, 484
Trade-driven markets, 121
Trade Reporting Facilities, 135
Trade-Through Rule, 138
Trade timing, impact, 353–354
Trading
  mechanics, 332–335
  priority rules, 332–334
  soft touch, 339
Trading costs
  minimization, 79
  taxonomy, 331–332
Traditional asset classes, 7
Traditional fundamental analysis, 153–154
Tranches, 518
  size, measurement, 531t
Transaction costs, 10, 171–172, 174–175
  identification, example, 346–347
  incorporation, 355–356
  liquidity, relationship, 347–349
  measurement, 349–350
  modeling, 352
  models, 356
  reduction, 392
  taxonomy, 340–347
Transactions, front-running, 337
Transferable assets, 800
Transfer agent, 733
Treasury bills, 488
Treasury bonds, 488
  futures, puts
    buying strategy, usage, 703t
    usage, 699
  futures, usage, 715
  futures contracts
    delivery options, summary, 686t
    features, 683–686

Index

pricing, 686–687
usage, 683–692
Treasury futures options, Black model, 697–698
Treasury inflation-protected securities (TIPS), 488, 502
Treasury issues, CBOT determination, 684
Treasury notes, 488
   futures contracts
      delivery options, summary, 686t
   features, 684–686
   pricing, 686–687
   usage, 683–692
Treasury securities, 487
   delivery, 695–696
   market, 487
   options valuation, Black-Scholes model (usage), 696–697
   types, 487–489
Treasury spot rates, 557
Treasury yield curve functions, focus, 556–557
Trinomial additive stochastic DDM, 259
Trinomial geometric stochastic DDM, 259–260
Trinomial model, 613
Trinomial stochastic DDM, 257
Trinomial stochastic models, 259–260
True-up mechanism, 545
Tversky, Amos, 80
12b-1 fee, 733
Two-asset portfolio
   portfolio risk, measurement, 24
   return variance, 28–29
Two-parameter model, 23
Two-period model, extension, 444–447
Two-period option pricing model, 444f
   illustration, 446f
Two-stage growth model, 255–256
Two-year corporate bond, pricing, 712
Two-year swap, PVBP, 711f

Unbundling, 755
Uncertainty
   assumption, 281
   level, measure, 280
Undated issues, 503
Underlying stock, price, 448f
Underweighting, 172–173
Unique risk, 99
United Kingdom, Financial Services Authority, 768
Unit trusts, 729
Universal life insurance
   elements, 755
   types, 753t
Unlisted market, 133
Unpredictability, statistical concepts, 282–286
Unsecured corporate debt obligation, 475
Unsystematic portfolio risk, 100f
Unsystematic risk factors, 91
Uptick trade, 143

Upward sloping yield curves, 560, 563
U.S. bankruptcy, 476–477
U.S. City Average All Items Consumer Price Index for all Urban Consumers (CPI-U), 488
U.S. creditor rights, 476–477
U.S. equity markets, 121
U.S. government bonds, 487
U.S. small-cap equity, inclusion, 49–51
U.S. stock markets, 125–133
   indexes, 150t
   overview, 126f
Utility function, 16–17

Valuation, lattice (usage), 622–625
Value-added strategies, 647–658
Value assets, store, 800
Value at risk (VaR), 76–77
Value company, 166–167
Value date, 484
Valued firm, project bases, 271–272
Value judgment, making, 274
Value Line Composite Index, 152
Value Line Investment Survey, The, 224
Value manager, 166
Value stocks, 6
Vanguard Total Bond Market Index Fund, 643–644
Variable annuities, 749, 756, 758–760
   characteristic, 761–762
Variable costs, fixed costs (contrast), 331
Variable life insurance, 749, 753–754
Variable universal life, 755
Variance, 22–26, 79
   addition, 667
   limitations (risk measure), 64–68
   usage, 23
Variance-covariance matrix, determination, 312
Variation margin, 370
   absence, 375
Vector autoregressive (VAR) model, 292
Venture capital
   fees, 786–788
   fund
      life cycle, 792–793
      illustration, 793f
      windup/liquidation, 793
   fund of funds, 791–792
   industry, specialization, 794
   investment vehicles, 789–792
Venture capitalists
   remuneration, 787
   roles, 786
   3(c)(1) funds, 789
   3(c)(7) funds, 789
Vertical common-size analysis, 220
Volatility
   absolute dollar terms, 689
   arbitrage, 783–784
   forecast, 814

Volume discovery, 137
Volume-weighted average price (VWAP), 349–350
  calculation, 350
Voluntary bankruptcy, 476

Wal-Mart Stores, Inc.
  cash flows, 229f
  net income, 229f
  operating profit, 229f
  revenues, 229f
Walt Disney Company, 100-year bonds, 458
Warrant trading, involvement, 783–784
Waterfall, 530
Wealth distribution, 48
Weighted average coupon (WAC), 513
  example, 514t–515t
Weighted average maturity (WAM), 513
  example, 514t–515t
Weighted average portfolio yield, 583–584
Weighting, perspectives, 172–173
White noise, 283
Wildcard option, 686
Wilshire indexes, 152
Working capital concept, 225

XS tranches, 536

Yield
  calculation procedure, 579
  decline, expectation, 657
  maintenance charges, 538, 539
  measures, 567, 576–583
  percentage change, natural logarithm, 810
  spreads, 656
Yield curve, 519
  exposure, measurement, 610–611
  risk exposure
    assessment, 664
    estimation, 663t–664t
  shapes, 556f
  spread, 556
  steepness, 560
  strategies, 650–651
Yield to call, 576, 578–580
  expression, 579
  measure, 580
Yield to first call, 579
Yield to maturity, 576–578
  calculation, iterative procedure (usage), 577t
  computation, 580
  ease, 578
  helpfulness, absence, 586–587
  impact, 596
  promise, 586
  realization, 582
  reinvestment risk, relationship, 581–583
Yield to par call, 579
Yield volatility
  calculation, 815–816
  Ho-Lee model, 816
  measuring/forecasting, 809
  modeling/forecasting, 814–825
  power function, proportionality, 816
  Vasicek model, 816
Y structure, 532

Zero-beta, 109–112
Zero-beta portfolio, 110–111
  construction, assumptions, 112
  selection, 111–112
Zero-coupon bonds, 460
  call schedules, 465
  periodic coupon payments, absence, 571
  price sensitivity, 469
  yield to maturity, computation ease, 578
Zero-coupon bullet-maturity bond, 517
Zero-coupon Treasury, 696
Zero-coupon Treasury security, 489–490
  investment, 558
Zero uptick trade, 143